THE SPEAKER'S INDEX

TO

40 Years

OF

GENERAL CONFERENCE

THE SPEAKER'S INDEX

TO

40 Years

OF

GENERAL CONFERENCE

A comprehensive guide to the General Conferences
of The Church of Jesus Christ of Latter-day Saints
from October 1968 through April 2010

BY

JAMES E. KERNS

ISBN 13: 978-1-59955-414-3

Published by CFI, an imprint of Cedar Fort, Inc., 2373 W. 700 S., Springville, UT 84663
Distributed by Cedar Fort, Inc. www.cedarfort.com

Cover design by Angela D. Olsen
Cover design © 2010 by Lyle Mortimer

Printed in the United States of America

10 9 8 7 6 5 4 3 2 1

Printed on acid-free paper

Introduction

This volume has been many years in the making. It had its beginnings in about 1972 when I took a religion class at Brigham Young University called "Teachings of the Living Prophets." As a project, Professor Anderson had the class members index two conference issues of the Church magazines.

Up to that point I was regularly frustrated as I tried to find statements and ideas I'd remembered hearing in General Conference or reading in the conference reports. I spent many hours paging through Improvement Eras trying to locate a particular thought that I remembered which I could use in my upcoming lessons and talks.

Professor Anderson's indexing project was akin to a revelation to me. I completed the project, went back a few years to index the conferences containing all of my favorite lost thoughts, and then continued indexing conferences for over 40 years.

I have tried unsuccessfully to locate Professor Anderson to thank him for what he's done for me. BYU's alumni association, for some reason, hasn't been able to supply me with his name and address. I owe this project to his inspired idea.

I owe completion of this project to my incredibly wonderful daughter-in-law, Tia. I have wished many, many times that my dog-eared, torn, soiled, well-used index could be typed, reproduced, and distributed for others to use. I started the task of typing it many times, but never got past the first several pages. The job was just too daunting.

For some inexplicable reason Tia took it upon herself to type my index into the computer. Her enthusiasm spurred my own. While she typed, I worked hard to index the conferences that I'd neglected doing. In November 2004 we both finished, and submitted the manuscript to my uniquely talented son-in-law Kevin Bradford, who designed the cover and book layout, and who printed the first 30 copies for Christmas presents to our family members.

Over forty years of General Conference are now indexed herein. That's 84 conferences. Also included are the general Relief Society and Young Women conferences that typically precede General Conference.

Each talk was read and indexed with the thought in mind of how individual statements, stories, and thoughts might be used in future lessons and talks that I might give. Very rarely is any talk limited to just one topic. An individual statement on tithing, for example, might also have application to prayer and faith. That statement was, therefore, indexed under all three subjects.

Each General Conference talk has been scrutinized, taken apart, dissected and minutely indexed so that the user of this index can readily find the important things that our Church leaders have said on any given topic.

This has been a labor of love. It covers all but one and a half of the years I've been a member of the Church. I love the brothers and sisters who lead this Church. I've come to know them very personally as I've studied their words. The Apostles and their individual styles and manners of speaking are so familiar to me that I'd like to think that I can read a talk without knowing beforehand who wrote it, and identify the author.

The words of the Apostles are scripture. (D&C 68:4). General Conference is the best, most current, and most applicable scripture we have. This index opens these scriptures for use.

I love the Brethren. I love the Church. I love Jesus Christ whose Church this is, and who these leaders represent.

I hope this volume may be helpful to many people, and particularly to my family, as they strive to serve our Savior.

James E. Kerns

13856 Willow Creek Lane
Haines, Oregon 97833
(541) 856-3595

How to Use this Index

The *Ensign* (1971 to present) , and its predecessor, The *Improvement Era* (1968-1970), were used for this indexing project. The three-column pages of those magazines were divided into six sections—a through f—to make references quickly locatable.

Column one contains sections a and b.

Column two contains sections c and d.

Column three contains sections e and f.

An identifying phrase is given for each reference.

Any references containing stories are so noted.

Each identifying phrase is followed by the date of the magazine where the phrase is located, and the page number is followed by the letters "a" through "f" to indicate where on the page the referenced item is to be found.

Table of Contents

Delbert L. Stapley	History of Young Women's MIA	Dec 1969	62d
	History of Young Men's Mutual Improvement Association		64f
Thomas S. Monson	4 admonitions to bearers of ,		90a
Joseph Fielding Smith	Trains and schools one for higher blessings and duties	June 1970	66d
Joseph Fielding Smith	Preparatory priesthood to qualify us to make covenants	Dec 1970	27e
N. Eldon Tanner	Only one in 1,000 holds the ,		91d-e
Victor L. Brown	Feelings of James E. Talmage when ordained to , —story		109f-111a
	Feelings of Wilford Woodruff when a priest		112a-e
Vaughn J. Featherstone	3 groups of , holders	July 1972	45c
Joseph Fielding Smith	Quorum of 12 will never lead Church astray		88b
Victor L. Brown	An honor to be a priest —young man's outlook		90d
Paul H. Dunn	Paul H. Dunn as a deacon —story		93d
Harold B. Lee	Apostles maybe aren't the best but most qualified men		103f
A. Theodore Tuttle	Melchizedek Priesthood and , working together		120c
Harold B. Lee	Activity leaves no time for evil	Jan 1973	62a
Howard W. Hunter	Apprenticeship for leadership		65d
Gordon B. Hinckley	Cannot afford immorality		92b
	Holds keys of ministering of angels		93b
N. Eldon Tanner	Position of Quorum of 12 upon president's death		100f
Victor L. Brown	Potential of new MIA —Lee and Joseph F. Smith	July 1973	80b
	Mutual Improvement Association not an auxiliary anymore		80f
	How new MIA is to be organized		81a
Robert L. Backman	Leadership of youth in new Aaronic Priesthood MIA		84d
	MIA youth leadership —story of Deacon's President		85d
N. Eldon Tanner	Actions and appearance of , when officiating		93f
Harold B. Lee	No topic has received more searching and prayer than MIA		96c
	Emphasis of MIA is priesthood and reaching the one		96c
Victor L. Brown	Services performed by youth in APMIA	Jan 1974	108e
	Five goals of Aaronic Priesthood MIA		109a
Victor L. Brown	The presidency of the , - Bishops	May 1974	74b-e
	The origin of Aaronic Priesthood MIA		74e-f
	Quorum presidencies and bishops - their relationships		75b-76b
Vaughn J. Featherstone	, should prepare sacrament before meetings begin	May 1975	68c
N. Eldon Tanner	The boy who became a 100 percenter —story		77a-b
Spencer W. Kimball	When the Apostles pass sacrament		79e-f
Victor L. Brown	How quorums should be run - require sacrifice	Nov 1975	66b-68f
Spencer W. Kimball	All , members should know Articles of Faith —story		77d-79e
N. Eldon Tanner	Murderer fell dead at his feet —story	May 1976	42c-43a
Thomas S. Monson	How advisor held regular interviews with president —story	May 1979	36b-f
Spencer W. Kimball	Account of W. Woodruff's mission as a priest —story		48d-49e
N. Eldon Tanner	How a member of Quorum of 12 is chosen —story	Nov 1979	44a-e
Thomas S. Monson	Entitled to the ministering of angels —story	May 1980	8d-f
	Stammering , holder baptized without a flaw —story		8f-9b
Boyd K. Packer	President Woodruff's mission as a priest —story	Nov 1981	30c-e
	Sacrifice and sacrament administered by ,		31a-b

Boyd K. Packer	Explanation of , —entire talk	Nov 1981	30b-33f
Victor L. Brown	Presidents in , to be called by bishop	May 1982	35e
	Inactive boy was asked to pray —story		36b-c
	Fun and games will not save any boy —story		36d-f
Robert L. Backman	Activating inactives in ,	Nov 1982	38c-d
	, presidencies should visit members		38d-e
	Advisors: Qualities to look for		38e-f
Gordon B. Hinckley	John the Baptist did not talk down to his "Fellow servants"		44f-45a
	Ministering of angels —W. Woodruff wagon story		45d-46c
Gordon B. Hinckley	Ministering angels about you to protect you	May 1983	46f-52e
Thomas S. Monson	All 45 priests filled missions —story	Nov 1984	43d-e
	Bishop found boy hiding in grease pit —story		43e-f
Rex D. Pinegar	, holders must protect girls' virtue	Nov 1985	41d-e
Gordon B. Hinckley	What worthiness at the sacrament table entails	May 1988	46e-f
Joseph B. Wirthlin	, Young Men have a greater challenge than any before	Nov 1988	35b
Robert D. Hales	What the , is not	May 1990	39b
Richard P. Lindsay	How his , advisor handled the quorum	May 1994	45b-f
Henry B. Eyring	Assignment by deacon's president saves boy —story	Nov 1995	38a-c
James E. Faust	Sacred responsibility of , to protect women		47b
Keith B. McMullin	Manhood begins with ordination, not age	Nov 1997	41c-d
	Has more power and authority than any others		41d-f
	A creed for , —excellent		41f-42a
Dallin H. Oaks	How , holds keys to ministering of angels	Nov 1998	37f-38a
	Principle of non-distraction by , during sacrament		39c-40b
D. Todd Christofferson	Course of study for , quorums in times past		41d-f
Thomas S. Monson	How an advisor trained a presidency —story		49d-f
	Purposes of the ,		50a
Thomas S. Monson	Priest memorized sacrament prayers —story	May 1999	49b-e
Robert D. Hales	Earn Duty to God and Eagle awards	Nov 2001	38d-39a
Spencer J. Condie	Receive and be ministering angels	May 2002	45b-c
	No difference if a man is priest or Apostle — Woodruff		46a
Gordon B. Hinckley	Avoid immorality to have angels attend	Nov 2002	58f-59f
Russell M. Nelson	5 personal objectives for young men	Nov 2003	46d-e
Monte J. Brough	Priests quorum got many referrals		49b
	Quorum had lessons in inactives' homes		49d
Thomas S. Monson	Helping Louis take sacrament —story		56f-57b
James E. Faust	Functions in 2 ordinances related to Atonement	Nov 2004	53f
	Ward had to use , to fullest - results		53f-54f
Thomas S. Monson	Adviser had regular interviews —pigeon story		56f-57e
Thomas S. Monson	Passing sacrament to Louis —story	Nov 2005	56c-d
	Stuttering priest baptized flawlessly —story		58a-d
James E. Faust	Older men administer sacrament reverently	May 2006	50d-51a
	Ministering angels		51b-52d
	Obligations of holders of , listed		52d-e
Thomas S. Monson	, holds keys of ministering angels —story		55d-56b

Aaronic Priesthood

Thomas S. Monson	Handicapped priest blessed sacrament —story	May 2006	56f-57b
	Dying deacon passed sacrament —story		57b-e
Henry B. Eyring	Deacon recorded lesson for another	Nov 2006	44a-c
	Assignment by deacon's president saves boy —story		44d-f
	Unity changes how basketball is played		44f-45b
Gordon B. Hinckley	Entitled to ministering of angels		60b
Gordon B. Hinckley	Equal protection as Priest or Apostle —Woodruff	May 2007	84d-f
L. Tom Perry	Deacon's president took the challenge —story		85d-f
	O. Cowdery's account of restoration of ,		87b-f
Thomas S. Monson	Duty to prepare for Melchizedek Priesthood and mission	Nov 2007	59d-e
Jay E. Jensen	Appearance of , during sacrament must not distract	Nov 2008	48e-49a
Michael A. Neider	Quorum president activated boys —story	May 2009	15f-16d
Boyd K. Packer	Kings and magistrates can't hold ,		49d-e
Henry B. Eyring	How home teaching helps future of , holders		65a-66e
Thomas S. Monson	Yours is a vital role in the ward		67d
	Called to speak extemporaneously as deacon —story		67d-e
M. Russell Ballard	Three ways to improve relations with father	Nov 2009	47f-48e
Henry B. Eyring	Bishop's policy: No lights out		61a-d
David L. Beck	Non-member describes his friend	May 2010	54b
	New Duty to God program		54e-55a
	Taking sacrament to a sick man —story		55a-b
	Lord: "I have a work for you"		55d
	Will change people and the world		56a-b
Henry B. Eyring	Deacon drew out plan for passing sacrament		60b-e
	First Presidency message to ,		61a
	Sacrament: Same job Lord gave Apostles		61a-d
Robert D. Hales	Do Duty to God program with parents		96d-e

Ezra Taft Benson	, jeopardizes exaltation	Dec 1970	46d
Sterling W. Sill	Slaughter of the innocents as Herod did	June 1971	44c
Ezra Taft Benson	We oppose this damnable practice	July 1973	41a
	Will bring wrath and judgment of God		41c
N. Eldon Tanner	Mentioned as a sin to be handled by Church		94f
Spencer W. Kimball	Could only be justified in very rare cases	May 1974	7b-c
Spencer W. Kimball	One million U.S. , each year	Nov 1974	7d-e
	Retribution for , is sure		9a
Spencer W. Kimball	Church policy regarding ,	May 1975	7d
James E. Faust	Promoter of , resigned after 60,000 deaths		28a-b
	Should , be performed if child to be handicapped?		28d-e
	1,000,000 U.S. , per year		28f-29b
Spencer W. Kimball	Statistics on , - One of the most grievous sins	Nov 1976	6b-c
John H. Groberg	Don't be swayed by cries of those who don't know —story		44b-45b
Spencer W. Kimball	Over 1 million in 1974	May 1978	5e
Spencer W. Kimball	Crime next to murder	May 1979	6d

Abortion, cont'd
Related Topics: Birth Control

Theodore M. Burton	Was feeding children to Molech any different?	May 1979	73d
Spencer W. Kimball	, has reached plague proportions	Nov 1980	4d-e
Vaughn J. Featherstone	34-year-old case of , forgiven —story		30f-31c
Russell M. Nelson	Those who advocate , have already been born	Nov 1984	31d-e
Russell M. Nelson	, —excellent talk	May 1985	11c-14b
Boyd K. Packer	A sin leading civilization to destruction	Nov 1986	16f-17a
Russell M. Nelson	, provokes the wrath of God	Nov 1987	89d
Boyd K. Packer	A spiritually dangerous life-style	Nov 1990	84c
	The rights of one affect the rights of others		84f
	Three lives are involved		85a-b
	Forgiveness possible even for ,		85e-86f
Boyd K. Packer	Pro-choice argument would have us remove traffic signs	May 1992	66f
	, is repentable		68e-f
Dallin H. Oaks	Why , is such a serious sin	Nov 1993	74d-e
Gordon B. Hinckley	Adoption - not abortion	Nov 1994	53e
Gordon B. Hinckley	Statistics and the Church's stand on ,	Nov 1998	71d-e
	Evil and repugnant		99c-d

Activation
Related Topics: Activity, Fellowshipping, Inactivity

Ezra Taft Benson	Statistics showing magnitude of reactivation problem	May 1983	43f-44d
	What some stakes have done concerning reactivation		43f-44d
David B. Haight	Presidency statement on reactivation and home teaching	Nov 1983	41a-c
Joseph B. Wirthlin	4 stories of reactivation —stories	May 1984	40d-41b
Robert D. Hales	A missionary couple's great success in England — story	May 1987	77b-e
M. Russell Ballard	Results of feeding missionaries in S. America —story	Nov 1987	78f-80a
Thomas S. Monson	Dying man activated many brethren —story	May 1991	49e-f
Thomas S. Monson	Stake activated 87 men in one year —story	May 1994	52a-c
Henry B. Eyring	Deacon activated boy despite shyness —story	May 2001	38f-39b
	Elder's president activated quorum —story		40b-e
Thomas S. Monson	You're responsible for those you might have saved —story		48d-f
	, through being a friend —stories		49f-50e
Thomas S. Monson	100 men activated in one year —story	May 2003	55f-56b
	All 29 inactive men went to temple —story		56b-e
	Visit bears fruit years later —story		56f-57c
Mervyn B. Arnold	Persistent Brazilian rescued surfer —story	May 2004	46d-48f
Thomas S. Monson	Visit was rejected, but caused guilt —story	May 2005	55a-f
Silvia H. Allred	When a shepherd cares, many will return	Nov 2007	114f
Susan W. Tanner	Inactive woman activates 16 girls —story	May 2008	114f-115d
Eduardo Gavarret	, in Peru through visits —entire talk	Nov 2008	98d-99b
Boyd K. Packer	Must activate tired, worn out, lazy, guilty	May 2010	9b

Activity
Related Topics: Activation, Inactivity

Paul H. Dunn	The blessings of , —humorous	June 1971	102a-b
N. Eldon Tanner	Blessings coming from ,	Dec 1971	111e-f
Harold B. Lee	A pillar holding up a weight can't be pushed over		113b

Harold B. Lee	, is the soul of spirituality	Dec 1971	113c
Boyd K. Packer	, programs do not nourish	Jan 1973	89d
Delbert L. Stapley	Challenge to be active for one year trial	July 1973	101f
Marvin J. Ashton	All 10 virgins in the parable were church members	May 1974	35f-36c
Paul H. Dunn	Honoring those who died in the service —story	Nov 1977	24f-25a
Spencer W. Kimball	Difference between "anxiously engaged" and busy work.	May 1978	101b-c
	Bishops to budget members' time		101b-c
John H. Groberg	Hawaiian overcame challenge - family stayed active —story	May 1980	49a-f
Victor L. Brown	Reduce unnecessary , in wards —suggestions	May 1981	38f-39f
H. Burke Peterson	Some are engaged in "the thick of thin things"		81c
Marion G. Romney	He can only guide our footsteps when we move our feet		91b
Marvin J. Ashton	A 1,000 mile journey begins with first step	May 1983	31a
Marvin J. Ashton	Those who fall out of Church weren't in far enough	Nov 1983	63a-b
Thomas S. Monson	German Temple built for 5,000 members. Levels exceed all	Nov 1985	34b-35a
Ezra Taft Benson	Are we using of the aids the Church has put out?	May 1986	4e
Marvin J. Ashton	A member in good standing or in good coming?	May 1987	66f-67a
Thomas S. Monson	The credit goes to the man in the arena —T.R. Roosevelt		69a
Robert J. Whetten	Most inactives still believe	May 2005	92f-93a
Paul K. Sybrowsky	How he was brought into , —story	Nov 2005	35e-36b
Thomas S. Monson	Couple returned to , because of visit —story	Nov 2006	57d-58b
Julie B. Beck	Limit children's , outside the home	Nov 2007	77f-78a
Dieter F. Uchtdorf	Discipleship is not a spectator sport	May 2009	76f-77a
	It is never too late		77a-78a
Dallin H. Oaks	Go to church with intent of being active		96c-e
Yoon Hwan Choi	Nine Korean youth joined Church —story	Nov 2009	53b-55b
Barbara Thompson	Has made all the difference in her single life		119b-f
Boyd K. Packer	Must activate tired, worn out, lazy, guilty	May 2010	9b

Adam
Related Topics: Creation, The Fall

Alvin R. Dyer	Location of Garden of Eden was in America	Dec 1968	44c
	Meaning of Adam-ondi-Ahman		44e
Marion G. Romney	Curse placed upon ground not ,	Nov 1976	125a
Mark E. Petersen	Who Adam is and was - Refutes Adam-God theory	Nov 1980	16b-18f
Bruce R. McConkie	Participated in creation of earth	May 1982	32f
Russell M. Nelson	, is next to Christ in authority	Nov 1987	86f

Adultery
Related Topics: Chastity, Immorality, Morality, Virtue

David O. McKay	Spirit won't strive with man who breaks up another's family	June 1969	29b-30a
Spencer W. Kimball	No essential distinctions between any sex sin	June 1971	19b-c
	Locks doors to temples		19c
Milton R. Hunter	New sex code proposed by a church		41d-e
	Biblical men who were broken by ,		41f-42b
Richard L. Evans	Commandment against , includes lesser infractions	Dec 1971	57d-58a
Bernard P. Brockbank	The sin of , includes fornication —definition		62e
Harold B. Lee	Sin second only to murder	Jan 1973	106c

Adultery, cont'd
Related Topics: Chastity, Immorality, Morality, Virtue

Harold B. Lee	Men, don't prostitute ability as a creator - Leads to divorce	Jan 1974	101a
Marion G. Romney	Its self-executing penalty is spiritual death	May 1974	82a
Elray L. Christiansen	Statement of First Presidency on ,	Nov 1974	24c-e
Gordon B. Hinckley	85% believe , is wrong but only 51% of movie writers do	Nov 1983	45c-46c
L. Whitney Clayton	David - Saddest story in scriptures	Nov 2007	51f-52c

Affliction
Related Topics: Problems, Trials

Marion G. Romney	Man must endure , to prove self	Dec 1969	67b
	Develops souls		67e
	Comforting words for ,		67f
	His greatest growth made in ,		69c
	Man must endure , to prove self		67b
	Develops souls		67e
	Comforting words for ,		67f
	His greatest growth made in ,		69c
Alvin R. Dyer	We have met the enemy and he is us	Dec 1970	124f
Marion D. Hanks	We came here to undergo experiences	July 1972	105e
H. Burke Peterson	Given to keep us in remembrance —story	Jan 1974	18c
	From trial comes refined beauty		18f
N. Eldon Tanner	Some may come as punishment for disobedience		93e
Loren C. Dunn	Wind blew one tree over but not another —story	May 1974	27d-e
Loren C. Dunn	Frustration is high on Americans' list of ,	Nov 1974	11e
Marion D. Hanks	God will temper the wind to the shorn lamb	May 1975	13c
Marion D. Hanks	Children mocked handicapped girl. What she did—story	Nov 1976	32f-33a
David B. Haight	Aurelia Spencer Rogers' history —story	May 1978	24a-d
George P. Lee	His brothers taunted him as he prayed		27e
	His brothers tried to pour alcohol down his throat		28b-e
Howard W. Hunter	Resistance creates a boat's forward movement —story	May 1980	24d-25a
	Members at peace become indifferent —Brigham Young		25d
	Suffering can make saints of people —Kimball		26e
	The flame shall not hurt thee		26f
Marvin J. Ashton	Man lost a hand —story	Nov 1980	54f-60a
	Mother's , were so she could measure herself		60a
	Joseph's character shaped by , - Jesus' too		60b
	Oyster makes pearls from ,		60e
Charles Didier	, show whether we are full of integrity or not	Nov 1981	52e
Rex D. Pinegar	Unpleasant things are not interruptions of life	Nov 1982	24e-f
	Others' , don't seem as hard as ours —story		25f-26d
Vaughn J. Featherstone	Gethsemane —great poem		72f
James E. Faust	Many have not known blessings of economic ,		87d
	The difference between recession and depression		87d
	Some calamities become great blessings		87f-88a
	Same , may chasten one and embitter another		88e
	Lord's best soldiers come from highlands of ,		88f
	Be glad there are big hurdles in life		89a

Affliction, cont'd

Related Topics: Problems, Trials

Boyd K. Packer	Purpose of , unclear without knowledge of premortal life	Nov 1983	16b-18f
James E. Faust	Caring for the handicapped —entire talk	Nov 1984	54b-60e
Dallin H. Oaks	, is consecrated for one's gain	Nov 1985	63d
Joseph B. Wirthlin	List of Paul's ,	May 1987	31b
L. Tom Perry	Kimball and Young leaving on mission —story		34f-35c
Neal A. Maxwell	Remember who wore the crown of thorns		72c
L. Aldin Porter	The rains descended on both houses	Nov 1987	74d-e
Hugh W. Pinnock	How a young man handled his disease —story	May 1989	11a-b
Marvin J. Ashton	Things that hurt, instruct —Franklin		22b
Ronald E. Poelman	Purposes of adversity —entire talk		23a-25b
Carlos H. Amado	Our adversities help us help others score	Nov 1989	29c-30a
Marvin J. Ashton	Runner practiced on beach and mountains —story		37a-b
Dallin H. Oaks	, shall work together for your good		67f
Joseph B. Wirthlin	A single mother of 8 —service story	May 1990	32f-33a
Jeffrey R. Holland	Pigs and cows supporting missionary died —story	May 1995	40a-f
Monte J. Brough	Eloquence and humor in , —stories		41f-42b
	Sister felt highly honored in , —story		42e
Susan W. Tanner	Gospel is a rock - not an umbrella —story	May 2005	106a-e
Keith B. McMullin	, does not control our personal world	Nov 2005	11d-f
	Purpose of , and how to deal with it		10b-12f
Dallin H. Oaks	List of heavy , we carry	Nov 2006	6b
	Atonement heals or lightens ,		6b-9b
David S. Baxter	Stand steady: Storms hit the wise man, too		14d-f
Joseph B. Wirthlin	Sunday will come		30a-b
Richard G. Scott	Temporary stepping stones to accelerate progress		41b-f
Don R. Clarke	Sudden blindness —story		97b-98b
	Peace about blindness came after prayer		98f
Keith R. Edwards	Son's injury likened to atonement —story		99f-101b
	Scriptural people who were steady through ,		100c-f
Gordon B. Hinckley	Single mother didn't want to go home —story		117b-d
Thomas S. Monson	4 children with muscular dystrophy —story	May 2007	24a-f
Bonnie D. Parkin	Blessing basket helped through ,		34e-f
Julie B. Beck	Orphan girl became Young Women general president		109d-110b
Richard C. Edgley	How ward helped a family in tragedy —story	Nov 2007	9d-10a
	Lessons that come from , —entire talk		9d-11b
Dieter F. Uchtdorf	Church came to his family amid war —story		18f-19a
Henry B. Eyring	Jesus' life was never easy		57e-f
Thomas S. Monson	Runner lost shoe, continued, finished third		59e-f
Octaviano Tenorio	Baby's death made conversions —story		96e-97f
Steven E. Snow	Cancer: A disease of love		102b-d
Joseph B. Wirthlin	He spoke up for the handicapped boy —story	May 2008	18d-f
Susan W. Tanner	Abraham didn't know there'd be an angel and a ram		82f-83a
	Jesus didn't come until the fourth watch		83a
Boyd K. Packer	Hard to be an Apostle's wife		86d-e
L. Tom Perry	The best is yet to be	Nov 2008	7b-c

Affliction

Affliction, cont'd

L. Tom Perry	Dealt with , by visits to Walden Pond	Nov 2008	7c-8b
Neil L. Andersen	Missionary was convinced to stay on mission —story		13e-f
Joseph B. Wirthlin	Can be times of greatest growth		26b-e
	Part of our on-the-job training		27d-f
	Every tear will be compensated —Autism story		28a-d
	If handled right , can be a blessing		28f
Jeffrey R. Holland	Rescued by worried father —story		30c-31c
	The ministry of angels —entire talk		29b-31f
Dieter F. Uchtdorf	Walked 22 miles on artificial leg —story		55d-56a
Thomas S. Monson	The missionary who couldn't learn Spanish —story		60d-e
Keith B. McMullin	, not always taken away, but prayer always answered		76f-77a
Thomas S. Monson	Grateful for her peephole of sight —story		87a-c
Quentin L. Cook	Stranded in a June snowstorm —story		102d-f
	Things that are best for us are often bitter —H.B. Lee		102f-103d
	2 women's views about leaving Nauvoo		103d-104c
	We won't suffer any more than for our good		104c-d
	Every cloud doesn't result in rain		104d
	Be prepared for June snowstorms		104e-f
	Comforted by perpetrator's grieving family —story		105a-d
Dieter F. Uchtdorf	How to rid self of discouragement and weariness		120e-f
D. Todd Christofferson	Faith to persevere comes through covenants	May 2009	21b-f
	Let covenants be paramount and obedience exact		22f
Henry B. Eyring	Common - even to those who don't seem deserving		23d-f
	Evidence of God's infinite love		23f-24b
	Couple lost employment but had faith		25b-f
Quentin L. Cook	Pioneer's eternal goal lay through ,		37d-f
Rafael E. Pino	Daughter's drowning softened by covenants —story		41b-d
	Six family deaths were a spiritual experience —story		41e-f
	Nothing goes permanently wrong if... —H.W. Hunter		42e
	The winds blew against both houses		42e-f
Boyd K. Packer	He had polio at age 5 —story		50b-c
L. Whitney Clayton	Comes from three sources	Nov 2009	12d-13c
	Provides opportunities to practice virtues		13d
	Four blessings that can come from ,		13d-14b
Dieter F. Uchtdorf	His life as an 11-year-old refugee —story		55-56b
	His early life shaped him for the future		58e
Boyd K. Packer	Never been easy to live the gospel	May 2010	7b-c
Wilford W. Andersen	Saints were happy as they left Nauvoo		16a-e
	Haitian saints happy after earthquake		16e-17a
Dieter F. Uchtdorf	Will only be understood in future		58f
Donald. L. Hallstrom	Joseph Smith: A model in handling ,		50b-d
James B. Martino	Small pains now protect from larger ones		101f-102a

Affliction

	Agency		
	Related Topics: Choices, Decisions, Freedom		
John H. Vandenberg	Freedom to discipline self is true freedom	Dec 1968	59a
Marion G. Romney	Preservation of , more important than life		73e
Alvin R. Dyer	The evils of sensitivity training	June 1969	40e-41a
David O. McKay	Distinguishes man from animals	Dec 1969	30e
Hartman Rector, Jr.	Three independent principles - man, God, Satan —Smith	June 1970	102f
Harold B. Lee	Greatest gift next to life itself	Dec 1970	29d
Robert L. Simpson	No , to make own rules in football game		95d-96a
William H. Bennett	No , to determine consequences		123d
Richard L. Evans	You have limitless possibilities	Dec 1971	57b-c
Harold B. Lee	Limitations upon what is defined as ,	July 1972	31b
Harold B. Lee	Paramount duty to proclaim freedom	Jan 1973	60e
N. Eldon Tanner	So-called Constitutional rights and ,	July 1973	10b
John H. Vandenberg	Every day is election day		32d
	Without , man is less than a man		33b
Harold B. Lee	Does not give license to do as we please	Jan 1974	5e
David B. Haight	Does not mean license		41f
William H. Bennett	No one can choose the consequences of our choices		65f
Ezra Taft Benson	No man is free who is in financial bondage		69d
Spencer W. Kimball	No compulsion in any part of the gospel	May 1974	87d-e
Delbert L. Stapley	4 principles involved in ,	May 1975	21c-d
	Can't be permitted to do as we please in all things —Young		21f-22a
	Lower kingdoms have , abridged —Brigham Young		22a
	God does not force righteousness —Talmage		22b
Marion G. Romney	Every wrong decision further restricts our ,	Nov 1981	45b,d,f
Boyd K. Packer	No true freedom without responsibility	May 1983	66c
Victor L. Brown	I am the only person that can save myself	May 1985	15b-d
James E. Faust	Nothing is mandatory in this Church	Nov 1985	8f-9a
Marion D. Hanks	God's greatest gift to man	Nov 1986	11c-d
Robert L. Simpson	The times we all exercise our ,	May 1987	40e-41b
James E. Faust	Private choices are not private		80d-e
Boyd K. Packer	Satan cannot destroy us without our consent	May 1988	71b-c
Boyd K. Packer	Addiction nullifies agency	Nov 1989	14c-e
Joseph B. Wirthlin	Not free to choose consequences		75d
Kenneth Johnson	Never again will I let someone else control my life —story	May 1990	42c-e
Boyd K. Packer	"Free Agency" is not scriptural	May 1992	67a
Neal A. Maxwell	We are choosing for the next generation	Nov 1992	65f-66a
Russell M. Nelson	, was activated by the Fall	Nov 1993	34d
Neal A. Maxwell	Our wills are the only gifts we can give the Lord	Nov 1995	24f
Henry B. Eyring	Ignoring God's counsel means choosing another influence	May 1997	25b-26c
James E. Faust	Loud voices call for no restraints in conduct	May 1999	45b
	President McKay's horse wanted freedom —story		45b-e
Richard G. Scott	Why was , given? - Pleasure or accomplishment	May 2001	7f
Gerald N. Lund	He surrendered his desires for God's —story	May 2002	85b-f
Neal A. Maxwell	Must allow our wills to be swallowed up in His will	Nov 2002	18e-f
Neal A. Maxwell	The only gift that is yours to give	May 2004	46b

Agency, cont'd
Related Topics: Choices, Decisions, Freedom

James E. Faust	Instant rewards and punishment would destroy ,	Nov 2004	19a-c
Thomas S. Monson	Statements by Woodruff and Young		67c-d
Gordon B. Hinckley	Give spouse wings to fly		84f-85a
Anne C. Pingree	The only gift you can give Jesus	Nov 2005	112c
Robert D. Hales	Satan can't influence us unless we let him	May 2006	6d
	Entire talk		4b-8b
Henry B. Eyring	Answer came when he submitted his will to Lord's		16c-e
Wolfgang H. Paul	A law which will always exist —Brigham Young		35a
James E. Faust	Addictions destroy ,	Nov 2007	123d-124a
James J. Hamula	We need to do what we did before - choose	Nov 2008	50f-51b
Dallin H. Oaks	Won't be abridged, even when harming others	Nov 2009	27f-28c
Quentin L. Cook	We are accountable for our ,		91e
Joseph W. Sitati	Some traditions restrict exercise of ,		105a-b
D. Todd Christofferson	All possess gift of moral , - Self discipline		105d-f
	Intelligent use of , requires knowledge		107d

America
Related Topics: Constitution, Freedom, United States

Alvin R. Dyer	True destiny of , is religious, not political	Dec 1968	42d
	The land of man's earthly beginning		43d-e
	America as Zion will not fail		45c-e
Gordon B. Hinckley	Reform of , begins with self and family		69b
Mark E. Petersen	The sex revolution is destroying us	June 1969	75b-d
	Rejection of morality will bring fall of ,		79c
Ezra Taft Benson	List of troubles in ,	Dec 1969	69d
Marion D. Hanks	The best lack conviction, the worst are intense		93a
LeGrand Richards	Moses called , precious 5 times in 4 verses	Dec 1970	70c
Sterling W. Sill	, will survive if religious —D. Webster		82c-e
Harold B. Lee	Pray for nations' leaders	July 1972	33a
Ezra Taft Benson	Quote by Alexis de Tocqueville	July 1973	39b
	Comparisons between , and Rome —amazing		40b
	Gibbon's reasons for fall of Rome		40e
	Greatest danger during greatest success		40f
Spencer W. Kimball	Crime, immorality and abortion in ,	Nov 1974	7d-e
Loren C. Dunn	, built upon foundation of its homes		9e
Vaughn J. Featherstone	Son: "Why didn't you tell me you loved ," —story	Nov 1975	7d-f
	Give me your tired, your poor... —poem		10a
Marion G. Romney	The history and destiny of , —entire talk		35b-37e
Paul H. Dunn	Purpose of , was to provide for Restoration		54f
N. Eldon Tanner	Columbus said he was inspired by Holy Ghost	May 1976	48f-49a
	, has a moral and spiritual destiny - lacked by past nations		50d-51b
	George Washington's elegant prayer for ,		51d-e
Ezra Taft Benson	Warning to , concerning communism and Monroe Doctrine	Nov 1979	31b-33f
Thomas S. Monson	19 of 21 civilizations died from within —Toynbee		67b-c
J. Richard Clarke	6 reasons the great civilizations fell	Nov 1980	82d-e
L. Tom Perry	President Washington rejected a lofty title	Nov 1983	12f

Ezra Taft Benson	The fate of Signers of Declaration of Independence	Nov 1987	4f
	Signers' testimonies of God's guidance		5a-6a
	Signers' appearance to President Woodruff		6b-d
David B. Haight	Government by reflection and choice or accident and force		13e-f
David B. Haight	, raised up to establish Church and freedom —J.F. Smith	May 1990	24b
Joseph B. Wirthlin	Washington took no pay - only expenses		32a
Gordon B. Hinckley	Statistics on deteriorating standards	May 1992	69f-70b
Gordon B. Hinckley	Columbus' 500-year anniversary	Nov 1992	52a-c
Joe J. Christensen	Media is rotting foundations of society	Nov 1993	11b-e
Gordon B. Hinckley	Statistics on deteriorating conditions		54f-59a
Boyd K. Packer	Church's response to brutality of ,	Nov 2008	88d-91f

Apostasy

Harold B. Lee	In all ages, worst enemies come from within	Dec 1968	71f
Ezra Taft Benson	There are many wolves among the flock	June 1969	42b-43b
	Apostate act to publish criticism of authorities		43c-d
Boyd K. Packer	Having a hobby doctrine and neglecting others leads to ,	Dec 1971	42b-c
Ezra Taft Benson	Ravening wolves among us —J.R. Clarke	July 1972	61e
Marion G. Romney	Elements lacking in other churches	Jan 1973	30d
Harold B. Lee	Today's , foreseen		60b
	Cults within Church		63d
	Wolves among our flock		104e
	Designing men in the Church		105c
	Judases among our ranks		107c
LeGrand Richards	Three quotes on , by non-members		109e
M. E. Petersen	God doesn't abandon people - vice versa		117c
Mark E. Petersen	History of , following Christ - groups named	July 1973	108f
	Modern apostate groups cite D&C 85		110b
	Apostates' fate —Brigham Young's excellent analogy		110d
	Salvation not in splinter groups		110f
	Excommunication revokes all rights		110f
Spencer W. Kimball	Where there is no ear, there is no voice	Nov 1976	111d-f
Spencer W. Kimball	If people are unreachable the Lord does nothing	May 1977	76f
	Total , will never again happen		77f
N. Eldon Tanner	Nicene creed quoted and commented upon	Nov 1978	47c-e
Mark E. Petersen	30 factions: their names and beliefs in the 1st Century	May 1979	21f-22c
Carlos E. Asay	Apostate cited changes in Church publications —story	Nov 1981	67e-f
Marvin J. Ashton	Those who stir up waters create their own whirlpools	May 1983	31f
James E. Faust	If I had been paying tithing, I'd quit		40c
Marvin J. Ashton	Those who fall out of Church weren't in far enough	Nov 1983	63a-b
Gordon B. Hinckley	The , and return of Thomas B. Marsh —story	May 1984	81d-83e
James E. Faust	Longer one stays away the more alienated he becomes	Nov 1985	9e-f
Boyd K. Packer	Obedience to priesthood authority prevents ,	May 1989	15b-e
Russell M. Nelson	Prepare your backs for a whipping —T.B. Marsh		70b-c
Boyd K. Packer	Warnings about secret groups	Nov 1991	21d-f

Apostasy, cont'd

Gordon B. Hinckley	Not one from handcart companies apostatized	Nov 1991	54c-d
Charles Didier	How to become an apostate		63e-f
Neal A. Maxwell	"Christianity did not destroy paganism; it adopted it"	Nov 1993	18b-20f
James E. Faust	When differences with authorities become ,		38b-e
L. Aldin Porter	The steps to , —Spencer W. Kimball	Nov 1994	63d-64c
M. Russell Ballard	The , described		65d-66e
James E. Faust	Oliver Cowdery's story —story	May 1996	5b-6c
	Thomas B. Marsh's story —story		7a-c
	Church has an open door for apostates		7c-d
Neal A. Maxwell	They leave Church but can't leave it alone		68e-f
Boyd K. Packer	The curse that comes upon apostates	Nov 1996	7d-f
Boyd K. Packer	Ordinances were changed or abandoned	May 2000	8a-c
James E. Faust	Samuel Brannan's life —story	Nov 2002	50f-51d
James E. Faust	Definition of secularism	Nov 2005	20f-21b
James E. Faust	Apostate apostle was never happy again		54b-c
	Luke S. Johnson returned to Church		54d-f
Merrill J. Bateman	The , recounted		74b-f
Richard G. Scott	From introduction of truth to , is a dispensation		79b-c
Gordon B. Hinckley	O. Cowdery was shorn of his strength	May 2006	58f-59b
James E. Faust	The great , outlined		61e-62d
	List of precious doctrines that were changed		61f-62a
	Roger Williams' quote on need for apostles		62c-d
Gordon B. Hinckley	Evolvement of understanding of God	Nov 2007	84e-f
Henry B. Eyring	Cause of "the Apostasy"	May 2008	20f-21a
Boyd K. Packer	Most precious thing lost in the , was keys		84e
Gerald Causse	Rejection of simplicity is the origin of ,	Nov 2008	32f-33a
M. Russell Ballard	Cycle of , ends with a collapse of morality	May 2009	32b-f
Tad R. Callister	To whom will you go if you turn away?	Nov 2009	37b-e
Thomas S. Monson	Thomas B. Marsh's , —story		68b-f
Jeffrey R. Holland	Book of Mormon is a barrier to those thinking of ,		89f-90c
Donald L. Hallstrom	Simonds Ryder: From convert to , —story	May 2010	79e-80a

Apostles
Related Topics: First Presidency, General Authorities, President, Prophets

Joseph F. Smith	Fate of early ,	Dec 1969	37c
Harold B. Lee	Do not lose positions when they die	June 1970	29e-f
Boyd K. Packer	Have the , seen Christ?	June 1971	87d-e
	Have the , seen Christ?		88c
	Have the , seen Christ?		88e
Spencer W. Kimball	One of greatest blessings is to be ordained an ,	Jan 1974	15b
N. Eldon Tanner	Early , received all keys - could have been president	May 1974	82f
Ezra Taft Benson	The sweetest assoc. of men this side of heaven		104b
David B. Haight	Supposed to be eye and ear witnesses	May 1976	21b-c
Rex D. Pinegar	President Kimball bore witness of his own calling	Nov 1976	68d-69d
Delbert L. Stapley	Responsibilities of the ,		91f-92a
Boyd K. Packer	Don't discuss sacred interviews which qualify them	May 1980	65a

James E. Faust	Jesus stood in midst of , unnoticed —story	May 1981	8b-c,10c
Gordon B. Hinckley	The calling of elders Nelson and Oaks	May 1984	49d-f
	, not found in other churches		50b
	The calling of the first , in this dispensation		50f-51c
	86 , called so far in this dispensation		51d
	Perfect unity among First Presidency and ,		51d-e
Boyd K. Packer	A sacred, little understood brotherhood	Nov 1985	80d-e
James E. Faust	Decisions by , must be unanimous	Nov 1989	10f
Dallin H. Oaks	One of those guys who hangs on the wall at seminary		65d-f
Gordon B. Hinckley	One president of , but 7 of the Seventy. Why?	Nov 1990	48d-f
Boyd K. Packer	He is a witness of after-life	May 1991	9f
Russell M. Nelson	I know by experiences too sacred to relate	May 1992	74f
M. Russell Ballard	Melvin J. Ballard's vision of Jesus —story		75f-76e
Gordon B. Hinckley	Hold all keys. Complete unanimity.	Nov 1992	53b-60b
Howard W. Hunter	Called to wear out lives in Jesus' service		96b-d
Boyd K. Packer	Many unpublished visitations to temple	May 1993	20a
Russell M. Nelson	A living linkage between heaven and earth		38d-e
	The title "Apostle" is sacred		38e-f
	, have all keys of priesthood authority		39b
	Seniority is honored among , —story		40e-f
Neal A. Maxwell	Have all keys that ever were —Joseph Smith		78b
	Get ahead of leaders and be in danger		78d
Gordon B. Hinckley	Promise that , will never lead Church astray	Nov 1993	54e
M. Russell Ballard	Sustaining the council leader's decision —story		78c-d
Gordon B. Hinckley	How , are chosen and function	May 1994	53f-59c
Robert D. Hales	His calling as an , is a process		78d-f
Howard W. Hunter	Total unanimity in all decisions	Nov 1994	7e
	One man should not have all power - It is shared by all ,		7f-8b
Jeffrey R. Holland	His feelings on being called as an ,		31d-f
L. Aldin Porter	Will never lead Saints astray		62f-63b
	Have a special gift given to no other		63b-d
	Any document from , is from the Lord		65a-b
James E. Faust	Stay with majority of , and never go astray		72c
	How Joseph got the keys		72d
	Keys will stay with , until Second Coming		73b-d
	History of Valdensians - believers in , —story		73f-74c
Boyd K. Packer	A special endowment as prophets, seers...	Nov 1996	6e-f
	Spirit limits what , may say		8e
	The Twelve , —entire talk		6b-8f
Henry B. Eyring	His powerful apostolic testimony		33b
James E. Faust	Overpowering witness of an ,	Nov 1997	59e
David R. Stone	Watch and warn against spiritual hurricanes	Nov 1999	31b-32f
Boyd K. Packer	Old men: 1,161 years of experience!	May 2003	84a-b
Thomas S. Monson	Addressing the quorum as newest Apostle —story	Nov 2003	57b-d
Gordon B. Hinckley	The sustaining of Uchtdorf and Bednar	Nov 2004	4b-c

Apostles

Jeffrey R. Holland	Affection stronger than death among ,	Nov 2004	6d-f
	The purpose of ,		6f-7c
	Roger Williams' statement on need for new ,		7d-8a
	Elder Hinckley was 75th , named		8e-9b
Cecil O. Samuelson, Jr.	What eyewitnesses said of Jesus		51b-c
Thomas S. Monson	1980 Proclamation by ,		56e-f
Thomas S. Monson	The calling of Peter and Paul		68f-69c
Dieter F. Uchtdorf	His first talk as an Apostle		74b-76b
David A. Bednar	His first talk as an Apostle		76d-78f
Joseph B. Wirthlin	Talmage cared for diphtheria family —story	May 2005	28b-d
Dieter F. Uchtdorf	Hasn't seen family since his calling		36d-e
David A. Bednar	Teach with clarity - Testify with authority		99b
James E. Faust	One of 7 "blockbuster" doctrines	Nov 2005	22a
James E. Faust	102 , called in this dispensation		53c
	Stick with the Brethren - Unity		53d-f
James E. Faust	Roger Williams' quote on need for ,	May 2006	62c-d
Jeffrey R. Holland	Most "in touch" group in the world	Nov 2006	105f-106b
Thomas S. Monson	His calling to be an ,	May 2007	41e-42a
	This is his 102nd talk as an , in the Tabernacle		42b
Boyd K. Packer	Testimony of , no different than ours —story	Nov 2007	7f-8d
	President Romney's testimony as strong as when an elder		8d-e
Russell M. Nelson	What the ministry of the , is	May 2008	7f-8a
D. Todd Christofferson	Eloquent commitment to be one of the ,		76b-c
	Short history of his life		76f
Boyd K. Packer	Seventy do whatever , direct them to do		83f
	What happened to first ,		84e
	Christofferson is 96th , to serve in quorum		84f-85a
	President Kimball testified of keys and ,		85a-d
	Backgrounds of current , - Ordinary men		86b-c
	Wear selves out in service to the Lord		86d
	Must travel to impart keys		86e
	Account of his 47 years of travel		86f
	They have that witness		87a
Thomas S. Monson	44 years as an Apostle		87d
	Were prepared by the Lord		88d-e
Richard G. Scott	Their responsibility as special witnesses	Nov 2008	47a-b
Henry B. Eyring	When he felt overwhelmed as an ,		59a-d
Thomas S. Monson	Neil L. Andersen sustained	May 2009	4b-c
Dieter F. Uchtdorf	Elder Andersen is 97th , in this dispensation		28f
Boyd K. Packer	Account of his entering Air Force		51b-52a
Neil L. Andersen	Never seen any anger, selfishness or positioning		79d-e
	His call as an , —entire talk		78d-80f
Neil L. Andersen	Hugged by President following his call	Nov 2009	40b-d

Victor L. Brown	Polynesians wore jackets though very hot —story	July 1972	90b
Spencer W. Kimball	Dressing like opposite sex is reprehensible	Nov 1974	8b-d
A. Theodore Tuttle	Improving , improves you inside too		71f
N. Eldon Tanner	We behave in accordance with the way we look and speak		86f-87a
Victor L. Brown	Modesty in dress is a quality of mind and heart		104f
Spencer W. Kimball	Report on cleanup and planting projects	Nov 1975	5b-6a
Marvin J. Ashton	Why run the risk of looking like something you're not?	Nov 1976	84c-e
	, includes voice, manners, language, etc.		85e-86b
Victor L. Brown	Follow , of present prophets - no beard —story	May 1977	37e-38d
Gordon B. Hinckley	Clean grooming is a badge of honor	May 1996	48f-49a
Harold G. Hillam	Don't disfigure body. Leave sloppy dress craze behind	May 2000	10d-f
Margaret D. Nadauld	Outward , reflects what's inside	Nov 2000	14f-15b
H. David Burton	Dress standards spelled out	Nov 2001	66b-d
M. Russell Ballard	Scruffy convert family changed , —story	May 2002	88f-89d
Margaret D. Nadauld	Boy was proud of date in prom dress —story		97a-b
Spencer V. Jones	8 youth at fireside had poor , —story	May 2003	88e-f
Dallin H. Oaks	Pagan piercing of body parts	May 2004	9f
Gordon B. Hinckley	Counsel on girls' ,		114b-c
James E. Faust	What about the light in their eyes? —story	Nov 2005	20b-d
	You had a light in your face —story		22b-e
Jeffrey R. Holland	No bare midriffs		29a-b
	Best dress, not beach attire, for church		29b-d
	The folly of obsession with physical ,		29d-30d
Elaine S. Dalton	It will show in your face —poem	May 2006	109b-c
L. Tom Perry	What , should entail	Nov 2007	48c
Dallin H. Oaks	Can't be a lifesaver looking like others on the beach	May 2009	95a
M. Russell Ballard	Talk to daughters about , and model it	May 2010	20e-f
Thomas S. Monson	Dress to bring out best - Avoid extremes		64f-65a
Elaine S. Dalton	, of Sister McKay —story		121d-122b
	Deep beauty stems from virtue		122b-d
	Holy Ghost develops beauty		122d-e
	Girl realized she was beautiful		122e-f

Ezra Taft Benson	War against religion in U.S.	Dec 1969	70e
	Union of state and , in U.S.		70f
	Atheism now here		72b
	Statistics on ,		72c
Howard W. Hunter	An argument to throw at atheists	June 1970	34e
Ezra Taft Benson	Free, public education promotes ,	Dec 1970	49a-b
Bernard P. Brockbank	An argument to throw at atheists	June 1971	85b
Boyd K. Packer	Carol Lynn Pearson's short poem to atheists —poem	Dec 1971	40a-b
John H. Vandenberg	Can't look at heavens and say there is no God —Lincoln		115c
Howard W. Hunter	Disbelief just because we haven't bothered to find Him	Nov 1974	96f-97a
Thomas S. Monson	Hopelessness of death as viewed by atheists	May 1976	10d-e

Atheism, cont'd
Related Topics: Other Churches

Spencer W. Kimball	Neglect cannot prove God's non-existence	Nov 1978	6b-c
Wm. Grant Bangerter	Galileo forced to say earth did not turn ("And yet it turns")	Nov 1979	9f-10a
Neal A. Maxwell	Bleak statements by an atheist	May 1983	9e
Robert E. Wells	Sophisticated atheistic lady lawyer is baptized —story	Nov 1985	29c-e
James E. Faust	Definition of secularism	Nov 2005	20f-21b
Thomas S. Monson	Statements by Darrow and Schopenhauer	May 2007	23b
	Wife's death changed atheist's mind —story		23b-d
M. Russell Ballard	This is an era that scoffs at religion	May 2009	33a
Quentin L. Cook	Religious war with London bus ads —story		35d-f
	Find miracles hard to accept		35f-36a
Robert D. Hales	Invitation to atheists to gain a testimony	Nov 2009	29d-32f

Atonement
Related Topics: Jesus

Marion G. Romney	Lord's intense suffering in ,	Dec 1969	67a
N. Eldon Tanner	World's most important event	Jan 1973	28e
N. Eldon Tanner	Jesus suffers more than once for some	Nov 1974	86e
Marion G. Romney	Jesus and the , —whole talk	May 1982	6a-9b
Bruce R. McConkie	Sufferings of Gethsemane returned on Calvary	Nov 1982	33f
Bruce R. McConkie	The , —entire talk excellent	May 1985	9b-11b
James E. Faust	Jesus and the , —entire talk		30d-32f
Neal A. Maxwell	The incredible weight Jesus had to bear		72f-73b
Neal A. Maxwell	Jesus shed much blood even before the scourging	May 1987	72c-e
Howard W. Hunter	What Jesus suffered and paid for	May 1988	16e-17a
Gordon B. Hinckley	The , and resurrection —entire talk		65b-68f
Boyd K. Packer	Appears once in New Test. - 55 times in Book of Mormon		69e-70c
J. Richard Clarke	Only Mormons extend , beyond grave	May 1989	60d
Dallin H. Oaks	What an excommunicated member learned	Nov 1989	66a
	Abuser forgiven because of , —story		66b-c
Marion D. Hanks	Free - but must be received as Jesus prescribed	May 1992	9f-10b
J. Richard Clarke	5 conclusions about the ,	May 1993	10d-f
Russell M. Nelson	The third pillar of God's plan	Nov 1993	34d-f
Ronald E. Poelman	The , and divine forgiveness —entire talk		84b-86b
Richard G. Scott	, saves us after all we can do —Lee		88c
Merrill J. Bateman	Jesus' , bridges the gap - Optician's conversion —story	May 1994	65f-66a
Merrill J. Bateman	, is intimate and infinite	May 1995	14f
M. Russell Ballard	, is conditional and unconditional		22f-23a
Richard G. Scott	We can do nothing of ourselves to satisfy justice		75d
Robert E. Wells	The center, heart and core of religion	Nov 1995	65e
Jeffrey R. Holland	The , —excellent talk		67b-69f
Russell M. Nelson	Enables bodies to again function without blood	Nov 1996	34b
	Meanings of the word ,		34d-f
	How animal sacrifices pointed to ,		34f-35a
	Appears once in Bible - 35 times in Book of Mormon		35a
	Infinite aspects of ,		35a-b
	Extends to other worlds created by Jesus		35b

Russell M. Nelson	The ordeal of the ,	Nov 1996	35b-d
	Enabled purpose of Creation to be accomplished		35e-f
James E. Faust	All inequities shall be compensated		52d-f
Boyd K. Packer	An understanding of , is of very practical value	May 1997	9c
	The power of , begins working the day you ask		10c
	The , —Packer's poem		10f-11b
	"Washed Clean" —wonderful talk and story		9b-11b
Neal A. Maxwell	His entitlement to blessings was settled in court of small claims		11d
	The central act of all human history		12b-d
Thomas S. Monson	A concise statement about the , —good		52e
Richard G. Scott	Contingent upon keeping commandments and ordinances		54b-c
	, will resolve all inequities of life		54b-c
James E. Faust	One of 2 pivotal events in history	May 1999	17b-e
Henry B. Eyring	, washes away all effects of sin —story	Nov 1999	35b-f
Joseph B. Wirthlin	Through repentance , becomes operative		40f
Russell M. Nelson	Mentioned 39 times in Book of Mormon		70b-e
Russell M. Nelson	One of 3 components of plan of salvation	May 2000	84c-e
	Ancient Egyptian manuscript explains ,		84e-f
Marlin K. Jensen	The greatest act of humility and submissiveness	May 2001	10c
Boyd K. Packer	"The Touch of the Master's Hand" —entire talk		22d-24f
	A power to call upon in everyday life		22d-24f
Russell M. Nelson	The heart of the plan of salvation		32e-f
Charles Didier	Compared to bridges —a favorite talk	Nov 2001	10b-12b
James E. Faust	Big boy took small boy's licking —story		18e-f
	Description of the , —good		19a-c
	Things the , did		19c-d
	Compared to climbing Mount Everest		19f-20a
Coleen K. Menlove	Child taught father about , —story	Nov 2002	15b
Robert K. Dellenbach	World's crowning event		34e
Spencer V. Jones	Skunk smell would not come off —story	May 2003	88b-89f
Lynn A. Mickelsen	The atonement, repentance and dirty linen	Nov 2003	10d-13b
Boyd K. Packer	Wayward people will receive a salvation	May 2004	80d
M. Russell Ballard	Infinite , is applied one by one		84d-87f
Bruce C. Hafen	Enables learning from experience without condemnation		97d-e
	Christ gave all - We must too		97f-98d
	Christ carries us the rest of the way		99a-b
	The , —excellent talk		97b-99f
Dale E. Miller	Jesus died for us as individuals	Nov 2004	13c
David A. Bednar	Grace strengthens and enables		76d-78f
Merrill J. Bateman	Accomplished for us individually	Nov 2005	75e-76b
Jeffrey R. Holland	Lifts disappointments and sorrows too	May 2006	70f-71a
Earl C. Tingey	Meaning and depth of ,		73d-74a
Dallin H. Oaks	Is for all men everywhere		77c-78b
Dallin H. Oaks	Pays for sin and heals every affliction	Nov 2006	6f-7a
	Heals and gives strength —entire talk		6a-7b

Atonement, cont'd
Related Topics: Jesus

Dallin H. Oaks	Heals or gives strength to bear the burden	Nov 2006	9a-b
Richard G. Scott	The roles of justice, mercy and grace		41f-42f
Keith R. Edwards	Son's injury likened to , —story		99f-101b
Gordon B. Hinckley	The keystone of our existence	May 2007	84d
Russell M. Nelson	Mentioned more in Book of Mormon	Nov 2007	44f & 46b
David A. Bednar	Cleanses, redeems, sanctifies, strengthens		82c
Russell M. Nelson	Objectives in Moses 1:39 enabled by ,	May 2008	8f-9a
Carlos H. Amado	Jesus came here to give his life		35b-c
Dieter F. Uchtdorf	Repentance shows gratitude for ,		60a-b
Jay E. Jensen	Does not apply only at end of life —Packer	Nov 2008	49d-f
	"Arms of Safety" —entire talk		47d-49f
Henry B. Eyring	Savior learned how to succor us through ,	May 2009	24b-25a
Quentin L. Cook	Most taught , would save but few		36f-37a
Rafael E. Pino	No infirmity, affliction or adversity not felt by Christ		41f-42d
Jeffrey R. Holland	Vivid description of Jesus' last days —entire talk		86b-88f
L. Tom Perry	Full blessings of , only available to members		110f
Mary N. Cook	Makes virtue possible		118c
Richard G. Scott	Does not cover some people	May 2010	76b
	3 challenges Savior faced during ,		76f-77a
	Accomplished , completely on His own		77a-b
	Entire talk		75c-78b
Donald L. Hallstrom	Has broader purpose than overcoming sin		80f
Thomas S. Monson	Description of the , —good		88e-89b
Russell M. Nelson	Fulfilled both of Father's objectives		91c-92b

Attitude
Related Topics: —

John H. Vandenberg	Treat others like the persons they should be	Dec 1970	35d-36a
	Some die at 30, but aren't buried until 70		36e
Marvin J. Ashton	Do we act or react? (whole talk too)		59b-f
Marvin J. Ashton	Some are ahead, some behind, but no one is losing —story	Nov 1974	41b-d
	Christ's , during last week		42f-43b
Spencer W. Kimball	The altitude of your attitude		80b-c
Marvin J. Ashton	The set of the sails determines ship's direction —poem	May 1979	68e
Marvin J. Ashton	We can change circumstance by changing ,	Nov 1979	62a
Loren C. Dunn	Faith and happiness can't exist with cynicism and hate	May 1981	26f
Barbara B. Smith	One saw mud, the other stars —poem and story		83e-84a
M. Russell Ballard	A good , produces good results - Make your circumstances.		86a
James E. Faust	The best of times and the worst of times —Dickens	Nov 1982	88b
	When all was hopeless the man built a church		88b
	Same situation chastens one and embitters another		88e
	Two buckets in the well —story		88e
Royden G. Derrick	Circumstances can be changed by changing ,	May 1983	24c
Ted E. Brewerton	We should be incurable optimists		73c-74a
	First Presidency is never heavy-hearted		74a
Thomas S. Monson	Non-productive town became most productive —story	Nov 1983	20a-e

Paul H. Dunn	Successful old people retained enthusiasm	Nov 1983	25d-f
H. Burke Peterson	One POW was not emaciated because of , —story		60a-b
Gordon B. Hinckley	Lower your voice of criticism and negativism		76b
Angel Abrea	Nephi's , had no room for excuses	May 1984	70e-71a
	We need more guiding lights and fewer excuse-makers		72e-f
Robert D. Hales	A gloomy mind in a leader is unpardonable	Nov 1988	11b-c
Hugh W. Pinnock	How a young man handled his disease —story	May 1989	11a-b
Thomas S. Monson	Knowing you're made in image of God brings strength		44a
	Never give up. Last baseball player chosen —story		44b-d
Gordon B. Hinckley	His , in a world of ugliness		65b-e
James E. Faust	The last of human freedoms	May 1992	8c-d
Thomas S. Monson	The smile that shines thru tears —poem	Nov 1992	70b
H. David Burton	Boy with muscular dystrophy had good ,	May 1994	67d-f
Richard C. Edgley	Developing confidence —great talk	Nov 1994	39d-41b
Lance B. Wickman	Gloom turned to hope —story		82d-f
Russell M. Nelson	A cheerful and loving , as death neared	May 1995	32c
Gordon B. Hinckley	He does not feel old		70e
	No room in Church for gloom and doom		71a-72b
	Burned out, drowned out, sold out, still here		72e-f
Russell M. Nelson	, is elevated by lowering heads in prayer	May 1996	16a
Richard G. Scott	In a sea of problems are you a rock or a cork		24e-25a
	It's harder for Lord to bless us if , is wrong		25a
Bonnie D. Parkin	Story of Caleb and Joshua changed , —story		90d-91a
David B. Haight	Enthusiasm - Throwing duds or hand grenades	Nov 1996	15d
Neal A. Maxwell	Partaking of a bitter cup without becoming bitter	Nov 1997	22f
	Count your blessings and make them count		24b
James E. Faust	Focusing on wrongs rather than rights		54e
Jeffrey R. Holland	The Lord deplores pessimism	Nov 1999	37a
Coleen K. Menlove	Things will straighten out —Boyd K. Packer	May 2000	12e-f
	Accentuate the positive —G.B. Hinckley		13a
Wayne S. Peterson	Choosing one's , in concentration camps	Nov 2001	83e-f
	Jesus: Perfect example of emotional control		84e-f
H. Ross Workman	The evils of murmuring —entire talk		85b-86f
Coleen K. Menlove	Exclamation marks - 14 in one verse	Nov 2002	13b-d
Thomas S. Monson	President Hinckley is the model of optimism		62b-d
Keith B. McMullin	President Hinckley's optimism	May 2004	33b
Richard G. Scott	Good or evil - You see what you look for		100d-e
James E. Faust	He is optimistic about future	Nov 2004	55c-e
Joseph B. Wirthlin	An invincible summer lies within me	May 2006	101d-102b
Jeffrey R. Holland	A commandment to "be of good cheer"	May 2007	18a-b
	Grumbling that everything is too yellow		18b
	Hit me again. I can still hear you.		18b
	Whining makes it worse		18c
Henry B. Eyring	"I never had a poor companion" —story	Nov 2008	58f-59a
Thomas S. Monson	The elder who couldn't learn Spanish —story		60d-e

Attitude

Attitude, cont'd
Related Topics: —

Steven E. Snow	The trials of a pioneer and his , —story	May 2009	82e-83f
Thomas S. Monson	Troubled times, but good , will pull us through		89b-d
Boyd K. Packer	We have very positive feelings about future	May 2010	6f
James B. Martino	"What a pitcher!" —story		101a-b
	Trials become blessings if we don't murmur		102b-c

Authority
Related Topics: Priesthood

LeGrand Richards	Others take , from reading their Bibles	Dec 1971	84f
Bruce R. McConkie	No saving religion without ,	Jan 1973	37e
Harold B. Lee	Test , to detect imposters		105c
Gordon B. Hinckley	Endures as long as the jurisdiction of the agency	May 1974	23e
Boyd K. Packer	No , unless sustained and set apart. Beware of "secret" ,	May 1985	33b-35f
Dallin H. Oaks	Those without , use name of Lord in vain		81a
Boyd K. Packer	Keys of presidency don't pass like baton in relay	May 1995	7d
	Joseph's prophetic statement about keys and martyrdom		7d-e
	Pres. Kimball bore testimony that he held the keys —story		8a-d
Thomas S. Monson	How does Church differ from others? —McKay	May 2006	54f
	Definition of priesthood by two prophets		55b-d

Baptism
Related Topics: Work for Dead

Joseph Fielding Smith	Baptism does not grant us exaltation	June 1969	38f-39a
Joseph Fielding Smith	At , we become children of Christ by adoption	June 1970	26f
James A. Cullimore	Covenants made in , - D&C 20:37		88b
	Responsibilities accompanying membership —McKay		88d-f
Howard W. Hunter	Vicarious , for dead. Christ also did vicarious work	Dec 1971	71f
LeGrand Richards	Next step after repentance	Jan 1973	11e
Paul H. Dunn	Warning by Baptist minister —funny story		86a
O. Leslie Stone	We must do more than believe	July 1973	60b
Marion G. Romney	Renew baptismal covenant weekly thru sacrament	Nov 1975	73d-e
LeGrand Richards	Infant , isn't an act of the child himself	Nov 1977	22f-23a
Spencer W. Kimball	Jesus participated in , Father said "I am well pleased"	May 1978	6e
H. Burke Peterson	Girl received her hearing at , —story	Nov 1981	35e-36f
M. Russell Ballard	, is a sign to God —Joseph Smith	Nov 1984	16a-b
Derek A. Cuthbert	Minister wanted to know about , for dead —story	Nov 1985	25e-f
Boyd K. Packer	, of little children a false doctrine	Nov 1986	17a-e
Boyd K. Packer	Preacher chastised dead boy's parents for no , —story	Nov 1988	18b-d
Ted E. Brewerton	Granny's deafness healed at , —story	Nov 1991	12b-f
Marion D. Hanks	Free atonement must be received the way Jesus prescribed	May 1992	9f-10b
L. Tom Perry	My Three White Dresses —poem	Nov 1993	67f-68a
Hartman Rector, Jr.	Three things to do after , - Enduring to end	Nov 1994	26b-f
Russell M. Nelson	Necessity of , for the dead		84c-85a
	, for dead not done before Christ		85a
	, for dead in Nauvoo Temple in 1841		87a
Russell M. Nelson	Adopted as children of Christ at ,	May 1995	34b
Richard G. Scott	Baptism is not enough	May 1997	54c-d

Russell M. Nelson	, is important but only initiatory	May 1997	72a
Boyd K. Packer	, is a call to lifelong service	Nov 1997	6c
Dallin H. Oaks	Keys to , held by Aaronic Priesthood	Nov 1998	37f-38a
David E. Sorensen	Vicarious , adds family members to Church —story		65e-f
Carol B. Thomas	Four things happen at ,	May 1999	91f-92a
Boyd K. Packer	"What shall we do?" - Repent and be baptized	May 2000	8d-e
Robert D. Hales	In , we cease sustaining wickedness	Nov 2000	7d-e
James E. Faust	Paralyzed man healed at , —story	May 2001	54f-55d
	Entire talk excellent		54b-58f
Charles Didier	The other end of the bridge to eternal life	Nov 2001	10b-12b
Mary Ellen W. Smoot	At , we leave neutral ground and can't return		91e-f
Boyd K. Packer	Steps after , must not be too high —story	May 2002	9b-d
Bonnie D. Parkin	An icy , at midnight —story	Nov 2002	103d-e
David B. Haight	His boyhood , described —story	May 2003	43d-f
Henry B. Eyring	I'm clean. I felt fire go down my body.	May 2005	77b-d
David A. Bednar	, by water is but half a , —Joseph Smith	May 2006	29d
James E. Faust	He was baptized in the Tabernacle	May 2007	39c
Thomas S. Monson	He was baptized in the Tabernacle		41c-d
	Girl was baptized because of his talk —story		42b-e
L. Tom Perry	O. Cowdery's account of John the Baptist's visit		87b-f
Charles W. Dahlquist, II	A , amid a shower of stones —story		94f-95b
Claudio D. Zivic	Being baptized and confirmed is not enough	Nov 2007	98b-d
	, made convert the happiest man in world —story		99b-d
Douglas L. Callister	No hope for unbaptized infants —story		100e-f
	Baptized after earnest prayer —story		100f-101b
James E. Faust	Special feelings at , - Fresh start		122e
Carlos H. Amado	Teaching and serving - responsibilities accepted at ,	May 2008	35e
L. Tom Perry	The double mission of , - Promises made at ,		46a-d
D. Todd Christofferson	Meaning of "born again" and significance of ,		77a-78e
	Excellent explanation of purpose of ,		79b
D. Todd Christofferson	Our foundational covenant - Done individually	May 2009	20b-d
Boyd K. Packer	Sacrament is a renewing of covenant of ,		51a-b
David A. Bednar	Points toward temple		97e-98e
L. Tom Perry	Covenant of , includes sharing gospel	Nov 2009	75c

Ezra Taft Benson	Thoughts on evils of , —good	June 1969	43d-44b
A. Theodore Tuttle	Bearing children is highest of human duties		101d
Ezra Taft Benson	, jeopardizes exaltation	Dec 1970	46d
Spencer W. Kimball	Couple practiced , - no children - miserable old age —story		75c-d
Spencer W. Kimball	Proponents of , never thought of continence	June 1971	17b-c
Joseph Fielding Smith	We must not prevent child birth		50a-c
Harold B. Lee	Grievous sin in poor countries	Jan 1973	62e
Ezra Taft Benson	We do not fear phony population explosion	July 1973	40a
	Procreation first great commandment		41a

Birth Control, cont'd
Related Topics: Abortion

Ezra Taft Benson	Will bring wrath and judgment of God	July 1973	41c
Spencer W. Kimball	Surgery for , leaves him aghast	Nov 1974	9a
Hartman Rector, Jr.	Living Word of Wisdom would enable us to feed the world	Nov 1975	11e-12b
	How Singapore forces ,		12b-d
Spencer W. Kimball	Husband's consideration for wife's health is first duty.	Nov 1976	6f-7b
	How France encourages more children		7b-d
John H. Groberg	Don't be swayed by cries of those who don't know —story		44b-45b
Spencer W. Kimball	, an act of extreme selfishness	May 1979	6d
N. Eldon Tanner	God said "multiply" not just "replenish"	May 1980	16a
	Our glory: To bring to pass the mortality of children of God		17d-e
	Theodore Roosevelt's statement against ,		17e-f
Ezra Taft Benson	Children should not be postponed for an education	Nov 1987	49a-b
Dallin H. Oaks	Have as many children as you can care for	Nov 1993	75a-c
J. Ballard Washburn	Preventing birth is breaking covenants	May 1995	12b-c
	Few women asked about , 35 years ago		12c-d
Boyd K. Packer	First commandment: Multiply and replenish	May 2009	52d
Dallin H. Oaks	Leaders rejoice when couples are willing to have children		93f

Bishops
Related Topics: —

James A. Cullimore	Has right to inspiration when giving counsel	June 1969	68e
Victor L. Brown	The office of Presiding Bishop	May 1974	74b-e
	The office of Bishop		75a-b
	The relationship of , to quorum presidencies		75b-76b
	Bishops and their families		76b
H. Burke Peterson	Primary responsibility is to youth	Nov 1974	69f-70e
N. Eldon Tanner	Members' sins not dealt with will be borne by ,		78b-f
Franklin D. Richards	Results when youth challenged to be peacemakers in home		106c-f
Spencer W. Kimball	, must bear sins of others which are ignored	May 1975	78b-e
Victor L. Brown	Welfare the duty of , — Actions not called into question	Nov 1976	112d-e
Ezra Taft Benson	, has sole responsibility for helping needy	May 1977	82f
J. Richard Clarke	Independent child placements are often illegal		86d-e
L. Tom Perry	Bishop was friend to old man —story		90a-b
Marion G. Romney	An inactive , does not hold weekly welfare meetings	Nov 1977	80c
Boyd K. Packer	Use care doling out counsel. Revelation may be impeded	May 1978	91a-93f
Boyd K. Packer	Bishops keep confidences —story	May 1979	81b-d
Marion G. Romney	Role of , in welfare program —entire talk	Nov 1979	94b-96f
A. Theodore Tuttle	Responsible for broken covenants if people not taught	May 1980	41d
Vaughn J. Featherstone	, does not remember your confessed sins	Nov 1980	30d
	Confess a sin—lift it from your priesthood leader's soul		30f
	, does not remember your confessed sins		31c
Victor L. Brown	Bishop should call Aaronic Priesthood president	May 1982	35e
L. Tom Perry	Names are approved in temple	Nov 1982	29b-c
	The love that develops in a bishopric —stories		29c-e
	Scriptures relating to ,		29f-30a
	No position will bring greater blessings —G.A. Smith		30b-c

L. Tom Perry	Support of wife and children evaluated before , is called	Nov 1982	30d-f
	How members can help ,		31d-32b
C. Frederick Pingel	How to build young men —entire talk		35b-36f
Robert L. Backman	, must participate in youth activities. His duties with youth		38f-39e
Robert D. Hales	Men willing to enter javelin-catching contest	May 1985	28d
	The power of discernment , has		28e-29a
	Everything above the , is all talk		29b
Ezra Taft Benson	Foremost responsibility is youth	May 1986	46a-b
Ezra Taft Benson	Responsibilities toward young women	Nov 1986	85a
Joseph B. Wirthlin	His , knew his name when he was 5	Nov 1988	34f
Gordon B. Hinckley	Counsel to bishops		48b-51f
Dallin H. Oaks	Some , aren't interviewing women leaders	May 1992	36f-37a
James E. Faust	, will bear sins if not dealt with	Nov 1993	37c-e
	The humble occupations of his ,		38e
Dallin H. Oaks	"Bishop help!" a boy yelled —story	May 1997	22b-c
	Duties of a ,		22c-23a
	Bishops are not specialists		23a
	Voice of , is the voice of the Lord		23b-c
	How we can help the ,		23c-24b
James E. Faust	, will have endowments of wisdom, insight, and inspiration		42d
Gordon B. Hinckley	What a , must be and do	May 1999	52b-53f
Boyd K. Packer	, left horses standing in furrow —story		57b-d
	Duties of the ,		57d-f
	Not voluntary service but a calling		57f-58a
	, and revelation can't be separated —story		58b-d
	Never turn down counsel or calling from ,		58e
M. Russell Ballard	Unlimited flexibility - not bound by rules	Nov 2000	76c
Jeffrey R. Holland	Sacrifice of bishop and wife to answer phone —story	Nov 2002	37a-38d
Henry B. Eyring	Recently released bishop had no counsel to give —story		77a-b
Gordon B. Hinckley	Counsel to bishops —entire talk	Nov 2003	60b-62f
Joseph B. Wirthlin	Poorest bishop we've ever had —story	May 2005	27f
James E. Faust	Overlook their warts and spots	Nov 2005	54f-55a
	Good sport , allowed dunking —story		55b-d
Richard G. Hinckley	, asked inactives to speak in Church	May 2006	49a-d
David A. Bednar	Visiting inactives who have been offended	Nov 2006	89b-f
Dallin H. Oaks	Do not counsel for divorce	May 2007	71f
Thomas S. Monson	Called at age 22	Nov 2007	60a-e
Susan W. Tanner	Bishop called smoker to be Laurel advisor —story	May 2008	114f-115d
Richard G. Scott	Must be sensitive to needs of women	Nov 2008	46b-c
Henry B. Eyring	Can see the wounded and the wounds	May 2009	63f-65a
Henry B. Eyring	Bishop's policy: No lights out	Nov 2009	61a-d
Henry B. Eyring	His wife always there ahead of ,		123f

Bishops' Courts
Related Topics: Abortion

Robert L. Simpson	Excommunicated man returns —story	July 1972	48e
	Courts of love, not retribution		49a
	Excommunication can be first step back		49e
N. Eldon Tanner	Bishops to bear men's iniquities if action not taken	July 1973	94d
James A. Cullimore	Not taking action against offenders is very unkind	May 1974	30d
N. Eldon Tanner	Bishops who have never excommunicated anyone	Nov 1974	78b-f
	Sins bishops must deal with		78f-79a
Spencer W. Kimball	Bishops will bear penalties which are waived	May 1975	78b-e
N. Eldon Tanner	, not always necessary for old transgressions	Nov 1978	43a
Theodore M. Burton	How we should treat those disciplined in ,	May 1983	71d-f
Theodore M. Burton	How to treat excommunicated members and their families	Nov 1985	64e-66b
Gordon B. Hinckley	The exquisite pains excommunication brings	May 1986	48e

Body
Related Topics: —

Russell M. Nelson	Amazing abilities of ,	Dec 1968	87f
Paul H. Dunn	Reply of thin boy to fat ones —story	Dec 1970	38f
Hartman Rector, Jr.	Relation of spirit to , —good explanation		76a-c
Richard L. Evans	Must last a mortal lifetime - don't abuse it	June 1971	74a
Theodore M. Burton	Hell is having a body which can't be used	July 1972	78d
Boyd K. Packer	One of reasons for earth life	July 1973	51d
	Purpose of ,		51e
	Death a separation of , and spirit		51f
Ezra Taft Benson	Conditions of , can affect spirit - health and scriptures	Nov 1974	66e
Boyd K. Packer	Only 20% of the doctor's ailments were of the ,	Nov 1977	59c
M. Russell Ballard	As , becomes aged and slower - spirit does opposite	Nov 1978	66e-67a
Boyd K. Packer	Bodies grow weaker, spirits stronger with age	May 1983	66f-67a
James E. Faust	Caring for the handicapped —entire talk	Nov 1984	54b-60e
Russell M. Nelson	, must be treated with reverence	Nov 1985	30d-e
Russell M. Nelson	Repentance is best achieved while one still has a ,	Nov 1988	8a-b
Howard W. Hunter	The miracle: Restoration of sight or sight at all?	May 1989	16a-c
Boyd K. Packer	Whether well-formed or not, it is a testing		59c-d
Dean L. Larsen	, compared to wind-up clock	Nov 1989	61e-62a
Russell M. Nelson	President Kimball advised to care for , —story	Nov 1990	74d-e
Boyd K. Packer	Deformities are not the result of sin	May 1991	7f-8a
	Girl mimicking handicapped was stricken —story		8b-e
	Spirits are perfect and unimpaired		8f-9a
Boyd K. Packer	Pranks of nature cause abnormalities	Nov 1993	21e
F. Enzio Busche	Spirit and , engaged in fight for life or death		24d-f
H. David Burton	Boy with muscular atrophy —story	May 1994	67d-f
Howard W. Hunter	His , is old, but his spirit is young	Nov 1994	7d-e
Janette Hales Beckham	Accounts of disabled people —stories	Nov 1995	11d-13b
W. Craig Zwick	Accounts of disabled people —stories		13d-14f
Boyd K. Packer	Offer an unpolluted , to your companion	May 1996	19d-f
Gordon B. Hinckley	Sacred and a miracle - Obey Word of Wisdom		48a-c
Rulon G. Craven	, may overcome spirit —Brigham Young		76d

Russell M. Nelson	Self-healing properties of the ,	Nov 1996	33d-34a
	The blessing of aging		34a-b
Richard G. Scott	Progress more rapidly with , than in spirit world	May 1997	54f
Russell M. Nelson	The marvel that is our physical ,	Nov 1998	85b-86d
	Physical challenges may bring spiritual strength		86f-87a
Harold G. Hillam	Don't disfigure , - Avoid sloppy dress	May 2000	10e-f
Dallin H. Oaks	Mortal deficiencies are only temporary		15f
Neal A. Maxwell	Use the stretch in our tethers		72d
	Girl will have her hand in heaven —story		74f
Margaret D. Nadauld	Never deface or open temples to view	Nov 2000	14f-15b
Gordon B. Hinckley	No tattoos and only one pair of earrings		52c-e
Boyd K. Packer	Having a , is the great principle of happiness		72e-f
	Tattoos: You wouldn't put graffiti on a temple		73a
Gordon B. Hinckley	Church position on tattoos and earrings		99c-e
Claudio R. M. Costa	Life without a leg is still happy —story	Nov 2002	93c-94a
Gayle M. Clegg	Crack is where light comes through —story	May 2003	111d-112f
W. Douglas Shumway	Blind boy became top hurdler —story	May 2004	96b
Gordon B. Hinckley	No tattoos		114d
Susan W.Tanner	The sanctity of the , —good talk	Nov 2005	13b-15f
Elaine S. Dalton	All Satan's attacks are directed to ,	May 2008	117b
Neil L. Andersen	Handicapped child comforted another —story	Nov 2008	14e-f
Boyd K. Packer	He had polio at age 5 —story	May 2009	50b-c
	Don't fall into trap of envying others		50e-f
	No tattoos or body piercings for men		50f
	Beings with bodies have power over those who don't		51a
Claudio R. M. Costa	40-minute walk to church - Handicapped —story		57f-58b
Elaine S. Dalton	A woman should be queen of her own , —McKay		121b-d
Thomas S. Monson	Popular girl reached out to handicapped girl —story		124d-125b
Boyd K. Packer	Beings with bodies have power over those who don't	Nov 2009	45f-46a
Thomas S. Monson	Keep your temple clean and pure	May 2010	65f-66b

Bernard P. Brockbank	How to gain testimony of , —story	Dec 1968	61b-62f
Milton R. Hunter	Ways in which the , is unique	June 1969	87f-88b
Milton R. Hunter	Indian books which sustain , —Ixlilxochitl cited	June 1970	100b-101f
Marion G. Romney	The Keystone of our Religion —Joseph Smith	Dec 1970	51b
	Authenticity rests upon Joseph Smith and revelation		51b-d
	Bears within self evidence of own authenticity		54e
LeGrand Richards	If found by plowman , would have been great		70c
	Testimony of , by non member preacher —story		70c-d
Mark E. Petersen	Ancient Americans and visit of Great White God		118a-120e
Loren C. Dunn	Read , even to young children	Jan 1973	85f
Vaughn J. Featherstone	He gained testimony from passage in ,		95d
LeGrand Richards	Those who haven't read it criticize most	July 1973	78e
Harold B. Lee	The keystone of our religion —Joseph Smith	Jan 1974	126f

S. Dilworth Young	Prophecies of coming forth of ,	May 1974	59f-60b
Boyd K. Packer	Parable of the boy and the diamond he found		93e-94b
	Changes which have occurred in the ,		94c-95a
	Formulas for reading the ,		95a-b
Rex D. Pinegar	How , made a convert —story	Nov 1974	44f-45a
Ezra Taft Benson	, may solve any objection to Church - tells how	May 1975	64e-65a
	President Romney read , each year for 9 years —story		65f
Gordon B. Hinckley	The testament of the New World		93a
James A. Cullimore	One of greatest modern books. It has changed America	May 1976	85a-d
	How , affected B. Young and Parley P. Pratt		85f
	How , affected 2 families —2 stories		85f-86c
Mark E. Petersen	Description of gold plates	Nov 1977	12b-c
Gordon B. Hinckley	P.P. Pratt's first encounter with , —story	Nov 1979	7b-d
Marion G. Romney	Promises if we daily read , in our homes	May 1980	67e-f
Marvin J. Ashton	Man traded week of food for , —story	May 1981	23d-e
James E. Faust	, is the basis for testimony about other things	Nov 1983	9f-10a
	Noticeable difference in those who have read the ,		10b
	What the , is not		10b-c
	Test for understanding , is spiritual		10e
	Why the hostility to the , ?		11a
Mark E. Petersen	, and revelation —good discussion		29b-31f
Bruce R. McConkie	How 4 ministers reacted to invitation to read , —story		72b-73a
	Teachings in , transcend teachings in Bible		73f
J. Thomas Fyans	J.F. Smith read , twice by age 10 —story	May 1984	38d-e
Ezra Taft Benson	An infrequent reading of , is not enough	Nov 1984	6f-7a
	President Romney read , 30 minutes each day		7a
	Those who know , never will fall away		7b-c
	A great harvest of souls depends on using ,		7d
	More people will be saved by , than by Bible		7d-f
	, verifies and clarifies the Bible		8b
Gordon B. Hinckley	One of the 4 cornerstones of the Church		51a-d
	What it is. His testimony of it.		52c-d
Wm. Grant Bangerter	Don't read , to see what is wrong with it —story	May 1985	64e-65a
Ezra Taft Benson	The power, promises and warnings of ,	May 1986	5b-6d
Boyd K. Packer	A warning about the Isaiah barrier		61b-c
	What the , is —entire talk		59b-61f
Ezra Taft Benson	Promises if we daily read ,		78b-f
Ezra Taft Benson	One of the greatest gifts given to mankind	Nov 1986	4b
	7 things about , the Lord has borne witness of		4c
	Parts of the Restoration that preceded ,		4d-e
	We're under condemnation unless we use ,		4e-5a
	The Keystone of our religion		5a-6c
	Written for our day - not for the Nephites		6c-7a
	Great promises if we study the ,		7a-7f
Ezra Taft Benson	The power of , and how it is a keystone		80b-c

Book of Mormon

Russell M. Nelson	What , can do for you	Nov 1999	71d
L. Tom Perry	Convert read , because of uneducated author —story		76f-77a
James E. Faust	Testimony of David Whitmer to J.H. Moyle	Nov 2000	54b-d
L. Aldin Porter	Testimony of Jesus comes from reading ,	May 2001	30b-32b
Gordon B. Hinckley	P.P. Pratt's first reading of , —story		68c-d
John K. Carmack	Nahom discovered in Arabia		76f
	Chiasmus and multiple authors in ,		76f-77a
	Our pathway to Savior is through ,		77f
Boyd K. Packer	Obscure first printing to 109 million copies	Nov 2001	62b-d
	Destitute German family converted by , —story		62d-63e
	His first reading of ,		63f
	Student changed test and bore testimony —story		63f-64a
	You have everything crossed out —story		64c
	Can heal starving spirits		64c-d
Richard G. Scott	Romney's son cried while reading , —story		88c-d
Gordon B. Hinckley	Cannot understand why Christians don't accept ,	Nov 2002	81a
Anne C. Pingree	Disabled man took 7 years to read , —story		109d-f
Gordon B. Hinckley	One of 20 most influential books	Nov 2004	6a-b
H. Bryan Richards	Experiences with and testimony of ,		95b-97f
Gordon B. Hinckley	87 languages in 1995 - 106 today	May 2005	5d
Boyd K. Packer	Translation took 65 days		6f
	Understanding insights in , came later		7c-e
	Read , when weak, depressed or afraid		8b-c
	Purpose of , and things learned therein		8f-9d
	Entire talk		6d-9f
Gordon B. Hinckley	51 million copies in last 10 years		81b-82b
L. Tom Perry	President Hinckley's challenge to read ,	Nov 2005	6d-f
	Written for future generations		6f-7a
	Describes today's conditions		7a-d
	Written for us today —E.T. Benson		7d-f
	Not a history book		7f-8a
	Why were stories and events included?		8a-b
	More valuable than property		8e-f
	Whole Christian world should welcome it		9d-f
James E. Faust	One of 7 "blockbuster" doctrines		22a
C. Scott Grow	Mexican waited 12 years —story		34b-f
Henry B. Eyring	President Hinckley's promise if reading ,		38f-39b
Boyd K. Packer	106 languages with 49 under way		72e
Gordon B. Hinckley	Hated , until he read from it —story	May 2006	59b-60d
Vicki F. Matsumori	Boyd K. Packer's first attempts to read ,	May 2007	76e
M. Russell Ballard	Companionship of Bible and , —good		82b-c
L. Tom Perry	Translated in 60 working days		86d-87b
Gary J. Coleman	One of 3 essential restored truths		93b-94a
Russell M. Nelson	Complements - not competes with - Bible	Nov 2007	43e
	Mentions resurrection more than Bible does		44d & 46a

Book of Mormon

Russell M. Nelson	Mentions atonement more than Bible does	Nov 2007	44f & 46b
	Changes 234 of 433 Isaiah verses		46a
	Entire talk		43b-46b
Christoffel Golden Jr.	Reactivates man inactive 45 years —story		78d-80b
Gordon B. Hinckley	A second witness declares divinity of Christ		84b-d
	Only book which carries promise…		84d
	Every attempt to explain origin fails but one		84f-85b
	133 million copies - 105 languages - etc.		85d-f
Craig C. Christensen	, authenticates mission of Joseph Smith	May 2008	107c-e
	Five important aspects of ,		105d-107f
Silvia H. Allred	A daily race home to read , —story	Nov 2008	10e-11d
Marcos A. Aidukaitis	"Because my father read the ," —story		15b-f
	A promise without reservation —Hinckley		15f-16c
	If , is true, so are many other things		16c-d
	Would you refuse to open a letter from your father?		16d-f
Walter F. Gonzalez	Using , makes more powerful priesthood holders	Nov 2009	50d-51a
	No literary work compares - Shepherded by God		51b
	He became member of Church because of ,		51b-e
	Application of , requires ordinances and covenants		51e
	Making , best-read and best-applied book		51f-52f
Jeffrey R. Holland	Joseph's and Hyrum's dying testimony of ,		88f-89d
	Withstood all attacks for 179 years		89d-f
	No wicked man could have written it		89f
	A barrier to anyone wishing to apostatize		89f-90c
	His powerful testimony of ,		90c-f
	Amazing talk on , —entire talk		88b-90f
David A. Bednar	Value of reading , with children	May 2010	41d-42a
	Promise if , read with children		43f
David L. Beck	Book made possible by two young men		54c-e

Boyd K. Packer	Should be neither sought nor declined —Clark	Dec 1968	80d
Thomas S. Monson	Pray for powers to equal tasks		83f
Spencer W. Kimball	A , refused was always regretted —story	Dec 1970	74f-75a
Thomas S. Monson	His unexpected , to stake presidency —story		99b-d
Harold B. Lee	All hell can't push us over if we have a responsibility	Dec 1971	113b
	Everyone should have a ,		113b
Gordon B. Hinckley	Assigned to talk to belligerent editor —story		124e-125b
N. Eldon Tanner	Let inactives decide if they want , - give opportunity	July 1972	34d
Loren C. Dunn	Meaning of the action of sustaining		43a
	Prophet accountable to Lord, Apostles to prophet, etc.		43c
	Person has right to know his , is of God		44a
H. Burke Peterson	Relates his , as General Authority		47a
Joseph Fielding Smith	Lord called Brethren then him		87a
Harold B. Lee	Lord looks around for most qualified man		103f

Callings, cont'd
Related Topics: —

Spencer W. Kimball	It's reassuring that Lee was called and not elected	Jan 1973	33d
	No errors, no ambitions allowed		33e
	No , if office sought		35f
James E. Faust	Called of Lord because no one else would have		81e
Gordon B. Hinckley	No unimportant , in Church		92f
N. Eldon Tanner	Of President of Church		101b
	Contrast with national elections		101c
	Leaders' , came because of diligence		103b
Thomas S. Monson	Divine approval of , —story		121c
Harold B. Lee	Of new Brethren came by prophecy		133a
Thomas S. Monson	Accept unimportant , —neat poem	July 1973	44a
Gordon B. Hinckley	Become opportunities if testimony strong		49e
Marion G. Romney	Callings should not be sought —story		90b
	Salvation does not depend upon height of ,		90c
Harold B. Lee	Lord makes one equal to the tasks		123f
Hartman Rector, Jr.	You get the Spirit of the calling only when you act	Jan 1974	107b
John H. Groberg	Much to be felt, but little to be said - Reaction to calling	May 1976	39a
Neal A. Maxwell	Willingness to serve —well stated	Nov 1976	12d
Robert L. Simpson	Don't seek or turn down , —story		100f-101a
	The Lord's Support System —entire talk		100b-101f
J. Richard Clarke	Families of Church leaders live in glass houses		109d-e
N. Eldon Tanner	What happens when there is a dissenting vote	May 1978	19a
Marvin J. Ashton	Forlornness about , turned to great joy —story	Nov 1978	50d-e
Thomas S. Monson	Calling to stake president —humorous anecdote	May 1979	35b-c
N. Eldon Tanner	Inspiration at , of a stake president —story	Nov 1979	45a
Marvin J. Ashton	Don't be offended by someone learning his job		63d
	The , we hoped never to get becomes ours		63d
Adney Y. Komatsu	New stake president made employment sacrifice —story		69a-c
Wm .Grant Bangerter	2 men resisted , but Spirit changed their minds —story	May 1980	46c-f
James E. Faust	Ancient columns still standing have weight on top	Nov 1980	35a
	Leaders honored because of position, not selves —story		36a
G. Homer Durham	Hole in the Rock episode —Church history story	May 1982	67b-68a
Thomas S. Monson	Kimball called a man without hands as patriarch —story	Nov 1983	20f-21b
Ezra Taft Benson	Accept and serve in , - Spirituality will increase	May 1984	7e
Marvin J. Ashton	New bishop had been married 3 weeks —story		9b-c
Victor L. Brown	Account of his , —humorous	May 1985	14d
Glenn L. Pace	His , as a General Authority		78b-79f
Boyd K. Packer	Men must be called by prophecy	Nov 1985	80d-e
Gordon B. Hinckley	How mission presidents respond to their calls		83f-84f
Thomas S. Monson	Whom God calls, God qualifies	May 1987	44f
Lynn A. Sorenson	Called not for what we are but for what we may become	Nov 1987	77d-e
Thomas S. Monson	When we are on the Lord's errand we're entitled to help	May 1988	41f
	Whom the Lord calls, the Lord qualifies		43e
Joseph B. Wirthlin	Greater tasks depend on how well you do the lesser ones	Nov 1988	35a
Monte J. Brough	Account of his , as a General Authority —story		40b-c

Callings

Albert Choules, Jr.	Circumstances preceding his , —story	Nov 1988	41b-e
Gordon B. Hinckley	Definition of magnify	May 1989	46f
	As he magnified , he was magnified —story of O. Cowdery		47d-48d
Russell M. Nelson	Sustaining makes known who has authority	Nov 1989	20b
Jeffrey R. Holland	Meaning of sustaining		25c
Marlin K. Jensen	He made his leaders look good - sustaining		28c
Gordon B. Hinckley	Each person's , helps create a perfect tapestry		52f-53c
	Weave beautifully your small thread in the tapestry		54d-f
Dallin H. Oaks	We serve because we're under covenant		65d-f
Jayne B. Malan	The Summer of the Lambs —story		78b-79f
Neal A. Maxwell	Confidence in leaders who keep confidences - sustaining		82f
Julio E. Davila	His first calling: Pictures Supervisor	Nov 1991	23f-24a
Russell M. Nelson	Help comes to ordinary souls given extraordinary callings		59f
Chieko N. Okazaki	We don't need , to be kind or thoughtful		89d
Thomas S. Monson	Responsible for those you might have saved —Taylor	May 1992	48d-e
Russell M. Nelson	Accountability of the one extending ,	May 1993	39f
Jacob de Jager	His first calling - In charge of hymn books	Nov 1993	32b
Virginia H. Pearce	, involve us in others' lives as we forget selves —story		80e-f
Richard P. Lindsay	Lambs died because of neglect —story	May 1994	46e-47b
Thomas S. Monson	Responsible for those you might have saved —Taylor		51a
	All stake members were blessed by president —story		52c-d
Gordon B. Hinckley	The principle of sustaining		53d-f
Robert D. Hales	New , are like acorns dropping - New beginnings		78d-f
David B. Haight	3 purposes for holding solemn assemblies	Nov 1994	14d-15c
James E. Faust	He neglected his duty and lost his lamb —story	May 1995	46a-d
Gordon B. Hinckley	The meaning of sustaining		51b-d
	Announcement of , of area authorities		51e-52c
	Our , is as important as his		71a-b
Henry B. Eyring	Your , is as important as President Hinckley's	Nov 1995	37d-38a
Thomas S. Monson	Whom the Lord calls, the Lord qualifies		50b
David B. Haight	His , as a general authority —story	May 1996	22f-23c
Thomas S. Monson	Responsible for those you might have saved —Taylor		43e
	Whom the Lord calls, the Lord qualifies		44b
David B. Haight	Enthusiasm - Throwing duds or hand grenades	Nov 1996	15d
Joseph B. Wirthlin	Never released from , to care for own soul	May 1997	16d
Dallin H. Oaks	Bishops call, but should not have to beg or push		23d
Monte J. Brough	Called by revelation, not aspiration		27f
	Afflictions accompany , for which we are chosen —story		27b-28f
Jeffrey R. Holland	Be sensitive toward young mothers		35e-f
Thomas S. Monson	New converts should have a ,		45a-b
Boyd K. Packer	How to issue ,	Nov 1997	7a-f
	Neither sought nor declined		7a-f
	President Kimball issued , right the second time —story		7f-8c
	Belle S. Spafford could not get released from , —story		8c-e
Mary Ellen Smoot	Pioneers did not go inactive while crossing plains		14a

Callings, cont'd

Richard D. Allred	Purpose of office of Patriarch	Nov 1997	27e-f
Joseph B. Wirthlin	Respond as if Lord called you - He did		33b
Thomas S. Monson	The first , of a man or woman is parenthood		96a-b
	Magnified , as ward magazine representative —story		96c-97b
Boyd K. Packer	Parenthood is most important , —important talk	Nov 1998	22b-24f
Boyd K. Packer	Not voluntary service but callings	May 1999	57f-58a
	Never turn down a , from your bishop		58e
Joseph B. Wirthlin	We grow into our ,	Nov 1999	41d-f
Thomas S. Monson	What it means to magnify a ,		51b-c
Gordon B. Hinckley	His first experience , a stake president —story	May 2000	49e-50e
	The office of stake president		50e-51f
Henry B. Eyring	2 million new , last year		66c-d
	, of a young, inexperienced stake president —story		66f-67c
Jeffrey R. Holland	Would a piece of granite from building be missed		85f-86a
Jeffrey R. Holland	A tragedy if unprepared when , comes	Nov 2000	40a
Mary Ellen Smoot	Each , is an opportunity to do good		90a
	Band instruments differ in size, shape, sound		90b-c
Henry B. Eyring	If we don't perform our , ...	May 2001	39f-40a
Thomas S. Monson	Responsible for those you might have saved —story		48d-f
Joseph B. Wirthlin	Fasting will bring spirit of ,		73f
Keith K. Hilbig	One neither seeks nor declines , —Clark	Nov 2001	46b
Joseph B. Wirthlin	Leaving our nets to follow Jesus	May 2002	15b-17f
Thomas S. Monson	New patriarch had no hands —story		51b-f
Jeffrey R. Holland	Sacrifices in , of early missionaries	Nov 2002	36d-37a
	Sacrifice of bishop and wife to answer phone —story		37a-38d
	His thanks for all who sacrifice in ,		38d-f
James E. Faust	"Where Shall I Work Today" —poem		52c
Henry B. Eyring	God calls, guides and magnifies you in ,		75d-78b
Dallin H. Oaks	General Authority became bishop's counselor	Nov 2003	38f-39a
Gordon B. Hinckley	Don't nag yourself with a sense of failure —story		113e-114b
Thomas S. Monson	Tend this tiny spot —poem	May 2004	20e
	Magazine representative saved men —story		22d-23d
Jeffrey R. Holland	Stake president had feet and faith but no car		30f-31a
Kathleen H. Hughes	Magnify , by doing service that pertains to it —Monson	Nov 2004	109f-110d
Thomas S. Monson	How to magnify a ,	May 2005	54f
Henry B. Eyring	A , to serve is a , to come to love the Lord	May 2006	16f-17a
M. Russell Ballard	Some become too unbalanced and energetic in ,	Nov 2006	18b-d
	Focus on people and principles - not programs		18d-f
	Be innovative but don't complicate ,		18f-19a
	Guilt is not a proper motivational technique		19c-e
	You're never done - so pace yourself		19f
Joseph B. Wirthlin	No time to pray about it —story		28b-d
Stanley G. Ellis	Parable of talents related to his ,		52d-f
Thomas S. Monson	Magnify , by doing service which pertains to it		58d-e
Don R. Clarke	Helped blind man - no , necessary —story		97b-98b

Callings

Thomas S. Monson	Sustained without being called —story	May 2007	57d-f
Susan W. Tanner	A testimony of her, came		109a-b
Boyd K. Packer	Neither seek nor decline, —J. Reuben Clark	Nov 2007	6f
	Brigham Young no better than my grandpa —story		7b-f
	His calling to be a General Authority —story		7f-8d
Henry B. Eyring	Fear as a deacon and speaking to ministers —story		55d-57a
Quentin L. Cook	Testimony: Most important qualification		70b-c
Robert D. Hales	Experiences calling 4 stake presidents —story		87a-88b
Steven E. Snow	Don't be too busy in, for quiet service		103d
Dallin H. Oaks	Magnify does not mean embellish - Simplify		106d-107a
Dieter F. Uchtdorf	Account of his, to First Presidency	May 2008	57d-f
Dieter F. Uchtdorf	Neither seek nor decline,		68d-e
D. Todd Christofferson	Previous, a pleasant experience in comparison		76b
Susan W. Tanner	Called as Laurel advisor while smoking —story		114f-115d
Dieter F. Uchtdorf	Should not seek to either lead or hide	Nov 2008	54a-d
	Walked 22 miles on artificial leg to fulfill, —story		55d-56a
	No, is beneath us. Each is an opportunity		56b
	Response to those who think they should receive,		56b-c
	President Monson could do your, but shouldn't		56d-e
Henry B. Eyring	When you feel overwhelmed in your, …		57b-f
Thomas S. Monson	Responsible for those we might have saved		62e
Barbara Thompson	Angels cannot be restrained as associates —Smith		116c
Russell M. Nelson	No, is intended for personal benefits	Nov 2009	83a-b
Henry B. Eyring	A pattern of rescue and rescuers —story	May 2010	23d-24b
Ronald A. Rasband	Apostles' process calling+B71 missionaries —story		52a-53b
Richard G. Scott	Never released as parents		77d-79a
Quentin L. Cook	Leader rescued children from tsunami —story		85f-86c

Celestial Kingdom
Related Topics: Eternal Life, Exaltation, Heaven, Salvation

Joseph Fielding Smith	The whole law must be kept to enter,	June 1969	38d
Bernard P. Brockbank	Takes more than purity to enter,	Jan 1973	44f
Elray L. Christiansen	The kingdom of families	May 1974	25f
Bruce R. McConkie	All upright members won't go to,	Nov 1974	34b
Sterling W. Sill	Why, is indescribable	Nov 1976	47b-48b
Marion G. Romney	, won't be obtained by works of someone else		124e-125a
Gordon B. Hinckley	3 boys earned place in, by one noble act —story	Nov 1981	42d-f
Mark E. Petersen	Earth will be, - Father will visit it from time to time	May 1983	63f-64a
Russell M. Nelson	Highest degree only available through marriage	May 1993	40b
Quentin L. Cook	Goals for, get sidetracked by telestial distractions	Nov 1996	29a
Richard G. Scott	False statements at funerals about,	May 2001	9a
Dieter F. Uchtdorf	Will be filled with the repentant	May 2008	60b-c

Character
Related Topics: Virtue

Paul H. Dunn	The cult of the common man is developing	Dec 1968	67f
Marion D. Hanks	The evils of an ill temper		97a-c

Character, cont'd

Hugh B. Brown	All things work for you if you're building ,	June 1969	99f
David O. McKay	Foundation of , is honesty	Dec 1969	31f
Hugh B. Brown	Building , life's problem		32e
Paul H. Dunn	King and Wedding Guest parable —explanation	June 1971	103f-104e
Delbert L. Stapley	Thoughts—actions—habits—character	Nov 1974	20b-c
	Great moments of test and trial is not when , is built		20d-e
	Not easy to obtain , - A reward from honest toil		21f-22a
	When a man boasts of his bad habits…		20f
N. Eldon Tanner	, determined by extent of our self mastery	May 1975	75c
Spencer W. Kimball	Thoughts of boyhood determine , of man		80d-e
	One's life and thoughts register in face —story		80e-81b
O. Leslie Stone	Reputation more valuable than money —story	Nov 1975	40f-41a
	What have you done with my name? —story		41b-f
Marvin J. Ashton	Showing , through personal conduct —entire talk	Nov 1976	84b-86b
N. Eldon Tanner	What is integrity?	May 1977	14c-f
	Integrity makes other virtues useless		16a
David B. Haight	To surrender what you believe is worse than dying	Nov 1977	58e-f
Robert E. Wells	In God we Trust - can God trust us?	Nov 1978	24b
Boyd K. Packer	Well-kept home got father the loan —story	May 1982	86c-e
Royden G. Derrick	Definition of integrity	Nov 1984	62f-63a
J. Richard Clarke	Serviceman couldn't be forced into sin —story	May 1985	75a-b
	Student set example for others —story		75d-f
Dean L. Larson	Questions we should ask ourselves about integrity	Nov 1985	68d-e
Joseph B. Wirthlin	Being without guile - integrity	May 1988	80b-83b
Richard G. Scott	, is woven from threads of hundreds of correct decisions	May 1989	36f-37a
Joseph B. Wirthlin	George Washington elected for , and integrity	May 1990	32a
Neal A. Maxwell	Selfishness —entire talk	Nov 1990	14b-16f
George I. Cannon	"No wonder you're honest - you're Mormon" —story	Nov 1991	13e-f
Julio E. Davila	Trials develop ,		24d-e
Neal A. Maxwell	Goodness is the key	May 1995	66d-f
Russell M. Nelson	, is elevated by lowering heads in prayer	May 1996	16a
Neal A. Maxwell	We must have both covenants and ,	Nov 1997	24a-b
James E. Faust	Members should be preferred employees	May 1998	43f-44a
	Abraham's integrity		44b-c
Robert S. Wood	Light speeches and light-mindedness obscure light	Nov 1999	83b-84f
Carol B. Thomas	Integrity —entire talk	May 2000	91a-92f
James E. Faust	What lies within us matters most —Emerson		97c-d
Wayne S. Peterson	Sow , and reap destiny —quote	Nov 2001	84b
F. Melvin Hammond	, of sons determined by how Dad treats Mom	Nov 2002	98d-99a
Richard G. Scott	Not developed in moments of great challenge	May 2003	77b-f
James E. Faust	Virtue is the noblest ornament of man		108e
D. Todd Christofferson	Integrity even if you lose your home	Nov 2006	47d-48a
Richard G. Scott	The relationship between faith and ,	Nov 2007	92c-e

Character

James J. Hamula	Youth counseled to be sober - Definition	Nov 2008	51d-f
H. David Burton	Integrity: The light of a disciplined conscience	Nov 2009	78a-b
Dieter F. Uchtdorf	Trials build ,	May 2010	58f

Charity
Related Topics: Kindness, Love

Marion G. Romney	Eternal life dependent on ,	Jan 1973	98c
N. Eldon Tanner	Laboring for strangers is the real test of ,	May 1977	47c-e
Gordon B. Hinckley	Help sent to handcart company —story	Nov 1981	97b-e
Robert L. Backman	Ostracized girl accepted by peers —story	Nov 1985	12d-f
W. Eugene Hansen	The opposite of selfishness	Nov 1989	24a
Marvin J. Ashton	Greatest examples of ,	May 1992	18f-19a
	Women's response to outburst of anger —story		20c-d
Howard W. Hunter	Greatest of all divine attributes		61e-f
	Thief was baptized —story		62b-f
C. Max Caldwell	We have , for those we serve	Nov 1992	30d-e
	The word , is not in the Old Testament		30e-f
Hartman Rector, Jr.	Means being nice and serving	Nov 1994	26b-f
Neal A. Maxwell	Faith, hope and , - A triad tied to Christ		35c-d
Thomas S. Monson	How much should a man give?		43f
Elaine L. Jack	A gift that multiplies as it is used	Nov 1996	92e
	"To give of oneself is a holy gift" —Kimball		92f
Dallin H. Oaks	Not an act but a state of being	Nov 2000	34a-b
Gene R. Cook	There is a difference between love and ,	May 2002	82d
	Charity is greater than love		83d-e
	Entire talk		82b-83f
Bonnie D. Parkin	Elder Ashton's definitions of ,	Nov 2003	105f
	Charitable attitude disappears when cumbered		106b
Don R. Clarke	Greatest principle in existence —J.F. Smith	Nov 2006	98d
Joseph B. Wirthlin	Joseph Smith's treatment of visiting boy —story	Nov 2007	29b-d
	The central object of our existence		30d
	Entire talk		28b-31b
Henry B. Eyring	President of U.S. called Hinckley to thank him for ,	May 2008	63d-f
Dieter F. Uchtdorf	How faith, hope and , complement each other	Nov 2008	23b-24a
Dallin H. Oaks	, will always secure heaven for us —Mother Teresa	May 2009	95f
Henry B. Eyring	Relief Society motto will serve forever	Nov 2009	121e
	His wife always there ahead of bishop		123f

Chastity
Related Topics: Adultery, Homosexuality, Immorality, Morality, Pornography, Purity, Sex, Virtue

David O. McKay	Ringing words on ,	June 1969	2f-3d
	No double standard in Church		5e
	Chaste girl - The pride of a young elder's heart.		28e-29a
	Men have no right to look at other women		28e-29a
Alvin R. Dyer	The judge advocated trial marriages		41a-b
Mark E. Petersen	Humanity will rise or fall because of ,		75b-d
	Must be willing to even die a social death to protect ,		79c

David O. McKay	Source of harmony in home	Dec 1969	30f
Loren C. Dunn	Suppression is not wrong —McKay		44b
	Though forgiven of sin, consequences may yet follow		44d-44f
Spencer W. Kimball	Is , outmoded - responses to questions	June 1971	17a
	Civilization based upon ,		19b
Harold B. Lee	Not taught by teaching about sex	July 1972	32e
Harold B. Lee	A serviceman nearly lost his , —story		102a
	How fathers are to teach chastity to boys		102f
Boyd K. Packer	Sex and chastity —excellent discussion —rest of talk		111d
Gordon B. Hinckley	Can never be restored —story	Jan 1973	92b
Marion D. Hanks	Some surrender because they're alone —story		128d
Hartman Rector, Jr	7 personal commandments to protect		131d
N. Eldon Tanner	How young men must treat women	July 1973	95a
Spencer W. Kimball	Civilization is based upon , —J.R. Clark	Nov 1974	8d
N. Eldon Tanner	, lost is gone forever	Nov 1976	82b
Ezra Taft Benson	President Kimball's denunciation of unchastity	Nov 1977	31a-c
David B. Haight	Emotion can override intellect		58b
Marion G. Romney	Better dead clean than alive unclean —story	May 1979	41e-42d
Paul H. Dunn	Do you want a penny now or a diamond later? —excellent	Nov 1981	72b-f
Rex D. Pinegar	Young priesthood holders must protect virtue	Nov 1985	41d-e
Gordon B. Hinckley	AIDS and how to combat it	May 1987	47e-48b
Boyd K. Packer	, is your key to happiness	May 1989	54e-f
Robert L. Backman	Contrasting feelings between , and immorality —story	Nov 1989	38b-e
	The foundation of manhood, home and progress		40b
M. Russell Ballard	The need for , among youth	Nov 1990	35d-38b
James E. Faust	Lose something sacred when , is abused	Nov 1995	47b
Russell M. Nelson	, is depicted as unhealthy and dehumanizing	May 1996	15a-b
James E. Faust	Youth's most precious possession	May 1998	95d
Richard G. Scott	Straight talk about sexual intimacies	Nov 1998	69a-f
Jeffrey R. Holland	Why be morally clean —entire talk great		75d-78b
M. Russell Ballard	, before marriage and fidelity ever after	May 1999	85f-86a
Richard G. Scott	Let no one touch sacred parts of body	Nov 2000	26f-27a
Gordon B. Hinckley	Nothing as magnificent as virtue	May 2001	95a-d
James E. Faust	A sacred passport to self-respect and happiness	May 2003	109a-b
Boyd K. Packer	Standards of , will not change	Nov 2003	26b
Susan W. Tanner	The sanctity of the body —good talk	Nov 2005	13b-15f
Elaine S. Dalton	Unfurling standard for virtue - Definition	Nov 2008	78f-79a
	President Monson's statement on virtue		79a-b
	Desensitized by degrees —good		79b-f
	Great list of scriptures promoting virtue		80a-c
Elaine S. Dalton	The core of a virtuous life	May 2009	120f-121a
Thomas S. Monson	A plea for ,		125b-126a

Gordon B. Hinckley	The advantages children should be given	Dec 1968	69b-d
Russell M. Nelson	Furniture marred by , a blessing		86d-f
Marion D. Hanks	What discipline to give ,		96e
David O. McKay	Training , is mainly responsibility of home	June 1969	4b-c
	Needs of ,		4d-e
Loren C. Dunn	Simple step for , to love God if parents godlike		52e
Loren C. Dunn	, deserve to be taught obedience —McKay		52e
Delbert L. Stapley	, can only be taught by example		70e-72a
Richard L. Evans	18-36 months is most curious age		80e
	Parents who are bad examples will have , who are worse		80e-f
	Don't try to hide your heart from ,		82a-c
	, —good quotes		82e-f
	, —poem		82f-83c
A. Theodore Tuttle	Bearing , is highest of human duties		101d
Robert L. Simpson	Song of a child brought back inactive father —story	Dec 1969	40f
Franklin D. Richards	Surest way to make it hard for , is to make things easy		103b-c
A. Theodore Tuttle	Ages 1-5 the most important. Mother must be there.		107e
Marvin J. Ashton	, learn love as they experience it	June 1970	42c
A. Theodore Tuttle	Points of advice in raising ,		81b-c
Ezra Taft Benson	Take nothing for granted about your children	Dec 1970	46d-e
Delbert L. Stapley	Parents love , more than , love parents		65f
Spencer W. Kimball	Sad fate in old age of couple who wanted no , —story		75c-d
Gordon B. Hinckley	Young trees are easily trained and bent —story		97b-98e
Boyd K. Packer	Changing wayward , begins in parents		106e-f
Marvin J. Ashton	We have not failed until we quit trying	June 1971	31f-32a
Harold B. Lee	It would be worth it if it were my boy —story		61b-d
Marion D. Hanks	The love of a boy for his brother —story		91d-f
James A. Cullimore	Three fundamental needs of ,		94c
Paul H. Dunn	How does it feel to have all my sins…		102c-d
Spencer W. Kimball	Kimball's observations of a family with good , —story	Dec 1971	37a-38b
	Childless Indian couple took 18 orphans —story		38c-e
Loren C. Dunn	Son had to ask family prayer when he came in —story		48c-49a
	Grown before you know it —poem		49b-e
LeGrand Richards	Account of the death of 2 of his , —story		84a-c
Marvin J. Ashton	Girl in detention home wanted to be wanted —story		101b-c
	Righteous , greatest joy - 3 John 4		101f
John H. Vandenberg	The Child's Appeal —poem		116d-e
S. Dilworth Young	Helps in raising sons —excellent, entire talk	July 1972	76a
David B. Haight	A sacred trust —good thought		108b
	Gifts from God —James E. Talmage		108e
Boyd K. Packer	, - The only way we love someone more than selves		113d
Spencer W. Kimball	Train and discipline each other	July 1973	15b
	Fewer divorces in families with ,		15e
	Faith and character begin in infancy		16e
	If taught well , can't go wrong		16f

Spencer W. Kimball	Which , to give away —good poem	July 1973	17e
Ezra Taft Benson	Encourage the having of ,		41a
Boyd K. Packer	Address directed to children —excellent		51a-54e
Marion D. Hanks	Mother of 14 had no favorites		112f
N. Eldon Tanner	Nation's problems would vanish with one good generation	Jan 1974	10a
Boyd K. Packer	Don't grab: trade , for things they shouldn't have		27a
LeGrand Richards	Cows forget calves but mothers never forget , —story		57d
	Huge ransoms are paid to keep , in mortality		59e
A. Theodore Tuttle	Son had to be in before alarm clock rang		68a
H. Burke Peterson	Not a gift but a precious loan	May 1974	32f
N. Eldon Tanner	What mother does not envision her infant as president?		84e-f
L. Tom Perry	Teach them the names of the General Authorities		98b-c
Vaughn J. Featherstone	Mother cares for , but grown , won't care for mother	Nov 1974	29e
	, must care for aged parents as they cared for babies		30d-e
LeGrand Richards	Wife saw an angel bring her child		52e
Marion D. Hanks	6-yr-old helped 3-yr-old when prayer faltered —story	May 1975	14a-b
Spencer W. Kimball	Give , assignments in the home and yard	May 1976	5b
Vaughn J. Featherstone	Mike will come back won't he? —story	Nov 1976	104c-e
	Every bird came back —story		105d-f
H. Burke Peterson	A success pattern for raising healthy ,	May 1977	68d
Thomas S. Monson	Wise mother taught child selflessness —story		72d-73b
Gordon B. Hinckley	In Feb. you can determine Sept.'s fruit —pruning	Nov 1978	18b-d
	When God wants a great work done, he has a baby born		18d
	Harsh society is outgrowth of harshness on children		18e
	Treat them with mildness —Brigham Young		19a-c
J. Richard Clarke	2 sons: One wanted father to come, one didn't	Nov 1981	81f-82b
Gordon B. Hinckley	Provide , with good reading material	May 1982	42a-d
Boyd K. Packer	Boys get tools for Christmas - girls learn womanly skills		86e-f
H. Burke Peterson	Treat , like adults but don't expect him to act like one	Nov 1982	44a
Gordon B. Hinckley	Most important thing fathers can do for , —McKay		77a
Carlos E. Asay	Interviewing , - wet or dry? —story	Nov 1983	14b-c
	Interview between Helaman and Alma		14d-15a
	3 question interview laid parents' fears to rest —story		15a-c
Howard W. Hunter	If , don't become overachievers we think we've failed		65a
	Some , would challenge any set of parents		65b
A. Theodore Tuttle	Things done in past to protect , are no longer sufficient	May 1984	23f
Angel Abrea	Parental words and example give distorted impressions		72b-e
James E. Faust	Caring for the handicapped —entire talk	Nov 1984	54b-60e
Dallin H. Oaks	I'm raising boys, not cows —story	Nov 1985	62a
Boyd K. Packer	Child got in bed with house guest - trust —story	Nov 1986	16b-c
	4 sins causing , to suffer		16f-17a
	Baptism of little , a false doctrine		17a-f
	Abuse of , yields to repentance		18e-f
Ezra Taft Benson	Don't postpone , for an education	Nov 1987	49a-b
Russell M. Nelson	Babies don't keep —poem		88a

Children

Ezra Taft Benson	How to reclaim lost ,	May 1988	5d-f
Ezra Taft Benson	If you limit , you will feel the loss		52d
Richard G. Scott	To Help a Loved One in Need		60b-61f
Dwan J. Young	Teach , to listen to the right voices		78e-f
	What would become of girl since family not sealed		79a
L. Tom Perry	How to train up a child to be a better person —good	Nov 1988	73b-75f
Ezra Taft Benson	To the , of the Church —entire talk	May 1989	81d-83f
Neal A. Maxwell	Twigs are bent, not snapped, into shape	May 1990	34e
Kenneth Johnson	First so good, we weren't blessed with more		42e
Thomas S. Monson	Benson: , aren't to be called "kids"		53e
	Description of small , —poem		53e-f
	A child and the Christus statue —story		54e-f
James E. Faust	Discipline , or public will do so	Nov 1990	34a-b
	A possible jungle of weeds —L. Burbank		34d
	Some could tax Solomon's wisdom and Job's patience		34d-e
	Affluent , are a special challenge		34e
	Will follow parental example if taught		34e-f
Russell M. Nelson	Parents don't own , —story	May 1991	22b-e
Thomas S. Monson	The Kingdom of God and , —poem	Nov 1991	68f
Thomas S. Monson	Capable of understanding deep concepts		87d-f
Boyd K. Packer	Wayward , will return	May 1992	68b-e
Janette C. Hales	Learn the names of ,		80f
Merrill J. Bateman	Handcart boy lost in storm —story	Nov 1992	27d-f
Neal A. Maxwell	Small equivocations lead to large deviations in ,		65f-66a
Michaelene P. Grassli	Teaching and helping , —great talk		92d-94f
Howard W. Hunter	We are God's first priority		95d
John K. Carmack	Things that destroy faith are not in ,	May 1993	43a
Joseph B. Wirthlin	Statistics on troubled children		68f-69a
	Do not let your , out to specialists —J.F. Smith		70f
Joe J. Christensen	Raising , in a polluted environment	Nov 1993	11b-13b
Boyd K. Packer	Don't let , out to others - Keep mother in home		22e-23c
Ben B. Banks	Stake mobilized to find lost boy —story		28d-f
	Suggestions for raising ,		28d-30b
Russell M. Nelson	First commandment was to beget ,		34b
Gordon B. Hinckley	The sapling could have been straightened —story		59c-f
	, need love, patience, encouragement, prayers		60b-f
Dallin H. Oaks	Have all the , you can care for!		75a-c
	, are the ultimate treasure		75a-c
Virginia H. Pearce	, want praise —story		80c
Aileen H. Clyde	Orphans thrived when given love —story		93b-e
Albert Choules, Jr.	, don't have to be commanded to love —story	May 1994	13c-e
Kenneth Johnson	Imperfect paint job was ok —story		30b-e
Merlin R. Lybbert	The special status of children —entire talk		31b-32f
Neal A. Maxwell	Sobering statistics on , in America		88f-89a
Jeffrey R. Holland	A father's best friends and examples	Nov 1994	32a

Children, cont'd

Gordon B. Hinckley	A rod is not necessary to discipline ,	Nov 1994	53f-54a
Gordon B. Hinckley	, honor parents with goodness of lives	May 1995	70d
Richard G. Scott	Haven't learned to be sad over what they don't have	May 1996	25b-d
Neal A. Maxwell	Boy knew a girl would be adopted —story		69f-70a
	"I love you anyway" —surgery story		70a-b
	A dying child's blessing and song —story		70e-f
Bruce C. Hafen	No children, no misery	Nov 1996	26e
	Raising , can be best religious experience		26e
Russell M. Nelson	, and trials of life go together		33d-e
Richard G. Scott	We have a responsibility to bear ,		73f
James E. Faust	Were difficult Sundays with , worth it?		96a-b
Thomas S. Monson	What is placed in brain in first 8 yrs is there to stay	Nov 1997	17d-e
Eran A. Call	Less than half raised in intact families		28e-f
Janette Hales Beckham	Must be moved - not titillated - repetition good		76b-c
Anne G. Wirthlin	Read scriptures to , —G.B. Hinckley	May 1998	11a-b
W. Eugene Hansen	Most precious asset —G.B. Hinckley		63f
Gordon B. Hinckley	Church's stand on abuse of ,	Nov 1998	72b-c
Joe J. Christensen	Overindulging , —excellent advice	May 1999	9f-11a
Robert D. Hales	Though , wander, they will return —O.F. Whitney		34c-d
Gordon B. Hinckley	No greater blessing and no greater responsibility		89a
James E. Faust	Master pianist put arms around student —story	Nov 1999	101b-c
Gordon B. Hinckley	Nothing in this world more precious than ,	Nov 2000	98b-c
Carol B. Thomas	Teach your , to deny themselves	May 2001	63f
Sharon G. Larsen	Love is listening when , are ready to talk —story	Nov 2001	67e-68a
Russell M. Nelson	Don't cling to , but to Jesus —raft story		69b-e
Boyd K. Packer	Encounters with orphan and disabled , —story	May 2002	7d-8c
	, must be cared for and not abused		8d-9a
	Most valuable lessons parents learn are from ,		9f-10b
Gordon B. Hinckley	How to deal with abuse of ,		54d-59a
Coleen K. Menlove	Tune , to hear and feel —Primary art story	Nov 2002	13d-f
	Primary held for just one child —story		13f-14b
	Learning from , —story		15b
	No other joy equals happy parenthood —Hinckley		15d-e
Kathleen H. Hughes	Temple marriage seals , . They will return —B.K. Packer		107d-e
James E. Faust	Some , would challenge any parents	May 2003	61e
	Sealed , will return		62b-f
	Comfort to parents with wayward ,		61b-68b
Susan W. Tanner	, learn best from love - not criticism		74d-75b
Jeffrey R. Holland	Off-course parents will be exceeded by ,		86a-d
Gordon B. Hinckley	His prayer for the ,		119f
Gordon B. Hinckley	What to teach your ,	Nov 2003	114e-115b
Russell M. Nelson	, follow example of parents	May 2004	27c-e
Thomas S. Monson	Son finally visited mother —story		57d-e
L. Tom Perry	Do not let your , out to specialists		71f-72b
Boyd K. Packer	Don't be afraid to bring , into world		79d-e

Children

W. Douglas Shumway	Having , : the first commandment	May 2004	95b
	Cherish , while you have them		95d
	Expense worth it if one is saved —story		95d-f
Thomas S. Monson	A newborn is like an empty computer	May 2005	19e-f
	Advice about raising ,		20d-21b
	, taken to circus —story		20f-21a
Paul K. Sybrowsky	The 2-year-old knew the answer —story	Nov 2005	35d-e
Bonnie D. Parkin	Good advice on parenting ,		109a-b
Richard H. Winkel	Excited son woke Dad at 2:00 a.m. —story	Nov 2006	9f-10d
	Sealed wayward , will return—quote		10d-f
James E. Faust	Salting cattle with Grandfather —story		53b-c
Margaret S. Lifferth	Protect from overindulgence, over scheduling , etc.		74e-f
	Non-member boy brought brothers and friends		75d-f
	We are to encircle , like Jesus did		75f-76a
Boyd K. Packer	, should be welcomed and treasured		87f
Gordon B. Hinckley	Sacrifice of parents for , —poem		116e-f
	Old age worries only about how , turned out		116f
Jeffrey R. Holland	Be constructive in all comments to ,	May 2007	17d-f
Quentin L. Cook	Will be righteous if 4 guidelines followed	Nov 2007	72b-d
Julie B. Beck	Commandment to bear , remains in force		76d-e
	Limit activities of , away from home		77f-78a
Douglas L. Callister	Can't be saved - Another church's viewpoint —story		100e-f
Dallin H. Oaks	Which activity son liked best		105d
	Beware overscheduling ,		105d-f
	Importance of family mealtimes		105f-106b
	Beware team sports and technology toys		107a-b
	Commandment to have , remains in force		110e-f
Thomas S. Monson	Being educated by the media		118f-119a
Russell M. Nelson	How correction is to be given	May 2008	9a-10a
M. Russell Ballard	Don't overschedule - 29 weekly commitments		109d-110a
	What , can do for mothers		110d
Neil L. Andersen	Handicapped child comforted another —story	Nov 2008	14e-f
Gerald Causse	Even , can understand Plan of Salvation		32b-34b
Thomas S. Monson	Busy father took , to circus —story		85b-86a
Barbara Thompson	, prayed for bishop's broken eyes —story	May 2009	84d-f
Dallin H. Oaks	Couple chose to have a dog instead of ,		93e-f
Dallin H. Oaks	Dealing with wayward , including cohabitation	Nov 2009	28d-29b
M. Russell Ballard	How fathers see , - Improved versions of selves		47e
Henry B. Eyring	Wayward , will return —Orson F. Whitney		71f-72c
	Blessings for honoring parents		72c-d
	Becoming like , - Becoming like Jesus		72e-73b
D. Todd Christofferson	Make converts of , while they are with you		107c
	Mother put early end to his life of crime —story		107e
Henry B. Eyring	No mists of darkness until age 8	May 2010	23a-b
	Strong Primary workers prevent future trouble		23b

Children, cont'd
Related Topics: Family, Home, Parents

Henry B. Eyring	Lost boy remembered to pray —story	May 2010	23d-24b
David A. Bednar	Spontaneously bearing testimony to ,		42b-e
Cheryl C. Lant	Bringing , to Christ		81a-83b
Robert D. Hales	Take advantage of teaching moments		95d-e
Neil L. Andersen	Cannot be casual as we teach them		108e
	Teaching of , - Like a wind across embers		18f-109a
	Are stories of Jesus embedded in , ?		109b-e
	If not listening, don't despair		110c-e
	Young Dallin Oaks spent evenings reading		112b

Choice
Related Topics: Agency, Decisions

Hartman Rector, Jr	Doing the right thing for wrong reason	Dec 1968	48f
Richard L. Evans	Quotes on roads —good		65a
	Another quote on roads		66c
Marion G. Romney	Good short poem on , —poem		75c
David O. McKay	No greater gift	Dec 1969	30e
Richard L. Evans	More complex today		73b
Richard L. Evans	You have limitless possibilities if you choose	Dec 1971	57b-c
N. Eldon Tanner	Choices shape destiny	July 1973	7a
	Wrong choices bring slavery —story		8b
John H. Vandenberg	Depends on heart —story		32a
	An element of human dignity		33b
Boyd K. Packer	The greatest , is between good and evil	Nov 1980	21d-e
James E. Faust	Private choices are not private	May 1987	80d-e
Ezra Taft Benson	Neither immediate blessings or cursings for actions	May 1988	6b-d
Thomas S. Monson	Choose your love; love your choice	Nov 1988	71a
Marion D. Hanks	Deacon kept Sabbath before his death —story	Nov 1990	39f-40b
	He who picks up one end of the stick...		40b-c
Russell M. Nelson	How to make choices —entire talk		73b-75f
Boyd K. Packer	Choices bump up against rights of others		84f-85a
Jack H. Goaslind	Yagottawanna	May 1991	45d-47b
Joseph B. Wirthlin	Learn to choose between good and evil	May 1992	86d
Neal A. Maxwell	We are choosing for the next generation	Nov 1992	65f-66a
Aileen H. Clyde	We don't need revelation in every ,		88f-89a
L. Tom Perry	Why mission president wore CTR ring —story	Nov 1993	66b-e
Gordon B. Hinckley	The , we make form the fabric of our lives	May 1995	53d
Boyd K. Packer	, is not independent of consequences	May 1996	17d-e
Richard G. Scott	Right of , is not given so that you can get what you want		25b
Chieko N. Okazaki	We choose hope or despair and meaninglessness	Nov 1996	90d-91a
Boyd K. Packer	Study of doctrines improves behavior	May 1997	9b
4 speakers	Choices Young Women made —many stories		88b-92f
Russell M. Nelson	Everything hinged upon President Hinckley's mission	Nov 1997	15a-b
Janette Hales Beckham	Bitterness or trust when father died —story		76c-d
Duane B. Gerrard	Every decision can be made correctly		77f
Richard G. Scott	2 patterns for making decisions	Nov 1998	68e-69a

Sharon G. Larsen	Some would keep a summer home in Babylon	Nov 1999	12e
	Choose God first or it won't matter		13a
L. Aldin Porter	Commandments give us , and ability to follow plan		65b-66f
James E. Faust	Results of Adam's and Eve's ,		101d-f
Richard G. Scott	Why was moral agency given?	May 2001	7f
	Each choice narrows our future		8a-c
Henry B. Eyring	We're here to see if we'll freely choose God	Nov 2001	16c-d
Wayne S. Peterson	Acting instead of reacting —story		83b-d
	Choosing an attitude in concentration camps		83e-f
Sharon G. Larsen	Girl had , of popular friends or standards —story	May 2002	91f-92c
James E. Faust	Iguacu Falls and staying on Lord's side	May 2003	51b-e
James E. Faust	Peer pressure and near-fatal dive —story	May 2004	51e-52d
	Not making a , is making a ,		52f-53a
	No greater , than marriage		53a
	Decide once - Russian vodka toast —story		53a-d
	Sin is sin even when all do it		53d-f
Gordon B. Hinckley	The perilous choices of mankind throughout history		81b-84b
Thomas S. Monson	Alice in Wonderland's , of roads	Nov 2004	68a-b
David A. Bednar	We become chosen by choosing	May 2005	100f-101e
Paul B. Pieper	A small , by one affected thousands	Nov 2006	12e-f
David A. Bednar	Being offended is a , we make		90b-91c
Neil L. Andersen	Couldn't do right because he lost CTR ring	May 2007	74a
Charles W. Dahlquist, II	Courageous , of Nephi and David		95b-e
Claudio D. Zivic	I choose not to be an ordinary man	Nov 2007	98b-d
Dallin H. Oaks	Good, Better, Best —entire talk		104d-108b
Henry B. Eyring	, of friends leads to light or away	May 2008	123f-124e
Neil L. Andersen	Faith is not only a feeling; it is a , —story	Nov 2008	13f-14b
James J. Hamula	We need to do again what we did before		50f-51b
Thomas S. Monson	Don't let less important things take priority		85a
	It is our , which secret garden we will tend		86f
M. Russell Ballard	Don't exhaust spiritual strength repeating mistakes	May 2009	31f-32b
	Our , results in spiritual consequences for posterity		32b-f
	Follow Nephi - not Laman - learn from the past		33b-34a
Henry B. Eyring	Choose sin and Holy Ghost becomes faint	Nov 2009	60e
Thomas S. Monson	No one can make us angry. It is our ,		67f-68a
Henry B. Eyring	Gravestone: "Please, no empty chairs"		71b-d
D. Todd Christofferson	A , - Yoke of Christ or yoke of Caesar		106f-107a

Church (of Jesus Christ of Latter-Day Saints)
Related Topics: —

David O. McKay	465 stakes and 84 missions	Dec 1968	34b
	The gospel makes all other blessings operative		35e
Joseph Fielding Smith	Has never been led by a man		41c
LeGrand Richards	2 reactions of non-members to the , —story		45e-f
	2 more reactions of non-members to the , —story		46d
S. Dilworth Young	4,226 wards		77b

Church (of Jesus Christ of Latter-Day Saints), cont'd
Related Topics: —

Robert L. Simpson	Promises made by living doctrines of ,	Dec 1968	89b
N. Eldon Tanner	Demands too much? —Tanner's response		92a-c
Ezra Taft Benson	Many wolves among the flock	June 1969	42b-43b
	Three threats to ,		44c
	Breach between , and world should be widening daily		47c-e
Marion D. Hanks	Early Roman found peace amid turmoil —letter		53d-54a
Henry D. Taylor	, tells us how to love one another		64c
Delbert L. Stapley	If this , is worth anything it is worth everything		72b
Gordon B. Hinckley	Makes bad men good and good men better —McKay		74f
A. Theodore Tuttle	, does not remove problems but gives courage to face them		100c
Paul H. Dunn	Navy officer: The world will look to you for direction		114a-d
David O. McKay	Preeminently a social religion		117a
David O. McKay	Purpose of , welfare of man	Dec 1969	31e
LeGrand Richards	This , has most to offer		54a
	Testimony of , by non-member		54c
	Testimony of , by non-member		54d
	Story about Marion D. Hanks —story		54d
	Testimony of , by non-member		54e
	Statements at Visitors Center		54f
	Statements at Visitors Center		55c
Eldred G. Smith	Times established		60a
Richard L. Evans	Prove love for , by service		74e
Gordon B. Hinckley	Opposition against , will intensify	June 1970	40a
	A pioneer story of hardship —story		40f-41e
Ezra Taft Benson	Report on the , in Asia		96c-97f
LeGrand Richards	The kingdom Daniel saw in vision —story		109b-d
Ezra Taft Benson	Family will outlive Church	Dec 1970	46a
Marion G. Romney	Authenticity of , rests upon revelation and Joseph Smith		51b-d
Marion D. Hanks	Every man a priest, and every home a parish		66d-67a
	Records: Purpose is not counting sheep but feeding them		68a
	Purpose of , programs		68e
Harold B. Lee	How new , programs come into being		103d-f
	, has some tight places to go through		126b-d
Harold B. Lee	A liberal , member —defined	June 1971	7c-d
Victor L. Brown	I hope I never meet a dishonest Latter-day Saint —story		56c
	A point of distinction to be a Latter-day Saint		56c-d
	Latter-day Saint wanted to pick in pineapple fields		56d-e
Paul H. Dunn	The secret of our success —funny		102a-b
Boyd K. Packer	Answer to objections that only our , is right	Dec 1971	40a-b
	Plays the full keyboard, not just one note		41c-e
Theodore M. Burton	Overflowing - not empty - churches is our problem		80c
Delbert L. Stapley	Non-member: I believe the Church will save the world!		95b
Dallin H. Oaks	Signs follow them that believe		110a-c
Joseph Fielding Smith	Here to stay	July 1972	28f
Mark E. Petersen	Achievements in world by some , members		41e

Church

Loren C. Dunn	Organized from top down unlike man-made	July 1972	43e
Ezra Taft Benson	Unconverted friends of , do most good outside		59d
	Communist take over would attack , leaders		61a
Victor L. Brown	Position of , is to aid parents not replace them		90f
LeGrand Richards	Mormons don't know strength of own position —story		114f
Spencer W. Kimball	History of , membership numbers	Jan 1973	33a
Ezra Taft Benson	Lord wants , to be independent		59d
Howard W. Hunter	Has always had a prophet		65d
A. Theodore Tuttle	This is a family Church		66d
N. Eldon Tanner	Source of guidance for ,		101e
Harold B. Lee	Most needed during problems		133d
Harold B. Lee	Has spread over world - 78 countries	July 1973	5a
Paul H. Dunn	Programs of , exist to help people		31d
Gordon B. Hinckley	Rev. Kelley says Mormon , is fastest growing		48f
LeGrand Richards	Bible is a blueprint fitting no other , —story		79c
Victor L. Brown	Exists to help parents		80f
Boyd K. Packer	Cannot be changed to keep it in the path of the wayfaring	Jan 1974	25d
Vaughn J. Featherstone	Poem on Statue of Liberty applies to ,		86c
N. Eldon Tanner	Demands too much? —Tanner's reply		94e
Theodore M. Burton	Why can , members recognize each other?		114a
Spencer W. Kimball	Rapid growth is greatest problem of ,	May 1974	4e-f
	World is second greatest problem of ,		5d
John H. Vandenberg	"Mormon" is not the proper name of the ,		11d-e
—	Statistical and Financial Reports for 1973		20a-21e
Marvin J. Ashton	All 10 virgins in the parable were , members		35f-36c
N. Eldon Tanner	Proceedings of Solemn Assembly 1974		38a-45b
Spencer W. Kimball	History of Solemn Assemblies		45d-46a
Mark E. Petersen	Solemn Assembly held as in Israel —J. Taylor		56a
Neal A. Maxwell	Membership is not passive security but opportunity		112f
Spencer W. Kimball	Growth of , from 1943 to present	Nov 1974	4b-c
Robert L. Simpson	LDS doing wrong don't do it because of ,		46f-47a
Boyd K. Packer	Not an easy , to join —story		88a-e
	Only real problem of , is its tremendous growth		88f-89a
Gordon B. Hinckley	A compliment when media points out wrongdoers are LDS		99e-100b
	Members of , will become more and more distinctive		100b-c
—	Statistical Report 1974	May 1975	18a-19a
Vaughn J. Featherstone	Don't leave meetings early —story		67c-e
N. Eldon Tanner	All in conference were new converts —story		74f
A. Theodore Tuttle	Greatest problem in , is growth - One chapel per day		90e
	Why , appeals to people		90e-91a
Gordon B. Hinckley	Why , does not use the cross		92d-f
James A. Cullimore	The , exists to assist the family —First Presidency	Nov 1975	27f
James E. Faust	The astounding growth of the , in South America		55d-f
Mark E. Petersen	What kind of people are the Mormons —entire talk		63a-65f
N. Eldon Tanner	Bears testimony that he was never embarrassed by ,		75e

Howard W. Hunter	History of the 100-yr-old Tabernacle	Nov 1975	94b-96f
Boyd K. Packer	Scope of miss. work impossible? We'll do it anyway		97d-e
	Scope of work for dead impossible? We'll do it anyway		99b
Spencer W. Kimball	Growth of , in numbers of stakes and missions	May 1976	4d
N. Eldon Tanner	Comparison of , to army		44f
Spencer W. Kimball	1947-First million, 1963-second, 1972-third, etc.	Nov 1976	4d-e
	Sacrament attendance used to be 19%		4e
Bernard P. Brockbank	Growth of , in England 1960-1976	May 1977	26c-d
Ezra Taft Benson	Sacrament attendance 20% in 1943 - 41% today	May 1978	32b-c
Gordon B. Hinckley	The changes he's seen in 20 years as a General Authority		58d-e
Marion G. Romney	Mormon vs. proper name of ,	May 1979	50d-51a
Spencer W. Kimball	, poised for major progress if individuals will move		82b-f
N. Eldon Tanner	, administration —entire talk excellent	Nov 1979	42b-48a
David B. Haight	The greatest power the world has known —Tolstoy story	May 1980	11e-f
N. Eldon Tanner	Near broken family became eternal —story		18f
LeGrand Richards	, is the kingdom Nebuchadnezzar saw —story		23c-e
Ezra Taft Benson	No one will stand neutral about ,		33e-f
Proclamation	, beliefs and positions —excellent statement		52a-53e
L. Tom Perry	From rags to beautiful Nauvoo in 5 years		74b-75a
	, has given him his best education		75f
Neal A. Maxwell	No other plan of happiness - Only multiple choice misery	Nov 1980	15c
James E. Faust	Exchanged his money because he was LDS —story		36d-e
Spencer W. Kimball	Mission of the , is threefold	May 1981	5e-f
Spencer W. Kimball	If this were not the Lord's work, Satan would ignore us		79a
Ezra Taft Benson	How long it took for , to achieve each million	Nov 1981	63b-c
Ezra Taft Benson	3 dangers that threaten the , within	May 1982	63e
J. Richard Clarke	Church tried and refined many times		77d-e
Boyd K. Packer	Things , must do. Starting schools is not one of them		85d-86c
Gordon B. Hinckley	, will be involved in few worldly campaigns	May 1983	7f-8a
Ted E. Brewerton	What Catholic study learned about ,		74c-d
Gordon B. Hinckley	Members had instant friends in Japan - no cultural shock		79f-80a
Gordon B. Hinckley	Growth of , in Chile 1956-1983	Nov 1983	52b
Ezra Taft Benson	Growth of , since 1943	May 1984	8d
Gordon B. Hinckley	The miracle which is the , —entire talk		46b-48f
Gordon B. Hinckley	The 4 cornerstones of the ,	Nov 1984	51a-d
Royden G. Derrick	, makes evil men good and good men better		61b
Ronald E. Poelman	Difference between the , and the gospel		64c-d
	Procedures may change but principles do not		64f-65c
Bruce R. McConkie	Like a great caravan		85b
Ezra Taft Benson	Growth statistics of ,	May 1985	6d-e
	World will be filled with stakes and members		8f
Gordon B. Hinckley	$6,025,656 given to African famine victims		53d-59b
Ezra Taft Benson	Takes slums out of people — take selves out of slums	Nov 1985	6e-f
James E. Faust	, is one of few things worthy of one's complete confidence		9f
Gordon B. Hinckley	Assets are mostly buildings - Money-consuming assets		49f-50c

Church

Gordon B. Hinckley	Why does the , have commercial businesses?	Nov 1985	50d-f
	, has no obligation to help its critics		52c-e
Boyd K. Packer	Why the , does not join with others		82e-f
Ezra Taft Benson	List of helps the , has put out	May 1986	4e
Joseph Anderson	Wentworth letter - Nothing can stop the ,	Nov 1986	39e
Wm. Grant Bangerter	Mormon, cult, sect, Saint, born again Christian	May 1987	11b-f
Gordon B. Hinckley	The miraculous growth of the ,		52b-53a
M. Russell Ballard	Building meetinghouses simplified in South America	Nov 1987	78d-e
Franklin D. Richards	Growth of , in Mexico and South America		81e-f
James M. Paramore	Police chief organized department like ,	May 1988	11a
Ezra Taft Benson	List of things members of , should do		84d-85b
Gordon B. Hinckley	The foundation stories of our,	Nov 1988	48d-e
Thomas S. Monson	History of the , in Germany	May 1989	50b-53b
Gordon B. Hinckley	Statistics thru 8 years of growth		65e-66a
Gordon B. Hinckley	Audacious, unbelievable vision of pioneers	Nov 1989	51d-52e
	1852: 98 called on "short" missions of 3 to 7 years		53c-e
	Comments of non members about Temple Square		53f-54c
	, is least provincial of any group in world		54c
L. Tom Perry	Appearance of abandoned Nauvoo —story		70d-71a
M. Russell Ballard	Simple condition of , in South America	May 1990	6c-e
	4 Caribbean countries dedicated		6f-7b
Russell M. Nelson	Name of , —excellent discussion		16b-18f
	Avoid using nickname "Mormon"		16b-c
	Bible mentions "Saints" 98 times and "Christians" just 3		16d-e
Gordon B. Hinckley	Church President used to sign all recommends		50e-f
Elaine L. Jack	Growth of , dependent upon women		78e-f
James E. Faust	Places of peace for , members		86b
Boyd K. Packer	, to pay budget expenses of local units		89b-91f
Thomas S. Monson	Steps implementing financial relief		92d-e
	No more moose heads in rented halls —story		92f-93a
	Principles governing budget allowance		93b-d
	Local unit budget allowance program		92b-94f
Gordon B. Hinckley	Financial progress of ,		95e-96b
	Comments on new budget program		95b-97f
Harold G. Hillam	World's best shoeshine man dies alone —2 stories	Nov 1990	24d-25f
Dallin H. Oaks	Jesus was not mentioned in sacrament meeting		30a
	Fundamental principle of , is Jesus		30a-b
Gordon B. Hinckley	His service as proxy to presidents		50c-51b
	Discussion of the nickname "Mormon"		51f-52c
	Salt Lake City number one city in U.S. for business		54e-f
Jacob de Jager	Mormon "irrigation" to flood the earth	May 1991	45a-b
Gordon B. Hinckley	520 new chapels last year		52c
	Assets are money-consuming not producing		54b-c
Howard W. Hunter	Organization of , ranks among important events		63b-e
Janette C. Hales	Book of Mormon prosperity cycle and Church today		84f-85a

Church

George I. Cannon	"No wonder you're honest - you're Mormon" —story	Nov 1991	13e-f
Gordon B. Hinckley	, statistics in his 30 years as an apostle		49b-e
Marvin J. Ashton	No unhallowed hand can stop... —Joseph Smith		72f
Chieko N. Okazaki	Our wonderful diversity		88f-89b
M. Russell Ballard	Major growth of , coming because of women		96f-97a
Marion D. Hanks	Central mission of , is bringing people to Christ	May 1992	9a-c
F. Michael Watson	1991 statistical report		22e-f
Gordon B. Hinckley	When will , join mainstream America?		69f-70b
Glenn L. Pace	, compared to a train —great analogy	Nov 1992	11f-12b
L. Tom Perry	Utah's amazing statistics		16c-d
Dean L. Larsen	Only a small percent of members pay tithing		42e
	More prospective elders than elders		42f
Gordon B. Hinckley	The Tabernacle		50b-51c
Boyd K. Packer	Gathering place is now in native country		71d-e
David B. Haight	Not a democracy: A Kingdom		74b
Boyd K. Packer	Left Nauvoo in endless procession	May 1993	18f-19a
	Given exactly 10 years in West to recoup		19d-e
V. Dallas Merrell	The purpose and goal of ,		28e
	, will prevail over all difficulty —story		29b-f
Gordon B. Hinckley	Promise that leaders will never lead , astray	Nov 1993	54e
David B. Haight	Will sweep every nation —Joseph Smith quote		62a-b
	Nations will flock to standard of ,		63b
Virginia H. Pearce	What wards do for us —entire talk		79b-81b
Boyd K. Packer	The purpose of every , teaching	May 1994	19e
Marlin K. Jensen	Why we build meetinghouses rather than hermitages		49b
Gordon B. Hinckley	How , functions when president is indisposed		53b-60b
	Christ is at the head of the ,		59c-60b
Howard W. Hunter	Is becoming a welcome refuge from world	Nov 1994	9a
L. Tom Perry	Proceedings at meeting organizing the ,		17d-f
James O. Mason	Status of the , in Africa		30b-31b
	"No unhallowed hand can stop..." —Joseph Smith		31b
Joseph B. Wirthlin	Feed soul through , attendance		75d
Patricia P. Pinegar	Intertwined redwood roots hold trees up		78b-c
Joseph B. Wirthlin	Growth of , during President Hinckley's service	May 1995	20c
Russell M. Nelson	Why we are called brothers and sisters		34b
James E. Faust	Look beyond any irritations caused by , bureaucracy		47f-48a
Gordon B. Hinckley	Largest programs in world —list		52d-53c
Gordon B. Hinckley	Report on growth of ,	Nov 1995	53b-f
	, saves a portion of budget each year		54b
	96,484 volunteers now serving		54b-c
	From 150 to 2,101 stakes in 50 years		54d-e
Thomas S. Monson	East Germany - from fear to a temple		61a-b
Robert E. Wells	Restoration of , essential to second coming		66d-f
Gordon B. Hinckley	More members outside U.S. by Feb 1996		70f
James E. Faust	Will never be destroyed by apostasy	May 1996	5b

Church

Speaker	Topic	Date	Ref
David B. Haight	Destined to be world's greatest power —Tolstoi	May 1996	22d-f
Jeffrey R. Holland	Holds answer to every problem		31a-b
Joseph B. Wirthlin	Grows because it is a demanding religion		32e-f
	Makes ordinary people great —J.E. Faust		34d-e
	Talk recounts story of Nauvoo and pioneers		32b-34f
L. Tom Perry	Account of organizational meeting		54c-e
Gordon B. Hinckley	Announcement of plans for Conference Center		65b-e
	Grows by equivalent of 100 new stakes per year		66d
	Will never be led astray		92a-b
M. Russell Ballard	Number of pioneers who crossed plains	Nov 1996	23f-24a
	Joseph's prophecy of move to Rocky Mountains		24b-d
	Saints introduced alfalfa to the West		25c-d
	Our pioneer legacy —entire talk, stories		23d-25f
Joseph B. Wirthlin	We meet the definition of Christian		70d-f
Gordon B. Hinckley	Rescue of handcart pioneers —story		85d-86f
Aileen H. Clyde	Mary F. Smith letter on trials		87e-88c
Gordon B. Hinckley	Organization of new Quorum of Seventy	May 1997	5d-6e
James E. Faust	4,000 pioneers died crossing plains		18c
	To go to Rocky Mountains and fill world —Joseph Smith		19a-b
David B. Haight	The , in 1906 —statistics		38a
L. Tom Perry	The first , meeting in 1830		69a-b
Russell M. Nelson	Two most important relationships are by covenant		71d-e
Gordon B. Hinckley	Don't look to press for doctrines of ,	Nov 1997	4b-f
Keith B. McMullin	Good definition of the gospel		40f
Gordon B. Hinckley	A friend, a refuge, a pillar, a cloud		52e-f
Gordon B. Hinckley	10 million members in 1997		67c-d
	Examples of growth in South America		67e-f
	No city in Americas without a congregation		67f-68a
	The wonderful future of the ,		68a-69a
Sheri L. Dew	"Grandma, what if the , isn't true?" —story		91d-f
Thomas S. Monson	, cannot take place of home		96a-b
David B. Haight	Conditions in P. Whitmer home	May 1998	6d-7a
James E. Faust	Twice as many percentage-wise now attend		18c
	Members should be preferred by employers		43f-44a
Richard E. Turley	Non member spent day with members —story		83b-e
Gordon B. Hinckley	Building replacement for Tabernacle	Nov 1998	4c-f
Virginia U. Jensen	Ironclad guarantees found only in ,		13d
Boyd K. Packer	, must not over schedule families —important talk		22b-24f
David E. Sorensen	, will fill the world —Joseph Smith prophecy		64b-c
Richard G. Scott	You don't fit where you don't belong		70a-b
Gordon B. Hinckley	Why the , is growing - much expected		72a-b
Russell M. Nelson	Primary children know who they are —story		85b
Sheri L. Dew	Depressing speaker said gospel is hard —story		94e-f
Gordon B. Hinckley	60,000 missionaries - 137,629 volunteers	May 1999	4c-d
L. Tom Perry	History of organization of Sunday School		6b-e

Church

Joe J. Christensen	Comforts afflicted and afflicts the comforted	May 1999	9b
James E. Faust	The favored people in the favored day —Joseph Smith		17b-e
	Religion is more than ritual - it is righteousness		18c
Statistical Report	1998 Statistical Report		22a-e
Boyd K. Packer	The , is no bigger than a ward		58f-63a
	Purpose of , is to shelter families		63a
	, must not compete with families		63b-c
	Families, like wards, grow and divide		63d
	, will fill earth - but be no bigger than the ward		63d
	What , provides		63d-e
	Sheltered within ward, families will be safe		63f
James E. Faust	Responsible for all who have lived on earth	Nov 1999	48d-e
Thomas S. Monson	Letter from excommunicated member		51a-b
Gordon B. Hinckley	Why , has BYU, businesses, and legislative involvement		52b-54f
L. Tom Perry	Members can be known by their buoyancy		77d-f
Gordon B. Hinckley	History of Tabernacle - reasons for Conf. Center		90b-91f
Sheri L. Dew	Why members are unique —good		98e-f
	Our uniqueness is a light to the world		99b-e
Gordon B. Hinckley	The Conference Center and its pulpit —report	May 2000	4b-6f
M. Russell Ballard	300,000 in 1900 - 11 million in 2000 - fill the earth		31b-f
David B. Haight	The Peter Whitmer cabin and , beginnings		34c-f
Thomas S. Monson	LDS sailors there after other religions dismissed —story		53f-54b
Jeffrey R. Holland	Early , was small but they saw our day		75d
Robert D. Hales	We separate - not isolate - selves from world	Nov 2000	8e
D.B. Neuenschwander	, will never accommodate to the world		42a
Thomas S. Monson	We are winning —G.B. Hinckley		47e
Thomas S. Monson	"I'm home" —abducted boy story		66d-f
Gordon B. Hinckley	1 million in 1947 - 11 million today		67d-e
	History of Conference Center and dedicatory prayer		68b-71f
Statistical Report	11,068,861 members - 2,581 stakes	May 2001	22b
L. Tom Perry	We don't appreciate its true value —story		35d-36b
John K. Carmack	Quietly moving forward in crescendo		76d
Bruce D. Porter	The most important class in Cambridge —story		80b-d
Gordon B. Hinckley	We have only seen the foreshadowing	Nov 2001	5d
David B. Haight	, history and Brigham Young's leadership		22f-24b
Walter F. Gonzalez	30-year growth of , in South America		31d
Jeffrey R. Holland	Growth of , since his teenage years		33b-c
	No fund raising assessments - A leap of faith		33d-e
Russell M. Nelson	The , exists to exalt the family		70e
Gordon B. Hinckley	From 6 members to 5th largest in U.S.	May 2002	4b-d
	Report on Winter Olympics		4d-6d
	Brigham Young's prophecy on Church growth		6d-e
Dallin H. Oaks	What , does for people —Brigham Young		34e
	No monopoly on good people but a concentration of them		34f-35a
Dieter F. Uchtdorf	Spiritual pioneers and ancestors then and now —story	Nov 2002	10f-11d

Gordon B. Hinckley	Brethren took , apart in attempt to simplify	Nov 2002	56d-f
Dallin H. Oaks	No paid ministry - a characteristic of ,		69d
Keith B. McMullin	Help build Zion, and vexations about time will disappear		95a-f
	, is the kingdom of God and will be Zion		96e
Bonnie D. Parkin	Meetings are where oil goes from vessel to vessel		102d
Gordon B. Hinckley	Sacrament attendance rising	May 2003	4d
	400 chapels constructed yearly		6b
	Be loyal to , and its positions		60a-e
Susan W. Tanner	, is a supplement to home		73c-e
Gordon B. Hinckley	Sun never sets on the ,	Nov 2003	7a
Sheldon F. Child	"The freeze" in Ghana - locked buildings		9f-10b
James E. Faust	Could join , if Joseph Smith taken out		19f-20b
	No errors in the doctrine		21f-22c
Quentin L. Cook	What it means to be a Saint		95b-96f
Gordon B. Hinckley	Almost 12 million members	May 2004	4c
	Revocations of Missouri and Illinois edicts		5b-d
Earl C. Tingey	"For the Strength of Youth" opens African country		50d-f
Gordon B. Hinckley	451 meetinghouses under construction	Nov 2004	4d-f
L. Tom Perry	The genius of , government is councils		24f
Henry B. Eyring	Federal official tried to take over —story		28e-29a
Thomas S. Monson	1980 Proclamation on Restoration		56e
Boyd K. Packer	The , was a family eating cold corn on a curb		87d-f
	Only 2 Americans among 47 , authorities		88c
Gordon B. Hinckley	Progress of , during Hinckley's 10 years	May 2005	4f-5f
Gordon B. Hinckley	8 doctrines unique to the ,		80d-82f
Julie B. Beck	Amazing growth of , in Brazil		107f-108f
Gordon B. Hinckley	Sun never sets on , - A new empire	Nov 2005	4b-d
	Growth has only scratched the surface		4d
Keith B. McMullin	, provides solutions to every ill		11f
James E. Faust	The light in members' eyes —story		20b-d
	7 "blockbuster" doctrines		21d-22b
Dallin H. Oaks	, and family must be mutually considered		25b-f
	Differences in priesthood in , and family		26b-27b
	Why this is a family , —good		27c-d
C. Scott Grow	Mexico's amazing growth in 36 years		33b-e
James E. Faust	Will always be led by old men		53b-c
Boyd K. Packer	Curriculum restructured to center on 4 things		72f
	Revelations to , in recent years		73a-c
Richard G. Hinckley	Bishop asked inactives to speak in ,	May 2006	49a-d
	What his membership means to him		50b
Thomas S. Monson	Why is , so wealthy? —story		54d-e
	How does , differ from others? —McKay		54f
James E. Faust	We care about all who ever lived		61d-e
Gordon B. Hinckley	Phenomenal increase in satellite downlinks	Nov 2006	4b-c
Gordon B. Hinckley	Handcart pioneers and text of Brigham's talk		83b-84d

Gordon B. Hinckley	The price they paid for the comforts we enjoy	Nov 2006	84d-e
Boyd K. Packer	160 nations and over 200 languages		86f
	Stakes are self-contained with everything needed		87a
	There is safety and protection in the ,		88b
	Willingly defend the history of the ,		88d
	Will prosper and prevail - certain		88f
	A defense and refuge from the storm		85d-88f
Gordon B. Hinckley	LDS stands for love, devotion, service		115f
David A. Bednar	Parable of the Pickle - Immerse self in ,	May 2007	19b-22b
Boyd K. Packer	The Spirit of the Tabernacle —entire talk		26b-29b
H. David Burton	Renovation of and significant events in Tabernacle		32b-34b
Marlin K. Jensen	Church historian speaks of value of remembering		36d-38f
James E. Faust	No early meetinghouses - prototype of Tabernacle		39b-40f
Gordon B. Hinckley	Re-dedicatory prayer for Tabernacle		44b-f
	Renovation and history of Tabernacle		43b-44f
Gordon B. Hinckley	Statistical progress of , in last 12 years		60d-e
Gary J. Coleman	"Mom, are we Christians?"		92b-94b
Boyd K. Packer	Moves upon shoulders of ordinary people	Nov 2007	9a-b
Enrique R. Falabella	Why he's a member of the ,		14b-15f
Dieter F. Uchtdorf	Joining , brought joy amid war —story		18f-19a
M. Russell Ballard	Excellent concise list of facts about ,		25b-27f
Joseph B. Wirthlin	The quality that best defines , members		30e
Jeffrey R. Holland	Others shouldn't wonder if LDS are Christian		40b-d
Quentin L. Cook	Philippines: 600,000 members in 46 years		71d-e
	25% of Polynesians are members		71e-72b
Gordon B. Hinckley	13 million in 176 nations		83d-e
	4th or 5th largest in U.S.		84a-c
	Most important work on earth		85f-86b
Daniel K. Judd	People come to , to be nourished		93d-e
Henry B. Eyring	Church is true because of keys	May 2008	20f-21a
	Church will become better		21d
F. Michael Watson	13,193,999 members		25b
Dieter F. Uchtdorf	Conference in 92 languages and 96 nations		59b
Thomas S. Monson	A network of influence for youth in ,		66e-f
Dieter F. Uchtdorf	His ancestors didn't cross plains, but legacy is his		70b-d
D. Todd Christofferson	The Seventy: most profound miracle in ,		76d-77a
James J. Hamula	God's kingdom will not be lost again	Nov 2008	50e-f
Henry B. Eyring	Compliments to , from government leaders		71e
M. Russell Ballard	Joseph's prophecy that , would go west		81b-c
	Growth of , in South America		82d-f
	Contrasting challenges of pioneers and us		83f-84b
	The growth of , described and enumerated		81b-84b
Boyd K. Packer	Sun never sets on congregations of the ,		91d-e
	Response of , to America's cruelties		88d-91f
Thomas S. Monson	The lifeblood of the , is continuous revelation		107d

Church

Church (of Jesus Christ of Latter-Day Saints), cont'd

Related Topics: —

D. Todd Christofferson	A community of Saints who encourage one another	May 2009	21a-b
Quentin L. Cook	Charles Dickens' astonishment at Saints —story		34f-35d
Dieter F. Uchtdorf	Discipleship is not a spectator sport		76f-77a
Neil L. Andersen	Fulfilling ancient prophecies - List		79f-80b
Dallin H. Oaks	Members can't walk, talk and do as other men		95a
	Don't go to , for self but for others		96c-e
David A. Bednar	Difference in members who consistently go to temple		99b
L. Tom Perry	Over 50% of non-members don't know about ,		110b
Tad R. Callister	Supplies other 900 pieces of the puzzle	Nov 2009	36d-f
L. Tom Perry	The Manti Miracle Pageant		73d-e
	Manti Temple built without power tools		73e-f
	Settling Sanpete County and building temple		74a-75c
Quentin L. Cook	Jewish leaders' reaction upon visit to ,		91b-d
	Martin Luther King III's reaction to ,		93f
Brent H. Nielson	"The truth of God will go forth boldly..." —quote		96b
	Growth of , in 35 years		96b-c
Joseph W. Sitati	Alaskan and African ministering together		103b-c
	Does away with tradition of a dowry		105a-b
Silvia H. Allred	Growth of , will come because of women —Kimball		115d-e
Boyd K. Packer	Battle plan is not our own	May 2010	6d
	Will influence all of humanity		7b-d
	Must support not supplant family		7f-8a
	Work of the Lord will prevail		9d
	Object is perfection of individual and family		9f-10a
Julie B. Beck	Growth to come from example of women		12d-e
M. Russell Ballard	Is a help and support to home		21d
Statistical Report	13,824,854 members - 2,865 stakes		28a
Bruce A. Carlson	Safety of , is in keeping commandments		38d
Ronald A. Rasband	8 Quorums of the Seventy		51b
Quentin L. Cook	Fundamental principles of , are...		84a
Russell M. Nelson	Proclaims, promotes, protects family		91c-92b
Thomas S. Monson	Look to lighthouse of the Lord		113b-d

Commandments

Related Topics: Obedience

N. Eldon Tanner	Too hard? —Tanner's reply	Dec 1968	92a-c
S. Dilworth Young	His simple , are guides to men's relationships	June 1969	84c-e
N. Eldon Tanner	Will bring joy if lived	Dec 1969	35f
	Keeping , whole duty of man		36f
Eldred G. Smith	Loving and tender advice of an all-wise Father	Dec 1970	43e
Franklin D. Richards	Testimony alone will not save us, but...	June 1971	47c
Richard L. Evans	Men tell untruths if they say , may be set aside		73f-74a
	Every , given for our happiness, health and peace		74b
	We cannot break the , ...—Cecil B. DeMille		74c
	God will tell us more as we keep the ,		74f
Hartman Rector, Jr.	Do not know , - no penalty then but no blessing either		79b-d

Commandments, cont'd
Related Topics: Obedience

Joseph Fielding Smith	Keeping , the supreme act of worship	Dec 1971	27b
N. Eldon Tanner	Most unhappiness caused by not keeping ,		34a
Richard L. Evans	, should not be rewritten but reread		57a
Sterling W. Sill	Entire talk —great		92a-94e
	The minister thought the 10 , too harsh		93b
	Ignorance of 10 , —funny story		93d
	Thou shalt not bear false witness —good thought		94c
Spencer W. Kimball	Lord's suffering means nothing unless we keep ,	July 1972	37c
Franklin D. Richards	When the Lord commands, do it —Joseph Smith	Jan 1973	72a
Sterling W. Sill	Keep the commandments —Lee as new President		82e
	Keeping , only road to celestial kingdom		82f
	Message of prophets through the ages		83e
Hartman Rector, Jr.	Set personal , as buffers for Lord's		131b
Harold B. Lee	Whoever keeps , will follow the Brethren	July 1973	99c
O. Leslie Stone	Doing will of Father prepares us for tomorrow	Jan 1974	39f
N. Eldon Tanner	Too demanding or hard? —Tanner's reply		94e
James A. Cullimore	Living , is a matter of will		121b
Joseph Anderson	Ministers teaching , outdated - Compare Matt. 5:18-19	May 1974	9e
O. Leslie Stone	If you want happiness keep the , —Kimball	May 1975	9c
Marion D. Hanks	Civility, gentility, forbearance, compassion, etc.	Nov 1976	32e
Spencer W. Kimball	Rain, harvest and peace promised if Sabbath kept	May 1977	4c-5f
James A. Cullimore	Doesn't matter where we live but how —H.B. Lee	May 1978	26d
Spencer W. Kimball	10 , set minimum standards of conduct	Nov 1978	6c-f
Spencer W. Kimball	The 10 , of President Kimball	May 1982	5b-c
Ezra Taft Benson	Knowledge comes by keeping all the ,	May 1983	54c-e
Ezra Taft Benson	List of , for LDS	May 1984	7f-8c
Angel Abrea	Nephi made no excuses when he received ,		70e-71a
	When the Lord commands, do it —Joseph Smith		71d-e
L. Tom Perry	The story of Daniel —story	Nov 1985	46e-48e
Gordon B. Hinckley	, we can live easily		85b-f
Hugh W. Pinnock	4 great ,	May 1987	62b
Robert D. Hales	Pilot fatality because training shirked —story	May 1990	39d-40d
Joseph B. Wirthlin	Like white lines on road in driving storm	Nov 1990	64d-f
Gordon B. Hinckley	Moses didn't bring 10 suggestions from Sinai	Nov 1991	51b-c
Russell M. Nelson	First , was to beget children	Nov 1993	34b
	Ten , cannot be amended		35a
M. Russell Ballard	All , directed toward happiness —Joseph Smith	May 1995	23c
Russell M. Nelson	Issue self , to "about face"	May 1996	15b
	Position in Church does not exalt - keeping , does		15f
Boyd K. Packer	Resistance to , may cause society to self-destruct		17d-e
	Word of Wisdom now a commandment		17e
Robert D. Hales	Why did the Lord give us , ?		36c-37a
Carlos E. Asay	The world is drifting —1916 quote		60f
Joseph B. Wirthlin	People try to serve the Lord without offending the devil	May 1997	16a
L. Tom Perry	List of leaders' concerns in 1856		68b-e

Commandments

James E. Faust	Later , emphasize DOs more than DO NOTs	Nov 1997	53c-e
James M. Paramore	Boy caught in quicksand —story	May 1998	42e-f
Thomas S. Monson	Not following , puts us in harm's way - ship sank —story		46d-47a
Sheri L. Dew	Keep , and we're led to promised land	May 1999	66f-67a
Joseph B. Wirthlin	, and ordinances make for happiness —Joseph Smith	Nov 1999	40b-c
L. Aldin Porter	, give us choice and the ability to follow the plan		65b-66f
Patricia P. Pinegar	, are like a kite string —story		67f-68a
Harold G. Hillam	Live , because you choose to	May 2000	11a-b
H. David Burton	, are safety restraints, not chains	May 2003	50b
James E. Faust	Rebelling against restraints —garage roof story		52a-c
Thomas S. Monson	Not the 10 suggestions	Nov 2003	68c
	Why don't you stay home and keep them?		68d
Clate W. Mask, Jr.	We only need to be pure	May 2004	93c
Bruce C. Hafen	Almost keep , - Almost receive blessings		98d-99a
David A. Bednar	Your work is to keep ,	May 2005	101f-102a
Boyd K. Packer	Basic , for Church members listed	Nov 2006	86d-e
Larry W. Gibbons	Rabbi: God cares what I have for lunch		102c-d
	Keeping a summer cottage in Babylon		102e
	Keeping one foot each in Church and world		102f
	Keeping , without offending the devil		102f
	We must stop drifting		102f-103a
	The 80:20 theory is OK for nutrition		103a-b
	Knowing won't save. Doing duty will.		103d-f
	Stay in middle of straight and narrow path		104a
Spencer J. Condie	List of exceeding promises if , are kept	Nov 2007	16e-17a
Joseph B. Wirthlin	Pharisees identified over 600 ,		28d-e
Dieter F. Uchtdorf	, are tests and navigational instructions	May 2008	60b
D. Todd Christofferson	Continual flow of blessings when keeping ,	May 2009	21a-b
	God designed all , for our happiness		23a
	When we obey , we seek more		23a
Thomas S. Monson	Not negotiable - Not the ten suggestions		125b-126a
Dieter F. Uchtdorf	Sometimes we amplify and add to ,	Nov 2009	21c-e
Dallin H. Oaks	God's and parental love do not supersede ,		26b-e
Thomas S. Monson	We will survive if we live the ,		109d-e
Boyd K. Packer	Never been easy to live ,	May 2010	7b
D. Todd Christofferson	Our protection against self-inflicted pain		34d
Bruce A. Carlson	Safety of Church is in keeping ,		38d
	3 reasons for not keeping ,		38d
	Martin Harris lost 116 pages —story		39d-f
Gregory A. Schwitzer	Keep , and prosper — repeated by prophets		105d-e
Ann M. Dibb	Obedience brings success		115b

Communication
Related Topics: Listening, Meditation, Prayer

Spencer W. Kimball	Analogies from burned telephone line in grass fire	July 1972	37d
	A marriage ruined from lack of , —story		38a

Communication, cont'd
Related Topics: Listening, Meditation; Prayer

Spencer W. Kimball	Returned missionary ruined from lack of , —story	July 1972	38b
	A marriage ruined from lack of , —story		39c
Sterling W. Sill	The African worshiped writing —story		125a
Marvin J. Ashton	7 points toward family , —entire talk	May 1976	52a-54f
Carlos E. Asay	65% of our , is non-verbal	May 1980	43a
Ted E. Brewerton	Talk in order that I may see you —Socrates	May 1983	72d
	Speak only positively - no negativism		73c-74a
Carlos E. Asay	Interviewing children - wet or dry? —story	Nov 1983	14b-c
	Alma's and Helaman's interview		14d-15a
	Short father-son interview dispelled fears —story		15a-c
Virginia H. Pearce	We discover and develop thoughts through ,	Nov 1993	80a
M. Russell Ballard	Eliminate "non-member" from vocabulary	Nov 2001	37d-e
H. David Burton	Eliminate "non-member" from vocabulary		66e
Thomas S. Monson	Good to commune with self —D.O. McKay	Nov 2004	68e-f
Russell M. Nelson	Man on plane ignored wife —story	May 2006	36b-c
Gordon B. Hinckley	Phenomenal increase in satellite downlinks	Nov 2006	4b-c
Joseph B. Wirthlin	"I knew who you was"		28e-f
Robert D. Hales	We can't afford it - , in marriage —story	May 2009	8b-9b

Communism
Related Topics: Government

David O. McKay	Pray that the Lord will frustrate ,	June 1969	30d
	The greatest satanical threat to peace		30d-f
Ezra Taft Benson	Seeks to destroy morals of a generation of youth		46e-47c
Ezra Taft Benson	Must warn against ,	Dec 1969	69b
	Revolution in America		69d
	Effective warning to America		69f
	Recognition of Russia a mistake		72b
Ezra Taft Benson	Gospel must be preached in communist countries	June 1970	96b
Sterling W. Sill	No other problems will matter if , takes over	Dec 1970	79b
David B. Haight	Communists asked "What is meaning of life?" —story	June 1971	53a
Ezra Taft Benson	Greatest threat to nation	July 1972	60e
	If , comes here there will be vacancies in leadership		61a
Spencer W. Kimball	, knows no God but force - tortures truth	May 1976	107f
Marion G. Romney	United Order is not ,	May 1977	94a-c
Ezra Taft Benson	Warning to America about , and Monroe Doctrine	Nov 1979	31b-33f
Bruce R. McConkie	There will be congregations in Moscow	May 1980	72c

Confession, cont'd
Related Topics: Forgiveness, Repentance, Sin

Ezra Taft Benson	Sensitivity training is not proper ,	June 1969	44e-46e
James A. Cullimore	Proper , —excellent explanation	Dec 1971	87b-c
LeGrand Richards	More than , required	Jan 1973	110f
	Other churches and ,		111e
Robert L. Simpson	A purpose of , is to provide a helper	July 1973	49d
James A. Cullimore	3 people to whom , must be made	May 1974	30f
Vaughn J. Featherstone	A tragedy when , is only partial	Nov 1980	30a

Vaughn J. Featherstone	42-year-old sin confessed - fornication —story	Nov 1980	30a-f
	34-year-old sin confessed - abortion —story		30f-31c
Marion G. Romney	To whom do we make , of various sins?		48a-c
F. Burton Howard	Ran from mission call. No peace until , made —story	May 1983	58f-59e
	Sins jeopardizing fellowship must be confessed		60a
Russell M. Nelson	To whom , must be made	May 2007	102f

Constitution
Related Topics: America, Freedom, United States

Ezra Taft Benson	Place allegiance to , not leaders —J.R. Clark	July 1972	60b
	Save , or have change of government		60d
Paul H. Dunn	, far exceeded the best efforts of its writers	Nov 1975	53e
	A divine document		54c
N. Eldon Tanner	Its writer said it was inspired - It's a miracle	May 1976	49b-e
Ezra Taft Benson	Interesting history behind the ,		91b-f
	A timeless document. Made for a moral people.		92a-c
	An urging for us to become familiar with ,		93d-f
	A sacred document akin to revelation		93f
Ezra Taft Benson	Fast approaching time when , will be on brink of ruin	Nov 1987	6d-e
	What we can do to maintain ,		6e-7f
David B. Haight	God's hand in , —quote by James Madison		13e
Boyd K. Packer	Cruelties came from corrupt administration not ,	Nov 2008	88d-91f

Contention
Related Topics: Quarreling

Theodore M. Burton	Anger must never be evident in discussions	Dec 1969	56e
	If we redden, tense, and get warm it is time to repent		56f-57c
Gordon B. Hinckley	Those who contend with other religions reap persecution	June 1970	40a
Elray L. Christiansen	Parents must avoid disputations	July 1972	55b
Marion D. Hanks	Farmer was wronged - spited self —story		105f
H. Burke Peterson	Must not be allowed in home	Jan 1973	114b
	Starts and stops with parents		115e
Boyd K. Packer	A marriage with no cross words ever		89f
Marvin J. Ashton	Joseph and Hyrum never rebuked one another	Jan 1974	104c
Theodore M. Burton	, for evil or good both please Satan	Nov 1974	56a
Franklin D. Richards	Bishop challenged youth to be peacemakers in home		106c-f
Marvin J. Ashton	Slanderous pamphlet deserved no reply —story	May 1978	7d-e
	5 suggestions for alleviating ,		9f
Marvin J. Ashton	Those who stir up waters create whirlpools	May 1983	31f
Marvin J. Ashton	, a tool of adversary. Peace a tool of Savior.	Nov 1987	21f-22d
Ezra Taft Benson	, comes through pride	May 1989	6a
Russell M. Nelson	Better give your path to a dog than be bitten —A. Lincoln		68d
	The canker of contention —entire talk		68b-71b
Robert D. Hales	How to react to opposition	Nov 2008	72f-73e

Boyd K. Packer	A reporter interviewing a , at Conference	Dec 1968	79e-80a
Henry D. Taylor	"We love one another" started conversion —story	June 1969	64b-c
Gordon B. Hinckley	Fruits of a convert's labors —story	Dec 1969	98f
Marion G. Romney	She tried nearly every church —story	June 1970	67c-d
John H. Vandenberg	Home teachers' faithfulness made , —story	Dec 1970	36f-37e
LeGrand Richards	Converted by Articles of Faith bookmarker —story	Dec 1971	84d
Victor L. Brown	Stirring stories of 2 men converted in prison —story		88a-89f
Milton R. Hunter	Boy , loses inheritance and goes on mission —story	July 1972	50d
	Nurse , loses inheritance and goes on mission —story		50f
	Girl eavesdrops, and makes 50 , —story		51b
	Woman sees missionaries in dream —story		51c
Victor L. Brown	A Jew and a Mormon - disowned by family - funeral		90d
N. Eldon Tanner	Converted by example —story		100e
David B. Haight	How Brazil was opened —story	Jan 1973	74f
Harold B. Lee	Price paid by a ,		108e
Gordon B. Hinckley	An Asian , - great sacrifice —story	July 1973	48b
	Praying wife converts rebellious husband —story		50a
	Woman drawn by appearance of Elders —story		50d
Sterling W. Sill	Must be a , before you can be a disciple or leader		104b
Franklin D. Richards	Air Force cadet converted - changed by Spirit		117a
Gordon B. Hinckley	Filipino converted by fact that we had a prophet —story	Jan 1974	122c
	A Christian turned Jew turned LDS —story		124b
	Young man on plane was reading an LDS book —story		124d
L. Tom Perry	Convert reconverts his missionary —story	Nov 1974	18d-f
Rex D. Pinegar	How Book of Mormon made a convert —story		44f-45a
Robert L. Simpson	Children went from reform school to missions —story		46d
	Black man found Church in prison —story		46d-e
	Stewardess anxious to be baptized —story		46e
Robert L. Simpson	Family converted through Primary —story		46e-f
	Fasting by non-member wife softened husband —story		46f
James E. Faust	Conversion of a young missionary —story		60c-d
H. Burke Peterson	The youth was disowned —story		68b-e
N. Eldon Tanner	A young , —story		76b-77c
Boyd K. Packer	Woman marveled over change in 2 nephews —story		87d-e
	Man could not accept tithing —story		88a-e
	When you know truth you won't want bad habits		89b-c
Thomas S. Monson	Father was missionary's final convert —story		108f-109e
A. Theodore Tuttle	Something was missing in life —story	May 1975	90d-e
LeGrand Richards	Statements of 2 converted ministers		97b-c
Adney Y. Komatsu	His conversion —story		100b-d
Joseph B. Wirthlin	Telephone call made convert —story	Nov 1975	105e-106a
James A. Cullimore	Converts made by 2 Books of Mormon —2 stories	May 1976	85f-86c
Hartman Rector, Jr	Conversion of Lutheran pastor —story	Nov 1976	97d-99b
Loren C. Dunn	Warm spot in heart told him it was true —story	May 1977	31c-32b
Carlos E. Asay	Hawaiian eager of news of a living prophet —story	Nov 1978	54a

N. Eldon Tanner	Statements by a Protestant minister convert	May 1979	19d-f
Yoshihiko Kikuchi	Baptism healed man who couldn't walk —story	Nov 1979	29d-30e
N. Eldon Tanner	Tracts in shoes converted Widtsoes —story		50b-e
N. Eldon Tanner	Near broken family became eternal —story	May 1980	18f
F. Enzio Busche	Join Church only if he would never be asked to give a talk		27b-c
Robert E. Wells	Elder apologized for meeting - no need to —story	Nov 1980	12e-13a
Marvin J. Ashton	Man traded week of food for Book of Mormon —story	May 1981	23d-e
David B. Haight	Temple visitors' children ushered into primary —story		40c-e
	Annapolis senior asked freshman for B of M —story		40e-f
Bruce R. McConkie	Would you have believed had you lived 2000 years ago?	Nov 1981	46b-48f
Yoshihiko Kikuchi	Oriental woman impressed by son's baptism —story		70b-d
	7-year-old Oriental sent Daddy Book of Mormon —story		70d-e
Marion D. Hanks	My specialty is mercy —story		73e-74e
	Woman vowed she'd never speak again —story		75a-b
James M. Paramore	Couple moved and were besieged by love —story	May 1983	28c-d
Vaughn J. Featherstone	Catholic boy committed to serve mission —story	Nov 1983	37a
Devin G. Durrant	Spanish boys , serve mission —story	May 1984	35f-36e
	Persuasive elder failed - Silent elder's love did it —story		36f-37b
Robert L. Simpson	How gospel changed East Indian saints		60e-f
	Sir, do you love the Lord? —story		61b-d
	I wouldn't be dishonest. I'm a Mormon. —story		61d-f
Wm. Grant Bangerter	Conversion of Helio da Rocha Camargo —story	May 1985	64e-65a
Ezra Taft Benson	Discussion of being "born again"	Nov 1985	5e-6d
	Christ takes slums out of people—take selves out of slums		6e-f
	Celestial people must truly be born again —dream		7b
Rex D. Pinegar	Man supported Church 47 years - was baptized —story		40e-41a
Gordon B. Hinckley	Divinity student joins Church —story	May 1986	41c-42e
Marvin J. Ashton	Buddhist family nearly divorced, then converted —story		67a-f
Joseph B. Wirthlin	Nun in Portugal —story	Nov 1986	60b-e
Thomas S. Monson	Converted by church-going son —story	Nov 1987	43a
	Converted by missionary son's letters —story		43e-44b
Lloyd P. George	100-yr-old waited 80 years for baptism—story	Nov 1988	42c-e
Thomas S. Monson	Australian told to never give up on husband —story		72b-f
Joseph B. Wirthlin	Abinadi had just one convert	May 1989	10a-b
Hugh W. Pinnock	, bring selves into Church. Missionaries don't.		10f-11a
Royden G. Derrick	Views of a Hindu convert		76b-c
Ben B. Banks	Sister missionary's parents become , —story	Nov 1989	41f-42a
Gordon B. Hinckley	, must wait 1 year before temple	May 1990	49f-50b
Robert K. Dellenbach	His conversion aboard ship —story	Nov 1990	23b-c
Helvecio Martins	Converted by others' testimonies —story		26b-f
Gordon B. Hinckley	Worldly man read Book of Mormon and cried —story		52e-f
Thomas S. Monson	Dog-eared Bible and healing at baptism —story		68c-e
Julio E. Davila	His conversion by B.K. Packer's son	Nov 1991	23d-24d
	Converted when we see, hear, and understand		24d
Joseph C. Muren	His conversion by fasting missionaries		29b-e

Converts

Marvin J. Ashton	How to tell if someone is converted	May 1992	19d-20b
James M. Paramore	Church changed everything in life	Nov 1992	10e
J. Richard Clarke	Insect's permanent metamorphosis like ,	May 1993	9d-e
	Letter from prisoner		10b-c
Chieko N. Okazaki	Her conversion —story		84b-85f
Tai Kwok Yuen	His Hong Kong conversion —story		86b-87f
Lowell D. Wood	What God can do for a life —E.T. Benson		89a
Boyd K. Packer	, will become a flood	May 1994	21b-f
Charles Didier	His conversion story		42f-44d
Merrill J. Bateman	Japanese optician suddenly could see —story		65f-66b
Hartman Rector, Jr	His conversion story	Nov 1994	25c-f
Dieter F. Uchtdorf	His family's conversion in Germany		41d-f
Merrill J. Bateman	Paralyzed Korean girl has change of heart —story	May 1995	14b-f
Henry B. Eyring	Family read daily - recognized gospel —story		25f-26a
Helvecio Martins	Home teachers assigned in 2nd week of investigation		44b-45b
Thomas S. Monson	Plane conversation with flight attendant —story		50b-f
Keith B. McMullin	"Don't argue with me - ask the Lord" —story	May 1996	8d-9e
W. Mack Lawrence	What true conversion entails		74b-75f
Virginia H. Pearce	Will , stay or drift away?	Nov 1996	11d-12a
	Her convert was called to teach —story		14a
Wm. Rolfe Kerr	Kicked out of home - 100's of descendants —story		81b-f
Henry B. Eyring	Keep reaching out to new , - persist —story	May 1997	26c-e
Thomas S. Monson	All new , should receive callings		45a-b
	Unknowingly, family joined simultaneously —story		45b-d
	At conference , wore white carnations —story		45e-f
Gordon B. Hinckley	321,385 , in 1996		47b
	Every convert needs 3 things		47b-c
	His convert and failure —story		47c-48a
	What we need to do to retain ,		48a-e
Thomas S. Monson	The convert who became ancestress of Jesus		50f-51a
Thomas S. Monson	Czech girl made dozens of , —story		94a-b
Carl B. Pratt	Differences between wards greeting new ,	Nov 1997	11b-12b
Mary Ellen Smoot	Man has 2,000 LDS descendants - brother has 1		12e-13a
	Pioneer convert's reply to plea to leave Church		13f-14a
Joseph B. Wirthlin	The effect of conversion —G.B. Hinckley		33e-f
Richard G. Scott	Social conversion more difficult than doctrinal		35e-f
Gordon B. Hinckley	Letter from a , - we must do better —story		50b-51d
Dallin H. Oaks	Fellowshipping at its finest		73c-d
Henry B. Eyring	The necessity of and how to feed ,		82b-84f
Jeffrey R. Holland	, will stay if taught and nourished	May 1998	26f-27a
Richard E. Cook	, come alive in all areas of their lives		28d-e
Gordon B. Hinckley	Gospel lifted , out of poverty —story		70d-f
Richard G. Scott	Advice to set aside incorrect heritages		85b-87b
M. Russell Ballard	Poignant letter about need to nurture ,	Nov 1998	7d-8a
H. David Burton	The 5 "I's" for including ,		11b-c

Converts

Ronald T. Halverson	Searching for peace , found Book of Mormon —story	Nov 1998	78d-79a
Richard G. Scott	His non member father became a sealer —story	May 1999	27b-c
Ned B. Roueche	Invitation to serve brought him back —story		42b-e
David B. Haight	He sealed the stewardess —story		68d-f
Henry B. Eyring	Girl was jailed for teaching —story		74d-75f
Gordon B. Hinckley	Finding and keeping , —important talk		104b-110f
Ben B. Banks	3 things , need —G.B. Hinckley	Nov 1999	10c
James E. Faust	Seeds and the soils they fall into		46b-47b
L. Tom Perry	Read B of M because of uneducated author —story		76f-77a
Richard H. Winkel	, compared to redwoods' intertwining roots		81b-82f
James E. Faust	Master pianist put arms around student —story		101b-c
Yoshihiko Kikuchi	She became one of those weird Mormons —story	May 2000	78b-79c
John B. Dickson	10 points to help , understand Church		82b-83f
Dallin H. Oaks	Conversion is far more than testimony —entire talk	Nov 2000	32a-34f
L. Tom Perry	Remarkable conversion of ancestor —story		61e-62b
M. Russell Ballard	Church-going child reactivated father —story		76d-e
Robert C. Oaks	300,000 , per year is not nearly enough		81c
Virginia U. Jensen	Emma Smith's , number in the thousands —story		92e-93b
Jeffrey R. Holland	People join because of what they feel and see	May 2001	14f
Boyd K. Packer	Destitute German family , —story	Nov 2001	62d-63e
Thomas S. Monson	Woman would not renounce Church —story		98f-99a
Earl C. Tingey	Counsel to , to pay tithing	May 2002	11f-12b
Mary Ellen W. Smoot	Handcart woman became a different person —story		13c-e
Joseph B. Wirthlin	Convert persecuted by family —story		17a-c
Richard G. Scott	Meaning of the word "conversion"		24f-25c
Henry B. Eyring	Being a true friend to , —entire talk		26d-29b
Spencer J. Condie	Make friends' cause your own —Browning poem		45f-46a
Gordon B. Hinckley	Rude investigator now a stake president —story		73a-c
	Green wood can't burn if removed from fire		74f
M. Russell Ballard	Scruffy family of , changed appearance —story		88f-89d
Dieter F. Uchtdorf	Lost everything twice, but found gospel —story	Nov 2002	10f-11d
Lance B. Wickman	Nurse heard blessing and sought missionaries —story		31e-32c
Dallin H. Oaks	Difficult mission converted proud elder —story		70b-f
Bonnie D. Parkin	An icy baptism at midnight —story		103d-e
M. Russell Ballard	450 , in one branch in one year —story	May 2003	38f-39a
Neal A. Maxwell	A labor which takes more than an afternoon		70d-e
Sheldon F. Child	Woman asked why we don't have prophets —story	Nov 2003	8f-9d
James E. Faust	Inactive member became , —story		21d-f
Dallin H. Oaks	Surfer became stake president		37b-d
Monte J. Brough	"No one ever asked me" —story		49a-b
D. Todd Christofferson	Becoming converted in your heart	May 2004	11b-13f
Jeffrey R. Holland	At his funeral he'll ask about retention		31d-f
Bruce C. Hafen	Flowers replaced weeds in life		97e-f
Richard G. Scott	Gospel changed poor Bolivian town		101d-102b
Dale E. Miller	Conversion and membership not the same	Nov 2004	12d-e

Thomas S. Monson	Man baptized through home teaching —story	Nov 2004	57e-58d
Dieter F. Uchtdorf	The conversion of his family —story		75e-f
Thomas S. Monson	Wife converted husband —tender story		115b-116a
Richard C. Edgley	African's heart was throbbing —story	May 2005	10b-f
Henry B. Eyring	Over half of Church is ,		77b
	I'm clean. I felt fire go down my body.		77b-d
L. Tom Perry	Convert progressed when focus was on Jesus		85d-f
	Missionaries sent in answer to prayers —story		86b-f
C. Scott Grow	Mexican waited 12 years —story	Nov 2005	34b-f
Thomas S. Monson	Nonmember: No one ever visits us —story		59b-d
Russell M. Nelson	True conversion brings healing		86d-87a
Gordon B. Hinckley	Hated unfriendly LDS. Friend changed that —story	May 2006	59b-60d
Dallin H. Oaks	Examples of amazing , from all nations		78b-79b
Susan W. Tanner	Example of Romanian girl , family —story		105b-d
James E. Faust	Girl's smiles make , —story		113a-d
Paul B. Pieper	One convert's decision affected thousands	Nov 2006	12e-f
	The first generation: A chosen generation		11d-13b
Jeffrey R. Holland	A hike and General Conference makes , —story		104d-105a
David A. Bednar	Parable of the Pickle - Conversion process	May 2007	19b-22b
Vicki F. Matsumori	Missionaries took bandages off woman's eyes		77b
Glenn L. Pace	A testimony from Holy Ghost at age 11 —story		78b-d
	Something spectacular doesn't need to happen		78e
	Intellectual woman couldn't deny feeling —story		78e-f
Gary J. Coleman	Three truths he learned as a convert		92b-94b
Dieter F. Uchtdorf	Church came to his family amid war —story	Nov 2007	18f-19a
Michael J. Teh	From rock thrower to convert —story		36f-37b
L. Tom Perry	Missionary doesn't convert - Spirit does		49a
Octaviano Tenorio	Plan to convert father worked —story		95f-96e
Claudio D. Zivic	Prayed to know - began to cry —story		99b-d
James E. Faust	Saul's conversion described		122b-d
	Special baptismal feelings - Starting fresh		122e
	Brutal alcoholic became convert —story		122e-123a
Russell M. Nelson	King offered to have his people baptized	May 2008	8c-d
Dieter F. Uchtdorf	Conversion of his wife's family —story		70e-75a
Silvia H. Allred	Her conversion and that of her family —story	Nov 2008	10e-11d
	Generational effects of her conversion —story		11d-12a
	Second-grade girl makes a convert —story		12e-f
Marcos A. Aidukaitis	Because father read the Book of Mormon —story		15b-f
Carlos A. Godoy	Nothing dramatic happened as he gained a testimony		100d-102b
Allan F. Packer	Conversion is to do and to become —D.H. Oaks	May 2009	17f
Quentin L. Cook	Wanted a more liberal salvation for man —story		36c-e
Thomas S. Monson	Missionaries appeared following prayer —story		68f-69c
Thomas S. Monson	Scottish , immigrated despite trials —story		89d-90b
Yoon Hwan Choi	Nine Korean troublemakers joined Church —story	Nov 2009	53b-55b
Russell M. Nelson	"I'd be honored to perform that sealing" —story		82d-f

Converts

Dale G. Renlund	Heart transplants - Physical and spiritual	Nov 2009	97d-98e
Michael T. Ringwood	Eph Hanks saving brother from Mormons —story		101a
D. Todd Christofferson	Make , of your children while they are with you		107c
Statistical Report	280,106 , in 2009	May 2010	28a
Koichi Aoyagi	His conversion —story		36c-37b
Dieter F. Uchtdorf	Welcome even Canned-Food Mormons —story		68d-f
Francisco J. Viñas	Make , of children by teaching		106a-108b

Counsel
Related Topics: Interviewing

James A. Cullimore	Bishops have right to give inspired ,	June 1969	68e
	It is sin to not follow , of brethren		68f
Theodore M. Burton	Don't give , until it is asked		109d-f
Richard L. Evans	Don't waste time looking for what has already been found	Dec 1971	58f
Harold B. Lee	Ignoring , brings fall	Jan 1973	107f
A. Theodore Tuttle	Disregard , never prosper	July 1973	19c
Vaughn J. Featherstone	Girl couldn't recognize answer to prayers —story	May 1975	68a-c
Robert D. Hales	Don't ask , of someone who is disoriented himself	Nov 1975	92f
Boyd K. Packer	People seeking too much , may lose ability to receive revelation	May 1978	91a-93f
M. Russell Ballard	Lord helped him , bereaved young man —story	Nov 1980	23c-f
Loren C. Dunn	I have no , for you because you won't heed it —story	May 1981	27a
Russell M. Nelson	, to learn English yielded 2 missions —story	May 1991	23f-24a
M. Russell Ballard	Too many murmur at , —Joseph Smith	Nov 1991	7d
Boyd K. Packer	Need for , will decrease with more reverence		23a-b
M. Russell Ballard	Follow , like Hyrum Smith did —story	Nov 1995	7f-8d
W. Eugene Hansen	Sheep ignored shepherd - 2 were killed —story	May 1996	38d-f
Rulon G. Craven	Yielding to temptation is going against ,		76f-77a
Thomas S. Monson	Always listen to your wife —story	Nov 1996	44f-45c
Joseph B. Wirthlin	Purpose is to teach and prepare for final judgment	May 1997	16f
Henry B. Eyring	Savior calls us by many means		24d-e
	Jacob Haun ignored prophet's , —story		24f-25a
	Rejecting , of prophets means choosing another influence		25b-26c
	When we follow , we save others —Handcart story		26c-e
	77 rescue wagons turned back by those not following ,		26c-e
	Treasure , like you would gold		26f
Boyd K. Packer	Never ignore , from your bishop	May 1999	58e
Henry B. Eyring	Recently released bishop found no , to give —story	Nov 2002	77a-b
Gordon B. Hinckley	Chinese woman blessed for following , —story	Nov 2006	118d-f
Richard G. Scott	Healing the consequences of abuse	May 2008	40b-43f
Thomas S. Monson	, given by Vietnam prisoners	Nov 2008	86d-e
M. Russell Ballard	Heed , of parents —Edsel dealership story	May 2009	31b-e
Boyd K. Packer	, to young men —entire talk		49d-52f

Courage
Related Topics: Fear

N. Eldon Tanner	Missionary resisted going out on town —story	Dec 1968	92f-93a
	Girl baptized in spite of opposition —story		93c-e

Boyd K. Packer	, begins when you know and face the truth —story	Dec 1970	106d-e
Thomas S. Monson	, to live decently better than , to die	July 1972	74a
Spencer W. Kimball	Fear develops into ,	July 1973	16e
	Fear that has said its prayers		16f
Boyd K. Packer	Faith is the one essential ingredient of ,	Jan 1974	28f
H. Burke Peterson	Some stayed, some left the movie —story	Nov 1974	69b-d
Marion G. Romney	, in the face of persecution —J.F. Smith story		74d-e
	Lincoln lost Senate race because of , —story		74e-75c
Spencer W. Kimball	David and Goliath retold —story		80e-82d
Marion G. Romney	Courage and majesty in chains at midnight —story	May 1975	72d-f
	, brings peace - cowardice brings regret		74a
	Through cowardice he ignored the Spirit —story		74b
Joseph B. Wirthlin	, to bear testimony changed spirit of meeting —story	Nov 1975	104e-105e
Gene R. Cook	Woman spoke up and touched a heart —story	May 1976	103d-e
N. Eldon Tanner	Boy could not be induced to open gate —story	May 1977	15c-e
Paul H. Dunn	British at Waterloo had , just 5 minutes longer	May 1979	9b-c
John H. Groberg	Hawaiian overcame insult - returned to church —story	May 1980	49a-f
Gordon B. Hinckley	3 boys carried pioneers through icy stream —story	Nov 1981	42d-f
James E. Faust	Sentenced to die for refusing to denounce Joseph —story	May 1982	47e-f
	Man shot while guarding the Brethren —story		48b-d
Robert L. Backman	Girl stood up for ostracized friend —story	Nov 1985	12d-f
L. Tom Perry	The story of Daniel —story		46e-48e
Thomas S. Monson	Scriptural examples of ,	Nov 1986	41a-c
	, is the determination to live decently		41d
	Paralyzed missionary returned to field —story		41f-42b
Dallin H. Oaks	19-year-old boys spied on murderers' meeting —story	May 1987	38e-39d
Marvin J. Ashton	Kayaking without a good right arm —story	Nov 1988	16b-f
Thomas S. Monson	Healing of Guatemalan missionary —story	May 1989	45b-46b
Boyd K. Packer	, sometimes means running away		54f
Thomas S. Monson	3 boys carried pioneers across river —story	May 1990	46f-47a
Ardeth G. Kapp	More , required than by pioneers —excellent talk	Nov 1990	93b-95b
Jack H. Goaslind	Young woman turned off movie —story	May 1991	47a-b
Thomas S. Monson	Czech man got Church recognized —story	Nov 1991	48b-e
Gordon B. Hinckley	Call to rescue handcart companies —N. Unthank story		52d-59b
Carlos E. Asay	E.T. Benson bore testimony in Moscow	May 1992	41d-f
V. J. Featherstone	The , to keep going —J.F. Smith		44d-f
Virginia H. Pearce	How to conquer our fears —good advice	Nov 1992	90b-92b
Marlin K. Jensen	Joseph rebuking guards —P.P. Pratt quote	May 1994	47e-48b
H. David Burton	Courageous man finds a way, not an excuse		67f-68a
Richard C. Edgley	Developing confidence —great talk	Nov 1994	39d-41b
Jeffrey R. Holland	Rudger Clawson's , as companion was shot —story	May 1995	39b-f
	Financial adversity - missionary's pigs and cows died —story		40a-f
Thomas S. Monson	Soldier gave water to wounded enemy —story		54c-59a
James E. Faust	Joseph F. Smith facing mobbers —story	Nov 1995	46e-f
Joe J. Christensen	"Come have lunch with us" —handicap story	Nov 1996	39c-d

Courage

James E. Faust	"I'll turn any cheaters in" —Med. school story	Nov 1996	42a-d
	Hard questions asked for officer candidate school —story		42e-43b
Neal A. Maxwell	Not shrinking is more important than surviving	Nov 1997	22f
M. Russell Ballard	J.F. Smith meeting the ruffians —story		37e-f
	Whistling and whittling to rid town of villains —story		39a-d
James E. Faust	Action is inhibited by fear		43d
	Panicked speaker mustered , —story		44d-e
Dallin H. Oaks	Two boys who spied for Joseph —story		73f-74e
Richard C. Edgley	Athlete left pornographic movie —story	Nov 1999	42f-43a
James E. Faust	Peter's denials led to strength		61a-d
James E. Faust	What a young woman endured —story	May 2000	97a-c
Joseph B. Wirthlin	Blind man climbed Everest —story	Nov 2001	25d-26a
Thomas S. Monson	Joseph Smith was the model of ,	Nov 2002	62a-b
Thomas S. Monson	Entire talk	May 2004	54d-57f
Thomas S. Monson	Young Joseph Smith's leg operation —story	Nov 2005	67b-f
David R. Stone	The basis for all other virtues	May 2006	92e-93a
James E. Faust	Rollins girls saving D&C pages —story		111f-112a
Boyd K. Packer	Future events will tax our , and extend faith	Nov 2006	88d
Thomas S. Monson	Sustained without being called —story	May 2007	57d-f
Charles W. Dahlquist, II	Baptized amid shower of stones —story		94f-95b
	Nephi and David - Two youths with ,		95b-e
Thomas S. Monson	Have , to stand alone	May 2008	65e-f
Susan W. Tanner	Youth individually resisted peer temptations		113f-114b
Elaine S. Dalton	Only one opposed to premarital sex —story		116e-117a
Henry B. Eyring	Give all in priesthood service, and Lord gives ,	Nov 2008	60a-b
Robert D. Hales	Jesus endured mocking with silence		72b-e
	Joseph Smith did not retaliate		72e
	Christian courage - How to face opposition		72b-75b
Henry B. Eyring	Rangers lost lives saving downed pilot —story	May 2009	63c-f
Thomas S. Monson	Have , against mocking and persecution		126b-127a
	Story of Queen Esther —story		127a-e
Ann M. Dibb	Teacher attacked girl's view —story	May 2010	116d-e

Covenants
Related Topics: —

David O. McKay	Don't go to temple unless you will keep ,	June 1969	28e-29a
Joseph Fielding Smith	What the temple , entail	June 1970	66c-d
Joseph Fielding Smith	Definition of ,	Dec 1970	26d-e
Elray L. Christiansen	New and everlasting , embraces all former ,	Jan 1973	50b
William H. Bennett	, made in temple and consequences of disobeying —story	Nov 1975	46d-47b
Marion G. Romney	Inactivity caused by failure to appreciate ,		72e-73a
	Renew baptismal , weekly through sacrament		73d-e
	4 important , - we are accountable when others break ,		73e-f
Boyd K. Packer	Good conduct with , will not redeem nor exalt	Nov 1985	82a
Gordon B. Hinckley	Priesthood holder was not ready for commitments —story	Nov 1986	44e
Boyd K. Packer	Can keep , as a home teacher as well as in a high position	May 1987	23f-24b

Covenants, cont'd
Related Topics: —

Boyd K. Packer	Our credentials for admission to God's presence	May 1987	24c-e
Charles Didier	Ordinances convey power —Widtsoe		27c
Dallin H. Oaks	We serve because we're under ,	Nov 1989	65d-f
Russell M. Nelson	Ordinances and , available only in Church	May 1990	18b-d
James E. Faust	Blessings come to children because of parents' ,	Nov 1990	35b
Joseph B. Wirthlin	Like white lines on road in driving storm		64d-f
Boyd K. Packer	Sacrament is a covenant		84b
	Keep , and you will be safe		84d
Russell M. Nelson	, are his most important accomplishment —story	May 1992	74c-d
Dallin H. Oaks	Many of us made , in pre-earth life	Nov 1993	72e
Elaine L. Jack	The road signs to eternal life	May 1994	15e-f
J. Ballard Washburn	Marriage , includes willingness to have children	May 1995	12b-c
	We go to temple to make , but home to keep them		12d-e
Russell M. Nelson	The Abrahamic Covenant		33a-d
	Meaning of "born in the covenant"		33e-f
Bonnie D. Parkin	, —good talk		78b-79f
Carlos E. Asay	, are a sextant to keep us on course	May 1996	60e-61c
Henry B. Eyring	God will keep , to gather family		64d-f
Henry B. Eyring	We home teach because of , —story	Nov 1996	30d-31c
	The fruit of keeping ,		32f
Elaine L. Jack	Living , in midst of flood —story		76b-e
Richard G. Scott	Ordinances and , are essential	May 1997	53f-54c
	Must be accomplished before departing earth		54e
	Keeping , is not hard if done willingly		54d-59a
Russell M. Nelson	Two most important relationships are by covenant		71d-e
	4 "f's" must not be loved more than ,		72c
Neal A. Maxwell	We must have both , and character	Nov 1997	24a-b
Richard G. Scott	Ordinances and , assure happiness	Nov 1998	68c
Neal A. Maxwell	Willing to break , to fix appetites		24b-c
M. Russell Ballard	Governed by , or convenience?	May 1999	86d
Sheri L. Dew	, and ordinances bind us to each other and to God	Nov 1999	98e-f
Richard G. Scott	No celestial kingdom unless , are kept	May 2001	9a
Russell M. Nelson	Breaking , is worse than not making them		32f
	The endowment —explanation		33a
	Obedience to temple , qualifies us for exaltation		33a-b
	, are not restrictive but protective		34b
	Proper succession of ,		34b-d
	Our credentials for admission to God's presence		34d
	We'll be judged according to our ,		34e
Keith B. McMullin	Living 3 or 4 , would solve all our problems —Hinckley		62a-e
Bonnie D. Parkin	I serve because I made ,	Nov 2002	103c-d
	"None but God heard my covenant" —story		103d-e
	What , do for us		104b-105a
Kathleen H. Hughes	Temple marriage seals children. They will return —Packer		107d-f
	Grandmother was one of last in Nauvoo Temple		108a-b

Covenants

Covenants, cont'd

James E. Faust	Sealed children, though wayward, will return	May 2003	62b-f
Susan W. Tanner	Money given in accident because of , —story		102d-f
James E. Faust	No other church claims keys to ,	Nov 2003	21a
Robert D. Hales	, will bring children back —O.F. Whitney	May 2004	91c-d
James E. Faust	A righteous person makes and keeps ,	Nov 2004	52d-53b
	Temple , by which we'll be organized and exalted		55a-b
Richard J. Maynes	The most important thing is to keep ,		93b
Susan W. Tanner	, sustained family during loss —story	May 2005	106a-e
Henry B. Eyring	Priesthood presidents are to teach ,	Nov 2006	43e-f
Robert D. Hales	Temple , more important than a mission	May 2007	49e-f
Spencer J. Condie	List of exceeding promises if , are kept	Nov 2007	16e-17a
Dieter F. Uchtdorf	, are tests and navigational instructions	May 2008	60b
D. Todd Christofferson	The law of the celestial kingdom is ,	Nov 2008	38f-39b
Silvia H. Allred	Our credentials for admission to God's presence		113b
D. Todd Christofferson	Sustained family through earthquake —story	May 2009	19d-20b
	Our access to God's power		20b
	Done individually		20b-d
	Obtain all God's divine possibilities through ,		20d
	Definition of new and everlasting ,		20d-f
	A continual flow of blessings comes through ,		21a-b
	Produce faith necessary to persevere		21b-f
	Empowering blessings, faith, divine power		21f-22a
	Endows with powerful instrument for good		22a-e
	In times of distress let , be paramount		22f
	Become a powerful instrument for good through ,		22f-23a
Richard G. Scott	, sustain him - Wife and 3 children died —story		45a-f
Dallin H. Oaks	Selfish people become disconnected from ,		95b-c
Walter F. Gonzalez	Application of Book of Mormon requires ,	Nov 2009	51e
Henry B. Eyring	Putting welfare of spouse at center of life		70f-71b
Boyd K. Packer	Priesthood power comes through honoring ,	May 2010	9d-e
M. Russell Ballard	Youth keep , if Spirit can be recognized		20f-21a
	Safest road to happiness is keeping ,		21a
Dieter F. Uchtdorf	Lord's promises not swift but certain		58d-e

Creation

Neal A. Maxwell	More stars than grains of sand	Nov 2003	100b-d
Keith B. McMullin	Jesus created millions of worlds	May 2004	34b-d
	Savior of other worlds —Joseph Smith		35a-c
Gordon B. Hinckley	All things were made by Jesus	May 2007	83e-84c
Richard G. Scott	Vast extent of God's , - From quarks to space	Nov 2007	90e-91d
	God's , revealed to prophets		91e-92c

Criticism

Franklin D. Richards	There is no salvation in ,	June 1970	35f
Robert L. Simpson	The saints are just the sinners who are trying hard	Dec 1970	97c-e

Harold B. Lee	True conversion means overcoming ,	June 1971	8d
Harold B. Lee	Evils of political ,	July 1972	29b
	Of America's leaders —story		29c
Franklin D. Richards	Criticism is judging	Nov 1974	106b
Neal A. Maxwell	Satan delights in self-criticism	Nov 1976	14d
N. Eldon Tanner	One cell of battery foamed and fumed —story		74e-75b
James E. Faust	Class criticized leaders for handcart trek —story	May 1979	53b-e
Boyd K. Packer	Those who criticize Church for wrongdoing of members		79d-80e
J. Richard Clarke	Some people have a problem for every solution	Nov 1980	84d
Marvin J. Ashton	It's easier to be a critic than a servant	Nov 1981	38b
Gordon B. Hinckley	People with heavy responsibilities do not need ,		98b-c
Gordon B. Hinckley	Our society feeds on ,	May 1982	46d
Ezra Taft Benson	Tempted to be critical of Joseph for 30 seconds —story		64d-e
H. Burke Peterson	Let sons see in fathers one who doesn't criticize	Nov 1982	43e-f
Marvin J. Ashton	Man resisted , - gave service instead —story		65d-e
Gordon B. Hinckley	Church's critics are savoring a pickle	Nov 1983	46c-d
H. Burke Peterson	Lives are changed by love quicker than by ,		60f
Marvin J. Ashton	Critics go to tree not for fruit but looking for scars		62c-d, 63a
Gordon B. Hinckley	Mocking that which is sacred to others is deeply flawed		74f-75b
	Lower your voice of , and negativism		76b
Neal A. Maxwell	Don't level , at prophets. They never claimed perfection.	Nov 1984	10d-f
	Historical details may differ but not major items		11d-e
Boyd K. Packer	To learn about a man, don't go to his enemies		66d-e
	When you know you're brothers, you can't belittle		67a
	Critics of Church move our work a little faster		69d-e
James E. Faust	, is often a symptom of the critic's own problems	Nov 1985	7d-e
	Publicly criticizing basic doctrines puts one in peril.		8b-d
	The effect , has had upon the Church		9b-c
Robert L. Backman	Ostracized girl accepted by peers —story		12d-f
George P. Lee	Should they welcome us if they rejected Jesus and Joseph?		22e-f
Gordon B. Hinckley	Tithing funds won't be used to help critics		52c-e
	We don't need critics standing on the sidelines		52f
Thomas S. Monson	It's not the critic who counts —T.R. Roosevelt	May 1987	69a
Paul H. Dunn	Children hear 100,000 negative messages and few positive		73b-c
James E. Faust	, can be worse than the conduct we try to correct	Nov 1987	35c
Marvin J. Ashton	4 comments on , —good	May 1988	63a-d
Hugh W. Pinnock	It is wrong to blame others and conditions	May 1989	10d-e
Glenn L. Pace	, by non-members is harmless: We are odd		25f-26a
	, by former members reveals their character		26b-c
Dallin H. Oaks	How Church responds to ,		27d-29a
Gordon B. Hinckley	O. Cowdery looked through wrong end of lens		47f
Gordon B. Hinckley	A proclamation to world in response to ,	Nov 1989	53a
Neal A. Maxwell	Murmur not —entire talk		82b-85b
Gordon B. Hinckley	Stop this , of handcart leaders —story	Nov 1991	54c-d
Thomas S. Monson	Difference between a lady and others is how she's treated	Nov 1992	97e-98a

Criticism

Gordon B. Hinckley	If Church without , we'd be concerned	Nov 1993	54e-f
Virginia H. Pearce	, stabilizes negative behaviors		80c
Gordon B. Hinckley	Critics fade after brief days in the sun	May 1994	60a-b
Joe J. Christensen	Grapefruit syndrome —marriage story	May 1995	64f-65b
Boyd K. Packer	The curse that comes upon critics of Church	Nov 1996	7d-f
Bruce C. Hafen	How , affects self-esteem —2 stories		26f-27a
Neil L. Andersen	Whining of skeptics at battle of Jericho	Nov 1999	16e
Gordon B. Hinckley	The Church is trapped by its history?	Nov 2002	80f
Susan W. Tanner	Children learn best from love - not ,	May 2003	74d-75b
Neal A. Maxwell	Chewing on old bones in outer courtyard	Nov 2003	99d
	Need spiritual Teflon against fiery darts		102b
Thomas S. Monson	Paperboy took own life because of , —story	May 2005	22d-e
Joseph B. Wirthlin	Poorest bishop we've ever had —story		27f
James E. Faust	Look past leaders' warts and spots	Nov 2005	54f-55b
Robert S. Wood	How to criticize or write a critique	May 2006	94d
	Dangerous ground when criticizing		95b
Boyd K. Packer	We do not attack or criticize or oppose	Nov 2006	87a
	Cannot lift self by putting others down		87b-c
Jeffrey R. Holland	Don't speak or think negatively of self	May 2007	17f-18a
	Grumbling that everything looks yellow —humor		18b
	Hit me again. I can still hear you.		18b
	No misfortune so bad that whining won't make it worse		18c
W. Craig Zwick	Laughter of world is trying to reassure itself	May 2008	98d-e
Robert D. Hales	, may be an opportunity - How to react	Nov 2008	72f-73e
Dieter F. Uchtdorf	Don't let voices of , paralyze you. Yours too		118e-119d
Quentin L. Cook	Dickens found , of Saints unfounded —story	May 2009	34f-35d
	Religious war with London bus ads —story		35d-f
	No , of other churches - Live with respect		37b-d
Thomas S. Monson	Have courage to not find fault		124b-c
Tad R. Callister	Miss mark by focusing on Peter's faults	Nov 2009	35b-c
Dieter F. Uchtdorf	Called to support and heal - Not condemn	May 2010	69f-70b

L. Tom Perry	Girl required each date to agree to her standards —story	Nov 1979	36a-c
N. Eldon Tanner	Would you loan your car to any stranger? —good	May 1980	16f-17a
Spencer W. Kimball	Dating standards of Church explained	Nov 1980	96e-f
Gordon B. Hinckley	Date members of the Church	Nov 1981	41d
William R. Bradford	Don't hold him back from mission. Serve one yourself		50e-f
Ezra Taft Benson	Don't date non-members	May 1986	45e
Ezra Taft Benson	Avoid steady dating before mission	Nov 1986	82f-83a
	Don't take chance of , non-members		84b-d
James E. Faust	His date's father waited up —story	May 1988	37e-38a
Kenneth Johnson	I couldn't marry you unless in the temple —story	May 1990	42e
Thomas S. Monson	Standards for , reviewed	Nov 1990	45f-46a
Gordon B. Hinckley	Do not get involved in steady ,	Nov 1997	51e-f

James E. Faust	What young women should look for in Young Men	May 2000	97d-e
Bonnie D. Parkin	Went looking for late children	Nov 2005	109a-b
Charles W. Dahlquist, II	Found mother upon knees —story	May 2007	96b-c
Joseph B. Wirthlin	The wrong blind date —story	Nov 2008	26f-27c
Elaine S. Dalton	Virtuous men are attracted to virtuous women	May 2009	120b-e
Thomas S. Monson	Do not date until 16 - Standards	May 2010	64f
Dieter F. Uchtdorf	The courtship of his wife —story		125f-126c

Death
Related Topics: —

Spencer W. Kimball	Tomb not a blind alley but a thoroughfare	June 1969	58f
LeGrand Richards	Funeral held no hope for bereaved parents —story		93a
Thomas S. Monson	To understand , we must understand life		102d
	God, too, had a Son who died		103e
James A. Cullimore	His elderly parents passed away quietly together	Dec 1969	79b
	The problem of , is the regret of not having lived		79c
Hartman Rector, Jr.	No miraculous change in character at ,	Dec 1970	76d-e
	We are here to get in condition to leave		76e-f
Sterling W. Sill	Give life for something worthwhile —poem		79f
Ezra Taft Benson	Like a child waking in his own bed —story	June 1971	33e-f
LeGrand Richards	Account of , of 2 of his children —story	Dec 1971	84a-c
Gordon B. Hinckley	Funeral: we come to comfort and not to mourn	July 1972	73b
Boyd K. Packer	Hand and glove demonstration of ,	July 1973	51e
	Explanation of , to children		51f
	How to overcome , —explained to children		53d
Franklin D. Richards	Two women comforted by Spirit when husbands die		117d
Harold B. Lee	A dying woman's outlook on , —story	Jan 1974	6b
	Put time to work. Death may be near —story		6c
Ezra Taft Benson	There is no untimely passing of a prophet	May 1974	104c
Vaughn J. Featherstone	Prayer with wife brought peace at man's death —story	Nov 1974	29e-30b
Marion G. Romney	Where do all souls go immediately after ,?		38f-39a
Marion G. Romney	Why Jesus had power over ,	May 1975	83c-84a
Boyd K. Packer	, no more an ending than birth is a beginning	Nov 1975	98f
Thomas S. Monson	Hopelessness of , as viewed by atheists	May 1976	10d-f
Bruce R. McConkie	Birth and , both essential steps	Nov 1976	107a
	Scriptures concerning ,		107d-108a
Sterling W. Sill	Worse than losing a child is to never have one —poem	May 1978	66e-67a
Proclamation	Transition to another sphere of purposeful activity	May 1980	52e
M. Russell Ballard	Youth miraculously helped after , of mother —story	Nov 1980	23c-f
Thomas S. Monson	The family lost 3 sons at once —story	Nov 1981	17b-18b
Neal A. Maxwell	, is a comma, not an exclamation point	May 1983	11f
Boyd K. Packer	"Dead" does not describe the departed	May 1987	25a-b
Gordon B. Hinckley	A poem about , by Hinckley —poem	May 1988	66c
Boyd K. Packer	Preacher consigned unbaptized boy to hell —story	Nov 1988	18b-d
	The Fall brought blood in veins - and death		18e-f
	Instructions for funerals		19a-21b

Michaelene P. Grassli	How a 7-year-old handled her mother's , —story	Nov 1988	78b-c
Wm. Grant Bangerter	An atheist's experience at death —story		80d-e
Merrill J. Bateman	Lessons taught by ,	May 1989	13c-e
Joy F. Evans	I've come to clean your shoes —story		74d-e
David B. Haight	Elder Haight's near death experience —story	Nov 1989	59e-61b
Denn L. Larsen	Body and , compared to wind-up clock		61e-62a
Horacio A. Tenorio	How they bore the , of their grandson —story	May 1990	79f-80f
Marion D. Hanks	Deacon kept Sabbath before his death —story	Nov 1990	39f-40b
M. Russell Ballard	Joseph wished to be buried by father	Nov 1991	5e
Russell M. Nelson	The only way to take sorrow out of ,	May 1992	72d
	We were born to die		72e
	, is essential to happiness		72f-73a
	, is not permanent		73f-74b
	His near-death experience —story		74c-d
	, is not an enemy		74f
	Loved ones are as close as next room		74f
Carlos E. Asay	Not a period but a comma in life	May 1994	12e
Thomas S. Monson	Letter from Civil War soldier facing ,		62f-63b
Dallin H. Oaks	Prayed wife's , would not affect children's faith —story		100c-d
Thomas S. Monson	Widow lost her children during 1,000 mile walk —story	Nov 1994	68d-69b
Wm. Grant Bangerter	Funeral material —entire talk good	May 1995	80b-82b
Dallin H. Oaks	Funerals should convey powerful ideas	Nov 1995	25b-c
Thomas S. Monson	Dust thou art; Not spoken of the soul —poem		60f
Boyd K. Packer	Obey Word of Wisdom and escape spiritual ,	May 1996	19b-c
F. Burton Howard	Safely dead with a testimony still burning		28f
Henry B. Eyring	Grandma's uncomplaining , showed testimony		64a-d
Gordon B. Hinckley	Only mitigated by promise of resurrection		66e-67f
Russell M. Nelson	A blessing to not be stranded on earth	Nov 1996	34a-b
James E. Faust	Pioneer woman's husband died during night —story		54c-d
Robert D. Hales	Name not mentioned at funeral —story		66e-f
	Man made videos for children before ,		66f-67a
Chieko N. Okazaki	, has no dominion over us because of Christ		90d
Neal A. Maxwell	Our exit routes vary. So does the timing.	May 1997	11f
Neal A. Maxwell	Granted a delay en route	Nov 1997	22b
Carol B. Thomas	, is like walking into another room	May 1998	91d
M. Russell Ballard	W. Woodruff's vision of Joseph and others hurrying	Nov 1998	6d-e
Robert D. Hales	The purpose of pain —excellent talk		14d-17b
Thomas S. Monson	Comfort for those who lose children —story		19d-20f
Russell M. Nelson	Death is a joy and a part of life		86d
Gordon B. Hinckley	Powerful testimony of Jesus' victory over ,	May 1999	70b-72f
Thomas S. Monson	At , family and love is all that matters	Nov 2000	65f-66a
Henry B. Eyring	Mother met daughter-in-law at , —story		87b-d
Sheri L. Dew	Funeral dedicated to testifying of Christ —story		94e-95a
	We are sad, but don't worry as much		95a
Richard G. Scott	False statements made at funerals	May 2001	9a

Death, cont'd

Debt

M. Russell Ballard	1/3 of American families are overextended	May 1981	85d-e
	6 steps to overcoming ,		87a-b
Marvin J. Ashton	A financial tool - not a magic carpet	Nov 1981	90d-e
	Difference between recession and depression		90f
Marvin J. Ashton	Advice to help avoid bad business promotions	May 1982	10d-f
	, not an inconvenience. It is a calamity		11a-b
James E. Faust	Counsel against speculation		48d-e
James E. Faust	Difference between recession and depression	Nov 1982	87d
James E. Faust	J. R. Clark's statement about interest	May 1986	21a-b
L. Tom Perry	Counsel against status symbol homes and consumer ,	Nov 1986	63a-b
Russell M. Nelson	He bled his wife between two jobs —story	Nov 1987	88e-f
Thomas S. Monson	Pay thy debt and live	Nov 1988	46f
Ezra Taft Benson	Avoid , and co-signing notes	Nov 1989	5f
L. Tom Perry	Interest: Thems that understands it earns it... —story	Nov 1991	66e-f
Joe J. Christensen	Spending $50 less than you make equals happiness	May 1995	65f-66a
L. Tom Perry	Selling produce and avoiding unnecessary purchases	Nov 1995	36c-d
	"Live within your means: —J.R. Clark		36d-e
	"Interest never sleeps..." —J.R. Clark		36e
	Those that understand interest get it; those that don't pay		36e-f
Gordon B. Hinckley	Church has no ,		53f-54b
W. Eugene Hansen	"Use it up, wear it out..."	May 1998	63d
Gordon B. Hinckley	To get out of , —excellent counsel	Nov 1998	52e-54b
Joe J. Christensen	Grinding debt —H.J. Grant quote	May 1999	11b-c
Gordon B. Hinckley	Basic principles - no , and a fixed percentage of savings	May 2001	53d-54a
Jeffrey R. Holland	Paying tithing is discharging a ,	Nov 2001	34e
Gordon B. Hinckley	Get free of , where possible		73b-d
Bonnie D. Parkin	Missionary more in , to Lord than before	May 2002	84f
Thomas S. Monson	Don't allow yearnings to exceed earnings	Nov 2002	53f-54a
Gordon B. Hinckley	Get out of ,		58e-f
Joseph B. Wirthlin	Some , is necessary - but not consumer ,	May 2004	40f-41a
	J.R. Clark's statement about interest		41b
	Prophets' statements about ,		41b-d
	No bankruptcy - Debt paid —story		42e-f
	5 key steps to financial freedom		41f-43a
	Jesus paid , He did not owe to free us from , we can't pay		43d
Thomas S. Monson	Interest never sleeps -J.R. Clark	May 2005	19f-20b
	Appalled at home equity loans		20b-d
Thomas S. Monson	Warning about , and home equity loans	May 2006	19d-f
L. Tom Perry	Most troubles caused by , —excellent counsel	Nov 2008	9d-f
Robert D. Hales	We can't afford it - Where would I wear it —story	May 2009	8b-9b
	Don't spend money for things of no worth		10d-e
	Entire talk		7b-10f

Decisions
Related Topics: Agency, Choice

Marion G. Romney	Each , expands or contracts area for future ,	Dec 1968	73f
Franklin D. Richards	It is our own , that make or break us	Dec 1970	83c
Elray L. Christiansen	Never make , while angry	June 1971	37d-e
Sterling W. Sill	Yes and no answers leave us open to mistakes	Dec 1971	92d-e
Gordon B. Hinckley	Lives determined by little ,	Jan 1973	91c
	Impact of little , on lives		91d
	Lives determined by little ,		91f
Bruce R. McConkie	How he decided upon his talk	July 1973	27b
John H. Vandenberg	Dependent upon persuasion of heart —story		32b
	Every day is election day		32d
N. Eldon Tanner	One , can alter course of whole life —story	Nov 1975	75f-76c
Spencer W. Kimball	Certain , need be made but once	May 1976	46b-c
L. Tom Perry	Girl required each date to agree to her standards —story	Nov 1979	36a-c
	As a boy President Kimball decided he'd never smoke, etc.		36c-e
Joanne B. Doxey	Decisions determine destiny	Nov 1987	91b
James E. Faust	, by leading quorums must be unanimous	Nov 1989	10f
Robert L. Backman	How to make , - Questions to ask		39b-c
Russell M. Nelson	3 questions to ask when making ,	Nov 1990	73d-e
Rex D. Pinegar	What would Jesus have you do? - Sunday campout —story	Nov 1991	41a-b
L. Tom Perry	Make , just once —Spencer W. Kimball	Nov 1993	67d-e
	My Three White Dresses —poem		67f-68a
Ruth B. Wright	She wanted to drop typing class —story	May 1994	85a-b
Howard W. Hunter	Total unanimity among Apostles in all ,	Nov 1994	7e
L. Tom Perry	"Say no to the offer" —story	May 1997	69d-70a
Richard G. Scott	2 patterns for making ,	Nov 1998	68e-69a
Henry B. Eyring	Go to meetings with an open mind	Nov 2000	86b-c
Richard G. Scott	Each choice narrows our future	May 2001	8a-c
James E. Faust	Decide but once about temptations —Kimball	May 2002	47b
James E. Faust	The grand key: D&C 9:7-9	May 2004	53f-54a
Paul B. Pieper	Small , by one affected thousands	Nov 2006	12e-f
Robert D. Hales	Your 20's - The decade of decision	May 2007	48d-e
	Not preconditioned, pilot died in crash —story		48e-f
	Not making , can be deadly		48f-49b
Richard G. Scott	Truth is needed to make ,	Nov 2007	90b-c
Neil L. Andersen	Faith is not only a feeling; it is a decision —story	Nov 2008	13f-14b
Gregory A. Schwitzer	Worldly judgment causes missed blessings	May 2010	104f
	4 guides in making ,		105a-f

Diligence
Related Topics: Excellence

Paul H. Dunn	Makes the difference between two men	Dec 1968	67a
	I'd give anything to play the piano like that		67d-e
Thomas S. Monson	Finish what you begin —good poem	July 1972	69f
Gordon B. Hinckley	Brethren leaders because of ,	Jan 1973	92f
N. Eldon Tanner	Leaders first showed ,		103b
	Boyhood , of presidents		103c

		Diligence, cont'd		
		Related Topics: Excellence		
Hartman Rector, Jr.	Failure ceased to exist in the face of persistence	Jan 1973	130b
Rex D. Pinegar	Scriptural examples of ,	Nov 1974	44a-d
	Lady missionaries tried one more day —story		44f
Sterling W. Sill	Marie Curie's , —story		62f
Spencer W. Kimball	Abraham Lincoln failed and failed but kept trying —story		80c-e
Marvin J. Ashton	From polio to Gold Medal —story	May 1975	86a-c
	Saints are sinners who kept trying		86d
Paul H. Dunn	He asked again and made the team —story	Nov 1976	54d-55c
Paul H. Dunn	Well-turned phrase on failing to try again	May 1979	9c
Thomas S. Monson	Stick to your task —poem		37a
Gordon B. Hinckley	Account of Peter denying Christ —story		65b-e
	Account of Peter's repentance of above —story		66d-67a
	Tragedy of men of high aim and low achievement		65e
	Convert went back to tobacco —story		66a
	Many get to third base but fail to score		66b
Marvin J. Ashton	Great souls have wills; feeble souls have wishes	Nov 1979	62e
Rex D. Pinegar	Worked at music until it worked for him —story	Nov 1980	72e-f
Robert D. Hales	Examples of President Kimball's , —stories	Nov 1981	19b-21b
Thomas S. Monson	The sinking of the Bismarck —story	May 1982	59d-60a
Boyd K. Packer	Learning piano, language or gospel requires ,	May 1983	67a-f
Vaughn J. Featherstone	Piano practice required mother's , —funny story	Nov 1983	37c
Marvin J. Ashton	Striving can be more important than arriving	May 1984	11f
Joseph B. Wirthlin	Unless we do all we can, we do less than we ought		40a
Russell M. Nelson	List of "endure to the end" scriptures	Nov 1985	32f
Thomas S. Monson	Editor rejected Robert Frost's poems —story	May 1987	68f-69a
	Handicapped youth finished race —story		69c-f
Joseph B. Wirthlin	Perseverance is active, not passive	Nov 1987	8b-d
Henry B. Eyring	, in home teaching develops godliness —entire talk	May 1988	39b-41b
Marvin J. Ashton	Kayaking without a good right arm —story	Nov 1988	16b-f
Thomas S. Monson	Never give up. Last baseball player chosen —story	May 1989	44b-d
Marvin J. Ashton	Man finished race without a shoe —story	Nov 1989	35d-36a
	Bruce R. McConkie's last words: Carry On		36a-b
	W. Churchill's statements about war		37b-c
Gordon B. Hinckley	Fill your responsibility with ,		52f-53c
Neal A. Maxwell	God's patient long-suffering with us	May 1990	33e
	Endurance is more than waiting		33f
	, is pressing forward - not pulling to side of road		34c
	Twigs are bent, not snapped, into shape		34e
Marvin J. Ashton	The first four-minute mile —story	Nov 1990	22a-e
Thomas S. Monson	Man finally joined Church —story	May 1991	50e-51f
Vaughn J. Featherstone	We can't lie down or stand still	May 1992	44d-e
Thomas S. Monson	17th letter got a response —story	May 1993	49f-50d
Marlin K. Jensen	Years of efforts wore down hostility —story	May 1994	48b-e
Hartman Rector, Jr.	3 components of enduring to the end	Nov 1994	26b-f
Gordon B. Hinckley	Use of time determines character —great talk— stories		46d-49b

Diligence

Monte J. Brough	Boy stayed on horse 80 miles —story	May 1995	41d-f
F. Burton Howard	Commitment —excellent talk	May 1996	27b-28f
David B. Haight	Enthusiasm - Throwing duds or hand grenades	Nov 1996	15d
Joseph B. Wirthlin	Some try to serve the Lord without offending the devil	May 1997	16a
Russell M. Nelson	Enduring to the end —entire talk		70d-73b
	Winners are declared at end of race - not before		71a
	"Stick to your task" —poem		71b
Virginia H. Pearce	Plug along - give time a chance —excellent talk		86b-87f
Robert D. Hales	Country sent him to finish the race —story	May 1998	76b-d
James E. Faust	Oliver Cowdery and Hyrum Smith contrasted	Nov 2001	46f-48b
Virginia U. Jensen	Duke ordered "stand firm"- history changed —story		94a-c
Thomas S. Monson	Convert would not renounce Church —story		98f-99a
Thomas S. Monson	Ruth - the model of loyalty - Nephi the model of ,	Nov 2002	61b-62a
Gayle M. Clegg	Boy finished assignment years later —story	May 2004	14b-c
	"The Finished Story" —excellent talk		14b-16b
Jeffrey R. Holland	Meaning of "abide in me"		31f-32f
Clate W. Mask, Jr.	Elders slosh through mud to get to meeting —story		92b-f
Bruce C. Hafen	Collapsed but still holding on to rod		99a-b
Gordon B. Hinckley	Player dropped ball once - Never forgotten —story		114e-115b
Donald L. Staheli	Do the very best you can —Hinckley	Nov 2004	37e-f
Boyd K. Packer	Can't always expect success, but must try		86b-e
Joseph B. Wirthlin	Elderly prophet prayed he would keep faith		102f-103a
	Enduring to the end		101b-104b
Thomas S. Monson	Wife converted husband —tender story		115b-116a
Coleen K. Menlove	3 tries required to write hymn —story	May 2005	15a-c
James E. Faust	I get up when I fall down		51d-e
	Marie Curie's 487th experiment —story		51e-f
	Entire talk		51b-53f
Thomas S. Monson	Last chosen but caught ball —story	Nov 2005	58e-f
Elaine S. Dalton	Learning to walk again —story	May 2006	109f-110d
Keith B. McMullin	Flunked chemistry class —story	May 2007	51d-f
Thomas S. Monson	Address located on 4th try —story		58f-60a
Dieter F. Uchtdorf	Meaning of "enduring to the end"	Nov 2007	20d-21a
Keith K. Hilbig	Path to exaltation is an upward incline		37f-38d
Thomas S. Monson	Runner lost shoe, continued, finished third		59e-f
L. Tom Perry	How to endure to the end	May 2008	46d-f
Susan W. Tanner	Girl took self to church - General R.S. President		114d
Elaine S. Dalton	Fought discouragement of marathon —story		117d-118d
Henry B. Eyring	Former bishop endured through trials —story	May 2009	26c-27a
Claudio R. M. Costa	40-minute walk to church - Handicapped —story		57f-58b
Dieter F. Uchtdorf	Letting the unimportant distract —entire talk		59b-62f
Dieter F. Uchtdorf	Tried his counsel for a week. It didn't work —story		76d-f
Thomas S. Monson	German woman lost all but faith —story		91a-92f
David A. Bednar	Consistency in prayer, study, Family Home Evening	Nov 2009	19d-20e
Dieter F. Uchtdorf	Try and keep on trying		23a-d

Diligence

Henry B. Eyring	Be prepared at a moment's notice —entire talk	Nov 2009	59b-62b
Boyd K. Packer	Gideon's men were always alert	May 2010	6d-e
Dieter F. Uchtdorf	Never give up on others or self		58b
Henry B. Eyring	Will bring knowledge of God and revelation		60a-b
Mary N. Cook	Never give up - Advice to young women		117b-119f

Discipline
Related Topics: Bishop's Courts

John H. Vandenberg	Freedom to , self is only true freedom	Dec 1968	59a
Marion D. Hanks	What , to give children		96e
Marion D. Hanks	Thoughts on , and dating —story	June 1970	99d-100a
Gordon B. Hinckley	Discipline required in marriage - of self	June 1971	72b
Gordon B. Hinckley	A father's method of , changed upon conversion	July 1972	72e
James E. Faust	If we don't , children, society will	Jan 1974	23b
Marvin J. Ashton	Self , is the only kind that works	Nov 1976	85b-e
Gordon B. Hinckley	Determine in February the fruit you'll pick in September	Nov 1978	18b-d
	Harsh society is outgrowth of harshness on children		18e
	Treat children with mildness —Brigham Young		19a-c
Ezra Taft Benson	How to , children —Joseph F. Smith	May 1981	34e-f
F. Enzio Busche	Father's anger cooled before , of son —story	May 1982	70e-f
Jeffrey R. Holland	An experience in , of his son —good story	May 1983	36b-38b
Matthew S. Holland	How his mother disciplined him —story		38f-39a
Ezra Taft Benson	No child should fear his father	Nov 1983	42f-43a
Marvin J. Ashton	Advice to the excommunicated	May 1988	62b-64f
Thomas S. Monson	Bishop brought excommunicated member back —story	May 1990	48f-49b
Joe J. Christensen	Say "No" to children - set standards	Nov 1993	11e-12a
Ben B. Banks	, and punishment are not synonymous		29f
James E. Faust	Must be done in a spirit of helping		37c-e
Gordon B. Hinckley	The sapling could have been straightened —story		59c-f
Gordon B. Hinckley	, self to use free time wisely —stories	Nov 1994	46d-49b
Gordon B. Hinckley	Reared boys with a rod - a fishing rod		53f-54a
Neal A. Maxwell	Major problems solved by self denial	May 1995	68a-c
James E. Faust	, self to decide but once about temptation	May 2002	47b
F. Melvin Hammond	Lashes couldn't have cut so deeply —story	Nov 2002	99a-b
James E. Faust	Part of , is teaching to work	May 2003	67a
Gordon B. Hinckley	, self, not your companion	Nov 2004	84f
James E. Faust	What is a disciple?	Nov 2006	20d-f
	The blessings of discipleship		22e-23b
Russell M. Nelson	How parents are to , children	May 2008	9a-10a
Henry B. Eyring	How his father disciplined him	Nov 2009	61d-62a
D. Todd Christofferson	Self , - No double moral standard —Faust story		105d-f
	We are disciples of Jesus who is a disciple of Father		105f-106d

Dispensation
Related Topics: —

Alvin R. Dyer	The last , - the depository period for all truth	June 1970	50e-f
Alvin R. Dyer	Definition of ,	July 1972	52c

Dispensation, cont'd

| Russell M. Nelson | All previous , limited in time and location | Nov 2006 | 79f-80a |
| Gordon B. Hinckley | The final chapter - Opened with God's appearance | Nov 2007 | 84c-d |

Divorce
Related Topics: Marriage

David O. McKay	Type of person unworthy of a second temple marriage	June 1969	4f-5e
Gordon B. Hinckley	Statistics on ,	June 1971	71c
James A. Cullimore	Usually the result of not living the gospel		93d-e
	A man not worthy of a second temple marriage		94c
	How children are hurt in a ,		94c
Spencer W. Kimball	Less , in families with children	July 1973	15e
James E. Faust	Harder to cope with than death		86c
Harold B. Lee	Wife considered , for frivolous reason —story	Jan 1974	99f
	Marriage saved by young bishop and simple comment		100b
	Frightening flood of , - many stem from adultery		101a
Spencer W. Kimball	Most , comes from selfishness and immorality	May 1974	6f-7b
Spencer W. Kimball	Stiff questions to answer when child deprived of parent	Nov 1974	8f-9a
Spencer W. Kimball	Divorce is spelled SELFISHNESS	May 1975	7a-b
Spencer W. Kimball	Bishops must never counsel for ,	May 1976	47c
James E. Faust	The marriage wasn't as bad as the , —story	Nov 1977	9d
	1/2 of all marriages end in ,		9d-e
L. Tom Perry	Hurry away or you'll be getting a divorce too. —story		62e-f
Spencer W. Kimball	More than 1 million in 1975	May 1978	5c
Boyd K. Packer	Do not destroy a marriage - A monumental transgression	May 1981	14b-d
	, not typical. We hear of , because its the wreck		14f-15a
Robert L. Simpson	Statistics on ,	May 1982	21b-c
Barbara B. Smith	Divorced mother put kids to work - paid bills —story	Nov 1982	84b-85a
David B. Haight	Insights about , —good	May 1984	12e-13a
	Every , is the result of selfishness		13f
Robert E. Wells	Couple saved from , by missionaries' visit —story	Nov 1985	28f-29a
Gordon B. Hinckley	Fathers' obligations to pay child support		51d-f
Gordon B. Hinckley	None in his large school class divorced	May 1988	65c-d
Gordon B. Hinckley	Selfishness and Satan are the cause of ,	May 1991	71b-74f
	2,423,000 marriages - 1,177,000 divorces		72f-73a
James E. Faust	What constitutes just cause for ,	May 1993	36e-37b
Spencer J. Condie	Husband changed when she changed self —story	Nov 1993	17b-d
Gordon B. Hinckley	Brigham Young's counsel against ,	Nov 2000	53a
Gordon B. Hinckley	Selfishness is the leading cause of ,	May 2003	59a-d
Gordon B. Hinckley	No , if each spouse would…	Nov 2004	84c-d
Dallin H. Oaks	"Starter marriages" and commonplace ,	May 2007	70c-e
	Divorced people may marry again		70f
	Dead marriages need to be ended —examples		70f-71a
	Happiness is recovered quicker after a death		71b
	Bishops don't counsel for ,		71f
	Not the remedy for unhappy marriage		71b-72e
	The difference between , and healed marriage		72e-73a

Divorce, cont'd
Related Topics: Marriage

Dallin H. Oaks	2/3 of unhappy marriages were happy 5 yrs. later	May 2007	73a
Gordon B. Hinckley	Over half of marriages end before 25th year	Nov 2007	62f-63a
Jeffrey R. Holland	3 divorces caused by pornography	May 2010	44a-e

Doctrine & Covenants
Related Topics: Scriptures

Marion G. Romney	The , are the scriptures binding upon us	June 1969	95f
Marion G. Romney	We to be judged by ,	Jan 1973	97f
Henry D. Taylor	Why "Lectures on Faith" are no longer part of ,	Nov 1976	63c-e
Ezra Taft Benson	Discussion of the value of ,	Nov 1986	78d-80f
Ezra Taft Benson	, is the capstone of our religion	May 1987	83f
Boyd K. Packer	The book that will never be closed	May 1990	36d

Dress Standards
Related Topics: Appearance, Standards

Gordon B. Hinckley	Clean grooming is a badge of honor	May 1996	48f-49a
James E. Faust	Don't wear strange clothes and ornaments	Nov 1997	42f
Vaughn J. Featherstone	Earrings and tattoos on men	Nov 1999	13d-e
James E. Faust	Take care of appearance - keep femininity		101f-102a
Boyd K. Packer	Dress to show Lord how precious body is	Nov 2000	72f-73a
Russell M. Nelson	Follow grooming examples of prophets	Nov 2003	46b-c
Dallin H. Oaks	Pagan piercing of body parts	May 2004	9f
Susan W. Tanner	Why we dress modestly —good talk	Nov 2005	13b-15f
Jeffrey R. Holland	No bare midriffs		29a-b
	Best dress - not beach wear - at church		29b-d
Gordon B. Hinckley	Unbecoming to dress in slouchy manner	Nov 2006	60d
Gordon B. Hinckley	No tattoos	May 2007	62e
	Sloppy dress leads to sloppy manners		62e
Elaine S. Dalton	Good discussion on virtue and modesty		112d-113b
L. Tom Perry	Adopt the appearance of a missionary	Nov 2007	48c
L. Tom Perry	Casual manners always follow casual dress	Nov 2008	9a-d
Dallin H. Oaks	Appropriate dress for sacrament meeting		18f
	Administrators of sacrament wear white shirts		20d-e
Jay E. Jensen	Priesthood during sacrament must not distract		48e-49a
Boyd K. Packer	No tattoos or body piercings for men	May 2009	50f
Dallin H. Oaks	Can't be lifesaver looking like others on the beach		95a
Mary N. Cook	How a girl handles mocking of ,		119b-c
Elaine S. Dalton	Our , and everything else must be different		122a-f
M. Russell Ballard	Talk to daughters about , and model it	May 2010	20e-f
Thomas S. Monson	Dress to bring out best - Avoid extremes		64f-65a

Drugs
Related Topics: Word of Wisdom

Loren C. Dunn	50% try ,	June 1969	51b-d
	Group started , because of parental alienation		51d-f
Richard L. Evans	Mind and , —David Starr Jordan	Dec 1969	73d
N. Eldon Tanner	Alcohol #1 problem - kids imitate parents	Dec 1970	32c-d
Loren C. Dunn	Girl reformed because father never gave up on her —story		63b-c

Drugs, cont'd
Related Topics: Word of Wisdom

Loren C. Dunn	Boy reformed because of mother not giving up —story	Dec 1970	63d-64a
Marvin J. Ashton	Focus on the cause not the symptoms	June 1971	30c-31a
	Don't reject users of ,		31b-c
Marion D. Hanks	Drugs led to suicide —story	Dec 1971	106c
N. Eldon Tanner	Good boy went bad —story	Nov 1974	86b-e
	Good boy went bad - Family brought him back —story		86e-f
Marion D. Hanks	Friends drugged sailor and led him into iniquity —story	Nov 1986	12a-13a
David B. Haight	Priesthood leader tried crack, ruined his life —story		37a
Thomas S. Monson	The maka-feke of ,	May 2006	19b-c
Boyd K. Packer	Avoid deadly poison of narcotics	May 2009	50f

Earth
Related Topics: Creation

Ted. E. Brewerton	Celestial , will be like a star	Nov 1991	11a-b
Joseph B. Wirthlin	, and the incomprehensible cosmos	Nov 1993	6b-c
Richard G. Scott	Description of the earth's beauties —poem	May 1996	24b-e
Russell M. Nelson	Phases of creation may have been ages	May 2000	84f-85c
	The creation testifies of a creator		85c
	We must care for the ,		86b
Gordon B. Hinckley	An overview of history of the ,	May 2004	81b-84b

Education
Related Topics: Knowledge, Teaching

N. Eldon Tanner	Professors tearing down religion - an example	Dec 1968	39b-c
Harold B. Lee	False , - one of greatest threats to work of Lord		71a
Spencer W. Kimball	All knowledge will be required to be able to create		101e
Hugh B. Brown	The gospel is a system of continuing ,	June 1969	32d
	Salvation is an eternal quest for knowledge		34c
Ezra Taft Benson	Some higher , is a major investment in error		44b-c
S. Dilworth Young	We will have to learn eternal physics , etc.		85a-c
Ezra Taft Benson	One of chief means of destroying youth is ,	Dec 1970	46e-49a
	Why Marx wanted free, public education		49a-b
	Review what your children are taught		49b-c
Neal A. Maxwell	Why youth should attend colleges near home		92d-93a
	95% of institute graduates have temple marriage		94c-d
Harold B. Lee	We never overcome ignorance but many quit learning	June 1971	9b-d
Wendell J. Ashton	Striking changes in ,		57f
Bruce R. McConkie	The , of most profit		77f-78b
William H. Bennett	Limitations of , - why we need the Lord		106f-107a
Paul H. Dunn	There are 2 educations	Dec 1971	119c
Boyd K. Packer	Academic giants may be spiritual pygmies	May 1974	95c
Spencer W. Kimball	Men spend 20 years on , but just hours on God		119a
Paul H. Dunn	Where , fits in our priorities	May 1975	62a
	Don't delay families because of ,		62f-63a
N. Eldon Tanner	, without integrity is dangerous	May 1977	15f
LeGrand Richards	12 years preparing for life. How about eternal life?	Nov 1981	28d
Gordon B. Hinckley	, is a shortcut to proficiency		40e-f

Ezra Taft Benson	Utah stands first in , —statistics	Nov 1981	63c-d
	Women leaving home for , misguided idea		105d-e
Ezra Taft Benson	False ideas in , - one of 3 dangers to Church	May 1982	63e
James E. Faust	Secular knowledge may make B of M difficult to unlock	Nov 1983	10e
Neal A. Maxwell	Joseph could not compose a well-worded letter		54b-c
Gordon B. Hinckley	The need for women receiving an ,		80f-82a
Russell M. Nelson	There is danger in the misuse of ,	Nov 1984	30c-e
Royden G. Derrick	All inventions, wisdom, etc. come from God		60f-62b
	Stuffing the mind with facts is not ,		62d
	When shall we cease to learn? - Never		62f
	Some truths have little to do with exaltation—others essential		62f
James E. Faust	, involves some unlearning —humorous statement	Nov 1985	7e
	Our souls are at risk when we pursue only secular ,		9c
Don Lind	Opportunity to be an astronaut came—he was prepared		39f
Gordon B. Hinckley	Hugh Nibley read an entire library	May 1986	48b
James E. Faust	, changed his life —story	Nov 1986	8d-e
Ezra Taft Benson	Spiritual , takes precedence over temporal	Nov 1987	46e-47b
	Don't postpone a family for ,		49a-b
Ezra Taft Benson	Women should not delay marriage for degrees	Nov 1988	97a-b
Gordon B. Hinckley	Women counseled to get an ,	Nov 1989	96e-97b
James E. Faust	Students: Don't study on Sabbath	Nov 1991	34c-d
Thomas S. Monson	, enables a child to live well —D.O. McKay		67e-f
Russell M. Nelson	Obtaining an , is a religious responsibility	Nov 1992	6d
	How old will you be in 13 years if you don't pursue an ,		6d-f
	Ignorance of scriptures cost lives —story		7a-f
Boyd K. Packer	Why no more church schools		71b-73f
	Get an , and attend institute		71b-73f
L. Tom Perry	Gain an , and keep it up-to-date	Nov 1995	36b
Gordon B. Hinckley	Girls need all they can get	May 1996	92b
Gordon B. Hinckley	Get all the , you can	Nov 1997	52a
L. Tom Perry	Decades to learn spiritual - eternity for secular		60d-e
Harold G. Hillam	Technology may make us "ever learning but…"		63c-e
Thomas S. Monson	, opens windows on life and the universe		95a
	Black woman learned to read —story		95a-b
Gordon B. Hinckley	Educated men enable wives to stay at home	May 1998	50d-e
James E. Faust	Girls counseled to get an ,		96f-97b
L. Tom Perry	, pays. Statistics on income levels	Nov 1998	73f
James E. Faust	Acquire a skill and as much , as possible	Nov 1999	48a-c
	Boy bought 5 cent tomato for 2 cents —story		48c-d
Gordon B. Hinckley	Why Church has BYU. Why not others?		52d-53b
James E. Faust	Science and technology have become a theocracy	May 2000	17f-18a
	Man never discovered anything that God didn't know		18b
James E. Faust	Girls should get , and skill training		97d
Gordon B. Hinckley	Expected average earnings of graduates	Nov 2000	52b-c
Gordon B. Hinckley	The Perpetual Education Fund —announcement	May 2001	51b-53f

Education, cont'd
Related Topics: Knowledge, Teaching

Gordon B. Hinckley	A girl needs an ,	May 2001	95d-f
Gordon B. Hinckley	Report on Perpetual Education Fund	Nov 2001	52e-54f
Thomas S. Monson	Women urged to pursue ,		99b
Gordon B. Hinckley	Report on Perpetual Education Fund	May 2002	6f-7b
Gordon B. Hinckley	Report on Perpetual Education Fund	Nov 2002	57e-58a
Gordon B. Hinckley	8,000 in program. Income rises 4.5 times	May 2003	6d-e
Gordon B. Hinckley	Report on Perpetual Education Fund	Nov 2003	6d-f
Gordon B. Hinckley	10,000 students in 23 countries	May 2004	61a-b
Gordon B. Hinckley	Girls to get all the , they can		113b-f
Gordon B. Hinckley	Perpetual Education Fund assisting 18,000	May 2005	5b-d
Gordon B. Hinckley	Young women getting more , than men	Nov 2006	60f-61b
Gordon B. Hinckley	Relief Society stands for ,		116b
James E. Faust	Had it made at graduation?	May 2007	56a
	People used to be able to fix own car		56a-b
Gordon B. Hinckley	"Boys, get on with your , "		62f
Gordon B. Hinckley	Unlocks the door of opportunity		116d
L. Tom Perry	, to prepare for mission	Nov 2007	48d-e
Julie B. Beck	Avails women nothing if they can't make a home		76f-77a
Thomas S. Monson	Children being educated by the media		118f-119a
	Urges women to pursue their ,		119d-f
Dieter F. Uchtdorf	Cultivate the earth and your mind —Brigham Young	Nov 2008	119b-d
Thomas S. Monson	PEF increases income 3-4 times	May 2009	6b-c
Boyd K. Packer	Don't complain about , - Learn practical things too		51b-52a
Dieter F. Uchtdorf	Longed to have a desk of his own —story	Nov 2009	57e-58a
	Not the filling of a bucket but lighting of a fire		57f-58a
	Not just a good idea - A commandment		58a-e
Dieter F. Uchtdorf	Patience enabled his ,	May 2010	57a-e

Elijah
Related Topics: Family History, Work for Dead

Joseph Fielding Smith	Fullness of priesthood revealed by ,	June 1970	65d-f
LeGrand Richards	Jews have armchair hanging on wall for ,	Dec 1970	70f-71a
Eldred G. Smith	Joseph Smith's explanation of keys of ,	Jan 1973	56a
LeGrand Richards	Discussion of effect of Elijah's return	May 1977	63c-f
A. Theodore Tuttle	, returned on Jews' Passover day	May 1982	65e-66a
James E. Faust	Sealing power eliminates confusion and disorder in lives	May 1993	37b-f
Henry B. Eyring	The coming of ,	May 2005	78a-c

Employment
Related Topics: —

N. Eldon Tanner	LDS man hired from last of 10 applicants	Dec 1971	111f-112a
N. Eldon Tanner	Employer wanted upright man —story	July 1972	100f
Ezra Taft Benson	Men who work with hands will be in demand	Jan 1974	81d
James A. Cullimore	Man was made board chairman because he was LDS		121b
Howard W. Hunter	, should be honorable, challenging and enjoyable	Nov 1975	122f
	Definition of honorable ,		122f-123a
	4 steps to choosing or changing ,		123b-e

Howard W. Hunter	Each ward to have an , resource person	Nov 1975	123f
Vaughn J. Featherstone	How to get a job —entire talk	Nov 1976	118d-120f
H. Burke Peterson	The way , system should work in ward —entire talk	May 1977	113d-115f
J. Thomas Fyans	80% of all jobs filled by word of mouth	May 1982	83f-84a
Boyd K. Packer	Boys get tools for Christmas—girls learn to sew and cook		86e-f
	Give more work than you're paid for		86f-87a
	Formula for success in , —D&C 75:28		87b
Dallin H. Oaks	Engage in , upon which you may ask Lord's blessings	Nov 1986	21a
	Gray areas as employees and investors		22e-f
L. Tom Perry	Expect 3 or 4 career changes	Nov 1995	36f-37a
James E. Faust	One choice as good as another sometimes	May 2004	52f
James E. Faust	Choice of vocation doesn't matter	May 2007	56b-c
L. Tom Perry	, to prepare for mission	Nov 2007	48f-49a
Dallin H. Oaks	"I wish I'd spent more time with my job?"		105b-c
Henry B. Eyring	Couple lost , but had faith because of preparation	May 2009	25b-f
Richard C. Edgley	We are brother's keeper where , is concerned		53d-e
	All necessary helps are in each quorum		53e-f
	Retired executive helped 12 find , —story		53f-54f
	Quorum put mechanic back on feet —story		54b-e
	, helps the Church offers		54e-f
	If you need , speak up		54f-55b
Claudio R. M. Costa	One of men's fourfold responsibilities —Hinckley		56b-c
	Don't do Church work on employer's time		56f-57a

Joseph Fielding Smith	, is life in the presence of the Father and Son	June 1969	37b
Harold B. Lee	We will rule over our progeny		104c
Hugh B. Brown	More than continuing to exist	Dec 1969	32d
Victor L. Brown	A lesson on , touched a group of youth deeply —story		108f-109a
Delbert L. Stapley	Must be earned	July 1973	100d
Marion G. Romney	A difference between immortality and ,	Jan 1974	13f
Spencer W. Kimball	, a projection of this one	May 1974	118e-f
Delbert L. Stapley	No abridgment of free agency in ,	May 1975	22a
Joseph Anderson	Difference between immortality and ,		31a
Marion G. Romney	Difference between immortality and ,		84f-85a
Spencer W. Kimball	Definition of ,	Nov 1978	72c
James E. Faust	The difference between immortality and ,	Nov 1988	12e-f
Wm. Grant Bangerter	, depends on repentance, ordinances, enduring, service		81b-82b
Henry B. Eyring	Tests here prepare us for trust of endless posterity	May 2009	23f-24b
Quentin L. Cook	Available only through obedience		37d-f
Jorge F. Zeballos	Perfection and , are not impossible	Nov 2009	33b-34f

Mark E. Peterson	Can believers in , have lofty aspirations?	Dec 1968	90c
John H. Vandenberg	, creates questions more profound than those answered	June 1970	59e

Evolution, cont'd
Related Topics: Creation

Henry D. Taylor	Dictionary resulting from explosion about as likely	Dec 1970	43d-f
Marion G. Romney	Relieves man of sense of responsibility	July 1973	14a
Bernard P. Brockbank	Self respect does not come from idea of ,	Jan 1974	116b
Mark E. Peterson	Belief in , is a denial of Christ	May 1983	64b-65a
Boyd K. Packer	God's children did not evolve from slime	Nov 1984	67e
Boyd K. Packer	Idea of , relaxes moral behavior	Nov 1986	18a-e
Boyd K. Packer	This world is based on choice, not chance	May 1988	71c-e
Boyd K. Packer	A mistake to teach that man is an animal	Nov 1990	85b-c
Larry W. Gibbons	God created us - Therefore guides us	Nov 2006	102b-c

Exaltation
Related Topics: Celestial Kingdom, Eternal Life, Heaven, Salvation

Harold B. Lee	We will only rule over our own progeny	June 1969	104c
	Will be a great work to learn our , beyond the grave —Smith		104f
Theodore M. Burton	A second salvation dependent upon works and grace	July 1972	78e
	Possible only with family		79b
A. Theodore Tuttle	No , without priesthood		119e
Sterling W. Sill	Will be awarded based upon type of life	Jan 1973	82f
Spencer W. Kimball	We will exceed the angels	Nov 1975	79e-80a
Marion G. Romney	Explanation of "more sure word of prophecy"	Nov 1976	73a-b
Spencer W. Kimball	An inextinguishable light is available		110d
Adney Y. Komatsu	Not possible without ordinances of temple	Nov 1983	28b-d
Ezra Taft Benson	, is an extension of righteous family life	Nov 1989	5d
Gordon B. Hinckley	Neither man nor woman exalted without the other	May 1991	71d-e
Jack H. Goaslind	Being married right is critical to ,	Nov 1995	10b
Neal A. Maxwell	Sins of omission may prevent ,		23a-c
Dallin H. Oaks	Life is for the sole purpose of ,		26a-b
Russell M. Nelson	Not a free gift like immortality	Nov 1996	35d-e
Dallin H. Oaks	"Have You Been Saved?" —good discussion	May 1998	55b-57f
John M Madsen	Eternal life: living forever as families in the presence of God	May 2002	78e
Neal A. Maxwell	Stars are not immortal, but we are!	Nov 2002	16d
James E. Faust	Wayward children will be saved but perhaps not exalted	May 2003	62b-f
Keith K. Hilbig	Path to , is an upward incline - not a plateau	Nov 2007	37f-38d
Russell M. Nelson	The highest state of happiness and glory	May 2008	8a-b
	A conditional gift		8f-9a
	Sealing of couples enables ,		9a
	Sealing ordinances are essential to ,		10b
	Salvation an individual matter - , a family matter		10d
L. Tom Perry	Difference between immortality and eternal life		44b-d
Dieter F. Uchtdorf	We will know the meaning of ultimate joy	Nov 2008	22f-23a
Russell M. Nelson	Salvation is an individual matter - , is a family matter		92d
Tad R. Callister	Can be found in only one place	Nov 2009	37f

Example
Related Topics: —

LeGrand Richards	Are you failing to let your light shine?	Dec 1968	45b-c
Marion D. Hanks	Son said , taught more than lectures		96c

Delbert L. Stapley	Three cardinal points for being a good teacher	June 1969	69d
	What you do thunders so loudly...		69f
	Convince a man he's wrong by doing right		70d
	No way to teach a child honesty but by ,		70d-e
	Teach children by , —Brigham Young		70e-72a
Richard L. Evans	Teachers must be what they teach		80b
	Parents who are bad, will have children who are worse		80f
Joseph F. Smith	A way to teach	Dec 1969	37b
David O. McKay	A duty no man can evade		87d
	Preach by , in the way you live		88f
Howard W. Hunter	Live to invoke best in others		96d
	Religion is practice and ,		96f
Gordon B. Hinckley	, is the most effective argument for Church	June 1970	40d
N. Eldon Tanner	Converts became inactive because of , of members	Dec 1970	33e-35a
Elray L. Christiansen	Parental , —short poem	June 1971	38b
Marion D. Hanks	Offbeat interpretation of "Practice what we Preach"		90b-d
Marvin J. Ashton	Astute observation about Jesus' example	Dec 1971	101f
Elray L. Christiansen	Parents teach best through , —short poem	July 1972	55a
William H. Bennett	Bad , is worst detriment to missionary work		83a
N. Eldon Tanner	Young man converted by , —story		100e
	The importance of setting a good ,		101a
Ezra Taft Benson	Follow Jesus' , —good thought	Jan 1973	57d
	Follow Jesus' ,		59e
Franklin D. Richards	People become like those they admire		71b
Hartman Rector, Jr.	If you make a mistake, you can always be a bad ,		130e
N. Eldon Tanner	Of parents to children	July 1973	8d
Robert L. Simpson	Savior's ,		23f
N. Eldon Tanner	Sister McKay's words about her husband		92e
Delbert L. Stapley	Greatest gift we can give another		100f
Paul H. Dunn	What you do thunders so loudly... —Emerson	May 1974	15b
	Teaching by , —good couplet		15b-c
Rex D. Pinegar	Father's , kept daughter from bad marriage —story		68a-d
	Told friend not to swear around his brothers —story		68f-69a
Marion D. Hanks	Boys need an , of a man at his best		79b
Marion G. Romney	Drinking boys discovered by non-member —story	Nov 1974	73f-74d
N. Eldon Tanner	, of 3 youth made a convert		76b-77c
	LDS are watched more than others		77e
Spencer W. Kimball	7 ward boys mimicked him in Church —story		79d-80b
	Younger children will do what the oldest does		79d-80b
Gordon B. Hinckley	Our , adds or detracts from Jesus' image	May 1975	94f
Victor L. Brown	The way children should learn from parental ,	May 1976	112f
Franklin D. Richards	I'm going on a mission to set an , for brothers	Nov 1976	16c
David B. Haight	May forget what you say but not how you made them feel		22b
Marion D. Hanks	Worked to pay mother's bill and converted druggist —story	Nov 1977	37b-f
H. Burke Peterson	Personal involvement and , most powerful teachers		88c-e

Example

L. Tom Perry	, of girl led to 37 converts —story	May 1978	52f-53b
Joseph B. Wirthlin	We are to be lights dispelling darkness from lives of others	Nov 1978	37b
Marion D. Hanks	Moistened left hand but turned pages with the right —story	May 1979	74d
Carlos E. Asay	, is the best service rendered to missionary effort	May 1980	43a
M. Russell Ballard	Little boy shared bread with lady - she converted —story	Nov 1980	23b
Paul H. Dunn	Girl did not want temple marriage because of , —story	Nov 1981	71d-72b
Gordon B. Hinckley	, the most persuasive gospel trait	May 1982	45a
James E. Faust	Chickens come home to roost and bring chicks with them		48b
H. Burke Peterson	Sons will follow fathers' example	Nov 1982	42c-e
Robert E. Wells	So live that false accusers will not be believed		70f
Ted E. Brewerton	I like myself more when I am with you	May 1983	74a
	First Presidency is never heavy-hearted		74a
Gordon B. Hinckley	85% of high achieving youth come from religious homes	Nov 1983	44d-e
Angel Abrea	Why is he breaking it now? —story of a sculptor	May 1984	70b-c
	We are accountable for our children's sins if we set a bad ,		72b-e
	We need more guiding lights and fewer excuse-makers		72e-f
J. Richard Clarke	Man gave him a personalized coat-of-arms —story	May 1985	74a-c
	Family was asked to let reporter live with them for 1 week		74d-e
	Guilty by association?		74f
	Serviceman was uncompromising —story		75a-b
	He is the finest practicing Christian I know		75b
	Other boys quit swearing around LDS boy —story		75d-f
Hugh W. Pinnock	Neighbors' , won motorcyclists —story	May 1987	62f-63b
Elaine L. Jack	A Beehive admired a Laurel —story	Nov 1989	88b-c
LeGrand R. Curtis	More children are punished for mimicking their parents	Nov 1990	12f
J. Richard Clarke	Son says "I thought you were better"	May 1991	42a-c
Janette C. Hales	Patterns: Sewing and in scriptures		83d-f
	, of sister and roommates taught prayer		84b-c
Ted E. Brewerton	We can reflect light into dark places	Nov 1991	12f
Robert D. Hales	Parental , —stories from his youth	Nov 1993	8d-10f
Thomas S. Monson	Youth at crossroads poem		48e
Gordon B. Hinckley	13-year-old quadriplegic paints with lips —story		54b-e
Albert Choules, Jr.	Children copy their parents' ,	May 1994	14e-f
Marlin K. Jensen	Palmyra's hostility worn down by , —story		48b-e
	Seeing Christ's image in others' faces helps us		49b
Howard W. Hunter	Jesus: The only perfect ,		64b-f
Rex D. Pinegar	Children are like wet cement - impressionable	Nov 1994	81b-c
Cecil O. Samuelson, Jr.	To see ourselves as others see us	May 1995	30e-f
Monte J. Brough	Good , not to be found in sports, movies, music		41b-c
Thomas S. Monson	Crossroads poem	May 1997	95a-b
Carol B. Thomas	Motherless girl learned from , of Young Women leaders	May 1998	92d
M. Russell Ballard	Are we keeping pace with President Hinckley?	Nov 1998	7a-b
Henry B. Eyring	Ministers listened because of neighbors' , —story		34b-c
Thomas S. Monson	Stories of boys affected by Hinckley and Monson —story		48b-e
Neal A. Maxwell	We are to be more loving, holy, courteous, etc.		63d

Example

Robert D. Hales	Love vs. force. Force depresses	May 1999	34b-c
Ben B. Banks	'Twas a sheep that strayed —poem	Nov 1999	10e-11a
Vaughn J. Featherstone	Children may carry parental , to extremes		14d
Thomas S. Monson	Son saw mother on knees —story		19f-20a
M. Russell Ballard	Our lives are magnifying glasses for others	May 2000	33c-d
Sharon G. Larsen	Best way to lead is by ,	Nov 2001	68a-b
	Girl noticed when leader removed extra earrings		68b-d
Margaret D. Nadauld	Sick girl reactivated family unknowingly —story	May 2002	97f-98c
Boyd K. Packer	Worthy youth of Church are , to world	Nov 2003	26c-f
Thomas S. Monson	Boy saw mother praying —story		69d-e
Gordon B. Hinckley	Your , will attract others		84d-e
Richard C. Edgley	, through enduring trials —2 stories		97b-e
Russell M. Nelson	Children follow parents',	May 2004	27c-e
Thomas S. Monson	Wife converted husband —tender story	Nov 2004	115b-116a
Thomas S. Monson	Father's prayer was powerful , —story	May 2005	22b-d
	Jesus' example —good quote		22f
M. Russell Ballard	The powerful , of our homes —good ideas	May 2006	85b-87b
Susan W. Tanner	, of Romanian girl converted family —story		105b-d
James E. Faust	Girl's smiles make converts —story		113a-d
D. Todd Christofferson	What Jesus did that we should emulate	Nov 2006	48b-e
Richard C. Edgley	Executive didn't pay for newspapers —story		73d-f
Henry B. Eyring	Peers' future shaped by you	May 2007	90c-d
Julie B. Beck	Orphan became Young Women general president		109d-110b
	Faithful member drank coffee and lost children —story		110b-e
Mary N. Cook	Brother's , resulted in family being sealed —story	Nov 2007	12f-13b
	Our responsibility to break cycle of bad family ,		13b
Henry B. Eyring	Ministers all knew a member they admired —story		55d-57a
Quentin L. Cook	Members must shed their camouflage		72d-e
Thomas S. Monson	Son saw mother at prayer —story		120a-b
Thomas S. Monson	Your , will influence generations —Tanner	May 2008	66a-b
	Boy imitated him but couldn't wiggle ears —story		66b-e
	Never do anything you wouldn't want son to do		66e
Mary N. Cook	, of girl reactivated mother and sister		122b-d
Henry B. Eyring	You will influence hundreds or thousands		125f
Thomas S. Monson	Popular girl reached out to handicapped girl —story	May 2009	124d-125b
Yoon Hwan Choi	Nine converts were , to his son —story	Nov 2009	53b-55b
Julie B. Beck	Church growth to come from , of women	May 2010	12d-e
M. Russell Ballard	Don't follow , of silly, worldly women		19b-c
	Follow , of mother		19d-e
	Young women behave like their mothers		19f
	Do your actions match your words?		20b
	Daughters must see modesty modeled		20e-f
Elaine S. Dalton	Don't be content to fit in - Shine forth		121b-c

Excellence
Related Topics: Diligence, Perfection

David O. McKay	What e'er thou art, act well thy part —story	June 1969	30b-c
Franklin D. Richards	No , without commitment		51c
Delbert L. Stapley	Choose to excel	Dec 1969	64b
Spencer W. Kimball	Hurdles give you chance to work way to head of crowd	Nov 1974	80e
	You start with all that the great have had—poem		83a-c
	You must not be just average		83f
William H. Bennett	Happiness and joy come from , —story	Nov 1976	30c-31b
Marvin J. Ashton	, in personal conduct —entire talk		84b-86b
Marion D. Hanks	I hope you see the five A's —story	Nov 1977	36d-e
L. Tom Perry	Joseph became the best prisoner also —story	May 1978	51d-52d
Victor L. Brown	Importance of , in all we do	Nov 1982	80f-81a
James E. Faust	Glad hurdles are higher than most people care to surmount		89a
Dean L. Larsen	Say "I am everything," then prove it	May 1983	35f
Marvin J. Ashton	Striving is more important than arriving	May 1984	11f
Peter Vidmar	Work just a bit harder than others —entire talk	May 1985	38b-40f
Ezra Taft Benson	Older almost always means better	Nov 1989	4e
Gordon B. Hinckley	We can do no less than our very best	May 1997	67c
Donald L. Staheli	Don't be satisfied with mediocrity —Hinckley	Nov 2004	37e-f
Thomas S. Monson	Can't be satisfied with mediocrity when , is within reach		58e
Boyd K. Packer	Can't always expect success, but must do our best		86b-e
Elaine S. Dalton	Inspired by a stone - She and McKay —story	May 2005	110e&111f
Keith B. McMullin	The sin that will cleave to us —Brigham Young	Nov 2005	12b
Joseph B. Wirthlin	Plowhorse became champion jumper —story	May 2006	99b-f
	Create a masterpiece of your life		101d-102b
Joseph B. Wirthlin	Don't be a scrub - Mother's saying	Nov 2006	28d-e
Dieter F. Uchtdorf	Desire makes the impossible possible —story		37b-f
Boyd K. Packer	, does not call attention to itself	May 2007	26d
Dieter F. Uchtdorf	A 2-degree error caused plane crash —story	May 2008	57f-58b
	A 1-degree error makes 500-mile difference		58f-59a
Dieter F. Uchtdorf	Cultivate a reputation for ,	Nov 2009	56f
Boyd K. Packer	Gideon's men were always alert	May 2010	6d-e

Excommunication
Related Topics: Bishop's Courts

Adney Y. Komatsu	Plan activities to bring people back	May 1992	29d-31b
James E. Faust	Invitation to come back	Nov 1992	86a-b
Neal A. Maxwell	, keeps the Church cleansed	Nov 1993	20d

Faith
Related Topics: —

Thomas S. Monson	United , of Tongans heals boy —story	Dec 1968	83a-b
David O. McKay	, —Edgar A. Guest —poem		86c-e
Franklin D. Richards	Commitment precedes effective ,	June 1969	51c
Harold B. Lee	Teach first principles of gospel first		104f-105a
Hugh B. Brown	Science based upon ,	Dec 1969	32b
	Of value here and now		32b
	Give youth , that life is eternal		32c

Hugh B. Brown	Sustaining power	Dec 1969	32d
	Man cannot live without ,		32e
	, —excellent definition		32f
	Only , saves from despair		33b
	Rich man desired , —story		33b
	Needed when suffering		33d
	Not substitute for truth		33e
N. Eldon Tanner	Comment upon Lazarus		34c
Alvin R. Dyer	Cures anything		40e
Howard W. Hunter	Principles of the gospel are taught by faith		97c
Mark E. Peterson	, in Christ easier now than past		99f
	Accept hard-to-believe doctrines		100c
	Accept Christ, accept teachings		100d
Delbert L. Stapley	Doubt cannot exist in a faith-filled heart	June 1970	74e
Henry D. Taylor	Why , is not blind	Dec 1970	44b
	Missionary rebuked the storm —story		44c-d
	Child prayed she wouldn't get spanked —story		44d-f
Harold B. Lee	Scriptures: "...I accept the rest on , " —A. Lincoln	June 1971	8a
	How one obtains learning by ,		10b-c
Richard L. Evans	Stake president had faith in words of father —story	Dec 1971	59a-c
Hartman Rector, Jr.	Excerpts from 6th lecture on faith		64f-65c
Thomas S. Monson	Faith and doubt cannot coexist	July 1972	69f
Harold B. Lee	Don't question what Lord says	Jan 1973	108c
Thomas S. Monson	Good , —short poem		121f
Spencer W. Kimball	Build faith before emergencies come	July 1973	16e
	Security born of unquenchable ,		17b
Hartman Rector, Jr.	Doubt and , cannot exist in same person —Joseph Smith		57d
O. Leslie Stone	Difference between , and belief		60a
	Right living is greatest , builder		60f
	Possibilities if faith lived up to		61d
Hartman Rector, Jr.	Defined - "a strong belief plus action"	Jan 1974	106f
Sterling W. Sill	Every man lives by some sort of , —example	Nov 1974	62f-63a
John H. Vandenberg	Living , of dead is the dead , of the living		93d
	, is not a leap in the dark		93e
	Without , mankind has no history		94e
Marion G. Romney	Laman knew he couldn't get the plates and proved it	May 1975	73a
Thomas S. Monson	, and prayer of dying girl answered —story	Nov 1975	20d-22f
A. Theodore Tuttle	Two kinds of ,		23d-e
Thomas S. Monson	, of Guatemalan missionary healed him —story	Nov 1976	53c-f
Spencer W. Kimball	Poem concerning God's power —poem		110e
Marion G. Romney	Guatemalan missionary walked again —story	Nov 1977	42a-b
Vaughn J. Featherstone	Missionaries gave food and returned to find groceries —story	Nov 1978	26d-e
Joseph B. Wirthlin	Lady healed when President Kimball shook hand —story		36b-e
N. Eldon Tanner	Believed gunpowder came from seeds— , in vain —story		46f-47a
L. Tom Perry	Required , for Lehi's sons to follow him	Nov 1979	34e-35c

John H. Groberg	Hawaiian overcame challenge - family stayed active —story	May 1980	49a-f
J. Richard Clarke	Trust enough to act first, receive confirmation later	Nov 1980	83b-c
	Red Sea not opened until its shores were reached		84d
Douglas W. DeHaan	Stake's corn harvested when priesthood stopped rain —story		87b-88f
Loren C. Dunn	Good scriptures and quote on ,	May 1981	25b-c
	Cannot exist with cynicism, skepticism, unforgiveness		26f
Carlos E. Asay	No answers for some things. Accept them on ,	Nov 1981	68f
Rex D. Pinegar	Faith - the force of life —Tolstoy	Nov 1982	25d-e
	, overcomes even multiple problems —story		25e-26b
Thomas S. Monson	Samoans knew General Authorities would bring rain—story	May 1984	18a-b
Angel Abrea	Nephi's , included no room for excuses		70e-71a
	If it cannot be done , and testimony can do it		71a-c
	Never be discouraged —Comment by Joseph Smith		71e
Marvin J. Ashton	Do you know who is holding you? —story	Nov 1985	69b&d
Ted. E. Brewerton	Boy wrestled champion at Joseph Smith's bidding —story	Nov 1986	30d-f
	200 routed a mob of 3500 —story		30f-31a
Ezra Taft Benson	The calling of his father to a mission —story		45f-46c
	The calling of his father to a mission —story		47f-48c
A. Theodore Tuttle	Faith financed his mission —story		73c-f
Robert L. Simpson	Man rolled up pant legs before walking on water —story	May 1987	40b-c
L. Aldin Porter	A call was rejected - Family left Church —story	Nov 1987	73e-f
Russell M. Nelson	Nothing is impossible —entire talk	May 1988	33b-35f
Richard G. Scott	Missionaries healed man with head wound —story	May 1989	35d-36a
Thomas S. Monson	Healing of Guatemalan missionary —story		45b-46b
Boyd K. Packer	Reason and , together will protect and redeem		54f
Gordon B. Hinckley	Alma Smith's hip socket healed —story	Nov 1989	97d-f
Thomas S. Monson	The , and service of a missionary with cancer —story	May 1990	59b-60b
Russell M. Nelson	Helped by repentance, obedience, prayer, effort	Nov 1990	74f-75c
Thomas S. Monson	"The Gate of the Year" —poem	May 1991	59d
Neal A. Maxwell	, in God's existence and redemptive capacity		90b
L. Aldin Porter	Heber C. Kimball's acceptance of mission call	May 1992	45c-e
Dallin H. Oaks	His encounter with a robber —story	Nov 1992	39b-40b
	Personal Protection —entire talk		37b-40b
Marion D. Hanks	What , is —good statement		65f
Virginia H. Pearce	How to conquer our fears —good		90b-92b
John K. Carmack	Nephi's ready, fire, aim approach	May 1993	42c
	, sometimes requires repentance first		42f-43a
	Things that block out ,		43a
Jeffrey R. Holland	Without , the world makes no sense	Nov 1993	13f-14a
John H. Groberg	Exercise , then go to work —rowboat story		26d-28b
Virginia H. Pearce	God knows you —excellent talk	May 1994	92b-94b
Janette C. Hales	Athletes require exercise and training - so does faith		97b
Dallin H. Oaks	Must have an object		98e-99a
	Cannot produce result contrary to Lord's will		100b-c
	Prayed wife's death would not affect children's , —story		100c-d

Faith

Neal A. Maxwell	Faith and hope are constantly interactive	Nov 1994	35c-d
Richard C. Edgley	Developing confidence —great talk		39d-41b
Boyd K. Packer	The flow of revelation depends on your ,		60f-61a
	Life - being led by Spirit, not knowing...		61f-62a
Joseph B. Wirthlin	Shallow roots allowed trees to fall —story		75b-c
Patricia P. Pinegar	Uprooted trees and intertwined redwoods —story		78b-c
Chieko N. Okazaki	Seek learning by study and , —entire talk		92b-94b
Boyd K. Packer	Shield of , not factory-produced but home produced	May 1995	8e-9b
Jack H. Goaslind	"Walk to the edge of the light..." —H.B. Lee	Nov 1995	10d-e
Gordon B. Hinckley	Where doubt is , has no power —Joseph Smith		72c
Carlos E. Asay	As long as Peter looked to Jesus he stayed on top	May 1996	60b-d
Henry B. Eyring	One's , is shown when tragedy strikes —story		64a-d
Chieko N. Okazaki	The opposite of hope is despair	Nov 1996	89e-f
Jack H. Goaslind	, and service of 20 young pioneers —story	May 1997	39d-40f
M. Russell Ballard	We have nothing to fear from the journey		60d-e
	Life and pioneer trek beautifully compared		61a-b
	Did pioneer trek require more , than ours?		61b-e
First Presidency	Presentation about pioneer journey west		62b-64f
Gordon B. Hinckley	Our inspiring pioneer heritage and present duty		65b-67f
Bonnie D. Parkin	11-yr-old girl left Sweden alone to go to Zion —story		84d-85b
	Step into darkness and light appears —H.B. Lee		85f
Russell M. Nelson	President Hinckley quote on prayer and work	Nov 1997	16b
Thomas S. Monson	A donated child's walker —story		19c-20a
James E. Faust	Essential things in which we must believe		43a-b
	, to follow leaders into the unknown		44f-45a
James E. Faust	Boy found cow through faith and prayer —story		59b-d
Dallin H. Oaks	The foremost quality of our pioneers		72e
Mary Ellen Smoot	, and doubt cannot be in mind at same time —story		87a-e
L. Tom Perry	History of Articles of ,	May 1998	23a-d
Neal A. Maxwell	, must be nurtured - unlike doubt and despair	Nov 1998	61d-e
Mary Ellen Smoot	A gift of God - A reward for righteousness		90c
Neal A. Maxwell	Those who demand signs quickly discount them	Nov 1999	8d-e
Jeffrey R. Holland	The light at the end of the tunnel is Jesus		36b-37c
H. Bruce Stucki	, of a sparrow raised by a girl —story		44d-45b
James E. Faust	Good things from missionary's shooting —story		59d-60c
	Woman's experience with , during miscarriage —story		60c-e
	, casts shadow of burdens behind us		60e
	Peter's denials strengthened his ,		61a-d
James E. Faust	The greatest undeveloped resource	May 2000	18d
	Like a supercharger in our lives		18e-f
	Intensifies and magnifies gifts and abilities		18f
	Flexible gristle replaced hip socket —story		19a-d
Thomas S. Monson	Better than light and safer than a known way —poem		54b-c
Joseph B. Wirthlin	, increases as we bear testimony	Nov 2000	24b-c
Gordon B. Hinckley	The miracle of , —entire talk	May 2001	67d-69f

Sharon G. Larson	Had Nephi ever seen a ship?	May 2001	86b-d
David B. Haight	, of a mustard seed	Nov 2001	24b-e
L. Whitney Clayton	Always moves its possessor to action		28d
	Is a step-by-step process		29f-b
Sharon G. Larson	Our small uncertainties produce large uncertainties in youth		68a-b
Neal A. Maxwell	Loss of , in immortality gives world a fatal moral problem		78e-f
Robert F. Orton	Love is the driving force behind ,		81e
Richard G. Scott	Unbelief does not alter reality		87b
Virginia U. Jensen	Duke ordered "stand firm" - history changed —story		94a-c
R. Conrad Schultz	It is not blind, because we can see	May 2002	29f-30b
Thomas S. Monson	Family sold car and quit job to go to temple —story		49f-50c
Gordon B. Hinckley	One step at a time and , lights the way		72d-73a
Thomas S. Monson	, and doubt cannot exist in same mind		100e
Lance B. Wickman	Believing is seeing - Not the other way around	Nov 2002	31d
	, during death or illness of a loved one		30b-32f
James E. Faust	"The Little Engine That Could" —story		49f-50b
Thomas S. Monson	Noah was the model of ,		60f-61b
	The , of the family of a deceased elder —story		62d-e
D. Todd Christofferson	Even Brigham's , was limited —Brigham Young quote		73a-b
Joseph B. Wirthlin	What is true faith?		82c
	, is confidence, action and obedience		83b-84d
	Darkness may be caused by lack of , —story		85b-d
Richard G. Scott	Janitor didn't believe in nuclear particles —story	May 2003	76b-e
James E. Faust	The moving cause of all virtues		108e-f
Russell M. Nelson	Boy prayed on operating table —story	Nov 2003	44b-d
Dennis E. Simmons	"But if not..." —entire talk	May 2004	73b-75b
Boyd K. Packer	, is best fabricated in a cottage industry		79a
Henry B. Eyring	, in those who hold keys —story	Nov 2004	26d-29e
Robert D. Hales	Finding , in Jesus Christ —entire talk		70d-73f
David A. Bednar	"Are you scared?" —BYU-Idaho story		77f-78c
Joseph B. Wirthlin	Pioneer children died of diphtheria —story		103c-f
Boyd K. Packer	Learn to walk into the darkness	May 2005	8a-b
Harold G. Hillam	If you doubt any doctrine, test it		32d-e
David E. Sorensen	Could not be officer because of mission —story		72b-73b
David A. Bednar	, qualifies us for tender mercies of the Lord		99b-102b
Benjamin De Hoyos	Convert quit job in cigarette factory —story	Nov 2005	31e-f
Henry B. Eyring	Great , has a short shelf life unless...		39b-f
Thomas S. Monson	First Vision and Joseph's ,		67e-68e
H. Bruce Stucki	Prayer and , found the boy's arrow —story	May 2006	96b-f
	Prayer and , accomplished brain surgery —story		97a-98b
David S. Baxter	What , does	Nov 2006	13e-14b
Thomas S. Monson	Like Canadian roads, our foundation must be deep		62b-69b
Gordon B. Hinckley	, of Joseph, Brigham and successors		82f-83b
	, of handcart pioneers - Brigham's talk calling for rescue		83b-84d
	Great-grandmother died entering valley		84d-e

Gordon B. Hinckley	, and prayer found lost ring —story	Nov 2006	84f-85a
Boyd K. Packer	Fear is the opposite of ,		87e-f
	Future events will tax our courage and extend ,		88d
Craig A. Cardon	"Move that mountain, Dad" —story		94d-e
Jeffrey R. Holland	Faith works by words	May 2007	16b-c
Bonnie D. Parkin	Gratitude is an expression of ,		35d-e
Neil L. Andersen	Faith is a decision		74f
Robert D. Hales	The key to revelation	Nov 2007	88f
Richard G. Scott	The relationship between , and character		92c-e
Russell M. Nelson	King offered to have his people baptized	May 2008	8c-d
David A. Bednar	Healing came only after prayer of , —story		96b-e
	, through meaningful prayer —entire talk		94d-97b
Neil L. Andersen	, is not only a feeling; it is a decision —story	Nov 2008	13f-14b
Dieter F. Uchtdorf	Hope is the foundation of ,		21f-22b
	The contrast between hope and despair		22b-d
	What hope is		22d-e
	Hope sustains and upholds us		23a-b
	How , hope and charity complement each other		23b-24a
Joseph B. Wirthlin	Healing eventually came —story		28d-e
D. Todd Christofferson	Lost everything in quake, but still smiling —story	May 2009	19d-20b
	Expands as we keep covenants through afflictions		21b-f
Henry B. Eyring	Couple had , through employment adversity		25b-f
Kevin W. Pearson	A principle of action and power - A spiritual gift		38e-f
	Requires an attitude of exact obedience		39a
	Spiritual photosynthesis using the Light of Christ		39b
	Six Destructive Ds to ,		40c-f
Thomas S. Monson	Not a time for fear but for ,		67f
Dieter F. Uchtdorf	The progressive path of ,		76b-d
Barbara Thompson	Children prayed for bishop's broken eyes —story		84d-f
Thomas S. Monson	Scottish converts immigrated despite hardships —story		89d-90b
	Future is as bright as your ,		92f
Boyd K. Packer	Girl prayed, then kicked trap to pieces —story	Nov 2009	46a-b
Michael T. Ringwood	Increases as we do seemingly insignificant things		102b-f
Boyd K. Packer	Fear is opposite of ,	May 2010	10a
Wilford W. Andersen	Saints were happy as they left Nauvoo		16a-e
	Haitian saints happy after earthquake		16e-17a
	Hope comes as a result of ,		17a-b
	Requires more than belief		17b-c
	Does anyone have problem with the Plan? —story		17f-18a
D. Todd Christofferson	Central purpose of scriptures is ,		34f-35b
	Matures as we feast upon the word		35a
Dallin H. Oaks	Other churches have , too —story		47e-48b
	Essential for healings		49a-b
	It's up to me now to exercise my ,		49b-c
	Enough , but not Lord's will		50d

Faith

Faith, cont'd
Related Topics: —

Dallin H. Oaks	Our , is not dependent on outcomes	May 2010	50e
Donald L. Hallstrom	Babies' deaths affected families differently —story		78c-79e
Ann M. Dibb	We have confidence in the result —Hunter		115b
	Teacher attacked girl's , —story		115d-e

Fall, The
Related Topics: Adam, Creation

Russell M. Nelson	Without , we would be stranded	Nov 1993	33f-34d
Dallin H. Oaks	Adam and Eve did not commit sin		72f-73f
Bruce C. Hafen	Not a tragic mistake	May 2004	97c-d
Earl C. Tingey	, brought about two deaths	May 2006	73a-d
Dallin H. Oaks	Not caused by sex but selfishness —C.S. Lewis	May 2009	95a-b

Family
Related Topics: Children, Home, Parents

Gordon B. Hinckley	Will we be grandfathers or grandsons of great men?	Dec 1968	70e
Marvin J. Ashton	Family members should be friends —story	Dec 1969	51b-f
A. Theodore Tuttle	A man's most important consideration		107b
Bruce R. McConkie	Decisions must be made on basis of how it affects the ,	June1970	43e-44a
	Heaven: A projection of an LDS , into eternity		44e
A. Theodore Tuttle	Advice for bringing , closer together		81b-c
Marion D. Hanks	As are families, so is society		98c
	5 suggestions for improving ,		98c-100e
Ezra Taft Benson	, will outlive Church	Dec 1970	46a
	Be a stick-together family —poem		50b-51e
Spencer W. Kimball	Man's 8 children all married in temple —story	Dec 1971	36c-37a
	Kimball's observations of a modest, ideal family —story		37a-38b
Loren C. Dunn	Priorities for fathers - family then Church		48a
	Plan and organize meetings to keep father in home more		48b
A. Theodore Tuttle	Questionable practices which weaken home		90f
Joseph Fielding Smith	Most important organization	July 1972	27e
Theodore M. Burton	Exaltation possible only with family		79b
	"Root nor branch" in Mal 4:1 —explanation		79d
A. Theodore Tuttle	A , Church designed to exalt ,	Jan 1973	66d
	Destiny of , to eternally live together		66e
Gordon B. Hinckley	Will you pass on good qualities?		92d
H. Burke Peterson	Eternal happiness will be in , unit		114a
Spencer W. Kimball	The great plan of life	July 1973	15b
	Society without , will disintegrate		15c
	A praying , —story		17b
	Everyone in , loved and important —poem		17e
L. Tom Perry	Gives encouragement and confidence		21d
Ezra Taft Benson	Abortion strikes at foundation of ,		41a
Hartman Rector, Jr.	Happy parents raise happy children		59c
N. Eldon Tanner	The most important thing in life		92c
Howard W. Hunter	What modern society has done to the ,	Jan 1974	55d
A. Theodore Tuttle	Best laboratory to practice celestial living		68e

Marvin J. Ashton	Joseph's praise of brother Hyrum	Jan 1974	104c
Elray L. Christiansen	The kingdom of families	May 1974	25f
Rex D. Pinegar	A religious institution. —Stephen L. Richards		67d-e
	Boy told friend not to swear around brothers —story		68f-69a
	Made that we might spend eternity with God		69b
Loren C. Dunn	America built upon foundation of ,	Nov 1974	9e
Theodore M. Burton	Families were planned in pre-existence		54f-55a
	Priesthood lineages planned in pre-existence		55b-c
Theodore M. Burton	Priesthood comes because of lineage	May 1975	69b-70a
	Your , will join Church because they are of correct lineage		70a-71f
Spencer W. Kimball	When the , falters, life falls apart	Nov 1976	8b
N. Eldon Tanner	One cell of battery foamed and fumed —story		74e-75b
Paul H. Dunn	Excitement - He was going home after 3 days	Nov 1977	25c
A. Theodore Tuttle	If isolated from Church, what would your children learn	Nov 1979	27f-28a
John H. Groberg	Hawaiian overcame challenge - , stayed active —story	May 1980	49a-f
Spencer W. Kimball	Only those deeply believing in , will be able to preserve it	Nov 1980	4e
Hartman Rector, Jr.	Lord designed greatest blessings to come thru ,	May 1981	73b
L. Tom Perry	Every , headed by executive committee and family council		88b-c
John H. Groberg	, prayer - sustained homesick missionary —story	May 1982	51a-52e
Ezra Taft Benson	Statistics on divorce, working mothers, single parents	Nov 1982	59d-e
Dean L. Larsen	Influence of , is greater than all others combined	May 1983	33b-c
James E. Faust	Lingering feelings should be settled quickly		42a
L. Tom Perry	Characteristics of strong families		79a-b
Vaughn J. Featherstone	They are all my children and it's no picnic	Nov 1983	36d-e
Ezra Taft Benson	No nation will rise above caliber of its homes	May 1984	6b-c
	Formula for successful ,		6e-7b
David B. Haight	The roles of fathers and mothers		12d-e
A. Theodore Tuttle	The influence of , for better or worse is overwhelming		24b-d
Gene R. Cook	Everyone belongs to a , - practice the principle		31a
Ezra Taft Benson	Most important friendships should be in ,	May 1986	43d-e
Ezra Taft Benson	Most important friendships should be in ,	Nov 1986	81f
James E. Faust	The glue that holds society together	May 1987	81a-d
Vaughn J. Featherstone	Older brother was girl's best friend —story	Nov 1987	28c-d
	Mentally unbalanced soldiers were from broken homes		28d
Dwan J. Young	Reasons families are breaking apart	May 1988	78d-e
Ezra Taft Benson	List of things members of Church should do in ,		84d-85b
Thomas S. Monson	The importance of , —quote from Margaret Thatcher	Nov 1988	69d
Michaelene P. Grassli	How to have children at peace		78f-79a
	What families do at family prayer time		79a
	A 9-year-old likened his , to Lehi's —story		79d-f
J. Richard Clarke	Why has Satan attacked the , ?	May 1989	60e
	The blessings of a close extended ,		60e-61a
Ezra Taft Benson	Elderly increasing faster than other age groups	Nov 1989	4e
	Older almost always means better		4e
	Eternity an extension of righteous , life		5d

Ezra Taft Benson	Responsibility of , to care for elderly	Nov 1989	6d-8b
Thomas S. Monson	Two forgotten elderly parents —stories		68a-c
Rex D. Pinegar	No genuine happiness apart from , —J.F. Smith	May 1990	9e
	Hurricane took house but not home —story		9e-f
	His chaotic , gathering —story		10f-11c
L. Tom Perry	, traditions we should keep		20e-f
Howard W. Hunter	Would you make your , like Capernaum?	Nov 1990	18d
James E. Faust	One per day , prayer no longer enough		33e-f
Dallin H. Oaks	Elderly parents are our responsibility	May 1991	15f
Graham W. Doxey	Children are internship - grandkids postgraduate education	Nov 1991	25b
James E. Faust	Promote more , togetherness on Sunday		34d-e
Thomas S. Monson	One of greatest fortresses against evil		87a-b
James E. Faust	Most important of all institutions	May 1993	35b
	Roles of fathers and mothers —excellent talk		35b-37f
L. Tom Perry	What , prayer and study did for Peru —story		90b-e
	A promise if , prayer and study is done daily		92f
Chieko N. Okazaki	Only 14% are a traditional American ,	Nov 1993	94c-d
Boyd K. Packer	Satan's ultimate purpose is to disrupt ,	May 1994	19e-f
	, is safe within the Church - will cause a flood of converts		21b-f
Kenneth Johnson	Same sociality there as exists here		30e-f
Neal A. Maxwell	Predates and will outlive nations		89e
	Build , upon gospel granite not secular sand		90f
Howard W. Hunter	Disintegration of , brings foretold calamities	Nov 1994	9a
Horacio A. Tenorio	Making our homes into fortresses		23b-24f
Howard W. Hunter	, transcends every other interest		50e-f
Rex D. Pinegar	Greatest challenge today is erosion of ,		81b
	Father's and son's view of day spent fishing —story		82b
	Simple acts will save , —entire talk		80b-82b
Boyd K. Packer	Too many out-of-home activities are not good	May 1995	8e-9b
Andrew W. Peterson	Six adoptions and then natural twins —story		80e-81b
LeGrand R. Curtis	Society's fatal sickness is instability of ,		82b
	Things to do around dinner table		82b-83f
L. Tom Perry	The need for , preparedness	Nov 1995	35e-36a
James E. Faust	The gospel operates through the ,		62e-f
Gordon B. Hinckley	Proclamation on the ,		100f-101e
Henry B. Eyring	Read scriptures aloud as a ,	May 1996	63c-d
	, prayer will touch hearts		63d-e
	God will keep covenant to gather ,		64d-e
Neal A. Maxwell	Adoption: A little girl is supposed to come to , —story		69f-70a
Susan L. Warner	Son was listening with eyes closed —story		79b-c
Robert D. Hales	The eternal , —entire talk	Nov 1996	64d-67b
Jerald L. Taylor	Widower with 6 married widow with 9	May 1997	33b-c
Jeffrey R. Holland	"The highest priority of all"		35e-f
Thomas S. Monson	, wanted to be there when mother awoke —story		94e
Mary Ellen Smoot	1 or 2000 descendants in Church? —story	Nov 1997	12e-13a

Family

Eran A. Call	, home and marriage —important quotes	Nov 1997	29b-e
Gordon B. Hinckley	Church's greatest concern is ,		69d-e
David B. Haight	Everything precious was in a sealing room —story		71d-f
Virginia U. Jensen	Law of harvest most evident in ,		90d-e
	Life is like a wheel - we're up as some are down		91a
Sharon G. Larsen	Premature baby recovered when put with twin —story	May 1998	94d-f
Virginia U. Jensen	Summary of Proclamation on the ,	Nov 1998	13e-f
Boyd K. Packer	Church must not over schedule , —important talk		22b-24f
Neal A. Maxwell	Leave your , clean earth to till		63c
Gordon B. Hinckley	The gift his wife gives to granddaughters		97d-e
Boyd K. Packer	Purpose of Church is to shelter ,	May 1999	63a
	Church must not compete with ,		63b-c
	Wards and , grow and divide		63d
	Sheltered in ward , will be safe		63f
Vaughn J. Featherstone	Boy cleaned kitchen for 3 hours —story	Nov 1999	15a-c
	Boy wanted prayer more than Thanksgiving —story		15c-16a
Neil L. Andersen	Presidency's counsel on prayer and Family Home Evening		17c-18a
Virginia U. Jensen	Satan's ultimate purpose is to destroy , —Packer		95e
	, is of utmost importance		96b-d
Russell M. Nelson	Earth created that families might be	May 2000	85d-f
Neal A. Maxwell	We learn to cope with world by coping with ,	Nov 2000	35f-36a
Thomas S. Monson	At death , is all that matters		65f-66a
Richard G. Scott	What an ideal , is	May 2001	6f-7b
	Draw as close as possible to being an ideal ,		7b-d
Russell M. Nelson	Earth, Church and temples created for ,	Nov 2001	69f
	The fundamental unit of the Church		70e
	Yielding to sin puts , at risk		71a-c
	The source of our greatest joy		71c
	The focus of our work and joy throughout eternity		71d
	Things that have highest priority in ,		71f
John M. Madsen	Eternal life is to live forever as families in presence of God	May 2002	78e
L. Tom Perry	President Kimball's formula for a successful ,	Nov 2002	8f
Dieter F. Uchtdorf	Responsibilities of , reiterated		12e-f
Coleen K. Menlove	Responsibilities of , reiterated —same quote		14b-c
James E. Faust	Good , destroyed fighting over inheritance		19c-d
Kathleen H. Hughes	God and one are a , —M.J. Ashton		106d-e
L. Tom Perry	Families are not yet ours —Brigham Young	May 2003	42d-e
	Helps for , through Church media		40d-43f
James E. Faust	Wayward, sealed children will return		62b-f
Susan W. Tanner	Elements making a successful ,		73c-e
M. Russell Ballard	, is Satan's main target	Nov 2003	18b-d
James E. Faust	No other church claims keys to bind ,		21a
Boyd K. Packer	Nothing more important to Church than ,		25a
	Chance for , is not past for righteous		25a-b
Joseph B. Wirthlin	Priorities: let , come first		81d

L. Tom Perry	Satan's vigorous campaign against ,	May 2004	69b-c
	Proclamation on the , —extensive quotes		70d-71a
Boyd K. Packer	Best protection against sin is a stable ,		79a
	Wayward members of , will be saved		80d
Robert D. Hales	, will be protected if righteous		88b
Richard J. Maynes	A Filipino family with 17 children	Nov 2004	93b-94d
Susan W. Tanner	Covenants sustain , during loss —story	May 2005	106a-e
Dallin H. Oaks	Church and , must be mutually considered	Nov 2005	25b-f
	Differences in priesthood in , and in Church		26b-27b
	Why this is a , Church —good		27c-d
M. Russell Ballard	First people we'll seek in spirit world		41b-d
	Mission statement: Build an eternal ,		41d
	Proclamation on , a prophetic document		41d-42a
	Contrasting worldly opinions on ,		42b-d
	World will be attracted to us because of ,		42d-f
	Never released from , relationships		42e-f
	No genuine happiness apart from ,		42f-43a
	How to strengthen ,		43a-f
	Put , first		43f
	A call to institutions to put , first		43f-44b
	Longest lasting and most important		44b
Boyd K. Packer	Curriculum restructured to center on ,		72f
Ronald A. Rasband	Are extra activities outside home worth it?	May 2006	47b-c
James E. Faust	Ministering angels are sometimes , members		51b-52d
H. Bruce Stucki	A good , is a sacred shield		98d-f
Susan W. Tanner	Kind to bus driver but not , —story		104b-d
Richard H. Winkel	Temple attendance increases love for ,	Nov 2006	9c-f
Margaret S. Lifferth	Obedience in , worship invites blessings		75b
Boyd K. Packer	A worthy LDS , is a standard to the world		87f
James E. Faust	Government of Church based on ,	May 2007	55d-56a
Gordon B. Hinckley	Closing counsel to families		105e
Boyd K. Packer	Work with , transcends anything in Church or out	Nov 2007	8f-9a
	Ultimate end of all Church activity is the ,		9a
Quentin L. Cook	Children will be righteous if 4 guidelines followed		72b-d
Julie B. Beck	A great and eternal organization		77b
Douglas L. Callister	Must bear testimony in ,		101d
	What if , can't light their lamps from ours?		101d-f
Dallin H. Oaks	"I wish I'd spent more time with my job?"		105b-c
	Which activity the boy liked best		105d
	Beware of overscheduling children		105d-f
	Startling importance of , mealtimes		105f-106b
	Beware team sports and technology toys		107a-b
Barbara Thompson	Nothing you have is more precious —Hinckley		116e
Russell M. Nelson	If families fail, other systems will also	May 2008	8d-f
Kenneth Johnson	67 years of happy family life		15f-16a

Family

Kenneth Johnson	The fabric that holds society together	May 2008	17a
Henry B. Eyring	Greatest joys center in , now and later		22b-d
	Those we'll bring with us when we go home		23b
D. Todd Christofferson	Eloquent tribute to his ,		76d-e
M. Russell Ballard	Don't overschedule - 29 weekly commitments		109d-110a
Dieter F. Uchtdorf	Judged more on time spent with , than on callings	Nov 2008	54f-55a
Russell M. Nelson	Exaltation is a , matter		92d
Boyd K. Packer	The foundation of human life and society	May 2009	52d
	4 grandsons came to announce engagements		52e
Claudio R. M. Costa	One of men's fourfold responsibilities —Hinckley		56b-c
David A. Bednar	Frequently bear testimony in ,	Nov 2009	18f-19c
M. Russell Ballard	Everything including temples focuses on ,		47b-c
Henry B. Eyring	The ideal setting in which to learn love		70f-71b
	Gravestone: "Please, no empty chairs"		71b-d
Quentin L. Cook	Will be asked about , in day of judgment		93a
Boyd K. Packer	Church must do more to assist ,	May 2010	7f-8a
	Ultimate end of all activity is a happy ,		9f
	Ultimate purpose is perfection of ,		9f-10a
M. Russell Ballard	Only LDS believe , continues beyond grave		21d-f
Henry B. Eyring	Has advantage in first 8 years		23a-b
David A. Bednar	Read and testify to bless future posterity		43f
Russell M. Nelson	Church proclaims, promotes, protects ,		91c-92b
Robert D. Hales	Mealtime interactions are important		95f-96b

Family History
Related Topics: Elijah, Work for Dead

Gordon B. Hinckley	Will we be grandfathers or grandsons of great men?	Dec 1968	70e
Theodore M. Burton	The importance of records in the judgment		81a-82e
Theodore M. Burton	Scriptures relating to ,	Dec 1970	57f-58c
	We become saviors		58d-e
	Power to do , rested with keys held by Elijah		58e-f
	An explanation of the power of Elijah by Joseph Smith		59a-e
LeGrand Richards	Jews have a chair hanging on wall for Elijah	June 1971	99d
Howard W. Hunter	Christ's work was vicarious, so why not ours	Dec 1971	71f
Theodore M. Burton	Explanation of "Root nor branch" in Mal. 4:1	July 1972	79d
A. Theodore Tuttle	Goals of , as administered by high priests		119f
Theodore M. Burton	Responsibilities, cursings, and saviors	Jan 1973	52c
	Our responsibility —Brigham Young		53e
	Goal of , —W. Woodruff		54a
	Individual responsibility —J.F. Smith		54b
L. Tom Perry	Lehi left this one essential behind as he fled	Jan 1974	51b
Eldred G. Smith	We promised ancestors we'd do , if they'd come first		63d
A. Theodore Tuttle	Don't bother about , if you don't know where kids were		68a
Theodore M. Burton	Succeeds no faster than the bishop's leadership		115f
Theodore M. Burton	Priesthood inheritance, and promises made to fathers	May 1975	69a-71f
Boyd K. Packer	, impossible in scope? We'll do it anyway	Nov 1975	99b

Boyd K. Packer	Missing records will be given by revelation	Nov 1975	99e
Eldred G. Smith	How the Lord makes it easier to do ,		107b-e
Mark E. Peterson	It matters not what else we do. , most important	May 1976	16b-d
John H. Groberg	We depend upon help from the departed		39b-c
Robert L. Simpson	Sure way to be ineligible for ultimate blessings is to ignore ,		58f-59c
Wm. Grant Bangerter	We are related to everyone —entire talk		69d-71f
Adney Y. Komatsu	Japanese couple married because of , research —story		102a-c
Jacob de Jager	Man he went to rescue turned out to be his brother —story	Nov 1976	56f-57e
Spencer W. Kimball	He feels same urgency about , as about missionary work	May 1978	4c
	2-fold emphasis—4 generation program and name extraction		4d-e
J. Thomas Fyans	Ours is a shared ancestry	Nov 1978	28d-f
	Our 4-generation assignment		28f-29a
	Purpose of name-extraction program —good analogy		29b-d
	At what rate are we progressing?		29f
Ezra Taft Benson	Family organizations		31b
	We'll live in temple and angels will give us names —Young		31c-e
Royden G. Derrick	Total names available since 1200 A.D. Where we stand	May 1979	27b-c
	Our responsibility now - 4 items		27e
A. Theodore Tuttle	, stays God from smiting earth with a curse	May 1980	40b-c
	Go forward by reaching backward		40e
	You will receive help from the dead		40f-41a
	Twin sheets, double sheets, family group sheets —joke		41b
	Broken covenants: leaders responsible if people not taught		41d
	We are their ONLY hope for salvation		41d-e
Spencer W. Kimball	One of the three missions of the Church	May 1981	5e-f
F. Burton Howard	Parable of the desert travelers —entire talk		71b-72f
Hartman Rector, Jr.	Elijah delivered the keys - We're to do the work		73e
	Writing family history will turn your heart to your fathers		74b-75a
Wm. Grant Bangerter	His , was "all done." Then they found 16,000 more	May 1982	71f-72a
Henry B. Eyring	Pass the heritage on undiminished	May 1985	77b-f
Boyd K. Packer	All can't devote the same time to ,	May 1987	24f-25a
	A veil, not a wall, separates us from Spirit World		25a-b
Vaughn F. Featherstone	Those worked for shall "embrace our knees" —J. Smith	Nov 1987	28b-c
Joanne B. Doxey	Help those on other side—receive help in all affairs of life		91f-92a
J. Richard Clarke	Most beautiful tree in forest of creation	May 1989	60b-c
	Only Mormons extend atonement beyond grave		60d
	I'm no longer the only member in my family		61d
	What was done on a "done" line —story		61f-62a
Richard G. Scott	, - Why and how —important talk	Nov 1990	5d-7f
David B. Haight	Elijah came during Paschal feast		60a-d
	The greatest responsibility —Joseph Smith		60f
David B. Haight	, records stored in granite mountain	May 1991	75d-f
	Family Search and Ancestral File explained		76f-77f
Russell M. Nelson	69 billion people on earth	May 1992	72f
Thomas S. Monson	Extraction and temple work for Civil War soldiers —story	Nov 1992	48b-f

Family History

Boyd K. Packer	The first , mission	May 1993	19f
David B. Haight	Our greatest responsibility —Joseph Smith		24d-e
	How to do ,		24e-25b
	Records on obscure ancestors will be found		25c-d
Russell M. Nelson	Revelation to do , announced in 1894	Nov 1994	85c-d
	History of genealogy and , in the Church		85d-f
	For whom will temple work be done?		86b-d
	We won't do temple work for everyone		87a-b
J. Ballard Washburn	Do , and take children to temple for baptisms	May 1995	11d-f
Monte J. Brough	Why Jews are interested in , —story		42f-43a
James E. Faust	You can't count the number of apples in a seed	May 1996	42d-e
Mary Ellen Smoot	Man has one descendant in Church - the other has 2000	Nov 1997	12e-13a
	Interesting ideas for using and doing ,		13a-e
Russell M. Nelson	Spirit of Elijah explained	May 1998	34d-e
	Joseph Smith quote: Not perfect without our dead		34e
	W. Woodruff revelation on , research		34f
	History of , Library		34f-35c
	, Source Guide and Vital Records Index explained		35d-f
	We are to be saviors on Mount Zion		36b
	20% of Internet use pertains to ,		36d
James E. Faust	Young Women project gave scrapbook to grandpa —story		97b-c
David E. Sorensen	Not only Church member after vicarious baptism —story	Nov 1998	65e-f
Carol B. Thomas	Youth prepared 10,000 names for temple	May 1999	13e-f
Thomas S. Monson	, work releases from bondage and darkness		56d-e
D.B. Neuenschwander	Efforts are futile if we don't know where we came from		84d
	, is a major factor in retention		83d-f
Stephen B. Oveson	Pioneers for ancestors and posterity	Nov 1999	30b
James E. Faust	, website has 7 million hits per day		48a
D. Todd Christofferson	Work for dead testifies of Jesus —entire talk	Nov 2000	9d-12b
Russell M. Nelson	, deserves commitment to a planned schedule	May 2001	34d-e
James E. Faust	Ancestors exert influence from other side	May 2003	62b-f
	Pull from ancestors grows as we age		67d
James E. Faust	You and , —entire talk	Nov 2003	53b-56b
Russell M. Nelson	Can't tell much about tree just from trunk	May 2004	27b-c
James E. Faust	What it means to be seed of Abraham	Nov 2004	54f-55b
Elaine S. Dalton	We did this for you - Two way exchange		89b-91e
Thomas S. Monson	Sacrifice of his pioneer ancestors —story	May 2005	21b-22b
Henry B. Eyring	Few if any will reject —W. Woodruff		78e
	After easy names, you'll be tempted to stop		79f-80a
	He saw a paper in a dream		80b
	Entire talk motivational and good		77b-80b
Gordon B. Hinckley	Duplication of work is troublesome	Nov 2005	5f-6a
Henry B. Eyring	Those we're to bring when we go home to God	May 2008	23b
Dieter F. Uchtdorf	His ancestors didn't cross plains, but legacy is his		70b-d
Russell M. Nelson	Our greatest responsibility —Joseph Smith	May 2010	92f

Russel M. Nelson	Refines those engaged in it	May 2010	93f
	Let us present an acceptable book —Joseph Smith		94b-d
	, and new Family Search —entire talk		91a-94f

Family Home Evening
Related Topics: —

Marion G. Romney	History of and promises in ,	June 1969	96c-d
	How to get , rolling in stakes and wards		96d-97a
Spencer W. Kimball	Admonition to hold ,	Dec 1969	50b
	Wards off spiritual foes		50d
A. Theodore Tuttle	Promises if , held regularly	June 1970	80f
Ezra Taft Benson	Vanguard for home instruction	Dec 1970	49d-e
Boyd K. Packer	A promise if , is held		108f
Elray L. Christiansen	Costs nothing, can have it at home —good statement	July 1972	54e
S. Dilworth Young	Some ideas for , —entire talk		76a
Harold B. Lee	How to increase % of home evenings		103b
David B. Haight	Don't give up trying to hold ,		108d
	The promise of Joseph F. Smith		108f
Ezra Taft Benson	Promise if held	Jan 1973	59b
Loren C. Dunn	Good place to bear testimony		85f
Rex D. Pinegar	Objectives and blessings of ,	May 1974	69a-b
L. Tom Perry	Teach children names of General Authorities		98b-c
James A. Cullimore	Examples of national attention , is getting	Nov 1975	28a-29b
Spencer W. Kimball	An outing only half satisfies the real need	Nov 1977	4b
Spencer W. Kimball	Church meetings are a supplement, not the only diet	May 1978	5a
Ezra Taft Benson	Daily devotionals are commendable	Nov 1982	60f
	Not one child in a hundred... —Joseph F. Smith		61b
Michaelene P. Grassli	It may be tough to start, but do it anyway	Nov 1988	78f-79a
Joseph B. Wirthlin	Edicts from First Presidency to hold ,	May 1993	70f-71a
	How his parents held ,		71a-c
Joe J. Christensen	Hold , every week	Nov 1993	12e-13a
L. Tom Perry	Counsel to hold , —entire talk	May 1994	36b-38f
Rex D. Pinegar	A simple thing yielding great blessings	Nov 1994	81c-d
Henry B. Eyring	Use testimony in ,	May 1996	63b
Susan L. Warner	Son was listening with eyes closed —story		79b-c
Henry B. Eyring	We have , because of covenants	Nov 1996	31d-32a
Neil L. Andersen	First Presidency's counsel on family prayer and ,	Nov 1999	17c-18a
Dieter F. Uchtdorf	Originated in 1915 and stressed now	Nov 2002	12e-f
Coleen K. Menlove	Casual and infrequent , are not enough		14d-e
Gordon B. Hinckley	Please reserve and use Monday nights for ,		58a-c
L. Tom Perry	Encouragement to hold ,	May 2003	41e-42a
	Avoid all other activities on Monday night		42f-43a
Russell M. Nelson	Subjects for ,	May 2004	27e-28a
W. Douglas Shumway	Secret friend , —story		96c-d
Thomas S. Monson	Cannot afford to neglect ,	May 2005	19e
H. David Burton	Inauguration of , - The promise if held	May 2007	33b-d

Gordon B. Hinckley	Use general conference as text for ,	May 2007	105d-e
Claudio R. M. Costa	A sacred duty of fathers	May 2009	56c-e
David A. Bednar	Consistency more important than content	Nov 2009	19d-20e

Fast Offerings
Related Topics: Fasting, Offerings, Poor and Needy, Tithing, Welfare Program

Henry B. Eyring	Knowing of , will help a child's fast	May 1996	63f
Thomas S. Monson	History of , and admonitions to pay	Nov 1996	45f-46e
	Collecting , —2 stories		46e-47a
Joseph B. Wirthlin	Poignant plea for , —story	May 2001	74d-f
	Give yourself into the kingdom of God		75a-d
Gordon B. Hinckley	Costs the giver nothing	Nov 2001	74b
Thomas S. Monson	Man saved from hunger pays , —story		99f-100b
Thomas S. Monson	Taking deacons to Welfare Square —story	Nov 2005	56f-57a
Keith B. McMullin	Chinese visitor gave , —story	Nov 2008	76b-d
Quentin L. Cook	Jewish rabbis were impressed about ,	Nov 2009	93b-c

Fasting
Related Topics: Fast Offerings

Thomas S. Monson	Fasting of Tongans saves boy —story	Dec 1968	83a-b
Hartman Rector, Jr.	How one man quit smoking though , —story	June 1970	103a-b
John H. Vandenberg	Origin and purpose of Fast Day —DHC and JD	June 1971	66b-67b
Henry D. Taylor	Double fast offerings: Increase prosperity	Nov 1974	14b
	What , should consist of		14d
	, as observed in President Young's day		14e
	Why fast day was changed to Sunday		15a
	A miracle wrought by , and prayer —story		15d-e
	Blessings associated with , —McKay		15e-f
	4 factors in a proper observance of ,		15f
Robert L. Simpson	, by wife softened husband and converted family —story		46f
Ezra Taft Benson	How to fast, how not to fast —good advice		67a
Victor L. Brown	, must be with a purpose —4 listed	Nov 1977	83b-c
Victor L. Brown	Purpose of , and blessings which come from ,	May 1981	37b-e
Gordon B. Hinckley	What fast offering funds did in 1983	Nov 1983	51d-f
Thomas S. Monson	Blessings coming from , —Isaiah 58:6-11	May 1984	17d-f
	5 non-member patients fasted for missionary —story		18d-f
Russell M. Nelson	Gives confidence that spirit can master appetite —story	Nov 1985	30f-31b
Howard W. Hunter	The history and purpose of ,		72b-74b
L. Tom Perry	3 purposes for ,	May 1986	31d-e
	If fast offerings would double, so would spirituality		32d-e
	The physical benefits of ,		32f-33a
	The spiritual benefits of ,		33a-c
Gordon B. Hinckley	Offerings cost nothing - could care for world	May 1991	52f-53a
Henry B. Eyring	Wise to fast when you want to listen		67a-d
Henry B. Eyring	Knowing of fast offering helps children ,	May 1996	63f
Joseph B. Wirthlin	How and why —entire talk	May 2001	73b-75f
	Blessings coming from ,		73e&75d

Fasting, cont'd
Related Topics: Fast Offerings

Joseph B. Wirthlin	, will bring spirit of calling	May 2001	73f
Spencer J. Condie	Will break yokes and bring revelation	May 2002	45e-f
Carl B. Pratt	Three aspects of a proper fast	Nov 2004	47b-c
	, is a commandment —J.F. Smith		47d
	Suggestions on how to conduct fast		47d-48d
	When should children begin to fast?		48d-f
	Explanation of Isaiah 58:6-11		48f-49b
Yoshihiko Kikuchi	Rain came because of tithing, temple and , —story	May 2007	97e-98d
Douglas L. Callister	Testimony came only after , —story	Nov 2007	100f-101b
Russell M. Nelson	, enhances prayer	May 2009	48a
	No wisdom in long fasts —Joseph F. Smith		48b-c

Fathers
Related Topics: Parents, Patriarchal Order

David O. McKay	If he doesn't help with kids he is untrue to marriage	Dec 1968	37d
Russell M. Nelson	Ways to exercise priesthood in home		87b-c
	Must father bodies and faith of children		87c-88c
David O. McKay	How , must conduct selves in home		109f
David O. McKay	No , has right to utter cross words in home	June 1969	116b-c
Marion D. Hanks	A neglectful yet loving father —story	June 1970	99c-d
Paul H. Dunn	Many , place business before children	June 1971	103b-c
A. Theodore Tuttle	Don't concentrate on material security for children	Dec 1971	90f-91a
Gordon B. Hinckley	A , methods of discipline changed upon conversion	July 1972	72e
Harold B. Lee	How , must teach their boys about sex		102f
Marion D. Hanks	The boy who tried everything but asking , —story		104f
N. Eldon Tanner	Good instructions to ,	July 1973	92c
	We'd rather be with our dad than anybody else		93b
	Blessing of children —Featherstone story		93e
Harold B. Lee	Admonitions to , concerning home		98f
James E. Faust	If , are heads of families juvenile delinquency stops	Jan 1974	22b
	Priorities , should have —H.B. Lee		23b
	General MacArthur greater as a , than as a soldier		23e
	Wife's tearful thanks to husband for temple sealing		23f
	I will go if my father will hold the rope —story		24c
	What , are for —Richard L. Evans		24e
A. Theodore Tuttle	The patriarch of the home, not the dictator		66b
	Should give fathers' blessings		67a
	Must guard home against intrusion of evil		67b
	Must promote peace at home - leave worries at office		67b
	Interview children regularly		67c
	Companions or strangers to children —story		67d
	A man needs the responsibility of a family		68c
	God himself chose to be known as Father		68e
Marvin J. Ashton	Companionship of elderly , a great blessing —Joseph Smith		104c

Author	Topic	Date	Page
Paul H. Dunn	A sacrifice made by his father to help him —story	May 1974	15c-e
Marion D. Hanks	It takes men to make men - Boys need men		76d-77c
	The father saw the C, but not the A's —story		78e
	The father helped his son give his talk —story		78f
	The father helped his disabled son do his duties —story		78f-79a
	Boys need an example of a man at his best		79b
Spencer W. Kimball	Should give sons blessings —story		89e-f
Mark E. Peterson	What , do affects eternal lives of wives and children	Nov 1974	51b-c
Marion D. Hanks	Believed in a loving Heavenly Father because of Dad —story	May 1975	14d-e
Joseph Anderson	Jesus always referred to God as Father		29f-30a
Spencer W. Kimball	Boys need idols; their fathers		79f-80a
H. Burke Peterson	How , holding priesthood should act in family	May 1976	33b-e
M. Russell Ballard	How , can better prepare sons for missions	Nov 1976	87c-88a
Spencer W. Kimball	Each must give a , blessing to his children	Nov 1977	4d
Ezra Taft Benson	Results when inactive dad was asked to bless son —story		31f-32b
Marion D. Hanks	Regular dads and imitation men —story		36c-f
L. Tom Perry	Husbands first - fathers second		63b
	Children chose house rather than him —story		63c-e
	All men must play with their children —story		64a-b
Ezra Taft Benson	How , are to discipline children —J.F. Smith	May 1981	34e-f
	, must put home first —David O. McKay		35a-b
	Children must be spiritually regenerated by ,		36b
	, must put homes in order —John Taylor revelation		36c-e
Paul H. Dunn	Some set example for temple marriage —story	Nov 1981	71d-72b
H. Burke Peterson	Sons will follow , examples	Nov 1982	42c-e
	Measure , at their fireside —good		44a-b
Gordon B. Hinckley	Most important thing , can do for children —McKay		77a
Jeffrey R. Holland	How to treat your children —2 good stories	May 1983	36b-38b
Matthew S. Holland	A , influence on son —story		39b-c
James E. Faust	Presence of , in home produces strong family		40d-e
	Chief responsibility of , is in home —G.A. Smith		41f-42a
Carlos E. Asay	Interviewing children - wet or dry? —story	Nov 1983	14b-c
	Alma's and Helaman's interview		14d-15a
	Interview with son dispelled parents' fears —story		15a-c
David B. Haight	The role of , —S.W. Kimball	May 1984	12d-e
Boyd K. Packer	Fatherhood taught him the important lessons	Nov 1984	67b
Ezra Taft Benson	First responsibility is to set the proper example	Nov 1985	35e
Ezra Taft Benson	A calling from which one is never released	Nov 1987	48d-e
	Your most important work		48e
	Must provide for family and allow mother to stay at home		48e-49d
	No child should fear his father		50e-f
	10 ways , can give spiritual leadership		50f-51b
Ezra Taft Benson	Home duties of , that would please God	May 1988	5d

J. Richard Clarke	He asked for a father's blessing —story	May 1989	61a-b
Gordon B. Hinckley	, prerequisites to temple recommends	May 1990	51f-52c
Marion D. Hanks	"Dad, are you looking at me?" —story	Nov 1990	39b-d
Durrel A. Woolsey	Excellent advice to ,		43b-44f
Jacob de Jager	The basic duties of ,	May 1991	43f-44b
Janette C. Hales	"Pattern" comes from "pater" or father		85a-b
Boyd K. Packer	Fathers should take toddlers out of meetings	Nov 1991	22c-d
James E. Faust	Are not optional family baggage	May 1993	35c-d
	Essential for establishing gender in children		35d-f
Gordon B. Hinckley	Put , back at head of home - his duties	Nov 1993	59f-60a
Boyd K. Packer	Responsibility as , transcends all else	May 1994	20f-21a
Kenneth Johnson	Never knew father until 5-yrs old —story		29b-f
Marlin K. Jensen	"Next time just send your father" —story		49a
Horacio A. Tenorio	The benefits of holding , interviews	Nov 1994	23f-24f
Jeffrey R. Holland	Children are a , best friends and examples		32a
Howard W. Hunter	Advice to husbands and ,		49d-51f
Rex D. Pinegar	Father's and son's view of day spent fishing —story		82b
James E. Faust	No greater responsibility	May 1995	46d-e
James E. Faust	, are patriarchs to their children	Nov 1995	62e
Lynn A. Mickelsen	Boy's father knew how to allay doubts —story		78f-79b
Jeffrey R. Holland	Fatherlessness: the central social problem	May 1997	35a
Gordon B. Hinckley	Nothing as valuable as love and respect of children	Nov 1997	52e-f
Boyd K. Packer	Exalting status of fatherhood comes as gift from wife	May 1998	73d-e
Boyd K. Packer	Most important calling —important talk	Nov 1998	22b-24f
Jeffrey R. Holland	The influence of ,	May 1999	15c-16f
Russell M. Nelson	Duties of ,		39f-40a
James E. Faust	Never without love and support of , —story	Nov 1999	100d-e
H. David Burton	Your most important and sacred responsibility	May 2000	40c-e
Loren C. Dunn	The influence of , in scripture		80b-81a
James E. Faust	Buried by earthquake, son knew father would come —story	May 2001	46d-e
Sharon G. Larsen	Father came looking for her —story		86f-87d
L. Tom Perry	Children chose house rather than him —story	Nov 2002	9b-f
Boyd K. Packer	As patriarchs to families , must give blessings		42f
M. Russell Ballard	, have responsibility to know children's worthiness		48b-f
F. Melvin Hammond	"Dad, are you awake?" —story		97d-f
	The duties of , in their homes		98b-d
	Character of sons determined by how men treat their wives		98d-99a
	Master self, and sons will be honorable		99b
Gordon B. Hinckley	Take stock of selves - Pray for guidance		100c-f
Thomas S. Monson	Father went to circus instead of meeting —story	May 2003	21b-d
L. Tom Perry	Satan's crosshairs are on ,	May 2004	69b-c
	A family needs a father to anchor it		70d-71a
	The head of the family		71a-d
	Father is a teacher		71f-72b

Fathers, cont'd

L. Tom Perry	Father is the provider	May 2004	72b-e
W. Douglas Shumway	Dad counseled sons —story		94d
	Dad made blind son a top hurdler —story		96b
H. David Burton	Families need less things and more , —Packer	Nov 2004	98c-d
Richard H. Winkel	Excited son woke Dad at 2:00 a.m. —story	Nov 2006	9f-10d
D. Todd Christofferson	Manhood defined by quality of fatherhood		46f-47b
Craig A. Cardon	"Move that mountain , Dad" —story		94d-e
Dallin H. Oaks	Which activity son liked best	Nov 2007	105c-d
M. Russell Ballard	Things husbands should do for wives	May 2008	110b-c
Thomas S. Monson	Don't let Daddy touch the microwave		111b
Marcos A. Aidukaitis	Because father read the Book of Mormon —story	Nov 2008	15b-f
Jeffrey R. Holland	Rescued by worried father —story		30c-31c
Claudio R. M. Costa	Each has a fourfold responsibility —Hinckley	May 2009	56b-c
	Duty to lead prayers, study, Family Home Evening		56c-e
Ann M. Dibb	Took girl 2500 miles to temple —story		116b-f
M. Russell Ballard	How , see sons - Improved versions of selves	Nov 2009	47e
	Model, mentor, hero, example and influence to sons		47e
	Three ways to improve relations with ,		47f-48e
	Three ways , can improve relations with sons		48e-50a
	Relations of , with returned missionary sons		50a-b
Henry B. Eyring	How his father disciplined him		61d-62a
Boyd K. Packer	Presides in home even if Apostle is present	May 2010	8a-b
	President declined to bless boy in favor of , —story		8b-d
	Made , ordain son —story		8d-f
	Your priesthood is a shield between home and adversary		9e
Neil L. Andersen	A special appeal to ,		110c

Fault-Finding

Marion G. Romney	They that watch for iniquity shall be hewn down	Dec 1971	76f
Harold B. Lee	Evils of name calling in politics	July 1972	29b
Spencer W. Kimball	Of Brethren, a deadly sin	Jan 1973	34e
Marvin J. Ashton	Change people by respect and esteem rather than through ,	Nov 1976	85b-e
Marion D. Hanks	I hope you see the five A's —story	Nov 1977	36d-e
Neal A. Maxwell	Difficult to carry cross and grudges too	May 1982	38d
	No cause too trivial once ego is committed		39b
	How Lorenzo Snow viewed Joseph's shortcomings		39b
Gordon B. Hinckley	Some found fault with A. Lincoln's looks		46e
Marvin J. Ashton	, required no talent, no brains —good quote	Nov 1982	63d
	None can prosper with , as their foundation		63e

Fear

Franklin D. Richards	Fear destroys faith	Dec 1968	94e
Joseph Fielding Smith	, of the Lord means love of the Lord	June 1969	39a
Thomas S. Monson	Confidence comes from knowledge	Dec 1969	90b
Gordon B. Hinckley	Parting words to missionary		98a

Fear, cont'd
Related Topics: Courage

Franklin D. Richards	Gospel living overcomes ,	June 1970	36a
Harold B. Lee	The greatest danger among us today is ,		65e
Spencer W. Kimball	Wholesome fear generates own antibodies	July 1973	16e
Ezra Taft Benson	, of criticism		38d
Marvin J. Ashton	Most never realize potential because of sense of inferiority	Nov 1976	84f
J. Richard Clarke	Not nervous but incredibly alert		109b
Marion G. Romney	, has come upon entire world —U.N. Secretary General	May 1977	51d-f
Gordon B. Hinckley	Nothing to , if we do these things...	May 1983	80e
Anne C. Pingree	Overwhelming , at mission call —story	Nov 2005	112d-114a
Jeffrey R. Holland	Peter began to sink when his glance left Jesus	May 2006	71a-c
Boyd K. Packer	We need not live in ,	Nov 2006	86f-87a
	Is there a place to move to escape? - No		87d
	The opposite of faith		87f
Henry B. Eyring	Lord will guide during scary assignments —story	Nov 2007	55d-57a
Quentin L. Cook	Less , about children if 4 guidelines followed		72b-d
	Members must shed camouflage		72d-e
	Choose a path out of , or follow Christ		73b
Dieter F. Uchtdorf	The contrast between despair and hope	Nov 2008	22b-d
Barbara Thompson	Next time try and have something to say —story		115e
Boyd K. Packer	You are not to be fearful	May 2009	51a
	"Do not be afraid! I do not fear."		52e
Thomas S. Monson	Not a time for , but for faith		67f
Thomas S. Monson	Troubled times, but be of good cheer and do not ,		89b-d
	Future is as bright as your faith		92f
Richard G. Scott	Overpowers Holy Ghost - Good example	Nov 2009	8e
Thomas S. Monson	We will survive if we live the commandments		109d-e
Boyd K. Packer	We have no , of the future	May 2010	10a

Fellowshipping
Related Topics: Activation, Friends

Paul H. Dunn	Removes fears - good story about his daughter	Jan 1973	86c
David B. Haight	How a home teacher reactivated a man —story	Nov 1975	59d-f
	An inactive convert brought back thru , —story		60f-61b
F. Burton Howard	Inaccessible couple asked for recommends —story	Nov 1986	76d-77a
Hugh H. Pinnock	Neighbors' love won motorcyclists —story	May 1987	62f-63b
M. Russell Ballard	Gen. Authority not recognized - ignored by ward —story	Nov 1988	28f-29a
	Results of , on two sisters —story		29a-c
	LeGrand Richards tipped his hat to everyone —story		30a
	Man helped neighbor with cement —story		30b
	, —good advice		30c-f

First Presidency
Related Topics: Apostles, President

Joseph Fielding Smith	Will never lead Church astray	July 1972	88b
	Follow counsel of , for peace and safety		88f
Harold B. Lee	Counselors are those the Lord wants		103d

N. Eldon Tanner	Reorganization of , —history	Jan 1973	100f
Gordon B. Hinckley	How , functions when president is infirm	Nov 1984	4f-5e
James E. Faust	Decisions by , must be unanimous	Nov 1989	10f
James E. Faust	His vision was limited until called to ,	May 1995	47e-f
William R. Walker	Picture of , hung in grandparents' entry —story	May 2008	37d-38a
	How , functions —Hinckley		39b-d
Boyd K. Packer	Reorganization of ,		83d-e
Thomas S. Monson	Reorganization of ,		87e

Ezra Taft Benson	Basic principles of welfare program —J.R. Clarke	Jan 1974	69c
	The righteous will have a year's supply		69d
	What and how much to store		69e
	Non-food items which should be stored		81c
	Have a cash reserve		81d
	You can't be spiritual if you're hungry		81e
	The hungry Saints of WWII Germany		81f
Theodore M. Burton	Share , and your cruse of oil will not fail	May 1974	61d-62c
Spencer W. Kimball	Be independent of every creature	Nov 1974	6c-e
Spencer W. Kimball	Members told to plant gardens	May 1975	5a-6a
Victor L. Brown	Signs of times indicate an urgency	Nov 1975	115d-e
H. Burke Peterson	30% of Church has a 2-month supply		116e
Vaughn J. Featherstone	What, how, when and should I share? —entire talk	May 1976	116b-118b
Marion G. Romney	Lord will help us provide, but won't give roast pigs —Young		123a-b
Spencer W. Kimball	Why call me Lord, and do not the things I say?		124b-125d
Barbara B. Smith	Pointers on ,	Nov 1976	121d-f
Bruce R. McConkie	Lord provides after we've done all we can —stories	May 1979	93e-f
Marion G. Romney	Others may take our , - so what? - we obeyed		94f-95a
J. Thomas Fyans	Linchpin is , not welfare projects —good illustration	Nov 1979	88a-b
Victor L. Brown	Church prepared to care for limited number for short time	May 1980	89c-d
	Survey on family preparedness		89d
Ezra Taft Benson	You will barter anything for food	Nov 1980	32e
	Good advice on ,		33a-c
	Do it now! I speak with urgency		33e
	Scenes from WWII Europe		33e-34a
	Prepare to feed others as well		34b
Victor L. Brown	Can't ask Lord to fight battles when we have the means		80b-f
J. Richard Clarke	Some wait to be sure the storm clouds really gather		82b
	Inflation reduces savings, but no savings buys nothing		84c
	Have life insurance and health insurance		84d
	We will yet live on what we produce		84e
Loren C. Dunn	Widow in WWII ate well because she had , —story	May 1981	26c-d
Mark E. Peterson	The Lord gives the harvest - we gather —squirrel story		62f-63a
	Most important storehouses are our own		63c

Food Storage, cont'd
Related Topics: Welfare Program

L. Tom Perry	Statistics showing unpreparedness of members	May 1981	87e-f
Ezra Taft Benson	, is even more urgent today	Nov 1987	49d-e
L. Tom Perry	The time to disregard counsel for , is over	Nov 1995	36f-37a
Gordon B. Hinckley	Counseled for 60 years to have ,	Nov 2001	73d
Gordon B. Hinckley	Start small, but do it	Nov 2002	58d-e
Keith B. McMullin	Parents are the family storekeepers —Faust	May 2007	52e
	A year's supply of debt and food free —Monson		52e-f
	Start small, but do it —Hinckley		52f
Quentin L. Cook	Be prepared for June snowstorms	Nov 2008	104e-f

Foreordination
Related Topics: Priesthood

Milton R. Hunter	All prophets were foreordained	Dec 1968	59b-60c
Spencer W. Kimball	Lee undoubtedly foreordained	Jan 1973	33e
N. Eldon Tanner	President Lee ,		101d
	All of us , for some purpose		103d
Joseph Anderson	Of Smith, Grant, McKay	July 1973	106f
Harold B. Lee	Joseph Smith said he and others had been ,	Jan 1974	4f
	Many , to greater states than they are prepared for		5a
N. Eldon Tanner	Testifies that President Kimball was foreordained	May 1974	50e
Bruce R. McConkie	President Kimball foreordained		71d-f
	, —excellent explanation		72b-73f
	All Israel and Church members foreordained		72e
N. Eldon Tanner	Each president foreordained		84a-d
Theodore M. Burton	Families were planned in pre-existence	Nov 1974	54f-55a
	Families and priesthood lineages were foreordained		55b-c
Theodore M. Burton	We are foreordained to receive priesthood	May 1975	69b-70a
N. Eldon Tanner	We have all been foreordained		77d
N. Eldon Tanner	All of us foreordained	Nov 1975	74d
Bruce R. McConkie	All who have calls to minister were foreordained	May 1982	32f
Ezra Taft Benson	Youth foreordained for birth in this day	May 1986	43b-c
Robert D. Hales	Many of us held in Spirit World —Woodruff	May 1995	16f
David B. Haight	President Hinckley foreordained		36b-c, 37b
	Joseph Smith and Gordon Hinckley foreordained		36d-f
Jeffrey R. Holland	President Hinckley foreordained		38b-d
James E. Faust	President Hinckley foreordained		45e
Joseph B. Wirthlin	President Monson foreordained	May 2008	17e-f

Forgiveness
Related Topics: Confession, Repentance, Sin

Joseph F. Smith	Strong admonition toward	Dec 1969	37d
Alvin R. Dyer	Brings release of tensions		39f
Franklin D. Richards	Blessed are the merciful - The reverse is true also	June 1970	36a
	If you would be forgiven, forgive		36e
Thomas S. Monson	Quarrel split father and son. Each forgave —story	June 1971	96c-e
Thomas S. Monson	Returning prisoner finds tree covered with ribbons —story	Dec 1971	132e-133a
Vaughn J. Featherstone	Must forgive every soul on earth —Lee	July 1973	36b

Food Storage | Foreordination | Forgiveness

Harold B. Lee	How to know when God has forgiven	July 1973	122a
Marion D. Hanks	Walk the second mile to relieve your anger	Jan 1974	20f
	He who takes offense is a fool —Brigham Young, good		21b
	Three instances where , was sought		21b
	Allow your cheek to be struck but not others'		21f
	Same sorrows and are equal at death; why not get along?		22a
James A. Cullimore	Justice must be satisfied before , comes	May 1974	29e
Franklin D. Richards	Forgetting is an important part of ,	Nov 1974	106b
Spencer W. Kimball	Many good stories of ,	Nov 1977	46b-48c
	, means to blot it from our minds		48d-f
Boyd K. Packer	His wife was killed by a doctor's infection —story		60b-e
Vaughn J. Featherstone	6 things necessary to obtain ,	Nov 1980	29f
	Punishment will be lightest possible. Rewards maximum		31c
Marion D. Hanks	Man demanded justice. Hanks gave mercy —story	Nov 1981	73b-e
	My specialty is mercy, said the convert —story		73e-74e
Gordon B. Hinckley	Mother of dead child could not forgive —story		97f-98a
Theodore M. Burton	We are forgiven to the extent we forgive	May 1983	71c
	He who cannot forgive has the greater sin		72a-b
Neal A. Maxwell	Joseph Smith's letter of , to W.W. Phelps	Nov 1983	55b-c
H. Burke Peterson	Girl lost leg because she killed the snake —story		59b-f
	One POW was not emaciated due to , —story		60a-b
	Depth of Savior's , —S.W. Kimball		60d-f
F. Burton Howard	Bishop forgot which priest had sinned —story	Nov 1986	77d-78b
Hugh W. Pinnock	Quarreling ranchers forgave —story	May 1987	62e-f
Boyd K. Packer	How to heal resentment or shame —entire talk	Nov 1987	16b-18f
	Man's wife was killed by the doctor —story		17b-18f
Marvin J. Ashton	Hurts heal more quickly if we avoid bitterness	May 1988	62e
Ezra Taft Benson	Withholding , is a form of pride	May 1989	6b
Dallin H. Oaks	Abuser forgiven because of Atonement -story	Nov 1989	66b-c
Dallin H. Oaks	Lincoln asked officer's , —story	May 1990	73b-c
M. Russell Ballard	Former sins return when done again	Nov 1990	38a-b
Neal A. Maxwell	We want private, painless, quick ,	May 1991	90f-91b
M. Russell Ballard	Letter from former drug addict	Nov 1992	32e-33a
Ronald E. Poelman	Obtaining divine , —entire talk	Nov 1993	84b-86b
Monte J. Brough	Man who had stolen livestock asked help —story	May 1995	42c-e
Thomas S. Monson	Lord will give maximum reward and minimum punishment		59b-c
	Brothers had divided room for 62 years —story		59d
	Don't persist remembering what Lord forgets —story		59f-60a
	Stolen key returned mounted on plaque —story		60b-c
	Who can't forgive breaks bridge over which he must pass		60c
Richard G. Scott	Finding forgiveness —entire talk good		75b-77f
Boyd K. Packer	No sin exempted from promise of complete , —entire talk	Nov 1995	18d-21b
	, does not necessarily assure exaltation		21b
Gordon B. Hinckley	Letter from single mother who forgave —story		99f-100e
Jeffrey R. Holland	Jesus still says "Forgive them, for they know not..."	Nov 1996	83d-e

Forgiveness, cont'd
Related Topics: Confession, Repentance, Sin

Jeffrey R. Holland	We don't want our sins remembered - so forgive	Nov 1996	83f
James E. Faust	Letters from W.W. Phelps and Joseph Smith	Nov 1997	54f-59b
Thomas S. Monson	Man didn't join Church because he couldn't forgive —story	May 2002	18e-19a
	Bishop forgot funeral - man forgave —story		19b-c
	Brothers never spoke for 62 years —story		20b-c
	Former friends reunited through service —story		20f-21b
Richard G. Scott	How to forgive one who has abused you	Nov 2002	88b-f
David E. Sorensen	Neighbors' quarrel became murder —story	May 2003	10b-11d
	Joseph forgave his brothers —story		12b-d
	Does not require us to tolerate evil		12d-e
	, keeps past from dictating future		12f
Kathleen H. Hughes	Peace came after much prayer —story		13d-e
Thomas S. Monson	Apology brought son home —story	Nov 2003	58a-d
Richard G. Scott	Innocent victims must forgive	Nov 2004	16e-17a
	Suffering does not bring , - Only faith		17d
	Not forgiving self is denying Atonement		17f-18b
Ned B. Roueche	We must forgive to be forgiven		30e-31a
Gordon B. Hinckley	The greatest virtue and most needed	Nov 2005	81f
	Assaulted by a frozen turkey —story		83f-84e
	Entire talk		81d-84f
James E. Faust	Women need to let go of the hurt		115b-d
Boyd K. Packer	What He made, He can fix	May 2006	28a
Gordon B. Hinckley	Joseph's letter of , to W.W. Phelps		60d-f
Jeffrey R. Holland	Change what you can, forgive the rest		70b
James E. Faust	The Amish and , —story	May 2007	67b-68a
	Grudges are wasted energy		68a-b
	Forgiving is wholesome and therapeutic		68b
	The healthful benefits of ,		68d-e
James E. Faust	Examples of ,		69e-70d
Dieter F. Uchtdorf	Wipes away anguish and torment —Kimball		100f
Richard G. Scott	Healing the consequences of abuse	May 2008	40b-43f
Jay E. Jensen	People are seeking , during sacrament	Nov 2008	48b-e
Neil L. Andersen	Overpowering , for riotous life —story	Nov 2009	40f
	No sin that cannot be forgiven		40f
Keith B. McMullin	Corrie ten Boom forgave cruel guard —story	May 2010	13b-f
James B. Martino	Don't pass blame for problems		103a

Freedom
Related Topics: Agency, America, Constitution, Government, United States

Franklin D. Richards	There are two freedoms...	June 1969	49d
Richard L. Evans	Liberty cannot be without morality		80d-e
Sterling W. Sill	No other problem will matter if , fails	Dec 1970	79b
Franklin D. Richards	We wear the chains we forge. Good comment on habits		83b
Spencer W. Kimball	People seeking to be free of all freedoms	June 1971	17a
Alvin R. Dyer	Gospel cannot find root where , forbidden	July 1972	52f
	Must precede gospel. Teaches good and evil		53c

Ezra Taft Benson	Good books on ,	July 1972	60d
	Godless conspiracy greatest threat to ,		60e
	Only blood will restore lost liberties		61a
	4 civic standards for saints		61f
Ezra Taft Benson	Killed by neglect as well as by attack	July 1973	39c
	If foundation is firm, the rest will stand —Coolidge		40a
N. Eldon Tanner	While seeking , they became slaves to their own bad habits	Nov 1974	85c
Ezra Taft Benson	Righteousness is indispensable to liberty	May 1976	92f-93c
N. Eldon Tanner	Strict obedience leads to , not to slavery —Brigham Young	May 1978	15b
	Greater knowledge makes one more free		16b
Marion G. Romney	Allowing government dole will destroy ,	May 1979	94d-e
Royden G. Derrick	, is not free - it must be earned	May 1981	66b
Thomas S. Monson	A. Lincoln's letter to mother who lost 5 sons	Nov 1981	16d-e
Boyd K. Packer	No true , without responsibility	May 1983	66c
Glenn L. Pace	Don't mistake lack of self control for ,	Nov 1987	40a-b
Thomas S. Monson	, has come to Eastern Europe	May 1990	4b-c
David B. Haight	, in Eastern bloc countries		23d-e
Joseph B. Wirthlin	Unbridled passions result in slavery	Nov 1991	16b
L. Tom Perry	Less self-reliance equals less ,		64f-65a
James M. Paramore	Freeing people from prisons —entire talk	Nov 1992	9b-11b
Gordon B. Hinckley	No , in pornography and addictions —letter		51d-52a
Richard G. Scott	, to choose acts but not consequences		60d-62f
Neal A. Maxwell	Gadarene swine racing downhill to their destruction	May 1993	77b
Boyd K. Packer	Obsession with , may self-destruct society	May 1996	17d-e
James E. Faust	Not , from restraints but , from doubts and anxiety	Nov 1999	102a
Russell M. Nelson	No one wants to be restrained	Nov 2001	70b
D. Todd Christofferson	More laws lead to diminished ,	Nov 2009	106f-107a

Friends

David O. McKay	One of life's most priceless possessions	Dec 1968	35a
Henry D. Taylor	Be kind to enemies: You made them	June 1969	62d
Marvin J. Ashton	Family members should be , —story	Dec 1969	51b-f
Marion G. Romney	Voice of , sweet during trials		67f
Delbert L. Stapley	Undesirable , seldom improve, but your standards lower	Dec 1970	65b
John H. Vandenberg	Strangers and neighborhoods —good quote	June 1971	67f
Gordon B. Hinckley	One's mate is the most precious friend		71e
Ezra Taft Benson	, of Church - Doniphan and Kane	July 1972	59d
Marvin J. Ashton	Best , remain under all circumstances	Jan 1973	41b
	Lincoln quote on destroying enemies		41b
	A possession we earn		41f
	Lord's , tried and tested		41f
	Only way to have a , —Emerson		43c
	Joseph Smith's measure of ,		43c
Marion D. Hanks	Rebels at Missionary Ridge surrendered because alone		128d
James E. Faust	40% of young people have no close ,	July 1973	89a

Friends, cont'd
Related Topics: Fellowshipping

Robert D. Hales	You can't do it alone	Nov 1975	92b-93d
N. Eldon Tanner	Never be found with those who lower standards	Nov 1976	82a
Ted. E. Brewerton	I like myself more when I am with you	May 1983	74a
Robert L. Backman	We don't have to leave our group , just increase our ,	Nov 1985	13b
Marion D. Hanks	False , drugged the sailor and led him into iniquity —story	Nov 1986	12a-13a
Ezra Taft Benson	Best , should be in family		81f
Richard G. Scott	Companions on oyster boat changed their opinions —story	May 1989	37b-d
Robert D. Hales	Two important elements in true ,	May 1990	40e
Malcolm S. Jeppsen	Phrases true , won't use		44e&45b
	True , make living the gospel easier		45b
James E. Faust	We want children to have , but not follow them	Nov 1990	34e-f
W. Eugene Hansen	Two sheep led others right through snakes —story	May 1996	38d-f
Thomas S. Monson	Poem about , not visited —poem		51d-f
	"Information Please" operator —story		51f-52c
Gordon B. Hinckley	"I need a friend" —handicapped girl story		92f
Thomas S. Monson	Temple marriage is determined by ,	May 1997	94f-95a
Joseph B. Wirthlin	Why we go two by two	Nov 1997	33a-b
James E. Faust	"All I ever wanted was to belong" —story		43d-f
Thomas S. Monson	Win people to cause by first being a ,		47b-c
Virginia U. Jensen	Life is like a wheel - we're up when some are down		91a
Sheri L. Dew	7 , traveled to Colorado to support her at funeral	Nov 1998	94d
Marlin K. Jensen	Friendship —entire talk	May 1999	64b-65f
Vaughn J. Featherstone	"I passed your house" - "Thanks"	Nov 1999	14b-c
Margaret D. Nadauld	, helped girl change friends —story	May 2001	91d-f
M. Russell Ballard	The doctrine of inclusion - How to treat others	Nov 2001	35d-38b
Henry B. Eyring	Being true , to converts —entire talk	May 2002	26d-29d
Spencer J. Condie	Make , cause your own —Browning poem		45f-46a
Sharon G. Larson	Moroni had angels and Holy Ghost for ,		91e-f
	Girl could choose , or standards —story		91f-92c
Gordon B. Hinckley	Be careful of your ,	May 2004	113f-114a
Anne C. Pingree	Lessons learned from a dying ,	Nov 2004	111d-113b
Kathleen H. Hughes	A grand fundamental principle —Joseph Smith	May 2005	76c
	Sorry to the amount of $5 —story		76d
Gordon B. Hinckley	Hated unfriendly LDS. Friend changed that —story	May 2006	59b-60d
Robert D. Hales	Birds of a feather flock together	May 2007	49d-e
Walter F. Gonzalez	Cut bad , off	Nov 2007	54f-55a
Henry B. Eyring	, lead either toward light or away	May 2008	123f-124e
Boyd K. Packer	Don't run with , that worry your parents	May 2009	50f
Jeffrey R. Holland	"None Were With Him" —entire talk		86b-88f

Future
Related Topics: Last Days, Today

Hugh B. Brown	You have a spotless ,	Dec 1969	95b
Sterling W. Sill	I haven't had my greatest experience yet —quote	June 1971	45c
	My interest is in the , because ...		45e
Marvin J. Ashton	The best of life is not in the , - it is now	May 1975	85d-e

Bruce R. McConkie	Turbulent , unavoidable	May 1979	93a-b
Victor L. Brown	Live each day providently and , will care for itself —story	Nov 1982	79d-f
Vaughn J. Featherstone	Today's youth will have little or no respite from the foe	Nov 1987	27f-28a
	Troubles will exceed those of pioneers		27f-28a
Gordon B. Hinckley	What happened to his classmates	May 1988	65b-e
Richard G. Scott	Enthusiastic about ,	Nov 1998	68c
James E. Faust	Assembly hall an expression of hope	Nov 1999	59b
Neal A. Maxwell	Fasten seat belts and hold onto principles	May 2004	44d
Boyd K. Packer	Don't be afraid of ,		77d-80f
Boyd K. Packer	Terrible days but he's positively optimistic	Nov 2005	70d-e
Thomas S. Monson	"When I have time: is a non-existent ,	Nov 2008	85a
	A wasteland of illusion if today not used		86f
Boyd K. Packer	Old men speak of past because they have no ,	May 2009	49d
	"Do not be afraid! I do not fear."		52e
Thomas S. Monson	Future is as bright as your faith		92f
Dieter F. Uchtdorf	"I am optimistic about the future"	Nov 2009	55d-e
L. Tom Perry	Want past way of facing the ,		73f-74a
Boyd K. Packer	We have very positive feelings about ,	May 2010	6f
	We have no fear of the ,		10a
Dieter F. Uchtdorf	Today's trials only to be understood in ,		58f

Spencer W. Kimball	LDS should not use playing ,	Nov 1974	6b-c
Spencer W. Kimball	The evils of gambling	May 1975	6c-d
Gordon B. Hinckley	The Church is opposed to lotteries - a tax on the poor	Nov 1985	52a-b
James E. Faust	Can morality be legislated? —D.H. Oaks	May 1987	80f-81a
Russell M. Nelson	Gambling provokes the wrath of God	Nov 1987	89d
Gordon B. Hinckley	Entire talk	May 2005	58b-61f
James E. Faust	Avoid every kind of addiction including ,	May 2006	53b-d
James E. Faust	Mind-altering - Destroys agency	Nov 2007	123d-124a
Dallin H. Oaks	An example of greed and selfishness	May 2009	95e-f

Bernard P. Brockbank	Japanese from tribe of Joseph	Dec 1970	120d
LeGrand Richards	Jews to be one of great movements of Church	June 1971	99f
Harold B. Lee	Each to gather in own country	July 1973	4e
Spencer W. Kimball	, effected when people remain in own land	May 1975	4f
J. Thomas Fyans	Prophecies concerning future of Lamanites	May 1976	12d-f
	Growth of Church in Mexico		12f-13a
	Fulfillment of prophecy concerning Lamanites		13a-d
Marion G. Romney	Book of Mormon scriptures concerning , —entire talk	May 1981	16b-17f
Russell M. Nelson	Takes place on both sides of veil	Nov 2006	80b & 80f
	Bible mentions Abraham 216 times—other scriptures 290		82a
	Israel dedicated for return of Jews by Hyde		82b
	Entire talk		79b-82b

General Authorities

Boyd K. Packer	The vocations, education and backgrounds of ,	Dec 1968	80a
	Speaking subjects not limited to religion		80b
	The weekly schedule of the ,		80b-c
Joseph Fielding Smith	Smith's praise of the ,	June 1970	27b-c
Marion G. Romney	What is so great about interviews with , —story		67a-b
Wendell J. Ashton	Elder Hinckley frightened of speaking in conference	June 1971	57b
Marion D. Hanks	The only one rained on while golfing —story	Dec 1971	104a
Joseph Fielding Smith	President Smith's attitude about his counselors		136a-b
Vaughn F. Featherstone	Qualities he observed in ,	July 1972	45b
A. Theodore Tuttle	No group of men like them on earth		120f
Spencer W. Kimball	Finding fault with the Brethren a deadly sin	Jan 1973	34e
Harold B. Lee	For safety, heed words of the Brethren		62b
	Revelation for Church only thru the Brethren		105c
L. Tom Perry	Tribute to , . Work hard in old age.	July 1973	20f
Harold B. Lee	Information to come from , not elsewhere		97d
	Look to , not to self-serving individuals		97d
	No greater men walk the earth		123f
Bruce R. McConkie	If Lord was to speak in conference He'd say what , say	Jan 1974	45b
N. Eldon Tanner	Sustaining of Church officers	Nov 1974	36a-37f
Wm. Grant Bangerter	His calling requires a complete life change	May 1975	39d
Spencer W. Kimball	Announcement that First Quorum of 70 to be organized	Nov 1975	4b
M. Russell Ballard, Jr.	Sitting in a big red chair —story	May 1976	38b-e
Loren C. Dunn	What the Brethren say is more important than scriptures		65f-66b
Spencer W. Kimball	Reconstitution of the First Quorum of Seventy	Nov 1976	9c-f
James E. Faust	The Brethren are ordinary men with a special gift		59e-f
Henry D. Taylor	Purest scriptures come from lips of living prophets		64b
N. Eldon Tanner	Announcement about emeritus status of ,	Nov 1978	16e-f
LeGrand Richards	What some , sacrificed to accept callings	Nov 1979	76c-77a
Robert E. Wells	Study testimonies of , to help know Christ —E. T. Benson	Nov 1980	12e
M. Russell Ballard	, presence in lunchroom touched boy —story		23c-f
Boyd K. Packer	, travel so much to convey keys of authority	Nov 1981	32b-c
Ezra Taft Benson	The only safety is in sustaining the Brethren	May 1982	64b-e
Gordon B. Hinckley	First Quorum of 70 to serve 3 to 5 years	May 1984	4d-5a
Boyd K. Packer	Ordinary sticks in a special position —Maeser	May 1985	35e
James E. Faust	Imperfect men with a divine commission	Nov 1985	8e
Gordon B. Hinckley	Living allowances come from other income, not tithing		50d-f
	Total unanimity of , required in decision		53d-54a
Theodore M. Burton	What do , do?		64b-e
Monte J. Brough	Account of his calling as a , —story	Nov 1988	40b-c
Gordon B. Hinckley	Appreciation expressed to released ,	Nov 1989	48d-49c
Han In Sang	Korea and his calling as a ,	May 1992	81b-82b
Russell M. Nelson	, are ordinary human beings —story	May 1993	39a-b
	Don't seek counsel from , —6 letters		40b
	If , enters meeting, consult with him —story		40c-d
	No one speaks following a presiding ,		40e

General Authorities

Gordon B. Hinckley	His testimony of ,	Nov 1993	53d-e
Monte J. Brough	, compared to David's 37 mighty men		63d-65f
Russell M. Nelson	, are not called to represent countries	May 1996	14f
David B. Haight	His calling as a , —story		22f-23c
Gordon B. Hinckley	Organization of new Quorums of Seventy	May 1997	5d-6e
Thomas S. Monson	Letter to , about starlings	Nov 1997	46c-e
Russell M. Nelson	Account of his wife's death	May 2005	16b-d
Gordon B. Hinckley	Nepotism and his son's sustaining		58b-c
Gordon B. Hinckley	, can no longer visit stake conferences	Nov 2005	6a-b
Richard G. Hinckley	Only , sustained with disclaimer from prophet	May 2006	48a
Boyd K. Packer	Testimony of , no different than ours —story	Nov 2007	7f-8d
	, are like all others - ordinary people		9a-b
Joseph B. Wirthlin	Each has suffered disappointment, sorrow and loss	Nov 2008	26b-e
Thomas S. Monson	Remember , in your prayers	May 2009	114b
Thomas S. Monson	Pray for me and ,	Nov 2009	110b
Boyd K. Packer	President declined to bless boy in favor of father —story	May 2010	8b-d

General Conference
Related Topics: —

Boyd K. Packer	Reason for holding , —McKay	Dec 1968	79b
	The first , and another reported on		79b
Harold B. Lee	15 degrees hotter in the tabernacle stands	Dec 1970	104a-c
Alvin R. Dyer	, used to be called feasts		124e-f
Harold B. Lee	Lord and angels at ,	Jan 1973	23d
	Feelings, not learning, important at ,		134b
	Lord present at ,		134d
	Get the spirit of ,		134f
Bruce R. McConkie	If Lord spoke in , He'd say what has been said	Jan 1974	45b
Harold B. Lee	Get copy of proceedings of , to learn Lord's will		128a
Paul H. Dunn	Enough taught in , to save entire world	May 1974	14d
Elray L. Christiansen	Subjects not assigned		25b-c
J. Thomas Fyans	What should , do in our lives?	Nov 1974	65a-b
Spencer W. Kimball	Purpose of , programs	May 1975	4d-e
Spencer W. Kimball	, has a definite bearing on our salvation	Nov 1975	112e
Robert L. Simpson	Letters from non-members watching Australian conference	May 1976	58d-f
Henry D. Taylor	Purest scripture comes from lips of living prophets —Lee	Nov 1976	64b
N. Eldon Tanner	Purposes of area conferences and how held		80b-f
Spencer W. Kimball	How affected him and should affect us	Nov 1977	75e-f
Victor L. Brown	, lights the way for 6 months ahead —story	Nov 1982	79e-f
James E. Faust	How to know what messages in , are for you	May 1986	22f
Marvin J. Ashton	Man reactivated by , —story	Nov 1986	15c-d
Ezra Taft Benson	Reports of , stand next to scriptures	May 1988	84c
Clinton L. Cutler	At 10 minutes to the hour there were still seats	May 1990	43b-c
John E. Fowler	Using , as our daily guide —good quotes	Nov 1992	78b-79f
Thomas S. Monson	Closing comments of , from 5 presidents		86f-87d
Dieter F. Uchtdorf	Updated sacred guidance	Nov 1994	42f

General Conference, cont'd
Related Topics: —

Gordon B. Hinckley	Subjects are not assigned	May 1995	87d
Gordon B. Hinckley	28 speakers - no assigned topics	Nov 1995	89b-c
W. Mack Lawrence	Can bring us into presence of God	May 1996	74b-c
Virginia H. Pearce	The Lord, his prophet and Holy Ghost come together in ,		85d-f
Russell M. Nelson	Subjects are not assigned	Nov 1997	14d
Gordon B. Hinckley	Purpose of ,	May 2001	85d
Gordon B. Hinckley	"It's all over but the work"	May 2003	99b
Gordon B. Hinckley	Broadcasts available to 95% of members	May 2004	4b-c
Gordon B. Hinckley	, should make us better people	Nov 2004	104d-f
Gordon B. Hinckley	, could have reached 95% of members	May 2005	102d
Lowell M. Snow	, is our Liahona	Nov 2005	96d-97b
Gordon B. Hinckley	Translated into 80 languages		103d
Jeffrey R. Holland	Listening to , on hike makes convert —story	Nov 2006	104b-105a
Gordon B. Hinckley	Use , as text for Family Home Evening	May 2007	105d-e
Neil L. Andersen	A spiritual symphony - A miracle	May 2010	108a-b

Gifts
Related Topics: Talents

Alvin R. Dyer	Give more than you receive —Indian Story	Dec 1970	124a-b
Bruce R. McConkie	Testimony a ,	Jan 1973	36b
Hartman Rector, Jr.	Sir Launfal and the Holy Grail —story	Jan 1974	107d
Rex D. Pinegar	Friend gave him most valued possession —story	Nov 1978	11a-b
Bruce R. McConkie	Covet to prophesy - seek the face of the Lord		61d-e
Thomas S. Monson	Jewels are substitutes for , —Emerson	May 1981	49b
Thomas S. Monson	Jewels are substitutes for , —Emerson	May 1983	56b
Dallin H. Oaks	An unwilling gift is a tax, not an offering	Nov 1984	14d
Marvin J. Ashton	A list of less evident ,	Nov 1987	20d
Thomas S. Monson	Self is the only true gift —Emerson	May 1992	102c
Gene R. Cook	Definition of grace	May 1993	80b
	Grace —entire talk		79d-81f
D. Todd Christofferson	How to give Jesus ,	May 2004	12d-f
James E. Faust	Joy, fulfillment and peace are ,	Nov 2005	21d
Anne C. Pingree	The only , you can give the Lord —Maxwell		112c

Goals
Related Topics: —

Paul H. Dunn	Everest conquered step by step	Dec 1968	67a
John H. Vandenberg	The Calf-Path —poem	June 1969	47b-f
Delbert L. Stapley	Easy to set , high. Hard to stay up there with them		72f
Robert L. Simpson	We're making good time, but we're hopelessly lost —story	Dec 1969	40d
Delbert L. Stapley	Set , and achieve perfection		64b
Thomas S. Monson	Ideals lead us to destination		92a
Richard L. Evans	If we don't change direction, we'll arrive...	June 1970	38b
	One small step at a time		38f
Robert L. Simpson	Reach for goals by living a day at a time	Dec 1970	96b
Paul H. Dunn	Work on the house stopped —story	June 1971	103d-f
Marvin J. Ashton	Intermediate goals are not destinations	July 1972	62a

Marvin J. Ashton	Temple marriage is not a final ,	July 1972	62c
	Satan says "You've reached , deserve rest."		63b
	A prisoner being released has , —story		63d
	Many , in Church but one destination		63f
John H. Vandenberg	Don't borrow , from others		128a
Spencer W. Kimball	Goals each youth should set	May 1974	86f-87c
	A scripture reading goal set in youth by Kimball		88a-b
	A Word of Wisdom goal set in youth by Kimball		88b-89a
N. Eldon Tanner	Definition of "wander"	Nov 1974	84b-d
N. Eldon Tanner	How great men achieve —poem	May 1975	76b
	The boy became a 100 percenter —story		77a-b
Thomas S. Monson	Hitchhiker held sign saying "Anywhere"	Nov 1976	51d-e
LeGrand Richards	Without , we might keep afloat but never make port	May 1982	29e
Marvin J. Ashton	A 1,000 mile journey begins with first step	May 1983	31a
Marvin J. Ashton	Striving is more important than arriving	May 1984	11f
M. Russell Ballard	Write down daily ,	May 1987	14e
Joseph B. Wirthlin	Set , in marathons and in life —story	Nov 1989	73c-f
Russell M. Nelson	Education is a religious responsibility	Nov 1992	6d-f
Thomas S. Monson	Set specific , —story	May 1994	50e-f
Quentin L. Cook	Distracted by Saturday morning cartoons —story	Nov 1996	29a-e
Joseph B. Wirthlin	Blind man climbed Everest —story	Nov 2001	25d-26a
	One Step After Another —entire talk		25b-27f
Thomas S. Monson	No , means life spent running up and down	May 2003	20d-e
Elaine S. Dalton	Envision where you want to be in 5 years		106d-e
John B. Dickson	Decide now - Decide early - Set ,	May 2007	14b-15f
Joseph B. Wirthlin	Don't take your eye off the ball —story		45c-46b
Gordon B. Hinckley	Woman did 20,000 temple endowments		85a-b
L. Tom Perry	High jumper kept raising the bar —story	Nov 2007	46e-47d
	Be certain you continually raise the bar		49b
Thomas S. Monson	Runner lost shoe, finished third, met goal		59e-f
Ann M. Dibb	Completed 79 of 80 Young Women , —story	May 2009	116a-f
Mary N. Cook	Young Women , - Prayer, study, smile		118d-e
Barbara Thompson	Her unfulfilled , as a single adult	Nov 2009	119b-f

God
Related Topics: Jesus

Hugh B. Brown	What , has been believed to be and what He is	June 1969	32a-b
	Our concept of , changes as we study and learn		33e-34a
LeGrand Richards	Christian creeds describe , as nothing		91f
	Why then do the scriptures say we will see , ?		92a-b
Harold B. Lee	, could not judge had He not been a mortal		104b
	Don't worry about origin of the Gods		104d-e
Bruce R. McConkie	Men to become as God —poem by L. Snow	June 1970	43b-c
Marion G. Romney	We have no peace in world because we don't know ,		68a-b
	, and man come from same mold		68b-c
	Not a spiritual something —convert's story		67c-d

Robert L. Simpson	How , feels about his children	June 1970	83b-c
Harold B. Lee	Role of Jesus in relation to ,	Dec 1970	29c
James A. Cullimore	First principle of gospel is to know , —Joseph Smith		61b-c
	, is an exalted man —Joseph Smith		62d-e
Delbert L. Stapley	God's love is greater because parents love children more		65f
Gordon B. Hinckley	Virtuous shall see , —good analogy here		72f-73c
Hartman Rector, Jr.	, can't force repentance		78a-c
N. Eldon Tanner	Not a prosecutor who is trying to convict us	June 1971	15d
Bruce R. McConkie	No salvation in worshiping a false ,	Dec 1971	129e-f
Marion D. Hanks	The car without an engine —story	July 1972	104b
Boyd K. Packer	Significant that He chose to be called Father		113e
Joseph Anderson	Times the Father has spoken	Jan 1973	47d
LeGrand Richards	Absurd concepts of , —good quote		111c
	Does not abandon people		117c
	Speaking today.		118f
Marion G. Romney	Man literal offspring of ,	July 1973	11a
Hartman Rector, Jr.	Tis only God may be had for the asking —poem		57f
LeGrand Richards	Has a wife		79c
Delbert L. Stapley	We have not progressed beyond need for ,		99b
	, has no pleasure in slaying wicked		100d
S. Dilworth Young	Only time , has appeared in person		115d
Spencer W. Kimball	Do not use name of , except in prayers and sermons	Nov 1974	7a
O. Leslie Stone	If you want to be where , is you must be like Him		32c-e
Marion G. Romney	, is a perfected, saved soul enjoying eternal life		38d-e
Howard W. Hunter	Can't say no , just because we haven't bothered to find Him		96f-97a
Delbert L. Stapley	There are but 2 parties on the earth —Brigham Young	May 1975	21d-e
Joseph Anderson	Jesus always referred to , as Father		29f-30a
Spencer W. Kimball	We use names of Deity too much	Nov 1975	80f-81b
LeGrand Richards	Fallacious concepts of , held by others	Nov 1976	65b-66b
Spencer W. Kimball	Faith in God's power —poem		110e
Bruce R. McConkie	We may see , while yet mortals	Nov 1977	34f-35a
N. Eldon Tanner	Nicene creed quoted and commented upon	Nov 1978	47c-e
	Not a minister could answer yes —story		48b-d
Ronald E. Poelman	God's love transcends our transgressions	May 1982	28f & 29b
Marion G. Romney	Lincoln called nation to remember ,	Nov 1982	50b-c
Robert E. Wells	The Holy Trinity is not a blur		70e
James E. Faust	, knows us better than we know ourselves		89b
Boyd K. Packer	One , or many? —good discussion	Nov 1984	68a-d
	Children of , may become like him —entire talk		66b-69f
Gordon B. Hinckley	The Father, Son, and Holy Ghost —entire talk	Nov 1986	49b-51f
Ezra Taft Benson	Love of , comes first —entire talk —good	May 1988	4b-6f
	, wants us to be like Him - Satan likewise		6b
Marion D. Hanks	God, are you looking at me? —story	Nov 1990	39b-d
Henry B. Eyring	, is our ancestor. He is close —story	May 1991	65d-66b
	We'll be startled to see how familiar God's face is—Benson		66b-d

Henry B. Eyring	How to draw close to ,	May 1991	66d-e
	Why and how , chastens us		67b-d
Graham W. Doxey	Every bush is afire with , —Browning	Nov 1991	25f
Angel Abrea	What knowing , consists of	May 1992	26f-27a
Boyd K. Packer	Most supernal teaching is that we are the offspring of ,		67d-f
David B. Haight	Either governed by , or tyrants	Nov 1992	74b-75b
Howard W. Hunter	We are his first priority		95d
Richard G. Scott	, must be first priority	May 1993	34f
Lowell D. Wood	What , can do for a life —E.T. Benson		89a
Joseph B. Wirthlin	The creations of , - The Cosmos	Nov 1993	6b-c
Jeffrey R. Holland	Without faith in , the world makes no sense		13f-14a
	What , is not		14a-b
	, weeps for us and is quick to answer		14b-f
Neal A. Maxwell	We can't know selves if we don't know ,		19f
Kenneth Johnson	Our service is not for God's benefit	May 1994	29f
Russell M. Nelson	Comprehension of , brings brotherhood of man		70f-71a
Gordon B. Hinckley	Man may become as ,	Nov 1994	48d
James E. Faust	Make , the center of our being —McKay	Nov 1995	47c
Thomas S. Monson	Who honors God, God honors		50f
Lynn A. Mickelsen	A graven image is anything pre-eminent over ,		79c
	We take name of , in vain by breaking covenants		79d
Russell M. Nelson	We may become like ,		87f-88b
Aileen H. Clyde	We must also be "adults of God"	Nov 1996	88d-e
L. Edward Brown	Lord's prayer teaches that we are children of ,	May 1997	78b-c
L. Tom Perry	Good explanation of Godhead	May 1998	23d-24a
Gordon B. Hinckley	Statement of our beliefs about ,	Nov 1998	70f-71b
Neal A. Maxwell	Moderns believe in a disabled Deity	Nov 1999	6d-7b
Russell M. Nelson	Old Egyptian manuscript explains love of ,	May 2000	84e-f
Thomas S. Monson	We have forgotten , —A. Lincoln	Nov 2000	64f
Neal A. Maxwell	What , has given us	May 2002	38b-c
Neal A. Maxwell	Has all things planned	Nov 2002	17f-18a
	God is in the details		18a
Gordon B. Hinckley	Why did both , and Jesus come to Joseph?		80d-e
Jeffrey R. Holland	God - His attributes and deep love	Nov 2003	70d-73b
Neal A. Maxwell	The scope of His creations		100b-101a
	Omnicompetent		101b
Dale E. Miller	First principle of gospel is to know ,	Nov 2004	14e
Gordon B. Hinckley	Compare First Vision with Nicaean Creed	May 2005	80f-81b
David A. Bednar	How to become God's chosen		100f-101e
James E. Faust	One of 4 "absolutes"	Nov 2005	21d
	Godhead is one of 7 "blockbuster" doctrines		21f
Richard G. Scott	Only appeared once in person		80b-d
Larry W. Gibbons	Created us - Therefore guides us	Nov 2006	102b-c
Richard G. Scott	Created numberless cosmos and worlds	May 2007	8c
Gordon B. Hinckley	The nature of , vs. the Nicene Creed		83b-e

God

God, cont'd
Related Topics: Jesus

Gary J. Coleman	A stunning awakening to learn nature of ,	May 2007	92b-93b
Joseph B. Wirthlin	Will never give up on us	Nov 2007	29f-30a
Jeffrey R. Holland	Godhead is one in every way except body		40d-e
	Harpers Bible Dictionary disputes Trinity		40e
	How can we strive to be like an incomprehensible , ?		40f-41c
	Scriptures showing separateness of Godhead		41d-42a
	No Christian can dismiss concept of an embodied ,		42a
Gordon B. Hinckley	Has only appeared once - Why? - Answered		84c-d
	He cannot understand Nicene Creed		84e-f
Richard G. Scott	Vast extent of His creations		90e-91d
	Makes us feel valuable, appreciated and dear		92e-f
Dallin H. Oaks	We have two channels to ,	May 2008	28e-29a
Robert D. Hales	The 4 times , introduced Jesus		30f
Elaine S. Dalton	Is only a prayer away —marathon story		117d-118b
Neil L. Andersen	Knowledge of God's love kept elder on mission —story	Nov 2008	13e-f
Dieter F. Uchtdorf	A , of creation, compassion and happiness		118d-e
Dieter F. Uchtdorf	Does not need us to love Him	Nov 2009	21f-22a
	What , has done for us		22c-e
	Eloquent description of God's love for each of us		22e-23a
	Diligently keeping commandments shows love for ,		23a-d
	How and where can we hear God's voice?		23d-24b
Robert D. Hales	Blasphemy to say man looks like God?		30a-b
	How we know , and Jesus are separate individuals		30b-31a
Walter F. Gonzalez	If , cannot lie then prophecy will be fulfilled		52d-e
Thomas S. Monson	He is personal and real		110b
D. Todd Christofferson	A tender parent who would spare us grief	May 2010	34a
	Some say, "If there is a , He'd…"		34b-d
Thomas S. Monson	The Grand Designer and creation		87f-88a
Russell M. Nelson	Love for His children is infinite		91c-92b

Gossip
Related Topics: Judging

David O. McKay	Poison to the soul	June 1969	30c-d
N. Eldon Tanner	Make world better by speaking good —poem	July 1972	34a
	How people excuse selves for ,		35c
	Worst form of judging. Tongue most dangerous		35e
	We gain nothing by defaming another		36b
Harold B. Lee	Confirm truth before spreading ,	Jan 1973	105b
Spencer W. Kimball	Poem about Hearsay —good poem	May 1975	81d-f
Marvin J. Ashton	A woman's response to one who wanted to , —story	May 1977	67e-f
Charles Didier	The best and worst part of man - the tongue	Nov 1979	25e
Virginia H. Pearce	Mutual murmuring can destroy a ward	Nov 1993	80a
Gordon B. Hinckley	, will only backfire to hurt you	May 1996	92e-f
Cree-L Kofford	Loving neighbor while gossiping behind back	May 1999	82d-f
Gordon B. Hinckley	Why "School Thy Feelings" was written	Nov 2007	62c-e
	Great advice in handling slanderous article		63a-b

Gordon B. Hinckley	"A little piece of string" —story	Nov 2007	63b-66a
Thomas S. Monson	Have the courage to not ,	May 2009	124b-c
M. Russell Ballard	Undermines a woman's nature to nurture	May 2010	20d

Government
Related Topics: Communism, Freedom, Law, Politics, United States

Ezra Taft Benson	How far separation of church and state should go	Dec 1968	51d-e
	, has no power of itself		51f
	, has only powers delegated by people —good example		51f
	Activities must be kept at most local level		52c
	Has no power to set up welfare programs		52d
	The danger of welfare state		52e
	Marxist , is materialistic - says man is an economic creature		52f-53a
	Redistribution of wealth will kill any ,		53a-b
	Complete socialism in our lifetimes unless...		53c-d
	How welfare state can be reversed		53d-e
Robert L. Simpson	Honor whatever , you're under	Dec 1970	97a-c
Harold B. Lee	Prayer that others might fashion their , after ours		105e
	Out of Zion shall go forth the law		105e
Hartman Rector, Jr.	One principle of gospel better than 1000 , programs	Nov 1975	11d-e
	Compensatory government programs		11d-e
	Men's , programs without Lord won't work		12e-f
L. Tom Perry	Impossible to govern without Bible —G. Washington		86d
L. Tom Perry	Suppose the Bible was a nation's only law?	May 1976	64c-e
Spencer W. Kimball	Limited, and unlimited opportunity	Nov 1976	6d
Marion G. Romney	We can't afford to become ward of the ,		124c
Ezra Taft Benson	People support , but , should not support the people	May 1977	84b-e
Spencer W. Kimball	Our civic responsibilities	May 1978	100c-e
	Why the Church doesn't involve itself in every matter		100e-f
George P. Lee	, and the Lord attack problems differently	Nov 1980	66e-f
Russell M. Nelson	Gambling, pornography, and abortion provoke God's wrath	Nov 1987	89d
David B. Haight	, is a delegated authority from God	Nov 1992	74b-75b
Neal A. Maxwell	The way secular , solves problems	Nov 1994	35a
Neal A. Maxwell	The state has become the church	May 1996	68b-e
L. Tom Perry	Priesthood: most perfect form of ,	Nov 2002	7d-e
Russell M. Nelson	We are to render loyalty to our countries		40c-d
Gordon B. Hinckley	Our obligations to , during war	May 2003	78d-81f
D. Todd Christofferson	Laws cannot replace self-discipline	Nov 2009	106d-e

Gratitude
Related Topics: —

Joseph F. Smith	Lack of , one of greatest sins	Dec 1969	38a
Paul H. Dunn	, is the memory of the heart	Dec 1970	41c
Angel Abrea	, for his blessings —excellent expression	May 1981	27d-28b
Marion G. Romney	A hog eating acorns not caring where they came from	Nov 1982	49b
	Men ascribe gifts and success to own genius - greatest sin		49e-f
	Lincoln called nation to acknowledge God		50b-c

Marion G. Romney	Commandment to be thankful is one of strongest	Nov 1982	50e-f
L. Tom Perry	Boy thanked God for priesthood blessing —story	Nov 1983	13b
Russell M. Nelson	Non praying people are like sullen goldfish	Nov 1986	69a
Hugh W. Pinnock	We show Savior our , through unity	May 1987	64e-f
Thomas S. Monson	Senile woman knew visitor and received words of , —story	Nov 1987	69b-f
Henry B. Eyring	Remembering poverty brought , —Orderville story	Nov 1989	11f-12c
	Prayers of , brings more ,		12f-13b
	Writing in journals brings ,		13c
W. Eugene Hansen	Ingratitude more serious than revenge		24b
Richard G. Scott	Most important part of prayer is , —story		32d-f
James E. Faust	Homemade bread and homemade soap	May 1990	85b-d
	A foundation for other virtues		86d-e
	Opens eyes to other blessings		87f
Helio R. Camargo	Enumerating our blessings —good talk	Nov 1990	80b-81f
Thomas S. Monson	The way to show , to Jesus —well phrased	May 1992	60e-f
Robert D. Hales	, is the foundation for repentance		63f
Thomas S. Monson	First thank you note in 50 years —story	May 1993	62e
	Lord has 2 homes: heaven and grateful heart		62e
Lloyd P. George	Ingratitude is one of the greatest sins	May 1994	27d-e
Thomas S. Monson	What the words "thank you" do	Nov 1998	17f
	Auctioneer bought bike for boy —story		18b-c
	Note to teacher was first in 50 years —story		18f
Gordon T. Watts	, begins with attitude —story, entire talk		83d-84f
	, is twin sister to humility —Talmage		83d-84f
Russell M. Nelson	As guilty as goldfish in a bowl		87a
Gordon B. Hinckley	Ingratitude is sharper than a serpent's tooth —King Lear	Nov 2000	100a
Steven E. Snow	First express , in prayer, then ask	Nov 2001	44b-e
Thomas S. Monson	Teacher's grave decorated each year —story		100d-f
Dallin H. Oaks	Give thanks in all things —entire talk	May 2003	95b-98f
Gordon B. Hinckley	Teacher never knew she'd answered prayer —story		117e-118b
Richard C. Edgley	Humility and , characterize happiness	Nov 2003	98d
Bonnie D. Parkin	Blessing basket helped through affliction	May 2007	34e-f
	Makes us more aware		35a
	2 little acts of kindness brought ,		35b-c
	, is an expression of faith		35d-e
	, for adversity —McKay		35f-36a
Henry B. Eyring	Journals help , and remembering	Nov 2007	66e-67b
Dieter F. Uchtdorf	Repentance shows , for Atonement	May 2008	60a-b
David A. Bednar	Prayers that only express , —story	Nov 2008	42d-43c
Thomas S. Monson	Don't focus on what's missing. Have , for abundance		86f
	Be grateful for what you have —Homer		86f-87a
	, for her tiny peephole of sight —story		87a-c
	One of noblest of virtues - 10 lepers		87c-e
	His , for the Savior		87f-88b

Gratitude

| Quentin L. Cook | Ingratitude close to unpardonable sin | Nov 2008 | 104f |
| Thomas S. Monson | Two most important words: Thank you | May 2010 | 87a |

Growth
Related Topics: Progression

Delbert L. Stapley	Quote by David Everett	Dec 1969	62b
John H. Vandenberg	Treat others like the persons they should be	Dec 1970	35d-36a
	Some die at 30 but aren't buried until 70		36e
Paul H. Dunn	Not what I ought to be, what I'm going to be, or what I was		41a-c
Harold B. Lee	Learning ceases for many	June 1971	9b-d
Sterling W. Sill	The tree that never had to fight... —poem		44d
Gordon B. Hinckley	We grow as we serve	July 1972	72a
	Convert grew from responsibility to responsibility —story		72b
Marvin J. Ashton	Simple acts are stepping-stones to ,	May 1977	67d-e
Marvin J. Ashton	You can change and grow all your life —good quote	Nov 1978	50f
John H. Groberg	Law of , requires constant effort and stretching		62b
Richard G. Scott	Constant upward change - leads to salvation	Nov 1979	71b
J. Richard Clarke	If at first you do succeed, try something harder	May 1982	78c
Neal A. Maxwell	Spiritual , requires calisthenics	Nov 1983	55d-e
Marvin J. Ashton	Either becoming person you should be, or don't want to be		62a
John B. Dickson	Real , comes with challenges —story	Nov 1992	45c-e
Lowell D. Wood	How God expands a person —E.T. Benson	May 1993	89a
Elaine L. Jack	No such thing as standing still —Cannon	May 1994	15d-e
Boyd K. Packer	High standards don't repel ,	Nov 2006	87d
David A. Bednar	Parable of the Pickle - Conversion process	May 2007	19b-22b
David A. Bednar	Repent first - then must continually grow better	Nov 2007	80d-82b
Joseph B. Wirthlin	Adversities can be times of greatest ,	Nov 2008	26b-e
	Adversities stretch, build and increase us		27d-f
Henry B. Eyring	Comes when you feel overwhelmed		57b-f
M. Russell Ballard	The , of the Church described and enumerated		81b-84b
Henry B. Eyring	Trials are invitations for ,	May 2009	25a
Ann M. Dibb	Did not understand magnitude of youthful experiences		114d-115a
Dieter F. Uchtdorf	Being a poor refugee was a great , experience —story	Nov 2009	55e-56b

Habits
Related Topics: —

Marvin J. Ashton	What is a lie?	May 1982	9c-e
	Chains of , too small to be felt until too strong to be broken		9f
	Why people lie		9f-10c
	Lying: accomplice to every other vice		11c-d
Marvin J. Ashton	The chains of , ... —Samuel Johnson quote	Nov 1986	14b
James M. Paramore	Freeing people from prisons of ,	Nov 1992	9b-11b
Neal A. Maxwell	We first endure, then pity, then embrace —poem	May 1993	76d
Spencer J. Condie	, are easily formed - make good ones	Nov 1993	16f
Wayne S. Peterson	Sow thoughts, reap habits and destiny	Nov 2001	84b
Mary N. Cook	Three Young Women daily , - Prayer, study, smile	May 2009	118d-e

David O. McKay	, here and hereafter depend on choice of mate	June 1969	3f
N. Eldon Tanner	Most unhappiness caused by not keeping commandments	Dec 1971	34a
John H. Vandenberg	The list of things bringing , didn't list peace of mind		116f-117a
Paul H. Dunn	Man looked like he was weaned on lemon juice		120a-c
Franklin D. Richards	Service made mission happiest time of life	Jan 1973	72e
O. Leslie Stone	Greatest , comes when living gospel		80e
L. Tom Perry	Home source of greatest , —McKay	July 1973	21d
Hartman Rector, Jr.	Material possessions bring no real happiness		58b
	The object and design of existence —Joseph Smith		58f
	Happy parents produce happy children		59c
Sterling W. Sill	Families and work should bring ,		104e
David B. Haight	Follows pure acts and thoughts	Jan 1974	42c
Spencer W. Kimball	Why members of Church are happy	Nov 1974	4d
Ezra Taft Benson	12 ways to fight depression		65d-67f
O. Leslie Stone	If you want , keep the commandments	May 1975	9c
William H. Bennett	, comes from doing one's best —story	Nov 1976	30c-31b
LeGrand Richards	Never saw tears of joy because of anything purchased		64e-65a
Marvin J. Ashton	Hard to make miserable a man with self respect —Lincoln		85a
Royden G. Derrick	, is a by-product of service	May 1977	58f
Paul H. Dunn	We think we'll find , when we reach some goal	Nov 1977	24c
H. Burke Peterson	Having something worthy to do and doing it well —Young		87e
L. Tom Perry	Saints are happy —Brigham Young quote	May 1978	52d-f
Alvin R. Dyer	No other plan of , only multiple choice misery	Nov 1980	15c
Joseph B. Wirthlin	, is a by-product rather than an end		70a
Loren C. Dunn	Man was cheated but looked at positive side —story	May 1981	26e-f
	Faith and , foreign to cynicism, skepticism, unforgiveness		26f
Theodore M. Burton	Hell is the absolute zero of ,		20f
Marvin J. Ashton	, is bound up with helpfulness	Nov 1982	65a
Alvin R. Dyer	Sadness and badness are mutually reinforcing	May 1983	9d
Richard G. Scott	, comes from serving and loving others	Nov 1983	71c
Marvin J. Ashton	Comes when we cease chasing it and turn to other things	May 1984	11d
Robert L. Backman	, is a by-product of service	Nov 1985	13d-f
Jack H. Goaslind	, is the object of our existence —Joseph Smith	May 1986	52f
Marvin J. Ashton	, comes from resisting temptation		68d-e
James E. Faust	Will I be Happy? —entire talk	May 1987	80b-82f
Glenn L. Pace	Mistaking telestial pleasure for celestial joy	Nov 1987	39d-41b
Thomas S. Monson	, is the object of our existence —Joseph Smith	Nov 1988	69b
Boyd K. Packer	Chastity is the key to your ,	May 1989	54e-f
F. Enzio Busche	Why aren't we happy? —good insight		72a-d
Joseph B. Wirthlin	All commandments promote , —Joseph Smith	Nov 1989	75b
Rex D. Pinegar	No genuine , separate from the home —J.F. Smith	May 1990	9e
Dallin H. Oaks	The object and design of existence —Joseph Smith	Nov 1991	73f
Russell M. Nelson	Death is essential to ,	May 1992	72f-73a
Joseph B. Wirthlin	The most optimistic and least pessimistic		87c-d
Marion D. Hanks	Half Hallels and deliverance from enemies	Nov 1992	63f-64a

Happiness

Boyd K. Packer	Plan of , requires marriage	Nov 1993	21d
Jacob de Jager	Positive ideas to help life be happy		32b-c
L. Tom Perry	, is the object of our existence —Joseph Smith		67b-c
Dallin H. Oaks	Plan of , explained —entire talk		72b-75f
W. Eugene Hansen	Life, liberty and the pursuit of ,		81d-e
	Has its roots in unselfishness		82b
	Pleasure is Satan's counterfeit for , —Talmage		82b-f
	How pleasure differs from , —Talmage		83d-f
M. Russell Ballard	All commandments directed toward ,	May 1995	23c
Joe J. Christensen	Pinnacle of , is in a unified marriage		66a-b
Alvin R. Dyer	Sensory , is illusory		67a
LeGrand R. Curtis	, is homemade		83a
Joseph B. Wirthlin	Holy Ghost is a way to maximize ,	Nov 1995	77d-e
Richard G. Scott	Never ends - Sadness does	May 1996	26d-f
Carlos E. Asay	The object and design of our existence —Joseph Smith		60b
Gordon B. Hinckley	Life is to be enjoyed, not just endured		94f
Elaine L. Jack	, in spite of losing possessions —story	Nov 1996	76b-e
Boyd K. Packer	, is inseparable from clean behavior	May 1997	10a-b
Patricia P. Pinegar	No joy equals that of happy parenthood		13f
Gordon B. Hinckley	We have found the key to a peculiar ,	Nov 1997	69e-f
Gordon B. Hinckley	No greater , than found in your home	May 1998	51f
Richard G. Scott	Ordinances and covenants assure ,	Nov 1998	68c
Gordon B. Hinckley	Why are we such a happy people? - Obedience		72f
Robert J. Whetten	Why are missionaries happy?	May 1999	31d
Thomas S. Monson	"Keep Right" to be happy		50e
Sheri L. Dew	Is , possible when life is hard?		67c-d
Joseph B. Wirthlin	Commandments make for , —Joseph Smith	Nov 1999	40b-c
L. Tom Perry	Members can be known for their buoyancy		77d-f
Boyd K. Packer	Having a body is the great principle of ,	Nov 2000	72e-f
James E. Faust	We don't have even a glimpse of potential ,	May 2002	47e-48a
Thomas S. Monson	The object and design of existence —Joseph Smith		99b
	Unhappiness will increase without repentance		99d-e
Claudio R. M. Costa	The difference between , and fun	Nov 2002	92b-94b
Gordon B. Hinckley	Life is easier if we'll be happy		100b
M. Russell Ballard	The sources of ,	May 2003	39f
Boyd K. Packer	Disrupt sex - disrupt plan of ,	Nov 2003	25b
Richard C. Edgley	Humility and gratitude characterize ,		98d
Thomas S. Monson	Pleasure is doing good work	May 2005	54f-55a
Keith B. McMullin	, is the object of our existence —Smith	Nov 2005	11f
James E. Faust	A gift of the Holy Ghost		21d
Benjamin De Hoyos	"Wanting to" is the determining factor		31b-32f
M. Russell Ballard	No genuine , apart from home —J.F. Smith		42f-43a
James E. Faust	Apostate apostle never again had ,		54b-c
Robert D. Hales	Satan can't have , unless we sin	May 2006	6b-c
Russell M. Nelson	Marriage brings greatest possibility for ,		36c-d

Happiness

Happiness, cont'd
Related Topics: Joy

Russell M. Nelson	, is predicated upon personal purity	May 2006	37a
Earl C. Tingey	World will not determine , if…		74a-b
Joseph B. Wirthlin	Happy people drink deeply of living waters		99f-100f
	No greater , than relieving distress of others		101d
Marcus B. Nash	, to the degree you live the gospel	Nov 2006	49b-50f
Boyd K. Packer	We are to be happy and positive		87e-f
Gordon B. Hinckley	A simple recipe for , and a promise	May 2007	115e&117f
Joseph B. Wirthlin	The grand key to , is love	Nov 2007	30f
Julie B. Beck	Women are happy when they embrace proper roles		110e-f
Susan W. Tanner	Things her soul delights in	May 2008	81d-83b
Joseph B. Wirthlin	Adversities can lead to greatest ,	Nov 2008	26b-e
	Learn to laugh at adversity —2 stories		26f-27c
Thomas S. Monson	Don't focus on what's missing but on what we have		86f
	Decided to be happy before she could see —story		87a-c
Russell M. Nelson	Must focus outside selves to find ,		94d
Dieter F. Uchtdorf	Creating and compassion make God happy		118d-f
	Our birthright and purpose is eternal ,		118e-119d
	Those who bring sunshine to others have ,		120b
	Achieve a life of meaning, grace and fulfillment by …		120e-f
D. Todd Christofferson	God designed all commandments for our ,	May 2008	23a
Dieter F. Uchtdorf	Many theories for , but only one plan is real		75e-f
Dallin H. Oaks	Satan has us seek , outside God —C.S. Lewis		95a-b
	Happy and fulfilled when we act and serve		96e
Thomas S. Monson	Man's greatest , comes from service —McKay	Nov 2009	85d
M. Russell Ballard	Safest road to , is keeping covenants	May 2010	21a

Healing
Related Topics: —

Thomas S. Monson	United faith of Tongans healed a boy —story	Dec 1968	83a-b
Harold B. Lee	Greatest miracles are , of sick souls	July 1973	123a
	His miraculous , —story		123d
Henry D. Taylor	Fasting and a 6-hour prayer brought , —story	Nov 1974	15d-e
James A. Cullimore	Call priesthood more, doctor less —Cannon		27f-28a
	Seek the power to heal		28c
	Why all are not healed —Kimball		28d-e
Wm. Grant Bangerter	Use priesthood for , of spiritual ills	Nov 1975	70a
Thomas S. Monson	, of Guatemalan missionary Randall Ellsworth	Nov 1976	53c-f
James M. Paramore	Daughter's earache instantly healed —story	May 1977	43a
Marion G. Romney	Guatemala missionary walked again —story	Nov 1977	42a-b
Joseph B. Wirthlin	Woman healed when Pres. Kimball shook hand —story	Nov 1978	36b-e
Thomas S. Monson	He gave a blessing as 60 sailors watched —story	May 1979	37b-e
Yoshihiko Kikuchi	Baptism healed man who couldn't walk —story	Nov 1979	29d-30e
Gordon B. Hinckley	Conditioned upon faith and will of God	May 1981	20e
H. Burke Peterson	Girl received her hearing at baptism —story	Nov 1981	35e-36f
James E. Faust	Man shot while guarding Brethren —story	May 1982	48b-d
L. Tom Perry	Boy thanked God for priesthood blessing —story	Nov 1983	13b

Thomas S. Monson	5 non-member patients fasted for missionary —story	May 1984	18d-f
Russell M. Nelson	Relation between blessings and medicine	Nov 1984	30f-31a
Gordon B. Hinckley	The , of Elijah Fordham by Joseph —story	Nov 1988	53b-f
	The , power of Christ —entire talk		52b-59b
Howard W. Hunter	Jesus restored physical and spiritual sight	May 1989	16d-17a
Richard G. Scott	Missionaries healed man with head wound —story		35d-36a
Thomas S. Monson	, of Guatemalan missionary Randall Ellsworth —story		45b-46b
F. Arthur Kay	Down's Syndrome baby was normal —story	Nov 1989	80b-c
	Blessing promised cystic fibrosis relief —story		80d-e
Gordon B. Hinckley	Alma Smith's hip socket healed —story		97d-f
Thomas S. Monson	Dying woman healed at baptism —story	Nov 1990	68c-e
Ted E. Brewerton	Granny's deafness healed at baptism —story	Nov 1991	12b-f
John B. Dickson	Cancer in bone should have been fatal —story	Nov 1992	45c-e
Rex D. Pinegar	Explosion - Healed by prayer —story	May 1993	65d-66b
	Explosion - Healed by prayer —story		68a-b
Carlos H. Amado	Donated corneas give girl eyesight —story	Nov 1993	44d-45a
Merrill J. Bateman	Paralyzed Korean girl healed within —story	May 1995	14b-f
Neal A. Maxwell	A dying child's blessing —story	May 1996	70e-f
Thomas S. Monson	Christ at Bethesda Pool —entire talk	Nov 1996	16d-19f
Russell M. Nelson	Self , properties of the body		33d-34a
James E. Faust	Flexible gristle replaced hip socket —story	May 2000	19a-d
Jeffrey R. Holland	New elder blessed boy struck by lightning —story	Nov 2000	38c-39a
Lance B. Wickman	Why some healings "don't work" —story	Nov 2002	30b-32f
W. Craig Zwick	Blessing a premature son —story	Nov 2003	34f-35e
Merrill J. Bateman	Back-to-school blessing was skipped —story		51a-52d
James E. Faust	Elder Dickson's bone cancer healed —story	Nov 2004	55b-c
James E. Faust	President Snow saved from drowning —story	May 2005	51f-52e
Russell M. Nelson	President Kimball's , through prayer —story	Nov 2005	85e-86c
	True conversion brings ,		86c-87a
	Resurrection: The consummate act of ,		87f-88a
Elaine S. Dalton	, a pioneer girl's frozen feet —story	May 2006	109f-110d
Dallin H. Oaks	Why some are not healed	Nov 2006	7d-8b
	Atonement provides , or strength to bear burden		9a-b
James E. Faust	Every missionary was healed —story		54e-55a
Thomas S. Monson	Blessing a sick sailor —story	May 2007	58b-f
Richard G. Scott	Healing the consequences of abuse	May 2008	40b-43f
David A. Bednar	, came only after prayer of faith —story		96b-e
Joseph B. Wirthlin	Through faith , eventually came —story	Nov 2008	28d-e
Keith B. McMullin	Miraculous , of girl run over by bus —story		77a-d
Thomas S. Monson	50 years with just a peephole of sight —story		87a-c
Thomas S. Monson	Food poisoning healed by two new elders —story	May 2009	69e-70e
	Blind man had light of the gospel —story		90b-91a
Henry B. Eyring	Keep oil handy - Be prepared —story	Nov 2009	59b-d
Dallin H. Oaks	Use priesthood and medical science	May 2010	47b-e
	Other faiths have , too —story		47e-48b

Healing, cont'd
Related Topics: —

Dallin H. Oaks	5 parts to a , administration	May 2010	48d
	Power passes through administrator		48f
	We aren't to boast of healings		48f
	The major element of , is faith		49a-b
	Avoid too frequent administrations		49b-c
	Words of blessing aren't essential		49c-50b
	Will of Lord is paramount		50b-c
	Girl was appointed to die		50d

Heaven
Related Topics: Celestial Kingdom, Eternal Life, Exaltation, Salvation

Robert L. Simpson	Associates in , will be just like you	Dec 1968	89e
Hugh B. Brown	Heaven or hell? Degrees of glory doctrine	June 1969	33a-e
Sterling W. Sill	A 5-minute look into heaven —Joseph Smith	Dec 1969	47c
Bruce R. McConkie	Heaven: A projection of an LDS family into eternity	June 1970	44e
Spencer W. Kimball	Glimpses of , on earth —entire talk —stories	Dec 1971	36a-39f
	, is a place, but also a condition		39d-e
Mark E. Peterson	Tis , alone that is given away —poem	Nov 1974	51c-d
Joseph Anderson	People work harder to reach hell than ,	May 1975	30b
Wm. Grant Bangerter	Quality hinges on repentance, ordinances, enduring, service	Nov 1988	81b-82b
Merrill J. Bateman	, only exists if families are eternal	May 1995	13e
Henry B. Eyring	Gravestone: "Please, no empty chairs"	Nov 2009	71b-d

Hell
Related Topics: —

Hugh B. Brown	Short, cute story	Dec 1969	95b
Theodore M. Burton	Sons of Perdition will have bodies but can't use them	Jul 1972	78d
Boyd K. Packer	Explaining second death to children	Jul 1973	53c
Marion G. Romney	To be shut out from presence of God	Nov 1974	40a
Delbert L. Stapley	Free Agency abridged in ,	May 1975	22a
Joseph Anderson	People work harder to reach , than heaven		30b
Theodore M. Burton	Description of , -cold and dark —story	May 1981	28d-29a
	, is the absolute zero of happiness		20f
Thomas S. Monson	Eternal exile from God	Nov 2008	107d-e
Quentin L. Cook	Common teachings about , are incorrect —Farrar	May 2009	36e-f
	No life shall be destroyed —Tennyson		36f
	Others teach most will go to ,		36f-37a
	Spirit prison or , will deliver up captives		37a-b

Holy Ghost
Related Topics: Light of Christ, Spirit

Bruce R. McConkie	Can't receive , without receiving revelation —J. Smith	Dec 1969	85a
Marion G. Romney	Why do people respond to meetings differently?	June 1970	67a-b
S. Dilworth Young	None of the 12 were converted before receiving ,	June 1971	39b-c
Henry D. Taylor	Testimony from , better than seeing —Smith		108d-e
	President Snow's reception of , —story		108f-109c
James A. Cullimore	The catalyst which unifies the Church	July 1972	56f
	Explanation of seriousness of sin against ,		57d

Author	Topic	Date	Page
James A. Cullimore	2 things necessary for companionship of ,	July 1972	57f
Ezra Taft Benson	Get witness of , concerning leaders —Brigham Young		61c
Hugh B. Brown	Heeding the promptings of the , —story		86a
Marion G. Romney	Brings spiritual rebirth	Jan 1973	31b
	Gives life to Church		31c
	Talks in Church are but words without ,	July 1973	11a
L. Tom Perry	How , inspires General Authorities		20f
Henry D. Taylor	Get the , —story by Wilford Woodruff		48a
Franklin D. Richards	Convert feels influence of , —story		117a
	Voice tells father to get up - finds fire —story		117c
Marion G. Romney	Discussion on the , —entire talk	May 1974	90a-92f
Elray L. Christiansen	Keep Satan out by keeping , in	Nov 1974	24e
Henry D. Taylor	Arrogant youth spoke without , —story	Nov 1975	62f
S. Dilworth Young	Four ways the , speaks to us	May 1976	22d-23a
Boyd K. Packer	Spiritual Crocodiles —entire talk		30a-32b
N. Eldon Tanner	Columbus said , inspired him		48f-49a
Paul H. Dunn	, —little poem	Nov 1976	54c
Loren C. Dunn	A more certain way of knowing than seeing	May 1977	31a-c
	Testimony a convert received through , —story		31c-32b
Marion G. Romney	Light of Christ, Holy Ghost, and Sure Word of Prophecy		43d-45f
James A. Cullimore	, will reveal what to do even in simplest matters —Snow	May 1978	26a-b
Gordon B. Hinckley	W. Woodruff told to move carriage —story	Nov 1982	45d-46c
James M. Paramore	He saved his daughter from drowning —story	May 1983	27d-e
James E. Faust	A way of knowing more surely than seeing	Nov 1983	11b
Thomas S. Monson	, told bishop to stop at inactive's house —story	May 1985	68f-69b
	Told him to see paralyzed friend - prevented suicide —story		69f-70b
Dwan J. Young	, told girl to move just before car accident —story	May 1988	78b-c
	TV program made boy feel dark inside —story		79b-c
Boyd K. Packer	, works in moments of quiet and reverence	Nov 1988	21a
James E. Faust	Difference between , and the gift of ,	May 1989	31e-f
	What , will do for a person		32f-33a
	What is the Holy Spirit of Promise?		33b-d
	Instructions of deceased Joseph Smith to Brigham Young		33e
Richard G. Scott	Your feelings, not the talk, are most important		37f
Boyd K. Packer	Dual alarm system: Pain and guilt		54f-59a
Ezra Taft Benson	When you do good, you feel good		82c
James E. Faust	Members must not blindly follow leaders	Nov 1989	11a
Boyd K. Packer	, speaks through feelings		14b-c
Dallin H. Oaks	Testimony must be rooted in ,	Nov 1990	30b-d
Henry B. Eyring	, whispers, not shouts	May 1991	67a-d
James E. Faust	A healthy conscience means a healthy spirit		68f
Graham W. Doxey	, speaks - but we're hard of hearing	Nov 1991	25e-f
	Suggested aids to our hearing		25f-26f
Thomas S. Monson	, would not let photos be thrown out —story	May 1992	49d-50a
Joseph B. Wirthlin	The , greatest blessing - What it does		88e-f

Holy Ghost, cont'd
Related Topics: Light of Christ, Spirit

Neal A. Maxwell	Helps recognize plain nonsense	May 1993	78f
Gordon B. Hinckley	Can teach things we can't teach each other		94d
Spencer J. Condie	Strives, entices, contends, persuades, - action verbs	Nov 1993	15f
Dieter F. Uchtdorf	Train self to hear , through static	Nov 1994	43d-f
Boyd K. Packer	Angels speak by power of ,		59e
	Promptings from , are strictly private		59f-60b
	Speaks through feelings		60b-f
L. Aldin Porter	Clamor and haste make immunity to ,		64d
Joseph B. Wirthlin	What , is and does		76b
Joseph B. Wirthlin	, is a way to maximize happiness	Nov 1995	77d-e
Keith B. McMullin	Years of experience can't compare to a moment with ,	May 1996	9b
Jeffrey R. Holland	, told two men the Hendrickses were starving —story		31c-f
Henry B. Eyring	How to give family the ,		62b-d
L. Aldin Porter	Does not teach the proud, indolent or doubter	Nov 1996	9f
	Most important knowledge comes from ,		11a
Thomas S. Monson	, told him to check woman in next bed —story		18f-19d
Dallin H. Oaks	Difference between , and gift of ,		60b-e
	What a convert felt when receiving ,		60e-f
	Use care to not take , for granted		60f
	Will leave spiritual feeling in home		60f-61a
	Comes a little at a time		61a
	Withdraws under profanity, sin, etc.		61a
	Told mother of daughter's new calling —story		61b-c
James E. Faust	Left meeting to check on woman —story		94f-95a
Dennis E. Simmons	Speaks through thoughts, impressions and feelings	May 1997	31f
	Scripture list of what , does		32e-f
James E. Faust	, told W. Woodruff not to board boat —story		42d-e
L. Tom Perry	, is as important to man as sun is to plants		69b-c
	"Say no to the offer" —story		69d-70a
	P.P. Pratt's wonderful description of what , does		70a-b
Neal A. Maxwell	, will preach from the pulpit of memory	Nov 1997	24a
James E. Faust	Boy found cow through help from , —story		59b-d
Duane B. Gerrard	Every decision can be made correctly through ,		77f
L. Tom Perry	Explanation of ,	May 1998	23d-24a
Dallin H. Oaks	Relationship of ministering of angels and ,	Nov 1998	37f-38a
	The most precious possession in mortality		38a-f
	Meaning of ministering of angels		38f-39c
Susan L. Warner	, bears testimony when we bear testimony		66e
Sheri L. Dew	"We Are Not Alone" —excellent talk		94d-96f
	We live far beneath our privileges —Brigham Young		95b
	Meeting was "Very Holy Ghost" —story		96e
James E. Faust	Voice told man to go help handcarts —story	May 1999	47b-f
Thomas S. Monson	Every man is given light of Christ —H.B. Lee		55d
Keith B. McMullin	A sensitive conscience indicates healthy spirit		80c
Neal A. Maxwell	A constant companion better than periodic miracles	Nov 1999	8d-e

Holy Ghost

Boyd K. Packer	The spirit of revelation —entire talk	Nov 1999	23b-25b
Joseph B. Wirthlin	Purpose of , and how to have it		40f-41b
Patricia P. Pinegar	, prompted mother how to save son —story		68a-c
Richard G. Scott	The range of help available through ,		87b-89f
Boyd K. Packer	Received , and knew it not	May 2000	8e-9a
	Can be smothered through sin and neglect		9b
Angel Abrea	The mission of the , —M.G. Romney		42d-e
Joseph B. Wirthlin	Influence of , on P. Pratt and J. Taylor —story	Nov 2000	22e-23a
Douglas L. Callister	How Brigham Young invited influence of ,		31a
	The effect of constant companionship of ,		31b-d
Sydney S. Reynolds	Listen to , - Clothes dryers were empty —story	May 2001	12d-e
James E. Faust	Gift of , at baptism discussed —good		55f-58f
Henry B. Eyring	The , is a cleansing agent	May 2002	28b-d
Robert R. Steuer	Joseph to Brigham in dream: "Get the , "		31d-e
	Carried 3 x 5 card to record messages from ,		32d
L. Tom Perry	Gift of , is a higher endowment —J.F. Smith		40b
	Joseph of Egypt and the , —story		40c-41f
	Heed , and angels will minister to you		41e
Spencer J. Condie	Teaches what men can't teach each other		45f
James E. Faust	, augments talents many fold		47e-48a
Sharon G. Larsen	You're never alone with ,		91d
	Moroni had company of the ,		91e-f
Thomas S. Monson	Conscience always warns before it punishes		100e
Thomas S. Monson	Conscience always warns before it punishes	Nov 2002	54d
	Heeding silent prompting led him to friend —story		55b-f
Kenneth Johnson	Cannot sin without overruling a warning		90c
	Stealing apples, smoking and guidance of , —story		89b-91f
Joseph B. Wirthlin	Light of Christ leads to ,	May 2003	26c-d
	Gift of , only for worthy members		26d-f
	Ministering influence of Godhead		26f-27a
	Confirmation gives the right to ,		27a
	, penetrates spiritual darkness		27a-b
	Message of deceased Joseph to Brigham		27f-28a
	How to have influence of , in home		28a-c
	Dramatic testimony came through , —story		28d-f
Thomas S. Monson	Prompting was followed. Fruit years later —story		56f-57d
Robert D. Hales	Times when , cannot be with us	Nov 2003	31a-b
Thomas S. Monson	"How did you know today is my birthday?" —story		58f-59d
James E. Faust	, gave teenager answer to teacher's question	May 2004	62f
	Avoiding spiritual dead spots		67a-d
	Receiving messages —excellent talk		61d-68f
Richard G. Scott	Explanation of Light of Christ	Nov 2004	15e-f
Dallin H. Oaks	, keeps one from being deceived		45d-46e
James E. Faust	The Lost Battalion —story		61d-f
Boyd K. Packer	How , works	May 2005	6f-7c

Holy Ghost, cont'd
Related Topics: Light of Christ, Spirit

Neil L. Andersen	Warned FBI agent about gun —story	May 2005	46b-e
David A. Bednar	Leader dreamed of young man —story		100b-e
James E. Faust	A light in members' eyes —story	Nov 2005	20b-d
	The source of lighted countenances		20d-f
	Joy, fulfillment and peace are gifts of ,		21d
	One of 7 "blockbuster" doctrines		22a
Henry B. Eyring	Answer came from , when he was quiet	May 2006	16c-e
David A. Bednar	Confirmation is a directive to receive ,		29d
	Baptism by water is but half a baptism		29d
	Intensity of influence is not constant		29f
	Liahona a type and shadow of ,		30c-d
	Keep the , - Joseph told Brigham in vision		31d-f
James E. Faust	Ministering angels are sometimes family members		51b-d
	Alma's conversion came by , not by the angel		52d
A. Roger Merrill	Testimony came while reading Book of Mormon	Nov 2006	92d-93b
	The necessity of receiving by the Spirit		92d-94b
Don R. Clarke	Carries a book in which to write impressions		99a-b
Boyd K. Packer	Still, small voice brought him peace	May 2007	26b-f
	Couldn't remember words, but can't forget feeling		27b-d
Thomas S. Monson	, told him to speak to girl in balcony —story		42b-e
Glenn L. Pace	Testimony from , came at age 11 —story		78b-d
	Those born in Church have always had feelings from ,		78e
	Intellectual woman could not deny feelings —story		78e-f
	Testimony from , more certain than angels		78f-79f
Keith K. Hilbig	Quench not the Spirit - Paul and Jacob	Nov 2007	37d-f
	, enhances our natural abilities		38d-e
	We determine how much the , will influence us		38e-39f
	Quickens all the intellectual faculties —P.P. Pratt		39f
L. Tom Perry	Missionary doesn't convert - , does		49a
Henry B. Eyring	Our task is to invite , into our lives		57f-58a
Henry B. Eyring	The key to remembering		68e-69a
	Spirit of Christ is given to everyone		69a-d
David A. Bednar	Cleanses, heals, purifies, washes garments clean		81d-f
Daniel K. Judd	, teaches with greatest effect		94d-95a
Gerald N. Lund	The relationship between the heart and ,	May 2008	32d-34f
Susan W. Tanner	, testified of Jesus to convert —story		113b-d
Henry B. Eyring	True servants and angels will help you		125f
Dallin H. Oaks	"The greatest gift that can be bestowed" —Woodruff	Nov 2008	17f
Jeffrey R. Holland	The ministry of angels —entire talk		29b-31f
David A. Bednar	Revelation is conveyed through ,		41d
Carlos A. Godoy	If preoccupied we may not feel whisperings —Packer		101a-b
Barbara Thompson	Angels will be our associates —Smith		116c
Dieter F. Uchtdorf	, can amplify your words		117f
Allan F. Packer	Heard voice of coach above the noise —story	May 2009	17d-f
	Notice the first intimation of revelation —Joseph Smith		18b-d

Holy Ghost

D. Todd Christofferson	List of what , is and does	May 2009	22a-e
Thomas S. Monson	Daily scripture study increases direction from ,		68a-e
Richard G. Scott	A principle of revelation when used —Joseph Smith	Nov 2009	6e
	Growth comes as you struggle to learn to use the ,		6f-7a
	More certain than what you see and hear		7a
	Gives inspiration and power to do		7b
	As taught by 2 different teachers —story		7b-8d
	Must authorize the , to teach you		8d-e
	Strong emotions will overpower , —good example		8e
	You can master principles of guidance by ,		9d-f
Vicki F. Matsumori	What the , feels like		10f
	8-year-old felt , for first time —story		11b
	Places where , is easy to feel - Make home the same		11c
	Must provide daily quiet time for , to speak		11d
	Feels like a warm blanket - Teaching tool —story		11d-f
	Felt Spirit as a young girl during a hymn		12e
Boyd K. Packer	Communicates through mind more than senses		44b-d
	W. Woodruff told to move carriage —story		44d-45a
	Operates equally with men, women and children		45b-d
	Mother knew son was in trouble —story		45d-f
Henry B. Eyring	Choose sin and , becomes faint		60e
Thomas S. Monson	Can't have , if we're angry		67f
Ann M. Dibb	Part of our safety equipment —Bridge story		79b-81b
Henry B. Eyring	Youth can be saved only by guidance of ,	May 2010	25a-d
D. Todd Christofferson	Inspires and accompanies scriptures		35b-c
Quentin L. Cook	Slow down, ponder, pray to hear ,		85c-e
Gregory A. Schwitzer	Peace must be external and internal to hear ,		105b-d
Mary N. Cook	Girl inspired to read Matthew 5 —story		119d-e
Elaine S. Dalton	Dismayed, discouraged, distracted, delayed, disqualified		121b
	Develops beauty of person, form, features		122d-e

Home
Related Topics: Children, Family, Parents

David O. McKay	Home then Church should teach children	Dec 1968	37d
Russell M. Nelson	Furniture marred by children a blessing		86d-f
Marion D. Hanks	The thing I remember best about , is ...		97c-d
Marion G. Romney	Rome fell because of undermining of ,	June 1969	96b-c
David O. McKay	No man has right to utter cross word in ,		116b-c
Sterling W. Sill	Sabbath breaking builds bars, not altars, in home	Dec 1969	46d
Eldred G. Smith	The only eternal organization		61c
Richard L. Evans	When one puts business or pleasure above , ...	June 1970	38b
Ezra Taft Benson	Importance of , —quotes	Dec 1970	46a-b
Alvin R. Dyer	, is the headwaters of humanity		95a
Marvin J. Ashton	We have not failed until we quit trying	June 1971	31f-32a
Marion D. Hanks	Things obtainable only in the ,		92d
A. Theodore Tuttle	Teaching by example in the ,	Dec 1971	91c-f

Joseph Fielding Smith	Make your , a heaven on earth	July 1972	27f
Elray L. Christiansen	Nations depend on home —good poem		55f
A. Theodore Tuttle	The loftiest spiritual unit we know	Jan 1973	66d
H. Burke Peterson	Satan's greatest efforts must be in home		114b
James A. Cullimore	The basis of a righteous life	-	126e
Marion D. Hanks	Must supply a place to go for support and love		128d
Spencer W. Kimball	Family unit organized by Lord	July 1973	15b
L. Tom Perry	Heaven a continuation of ideal ,		21d
	His , has a closet for prayer		21e
David B. Haight	Parents must teach in ,		56d
Hartman Rector, Jr.	Most important work is within one's walls —Lee		58e
N. Eldon Tanner	How President McKay acted in , —by Sister McKay		92e
Harold B. Lee	Keep , strong to protect youth		98f
Henry D. Taylor	No bickering if Spirit is to be there	Jan 1974	37b
Spencer W. Kimball	LDS homes and farms are to be cleaned up	Nov 1974	4e-f
Loren C. Dunn	America built upon foundation of homes		9e
Franklin D. Richards	What , can and should be —McKay		106b-c
	Results when youth became peacemakers in ,		106c-f
Spencer W. Kimball	Creating positive currents to fight negative ones in ,		110a-113f
Spencer W. Kimball	Clean up, plant gardens	May 1975	5a-6a
Thomas S. Monson	Kidnapped boy finds home by memory of bell —story		17e-f
Spencer W. Kimball	Report on cleanup and planting projects	Nov 1975	5b-6a
Gordon B. Hinckley	Influences to have in ,		39b-d
Spencer W. Kimball	Plant gardens and clean up place	May 1976	4e-5a
Marion D. Hanks	Small poem about	Nov 1976	31d
Vaughn J. Featherstone	Mike will come back won't he? —poem		104c-e
Paul H. Dunn	Excitement - He was going , after 3 days	Nov 1977	25c
Spencer W. Kimball	Home is the seedbed of Saints	May 1978	5a
Alvin R. Dyer	Deserting , is equal to removing fingers from dike		11a
Spencer W. Kimball	Success as Church depends on how we live gospel at ,		101f
A. Theodore Tuttle	Teach in , as if family isolated from Church	Nov 1979	27f-28a
Ezra Taft Benson	Home must be man's first priority —McKay	May 1981	35a-b
David B. Haight	2 youth ended oppositely because of teachings in , —story	Nov 1983	39d-40b
A. Theodore Tuttle	Influence of , for better or worse, is overwhelming	May 1984	24b-d
Gene R. Cook	Boy's house burned but not his , —story		30d-e
Thomas S. Monson	What , is —quote by Margaret Thatcher	Nov 1988	69d
Loren C. Dunn	Church exists to help home —Spencer W. Kimball		74a-b
Rex D. Pinegar	No genuine happiness separate from the , —J.F. Smith	May 1990	9e
	There is nothing temporal in an LDS , —McKay		9f-10b
	A , of love is more valuable than riches		11d
	A man's thoughts as he watched , burn —story		11d-f
James E. Faust	Place of peace for Church members		86b
LeGrand R. Curtis	Happiness is homemade —entire talk	Nov 1990	12d-13f
Thomas S. Monson	One of greatest fortresses against evil	Nov 1991	87a-b
Dallin H. Oaks	Greatest work of men or women is in ,	May 1992	36e-f

Home

Thomas S. Monson	Blind man, a sacrificing woman and an ideal , —story	Nov 1992	69d-70b
Joseph B. Wirthlin	Every , is a house of learning either for good or otherwise	May 1993	70b
	What , should be —entire talk		68d-71f
Chieko N. Okazaki	Only 14% is a traditional American ,	Nov 1993	94c-d
Boyd K. Packer	Satan's ultimate purpose is to disrupt ,	May 1994	19e-f
Neal A. Maxwell	The basis of a righteous life —McKay		89e-f
Horacio A. Tenorio	Making our , a fortress	Nov 1994	23b-24f
J. Ballard Washburn	Go to temple to make covenants but home to keep them	May 1995	12d-e
	Where would Elder Packer go if he could choose? - Home		12e
LeGrand R. Curtis	Go , to church where Spirit is accessible		83d-e
	Most important work is in , —H.B. Lee		83f
Anne G. Wirthlin	I like your , because I feel safe here —story	Nov 1995	82d-e
Eran A. Call	, and family —important quotes	Nov 1997	29b-e
Virginia U. Jensen	Creating places of security - like Captain Moroni		89b-91b
	The last and only sanctuary		89d-e
	Law of harvest most evident in , and family		90d-e
Thomas S. Monson	Foundation of society and primary institution of Church		96a-b
Gordon B. Hinckley	No greater happiness than found in your ,	May 1998	51f
Robert D. Hales	Angry voices cause Spirit to depart , —H.B. Lee	May 1999	33b
Vaughn J. Featherstone	Teaching in , important influence on youth	Nov 1999	14d-e
Virginia U. Jensen	Observations on birds and nesting —story		95e-96b
	, is of utmost importance		96b-d
	Have Savior in , not just His picture —story		96f-97b
Thomas S. Monson	Safety of nation depends on purity of ,	May 2000	54c
Thomas S. Monson	No other instrumentality can take its place	Nov 2000	64f
	Christ should be pleased to linger in your ,		66b-c
	Abducted boy remembered village bell —story		66d-f
Russell M. Nelson	The basis of a righteous life	Nov 2001	70f
Wayne S. Peterson	Should be a refuge of safety and love		84b-e
Bonnie D. Parkin	Our problems arise from , —Hinckley	Nov 2002	104f-105a
Joseph B. Wirthlin	How to have influence of Holy Ghost in ,	May 2003	28a-c
Susan W. Tanner	Elements making a successful ,		73c-e
Sheldon F. Child	Worship at , during "The freeze" in Ghana —story	Nov 2003	9f-10b
Thomas S. Monson	, is the basis of a righteous life…		58a
Boyd K. Packer	Best protection against sin is a stable ,	May 2004	79a
	Bring mothers ,		79f
Gordon B. Hinckley	McKay and Lee quotes on ,	Nov 2004	84e
Thomas S. Monson	Teaching is best done in , —D.O. McKay		115a
Thomas S. Monson	Nothing can replace , —good quote	May 2005	19e
M. Russell Ballard	No genuine happiness apart from , —Smith	Nov 2005	42f-43a
Russell M. Nelson	Famous quotes by McKay and Lee	May 2006	38d
Ronald A. Rasband	Are the extra activities outside , worth it?		47b-c
M. Russell Ballard	Creating a gospel-sharing ,		85b-87b
Boyd K. Packer	Our , will be a refuge against storms	Nov 2006	88b-c
Julie B. Beck	LDS women should be best , makers in world	Nov 2007	76f-77a

Home, cont'd
Related Topics: Children, Family, Parents

Julie B. Beck	A pre-missionary training center	Nov 2007	77b-d
Russell M. Nelson	God's laboratory of love and service	May 2008	8d
Dieter F. Uchtdorf	Create a beautiful, harmonious ,	Nov 2008	118e-119d
Gary E. Stevenson	Make your , a temple	May 2009	101f-102e
Vicki F. Matsumori	Make , a place where Spirit is easy to feel	Nov 2009	11c
Quentin L. Cook	Religious observance in , as important as food		93a-b
D. Todd Christofferson	Must be constant teaching in ,		107c
Boyd K. Packer	Church must support not supplant ,	May 2010	7f-8a
	Priesthood a shield between , and adversary		9e
	Adversary attacks , not meetings		9f
	Ultimate end of all activity is a happy ,		9f
M. Russell Ballard	Most important work is in , —H.B. Lee		20b-c
	Church is there to support ,		21d
Henry B. Eyring	Has advantage in first 8 years		23a-b
L. Tom Perry	Teaching in , adds layer of insulation		31f
Richard G. Scott	Teaching must be primarily in ,		77d-78a
Robert D. Hales	Greatest works will be in ,		97c-98a

Home Teacher
Related Topics: Home Teaching

Robert L. Simpson	Follow-up by , broke smoking habit —story	Dec 1969	43b
John H. Vandenberg	, activated husband and converted wife —story	Dec 1970	36f-37e
Harold B. Lee	How to make better home teachers	July 1972	103b
Boyd K. Packer	Guardians of family and individual	Jan 1973	88e
	"Only" a home teacher		90f
James A. Cullimore	Should be home guardians rather than , —Lee		125e
Harold B. Lee	Watch for signs of divorce or incorrigible children	Jan 1974	101a
David B. Haight	How a , reactivated an inactive member —story	Nov 1975	59d-f
Wm. Grant Bangerter	The , won't do it? —story		69d-e
L. Tom Perry	1 bishop to 108 families, 1 quorum leader to 60 , 1 , to 3	May 1981	89b-d
David B. Haight	Activated man resolved not to live Word of Wisdom —story	Nov 1981	59c-e
	, reactivated 86- and 84-year-old couple —story		59e-f
Ezra Taft Benson	Stopped in so I could tell bishop I made my calls —story	May 1987	50e
	Instruction on how to be a , —excellent		48d-51f
Henry B. Eyring	We don't worry about all people in world like God does	May 1988	39e
John R. Lasater	The , as a shepherd —Shepherd story		74b-75f
Dallin H. Oaks	, was a girl's lifeline	Nov 1989	67a
Helvecio Martins	His first priesthood assignment	May 1995	43e
	Always released from previous callings		43f
	No greater calling —Benson		43f
	His first , —a good dedicated example		44b-f
	Watchmen on the tower - happy - trainers		44f-45b
James E. Faust	He neglected his duty and lost his lamb —story		46a-d
Dallin H. Oaks	Should not have to be pushed	May 1997	23d-e
Thomas S. Monson	Two children playing , knocked on door —story	Nov 1997	19a-b
Thomas S. Monson	While you were gone we had a party at your house—story		48b-e

| James E. Faust | A , at age 100 | May 2005 | 53b |

Robert L. Simpson	Follow-up by , broke smoking habit —story	Dec 1969	43b
John H. Vandenberg	, activated husband and converted wife —story	Dec 1970	36f-37e
Harold B. Lee	How to make better home teachers	July 1972	103b
Boyd K. Packer	Guardians of family and individual	Jan 1973	88e
	"Only" a home teacher		90f
James A. Cullimore	Should be home guardians rather than , —Lee		125e
Harold B. Lee	Watch for signs of divorce or incorrigible children	Jan 1974	101a
David B. Haight	How a , reactivated an inactive member —story	Nov 1975	59d-f
Wm. Grant Bangerter	The , won't do it? —story		69d-e
L. Tom Perry	1 bishop to 108 families, 1 quorum leader to 60 , 1 , to 3	May 1981	89b-d
David B. Haight	Activated man resolved not to live Word of Wisdom —story	Nov 1981	59c-e
	, reactivated 86- and 84-year-old couple —story		59e-f
Ezra Taft Benson	Stopped in so I could tell bishop I made my calls —story	May 1987	50e
	Instruction on how to be a , —excellent		48d-51f
Henry B. Eyring	We don't worry about all people in world like God does	May 1988	39e
John R. Lasater	The , as a shepherd —Shepherd story		74b-75f
Dallin H. Oaks	, was a girl's lifeline	Nov 1989	67a
Helvecio Martins	His first priesthood assignment	May 1995	43e
	Always released from previous callings		43f
	No greater calling —Benson		43f
	His first , —a good dedicated example		44b-f
	Watchmen on the tower - happy - trainers		44f-45b
James E. Faust	He neglected his duty and lost his lamb —story		46a-d
Dallin H. Oaks	Should not have to be pushed	May 1997	23d-e
Thomas S. Monson	Two children playing , knocked on door —story	Nov 1997	19a-b
Thomas S. Monson	While you were gone we had a party at your house—story		48b-e
James E. Faust	A , at age 100	May 2005	53b

Victor L. Brown	Pornography can turn 12- and 13-year-olds to ,	June 1970	46d-e
Spencer W. Kimball	Attitude of other churches toward ,	June 1971	18b-d
Victor L. Brown	Develops when men don't act like men		55e
Harold B. Lee	Equally grievous as adultery	Jan 1973	106c
Robert L. Simpson	, overcome by a man	July 1973	23a
Spencer W. Kimball	There is no halfway	Nov 1974	8b
Vaughn J. Featherstone	Dad counseled son never to masturbate—never did —story	May 1975	66f-67a
Gordon B. Hinckley	Young man realized he'd have no son —story	Nov 1975	38b-d
J. Richard Clarke	Boy rejected by father becomes homosexual —story	May 1977	85b-e
	Will not occur where a normal father-son relationship exists		87c
Spencer W. Kimball	The cure for this evil is not through legislation to legalize it	Nov 1977	6a-f
Spencer W. Kimball	Church's stand on , explained - also masturbation	Nov 1980	97a-f
Gordon B. Hinckley	71% believe , is wrong—only 20% of movie writers do	Nov 1983	45c-46c

Homosexuality, cont'd
Related Topics: Chastity, Immorality, Pornography, Sex

Boyd K. Packer	A spiritually dangerous life-style	Nov 1990	84c
	Debunking current publications promoting ,		85c-d
	Life-long temptation, but repentance possible		85e-86f
Spencer J. Condie	, overcome through Book of Mormon —story	Nov 1993	16f-17b
Boyd K. Packer	Adam could not progress alone or with another man		21d
Richard G. Scott	Acts of , are evil and absolutely wrong	Nov 1994	38c
Gordon B. Hinckley	We cannot condone same sex immorality	Nov 1995	99c
Gordon B. Hinckley	The attitude of the Church towards ,	Nov 1998	71b-c
Vaughn J. Featherstone	, is wrong in spite of public opinion	Nov 1999	13f
Boyd K. Packer	Good discussion on ,	Nov 2000	73c-74f
Russell M. Nelson	Gender disorientation is poorly understood	May 2002	76e
Dallin H. Oaks	From darkness to love and gratitude	Nov 2006	8e-9a
Boyd K. Packer	Do not abuse self. No unworthy touching	May 2009	50f

Honesty
Related Topics: —

Gordon B. Hinckley	...One fewer rascal... —good quote	Dec 1968	69b
Marion D. Hanks	You forgot to look up —story		96b
Delbert L. Stapley	Example is only way to teach children ,	June 1969	70d-e
Hugh B. Brown	Honesty by serviceman —story		97d-98e
David O. McKay	Foundation of character	Dec 1969	31f
Theodore M. Burton	The more honest you are, the more successful	June 1970	84d
	No one is born honest or dishonest - We're taught		84d
	If each employee takes a pencil, how much is lost?		84e
N. Eldon Tanner	Definition of hypocrisy	Dec 1970	31f
	Two kinds of hypocrisy		33c
Victor L. Brown	3 quotes on , by David O. McKay	June 1971	56b-c
	He that telleth lies shall not tarry in my sight		56e
Delbert L. Stapley	We must correct mistakes made in our favor		105b-c
	Honest man - most enviable title —Washington		105f
Mark E. Peterson	, a principle of salvation - no salvation without ,	Dec 1971	72b-c
	Dishonesty stems from selfishness		72d
	No war nor crime if all were honest		72d
Spencer W. Kimball	Cheating your neighbor —Emerson	May 1974	89c
	The disgrace of shoplifting		89d-e
Sterling W. Sill	Mohandas Gandhi's , —story	Nov 1974	62b-c
	, of a little slave girl		62d
Spencer W. Kimball	The evils of gambling	May 1975	6c-d
Spencer W. Kimball	Don't avoid customs dues when traveling	Nov 1975	6f
Gordon B. Hinckley	A small leak will sink a great ship	May 1976	62e
Marion G. Romney	A lie is the handle that fits all sins	Nov 1976	36e
	6 aspects of lying		38b
O. Leslie Stone	Trust is a greater compliment than love		60b
N. Eldon Tanner	Boy would not leave sheep —story	May 1977	16e-17a
Vaughn J. Featherstone	Complained about shortage, but not overpayment —joke	Nov 1978	26f
James E. Faust	Money exchanged because other LDS showed , —story	Nov 1980	36d-e

James E. Faust	Bankrupt man eventually paid debts	May 1981	8f
Joseph B. Wirthlin	Builder built flawed house - for himself —story	May 1982	23f-24a
James E. Faust	Not cheating neighbor —quote by Emerson		47c-d
Robert L. Simpson	I wouldn't be dishonest. I'm a Mormon —story	May 1984	61d-f
J. Richard Clarke	Little girl confessed to breaking a compact —story		63e-64b
James E. Faust	Warning against seeking advantage over others	Nov 1986	10b-d
Dallin H. Oaks	Definition of fraud		20d-f
	, in lawsuits and to employees and employers		21a-d
	Don't victimize unwise buyers		21d-e
David B. Haight	, is the best and only policy	Nov 1987	15d
Richard G. Scott	Don't lie to self. Don't premeditate sin	May 1989	37a-b
Gordon B. Hinckley	Paying taxes is part of honesty	May 1990	51e-f
	Paying child support is part of ,		51f-52c
Thomas S. Monson	Cheating student turned pages with toes —story	Nov 1990	46b-c
George I. Cannon	"No wonder you're honest - you're Mormon" —story	Nov 1991	13e-f
Marvin J. Ashton	Those who tell white lies become color-blind		72a
James M. Paramore	Sharp business caused another to lose his —story	Nov 1992	9f-10c
Michaelene P. Grassli	Girl refused to cheat on test —story	Nov 1994	12f-13a
Thomas S. Monson	Stolen key returned mounted on plaque —story	May 1995	60b-c
Gordon B. Hinckley	A precious jewel	May 1996	49b
	Want operation done by doctor who cheated?		92a
James E. Faust	, is truth telling, truth living, truth loving	Nov 1996	41f
	Pioneer boy cut off tastes of meat —story		41f-42a
	Medical student warned cheating classmates —story		42a-d
	Stealing one's good name is the worst		43b-c
	I was under oath to say I'm the best —story		43c-d
	Breaking the rope climbing record —story		43d-44a
	President Hinckley's statement on ,		44a-b
Sheldon F. Child	Father's word as good as his bond —story	May 1997	29a-c
	Church members' creed of ,		29f
James E. Faust	His mother had to do the dishes —story	May 1998	44c-e
Thomas S. Monson	Sailors lied about ability to swim —story		47a-b
Thomas S. Monson	"Never lie," young serviceman said —story	Nov 1998	49f-50a
Thomas S. Monson	Sailors took swim test before liberty —story	Nov 2000	49a-c
James E. Faust	Girl corrected incorrect volleyball call —story	May 2003	108f-109a
Gayle M. Clegg	Boy finished story years later —story	May 2004	14b-c
Dallin H. Oaks	Many practice deception - repent	Nov 2004	45b-d
D. Todd Christofferson	Integrity even if you lose your home	Nov 2006	47d-48a
Richard C. Edgley	Three towels and a 25-cent newspaper —story		72c-73f
Joseph B. Wirthlin	Tempted to move ball 2 inches —story	May 2007	46b-e
Daniel K. Judd	Feeding horses dirt rather than grain	Nov 2007	93b-d
D. Todd Christofferson	Lack of , the cause of current recession	Nov 2009	106f-107a
	Mother put early end to his life of crime —story		107e
Thomas S. Monson	What will I think of myself?	May 2010	65b
	Cheater turned pages with toes —story		65b-d

Humility
Related Topics: —

William H. Bennett	He learned , through an inferiority complex	Dec 1970	123b
Alvin R. Dyer	Difference between , and meekness		125c
Marion D. Hanks	Humiliation must come before exaltation	Jan 1974	20e
O. Leslie Stone	, renders us teachable and easy to learn	Nov 1974	31e
	Meekness is not a weak, but a heroic quality		32a
Marvin J. Ashton	Be a team member first, a coach second	Nov 1976	85a
L. Tom Perry	G. Washington rejected a lofty title	Nov 1983	12f
Howard W. Hunter	If there was only one righteous, it would be me	May 1984	65e
Neal A. Maxwell	Blessed are the meek for they shall not be easily offended	May 1991	90e
L. Aldin Porter	H.C. Kimball's acceptance of mission call	May 1992	45c-e
Boyd K. Packer	"They'll never build the temple without me"	May 1993	19a-b
Howard W. Hunter	, is costly, but will take over the world		64f-65a
Spencer J. Condie	, is concerned with what is right - not who	Nov 1993	17d
Henry B. Eyring	Be humble by "always remembering Him"	May 1995	25b-26b
Monte J. Brough	When nice things are said about you, don't believe it	May 1997	27e-f
W. Eugene Hansen	Refresher courses in school of hard knocks	May 1998	63b
Marlin K. Jensen	Brigham's reply when rebuked by Joseph —story	May 2001	10b-c
	Atonement: greatest act of ,		10c
	Great statement of what , leads us to do		10f-11a
	The first test of a truly great man		11d
Neal A. Maxwell	Lord mentored Moses through the pronoun problem	May 2002	37f
Thomas S. Monson	John the Baptist was the model of ,	Nov 2002	60b-d
Dallin H. Oaks	J.R. Clark "demoted" to 2nd counselor		68b
	Perfect mission area humbled proud elder —story		70b-f
James E. Faust	Learn to say "I don't know" —good saying	May 2003	109b-c
Richard C. Edgley	, and gratitude bring happiness	Nov 2003	98d
	Joseph chastised Brigham as test of , —story		98d-e
	Greatness begins with ,		98e
	Entire talk —good		97b-99b
Thomas S. Monson	Humble couple served missionaries —story	May 2006	21b-e
Boyd K. Packer	Can't tell how high a frog can jump —story	Nov 2007	7b-f
Bruce D. Porter	Meaning of "broken heart and contrite spirit"		31d-32f

Humor
Related Topics: —

Hugh B. Brown	Cultivate a sense of ,	June 1969	97d
Hugh B. Brown	Short, cute story about hell —story	Dec 1969	95b
David B. Haight	You're not on a hill. Your rear wheels are off	Nov 1975	60f
Paul H. Dunn	Doctor touched his heart very deeply - Open heart surgery	Nov 1976	54b
J. Richard Clarke	Not nervous but incredibly alert		109b
Vaughn J. Featherstone	Talking to the wall —story		118d-f
Vaughn J. Featherstone	Man complained about short paycheck	Nov 1978	26f
Gordon B. Hinckley	Shortsighted man repaired building —story	Nov 1981	40b-d
Paul H. Dunn	The parachutist and the camper —story		71a-c
Marion G. Romney	Old man's response on reason for long life: Keep breathing	Nov 1982	91b
James E. Faust	If I'd been paying tithing, I'd quit	May 1983	40c

Jacob de Jager	Joke about balloonists and politicians —story	May 1983	75e
Vaughn J. Featherstone	They are all my children and it's no picnic	Nov 1983	36d-e
	Boy nearly drowned during high priest's prayer		37b-c
	To boy practicing piano "Is your mother home?"		37c
Thomas S. Monson	Bless Sister Lister	May 1984	17b-c
Elaine A. Cannon	I love holding the priesthood		25e
	Tell them, don't do it.		26b
Victor L. Brown	Humorous account of his calling —story	May 1985	14d
Robert D. Hales	Bishops: Man in a javelin-catching contest		28d
Jacob de Jager	Some finish listening before speaker finishes speaking	May 1986	71b
Wm. Grant Bangerter	His wife's first husband was perfect —story	May 1987	11f-12d
Robert L. Simpson	Man rolled up pant legs before walking on water		40b-c
Vaughn J. Featherstone	Teacher helping boy with too small boots	Nov 1987	27b
Robert L. Backman	The missionary no companion could get along with		62c
James E. Faust	Man went to ball game rather than wife's funeral	May 1988	36c
Glenn L. Pace	Why LDS people look odd to non-members	May 1989	25f-26a
Ben B. Banks	Missionary's magic trick backfired —story	Nov 1989	41d-f
James E. Faust	Homemade soap - Advantage of old age	May 1990	85b-d
James E. Faust	His mother asked "Where did I fail?"	Nov 1990	32e
	Work fascinates me. I can look at it for hours.		34c
Russell M. Nelson	Hearing test backfired on husband —story	May 1991	23a-b
Jacob de Jager	Behind every great man is a surprised mother-in-law		43d-e
Jack H. Goaslind	Lady Aster dreaded growing old		46c
David B. Haight	His first football game —story	Nov 1991	36c-e
Thomas S. Monson	"Blessed are the pacemakers"		87b-d
Vaughn J. Featherstone	"I can guess your age" —story	May 1992	43b-d
	"I don't like the looks of your husband"		43d
Stephen D. Nadauld	Twin ran into himself —story		82d-e
Thomas S. Monson	The finest missionary ever recommended —story	Nov 1992	47d
Richard G. Scott	"I'll show you how much fun it is" —story		60d-f
David E. Sorensen	Help us get married in the street —story	May 1993	30b-c
Gordon B. Hinckley	The boy who chewed his tie —story		53a
Joe J. Christensen	Boy practicing piano - "Is your mother home?"	Nov 1993	12d-e
Spencer J. Condie	If you're going to impersonate me, behave yourself		15d-e
Russell M. Nelson	"Give me the good old days - plus penicillin"		33b
H. David Burton	Captain ordered lighthouse to change course	May 1994	68d-e
Hartman Rector, Jr.	When a 70 becomes 70 he becomes emeritus	Nov 1994	25b
Monte J. Brough	The only commoner in his family	May 1995	41d
James E. Faust	Even his mother didn't dream he'd be in First Presidency		61b
Bonnie D. Parkin	Called to be general den mother		78b
Thomas S. Monson	Young want to change world - old change young		97c
Gordon B. Hinckley	Dancing stopped after they were married		99c
Harold G. Hillam	"I have never slept in a sleeping bag" —story	Nov 1995	41b-c
James E. Faust	"Which one of you is the accused?"		46c
David B. Haight	LeGrand Richards put hand over light		73b-c

Humor, cont'd

David B. Haight	Crossed Nevada going 100 MPH in Model T	Nov 1995	74a-b
F. Burton Howard	Why we can never get above 83% home teaching	May 1996	27e
	Definition of fanatic		27f
Gordon B. Hinckley	Urges us to have fun and laughter		94f
Bruce C. Hafen	"I'm at the end of my troubles"	Nov 1996	26b
	No children, no misery		26e
	That child will make Christians of us —story		27d-f
Joe J. Christensen	"Tell Jesus not to count on me"		39b
Monte J. Brough	People will say nice things about you - don't believe	May 1997	27e
Sheldon F. Child	We were blessed with enough land		29a
Jeffrey R. Holland	Humorous look at young married years		35d-e
	What we expect mothers to teach babies		36a
David B. Haight	His unevenly-matched football game —story		38e-39a
Richard B. Wirthlin	Letter terminating Medicare benefits	Nov 1997	9d-e
James M. Paramore	Dad taught son to swim	May 1998	41d-e
James E. Faust	Grandparents are overindulgent ...		95c
David B. Haight	Advanced age —joke and poem	Nov 1998	35d
Joe J. Christensen	Comfort the afflicted and afflict the comforted	May 1999	9b
	Humorous prayer for help		9b-c
James E. Faust	Humorous observation about time		17f-18e
Vaughn J. Featherstone	Thanks for passing my house	Nov 1999	14b
Joseph B. Wirthlin	"You'll grow into it" —story		38d-39b
James E. Faust	Poem for single women —poem		102b
James E. Faust	Honeyhives and mermaids	May 2000	95e-f
David B. Haight	Playing an out-of-tune violin —story	May 2001	70d-71a
Gordon B. Hinckley	Why he uses a cane		85b-c
Steven E. Snow	Hadn't seen Grand Canyon —story	Nov 2001	43d-e
Boyd K. Packer	You have everything crossed out —story		64c
Jeffrey R. Holland	His sacrifices compared to earlier missionaries'	Nov 2002	36b-d
Russell M. Nelson	Revenge will make us blind and toothless		39f
Gordon B. Hinckley	Long life attributed to fresh air	May 2003	59f
Russell M. Nelson	Senior missionaries: Hasten your shuffle	Nov 2004	79d
H. Bryan Richards	Read 150 pages in one day —story		95f-96b
Joseph B. Wirthlin	Poorest bishop we've ever had —story	May 2005	27f
M. Russell Ballard	Grateful to stand before you today	May 2006	84b
Joseph B. Wirthlin	50 cents for a dollar birthday present	Nov 2006	28e
	"I knew who you was"		28e-f
	"I couldn't hit what I couldn't see"		28f
Jeffrey R. Holland	Hit me again. I can still hear you.	May 2007	18b
	Whining makes it worse		18c
Gordon B. Hinckley	Old age attributed to fresh air	Nov 2007	66a
Gordon B. Hinckley	Speakers must have something new		83d
Richard G. Scott	Heavy man ordering doughnuts		92b-c
Claudio D. Zivic	No one ever died speaking in general conference		98b
Steven E. Snow	Mother: The travel agent for guilt trips		102b

Humor

Humor, cont'd			

Related Topics: —

Thomas S. Monson	Don't let Daddy touch the microwave	May 2008	111b
	"I forgot to mail our taxes" —story		111f-112b
Joseph B. Wirthlin	Getting lost and the blind date —2 stories	Nov 2008	26f-27c
	Autistic boy brought another baseball —story		28a-d
Boyd K. Packer	Youth speak of future because they have no past	May 2009	49d

Idleness

Related Topics: Welfare Program, Work

Alvin R. Dyer	I don't sleep long. I just sleep slow.	Dec 1971	120f
	An idle person has trouble resisting temptation		120f
	The parent of all vices		121a
	Life drives him hard who has nothing to do		121a
	Hours required for sleep varies		121d-e
Harold B. Lee	Ruins integrity	Jan 1973	61e
Robert L. Simpson	Measure of man is what he does with idle time		113d
Marion G. Romney	Human race would never survive if idle	Jan 1974	89b
	Idle mice turned into a mob —story		89d
	Will ruin any community —Brigham Young		89f
	List of scriptures on ,		89f
J. Richard Clarke	13 wasted min/day equals 2 weeks/year without pay	May 1982	78c
	Leisure is not ,		78e-f
Marion G. Romney	Sad day when a man works out a way to keep from working		87f-88d

Immorality

Related Topics: Adultery, Chastity, Homosexuality, Morality, Pornography, Purity

Mark E. Petersen	The sex revolution is destroying us	June 1969	75b-d
	Facts on , of servicemen in Asia		78d-79a
	Rejection of morality may bring fall of America		79c
David O. McKay	Statistics on premarital sex	Dec 1969	30f
	Most vicious enemy to homes		30f
Gordon B. Hinckley	Peace and freedom or enslavement and debauchery?	Dec 1970	71b-72c
	A new religion: Body Worship		72d-e
Neal A. Maxwell	, causes internal concussions and bleeding		94f
Spencer W. Kimball	Will destroy any group or nation	June 1971	19a
Mark E. Petersen	Statistics on venereal disease - now a plague		47b-d
Marion D. Hanks	Promise liberty but are servants of corruption	Jan 1973	127f
N. Eldon Tanner	, in movies —good comments	July 1973	8f
	Duty to speak out against ,		10b
Ezra Taft Benson	Greatest national problem		39a
David B. Haight	Pleasure at any price has replaced morality		56a
Spencer W. Kimball	, is totally selfish - causes 90% of divorces	May 1974	7b
Spencer W. Kimball	1/3 of firstborn children conceived out of wedlock	Nov 1974	7d-e
James E. Faust	, an epidemic plague		59b-d
N. Eldon Tanner	There are things worse than death —story		85d-e
Spencer W. Kimball	The idolatry of lust	May 1975	7a
Gordon B. Hinckley	4 ways to fight ,	Nov 1975	38b-40b
N. Eldon Tanner	The young future General Authority fled from the girl —story		75f-76c

Robert D. Hales	Letter from a girl who is making it back —story	Nov 1976	24d-26a
N. Eldon Tanner	Don't keep company with fornicators		82a
Spencer W. Kimball	No happiness if we condone , - Lift your voice	Nov 1977	5a-b
Spencer W. Kimball	Necking, petting, fornication explained	Nov 1980	94e-96e
Royden G. Derrick	, brings loss of freedom	May 1981	66b
Ezra Taft Benson	One of 3 threats to Church	May 1982	63e
Dean L. Larsen	Some youth premeditate , and eventual repentance	May 1983	34f-35f
Gordon B. Hinckley	, does irreparable damage	Nov 1983	44f-45a
Wm. Grant Bangerter	Coming through the mists —entire talk	May 1984	27b-28f
Russell M. Nelson	Misuse of sex leads to its loss	Nov 1984	31d-e
Russell M. Nelson	Who buys a minute's mirth to wail a week? —Shakespeare	Nov 1985	31e-f
Ezra Taft Benson	One of the three dangers the Church faces	May 1986	4f
Gordon B. Hinckley	Child abuse is a cause for excommunication		48e-f
Boyd K. Packer	Sins leading civilization to destruction	Nov 1986	16f-17a
	, deprives children of shelter and happiness		17f-18a
Russell M. Nelson	Joy's deadly poison		68e
Ezra Taft Benson	Petting is a form of fornication		83b-e
Gordon B. Hinckley	AIDS and how to combat it	May 1987	46e-47b
Robert L. Backman	Contrasting feelings between , and chastity —story	Nov 1989	38b-e
Thomas S. Monson	God counts women's tears	Nov 1990	47a
Russell M. Nelson	, abets the plague of AIDS	Nov 1992	8b-d
Dallin H. Oaks	We are solemnly responsible for ,	Nov 1993	74b-d
Richard G. Scott	Straight talk to young men about ,	Nov 1994	37b-39b
Howard W. Hunter	Lord forbids intimacy outside marriage		50b
Gordon B. Hinckley	The cost of teenage births —statistics		53d
Neal A. Maxwell	America's grossest national product	May 1995	67b-c
	A society which permits anything will lose everything		67d
	, desensitizes - past feeling		67f-68a
Gordon B. Hinckley	Statistics on out-of-wedlock babies and welfare	Nov 1995	99b
Gordon B. Hinckley	The term "adultery" includes fornication	May 1996	48d-e
	, will only lower self-esteem		92d-e
Gordon B. Hinckley	Some leaders have betrayed us	Nov 1998	98f-99a
Russell M. Nelson	, prevented man's donating blood to mother —story	May 1999	38d
Vaughn J. Featherstone	, is wrong even if majority accepts it	Nov 1999	13f
Gordon B. Hinckley	Why Church is involved in legislative issues		53f-54c
Neal A. Maxwell	Loss of faith in immortality gives rise to ,	Nov 2001	78e-f
	"The Seventh Commandment: A Shield"		78b-80f
James E. Faust	Just one look won't hurt?	May 2002	47b-e
Thomas S. Monson	Alexander Pope poem on embracing vice —poem	Nov 2002	54c
Gordon B. Hinckley	Plea to youth to avoid ,		58f-59f
Gordon B. Hinckley	There is no future in ,	May 2004	114a-b
Thomas S. Monson	The maka-feke of ,	May 2006	18d-e
James E. Faust	Don't approach edge of sexual enticement	May 2007	55b-d
Elaine S. Dalton	Only one opposed to premarital sex —story	May 2008	116e-117a
D. Todd Christofferson	, even in a non-TV non-Internet world	Nov 2008	38f-39b

Immorality

Dallin H. Oaks	Dealing with cohabiting children	Nov 2009	28d-29b
M. Russell Ballard	Immodest, immoral, intemperate women	May 2010	19b-c
D. Todd Christofferson	Complete reversal from a century ago		34b-d
Jeffrey R. Holland	Difference between love and lust		44e-45b

Inactivity
Related Topics: Activation, Activity

Robert L. Simpson	Song of his child brought him back —story	Dec 1969	40f
	Church music at cocktail party brought him back —story		42f
	73-year-old came back - never too late —story		43d
	The spark never goes out - fan it into flame		43e
N. Eldon Tanner	Testimony of a bishop activated by home teacher	June 1971	59f-60a
	Man having Word of Wisdom problem activated —story		60a-61a
Harold B. Lee	Statistics on inactive priesthood holders	Dec 1971	113a
	New program for bringing men out of ,		113c
	Testimony of a mother whose husband was activated		114a-e
	Wake up inactive fathers before it's too late		114e
Paul H. Dunn	Caused in 3 ways - 3 of Jesus' parables explained		119d-120a
N. Eldon Tanner	The more inactive we are, the more we criticize	July 1972	35d
Spencer W. Kimball	Ex missionary loses testimony from lack of study, prayer		38b
	2 couples reduced activity, prayer, and fell		39c
O. Leslie Stone	Himself once a prospective elder	Jan 1973	80b
Harold B. Lee	Number of inactives in church	July 1973	6b
Neal A. Maxwell	Your casualness may mean children's hostility	Nov 1974	12d-e
Spencer W. Kimball	Church got along without Oliver but not vice versa —story	May 1975	78f-79a
Marvin J. Ashton	No time for God —poem		86d
Boyd K. Packer	Come back—soon be like you never went away —story		104d-105b
Wm. Grant Bangerter	Quorum all qualified for temple recommend —story	Nov 1975	71a
Marion G. Romney	More brethren go , each year than are converted		71d
	, results from failure to appreciate covenants		72e-73a
Franklin D. Richards	Hold firesides for prospective elders	Nov 1976	16e-f
	Testimony of inactive who attended cottage meetings		17a-b
Gordon B. Hinckley	Letter from one crying for help		95b-c
	His missionary companion's reactivation —story		96d-97b
Thomas S. Monson	Man saved boy from planned , —story	May 1977	71f-72b
Spencer W. Kimball	6 steps to reduce ,	Nov 1977	45d-46b
Wm. Grant Bangerter	A great deal to throw away just to go fishing	Nov 1979	10b-c
John H. Groberg	Hawaiian overcame challenge - family stayed active —story	May 1980	49a-f
L. Tom Perry	Priests quorum met at bedside of inactive —story	Nov 1981	38d-39c
David B. Haight	Sheepherder asked conductor to sound an "A" —story		54a-c
	The road back after 16 years —story		59a-c
	Home teacher brought couple back —story		59c-e
	Home teacher brought back 86- & 84-yr-old couple —story		59e-f
Neal A. Maxwell	Good instruction on bringing people back from ,	May 1982	37b-38b
Gordon B. Hinckley	Letter from former inactive reporting on his life —story	Nov 1982	7e-8e
Robert L. Backman	How Aaronic Priesthood quorums should deal with ,		38c-d

Inactivity, cont'd
Related Topics: Activation, Activity

Vaughn J. Featherstone	Beautiful invitation to inactive to come home	Nov 1982	73a-b
Joseph B. Wirthlin	4 groups of inactives	May 1984	40b
	Spiritual conversion and social integration needed		40c
	4 stories of reactivation —story		40d-41b
L. Tom Perry	Church: I go in empty and come out full	Nov 1984	19f
Russell C. Taylor	Our duty is to be uncomfortable in complacency		23e
Thomas S. Monson	Prospective elders outnumber Mel. Priesthood holders		41f-42a
Ezra Taft Benson	Salt that has lost its savor —D&C 103:8-10	May 1985	7a
James E. Faust	Wilford Woodruff's plea to Lyman Wight	Nov 1985	9e-f
Henry B. Eyring	Light of faith is never extinguished —J.R. Clark	Nov 1986	74c-d
F. Burton Howard	Chased bishop off, later asked for recommend —story		76d-77a
L. Aldin Porter	A call was rejected - family left Church —story	Nov 1987	73e-f
Dwan J. Young	Dad, what will happen to me since we're not sealed?	May 1988	79a
Hugh W. Pinnock	Inactives activate selves. We don't.	May 1989	10f-11a
Thomas S. Monson	Elderly couple reactivated —story	Nov 1991	47e-48a
Adney Y. Komatsu	Plan activities to bring people back	May 1992	29d-31b
James E. Faust	Invitation to come back	Nov 1992	86a-b
Virginia H. Pearce	Will her convert stay or drift away?	Nov 1996	11d-12a
	Class drove man away - another brought him back —story		12d-f
Thomas S. Monson	Tithing is insurance against ,		45d-e
Thomas S. Monson	Missionaries should visit inactives	May 1997	45f-46a
Mary Ellen Smoot	Pioneers did not go into , while crossing plains	Nov 1997	14a
Thomas S. Monson	Ember goes out when alone —story		47f-48b
H. David Burton	The 5 "I's" for including the less active	Nov 1998	11b-c
Thomas S. Monson	Dam off the flow into , —story	May 1999	48d-e
Keith B. McMullin	Special meeting brought man back —story		80e-81a
Ben B. Banks	Lost lamb and lost people —story	Nov 1999	9b-10a
	Why members go into , —survey		10b-c
	Why inactives return —survey		10c
	3 things inactives need		10c
Thomas S. Monson	Former bishop brought man back —story	Nov 2001	50c-e
	He brought back a former quorum member —story		51a-f
Robert F. Orton	No one had ever said "I love you" to man —story		81f
F. Melvin Hammond	Visit to father brought family back —story	Nov 2002	97f-98b
Thomas S. Monson	Couple left , because of service assignment —story	Nov 2003	58f-59d
Dallin H. Oaks	Only half will be ready when Savior comes	May 2004	8b-d
Thomas S. Monson	, arrested by magazine representative —story		22d-23d
Russell M. Nelson	Fruit detached from roots can't survive		28a-e
Ned B. Roueche	The gratitude of one who was brought back —story	Nov 2004	30b-c
Joseph B. Wirthlin	Anger caused , - Kindness activated —story	May 2005	26b-d
Richard G. Hinckley	Bishop asked inactives to speak in Church	May 2006	49a-d
David A. Bednar	Visiting inactives who have been offended	Nov 2006	89b-f
Joseph B. Wirthlin	Counsel for those who are weary	May 2008	18e-19b
	"Restricted Entrance - Perfect People Only"		19b-f
	No apology to those with doctrinal concerns		19f-20a

Inactivity

Neil L. Andersen	"We are back, but we are back alone"	Nov 2009	42e-f
Yoon Hwan Choi	Nine Korean youth joined Church —entire talk		53b-55b
Bradley D. Foster	Distractions don't have to be evil —story	May 2010	99b-f

Gordon B. Hinckley	Reform the world by starting with self and family	Dec 1968	69b
Gordon B. Hinckley	Behavior of the masses is the behavior of ,	June 1969	74e
	Every great institution is the shadow of an ,		75a
Sterling W. Sill	We might feel like worshipping the most ordinary ,	Dec 1969	47c
Hartman Rector, Jr.	Every , is superior in some respect		82e
Robert L. Simpson	One important thing not here 10 years ago - me —story	June 1970	82b-c
Sterling W. Sill	Fight as though whole battle depended on you	Dec 1970	82a-c
Paul H. Dunn	Are lost in 3 ways - Explanation of 3 of Jesus' parables	Dec 1971	119d-120a
	Beggar shown worth, begs no more —poem		120e
Marion D. Hanks	Child who saw 17 important , in class —story	Jan 1973	127e
Paul H. Dunn	Teach toward , - red schoolhouse —story	July 1973	30b
	Programs exist to help ,		31d
	Saving a youth and losing property —story		31f
Eldred G. Smith	Concise statement showing importance of ,	Jan 1974	63e
Sterling W. Sill	Hearts can inspire other hearts with its fire —poem	Nov 1974	61e-f
Franklin D. Richards	Power of , in promoting peace in home		106c-f
Thomas S. Monson	A man with God is always in the majority	May 1975	15f
Robert D. Hales	Be self-sufficient but not independent of help of others	Nov 1975	91f
John H. Vandenberg	You are your greatest treasure	May 1976	25e
N. Eldon Tanner	Most pitiable is one who is uncomfortable in own company		44e
N. Eldon Tanner	One cell of battery foamed and fumed —story	Nov 1976	74e-75b
Marvin J. Ashton	Personal Conduct —entire talk		84b-86b
Paul H. Dunn	God is still concerned about the , —good story	Nov 1977	25b-c
Spencer W. Kimball	Time for , to move. Church poised for major progress	May 1979	82b-f
Boyd K. Packer	The Lord knew there was such a person as me —story	May 1980	63b-e
Robert L. Backman	You will never amount to a hill of beans —story	Nov 1980	40b-f
Marvin J. Ashton	I'm somebody cause God don't make no junk	Nov 1981	89b
Thomas S. Monson	Worth of the , —poem	Nov 1983	19c-d
Neal A. Maxwell	Can't know who we are without knowing where came from	May 1986	35a
David B. Haight	Human potential is most squandered resource	May 1987	60d-e
Thomas S. Monson	The five most important words build up ,	Nov 1987	68f-69a
Marvin J. Ashton	The worth of the , —G.Q. Cannon	May 1989	21b
Thomas S. Monson	The worth of a soul is its capacity to become as God	Nov 1989	45e-46b
	Joseph Millett story		46d-f
	Past stake president helped but died next day —story		47b-48a
David B. Haight	God knows names of stars and ,		59b-e
Howard W. Hunter	Can't change world but can change self	May 1990	61e
James E. Faust	Handcart girl took care of self —story		87a-d
Neal A. Maxwell	Selfishness - Excessive concern with self	Nov 1990	14b-16f
Russell M. Nelson	Who am I?		73e-74a

Individual, cont'd
Related Topics: Man, Nobody

George I. Cannon	A bee is not an eagle but makes honey	Nov 1991	14c
David B. Haight	You have the potential to become a god		37b
Thomas S. Monson	Only existing photos of family given to man —story	May 1992	49f-50a
Chieko N. Okazaki	, starts mass movements and revolutions		95f
Robert L. Backman	What to do with the golden years	Nov 1992	13d-15b
Dallin H. Oaks	Protection of guardian angels		39b
	His encounter with a robber —story		39b-40b
	Personal protection —entire talk		37b-40b
Thomas S. Monson	The Lord knew Joseph Millett —story	May 1993	61b-d
	Elderly need to belong and be loved		62b
	You will one day be old, too —folktale		62b-d
Chieko N. Okazaki	So interconnected that we must be kind to everyone —story		84b-85f
Boyd K. Packer	Gender did not begin at birth	Nov 1993	21b
Virginia H. Pearce	The ward knew the little boy's name —story		79f-80a
Chieko N. Okazaki	Crazy quilts or predictable patterns		94d-e
	Her life story		94f-95d
	Her changing circumstances through life		96b
Virginia H. Pearce	God knows you —excellent talk	May 1994	92b-94b
Thomas S. Monson	What is the worth of a soul? —story	Nov 1994	43c-e
Howard W. Hunter	A personal priesthood blessing from the prophet		88f
Russell M. Nelson	"Peculiar people" means "valued treasure"	May 1995	34b-c
Gordon B. Hinckley	Global Church still concerned with ,		52d-53c
Bonnie D. Parkin	Most important things in Church done as ,		78e-f
James E. Faust	The unimaginable potential of each ,	Nov 1995	47c-f
Thomas S. Monson	God placed him where he could rescue girl —story		48e-49b
Russell M. Nelson	We may become like God		87f-88b
Chieko N. Okazaki	Fruit in bottles or baskets - both are good	May 1996	13a-b
F. Burton Howard	An anonymous hero in scripture - Abram's servant		28b-e
Jeffrey R. Holland	Anonymous heroines in scripture - 2 widows		29b-f
Thomas S. Monson	Spirit told him to check woman in next bed —story	Nov 1996	18f-19d
Bruce C. Hafen	Destroying or building self-esteem —stories		26f-27a
Joe J. Christensen	You are a great work in progress		40b
Richard G. Scott	Gender existed before coming to earth		73d
Wm. Rolfe Kerr	Kicked out of home - 100's of descendants —story		81b-f
	The power of one person —entire talk		80b-81f
Boyd K. Packer	You by nature are good	May 1997	10a-b
Thomas S. Monson	, most influenced by teachers who care		46a-b
M. Russell Ballard	Ordinary people did heroic things		60b-c
Richard G. Scott	You don't fit where you don't belong	Nov 1998	70a-b
L. Tom Perry	We are "Junior angels"		74a-c
Thomas S. Monson	23 years of service blessing everyone —story	May 2000	54d-e
Russell M. Nelson	Would a piece of granite be missed from building?		85f-86a
Ronald A. Rasband	Mission president inspired to ask elder to pray —story	Nov 2000	29f-30b
Joseph B. Wirthlin	Don't have to be better than someone else	Nov 2001	27c
Jeffrey R. Holland	Jealousy and the other prodigal - We aren't competing	May 2002	62d-64f

Individual

Sharon G. Larsen	Alone and in good company —story	May 2002	91d
	Moroni was not alone - angels and Holy Ghost		91e-f
James E. Faust	"What's in it for me?" —selfish attorney story	Nov 2002	19b-c
	Selfishness —entire talk		19b-22b
Anne C. Pingree	Together individuals can alter the world		108d-f
Elaine S. Dalton	Choices affect generations —story	May 2003	105d
	Choices affect generations —story		106e
Dallin H. Oaks	Plan is based on , choice and effort	Nov 2003	39f-40b
Russell M. Nelson	Things only an , can do		44d-e
James E. Faust	We are the sum of our ancestors		53e-f
Sydney S. Reynolds	Mother was inspired to call —story		76c-d
	Portuguese testimony thwarted planned inactivity —story		76d-f
	Eye doctor noticed man and restored sight —story		76f-78a
M. Russell Ballard	, is known of God by name.	May 2004	84d-87f
	Infinite atonement applied one by one		84d-87f
Dale E. Miller	Jesus died for us as individuals	Nov 2004	13c
Boyd K. Packer	Church was a family eating cold corn on a curb		87d-f
	Oliver Granger and ordinary , are the Church		86d-88f
Harold G. Hillam	One of 1000 was active Church member	May 2005	32b-d
	The possible influence of one ,		32b-33f
David A. Bednar	How to become God's chosen		100f-101e
	Man's work and God's work		101f-102a
Elaine S. Dalton	God knows each , by name - a list		109f-110a
Merrill J. Bateman	Atonement accomplished for us individually	Nov 2005	75e-76b
David F. Evans	Hinckley's mission - Forget self	May 2006	32f-33d
Thomas S. Monson	What is the worth of a soul? —story		56b-c
Joseph B. Wirthlin	Plowhorse became champion jumper —story		99b-f
	Potential we can scarcely imagine		101d-102b
Paul B. Pieper	A small choice by an , affected thousands	Nov 2006	12e-f
M. Russell Ballard	Focus on people and principles - not programs		18d-f
Anthony D. Perkins	How to overcome feelings of inadequacy		76d-78f
Thomas S. Monson	Holy Ghost told him to speak to girl in balcony —story	May 2007	42b-e
James E. Faust	Each is a unique creation		56d-e
Gordon B. Hinckley	There is no limit to your potential		115d-e
Boyd K. Packer	Brigham Young no better than my grandpa —story	Nov 2007	7b-f
	Leaders have no more worth than ordinary members		8f-9a
	General Authorities are the same as ordinary people		9a-b
Thomas S. Monson	Non-member widow heard talk about herself —story		21d-24f
Henry B. Eyring	Forget self - Pray for others		57a-b
Claudio D. Zivic	I choose not to be an ordinary man		98b-d
Joseph B. Wirthlin	Jesus always sought the one	May 2008	18a
	Different? Orchestras don't value only piccolos		18b-c
Dean R. Burgess	"Do you know who you are?"		53b-55b
Dieter F. Uchtdorf	Monson focused on the one —story		69a-70a
D. B. Neuenschwander	The power of one - 3 scriptural examples		101d-103b

Individual, cont'd
Related Topics: Man, Nobody

Susan W. Tanner	Youth individually resisted peer temptations	May 2008	113f-114b
	Took self to church - Became general Relief Society pres.		114d
Elaine S. Dalton	Only one opposed to premarital sex —story		116e-117a
Henry B. Eyring	You will influence thousands		125f
Lawrence E. Corbridge	Any , can become like Jesus	Nov 2008	35f-36f
Dieter F. Uchtdorf	Sons of Helaman could not do it alone		56a
Henry B. Eyring	Unity cannot come to us as individuals		69d
Dieter F. Uchtdorf	Your spirit is a masterpiece		118e-119d
Claudio R. M. Costa	Responsibility of , to grow spiritually	May 2009	58d-e
Elaine S. Dalton	You are not common or ordinary		121a-b
	Everything about us must be different		122a-f
	You are being tapped on the shoulder —Churchill		123a
Dieter F. Uchtdorf	Eloquent description of God's love for the ,	Nov 2009	22e-23a
Quentin L. Cook	Stewards over bodies, minds, families, properties		91e
Julie B. Beck	Act as if everything depends on you —Joseph Smith		114d-e
Boyd K. Packer	Ultimate purpose of activities is perfecting ,	May 2010	9f-10a
Dieter F. Uchtdorf	Center of the universe syndrome		57d-e
Dieter F. Uchtdorf	Each , is a VIP to Heavenly Father		69b-d
	Crumpled, torn, but still worth $20		69d-e
Elaine S. Dalton	You are elect - Shine forth		121b-c
	I was born to be a king —story		121d

Intelligence
Related Topics: Knowledge

Joseph Anderson	Inventors receive , from God	Jan 1973	49c
Gordon B. Hinckley	Work of world not done by geniuses		91f
Elray L. Christiansen	Satan had knowledge but not ,	Nov 1974	22f
Angel Abrea	, is knowledge and its proper application	May 1988	26b

Interviewing
Related Topics: Counsel

N. Eldon Tanner	Advice and instruction on ,	Nov 1978	41c-43a
Carlos E. Asay	, children - wet or dry? —story	Nov 1983	14b-c
	Alma's and Helaman's ,		14d-15a
	Interview with son dispelled parent's fear —story		15a-c
Russell M. Nelson	Interviews are dress rehearsals for Judgment	Nov 1990	75e
Boyd K. Packer	Need for , will decrease with more reverence		23a-b
Gordon B. Hinckley	Substance of interview with Mike Wallace		48b-51f
Russell M. Nelson	Interviews are dress rehearsals for Judgment		75e
Gordon B. Hinckley	Substance of interview with Mike Wallace	Nov 1996	48b-51f
Joseph B. Wirthlin	Purpose is to teach and prepare for final judgment	May 1997	16f
Thomas S. Monson	His interview to receive Melchizedek Priesthood —story	May 2006	55d-56b
Richard G. Scott	A private priesthood interview with Elder Scott	Nov 2008	45a-f
M. Russell Ballard	How to monthly interview sons	Nov 2009	48f-50b

Hartman Rector, Jr.	Impossible to love him whom we do not know	Dec 1968	49c
Sterling W. Sill	Understands occupational and personal problems		104a-c
Marion D. Hanks	What , was and did —a summary	June 1969	54a-f
Gordon B. Hinckley	What relevance has , for us?		74a
	The conqueror of death - the master of life		74c
John Longden	What you think of , is largely what you will be —McKay		113f
Mark E. Petersen	Easier to accept now	Dec 1969	99f
	Church's testimony of Christ		100e
Joseph Fielding Smith	We are children of , by adoption	June 1970	26f
Harold B. Lee	Role of , in relation to the Father	Dec 1970	29c
Thomas S. Monson	Passed beneath all things to save all life	June 1971	97c
Joseph Fielding Smith	Love for , comes through study and keeping His law	Dec 1971	27e
Mark E. Petersen	Knows the burden of sin		74d
Bruce R. McConkie	I Believe in Christ —poem	July 1972	109c-e
Ezra Taft Benson	True greatness is closeness to ,	Jan 1973	57d
	Be as , - study His life		59e
Harold B. Lee	Present at General Conference		134d
Harold B. Lee	April 6, birthday of Christ	July 1973	2a
Boyd K. Packer	Explaining Christ and resurrection to children		53b
	His testimony of Christ to children		54b
S. Dilworth Young	Cannot know , unless we see Him		113f
	His suffering in Gethsemane		114d
Spencer W. Kimball	The soldier who turned , away —story	Jan 1974	14b
Spencer W. Kimball	April 6th the birthday of ,	May 1974	4b
Howard W. Hunter	Jesus' final days and hours —entire talk		17a-19f
Thomas S. Monson	6 paths , walked		48f-49c
S. Dilworth Young	Prophecies fulfilled by ,		59a-e
David B. Haight	What does , mean to modern man?		69f-70d
Spencer W. Kimball	The writing of Ben Hur —story		119c-d
	George F. Richards' dream of the Savior		119d-e
	George Q. Cannon saw him		119e-f
Spencer W. Kimball	, gives offense because of moral austerity	Nov 1974	7e
Marvin J. Ashton	Jesus' positive attitude during last week		42e-43b
Spencer W. Kimball	The hinge of history is on the door of a Bethlehem stable	May 1975	4c
	Born 6 April		4c
Joseph Anderson	, always referred to God as Father		29f-30a
Marion G. Romney	Why , had power over death		83c-84a
Gordon B. Hinckley	Why Church doesn't use the cross		92d-f
	Description of crucifixion —good		93c-e
Neal A. Maxwell	More intelligent than brightest mortals in every field	May 1976	26d-e
	Jesus' grip on himself was our hold on eternity		26e
	Shares his perfect work with imperfect us		27b-c
Eldred G. Smith	, created millions of worlds		67e-f
William R. Bradford	Are you following , ? —entire talk		97d-98f
Howard W. Hunter	Had capacity to sin	Nov 1976	19a

LeGrand Richards	Did , lay down his body twice?	Nov 1976	65b-66b
Loren C. Dunn	John Murdock's description of ,	May 1977	30d-f
Boyd K. Packer	The mediator —entire talk		54b-56f
Joseph B. Wirthlin	Theologians contend , not Son of God	Nov 1978	37b-c
Marion D. Hanks	Only 1 of the 3 men recognized , at the gate —story	May 1980	29e-30a
Robert E. Wells	23rd Psalm - Actor knew words, old man knew , —story	Nov 1980	12b-e
	Know , thru study, prayer, revelation —E.T. Benson		12e
	Am I loving, studying and serving enough to know ,		13f
Vaughn J. Featherstone	His punishments will be lightest possible—rewards maximum		31c
Marion G. Romney	2 great missions: Atonement and relief of suffering		92d
James E. Faust	, stood in midst of Apostles —story	May 1981	8b-c, 10c
Neal A. Maxwell	Beautiful declarations of who , is and what He did	Nov 1981	8d-10f
Bruce R. McConkie	Would you have believed , had you lived 2,000 years ago?		46b-d 48d-f
	Are Mormons Christians?		47b-48a
Marion G. Romney	The Resurrection of , —excellent talk	May 1982	6a-9b
George P. Lee	, His life and purpose —entire talk good	Nov 1982	73d-75f
Mark E. Petersen	Scriptures saying He is the creator	May 1983	64b-65b
G. Homer Durham	Meaning of the word "Jesus"	May 1984	14e-15a
	Man's search for "saviors" —Toynbee		16a-b
Russell M. Nelson	The fundamentals of our religion center on ,		53c
Howard W. Hunter	, created the waters, so He can calm them	Nov 1984	33b-f
Gordon B. Hinckley	The chief cornerstone of 4		51a-d
	A short synopsis of his life		51d-52a
Bruce R. McConkie	McConkie's account of the Atonement	May 1985	9e-10e
James E. Faust	, and the Atonement —entire talk		30d-32f
Ezra Taft Benson	Takes slums out of people—they take selves out of slums.	Nov 1985	6e-f
J. Thomas Fyans	Who may see ,		90d-e
Dallin H. Oaks	A sacred and powerful name	May 1986	51a
Ezra Taft Benson	Over 1/2 of verses and 100 names in B of M refer to ,	Nov 1987	83b-c
	Attributes of , as given in Book of Mormon		83c-f
	Book of Mormon convinces of and commits to ,		84a-b
	We must daily take His name upon us		85d-e
Howard W. Hunter	What , suffered and paid for	May 1988	16e-17a
Gordon B. Hinckley	His Atonement and resurrection —entire talk		65b-68f
Dallin H. Oaks	Teachings of other churches about ,	Nov 1988	65b-d
	I am the captain of my soul and Whitney's answer —poems		67a-c
Neal A. Maxwell	Withdrawal of Father's spirit made , fully comprehending	May 1989	64e
Jeffrey R. Holland	The last hours and the sacrifice of ,	Nov 1989	25b-26f
David B. Haight	Testimony of , resulting from near-death experience —story		59e-61b
Thomas S. Monson	What would He have me do?		69d-e
Neal A. Maxwell	Only , is both willing and able to take our sins		85a
Thomas S. Monson	, will reveal Himself in our trials and conflicts	May 1990	5f
Richard P. Lindsay	Christ or detours to doom - the choice		14e
Thomas S. Monson	A child and the Christus statue —story		54e-f
Russell M. Nelson	Summary of who He is		77e-f

Jesus

Howard W. Hunter	He is greatest whose life approaches ,	Nov 1990	18d-e
Dallin H. Oaks	, was not mentioned in sacrament meeting		30a
	, is fundamental principle of Church		30a-b
	People no longer have a fundamental belief in ,		31d-f
Francis M. Gibbons	Joseph Smith and Jesus compared	May 1991	32b-33f
Neal A. Maxwell	We naively expect , to come to us		90e
Gordon B. Hinckley	President Benson's testimony of Jesus' influence	Nov 1991	4b-5b
Robert L. Backman	More important than a king —story		8b-d
	Misquoted 23rd psalm puts , in perspective		8d-e
	, —excellent talk		8b-10b
Rex D. Pinegar	Third on list of most influential people		39b-d
	What would , want you to do? - Sunday campout —story		41a-b
Marion D. Hanks	Mission of Church is to bring people to ,	May 1992	9a-c
Thomas S. Monson	No room in the inn —beautiful phraseology		60e-f
Gordon B. Hinckley	Ezra Taft Benson's beautiful testimony of ,		89c-d
Howard W. Hunter	Peter only sank when his eyes left ,	Nov 1992	19a-f
Neal A. Maxwell	Each is an innkeeper deciding if room for ,		66f
Richard G. Scott	, must be first priority	May 1993	34f
Howard W. Hunter	The source of light, and life, and love		63f
Gordon B. Hinckley	President Benson's stirring testimony of ,		93c-e
Jeffrey R. Holland	Trust , - Family facing leukemia —story	Nov 1993	14f-15b
Howard W. Hunter	The only perfect example —good talk	May 1994	64b-f
Merrill J. Bateman	Jesus bridges the gap —Optician's conversion story		65f-66b
H. David Burton	Live so people can see , in you		68f
Gordon B. Hinckley	His resurrection is best attested event		72b-f
David B. Haight	Description of , last hours —entire talk		75d-78b
F. Melvin Hammond	Panoramic view of Jesus' life —good		82d-83f
Howard W. Hunter	His emphasis: Follow Jesus' example	Nov 1994	8d
Bruce D. Porter	We are all prodigal sons —great talk on , as our Redeemer	Nov 1995	15b-16b
Boyd K. Packer	Jesus' work is not finished		20f-21a
Neal A. Maxwell	We either serve , or other masters		22f-23a
Dallin H. Oaks	Whatever builds people serves ,		26f-27c
Robert E. Wells	First and Only Begotten - His role		65b-e
Carlos E. Asay	As long as Peter looked to , he stayed on top	May 1996	60b-d
Gordon B. Hinckley	His death and resurrection		66e-67f
Russell M. Nelson	An infinite being - in many ways	Nov 1996	35a-b
Joseph B. Wirthlin	What we believe about ,		70f-71c
M. Russell Ballard	Rescue of handcart company compared to our rescue by ,	May 1997	61e-f
L. Edward Brown	Moses learned there is power in name of ,		79a-d
	More than a way to end a talk or prayer		79f
Thomas S. Monson	Come unto me, come learn, come follow		94e
Neal A. Maxwell	Irony was one of His trials	Nov 1997	23c-d
Robert D. Hales	Where light of , is darkness must depart		26b
Jeffrey R. Holland	Need for , —beautiful talk		64d-66f
Sheri L. Dew	Our responsibility to know , and how to do it		91f-92e

Jesus, cont'd
Related Topics: Atonement, God, Resurrection, Second Coming

Russell M. Nelson	, did not finish his work when he was slain	May 1998	36b
Margaret D. Nadauld	Twin's compassion was like that of , —story		64c-e
Thomas S. Monson	Good testimony of how to be like ,	Nov 1998	51b
Gordon B. Hinckley	Statement about our beliefs about ,		70f-71b
Jeffrey R. Holland	The special relationship between , and God	May 1999	14d-15c
Stephen A. West	Examples of Christlike love —stories		28a-29f
Sheri L. Dew	Rescued by their father in blizzard —story		66d-e
	, is our only chance		66e-f
	What , does for us —a list		67a
	How we come to ,		67b-c
	Is it possible to be happy when life is hard?		67c-d
	Whatever , lays his hands upon lives —H.W. Hunter		67d-e
Gordon B. Hinckley	Powerful testimony of Jesus and resurrection		70b-72f
Jeffrey R. Holland	The light at the end of the tunnel is ,	Nov 1999	36b-37c
Russell M. Nelson	, is central focus of Book of Mormon		69b-f
Gordon B. Hinckley	Calendar based on greatest event in history		72d-73b
Sheri L. Dew	Come unto , by walking away from world		98a-b
	Litmus test: Does it lead us to , ?		98b-c
	Come unto , by giving up worldly indulgences		98f-99b
James E. Faust	Master pianist put arms around student —story		101b-c
Harold G. Hillam	Knowing , requires obedience, prayer and revelation	May 2000	11b-c
Joseph B. Wirthlin	A life centered on , cannot fail —H.W. Hunter		61b-c
Russell M. Nelson	Old Egyptian manuscript explains Atonement		84e-f
D. Todd Christofferson	5 things we believe about ,	Nov 2000	10b
M. Russell Ballard	Can we tell , we were too shy to do missionary work?		76f
L. Aldin Porter	A witness of , comes from reading Book of Mormon	May 2001	30b-32b
Charles Didier	Compared to a bridge —entire talk	Nov 2001	10b-12b
Russell M. Nelson	Don't cling to children but to , —raft story		69b-e
Dallin H. Oaks	"What's he done for me?" —story	May 2002	33d-f
John M. Madsen	Testimony of the Apostles on who , is		78f-79a
Gene R. Cook	Think about Him, act like Him, become like Him		83f
Gordon B. Hinckley	Critics say we don't believe in traditional ,		90f-91b
James E. Faust	A testimony begins with , and Joseph Smith	Nov 2003	19f
Shirley D. Christensen	The Testimony of the Apostles		34a-b
W. Craig Zwick	Blind man ran marathon —story		36d-f
Thomas S. Monson	The Bridge Builder —poem		70a-b
D. Todd Christofferson	How to give , gifts	May 2004	12d-f
Keith B. McMullin	Created millions of worlds		34b-d
	Description of his life and mission —good		34d-35a
	, —poem by Joseph Smith		35a-c
Joseph B. Wirthlin	Paid debt He didn't owe to free us from debt we can't pay		43d
Dale E. Miller	He died for us individually	Nov 2004	13c
Cecil O. Samuelson, Jr.	What eyewitnesses said of ,		51b-c
James E. Faust	A testimony of , is of inestimable value		52c-d
Thomas S. Monson	Jesus' example —good quote	May 2005	22f

Jesus

L. Tom Perry	Convert progressed when focus was on ,	May 2005	85d-f
David A. Bednar	Choice of hymn showed his tender mercy —story		99b-e
James E. Faust	One of 4 "absolutes"	Nov 2005	21d
Boyd K. Packer	Curriculum restructured to center on ,		72f
Merrill J. Bateman	Jesus' death a voluntary act		75b-e
Russell M. Nelson	His names and titles		85c
	Why did , have to suffer so much?		87a-f
Boyd K. Packer	What He made, He can fix	May 2006	28a
Jeffrey R. Holland	The need to "Come unto Jesus"		69b-f
	How to "Come unto Jesus"		69f-70f
	He knows the way because He is the way		70f-71a
	Fixes broken things —poem		71d-f
Earl C. Tingey	The condescension of , —John Taylor		73d-74a
Richard H. Winkel	Everything in temple testifies of ,	Nov 2006	11b
James E. Faust	What is discipleship?		20d-f
	Things , did which we can emulate		21b-e
D. Todd Christofferson	What , did that we should emulate		48b-e
Boyd K. Packer	The ensign to which we rally		88d
Thomas S. Monson	Description of His life and resurrection	May 2007	24f-25f
H. David Burton	Bruce R. McConkie's dying testimony of ,		33d-f
Gordon B. Hinckley	Jehovah - The Creator - The Messiah		83e-84c
Jeffrey R. Holland	How can we be like , if He is incomprehensible?	Nov 2007	40f-41c
	Christians can't claim , is unembodied		42a
Henry B. Eyring	In no instance was His life easy		57e-f
Robert D. Hales	The 4 times God introduced ,	May 2008	30d
	, created all things		31a
Carlos H. Amado	He came here to give his life		35b-c
	Things , cannot do		36b
Susan W. Tanner	Holy Ghost testified of , to convert —story		113b-d
Lawrence E. Corbridge	The way, the light, the resurrection, the Bread of Life	Nov 2008	34d-36f
Robert D. Hales	Endured mocking with silence and love		72b-e
Keith B. McMullin	How careful we must be with his name		77f-78a
Thomas S. Monson	His gratitude for ,		87f-88b
William D. Oswald	The Master Teacher		96d-e
Dieter F. Uchtdorf	Always helping others - Did not compete		120d
Rafael E. Pino	No infirmity, affliction or adversity not felt by ,	May 2009	41f-42d
Jeffrey R. Holland	Vivid description of His last days —entire talk		86b-88f
Robert D. Hales	How we know God and , are separate individuals	Nov 2009	30b-31a
Neil L. Andersen	Jesus' arms		40b-d
Boyd K. Packer	Be quiet while I untie the knot —poem		46d
Henry B. Eyring	Trying to be like ,		70b-f
	Becoming like , through love		70f-71b
	Becoming like , - Becoming like children		72e-73b
D. Todd Christofferson	Disciples of , who is a disciple of Father		105f-106d
	A choice: Yoke of , or yoke of Caesar		106f-107a

Jesus, cont'd
Related Topics: Atonement, God, Resurrection, Second Coming

D. Todd Christofferson	What , is imagined to be today	May 2010	34b-d
Jeffrey R. Holland	Our sins hurt family and ,		46b-c
Dieter F. Uchtdorf	Statue of , lost hands —story		68a-c
	He didn't just teach a class on love		70d-e
Richard G. Scott	3 challenges , faced during Atonement		76f-77a
	Accomplished Atonement totally on His own		77a-b
	Jesus and the Atonement — entire talk		75c-78b
Quentin L. Cook	Initiated 3 doctrines at Last Supper		83e-f
	The fundamental principles of our religion are…		84a
	Focus is on resurrected Lord —Farrar		84b
	LDS symbol of Christ is our faith and lives		84b
	Never prepared defense against accusers		84c-d
Thomas S. Monson	The creation, death, Atonement, resurrection		87a-90f
Bradley D. Foster	Last act was to care for mother		100e-f
James B. Martino	5 things we learn from His trials		101a-103b
Neil L. Andersen	Stories of , like wind over embers		108f-109a
	Counsel: Speak more frequently of ,		109f
	His life, Atonement, Resurrection, return are sure		111f
Thomas S. Monson	No fog so dense, no night so dark…		113b-d

Joseph Smith
Related Topics: —

Milton R. Hunter	Produced more scripture than any other	Dec 1968	60f
Marion G. Romney	Developed by tribulation	Dec 1969	67e
Paul H. Dunn	Observations on his call. Jeremiah was also 14.		106d
Gordon B. Hinckley	Poetical summary of work of , —P.P. Pratt	June 1970	39f-40a
Paul H. Dunn	Description of , - physical and spiritual		70f-73e
Marion G. Romney	Authenticity of Church and Book of Mormon rest upon ,	Dec 1970	51b-d
LeGrand Richards	, was the messenger spoken of in Malachi		69e-70a
S. Dilworth Young	Saw more than the original 12 saw	June 1971	39f
A. Theodore Tuttle	No greater prophet than ,		70a
	All are subject to accepting , to get to heaven		70b
Theodore M .Burton	After First Vision knew more than anyone about God	Dec 1971	80b
Spencer W. Kimball	Waited for priesthood	Jan 1973	33f
Marvin J. Ashton	An obscure boy but not a nobody	July 1973	26a
LeGrand Richards	Malachi speaks of ,		76f
	Spoken of in Book of Mormon		78e
Henry D. Taylor	Could not translate until he made up with Emma	Jan 1974	37b
Harold B. Lee	Those will be forgotten who revile ,		126a
Boyd K. Packer	Not a genius but an ordinary man	May 1974	94b-c
LeGrand Richards	Was the messenger spoken of in Malachi		116d-e
Robert L. Simpson	Your eternal life depends on ,	Nov 1974	47e
Marion G. Romney	Courage and majesty at midnight —story	May 1975	72d-f
Spencer W. Kimball	His youthful age during various events		80c
Bruce R. McConkie	Once or Twice in 1,000 years —entire talk good	Nov 1975	15d-18f
Bruce R. McConkie	Two letters: One orders that , be executed	May 1976	96e

LeGrand Richards	Doubters of , should try to write a revelation	Nov 1976	66c-e
Gordon B. Hinckley	, the man and what he accomplished —entire talk	May 1977	64b-66b
N. Eldon Tanner	2 statements about historical significance of ,	Nov 1979	51f-52a
J. Thomas Fyans	Could have told you what Adam looked like	Nov 1980	53d
Bruce R. McConkie	Do Mormons worship , ?	Nov 1981	47b-48a
James E. Faust	The life and accomplishments of , —entire talk		75d-77f
Neal A. Maxwell	, could not compose a well-worded letter	Nov 1983	54b-c
	A blessing given to , by his father		54c-d
	His letter of forgiveness to Phelps		55b-c
	Similarity of persecutions of prophets		55f
	His care of a neighbor's child —story		56a
	Two stories of , compassion —story		56b-c
James E. Faust	If First Vision a fraud , would have said Father taught him	May 1984	68c
	Impressions of , by his contemporaries		68d-69f
Neal A. Maxwell	, never claimed perfection	Nov 1984	10d-f
Gordon B. Hinckley	First Vision is one of 4 cornerstones of the Church		52a-c
Rex C. Reeve	Was foreordained to be a prophet	Nov 1985	78d-f
	Vermont snows forced his parents to move		79a
Neal A. Maxwell	, added nearly 900 pages of scripture	May 1986	34e
Ted E. Brewerton	, had 19-year-old throw the champion wrestler —story	Nov 1986	30d-f
Gordon B. Hinckley	Testimonies about , from those who knew him	May 1987	54a-59b
Carlos E. Asay	, and the Restoration —excellent talk	May 1990	62d-65b
Francis M. Gibbons	Jesus and , compared	May 1991	32b-33f
M. Russell Ballard	The family of , —excellent talk	Nov 1991	5d-7f
Neal A. Maxwell	"My Servant Joseph" —entire talk	May 1992	37d-39f
Carlos E. Asay	, rebuking guards —story		41f-42a
Joseph B. Wirthlin	Articles of Faith are evidence of his divine calling		86b-c
V. Dallas Merrell	Testimony of Jewish scholar about ,	May 1993	28b-c
Marlin K. Jensen	, rebuking guards —P.P. Pratt quote	May 1994	47e-48b
Gordon B. Hinckley	His life compared to Governor Ford's		72f-74b
L. Aldin Porter	Restored doctrines, powers, keys, priesthood, ordinances	Nov 1994	62f
James E. Faust	How , got the keys		72d
	Brigham's and Wilford's reaction to death of ,		72d-f
Robert K. Dellenbach	The miracle of the Book of Mormon translation	May 1995	9d-11b
M. Russell Ballard	A tribute to the life of Hyrum Smith	Nov 1995	6b-9b
Robert E. Wells	His accomplishments - Taught by angels		65f-66c
Keith B. McMullin	List of angels who came to ,	May 1996	9e-f
Dallin H. Oaks	Joseph, The Man and The Prophet —entire talk		71b-73f
Thomas S. Monson	Tyndale's prophecy of a ploughboy	May 1997	51c-e
L. Tom Perry	His preparation required a decade		69a-b
M. Russell Ballard	His appearance as he received revelation	May 1998	31c-e
David E. Sorensen	Church will fill the world —prophecy by ,	Nov 1998	64b-c
John K. Carmack	Our pathway to Savior is through ,	May 2001	77f
Virginia U. Jensen	His prayer in a grove was preceded by his mother's	Nov 2001	95b-d
Carlos H. Amado	Principles learned from , —story	May 2002	80b-81f

Joseph Smith

Joseph Smith, cont'd
Related Topics: —

Robert K. Dellenbach	The sacrifices of ,	Nov 2002	33f-34e
Gordon B. Hinckley	Restoration came through unschooled boy		80b-81f
James E. Faust	I could join your church if , was taken out	Nov 2003	19f-20b
	, said he wouldn't have believed his story		20b-e
	Strong witness of ,		20e-21a
	Prophecy about , has been fulfilled		22d
Neal A. Maxwell	The magnitude of his revelations		99d-102b
Keith B. McMullin	Jesus —a poem by Joseph Smith	May 2004	35a-c
Henry B. Eyring	His statement about sealing keys on Apostles	Nov 2004	27f-28b
James E. Faust	Testimony of , is of inestimable value		52c-d
Boyd K. Packer	, did not have the insights in the Book of Mormon	May 2005	7c-e
	Detractors of , face stern penalties		9d-f
	Book of Mormon, D&C and Pearl of Great Price defend ,		9f
Joseph B. Wirthlin	, cleaned mud from children's shoes —story		27b-c
Kathleen H. Hughes	Sorry to the amount of $5 —story		76d
Gordon B. Hinckley	"The Seer" —poem and song by John Taylor		83d-f
Susan W. Tanner	Moroni and , compared —entire talk		104b-106f
Thomas S. Monson	Young Joseph's leg operation —story	Nov 2005	67b-e
	First Vision recounted - Principles taught		67e-68e
	His death exemplified love		68f-69b
	Rejected elder returned to testify of , —story		69b-f
Richard G. Scott	Greatest prophet		80b-d
Joseph B. Wirthlin	His kindness to 8 Africans —story	May 2006	100f-101b
Glenn L. Pace	A testimony at age 11 from reading , story	May 2007	78b-d
	Challenge to read , story		78f-79f
Joseph B. Wirthlin	His quote about a man filled with love	Nov 2007	28f
	His treatment of a 14-year-old visitor —story		29b-d
Gordon B. Hinckley	Must have been stunned by Moroni's visit		83e-84a
	God only appeared once - and to a boy - Why?		84c-d
	Affirms the calling of , - He stands in wonder		85f-86b
D. Todd Christofferson	The preeminent revelator of Jesus Christ	May 2008	79a
Craig C. Christensen	Book of Mormon authenticates mission of ,		107c-e
Robert D. Hales	Did not retaliate	Nov 2008	72e
William D. Oswald	Learned of his prophetic role from Moroni		97d
Tad R. Callister	Missing mark by focusing on faults of , or Peter	Nov 2009	35b-c
	Four truths learned in sacred grove		35d-36a
	Doctrines not inventions of a creative mind		36b-d
	Angels and visions in former days too		36f-37b
	Restored powers, keys, teachings, ordinances		37f
Jeffrey R. Holland	Hyrum's and Joseph's dying testimony		88f-89d
	No wicked man could write Book of Mormon		89f
Bruce A. Carlson	Martin Harris lost 116 pages —story	May 2010	39d-f
Donald L. Hallstrom	A model in how to handle afflictions		80b-d

Spencer W. Kimball	All urged to keep a journal or diary	Nov 1977	4d
Spencer W. Kimball	He has 33 , — Every family must leave its memoirs.	May 1978	4e
	Book of Remembrance makes remembering Lord more likely		77f
Spencer W. Kimball	Repent and keep a ,	May 1979	84f
Spencer W. Kimball	Keeping of , a commandment	Nov 1979	5b&d
John H. Groberg	Become sensitive to spiritual things if we write about them	May 1980	48d
	Family histories become family scripture		48f
	Posterity calls man blessed. He recorded his feelings —story		49a-f
Boyd K. Packer	The Lord knew Joseph Millett —diary entry and story		63b-e
Hartman Rector, Jr.	Best way to turn children's hearts to you	May 1981	74b-75a
Neal A. Maxwell	Writing is greater than preaching	Nov 1983	55f-56a
Henry B. Eyring	Keeping , promotes gratitude	Nov 1989	13c
Russell M. Nelson	What you don't record won't be recorded in heaven —Smith	Nov 1994	85c
Henry B. Eyring	The legacy of Grandfather's ,	May 1996	62d-63a
Dallin H. Oaks	All are commanded to write	May 2006	80b-d
Marlin K. Jensen	Church historian speaks of value of remembering	May 2007	36d-38f
Henry B. Eyring	Writes daily - Helps gratitude and remembering	Nov 2007	66e-67b
Richard G. Scott	He wrote, meditated, and was given more —story	Nov 2009	7b-8d
Russell M. Nelson	Woke up, wrote, then couldn't read it —story		81e-f

Marvin J. Ashton	Righteous children greatest , - 3 John 4	Dec 1971	101f
Robert L. Simpson	Highest , comes through service	July 1973	23b
Jacob de Jager	Man he went to rescue turned out to be his brother —story	Nov 1976	56f-57e
LeGrand Richards	Never saw tears of , because of purchases		64e-65a
Theodore M. Burton	Hell is the "absolute zero" of ,	May 1981	30f
Glenn L. Pace	Mistaking telestial pleasure for celestial ,	Nov 1987	39d-41b
Dallin H. Oaks	Definitions of , and misery —good	Nov 1991	73b
	Recovery of boy lost in mine —story		73c-d
	Discussion of , —entire talk good		73d-75f
L. Aldin Porter	Heber C. Kimball's feelings as he left England	May 1992	45c-e
Howard W. Hunter	The path to , lies through trials	May 1993	63d-e
Lynn A. Mickelsen	Rabbi was amazed at 2 Nephi 2:25 —story	Nov 1995	78d-f
Richard G. Scott	, is not conditional for the Lord	May 1996	24e-25a
	Finding , in life —entire talk		24b-26f
Thomas S. Monson	Clean youth will have , unspeakable	May 1997	93c
Richard B. Wirthlin	Satan confuses location of ,	Nov 1997	10a
Thomas S. Monson	Auctioneer bought bike for boy —story	Nov 1998	18b-c
	Downs girl elected homecoming queen —story		19a-b
Ronald T. Halverson	Intense inner peace and happiness —story, entire talk		78d-79f
Sharon G. Larsen	Harvest time with children - No greater ,	Nov 2001	68f
Russell M. Nelson	Celestial marriage and family are greatest ,		71c
Coleen K. Menlove	No other , equals happy parenthood —Hinckley	Nov 2002	15d-e
Thomas S. Monson	Abraham's greatest sorrow instantly turned to ,		60d-e
James M. Dunn	, is the purpose of life	May 2003	35e

Joy, cont'd

Thomas S. Monson	Life is work. Work is , —poem	May 2005	54e
James E. Faust	A gift of the Holy Ghost	Nov 2005	21d
Russell M. Nelson	Real , awaits on the other side of sorrow		87f-88a
Robert D. Hales	Satan can't have , unless we sin	May 2006	6b-c
Joseph B. Wirthlin	Drink deeply of living waters to have ,		99f-100f
	No greater , than relieving distress of others		101d
Joseph B. Wirthlin	From despair to , in an instant	Nov 2006	30a
	Sunday will come		30a-b
Dieter F. Uchtdorf	Church changed viewpoint from war to , —story	Nov 2007	18f-19a
Henry B. Eyring	Greatest , centers in family now and hereafter	May 2008	22b-d
Dieter F. Uchtdorf	We will know the meaning of ultimate ,	Nov 2008	22f-23a
Thomas S. Monson	Find , in the journey - now		85a
Dieter F. Uchtdorf	Our birthright and purpose is ,		118e-119d
Dieter F. Uchtdorf	Obedience becomes a , rather than a burden	Nov 2009	21e-f
Henry B. Eyring	Greatest , and sorrow in family relationships		70f-71b

Judging

Hugh B. Brown	Understanding and judging —poem	June 1969	31d
Franklin D. Richards	If motives are understood we are less prone to judge	June 1970	35f
N. Eldon Tanner	Sister McKay reformed troublemaker —story	July 1972	34b
	Judged by friends, but man had tumor		34c
	Give inactives chance to serve. Don't decide for them		34d
	Judging bishop prejudices children		34e
	Can't judge others because of different positions		35b
	The further out of line we are, the more , we do		35d
Paul H. Dunn	He judged an ill-kempt missionary —story		95c
H. Burke Peterson	His last impression was vastly different than his first —story	Nov 1974	68b-e
Carlos E. Asay	The smelly young man had a reason —story	Nov 1976	43e-f
Boyd K. Packer	Answer to those who judge Church if members do wrong	May 1979	79d-80e
	Publicity about wrongdoing member is actually compliment		80b-c
	Fired policeman thought Packer to blame —story		80e-81a
	Principal took abuse to protect the man he fired —story		81a-b
Neal A. Maxwell	Focus on Peter walking on water or that he didn't continue?	May 1982	38f & 39c
Marvin J. Ashton	Peace comes when we refuse to pass judgment	May 1983	32b
H. Burke Peterson	We only see what a man hits, not his target	Nov 1983	60c
Marvin J. Ashton	Self judgment is a hazardous pastime	May 1987	67a-b
Paul H. Dunn	Boy released balloon for dead sister —story		74f-75a
Marvin J. Ashton	Unrighteous , of self is one of life's tragedies	Nov 1987	20b
Marvin J. Ashton	It is wrong to compare ourselves to others	May 1989	20e-21a
F. Enzio Busche	We are our own judges		72f-73a
Russell M. Nelson	Judgment day on thoughts and intents	Nov 1990	75d-e
Gordon B. Hinckley	Boy who chewed tie became success —story	May 1993	53a
James E. Faust	God will judge as lightly as He can	Nov 1996	53a
Thomas S. Monson	Why was the worker late? —story	May 1998	47e
Stephen A. West	Worn out scriptures are like people	May 1999	29b

Russell M. Nelson	The things for which we'll be judged	May 2001	34e
Neal A. Maxwell	He misjudged his bishop —story	May 2004	44f-45a
Thomas S. Monson	Paperboy took own life because of , —story	May 2005	22d-e
Henry B. Eyring	Speak well when asked opinion of others	Nov 2008	71a-c
Quentin L. Cook	Dickens found criticism unfounded —story	May 2009	34f-35d
Thomas S. Monson	Have courage to not find fault		124b-c
	If you judge, you have no time for love		124c
Dieter F. Uchtdorf	Extend to others what we want for selves	May 2010	68f-69b
	Can't gauge worth of another soul		69b-d
Gregory A. Schwitzer	Don't judge but use good judgment		103d
	Martha has been misjudged		103d-104e
	Doctor misjudged patient —story		104e-f

Judgment
Related Topics: —

Theodore M. Burton	Records will be our password	Dec 1968	81a
	The importance of records in the ,		81b-e
Sterling W. Sill	He who was judged shall judge		105c
Hugh B. Brown	We'll be looked over for scars not medals	June 1969	99a
Richard L. Evans	Every sin to be paid for	Dec 1969	73f
Hugh B. Brown	Made on scars not honors		95d
Richard L. Evans	No guilty man is acquitted by his conscience	June 1971	74a
Richard L. Evans	Every wrong act or word will be evened out —Emerson	Dec 1971	58a-c
Marion G. Romney	Made on care given the poor	Jan 1973	97b
N. Eldon Tanner	Disobedient will be punished	Jan 1974	93e
Spencer W. Kimball	Justice before sympathy and forgiveness	Nov 1974	9b
Marion D. Hanks	, of parents —a good, short scripture	Nov 1975	26a
Boyd K. Packer	, mercy, the Mediator and repentance —entire talk	May 1977	54b-56f
Gordon B. Hinckley	Must be universal opportunity if universal justice is to be	Nov 1985	59d-e
Boyd K. Packer	Temptations and conditions will be taken into account in ,	May 1989	59a-b
Cree-L Kofford	Our , - an allegory in a trial setting	Nov 1991	27b-28f
Marvin J. Ashton	Don't expect me to be perfect —Joseph Smith		72e
James E. Faust	Will give least punishment and greatest reward	Nov 2001	19d-e
Joseph B. Wirthlin	Won't be asked about callings or possessions	Nov 2007	30e
Dieter F. Uchtdorf	Based more on families than on callings	Nov 2008	54f-55a
	Both callings pleasing to the Lord —story		55d-56a
Dallin H. Oaks	How many people did you help? —Monson	May 2009	93d-e
Dallin H. Oaks	To be determined by law, not love	Nov 2009	28b-c
Quentin L. Cook	Rationalizations will be silly in day of ,		92e-f
	Will be asked about family in day of ,		93a
Gregory A. Schwitzer	Don't judge but use good ,	May 2010	103d
	Blessings missed because of worldly ,		104f

Keys
Related Topics: Priesthood

Joseph Fielding Smith	Definition of , —good	July 1972	87e
Spencer W. Kimball	Apostles hold , in suspension	Jan 1973	34b

Keys, cont'd
Related Topics: Priesthood

N. Eldon Tanner	President holds ,	Jan 1973	103a
N. Eldon Tanner	Will stay till Savior comes —Woodruff	May 1974	83e
David B. Haight	Conferred upon Peter, James and John at transfiguration	May 1977	9e-10b
Spencer W. Kimball	We don't yet hold all , . Keys of resurrection is one		49b-d
Russell M. Nelson	Trained as a surgeon, he could not practice until authorized	Nov 1987	36d-f
	The , given to Joseph Smith		38d-39a
Boyd K. Packer	, of presidency don't pass like baton in relay	May 1995	7c-d
	Joseph's prophecy about keys and martyrdom		7d-e
	President Kimball testified that he held the , —story		8b-d
Russell M. Nelson	Apostles do not hold , of resurrection		32d
Robert D. Hales	Joseph's relief when he conferred ,	Nov 2005	91d-e
James E. Faust	List of , restored	May 2006	62d-f
Henry B. Eyring	Church is true because of ,	May 2008	20f-21a
Boyd K. Packer	Only one man can exercise all of the ,		83d-e
	Most precious thing lost in the Apostasy		84e
	President Kimball testified that he held the , —story		85a-d
	Apostles must travel to impart ,		86e
Dallin H. Oaks	Sacrament authorized only by one holding ,	Nov 2008	20e-f
Thomas S. Monson	, held by the two priesthoods	May 2009	67b-c

Kindness
Related Topics: Charity

John H. Vandenberg	Treat people as they ought to be —good quote	Dec 1970	35d-36a
Gordon B. Hinckley	We seldom get into trouble when we speak softly	June 1971	72a-b
Boyd K. Packer	Unkind words —story	Jan 1973	89f
Marion D. Hanks	Be kinder than others are to you and you'll be happy —story	Nov 1976	32f-33a
Marvin J. Ashton	Encourage change with , rather than fault-finding		85b-e
Marvin J. Ashton	Compliment to prisoners changed attitudes —story	Nov 1979	61f-62a
Marion D. Hanks	My specialty is mercy —story	Nov 1981	73e-74e
Marvin J. Ashton	Power cannot command , nor can money buy it		91c
Robert L. Backman	Ostracized girl became accepted because of , —story	Nov 1985	12d-f
Paul H. Dunn	Husband's note kept wife from panic —story	May 1987	74f
Marvin J. Ashton	Those who argue and shout have ceased listening	Nov 1987	21d
Dallin H. Oaks	Surgeon didn't charge for caesarean —story	May 1988	29e-30a
	Treat non-members like members		32d-f
Marion D. Hanks	Be kinder and fairer, handicapped girl was told —story	Nov 1988	63b-d
Gordon B. Hinckley	"Blessed are the Merciful" —entire talk	May 1990	68b-70f
H. Burke Peterson	"Your ceiling's really clean" —story		83e
James E. Faust	Passengers sprang to aid of mother —story		86e-87f
Glenn L. Pace	Warn 1,000 times, but then help them	Nov 1990	8b-10b
Betty Jo Jepsen	Entire talk		91b-92f
Boyd K. Packer	Girl making fun of handicapped —story	May 1991	8b-e
	Class was marvelously blind —story		8e
Marvin J. Ashton	Mark Twain could live 2 months on one good compliment		18e-f
Thomas S. Monson	Baseball confiscator won over by , —story		49f-50e
Thomas S. Monson	No regrets for , —poem		61f

Kindness, cont'd
Related Topics: Charity

Thomas S. Monson	Acts of , healed animosity —story	May 2000	47d-48c
Thomas S. Monson	81 years of marriage attributed to ,		53a
	President Smith sent his own coat —story		53d-f
Sharon G. Larsen	"A certain girl fell among thieves" —parable		89b-e
	Can't make rainbows, but can show ,		90f
Thomas S. Monson	Samaritan couple saved hopeless young man —story	May 2001	18e-19a
M. Russell Ballard	The doctrine of inclusion - How to treat others	Nov 2001	35d-38b
Wayne S. Peterson	Reacting to rudeness with , —story		83b-d
	, in concentration camps remembered		83e-f
Thomas S. Monson	Woman wished for second chance to be kind —story	May 2002	20e
Gayle M. Clegg	Man made frozen girl run —story		68e-69a
M. Russell Ballard	Make me an instrument of thy peace —poem		89d-e
Neal A. Maxwell	Earnings shared with jobless friends —story	May 2003	70b-d
Susan W. Tanner	Money given to family who caused accident —story		102d-f
Gordon B. Hinckley	May each be a little more kind	Nov 2003	103d-f
Thomas S. Monson	Party fund given to family —story	May 2004	20f-22b
W. Douglas Shumway	Secret friend Family Home Evening —story		96c-e
Gordon B. Hinckley	Treat women with , —entire talk	Nov 2004	82d-85e
Thomas S. Monson	Criticism of boy leads to tragedy —story	May 2005	22d-e
Joseph B. Wirthlin	Anger sent man away - , brought him back —story		26b-d
	President Hinckley's , remembered for 60 years —story		26d-f
	Joseph cleaned mud from children's shoes —story		27b-c
	Talmage cared for family with diphtheria —story		28b-d
	What if people are rude? - Love them		28d-e
Kathleen H. Hughes	Loaned stranger a spare tire —story		74f-75b
Gordon B. Hinckley	No disciple of Christ makes racial slurs	May 2006	58b-e
	Hated unfriendly LDS. Friend changed that —story		59b-60d
Joseph B. Wirthlin	Joseph's , to 8 black people —story		100f-101b
Susan W. Tanner	Differing outlooks of two literary characters		103e-f
	Polite to bus driver but not family —story		104b-d
James E. Faust	Smiles convert family —story		113a-d
Bonnie D. Parkin	2 little acts of , greatly appreciated	May 2007	35b-c
Gordon B. Hinckley	Treat your children with great ,		105e
Michael J. Teh	Screwtape's advice about ,	Nov 2007	35f-36b
	Rock thrower becomes convert because of , —story		36f-37b
Joseph B. Wirthlin	He spoke up for the handicapped boy —story	May 2008	18d-e
Dieter F. Uchtdorf	Monson visited man at personal sacrifice —story		69a-70a
Neil L. Andersen	Handicapped child comforted another —story	Nov 2008	14e-f
D. Todd Christofferson	Man cut his table in half —story		39f-40d
Richard G. Scott	Express love and gratitude frequently to spouse		46f
Henry B. Eyring	Always speak well of others		71a-c
Thomas S. Monson	Will never regret , but will regret omissions		86b-d
Dieter F. Uchtdorf	Creativity and compassion make God happy		118d-e
	Lift others and rise higher yourself		119d-120a
Quentin L. Cook	No criticism of other churches - Live with respect	May 2009	37b-d

Kindness

Dallin H. Oaks	, will always secure heaven for us —Mother Teresa	May 2009	95f
Thomas S. Monson	Popular girl included handicapped girl —story		124d-125b
Thomas S. Monson	No regrets for being too kind —poem	Nov 2009	85f-86a
Quentin L. Cook	Jewish leader: Two reasons people engage in ,		91b-d
Julie B. Beck	Never suppress a generous thought		114c-d
Dieter F. Uchtdorf	Give others what we desire for selves	May 2010	68f-69b
	Each brother gave 1/3 of harvest to other —story		70b-d

Knowledge
Related Topics: Education, Intelligence

Spencer W. Kimball	What are "hidden treasures of , ?" —story	Dec 1968	99b-101a
	All , will be necessary to be able to create		101e
Hugh B. Brown	Salvation is an eternal quest for ,	June 1969	34c
Joseph Fielding Smith	Cannot be saved in ignorance of gospel		39a-c
Harold B. Lee	A great work to learn exaltation beyond grave		104f
Delbert L. Stapley	Wisdom is putting , to proper use	June 1970	73f
Thomas S. Monson	No ignorance so deep as willful ignorance	Dec 1970	103c-e
Harold B. Lee	We can't understand the creation	June 1971	8a
Sterling W. Sill	Tends to make men as God	July 1973	104a
	Man who wanted to be like Socrates —story		104c
Howard W. Hunter	Knowledge explosion not of man's creation	Jan 1974	56c
Hartman Rector, Jr.	Don't care how much you know until know you care		107f
N. Eldon Tanner	, without integrity is dangerous	May 1977	15f
Gordon B. Hinckley	For , go to the source. Don't ask Xerox about IBM —story		64e-f
N. Eldon Tanner	Greater , makes one more free	May 1978	16b
Marion G. Romney	, of God is the only , that can save us	Nov 1980	44c
	How to obtain a full , of the gospel		44e
Ezra Taft Benson	, will come by keeping all commandments	May 1983	54c-e
Royden G. Derrick	All , comes from God	Nov 1984	61f-62b
	Integrity without , is useless. , without integrity is dangerous		63c-d
Vaughn J. Featherstone	Fullness of , brings fullness of accountability	Nov 1987	27d
Wm. Grant Bangerter	Ministers amazed that he had answer for everything —story	Nov 1988	80f-81a
Dallin H. Oaks	Sacred , must come through revelation	May 1989	29b-30f
Russell M. Nelson	Wisdom can be lost in ,	Nov 1992	8b-d
Boyd K. Packer	You may know not that you know not	Nov 1994	59d
Elaine L. Jack	Converting light and truth to everyday action		91a
	Distinguishing between foolish notions and wise ideas		91d
L. Aldin Porter	Most important , comes from Holy Ghost	Nov 1996	11a
Richard B. Wirthlin	More , in a newspaper than in a 17th-century lifetime	Nov 1997	9d
Virginia U. Jensen	Ignorance is not bliss: it is dangerous		90d-e
Thomas S. Monson	It is spring time and I am blind —story	May 1999	54b-e
	Blind counselor led him through dark —story		54e-f
James E. Faust	New ideas: rate then and now	May 2000	18c
	Four absolute truths		19e
Russell M. Nelson	, to be poured out in latter days		85e-f
Dallin H. Oaks	Limited information wisely used —good	May 2001	82e-83f

Knowledge, cont'd
Related Topics: Education, Intelligence

James E. Faust	, without labor is profitless	May 2003	67a
Ronald T. Halverson	You know a thing because you live it	Nov 2004	32f-33a
James E. Faust	Priesthood holds key to all ,		52c-d
Joseph B. Wirthlin	Intellect must not rule over spirit		102b-c
Thomas S. Monson	The joy of learning to read —story		113f-114f
Dallin H. Oaks	Obedience enhances , and , encourages obedience	May 2008	28e-29a
Robert R. Steuer	Treasures of , are hidden - Require dedication		100d-e
Gerald Causse	Plan of Salvation is simple enough for a child	Nov 2008	32b-34b
Dieter F. Uchtdorf	Does away with darkness, anxiety and doubt	Nov 2009	58a-e
	Comes with patience	May 2010	58f
Francisco J. Viñas	Impart , and facilitate revelation		108a

Last Days
Related Topics: Future, Second Coming, Today

Harold B. Lee	Safety is where you are if you are pure in heart	June 1970	64e
Harold B. Lee	Old prophecies being fulfilled now	Dec 1970	28d-f
	We have some tight places to go through		126b-d
Harold B. Lee	Many false Christs around us	Dec 1971	30f-31b
	Peru earthquake. Those doing duty will be safe		31b-e
Joseph Fielding Smith	These are the , - Days of trouble	July 1972	27b
Harold B. Lee	Each dispensation equally as critical		29a
Marion G. Romney	Tribulations in the ,	Jan 1973	32a
Harold B. Lee	Days of complete frustration		60b
Sterling W. Sill	Comparisons with first days		83d
Harold B. Lee	Sources for accurate knowledge about ,		106d
Harold B. Lee	Satan has power over his dominion now	July 1973	4b
	Never before such a feeling of urgency as now		4d
David B. Haight	False Christs teaching permissiveness		55a
	Space-age Sodom and Gomorrah		56a
Ezra Taft Benson	A list of the calamities in the ,	Jan 1974	68f
	Lord provides a warning, a program, a refuge		69d
	The angels have been loosed to reap the earth		69d
	Calamities to come in not too distant future		81f
	The time is about ripe —Lee		81f
Harold B. Lee	Today is the day spoken of in Matthew 24		129b
Spencer W. Kimball	Be prepared and thus resist evil of ,	May 1974	6b
Bruce R. McConkie	Conditions won't be getting better	Nov 1974	35e
James E. Faust	Immorality: An epidemic plague of ,		59b-d
Theodore M. Burton	Atomic war and Word of Wisdom	May 1976	29e-f
Victor L. Brown	We will live on what we produce —Romney		111a
	Calamities will increase —Kimball		111a-b
Marion G. Romney	U.N. Secretary-General says all the world fears	May 1977	51d-f
	Predicted calamities are inevitable		53c
Ezra Taft Benson	No one will stand neutral about the Church	May 1978	32e
	Pressure on Saints will become great		32f
	Contrast between Church and world will increase		33b

Bruce R. McConkie	All sorrows of past are but a foretaste	May 1979	92d
	Enumerating the plagues to come		93a-b
	These trials not conditional		93b
	Lord doesn't tell us when—only says watch and be ready		93e
	Atomic holocaust a surety - all saints won't be spared		93f
LeGrand Richards	Nahum described cars in ,	May 1980	22c-d
	More calamities in his life than in rest of history		24a
Bruce R. McConkie	Entire talk		71a-73f
Ezra Taft Benson	It can't happen here?	Nov 1980	34a
Bruce R. McConkie	Men in our time will never find peace		51e-f
Bruce R. McConkie	Priesthood can stay the fall of atomic bombs	May 1982	34b
Neal A. Maxwell	141 wars since WWII	Nov 1982	67a-b
Dean L. Larsen	More temptations, less stigma	May 1983	34a-f
A. Theodore Tuttle	No one will be able to stand without individual testimony	May 1984	23f
H. Verlan Andersen	Lamanites joined Church prior to 1st Coming, too	Nov 1986	23e
Neal A. Maxwell	Prophecies may have rapid fulfillment	May 1988	7c-d
Gordon B. Hinckley	His positive outlook in a world of ugliness	May 1989	65b-e
Russell M. Nelson	, vs. latter days	May 1990	17b-e
Neal A. Maxwell	Events will be compressed in ,	May 1992	39f
Glenn L. Pace	Horrible storms are blowing out our moral fiber	Nov 1992	12b-e
	Not a time to panic, but to prepare		12e-f
M. Russell Ballard	Statistics on increasing earthquakes		31b-e
	Don't overreact or make extreme preparations		32b
Spencer J. Condie	Man tried to warn that bridge was out —story	Nov 1993	17e-f
Gordon B. Hinckley	Building replacement for Tabernacle	Nov 1998	4c-f
M. Russell Ballard	W. Woodruff's vision of Joseph and others hurrying		6d-e
Virginia U. Jensen	The best lies ahead —G.B. Hinckley		14a
James E. Faust	Next century will bring exponential advances	May 1999	17b-e
Boyd K. Packer	We need not fear in troubled times	May 2000	8c&e, 9d
Dallin H. Oaks	Signs preceding Second Coming	May 2004	7d-f
	Statistics on earthquakes and disasters		7f-8a
Cecil O. Samuelson, Jr.	Focus of prophets' concerns and aspirations	Nov 2004	49d
James E. Faust	Difficult days ahead - but optimistic		55d-e
Keith B. McMullin	How to be prepared for ,	Nov 2005	12a-b
Gordon B. Hinckley	Calamities are coming - Be prepared		60b-62f
Boyd K. Packer	Terrible days but he's positively optimistic		70d-e
Dallin H. Oaks	More scripture to come forth	May 2006	80d-f
Thomas S. Monson	Millions will die - Prophecy by G.A. Smith	May 2007	41d-e
Jeffrey R. Holland	Not a time to fear and tremble	Nov 2008	30b
James J. Hamula	Sodom did not exceed current wickedness		51b-c
Jeffrey R. Holland	Calamities of , will be personal too	Nov 2009	88b-c
	Mist of darkness descended on all travelers		88c-e
Thomas S. Monson	Swimming against tide, but we will survive		109d-e

Law
Related Topics: Government

Richard L. Evans	Respect for , begins with respect at home	June 1969	80f-82a
Joseph F. Smith	Live , no matter what	Dec 1969	37c
N. Eldon Tanner	Discussion on laws—bad laws must be obeyed until changed	June 1970	30f-31f
Robert L. Simpson	Laws in football games and life compared	Dec 1970	95d-96a
Harold B. Lee	A cause of disrespect for ,	July 1972	29b
	People who are , unto themselves		31b
Harold B. Lee	Obey laws of land	Jan 1973	106b
Neal A. Maxwell	Not enough policemen for those who won't restrain selves	May 1975	101d
N. Eldon Tanner	, is the application of truth	Nov 1975	82f
	Why all laws of the land must be observed		83c-e
L. Tom Perry	Suppose the Bible was a nation's only , ?	May 1976	64c-e
William R. Bradford	, must be known and applied to save —good example	Nov 1977	64e-f
N. Eldon Tanner	Church pays taxes like any corporation	Nov 1979	48b
Hartman Rector, Jr.	He stopped at 15 of 16 stop signs —story	May 1983	25f-26c
L. Tom Perry	Whatever , anyone keeps, it preserves him.	May 1990	20d
Boyd K. Packer	Man cannot change doctrine or natural , —story	Nov 1993	22d-e
Russell M. Nelson	Some , cannot be repealed by Congress		35a
Dallin H. Oaks	Judgment will be based on , not love	Nov 2009	27e-28c
D. Todd Christofferson	Cannot replace self-discipline		106d-e
	More laws diminish freedom		106f-107a
	What is legal is way below what is right		108e

Leadership
Related Topics: —

N. Eldon Tanner	, of one caused team to quit smoking —story	Dec 1968	92e-f
	Missionary resisted going out on town—saved 4 others —story		92f-93a
	Baptized in spite of parents and boyfriend - all joined —story		93c-e
David O. McKay	5 things a leader must be and do		109a-b
John H. Vandenberg	The Calf-Path —poem	June 1969	47b-f
John Longden	Janitor showed , to owner of lost wallet —story		113b-c
Gordon B. Hinckley	We lack leaders who will say "this I believe"	June 1970	40b-c
Thomas S. Monson	Power to lead is also power to mislead		90f-91a
Harold B. Lee	Anyone can be a leader —Eisenhower	June 1971	9d
Harold B. Lee	Leaders lighten their loads by activating others	Dec 1971	31f
Robert L. Simpson	Advice to bishops - delegation , etc.	July 1972	49c
Howard W. Hunter	Aaronic priesthood prepares for ,	Jan 1973	65d
Robert L. Backman	Church , built upon foundation youth are laying	July 1973	84d
	Of deacons' president —story		85d
Eldred G. Smith	To find who the leaders are, pour on the work	Jan 1974	63b
Harold B. Lee	Observations on the growth of local , in Mexico		97b
	New programs do as well as the bishops do		99c
Spencer W. Kimball	Leaders admonished to read their handbooks	May 1974	86e
Spencer W. Kimball	Many will follow, but few will lead	Nov 1974	79d-80b
N. Eldon Tanner	The leader who says hard things is loved	Nov 1975	77a

John H. Groberg	Follow experienced , —good sea story	Nov 1976	44b-45b
Thomas S. Monson	One stands at crossroads to help youth decide —poem	May 1977	72b-d
Wm. Grant Bangerter	Are leaders listening to prophet —examples	Nov 1979	11b-d
A. Theodore Tuttle	Responsible for broken covenants if people not taught	May 1980	41d
James E. Faust	Make assignments - Don't depend on volunteers	Nov 1980	34d-f
	Leaders not to be dictators but shepherds		35b
	Not honored because of selves but of position —story		36a
	, should make harmonious symphony not a loud solo		37a
Marion G. Romney	Report to your group on your stewardship		93b-c
Spencer W. Kimball	Limit meetings, make them effective	May 1981	45b-c
Angel Abrea	Failure to sustain , is a grievous sin	Nov 1981	24d-e
Vaughn J. Featherstone	How scouting developed his , ability —story	Nov 1983	37e-39a
	The Torchbearer —poem		39b
Rex D. Pinegar	Unrighteous leaders deny divine guidance to those they lead	Nov 1985	41f-42a
Glenn L. Pace	Methods may change with leaders	May 1986	24c
James E. Faust	Leaders have watch for our souls and must give account	Nov 1986	8b-c
John R. Lasater	Shepherds and , —Shepherd story	May 1988	74b-75f
Robert D. Hales	A gloomy mind in a leader is unpardonable - also impatience	Nov 1988	11b-c
Joseph B. Wirthlin	Lambs can't follow path if shepherd goes astray		35b-d
Gene R. Cook	How to bring Spirit into visits to homes		37d-39f
Hugh W. Pinnock	Courageous girl quieted class —story	May 1989	11b-c
Spencer J. Condie	Scriptural lessons on ,	May 1990	27b-28f
Gordon B. Hinckley	Why sustaining , is prerequisite for recommend		51c-e
George I. Cannon	Membership is a call to , —Spencer W. Kimball	Nov 1991	14b
Thomas S. Monson	Youth at crossroads poem	Nov 1993	48e
M. Russell Ballard	Instruction on using councils		76b-78f
Boyd K. Packer	Establish rule before dealing with exceptions	May 1994	20d-e
M. Russell Ballard	More instruction on using councils		24b-26f
Richard P. Lindsay	Lambs died because of neglect —story		46e-47b
James E. Faust	5 fundamental truths about ,	May 1996	7c-d
Russell M. Nelson	Position in the Church does not exalt		15f
	We can only lift from a higher plane		16a
W. Eugene Hansen	Sheep ignored shepherd - 2 were killed —story		38d-f
James E. Faust	Help is not helpful if others' responsibilities are usurped	May 1997	42c
Thomas S. Monson	Crossroads —poem		95a-b
	How one leader affected her Young Women —story		95c-e
Joseph B. Wirthlin	Noticing the insignificant —story	Nov 1997	33f-34b
Boyd K. Packer	Take care of the rule first - not exceptions —story	May 1998	73a-c
M. Russell Ballard	Are we keeping pace with President Hinckley?	Nov 1998	7a-b
James E. Faust	Master pianist put arms around student —story	Nov 1999	101b-c
Sharon G. Larsen	Best , is example	Nov 2001	68a-b
	Girl noticed when leader removed extra earrings		68b-d
Henry B. Eyring	Federal official tried to take over meeting —story	Nov 2004	28e-29a
Harold G. Hillam	Stake president delegated and interviewed	May 2005	33d-f
Thomas S. Monson	Making people glad to follow you		54f

Leadership, cont'd

Life

Delbert L. Stapley	Begins as pure stream then becomes polluted	Dec 1971	97b-d
Harold B. Lee	Desirability of a , without effort	July 1972	31d
Sterling W. Sill	Life expectancy through the ages	Jan 1973	82a
N. Eldon Tanner	Purpose is joy		103e
Marion D. Hanks	Purpose of , same as Christ's		127b
Rex D. Pinegar	The measure of a life —short quote	Jan 1974	32b
Elray L. Christiansen	No reruns to , - This , determines eternity	May 1974	26e
James E. Faust	He who saves one life saves a world —Talmud	May 1975	27d-e
Sterling W. Sill	What a blessing birth is		41c
Spencer W. Kimball	Not a , of luck, but one of pluck		80a
N. Eldon Tanner	One decision can alter course of ,	Nov 1975	75f-76c
Boyd K. Packer	Death is no more an ending than birth a beginning		98f
Spencer W. Kimball	One must be "born" again and again.	May 1976	108c
Bruce R. McConkie	, never was intended to be easy	Nov 1976	106e-f
Paul H. Dunn	We think we'll be happy when we reach a goal	Nov 1977	24c-d
	Life is a journey not a camp - many are camping		24d
Spencer W. Kimball	Counsel to not kill birds and animals	Nov 1978	44a-45d
Hugh W. Pinnock	3 sage observations on old age	Nov 1979	74d & 75b
Rex D. Pinegar	Unpleasant things are not interruptions of ,	Nov 1982	24e-f
	Nothing in , has meaning but faith —Tolstoy		25d-e
	We think others' problems aren't as hard —story		25f-26b
Derek A. Cuthbert	, should be beautifully simple - simply beautiful		54f
Victor L. Brown	Man who had everything considered suicide —story	May 1983	62a-c
Boyd K. Packer	, and trials unexplainable without knowledge of premortal life	Nov 1983	16b-18f
Jack H. Goaslind	, is a mission, not a career —S.L. Richards	May 1986	54e
Russell M. Nelson	, is not a smooth track but an obstacle course	Nov 1987	86c
Ezra Taft Benson	The great test, task, and commandment of ,	May 1988	4b-6f
Joseph B. Wirthlin	, compared to a marathon —story	Nov 1989	73c-f
Marvin J. Ashton	, must follow set patterns —entire talk	Nov 1990	20b-22f
Marion D. Hanks	Do they do this to make it fun for kids? —story		38e-f
Russell M. Nelson	The purposes of ,		74b-c
Boyd K. Packer	A microscopic drop of water in ocean	May 1991	9b-c
Wm. R. Bradford	Unclutter your , —good talk	May 1992	27d-29b
Russell M. Nelson	Only satisfactory , is , everlasting		72c
	We barely blossom on earth		72e
L. Lionel Kendrick	, is a trip and it needs a road map	May 1993	13b-c
Thomas S. Monson	What we do with , is our gift to God		63a
Tai Kwok Yuen	View from a peak is sometimes clear, sometimes foggy		86b-c
Lowell D. Wood	How God expands a , —E.T. Benson		89a
Boyd K. Packer	Eve should be praised for her decision	Nov 1993	21d
	The Fall had a twofold direction - downward, yet forward		21e
Russell M. Nelson	Blood began to circulate at the Fall		34c
Thomas S. Monson	4-point guide to ,		49d-f
W. Eugene Hansen	Learn lessons of , through joy or sorrow		83a-b
Chieko N. Okazaki	Her changing circumstances through ,		96b

Life, cont'd

Elaine L. Jack	Birth not by chance but by choice	Nov 1993	98e
H. David Burton	Live so that Jesus can be seen in you	May 1994	68f
Dallin H. Oaks	, is for the sole purpose of exaltation	Nov 1995	26a-b
	"Never take no cutoffs..." —story		27c-e
James E. Faust	Don't live , on the edge —cave story		45d-46c
Richard G. Scott	Description of the beauties of , —poem	May 1996	24b-e
	Purpose of , is not entertainment and pleasure		25a
Richard G. Scott	Don't let good things crowd out essential things	May 1997	53f-54c
	Don't give up what you want most for wants now		54d-59a
M. Russell Ballard	We have nothing to fear from the journey		60d-e
	, and pioneer journey beautifully compared		61a-b
Neal A. Maxwell	"For this cause came I into the world"	Nov 1997	22e
	We behave like hurried tourists		22f
	Some think they're auditing the course		23c
	Count your blessings but make them count		24b
Sheri L. Dew	, must not be a sight-seeing or shopping trip	Nov 1999	97d-f
James E. Faust	Today's , is more complicated	May 2000	17d
	, expectancy increased from 25 to 64 years		18c
Ben B. Banks	, compared to bicycle and canoe trips	May 2002	42b-43f
James M. Dunn	, is a mission, and not a career	May 2003	35b
	Joy is the purpose of ,		35e
Boyd K. Packer	The Golden Years - The value of age		82b-84f
Dennis E. Simmons	, is a test	May 2004	73d-e
Thomas S. Monson	Simple formula to guide ,	Nov 2004	70a
M. Russell Ballard	Mission statement of , is build eternal family	Nov 2005	41d
Richard G. Scott	Fundamental purpose of , is obedience		78d-f
Robert D. Hales	Giving and living our lives for the gospel		91f
Joseph B. Wirthlin	Don't go through , mourning - How to seek joy	May 2006	99f-100f
	This , is merely one small step		102a
	Create a masterpiece of your ,		101d-102b
Richard G. Scott	Compared to rock climbing - Don't go solo	Nov 2006	40b-41b
David A. Bednar	Not merely a sightseeing journey	Nov 2007	81d
Silvia H. Allred	Measure of , - Not what we get, but give		113f-114a
Lance B. Wickman	"They can't kill an old bird like me" —story	May 2008	103f-105a
	Not a time for getting and accumulating		105a
L. Tom Perry	4 necessities to , - Thoreau's , at Walden Pond	Nov 2008	7c-8b
	Obtain relief from stress by simplifying , —entire talk		7b-10b
M. Russell Ballard	Our lives contrasted with pioneers		83f-84b
Thomas S. Monson	Incremental changes in , become monumental		84d-85a
	Purpose of , is to learn what is important		85a
	What if you could return to , ? Enjoy each minute		86e-f
Dieter F. Uchtdorf	A , of meaning, grace and fulfillment achieved by...		120e-f
Henry B. Eyring	Can polish and perfect us	May 2009	27a
Steven E. Snow	Kindergartener needed to get on with , —story		81b-c
	The trials of a pioneer and his attitudes —story		82e-83b

Life, cont'd

Steven E. Snow	How to deal with changes in , —entire talk	May 2009	81b-83b
Elaine S. Dalton	A hike compared to a virtuous , —story		122a-f
Ann M. Dibb	We have a hazardous job description and duty	Nov 2009	79e
	We too strive to enter a land of promise	May 2010	114e
	4 guidelines to , from Joshua —entire talk		114a-116f
Elaine S. Dalton	Dismayed, discouraged, distracted, delayed, disqualified		121b
Dieter F. Uchtdorf	"Your Happily Ever After" —entire talk		124c-127f

Light

Joseph Anderson	Church has white , others have incomplete spectrum	July 1972	81e
L. Tom Perry	She radiates since she joined —story	May 1978	51b-d
Theodore M. Burton	Good discussion on , - what it is —story	May 1981	28d-29d
Ted E. Brewerton	Don't live on borrowed , —J.F. Smith	Nov 1991	11f-12b
	Like mirrors, we light up dark places		12f
Robert D. Hales	The conflict between , and darkness	May 2002	69d-72b
Coleen K. Menlove	Darkness had to leave —Primary art story	Nov 2002	13d-f
Joseph B. Wirthlin	His world was becoming dark —story		85b-d
Kenneth Johnson	, of Christ will lead us to the source		90f
Gayle M. Clegg	Crack in vase is where the , comes through —story	May 2003	111d-112f
Richard G. Scott	Explanation of , of Christ	Nov 2004	15e-f
James E. Faust	The , in members' eyes —story	Nov 2005	20b-d
	Holy Ghost is source of , in countenances		20d-f
	There was a , in your face —story		22b-e
Susan W. Tanner	Reading by combined , of glowworms	May 2006	104f-105a
	Holding up our , to families and the world		103b-105f
Douglas L. Callister	Eternity a long time to live without ,	Nov 2007	101d-f
Robert R. Steuer	Relation between , and truth	May 2008	99d-101b
Henry B. Eyring	Walk in the , —entire talk		123b-125f
Robert D. Hales	The high ground is where the , is	Nov 2008	74d-f
Thomas S. Monson	Blind man had , of gospel —story	May 2009	90b-91a

Light of Christ

Harold B. Lee	One's conscience	July 1972	32a
Marion G. Romney	, Holy Ghost and Sure Word of Prophecy discussed	May 1977	43d-45f
Robert D. Hales	The reason all men know good from evil	May 1979	78a
Vaughn J. Featherstone	, never goes out —J. Reuben Clark, Jr.	Nov 1982	73a-b
Royden G. Derrick	Guilt feelings at age 4 stemmed from , —story	Nov 1984	61c-e
Henry B. Eyring	, never wholly extinguished —J.R. Clark	Nov 1986	74c-d
James E. Faust	What is the , ?	May 1989	31e
Richard G. Scott	Explanation of ,	Nov 2004	15e-f
M. Russell Ballard	, is as universal as sunlight —Packer	May 2005	69f
James E. Faust	Holy Ghost is source of light	Nov 2005	20d-f
Richard G. Scott	Not a person - What it does		79d
Robert R. Steuer	Enlightens inventors, artists, etc. —Boyd K. Packer	May 2008	100b-c
Henry B. Eyring	The sense of right or wrong, true or false		123e

Light of Christ, cont'd
Related Topics: Holy Ghost

Kevin W. Pearson	Faith plus , produce spiritual photosynthesis	May 2009	39b
Jose A. Teixeira	Sin or misuse cause us to lose the signal		104e-105b
Boyd K. Packer	Every person is provided with ,	Nov 2009	43d
	Every man is given the Spirit of Christ		44b

Listening
Related Topics: Communication

Marion G. Romney	We don't lack a guide but a , ear	Dec 1971	75c
Gordon B. Hinckley	Listen for promptings of Spirit	Jan 1973	93f
A. Theodore Tuttle	Don't need more prophets but , ears	July 1973	19b
James E. Faust	What is the quality of prayers when only the Lord listens?	Nov 1976	58e
Vaughn J. Featherstone	Talking to the wall —story		118d-f
Boyd K. Packer	We hear what we're trained to hear —3 stories	Nov 1979	19d-20b
J. Richard Clarke	Recent widow just needed to talk —story	Nov 1981	80f-81a
H. Burke Peterson	Give more ear and less lip to your sons	Nov 1982	43c-d
Jacob de Jager	Some finish , before speaker finishes speaking	May 1986	71b
	Definition of logokophosis		71d-e
	Be doers and not hearers only		71f
Russell M. Nelson	Learn more by , to children —story	May 1991	22b-f
	Hearing test backfired on husband —story		23a-b
Virginia H. Pearce	Our baptismal covenant demands ,	Nov 1993	80a
Sharon G. Larsen	Love is , when child is ready to talk —story	Nov 2001	67e-68a
Thomas S. Monson	Pray and then listen for the answer	May 2009	68e-f
Dieter F. Uchtdorf	How and where we can hear God's voice	Nov 2009	23d-24b
M. Russell Ballard	Interview and listen to your sons		48f-49b
Robert D. Hales	"Grandpa! Are you in there?"	May 2010	96b
Gregory A. Schwitzer	Peace internal and external to hear Holy Ghost		105b-d

Love
Related Topics: Charity, Self-Respect

Hartman Rector, Jr.	Impossible to , him whom we do not know	Dec 1968	49c
Delbert L. Stapley	Things one won't do if he loves the Lord		54c-d
	Angels would visit those who keep first commandment		55f
Henry D. Taylor	Be kind to enemies: You made them	June 1969	62d
	Statement "We , one another" started conversion —story		64b-c
	Church tells us how to , one another		64c
	If personalities are eternal so is , —McKay		64d
	Love can be starved to death if not fed —McKay		64d-e
	Eisenhower's last words were of , for family and USA		64f
Gordon B. Hinckley	Psychedelic crowd's , is counterfeit		75c
Hartman Rector, Jr.	God loves us because He is good, not because we are good	Dec 1969	82a
Marvin J. Ashton	Children learn , as they experience it	June 1970	42c
N. Eldon Tanner	Our neighbor is anyone needing help	Dec 1970	32d
John H. Vandenberg	Treat others like the person they should be		35d-36a
Delbert L. Stapley	Power to , is the noblest gift to man		64b-65a
	Love flows downward. Parents love best		65f
Marion D. Hanks	Two tender examples of , —story		68c-d

John H. Vandenberg	We love that for which we sacrifice	June 1971	63f
	You get no closer to God than you do to fellowmen		68e
Thomas S. Monson	Quarrel caused son to leave. Love brought back —story		96c-e
Spencer W. Kimball	Childless Indian couple took 18 orphans —story	Dec 1971	38c-e
Marvin J. Ashton	The prisoner never had any family relationships —story		99f-101a
	Girl in detention home wanted to be wanted —story		101b-c
Marion D. Hanks	Must be unconditional —well phrased		106b-c
Harold B. Lee	Person who feels no one cares is in dangerous state		113e-114a
Thomas S. Monson	Prisoner returns to tree covered with ribbons —story		132e-133a
Harold B. Lee	Lee's , of members when called	Jan 1973	25d
Marvin J. Ashton	Greater , hath no man		43c
Boyd K. Packer	A people who care for others		88a
	Membership brings fellowship		88b
Harold B. Lee	Assurance that Brethren , members		134c
Spencer W. Kimball	Parents' love for children —good poem	July 1973	17e
Robert L. Simpson	A prisoner never told he was loved		23a
Vaughn J. Featherstone	Touch of the Master's Hand —good poem		35f
	Must love every soul on earth —Lee		36b
	Sugar beet story		36c
Thomas S. Monson	Yellow canary story		41b
Boyd K. Packer	Explanation of Father's , to children —good		53a
Harold B. Lee	If we lose self-respect we lose all love	Jan 1974	3c
Henry D. Taylor	Love can be starved to death —McKay		36e
Hartman Rector, Jr.	Don't care how much you know until know you care		107f
Elray L. Christiansen	Love is not earthbound	May 1974	25e
Loren C. Dunn	, can overcome many parental mistakes	Nov 1974	11a
Marvin J. Ashton	A great shock absorber in trials		42b
Marvin J. Ashton	Dead man never told son he loved him —story	May 1976	53b-d
Marion D. Hanks	An unharnessed power —two good quotes	Nov 1976	33a
Vaughn J. Featherstone	Every bird came back —story		105d-f
N. Eldon Tanner	Brotherhood is democracy at work	May 1977	46b-c
H. Burke Peterson	Missionary had never been told "I love you" —story		68e-69a
	We love him because he first loved us		69c-d
	The Daily Portion of Love —entire talk		68d-69f
J. Richard Clarke	Boy rejected by father becomes homosexual —story		85b-e
Rex D. Pinegar	Friend gave him most valued possession —story	Nov 1978	11a-b
Theodore M. Burton	A lack of personal selfishness	May 1979	72d-f
Boyd K. Packer	, is not divisible - each child gets it all	Nov 1980	22b
Marion G. Romney	Judgment turns on the hinge of loving neighbor as ourselves		93d-e
Marvin J. Ashton	We learn to , that which we serve	May 1981	24b-d
Jack H. Goaslind, Jr.	They do not , that do not show their ,		59f
David B. Haight	Tests to recognize ,	Nov 1982	11d-e
	Man passed life preserver to others —story		11f-12a
	, of one man may neutralize the hate of millions		12a
	A man filled with , is anxious to bless all		12b

Love

David B. Haight	Christ's method of promoting His cause	Nov 1982	12c
	Love is a verb		12e
Thomas S. Monson	Jewels are but substitutes for gifts —Emerson	May 1983	56b
L. Tom Perry	Must be constant as rising of sun, not seasonal like monsoon		78f
Vaughn J. Featherstone	The greatest power in the world	Nov 1983	37e
David B. Haight	How to tell when you're in ,	May 1984	14e-f
Robert L. Backman	We can't resist those who have genuine , for us	Nov 1985	13b
Robert E. Wells	No one ever cried when I entered a room before —story		29a-b
Thomas S. Monson	An outward expression of an inward conviction		34b
Howard W. Hunter	A man wrapped up in himself makes a small bundle	Nov 1986	35a
	Willard Richards refused to leave Joseph —story		35b-d
David B. Haight	Gentiles were not the Jews' neighbor	May 1987	59d-f
Hugh W. Pinnock	Neighbors' , won over motorcyclists —story		62f-63b
Paul H. Dunn	Song restored Thomas Moore's wife's self respect —story		74b-e
Thomas S. Monson	, isn't , until you give it away	Nov 1987	68d
	The most noble attribute		68e
	The single most important word		68f-69a
	, from primary president ended reverence problem —story		69b-f
Ezra Taft Benson	, of God comes first - all else fits into place	May 1988	4b-6f
	How to tell if you're in ,		53b
Marvin J. Ashton	The worse sin is not to hate but to be indifferent		62d
Yoshihiko Kikuchi	Hawaiian lived in leper colony to be with wife —story		76f-77c
Gordon B. Hinckley	, is the lodestar of life. A constant amid change	May 1989	66b-c
	Those who hate don't win unless you hate back		67b
	, can be nurtured & strengthened or starved & weakened		67d
W. Eugene Hansen	Which child did widow , most? —story	Nov 1989	24b-e
Thomas S. Monson	3 Young Men carried pioneers across river —story	May 1990	46f-47a
	Man gave street cleaner his coat —story		47a-b
	Samaritans bought room and food —story		48a-e
LeGrand R. Curtis	Discipline is organized ,	Nov 1990	12f
Thomas S. Monson	White ribbon on apple tree —story	May 1991	59f-60b
Howard W. Hunter	W. Richards willing to die for Joseph		64b-c
Loren C. Dunn	Coach united team and town —story		82e-83a
Howard W. Hunter	, transcends race, language and economics	Nov 1991	18c-f
Marion D. Hanks	Must learn , to inherit Kingdom with Jesus	May 1992	9a-11b
Vaughn J. Featherstone	"After we have mastered the winds, waves…"		43b
Howard W. Hunter	Thief was baptized —story		62b-f
	A more excellent way —entire talk		61b-63b
Russell M. Nelson	Only way to take sorrow out of death is to take , out of life		72d
C. Max Caldwell	We , those we serve most	Nov 1992	30d-e
Thomas S. Monson	, isn't , till you give it away	May 1993	61f
Aileen H. Clyde	Orphans began to thrive when given , —story	Nov 1993	93b-e
Albert Choules, Jr.	Children don't have to be commanded to , —story	May 1994	13c-e
Thomas S. Monson	When power of , replaces , of power		61b
Dallin H. Oaks	Must have an object - faith, too		98e-99a

Love

Joe J. Christensen	If I change my mind I'll let you know —story	May 1995	65b-c
Dallin H. Oaks	The most powerful force in the world	Nov 1995	25e-f
Neal A. Maxwell	"I love you anyway" —child's surgery story	May 1996	70a-b
James E. Faust	He insensitively let grandmother fill wood box —story	Nov 1997	59d-e
Margaret D. Nadauld	Injured 5-year-old helped by twin —story	May 1998	64c-e
Stephen A. West	Examples of Christlike , —stories	May 1999	28b-29f
Robert D. Hales	, vs. force. , is power. Force depresses		34b-c
James E. Faust	Better to be trusted than loved —D.O. McKay		46e-f
Vaughn J. Featherstone	11-year-old boy cleaned kitchen for 3 hours —story	Nov 1999	15a-c
Dallin H. Oaks	, of God and man is highest reason for service		79c
Russell M. Nelson	Old Egyptian manuscript explains , of God	May 2000	84e-f
Thomas S. Monson	At death nothing matters but who loved you	Nov 2000	65f-66a
Sharon G. Larsen	, is listening when child is ready to talk —story	Nov 2001	67e-68a
Robert F. Orton	, is the driving force behind faith		81e
	, is a natural consequence of service		82b
	The first and great commandment		81b-82f
Jeffrey R. Holland	Jealousy and the other prodigal —entire talk	May 2002	62d-64f
Gayle M. Clegg	Man made frozen girl run —story		68e-69a
Gene R. Cook	, shared is , multiplied		82f
Lance B. Wickman	Grief is the natural by-product of ,	Nov 2002	30c
F. Melvin Hammond	"Dad, are you awake?" —story		97d-f
Susan W. Tanner	Parental , makes the difference	May 2003	74d-75b
Thomas S. Monson	Quarrel made boy leave - , brought him back —story	Nov 2003	58a-d
W. Douglas Shumway	Is when comfort and security of another is more important	May 2004	95a
John H. Groberg	Starving missionary sustained by , —story	Nov 2004	10a-f
	Drowning missionary saved by , —story		10f-11f
	True , is a power —entire talk		9d-11f
H. David Burton	Elder couldn't memorize but had great , —story		100a-b
Thomas S. Monson	Widow's house renovated —story	May 2005	56a-e
David A. Bednar	Choice of hymn showed Jesus', —story		99b-e
	Letter arrived after husband's death —story		100a-b
Thomas S. Monson	Joseph's martyrdom exemplified , —story	Nov 2005	68f-69b
Joseph B. Wirthlin	The greatest of all the commandments	May 2006	100b
D. Todd Christofferson	A year without lunch to buy an Ironrite —story	Nov 2006	46b-d
Don R. Clarke	Helped blind man —story		97b-98b
	Uplifting others is our mission —J.F. Smith		98d
Gordon B. Hinckley	LDS stands for love, devotion, service		115f
Susan W. Tanner	She felt God's love for young women	May 2007	109a-b
Elaine S. Dalton	Man carried 5 packs for others —story		114b-d
Joseph B. Wirthlin	"A man filled with love ranges..." —J. Smith	Nov 2007	28f
	Comforts, counsels, cures and consoles		28f-29a
	, shown by J. Smith to visiting boy —story		29b-d
	Man painted invalid wife's nails —story		29d-e
	God never gives up on us		29f-30a
	Obedience ceases to be a burden when we ,		30a-c

Love, cont'd
Related Topics: Charity, Self-Respect

Joseph B. Wirthlin	The grand key to happiness		30f
	The one trait which will most improve us		31a
Steven E. Snow	One piece of candy shared among friends —story		103f-104b
Silvia H. Allred	When shepherds care, others return to fold		114f
D. Todd Christofferson	Man cut his table in half —story	Nov 2008	39f-40d
Robert D. Hales	Love your accusers		74f-75b
Thomas S. Monson	They do not , who do not show ,		86b-d
David A. Bednar	Must tell people we , that we , them	Nov 2009	17e-18f
Dieter F. Uchtdorf	Great list of what , is and does		21e-f
	God does not need us to , Him		21f-22a
	We have a vast capacity for ,		22b
	, of wrong things vs. , of good things		22b-e
	Eloquent description of God's , for each of us		22e-23a
	How to increase , for God		23a-d
	Why is , the great commandment?		24b-f
Dallin H. Oaks	Does not supersede commandments		26b-e
	God's anger is an evidence of His ,		26e-27d
	Judgment will be based on law, not ,		27e-28c
	Parental dealings with wayward children		28d-29b
Henry B. Eyring	Becoming like Jesus through ,		70f-71b
Jeffrey R. Holland	Differences between , and lust	May 2010	44e-45b
Dieter F. Uchtdorf	Jesus taught and showed ,		70d-e
	Excellent discussion of what , is		70f-75b
Russell M. Nelson	God's , for His children is infinite		91c-92b
Bradley D. Foster	Mother's , typifies Savior's		100e

Man
Related Topics: Individual

Hugh B. Brown	What is man? —Talmage	June 1969	31f-32a
John H. Vandenberg	You are your greatest problem and treasure		48e
S. Dilworth Young	May be creators of heavens		84a
David O. McKay	A dual being - an animal if only physical		116d-e
David O. McKay	Choice lifts , above animals	Dec 1969	30e
	Church exists for welfare of ,		31e
Hugh B. Brown	Called to help finish world		33a
	Nature divided against self		33a
Sterling W. Sill	God, angels, spirits and men are all same species		47d-e
David O. McKay	A dual being - physical, spiritual		110f
	Not living for self		111c
Bruce R. McConkie	Men to become as God —L. Snow's poem	June 1970	43b-c
Sterling W. Sill	We claim to be children of God and then act like orphans		45f
Ezra Taft Benson	Man is essentially good	June 1971	32d
Dallin H. Oaks	Comparison of world's and Church's view of , —good	Dec 1971	109a-c
John H. Vandenberg	3 examples on smallness of , —T. Roosevelt for one		115c-e
	All God's creations are for man		116a-b
Alvin R. Dyer	Man is what he thinks and does		122a

Marion G. Romney	May become like God	July 1973	11a
	, —essay by Pope		13f
	Evils of evolution theory of man		14a
	A God in embryo		14b
John H. Vandenberg	Earth created for ,	Nov 1974	93b-c
Boyd K. Packer	Children of God may become like him —entire talk	Nov 1984	66b-69f
Hugh W. Pinnock	Minister shown that , could become as God —story		73d-e
Ted E. Brewerton	The vastness of space and the individual's importance	Nov 1986	28f-30c
	What is man? —quote by James E. Talmage		31a-b
Carlos E. Asay	, is but a beast until he becomes spiritual	May 1992	41c
Boyd K. Packer	Most destructive teaching: man is just an advanced animal		67d-f
Russell M. Nelson	69 billion people on earth		72f
Boyd K. Packer	Complementing differences between , and woman	Nov 1993	21f
Russell M. Nelson	Don't deny rights because of race	May 1994	71d
Gordon B. Hinckley	, may become as God	Nov 1994	48d
David A. Bednar	How to become God's chosen	May 2005	100f-101e
	Man's work and God's work		101f-102a
Robert D. Hales	Blasphemy to say , looks like God?	Nov 2009	30a-b
Thomas S. Monson	Man alone received intelligence	May 2010	88b

David O. McKay	Happiness here and hereafter depend on choice of mate	June 1969	3f
	Warn against secret and hasty ,		3f-4a
	Primary purpose of , is to raise a family		4f-5e
LeGrand Richards	Not good for man to be alone before or after death		92e
Richard L. Evans	No more important commitment	Dec 1969	73b
A. Theodore Tuttle	A calling from which we're never released		107b
Bruce R. McConkie	Everything in Church centers around Celestial ,	June 1970	43e-44a
Harold B. Lee	Comments on being sealed by Holy Ghost	Dec 1970	105c-e
Milton R. Hunter	Greatest laws of gospel pertain to ,	June 1971	42b
Gordon B. Hinckley	Except the Lord build the house…		71d
	One's mate is the most precious friend		71e
	4 cornerstones for a ,		71e-72f
James A. Cullimore	Rearing a family is the purpose of ,		93b-c
	No eternal progress without eternal , —Smith		93c
	Apathy most dangerous in , —Lee		94b
	Constant confidence, counsel, compromise, courtship		94d
	Thoughts on continual courtship		94e-f
Milton R. Hunter	Express love for mate every day	Dec 1971	69b-c
LeGrand Richards	No other major church believes , is eternal —story		82c-83f
	The minister believed , was eternal —story		82c-83f
Spencer W. Kimball	A , ruined from lack of communication —story	July 1972	38a
	A , ruined from lack of communication —story		39c
Vaughn J. Featherstone	Positive and negative remarks to mate —funny story		45a
	Praise of his wife		45e

Marriage, cont'd

Elray L. Christiansen	Parents must avoid disputations	July 1972	55b
Gordon B. Hinckley	A , saved by a priesthood committee		71b
	Comments on "Till death do ye part"		72f
Boyd K. Packer	Discussion on chastity and sex in , —excellent		111d
James E. Faust	Thanks given to his wife	Jan 1973	81b
Boyd K. Packer	A , with no cross words ever —story		89f
LeGrand Richards	No other church believes in eternal , —story	July 1973	79b
Henry D. Taylor	Happiness does not begin at the altar —McKay	Jan 1974	36a
	Wise advice before or after ,		36b
	How to have a happy ,		36c
	Return to temple each anniversary		36f
	Repent - don't divorce or separate		37b
LeGrand Richards	No other major church believes , is eternal —story		57b
	The minister believed , was eternal —story		57c
	The minister believed , was eternal —story		57d
	Not good for man to be alone before death or after either		59a
	Scriptures supporting eternal ,		59b
Robert L. Simpson	Look for someone capable of perfection, not already there		88c
Harold B. Lee	No man who is unmarried is living his religion		99d
	Wife considered divorce for frivolous reason		99f
	Where to go for counsel when troubles come —story		100b
	Holders of priesthood have duty to marry —story		100b
Spencer W. Kimball	All strongly urged to get married and have children	May 1974	6c-d
Gordon B. Hinckley	Conversation with non-member couple about , —story		22e-23c
	Lasts as long as the jurisdiction of authority		23e
	I want you only for a little while —funny story		24d-e
Elray L. Christiansen	True love is not earthbound		25e
Spencer W. Kimball	All normal people should marry	Nov 1974	8d-e
Paul H. Dunn	Mission then ,	May 1975	62a
Spencer W. Kimball	Work out discipline and budget together	Nov 1975	6c
	If we cease , we are done for		112e
H. Burke Peterson	Priesthood fulfilled only with happy wife at side	May 1976	34a
James M. Paramore	For wife's sake, come home when you say you will —story	May 1977	42e-43a
L. Tom Perry	The most vital of all decisions		60b
Barbara B. Smith	Working together in partnerships —story		91f-92a
James E. Faust	6 questions you should ask before or during ,	Nov 1977	10b
	Payment of tithing helps ,		11a
	Most sublime happiness comes thru ,		11a
	, greatly enriched through parenthood		11b
O. Leslie Stone	Don't yell, keep order, help wife, be chivalrous	May 1978	56d-57a
N. Eldon Tanner	Scriptural supports showing , is meant to be eternal	May 1980	16b-d
	Advice Tanner gives to those approaching ,		17a-c
Robert L. Simpson	Each useless without the other —poem	Nov 1980	10f-11a
Rex C. Reeve, Jr.	Heaven is shut to him who comes alone		28c
Gordon B. Hinckley	A , ruined because of speaking of each others' faults		62d-e

Marriage

Boyd K. Packer	A monumental transgression to destroy a ,	May 1981	14b-d
	We hear of divorce because wreaks make headlines		14f-15a
	Dying wife urged husband to remarry soon —story		15b-c
Robert L. Simpson	Importance of communication in ,	May 1982	21c-f
	Importance of finances in ,		22a-f
	God commends and commands ,		23a
Bruce R. McConkie	It is an order of the priesthood		34a
J. Richard Clarke	Don't label jobs strictly male or female		78e
H. Burke Peterson	Measure a man by the way he treats his ,	Nov 1982	44a-b
Ezra Taft Benson	Only 2 whom we are commanded to love with all our hearts	Nov 1983	43e-f
Gordon B. Hinckley	Counsel to women who have civil ,		82d-e
David B. Haight	How to tell when you're in love	May 1984	14e-f
Russell M. Nelson	His wife supported him through schooling	Nov 1984	31b-c
	Couples bear and share priesthood		32b
Marion D. Hanks	The importance of friendship in ,		36f-37b
	Other covenants must precede covenants of ,		37b-c
Thomas S. Monson	Mission call came the day after ,		41e
Boyd K. Packer	, provides shelter for helpless, innocent children	Nov 1986	17f-18a
Russell M. Nelson	His wife didn't expect much, so was rarely disappointed		67f-68b
James E. Faust	Why not just live together?	May 1987	81a-d
Ezra Taft Benson	How wives should be treated —good	Nov 1987	49f-50e
Russell M. Nelson	One plus one is greater than two		89b
Ezra Taft Benson	If you limit posterity, you will feel the loss	May 1988	52d
	The greatest responsibilities and greatest joy		52d
Yoshihiko Kikuchi	Hawaiian lived in leper colony to be with wife —story		76f-77c
Thomas S. Monson	Eyes fixed on different stars won't bring happiness	Nov 1988	69f
	No enmity if couples pray together		70a
Ezra Taft Benson	Advice to single women about ,		96e-97a
	All blessings will come to faithful single women		97b
James E. Faust	What is the Holy Spirit of Promise?	May 1989	33b-d
Thomas S. Monson	Hugh B. Brown always waved handkerchief to wife —story	Nov 1989	67e-f
Kenneth Johnson	I wouldn't consider marrying you unless in the temple —story	May 1990	42e
Gordon B. Hinckley	Neither man nor woman exalted without the other	May 1991	71d-e
	Little sympathy for single young men		71f
	, is not perpetual bliss		72a-f
	Spouse is most valuable asset		74f
	, —excellent talk		71b-74f
Gordon B. Hinckley	Condemnation of domineering and unfaithful husbands	Nov 1991	51c-f
	The way a , should be		52a-b
Russell M. Nelson	Temple , - his most important accomplishment	May 1992	74c-d
Thomas S. Monson	Husbands never outgrow need for affection		101f
Thomas S. Monson	Waited 9 years to marry blind man —story	Nov 1992	69d-70b
Thomas S. Monson	Counsel for unselfishness in ,		98b
	President Brown waved white handkerchief —story		98b-c
	What gift do you want? - A temple sealing —story		99a-e

Marriage

Marriage, cont'd
Related Topics: Temple Marriage

Thomas S. Monson	Constant irritant became loving ritual —story	Nov 1992	99a-e
James E. Faust	Counsel for , —excellent	May 1993	36c-e
Russell M. Nelson	First priority of priesthood is to honor wife		40b
Spencer J. Condie	Husband changed when she changed self —story	Nov 1993	17b-d
Boyd K. Packer	Includes most beautiful experiences of life		21c
	Plan of happiness requires ,		21d
	Parable of the vault and the safe —parable		23c-f
L. Tom Perry	My Three White Dresses —poem		67f-68a
Dallin H. Oaks	Intimacy within , is pleasing to God		74b-d
	No exaltation without proper ,		74e-f
	Unmarried men are deficient in a sacred duty		74f-75a
	Have all the children you can care for		75a-c
Jeanne Inouye	, didn't happen until age 34 —story		96d-97c
Boyd K. Packer	Sexual powers must be protected until ,	May 1994	19d-e
	Man's responsibility in , transcends all else		20f-21a
Howard W. Hunter	The pattern for family life	Nov 1994	9a
Jeffrey R. Holland	"Wherever she was, there was paradise"		32a
Howard W. Hunter	Don't postpone sacred obligation of ,		49d-f
	No blessings withheld if no opportunity for ,		49f-50b
	Nothing takes precedence over spouse		50b
J. Ballard Washburn	Covenant includes willingness to have children	May 1995	12b-c
Joe J. Christensen	Numerous good thoughts —entire talk		64b-66b
Jack H. Goaslind	Proper , is critical to exaltation	Nov 1995	10b
David B. Haight	His parents' , and his travels to temple —story		73e-74c
Gordon B. Hinckley	Proclamation on the family		100f-101e
Boyd K. Packer	Offer an unpolluted body to your companion	May 1996	19d-f
Gordon B. Hinckley	Education better equips girls for ,		92b
Bruce C. Hafen	Difference between contract and covenant ,	Nov 1996	26b-d
	No children, no misery —humor		26e
	Can yield best religious experiences		26e
	Each , is tested 3 ways		26f-27b
Robert D. Hales	Eternal , doesn't just happen		64d-65f
Richard G. Scott	Takes 2 different halves to make a whole		73f-74b
Jeffrey R. Holland	Humorous look at young married years	May 1997	35d-e
Russell M. Nelson	Two most important relationships are by covenant		71d-e
	Magnify wife and magnify priesthood		71f
	Weak commitment to Lord causes weaker ,		72b
	4 "f's" must not be loved more than spouse		72c
Thomas S. Monson	, in temple is determined by friends		94f-95a
Eran A. Call	Statistics on , and divorce	Nov 1997	28e-f
	, and family —important quotes		29b-e
Richard J. Maynes	Very difficult to cram for mission or ,		30b-31f
Gordon B. Hinckley	Nothing as valuable as love of wife		52e-f
Thomas S. Monson	No blessing to be withheld from singles		96b-c
James E. Faust	From , springs all other relationships	May 1998	45a

Marriage

Gordon B. Hinckley	No greater happiness - most important choice	May 1998	51f
Gordon B. Hinckley	Polygamy unacceptable even where allowed	Nov 1998	71e-72a
Richard G. Scott	Qualities to seek in prospective spouse	May 1999	26a-c
Russell M. Nelson	Most important day of life		39c-e
	Nothing takes priority over wife		39c-e
James E. Faust	Mistake to think life begins with ,	Nov 1999	102b-c
Richard G. Scott	Counsel about sex in ,	May 2000	37c-d
James E. Faust	Don't take a secret shame to your ,		44e-f
Sheri L. Dew	The united roles of men and women	Nov 2001	12d-14f
Russell M. Nelson	Celestial , is source of greatest joy		71c
	No sacrifice too great to have eternal ,		71c-d
Boyd K. Packer	The value of a wife	May 2002	9f-10b
Dallin H. Oaks	Widowed mother made father a daily presence		35a
Gordon B. Hinckley	Man and woman are equals in ,		53f-54a
	Wife abuse nullifies man's priesthood		54a-b
F. Melvin Hammond	Sons will treat wives like Dad treated Mom	Nov 2002	98d-99a
Kathleen H. Hughes	Temple , seals children. They will return —B.K. Packer		107d-f
James E. Faust	Faithful single women will have , later		112e
Gordon B. Hinckley	Long life attributed to fresh air —humor	May 2003	59f
F. Burton Howard	The crowning gospel ordinance		92d-e
	What we give and get from eternal ,		92e-93d
	If lasting forever it is treated differently —silverware story		93f-94f
Boyd K. Packer	Chance for , is not past for righteous	Nov 2003	25a-b
Russell M. Nelson	A husband's foremost priority is his wife		46f
Gordon B. Hinckley	What to look for in a husband		114c-d
James E. Faust	Most important choice in life	May 2004	53a
L. Tom Perry	No president in , - coequals		71d-f
Gordon B. Hinckley	One is incomplete without the other	Nov 2004	84a-b
	The cure for marital troubles		84e
Dallin H. Oaks	Surprised that his mother was a widow —story	Nov 2005	27d-f
Richard G. Scott	Compensating opportunities postmortally		79a
Russell M. Nelson	Man on plane ignored wife —story	May 2006	36b-c
	, brings greatest possibility for happiness		36c-d
	Worldly definitions of , are contrary		36e
	A foundry, a fountain, a foundation		36f
	A commandment and an exalting principle		37a
	Doctrinal foundation for a joyful ,		36e-37b
	Foremost priesthood duty is to nurture ,		37b
	Appreciation, communication, contemplation		37d-38d
Gordon B. Hinckley	The man is an infidel if he won't work		58e-f
Richard G. Scott	A higher priority for girls than mission		88b-c
Joseph B. Wirthlin	A perfect ,	Nov 2006	28f
Jeffrey R. Holland	Speak no cold, caustic, unkind remarks to spouse	May 2007	16f-17d
James E. Faust	Government of Church based on , and family		55d-56a
Dallin H. Oaks	The trivializing of modern ,		70c-e

Marriage

Marriage, cont'd
Related Topics: Divorce, Temple Marriage

Dallin H. Oaks	Divorced persons may marry again	May 2007	70f
	Remedy for problems in , is repentance		71b-72e
	Healing was achieved 100% of the time		72e-73a
	2/3 of unhappy , were happy 5 years later		73a
Gordon B. Hinckley	Wife is your most precious possession		105e
Joseph B. Wirthlin	Man painted invalid wife's nails —story	Nov 2007	29d-e
Gordon B. Hinckley	Married 67 years - No quarrel		63a
	Old age attributed to fresh air —humor		66a
Julie B. Beck	Commandment to bear children remains in force		76d-e
Russell M. Nelson	Temple sealing enables exaltation	May 2008	9a
Kenneth Johnson	A soaring symphony from a simple melody		15f-16a
Henry B. Eyring	P.P. Pratt's feelings about eternal ,		62f-63c
M. Russell Ballard	Things husbands should do for wives		110b-c
Thomas S. Monson	Don't let Daddy touch the microwave		111b
	Grandfather left on mission 3 days after ,		111c-d
Richard G. Scott	A priesthood interview about your , covenants	Nov 2008	45a-f
	An equal partnership		45f-46a
	Wives are not to be owned or dominated		46d-e
	Express frequent love and gratitude		46f
Russell M. Nelson	"Patterns of the shopper" —parable		92b-d
	Celestial marriage —entire talk		92b-95b
Robert D. Hales	We can't afford it - Communication in , —story	May 2009	8b-9b
Neil L. Andersen	Trying to become what she thought I already was		79b
David A. Bednar	Must frequently express love to spouse	Nov 2009	17e-18f
Henry B. Eyring	Covenant to put welfare of spouse at center		70f-71b
	Father cared for mother in last illness		71d-f
Joseph W. Sitati	Church does away with tradition of dowry		105a-b
Dieter F. Uchtdorf	His courtship of wife —story	May 2010	125f-126c

Meditation (Pondering)
Related Topics: Communication, Mind, Thoughts

David O. McKay	Sit down and commune with yourself	June 1969	30a-b
Paul H. Dunn	We just sit and think, mostly sit. —story	Dec 1970	37d
Marion G. Romney	Discussion of the word "ponder" —good	July 1973	90e
Marvin J. Ashton	, solves problems more quickly than frantic force	Nov 1981	90c
M. Russell Ballard	Regularly find some quiet time to think	May 1987	14e
Marvin J. Ashton	Pondering is a gift and a commandment	Nov 1987	20e-f
Thomas S. Monson	Sit down and commune with yourself —D.O. McKay	Nov 2004	68e-f
Richard G. Scott	Lord prompts in quiet moments	May 2007	9d
Marlin K. Jensen	Church historian speaks of value of remembering		36d-38f
Walter F. Gonzalez	Pondering strengthens for future trials	Nov 2007	54b-f
William D. Oswald	Invites personal revelation - A teaching tool	Nov 2008	97f
Richard G. Scott	, brought further inspiration —story	Nov 2009	7b-8d

Military Service

Hartman Rector, Jr.	Young men away from home for the first time—observations	Dec 1968	47d-48e
Gordon B. Hinckley	Soldiers: moral coward and one who stood taunting —stories		69d-70a
Victor L. Brown	Why some must die		98c-d
Mark E. Petersen	The immorality of men in ,	June 1969	78d-79a
Hugh B. Brown	Canadian Mormons in WWI —stories (Word of Wisdom)		97d-98e
Boyd K. Packer	All Asian missions opened by servicemen	June 1970	52f
	Young men should be ready to serve in ,		54a
	Helps available to men entering ,		52c-54a
	When he was tempted to break Word of Wisdom		54c-e
	He gained his testimony in the ,		54e
Sterling W. Sill	Many of God's greatest men were military men	Dec 1970	79b-d
	Religion in , is an effective armor		79d-e
Robert L. Simpson	Is , and participating in war righteous?		97a-c
N. Eldon Tanner	, and prostitution	Dec 1971	112a-c
William H. Bennett	Three experiences with non-members in , —stories	July 1972	83b
Harold B. Lee	A man who nearly lost his chastity in , —story		102a
David B. Haight	Constant resistance of evil finally brought respect		107b
David B. Haight	7 LDS on tiny island base holding services	Jan 1974	41b
L. Tom Perry	He exchanged drinking companions for LDS —story	May 1974	98e-99b
David B. Haight	Importance of writing letters to men in ,	May 1975	10d-12b
Thomas S. Monson	He gave a blessing as 60 sailors watched —story	May 1979	37b-e
Paul H. Dunn	Soldiers caught him praying —story	May 1980	38f-39c
Thomas S. Monson	Gave youth that the world might grow old in peace —poem	May 1992	60c-d
Thomas S. Monson	Numbers of war dead at Normandy	May 1994	61a-b
L. Tom Perry	His WWII sacrament meetings —story	May 1996	53b-e
Thomas S. Monson	Family lost 4 sons in WWII —story	Nov 1999	20c-e
Boyd K. Packer	Calmness came through music in crises —story		23b-24b
James E. Faust	Some lowered standards - others did not	Nov 2000	45a-d
James E. Faust	Warning to persons in ,	May 2003	52e-53a
Gordon B. Hinckley	Our , obligations during war		78d-81f
Boyd K. Packer	His question about war answered by Book of Mormon	May 2005	7f-8a
David E. Sorensen	Couldn't be officer because of mission —story		72b-73b
D. Todd Christofferson	Faust's interview for officer school —story	Nov 2009	105d-f
Boyd K. Packer	President declined to bless man —story	May 2010	8b-d

Mind

Sterling W. Sill	Mind is what it feeds upon	Dec 1969	46c
	Mind is colored by what it holds		46e
Richard L. Evans	Finest mechanism in universe		73d
Joseph Anderson	The , is a library	Dec 1970	54b
Harold B. Lee	Gets hot in meetings because of mind —story		104a-e
Robert L. Simpson	Quality input fights efforts to control ,	Jan 1973	112b
O. Leslie Stone	The only eternal work of art	Nov 1976	61f-62a
LeGrand Richards	Unseen powers operate on minds of men	May 1977	63d
Boyd K. Packer	Only 20% of a doctor's ailments were of the body	Nov 1977	59c

Boyd K. Packer	Like a vacant corner lot the , collects trash —good	Nov 1977	59e-60a
Sterling W. Sill	How would you like to create your own , ?	May 1978	66d-e
Russell M. Nelson	Endowed with power to recall everything	Nov 1985	30e-f
Boyd K. Packer	Reason and faith together will protect and redeem	May 1989	54f
M. Russell Ballard	Minds are banks - what you put in comes back with interest		78e
Thomas S. Monson	Your , is a cupboard	May 2005	19e-f
James E. Faust	Addictions are , altering	Nov 2007	123d-124a
Boyd K. Packer	Holy Ghost communicates through , more than senses	Nov 2009	44b-d
	Keep , clean and free from clutter of the world		45b-d
Jeffrey R. Holland	Pornography can blast a permanent crater in ,	May 2010	44e

Mission
Related Topics: Missionaries, Missionary Work

David O. McKay	His , changed the course of his life	Dec 1968	34f-35a
Joseph F. Smith	All sent with a ,	Dec 1969	37b
Paul H. Dunn	Accent on youth but stress on parents when paying for ,	Dec 1970	38f
	What a , does for a boy		38f-39b
Spencer W. Kimball	Every worthy LDS male should fill a ,	May 1974	87c
A. Theodore Tuttle	I don't want to go - So what. "We need you"	Nov 1974	71b-d
	Nothing takes precedence over a ,		71d-e
	Things to do to prepare for a ,		71e-f
	Financial preparation for a ,		72a-c
	Will make a better marriage		72c
	How a , will make you feel		72f
N. Eldon Tanner	No business would send out an untrustworthy representative		77d-e
Spencer W. Kimball	Save for a mission! Fill One!		82f-83a
Loren C. Dunn	Too big a sacrifice? —stories in Samoa	May 1975	25d-27b
Hartman Rector, Jr.	Why do young men serve , - position, power, acclaim?		56e-57a
Paul H. Dunn	, then marriage		62a
	Cost of a ,		62c
J. Thomas Fyans	6 things fathers and young men can do to prepare for a ,	May 1977	39b-40f
A. Theodore Tuttle	A call for elderly couples to serve a ,	Nov 1977	55a-56b
Robert L. Simpson	Amazing personal blessings received from a ,	May 1978	36d-f
	All men to prepare for a ,		37a
Vaughn J. Featherstone	This time is the Lord's, not yours —story	Nov 1978	26b-c
Ezra Taft Benson	Why were you sent to earth under such favorable conditions	May 1979	33a
Wm. Grant Bangerter	How he changed minds of youth about serving a ,	May 1980	46f-47a
William R. Bradford	Purpose of , - to sanctify elder and make converts	Nov 1981	49f
Gordon B. Hinckley	Things to do to prepare for a ,	May 1982	42e-f
Royden G. Derrick	Every stake leader served a , - importance of ,	May 1983	24f-25a
Victor L. Brown	16-year-old won a car - used it to finance , —story		61e
Jack H. Goaslind, Jr.	Not an option	Nov 1983	33f-34a
Vaughn J. Featherstone	Catholic boy committed to serve , —story		37a
Devin G. Durrant	Promised he'd be better ball player when he returned —story	May 1984	35d-e
	Chickens laid better while , was served —story		35f
	Spanish boy converted - serves , —story		35f-36e

Devin G. Durrant	Love, faith and testimony more important than talents —story	May 1984	36f-37b
Boyd K. Packer	Every young man should serve a , —parable/story		41d-43b
Ezra Taft Benson	Missionary spoke on different subject —story		44b-f
	Every young man should serve a ,		45a
	All 11 children served a , —story		45c-e
Thomas S. Monson	Mission call came day after marriage	Nov 1984	41e
R. LaVell Edwards	Does a , and college athletics mix?		44b-46b
Ezra Taft Benson	How to prepare sons to serve ,	May 1985	7b-e
	The , tradition in his family		8e-f
	4 ways to prepare for ,		36c-e
	Didn't follow counsel—crowd roughed him up—story		36e-37f
M. Russell Ballard	Young man planning marriage called on , —story		42f-43b
Gordon B. Hinckley	A , is a tithe of one's life		49b
Gordon B. Hinckley	How men respond when called as , presidents	Nov 1985	83f-84f
Gordon B. Hinckley	Account of his own hesitancy about a , —story	May 1986	40c-41b
Ezra Taft Benson	Most important duty is to preach gospel —J. Smith		44d
	1/5 of young men serve a ,		44d
	We want men who begin their , on the run		45e-f
H. Verlan Andersen	The missions of his family	Nov 1986	24d-e
Ezra Taft Benson	The calling of his father on a , —story		45f-46c
	The calling of his father on a , —story		47f-48c
A. Theodore Tuttle	Faith financed his , —story		73c-f
Ezra Taft Benson	His feelings about young women serving a ,		83a
David B. Haight	! wish I'd be asked to do something really important —story	May 1987	61e
	The goal of every couple should be a ,		61e-f
Thomas S. Monson	Young man assigned to S. Africa —humorous story	Nov 1987	42f-43a
	Man called on , 3 days after marriage —story		43d
Robert L. Backman	A , is like being dipped in a big pot of love		62c
	How to prepare for a , —entire talk		60c-63b
William R. Bradford	The finest thing I have ever done		75e
Ben B. Banks	Preparing for bike trip compared to , —story	Nov 1989	40d-41b
	Sister missionary's parents converted —story		41f-42a
Joe J. Christensen	Young German banker called to Japan —story		43d-44d
Gordon B. Hinckley	1852: 98 called on "short" missions of 3-7 years		53c-f
L. Tom Perry	Account of his , interview	May 1991	39d-40e
Rex D. Pinegar	14-year-old thought he was called on , —story	Nov 1991	40d-e
Vaughn J. Featherstone	Serve a couple , and save your family	May 1992	44b-d
	Eloquent plea for couple missionaries		44e-f
	The need for couple missionaries		42d-44f
L. Aldin Porter	H.C. Kimball's , to England		45c-e
Thomas S. Monson	Couple's 5-year , to open Poland		48e-f
Thomas S. Monson	Marriage postponed for , —story	Nov 1992	47e-48b
Hugh W. Pinnock	Non-member general: A , is what it's all about	Nov 1993	42a-b
Gordon B. Hinckley	, funds donated when elder died —story		52e-f
David B. Haight	Baseball player would not sign contract —story		61f

Mission

Mission, cont'd
Related Topics: Missionaries, Missionary Work

Marlin K. Jensen	5-year , to Palmyra became 25 —story	May 1994	48b-e
Howard W. Hunter	Every able, worthy young man - couples too	Nov 1994	88e-f
Harold G. Hillam	Sons of Mosiah, Kimball and Young —stories	Nov 1995	41c-42b
	Sacrifice of Brazilian to serve , —story		42b-e
	No more majestic call than a ,		42f
Gordon B. Hinckley	The great blessings of a ,		51c-52c
James E. Faust	10 things to know about a ,	May 1996	40b-42f
Henry B. Eyring	Changes older couples, too	Nov 1996	32f-33a
Joe J. Christensen	Played basketball better after , —story		40f-41a
	Who should serve a , ?		41b
Richard C. Edgley	What a typical , entails		62e-f
Russell M. Nelson	Everything hinged upon President Hinckley's ,	Nov 1997	15a-b
Richard J. Maynes	Very difficult to cram for , or marriage		30b-31f
Richard G. Scott	, opportunities for couples		36d-37b
Gordon B. Hinckley	Relatively few young women should serve a ,		52b-e
Earl C. Tingey	"Short" 3-7 year ,	May 1998	39f-40a
	How to prepare for and serve a ,		40c-f
Gordon B. Hinckley	Serving a , makes a better husband		50f-51a
Gordon B. Hinckley	His , - to be out among the people		69b-e
H. Bryan Richards	Three statements that young men should serve ,	Nov 1998	43b-d
Gordon B. Hinckley	His promises to those who serve a ,		52d-e
David B. Haight	Examples of couples serving a ,	May 1999	69b-f
Richard G. Scott	Everything he treasures today began with his ,	May 2001	8a-c
Jeffrey R. Holland	Couple raised potato production from 50 to 550 sacks —story		15d-16c
	Family leased out home to finance ,		16c-e
James E. Faust	, may open other opportunities	Nov 2001	49a
Boyd K. Packer	Little ward spoke 15 languages —story		64d-e
L. Tom Perry	10 months and a war with same companion —story		77b-f
Spencer J. Condie	Account of W. Woodruff's missions —story	May 2002	44b-e
Dallin H. Oaks	Perfect , spot humbled proud elder —story	Nov 2002	70b-f
Thomas S. Monson	Prized violin sold to finance , —story	May 2003	19e-20c
Daryl H. Garn	Prepared for basketball but not , —story		46b-e
Richard G. Scott	Preparation for a ,	Nov 2003	42b-43f
Russell M. Nelson	Types of , available to senior couples	Nov 2004	82b
Robert D. Hales	That moment changed my life forever	May 2005	39b-c
	The 5 F's of serving a ,		39d-e
	Daughter's problems solved by parents' , —story		40a-d
	What part of life would you want to live over?		40f-41a
	Couple missions plant seed of service in family		41d
	Lord expects us to express our desires		41d
	Examples of couple missions		41f-42d
	Now is the time		42d-e
Jeffrey R. Holland	Kimball blessing family before , —story		44e-45b
James E. Faust	His , guided the rest of his life		51b-c
	Eight things a , teaches you		51c-d

Mission

James E. Faust	Elder was saved from drowning —story	May 2005	51f-52e
David E. Sorensen	Could not be officer because of , —story		72b-73b
Anne C. Pingree	Patriarchal blessing emphasized , —story	Nov 2005	112d-114a
David F. Evans	Hinckley's , changed his life	May 2006	32f-33d
	Changed his life - lifted the fog		34a-b
Richard G. Scott	Girls should not be pressured to serve		88b-c
	Effects of using Preach My Gospel		87d-88e
	His daughter's call and ,		88e-89a
	The far-reaching effects of his ,		89d-90a
	His wife's , was a great blessing		90a
	Young men may regret not serving		90b
Robert D. Hales	A tithing on first 20 years of life	May 2007	49e-f
Michael J. Teh	Took him a long time to decide to serve a ,	Nov 2007	36e
L. Tom Perry	Minimum qualifications to serve a ,		47d-48b
	How to prepare to serve a , —good		48b-49b
Thomas S. Monson	Responsibility to serve ,		59d-e
Julie B. Beck	Home: A pre-mission training center		77b-d
Silvia H. Allred	Elder Holland thinks of his , every day	Nov 2008	11d
Thomas S. Monson	Two-year , to Poland became five —story		60e-67a
Elaine S. Dalton	Focus changes during a ,	May 2009	120b-e

David O. McKay	One of his mission experiences - "What e'er thou art"	June 1969	30b-c
S. Dilworth Young	Elder Young's financial experiences as a ,	Dec 1969	61a-c
	Seventies financial help to , from foreign lands		61d-62c
Thomas S. Monson	Story of , from farm —story		89f
	Fear makes ineffective ,		90b
	Farm boy's testimony to proud man makes convert —story		91b-c
	Diligence of , converts parents		91d
Marion D. Hanks	13,000 in field		93c
Gordon B. Hinckley	Parting words to , —short story		98a
	Miracle of ,		98d
	1/3 have inactive parents		98e
Joseph Fielding Smith	Need many more , - old, young and sisters	Dec 1970	3e-f
Paul H. Dunn	Reply of thin , to fat , —funny story		38f
Henry D. Taylor	, stilled the storm —story		44c-d
Neal A. Maxwell	12,000 in field		92b
LeGrand Richards	14,000 in field	June 1971	99a
Spencer W. Kimball	Missionary gave blood to stay on mission —story	Dec 1971	39a-d
Marvin J. Ashton	Self-motivated missionary —story		101a-b
Dr. James O. Mason	Explanation of new Health Missionary Program		107a-108f
Spencer W. Kimball	Ex missionary loses testimony from lack of study, prayer	July 1972	38b
Milton R. Hunter	15,400 in field		50a
	Sacrifices made to go on missions		50a
	Mother of , softens attitude toward Church —story		50d

Missionaries, cont'd
Related Topics: Converts, Mission, Missionary Work

Milton R. Hunter	Professional ball contracts turned down —story	July 1972	50f
	Girl joins, disowned, becomes missionary —story		50f
	Eavesdropper converts 50. Elders had baptized nobody		51b
	2 , seen in dream - make convert —story		51c
	Mission President makes sacrifice to go —story		51d
Marvin J. Ashton	An honorable release is a commencement		62f
	An outstanding handicapped , —story		63c
Gordon B. Hinckley	You're not much…but you're all the Lord has.		72a
Paul H. Dunn	Appearance masked a noble spirit —story		95c
Howard W. Hunter	16,000 in field	Jan 1973	65c
Victor L. Brown	Stories of health , —stories		68b
Franklin D. Richards	Being a , had first priority —story		72e
Thomas S. Monson	Sacrifice of parent for , —story		120f
Harold B. Lee	17,000 in field	July 1973	5f
LeGrand Richards	Wouldn't trade $1,000,000 for their experience		78c
	Teaching doctrines non-members have never heard		79a
Loren C. Dunn	Conversation changed aims of homesick elder —story	May 1974	27f-28b
James E. Faust	Conversion of a young missionary —story	Nov 1974	60c-d
	Sacrifice of a missionary —story		60e-f
Boyd K. Packer	Less than 5% of 18,000 are age 21 or over		87f-88a
Thomas S. Monson	Father was missionary's final convert —story		108f-109e
Spencer W. Kimball	19,000 in field	May 1975	4f
Marion D. Hanks	Lord told father to plant onions to finance mission —story		14d-e
Spencer W. Kimball	21,000 in field - many native to their country	Nov 1975	6b
A. Theodore Tuttle	From 17,600 to 21,000 in 18 months		23f
Henry D. Taylor	Every young man should serve —comments by Kimball		61d-f
Mark E. Petersen	Number of , 10 years ago and today		63f
Howard W. Hunter	105 , called in Oct. 1875 - compared to 7,923 today		96c
Rex D. Pinegar	Young Brazilian found way to become , —story		102e-103c
Vaughn J. Featherstone	272 health and agricultural missionaries		119b-c
	Examples of accomplishments of health ,		119d-f
	Are there couples in your ward who could serve as , ?		120e
Spencer W. Kimball	23,000 in field	May 1976	4d
Bernard P. Brockbank	1% of world = 36,000,000. , urgently needed		75f
Franklin D. Richards	25,000 in field	Nov 1976	15d
M. Russell Ballard, Jr.	How , can better prepare themselves		86f-87a
	How fathers can better prepare ,		87c-88a
	How mothers can prepare better ,		88b-c
	How leaders can prepare better ,		88c-e
Franklin D. Richards	Over 25,000 in field	May 1977	19f
Adney Y. Komatsu	Brigham Young's account of leaving on his mission	Nov 1977	28c-d
Charles A. Didier	Letter to the inactive , who converted him —story		66d-68b
Statistical Report	25,300 in field	May 1978	17c
Robert L. Simpson	Mexican sent to New Zealand - finds Chileans —story		37b-e
Spencer W. Kimball	Interesting statistics concerning ,		102c

Missionaries

Spencer W. Kimball	26,606 missionaries	Nov 1978	4d
Vaughn J. Featherstone	Stories about , —stories		26f-28b
Thomas S. Monson	, trade three D's for three T's		56a
	Told to sell stamp collection. Kimball replaced it —story		56a-c
Spencer W. Kimball	28,000 in field	May 1979	4c
Howard W. Hunter	Account of W. Woodruff's , experiences —story		24d-f
Thomas S. Monson	How , are assigned —humorous story		35f-36a
N. Eldon Tanner	How , are called —story	Nov 1979	45f-46b
Spencer W. Kimball	29,000 plus in field		78e
Spencer W. Kimball	30,004 (79% young men, 13% young women, 8% older)	May 1980	4c-d
Wm. Grant Bangerter	What to do when contact decides against baptism		47b-c
Robert L. Backman	Young man invited non-member friends to his farewell	Nov 1980	40f
Joseph B. Wirthlin	, solved problems by baptizing banker and grocer —story		70a-c
William R. Bradford	30,000 missionaries, 82 nations, 48 languages	Nov 1981	49d
	If all served who could, we'd exceed highest expectations		49e
	Answers to excuses for not serving - Advice to girls		50a-51a
	Work will go on without you—what about your sanctification		51a-b
John H. Groberg	Family prayer sustained homesick , —story	May 1982	51a-52e
Ted E. Brewerton	8 Brazilian , in 1974 - over 500 in 1979	May 1983	74b
Thomas S. Monson	5 non-member patients fasted for missionary —story	May 1984	18d-f
L. Tom Perry	Letters from older , and a plea for more couples —good		79a-80f
Ezra Taft Benson	How many , do we need? - All of them —S.W. Kimball	May 1985	7b
Robert E. Wells	Experiences and encouragement for couple , —story	Nov 1985	27e-28c
	Man locked sister , in until he'd heard it all —story		28c-d
	An act of service by , softened a professor —story		28d-f
	Divorcing couple reconciled and baptized —story		28f-29a
	No one ever cried to see me enter a room —story		29a
	Sophisticated atheistic lady lawyer baptized —story		29c-e
Russell M. Nelson	His General Authority companion shined his shoes —story	Nov 1986	68b-c
L. Tom Perry	Kimball and Young leaving on mission —story	May 1987	34f-35c
David B. Haight	Thousands of couples are needed		60b
	Baptist couple ended up on mission —story		60c-d
	Couple revived a struggling branch —story		60f-61a
	Couple made cookies for elders —story		61b-d
Robert D. Hales	A couple's great success in England —story		77b-e
Douglas J. Martin	Experiences as a missionary couple in the Philippines	Nov 1987	23d-24f
Thomas S. Monson	Missionary meets one he unknowingly touched —story		41d-42c
	Regular letters home converted father —story		43e-44f
Robert L. Backman	The , no companion could get along with —funny story		62c
Thomas S. Monson	Testimony of , bore fruit 13 years later —story	May 1988	43c-d
M. Russell Ballard	35,700 in field	Nov 1988	28e
	2 older sister , activated 12-15 families —story		29c
Gordon B. Hinckley	Wealthy couple sold all to become , —story		52a-f
Marion D. Hanks	, serving in refugee camps		64d-e
David B. Haight	The great need for couple ,		83d-85f

Missionaries

Missionaries, cont'd
Related Topics: Converts, Mission, Missionary Work

Joseph B. Wirthlin	Abinadi had just one convert	May 1989	10a-b
L. Tom Perry	The lack of training for , in years past —story		13e-f
Richard G. Scott	Healed a serious head wound —story		35d-36a
	Two , saved from horseman —story		36b-c
Thomas S. Monson	Guatemalan , returned following earthquake injury —story		45b-46b
Gordon B. Hinckley	36,132 in field		65f
Ezra Taft Benson	Need for senior ,	Nov 1989	5a-b
M. Russell Ballard	Dangers to , but the work must continue		33b-35b
Dallin H. Oaks	Couple , - I only thought I could fish		64f-65a
L. Tom Perry	, state no political opinions		71e-f
Robert K. Dellenbach	His conversion as missionary on ship —story	Nov 1990	23b-c
Thomas S. Monson	Parents promised to never write —story		47f-48b
Gordon B. Hinckley	43,651	May 1991	52b
Joseph B. Wirthlin	44,000	Nov 1991	17a
D.B. Neuenschwander	Advice to , from a mission president		42b-43f
L. Tom Perry	A call for more , and couple ,	May 1992	23b-25b
L. Aldin Porter	What , must be and do —entire talk		45b-46f
Robert L. Backman	Experiences of couple , related	Nov 1992	14c-f
Thomas S. Monson	Finest , ever recommended —humor		47c
Richard G. Scott	The miracle of , willing to serve	May 1993	32b-d
	Best , have stay-at-home mothers		32e-33d
	Comments from , applications		33d-34c
John H. Groberg	Old man rowed , to appointment —story	Nov 1993	26d-28b
Carlos H. Amado	Elder with cancer serves until death —story		45c-f
Gordon B. Hinckley	49,000		52e
David B. Haight	Destiny of human family hangs on ,		62c-d
	Kimball's call for more and better ,		62d-e
Howard W. Hunter	Every able, worthy young man - couples too	Nov 1994	88e-f
Jeffrey R. Holland	Pigs and cows supporting , died —story	May 1995	40a-f
Thomas S. Monson	What kind of men , should be —John Taylor		49c
Thomas S. Monson	Adept trainers not available for leadership	Nov 1995	49f-50a
	Elder without talents answered questions —story		50b-e
Gordon B. Hinckley	Great promises to , and challenge to serve		51c-52c
Joseph B. Wirthlin	Opportunity to be , is open for short time		76b
Lynn A. Mickelsen	8-year-old Chilean couldn't promise to be a , —story		78f-79b
F. Michael Watson	48,631 full-time ,	May 1996	21f
James E. Faust	10 things , should know		40b-42f
Thomas S. Monson	Spanish seemed possible after Japanese —story		44b-d
L. Aldin Porter	52,000	Nov 1996	9f
	Their power comes from faith, prayer, humility		9f-10b
Thomas S. Monson	, can effectively visit inactives	May 1997	45f-46a
Joseph B. Wirthlin	56,000	Nov 1997	33c
James E. Faust	58,000	May 1998	18d
Earl C. Tingey	The 12 leaving as , to Great Britain		39d-f
	Statistics on today's ,		40b-c

Missionaries

Earl C. Tingey	47 , among his father's descendants	May 1998	41a-b
James E. Faust	Maintain good grooming after mission		45b-c
Thomas S. Monson	Gave destitute woman their money —story	Nov 1998	50c-d
Gordon B. Hinckley	Letter from a , about his growth		52b-d
Gordon B. Hinckley	60,000 , - 137,629 volunteers	May 1999	4c-d
Richard C. Edgley	Repentant , became best in Church —story	Nov 1999	43b-44a
James E. Faust	, left seed which became 60 members —story		47b-f
James E. Faust	Good came from missionary's shooting —story		59d-60c
Statistical Report	58,593 serving	May 2000	22e
Jay E. Jensen	, teach selves —Romans 2:21		28b
Loren C. Dunn	, from ranch was told to "cowboy up" —story		80f-81a
Statistical Report	60,784	May 2001	22a
Robert D. Hales	Many more couple , needed		25b-27f
John H. Groberg	, asked to heal lifeless Tongan boy —story		43d-44c
James E. Faust	, baptized one dirty little Irish kid —story		46f-47b
Carol B. Thomas	"If that girl comes home, the sheep are yours" —story		63d-e
David B. Haight	Accounts of 2 couple missions —story		72d-f
Statistical Report	60,850	May 2002	23c
Thomas S. Monson	Protected by angels in walk across frozen lake —story		50e-51b
Gordon B. Hinckley	Must never be separated from companion		53b
Russell M. Nelson	Missionary grateful for cancer —story		77c-d
Bonnie D. Parkin	Missionary more in debt to Lord than before		84f
M. Russell Ballard	The bar for , is being raised	Nov 2002	48a
	, service —great talk		46b-49b
	Instruction for returned ,		49a-b
Gordon B. Hinckley	Endorsement for raising the bar		57a
	No more , farewells		57a-d
	No open houses for ,		57d
	No , homecoming sacrament meetings		57d-e
Thomas S. Monson	Elder killed on last day of mission —story		62d-e
Dallin H. Oaks	The faith, service and multiple missions of couples		68b-69b
Statistical Report	61,638	May 2003	25d
Henry B. Eyring	How to be a member missionary		29d-32f
Daryl H. Garn	Bar has been raised in preparation and worthiness		46f-48a
H. David Burton	Raising the bar in athletics and for ,		48d-50f
Gordon B. Hinckley	California newspaper article on ,	Nov 2003	5b-f
Sheldon F. Child	Woman asked why we don't have prophets —story		8f-9d
Richard G. Scott	Why standards were raised for ,		41e-42b
Henry B. Eyring	Dan Jones and his Welsh mission		91f-92d
D. Todd Christofferson	, became invisible to evil men —story	May 2004	12f-13a
F. Michael Watson	56,237		26e
Jeffrey R. Holland	A living symbol of the Church		30b-c
	The sacrifices three , made —stories		30d-e
	Promise senior , experience of lifetime		30e-f
Richard G. Scott	, changed poor Bolivian town		101d-102b

Missionaries

Missionaries, cont'd
Related Topics: Converts, Mission, Missionary Work

John H. Groberg	Starving , sustained by love —story	Nov 2004	10a-f
	Drowning , saved by love —story		10f-11f
M. Russell Ballard	Abinadi made only one convert		41b-c
Russell M. Nelson	Senior , : Hasten your shuffle		79d
	Calls from President Grant and Hinckley for senior ,		81d
	4 concerns of senior ,		81b-82a
	Serving as senior , —entire talk		79b-82b
Richard J. Maynes	Triplet , serving from family of 17 children		93b-94d
H. David Burton	Slow elder had great testimony —story		100a-b
F. Michael Watson	51,067	May 2005	25c
M. Russell Ballard	Raising the bar		69b-d
	Bar raised for parents too		70b
	We need more , —Hinckley		70b-d
	Young women are not obligated to serve		70d-e
	Preparing , —entire talk		69b-71f
Joseph B. Wirthlin	One village was saved from tsunami —story	Nov 2005	16b-d
David A. Bednar	We are all ,		44d-f
	Become , long before the call		45a-46f
Thomas S. Monson	Rejected elder returned to testify of Joseph —story		69b-f
Richard G. Scott	Girls should not be pressured to serve	May 2006	88b-c
	, are matched to their missions		89b-c
James E. Faust	All the , were healed —story	Nov 2006	54e-55a
Jay E. Jensen	, were inspired to sing —story	May 2007	11f-12a
Gordon B. Hinckley	387,750 , in last 12 years - 40% of total		60d-e
Vicki F. Matsumori	, took bandages off woman's eyes		77b
Mary N .Cook	, letter resulted in his family's sealing —story	Nov 2007	12f-13b
L. Tom Perry	High jumper kept raising the bar —story		46e-47d
	Minimum qualifications for ,		47d-48b
	Physical qualifications for ,		48b-c
	Physical appearance of ,		48c
	Educational preparation of ,		48d-e
	Social preparation of , —good insights		48e-f
	Employment as a preparation for ,		48f-49a
	, teach but only the Spirit converts		49a
	Be certain you continually raise the bar		49b
F. Michael Watson	52,686	May 2008	25c
Thomas S. Monson	Faithfulness of an elder with cancer —story		67a-68b
David A. Bednar	Don't pray for , to do our work		95d
Thomas S. Monson	Grandfather left for mission 3 days after marriage		111c-d
	Uncle taught wife's father —story		111d-f
Thomas S. Monson	Urge members to pray for countries to open to ,	Nov 2008	6b-e
Neil L. Andersen	Elder was convinced to stay on mission —story		13e-f
Henry B. Eyring	A , who was assigned 13 companions —story		58f-59a
	Why we no longer have , farewells		59f-60a
Thomas S. Monson	The , who couldn't learn Spanish —story		60d-f

Missionaries

M. Russell Ballard	Numbers of , called in each decade	Nov 2008	81b-84b
Thomas S. Monson	53,000	May 2009	5f
Statistical Report	52,494		30c
Dallin H. Oaks	"Forget yourself and go to work" —Hinckley		93d
L. Tom Perry	An underutilized teaching resource - Members find		110b-d
M. Russell Ballard	Advice to returned ,		50a-b
L. Tom Perry	Teach three basic lessons	Nov 2009	76a
Statistical Report	51,736	May 2010	28c
Ronald A. Rasband	Heber C. Kimball's call to England		51b-c
	The , opportunity of a lifetime is yours		51e
	Lord needs every able young man		51e
	Apostles' process of calling , —story		52a-53b
	The most important work youth can do		53b-f
Thomas S. Monson	Elder got no letters from home —story		67a-f

Missionary Work
Related Topics: Converts, Gathering of Israel, Mission, Missionaries, Non-members

Joseph Fielding Smith	Gospel will be spread more and more rapidly	Nov 2008	41b
Bruce R. McConkie	The gospel will be preached in Russia and China	June 1969	112c
Boyd K. Packer	Thousands must be sifted to find one who will listen	Dec 1969	58e
David O. McKay	Challenge to make one convert		87b
	Responsibility of members		88f
	Many waiting for testimonies		88f
Thomas S. Monson	Trials and rewards from ,		90a
	Story of courage making convert —story		91b
Gordon B. Hinckley	Fruits of a convert's labor —story		98f
Franklin D. Richards	Extra mile brought 3 golden referrals —story		102e-f
S. Dilworth Young	The three aspects of ,	June 1970	56e-f
Ezra Taft Benson	Gospel must be preached in communist countries		96b
	Report on Asia		96c-97f
Joseph Fielding Smith	Most important duty is to preach —J. Smith	Dec 1970	4a
Paul H. Dunn	Nothing can stop progress of , —J. Smith		41e
S. Dilworth Young	, the responsibility of families as it formerly was	June 1971	40c-e
LeGrand Richards	Jews to be one of great movements of Church		99f
Joseph Fielding Smith	No work as important as ,	July 1972	27c
William H. Bennett	Examples of approaches used to open discussions		84b
Hugh B. Brown	Heeding Spirit and calling again makes converts —story		86a
Theodore M. Burton	Responsibility of Church —J.F. Smith	Jan 1973	54b
David B. Haight	Imagine the quantity of seed planted		74e
LeGrand Richards	Fourteen straight years of ,		109a
	Honest men will join if taught		109b
Ezra Taft Benson	If wicked not warned, their blood upon us	July 1973	38a
Rex D. Pinegar	Members and missionaries working together —story		75c
LeGrand Richards	Not a person who couldn't join - testimony		80e
Rex D. Pinegar	Bequeath Christianity to your family —Pat. Henry	Jan 1974	34c
William H. Bennett	Blind man in river yelled "which way to shore?"		64a

Missionary Work, cont'd
Related Topics: Converts, Gathering of Israel, Mission, Missionaries, Non-members

William H. Bennett	Many know not where to find truth	Jan 1974	64d
Ezra Taft Benson	The story of Samuel Harrison Smith	May 1974	104f
	Statistics on #'s of missionaries from 1830 on		105c
Rex D. Pinegar	Lady missionaries tried one more day —story	Nov 1974	44f
Boyd K. Packer	Imagine Father's joy when his child is saved —story		89c-90a
O. Leslie Stone	8 things we can do to be missionaries	May 1975	8b-d
Loren C. Dunn	Too big a sacrifice? —stories in Samoa		25d-27b
A. Theodore Tuttle	Let down your buckets where you are —story		90b-d
Robert L. Simpson	, through ward choirs	Nov 1975	13f-14a
Boyd K. Packer	Its scope impossible? We'll do it anyway		97d-e
Rex D. Pinegar	Two effective member-missionaries —stories		103e-f
Carlos E. Asay	Why missionary program succeeds —story	May 1976	37c-e
Jacob de Jager	If you have acrophobia don't get on roof - just preach		41a
Loren C. Dunn	Shouldn't go back to Maker without warning neighbors		66d
	World would open for , if we asked night and morning		66d-e
Spencer W. Kimball	Proper , by members can hasten Second Coming	Nov 1976	4e
David B. Haight	Reluctance of members holding back ,		20e
	The man knew his neighbors wouldn't listen —story		21e-22b
A. Theodore Tuttle	The great need to help finance potential missionaries		22d-24b
Carlos E. Asay	How we are affected ourselves by our ,		43d
Jacob de Jager	Man he went to rescue turned out to be his brother —story		56f-57e
Marion G. Romney	No storm could drive you from work if this is true —story		70b-d
N. Eldon Tanner	Voice of warning compared to Teton Dam disaster		82e-83e
LeGrand Richards	They will love you —2 stories	Nov 1978	32f-33a
	The fruits of his , as seen 70 years later		33d-e
Spencer W. Kimball	Pray constantly that countries may open to ,		45f-46b
Jacob de Jager	Two sources of light: seen and ,		68e
Hartman Rector, Jr.	Go beyond natural and easy proselyting —Kimball	May 1979	31b
Spencer W. Kimball	Being neighbors as usual? - Convert someone	May 1980	4b-c
Bruce R. McConkie	There will be congregations in Moscow and Peking		72c
Robert E. Wells	Elder needlessly apologized for poor meeting —story	Nov 1980	12e-13a
Rex C. Reeve, Jr.	Members: the sleeping giant of ,		27f-28b
	Heaven's gate is shut to him who comes alone		28c
Spencer W. Kimball	One of the three missions of the Church	May 1981	5e-f
Royden G. Derrick	He talked with father of 8 on plane —story		66f-67b
Teddy E. Brewerton	3 who each baptized hundreds —stories		69a-c
F. Burton Howard	Parable of the Desert Travelers —entire talk		71b-72f
Ezra Taft Benson	How long it took for Church to achieve each million	Nov 1981	63b-c
Ted E. Brewerton	I like myself more when I am with you	May 1983	74a
Thomas S. Monson	Non-baptizing town became most productive —story	Nov 1983	20a-e
Jack H. Goaslind, Jr.	Obligation to bring gospel to others' attention		32f-33a
	God will hold us responsible for those we might have saved		33d-e
	This call to , leaves us no option		33f-34a
M. Russell Ballard	Statistics about world population	Nov 1984	15d-16a
	Our own sins are more readily forgiven as we do ,—Kimball		16b-d

Missionary Work

M. Russell Ballard	Set a date for having someone ready	Nov 1984	16f-17b
Ezra Taft Benson	Nothing can stop the work —Wentworth letter	May 1985	6d-e
	Explanation of General Missionary Fund		7e-8a
	World will be filled with stakes and members		8f
Derek A. Cuthbert	10 questions one might ask about the Church	Nov 1985	24d-26f
M. Russell Ballard	History of the Church in South America	May 1986	12f-13e
M. Russell Ballard	4 letters from successful member missionaries	Nov 1986	32c-33a
	The 4 steps to member ,		33b-d
Gordon B. Hinckley	Comments from people at Visitor's Center	May 1987	53a-b
Alexander B. Morrison	3 African countries dedicated	Nov 1987	25c-d
M. Russell Ballard	Results in when members fed missionaries —stories		78f-80a
	Gen. Miss. Fund provides for thousands of missionaries		81a
Franklin D. Richards	Boy converts friend's family —story		82b-d
Dallin H. Oaks	Treat non-members like members	May 1988	32d-f
Yoshihiko Kikuchi	, in Hawaii began with a dream —story		76f-77c
M. Russell Ballard	We baptize in a year as many as are born in a day	Nov 1988	28e
L. Tom Perry	The commandment that unites us	May 1989	13d
	Two reasons for our reluctance to do ,		13e-f
	Three messages having the greatest appeal		13f-15b
Thomas S. Monson	Freedom has come to Eastern Europe	May 1990	4b-c
Glenn L. Pace	Warn people of the calamities to come	Nov 1990	8b-10b
Harold G. Hillam	World's best shoeshine man dies alone —2 stories		24d-25f
Thomas S. Monson	History of , in early Canada		67f-68c
	New church would need architect, plumber —story		68f-69c
Thomas S. Monson	Results of 5-year-old girl's , —story		97a-b
Augusto A. Lim	Progress of , in the Philippines	Nov 1992	82b-83f
F. David Stanley	The secret of , is work —E.T. Benson	May 1993	44f-45b
Gordon B. Hinckley	Mission funds donated at elder's death —story	Nov 1993	52e-f
David B. Haight	What , accomplished in 5 years		61f-62a
	Will sweep every nation —J. Smith quote		62a-b
Boyd K. Packer	Converts will become a flood	May 1994	21b-f
James O. Mason	"No unhallowed hand can stop…"	Nov 1994	31b
Russell M. Nelson	Temple work and , are the same effort		84b
Thomas S. Monson	The , opportunity of a lifetime is yours	May 1995	49b
Henry B. Eyring	, is done through quietly living the gospel	Nov 1995	37d-40f
Henry B. Eyring	Promises if we do our ,	Nov 1996	32a-d
Gordon B. Hinckley	Rescue of handcart pioneers compared to , —story		85d-86f
Thomas S. Monson	Czech girl converted dozens —story	May 1997	94a-b
Richard G. Scott	How important is , —scripture sequence	Nov 1997	35c-e
	How to do , without a call		36b-d
Gordon B. Hinckley	Essentially a priesthood responsibility		52b-e
Virginia U. Jensen	An exemplary life is the best gospel tract		90b
Richard E. Cook	Why we do , among "unspoiled" people	May 1998	28e-29a
	, is not an optional program		29b
E. Ray Bateman	Seed of Abraham should be easy to find	Nov 1998	28d-f

Missionary Work, cont'd
Related Topics: Converts, Gathering of Israel, Mission, Missionaries, Non-members

Henry B. Eyring	Warnings about dangers people can't see	Nov 1998	32d-f
	He taught widow - son joined later —story		32f-33b
	Next world: they will know that you knew —story		33c-e
	This is the third yard Mormons have put in for us—story		33e-34b
	Ministers listened because of neighbor's example —story		34b-c
	Even (especially) the simple can do it		34d-35b
Gordon B. Hinckley	Finding and keeping converts —important talk	May 1999	104b-110f
M. Russell Ballard	Could we tell Jesus we were too shy to do , ?	Nov 2000	76f
Robert C. Oaks	300,000 converts per year is not enough		81c
	Significant statements by each prophet		81d
	Four-step member-missionary work		81d-e
	Afraid of offending friends? Absurd		81e-82b
Jeffrey R. Holland	The need for members to do ,	May 2001	14b-e
	Being good members is best ,		14f-15a
	Pray daily for missionary experience		15a-b
	Listening is more important than speaking		15b-d
	Pass-along cards		15d
Dallin H. Oaks	Sharing the gospel —entire talk	Nov 2001	7b-9f
L. Tom Perry	Need army of returned missionaries reenlisted into service		77a
Spencer J. Condie	Nonmember wished youth would invite daughter —story	May 2002	45a-b
Henry B. Eyring	Impressed to take along a Book of Mormon —story	May 2003	31c-d
	How to do , as a member		29d-32f
M. Russell Ballard	Bar has been raised for members, too		37e-38b
	450 baptisms in one branch in one year —story		38f-39b
	Three simple things to help us do ,		38b-40b
	Our greatest and most important duty —J. Smith		40b
Monte J. Brough	"No one ever asked me" —story	Nov 2003	49a-b
	Priests quorum got many referrals —story		49b
Henry B. Eyring	Six things to teach those you love		89b-92f
Richard G. Scott	Introduction of Preach My Gospel book	May 2005	29b-31f
C. Scott Grow	Mexican waited 12 years —story	Nov 2005	34b-f
M. Russell Ballard	Invite people into your home —good ideas	May 2006	85b-87b
James E. Faust	Smiles convert a family —story		113a-d
L. Tom Perry	College student waitress and a truck driver —story	Nov 2006	69d-f
Jeffrey R. Holland	Called to rescue souls just like handcarters		106b-e
Erich W. Kopischke	Using Preach My Gospel	Nov 2007	33b-35b
Quentin L. Cook	How Polynesians find water in drought		71e-72b
	Members must shed their camouflage		72d-e
Octaviano Tenorio	Baby's death brings conversions —story		96e-97f
Henry B. Eyring	Those we're to bring when we go home to God	May 2008	23b
David A. Bednar	Don't pray for missionaries to do our work		95d
Craig C. Christensen	Presenting scriptures to a friend —story		105f-106e
Silvia H. Allred	Generational effects of , —story	Nov 2008	11d-12a
	A fourfold endeavor		12b
	Suggestions on how to do ,		12b-e

Missionary Work

Missionary Work, cont'd

Related Topics: Converts, Gathering of Israel, Mission, Missionaries, Non-members

Silvia H. Allred	Results of a second grader's ,	Nov 2008	12e-f
Henry B. Eyring	The gathering will accelerate		68d
M. Russell Ballard	Joseph's prophecy that the work would roll forth		81c-d
L. Tom Perry	Over 50% of non-members don't know about Church	May 2009	110b
	Elders are underutilized - Members must do finding		110b-d
	"Open your mouths" - What to say and testify of		111a-e
	"Bring Souls Unto Me" —entire talk		109b-112b
Thomas S. Monson	Pray for countries to open to ,	Nov 2009	6b
L. Tom Perry	Baptismal covenant includes sharing gospel		75c
	Focus is now at ward level - More effective		75c-76a
Brent H. Nielson	Prayer opened Russia and a Finnish town to , —story		95b-96b
	"The truth of God will go forth boldly…" —quote		96b
	Savior's last words to Apostles were about ,		96d-97a
	The field has never been whiter		97a-b

Morality

Related Topics: Adultery, Chastity, Immorality, Purity, Virtue

James E. Faust	Can , be legislated?	May 1987	80f-81a
Gordon B. Hinckley	Immorality is just plain wrong —Ted Koppel	Nov 1991	51b-c
Boyd K. Packer	Our polluted moral environment —entire talk	May 1992	66b-68f
Joe J. Christensen	Polluted moral environment will rot society	Nov 1993	11b-e
Richard G. Scott	Straight talk to young men about ,	Nov 1994	37b-39b
Boyd K. Packer	Avoid every kind of immorality	Nov 2006	86d-e
Elaine S. Dalton	Unfurling standard for virtue - Definition	Nov 2008	78f-79a
	President Monson's statement on virtue		79a-b
	Desensitized by degrees —good		79b-f
	Great list of scriptures promoting virtue		80a-c
M. Russell Ballard	Cycle of apostasy ends with a collapse of ,	May 2009	32b-f
	Boundaries of , pushed until no boundaries at all		33a
	Cycle of apostasy is repeating with a collapse of ,		33b
Elaine S. Dalton	Virtue is moral excellence, power and strength		120f-121a
Quentin L. Cook	Our duty to teach ,	Nov 2009	92e
D. Todd Christofferson	No double standard of , —Faust story		105d-f
	Recession caused by unethical behavior		106f-107a
	Mere wanting is no guide to moral conduct		107f
	Other churches don't talk about , any more		108f
D. Todd Christofferson	Korihor: No absolute moral standards	May 2010	33f-34b
Gregory A. Schwitzer	No such thing as "new" ,		105a-b

Mortality

Related Topics: Life

Boyd K. Packer	Beginnings and purpose of ,	July 1973	51d
	Second purpose of ,		53c
O. Leslie Stone	The purposes of ,	Jan 1974	39a
M. Russell Ballard	Mission statement of , is build eternal family	Nov 2005	41d
Richard G. Scott	Obedience is the fundamental purpose of ,		78d-e

Motherhood and Mothers
Related Topics: Parents, Women

Russell M. Nelson	How to show love and concern for wife	Dec 1968	87a-b
David O. McKay	Motherhood - a sacred obligation	Jun 1969	4b-c
Richard L. Evans	What his widowed , taught him	Jun 1970	38c
Sterling W. Sill	I had a mother who read to me —poem	Jun 1971	44e
John H. Vandenberg	Why mother love is greatest: sacrifice		63b
Paul H. Dunn	The World's Meanest Mom		102e-103b
Joseph Fielding Smith	Lies at foundation of happiness in home	Jul 1972	27f
A. Theodore Tuttle	The role of mother —good quote by J.R. Clark	Jan 1973	66f
James E. Faust	He still needs his mother's prayers		81b
N. Eldon Tanner	Satan working overtime to destroy ,	Jan 1974	7e
	Mothers have greatest influence on children		8b
	More joy in , than in any other vocation		10a
Thomas S. Monson	Aged and forgotten , —thoughts and a story		29b
	The blind man cried as he sang of mother		29f
	A toast to mother and the guilty slunk away		29e
	Opening a deceased mother's treasure box —story		31a
	Which Loved Best —good poem		31d
	One cannot forget mother and remember God		32e
LeGrand Richards	Cows forget calves but mothers never forget —story		57d
Spencer W. Kimball	The highest, holiest service assumed by mankind	May 1974	8d-f
H. Burke Peterson	There is no mommy at my house - Working , —story		31d-f
	The noblest office or calling in the world —McKay		31f-32b
	Working Mothers —entire talk is excellent		31d-33b
Rex D. Pinegar	Robert E. Lee's , molded his character		68d-e
Ezra Taft Benson	, have better chance of keeping their spirits up	Nov 1974	66d
Spencer W. Kimball	, is the greatest vocation	May 1975	7c
Sterling W. Sill	…I had a mother who read to me —poem		41f
Howard W. Hunter	No one expends more energy than ,	Nov 1975	124b
J. Richard Clarke	Working mothers and weekend fathers —story	May 1977	85f-86a
L. Tom Perry	, should not work unless husband incapacitated	Nov 1977	62f-63a
G. Homer Durham	What about the Pilgrim , ? —clever poem	May 1979	10e
N. Eldon Tanner	, the greatest glory that can come to women	May 1980	17d-e
M. Russell Ballard	34% of LDS women work outside home	May 1981	85d-e
Ezra Taft Benson	Statistics about working outside the home	Nov 1982	59d-e
Barbara B. Smith	Discouraged , gave children individual attention —story		82b-d
Matthew S. Holland	How his mother disciplined him —story	May 1983	38f-39a
Boyd K. Packer	Tired student didn't realize mom had to get up first —story		68a
Vaughn J. Featherstone	They are all my children and it's no picnic	Nov 1983	36d-e
	Making the child practice piano —humorous		37c
David B. Haight	The role of mothers —Spencer W. Kimball	May 1984	12d-e
Russell M. Nelson	Paralyzed mother still influenced home	Nov 1984	31a-b
Waldo P. Call	His mother's love saved him	May 1985	84b
Ezra Taft Benson	Full-time mother - Life's greatest career	Nov 1986	84f-85a
Vaughn J. Featherstone	Serious consequences when , laid aside	Nov 1987	28e-f
Ezra Taft Benson	Mothers should not work outside the home		48e-49d

Motherhood and Mothers

Author	Description	Date	Page
Russell M. Nelson	, priorities: Children. —Poem	Nov 1987	88a
Ezra Taft Benson	Not leaving the home pleases God	May 1988	5e
Monte J. Brough	, called mission president after tornado —funny story	Nov 1988	40c-e
Ezra Taft Benson	Those denied motherhood will be compensated		97b
Russell M. Nelson	Woman - of Infinite Worth —entire talk	Nov 1989	20b-22f
	When you teach a girl, you teach a generation		21c
	Any lawyer can care for my clients but only I can , this child		21f
W. Eugene Hansen	Which child did widow love most? —story		24b-e
Thomas S. Monson	10 suggestions for , —Ezra Taft Benson	May 1992	5b-e
Thomas S. Monson	God could not be everywhere, so He gave us ,		59a
Richard G. Scott	Best missionaries have stay-at-home ,	May 1993	32e-34d
	, with children should be in the home		34c
James E. Faust	No greater good than motherhood		35b
Boyd K. Packer	Priesthood for men - Motherhood for women	Nov 1993	21f-22c
	Motherhood is the highest, holiest service		22e-23c
	Keep , in the home		22e-23c
James E. Faust	Chief calling is motherhood		38f-39a
	An especially noble calling in last days		39a
Gordon B. Hinckley	Greatest blessing, mission and happiness		60b
Jeanne Inouye	Gave up lawyer career to be mother —story		96d-97c
Howard W. Hunter	Mankind's holiest service	Nov 1994	50d-e
	Allow , to stay in home		51c-d
James E. Faust	Even his , didn't dream he'd be in First Presidency	May 1995	61b
L. Tom Perry	Sister Hinckley's remarks about the greatness of full-time ,		74b-d
	Noblest and greatest of all callings		74e
Gordon B. Hinckley	Advice to and letter from single mother —story	Nov 1995	99f-100e
	No other work reaches so close to divinity		101f
Gordon B. Hinckley	A girl's best friend is her mother	May 1996	92f-93a
Virginia H. Pearce	Class on , demonstrated —story	Nov 1996	13b-14a
Gordon B. Hinckley	Upbeat letter from a single mother		68f-69c
	Counsel to working ,		69c-e
Richard G. Scott	Work together to keep , in the home		74e-75a
Patricia P. Pinegar	Not fulfilled? Where feelings come from?	May 1997	14e
Henry B. Eyring	3 prophets have warned that , must be in home		25a-b
Jeffrey R. Holland	No blessing withheld from childless woman		35b-c
	The difficult lot of young , —humorous		35d-f
	"You are magnificent"		36a-d
	The grand tradition of , and comfort to ,		36d-37a
Virginia U. Jensen	"Mom, choose me" —story (working moms?)	Nov 1997	90f-91a
Boyd K. Packer	Most important calling —important talk	Nov 1998	22b-24f
Russell M. Nelson	The highest and noblest work	May 1999	38e
	, should not need to issue orders		38e-f
	Letter from , saved elder from beating —story		38f-39b
Thomas S. Monson	What begins with M and picks things up —story		98c
Vaughn J. Featherstone	Boy cleaned kitchen for 3 hours —story	Nov 1999	15a-c

Mary Ellen Smoot	Not all women give birth to those they mother —story	Nov 1999	93e-f
Virginia U. Jensen	Observations on birds and nesting —story		95e-96b
Margaret D. Nadauld	Happenings in cradles more important than on battlefields	Nov 2000	15e-f
Sheri L. Dew	Premortally endowed with motherhood	Nov 2001	96e-f
	Motherhood as important as priesthood		96f-97a
	All women are , —excellent talk		96b-98b
Anne C. Pingree	Mother taught disabled son to read —story	Nov 2002	109d-f
Susan W. Tanner	Lord holds , in highest esteem —Kimball	May 2003	73f
Sydney S. Reynolds	Mother was inspired to call daughter —story	Nov 2003	76c-d
Gordon B. Hinckley	His kids phone and ask for mother		113d
	What to teach your children		114e-115b
L. Tom Perry	Allow mothers to stay at home	May 2004	72b
Julie B. Beck	The exalted role of , —good talk		75d-77b
Boyd K. Packer	Bring mothers home		79f
Thomas S. Monson	Feels for you more keenly than you do for self	Nov 2004	116a-b
Bonnie D. Parkin	The mother got a standing ovation —story	Nov 2005	108d-f
Gordon B. Hinckley	Single , didn't want to go home —story	Nov 2006	117b-d
Julie B. Beck	Should desire to bear children	Nov 2007	76d-e
	Women should be nurturers and homemakers		76f-77a
	Mothers are teachers		77b-d
	"Mothers Who Know" —entire talk		76b-78b
Steven E. Snow	The travel agent for guilt trips		102b
Julie B. Beck	Commandment to multiply remains in force		110e-f
Susan W. Tanner	Meaning of "nurture"	May 2008	82b-d
M. Russell Ballard	He and wife reversed roles —story		108b-d
	Most essential and eternal role		108e
	Priorities: God, husband, children		108e
	Simple things to make motherhood rewarding		109a-110b
	Joy of , comes in moments		109b-d
	Don't overschedule self or children		109d-110a
	Make time for self		110a-b
	Pray deeply about children		110b
	Things children should do for ,		110d
Dieter F. Uchtdorf	Train and children were gone when , returned —story	Nov 2008	21b-e
Dieter F. Uchtdorf	Creative talents culminate in motherhood		118e-119d
Mary N. Cook	Letter from , influenced life	May 2009	117b-d
	Satan makes , seem less important		117f
Boyd K. Packer	Mother knew son was in trouble —story	Nov 2009	45d-f
M. Russell Ballard	Model selves after ,	May 2010	19d-e
	Young women behave like ,		19f
	First line of defense against world		19f-20a
	Find joy in nurturing children		20b-c
	Nurturing: Love, correction, continuity		20d
L. Tom Perry	His , as a teacher —story		29d-30c
Bradley D. Foster	"Mother told me" —story		98d-f

Motherhood and Mothers

Bradley D. Foster	No greater good than motherhood —Faust	May 2010	98f
	Nurturing part of spiritual heritage		98f-99a
	Cows could lead lost calves —story		99b-f
	Tired children turn toward , —poem		99f-100d
	Love of , typifies love of Savior		100e
	Jesus' last act was caring for ,		100e-f
Neil L. Andersen	A promise to single ,		110a

Movies, TV and Media
Related Topics: —

Richard L. Evans	If not good for children it isn't good for adults	June 1969	80b-d
N. Eldon Tanner	Immorality and violence on ,	July 1973	8f
William R. Bradford	TV even if not for its evils is still a time drain	Nov 1979	37e-38a
Howard W. Hunter	Time robbed of worth by viewing or reading frivolous things		64c
Ezra Taft Benson	Children watch 25 hours per week	Nov 1982	60e
James E. Faust	TV robs families of time together	May 1983	41b-c
Gordon B. Hinckley	Entertainment writers have non-traditional values	Nov 1983	45c-46c
David B. Haight	Good is not rewarded nor evil punished	Nov 1986	37b
Ezra Taft Benson	Don't see R-rated movies		84a
Dwan J. Young	18-year-olds spent more time with TV than in school	May 1988	78e
Joseph B. Wirthlin	TV out of control. Fathers watch too much sports	Nov 1988	35f-36b
Joseph B. Wirthlin	It will get a lot worse	May 1989	9a-c
M. Russell Ballard	The effects of TV —entire talk		78b-81b
Joseph B. Wirthlin	Watching , to excess becomes sin	Nov 1990	65a-e
J. Richard Clarke	One standard of decency—Unfit for youth, unfit for parents	May 1991	42a-c
Jack H. Goaslind	Young woman turned off movie —story		47a-b
Gordon B. Hinckley	Don't idle away time watching ,	May 1992	71e
Neal A. Maxwell	Talk shows feature exhibitionism	May 1993	77a
	Soap operas are in need of soap		77a
Joe J. Christensen	, are rotting foundations of society	Nov 1993	11b-e
H. Burke Peterson	Powerful farewell address warns about ,		42d-44b
L. Tom Perry	Very few movies are worthy of seeing		67c-d
James E. Faust	Should be used for nobler purposes	May 1994	4f-5a
W. Don Ladd	Used to be rated on how good movie was	Nov 1994	28e
Gordon B. Hinckley	Pity the man who wallows in the mire		48c
Gordon B. Hinckley	Statistics on TV viewing by typical child	Nov 1995	99d-e
Joe J. Christensen	Do not watch R-rated movies	Nov 1996	40b-f
James E. Faust	Inappropriate entertainment desensitizes	May 2002	47b-e
L. Tom Perry	How the Church is using all the media	May 2003	40d-43b
M. Russell Ballard	The negative power of , —entire talk	Nov 2003	16b-18f
	7 things to minimize negative effects of ,		18f-19a
Gordon B. Hinckley	Two stations refused to air program		83f-84b
Dallin H. Oaks	What we accept as entertainment	May 2004	9c-10a
Russell M. Nelson	Man on plane ignored wife —story	May 2006	36b-c
L. Whitney Clayton	If not too bad, it isn't too good either	Nov 2007	52e-f
Julie B. Beck	Allow less media in our homes		77f-78a

Movies, TV and Media, cont'd
Related Topics: —

Dallin H. Oaks	Beware team sports and technology toys	Nov 2007	107a-b
Julie B. Beck	, teach individual fulfillment and self-worship		110d-e
Thomas S. Monson	Children educated by media - Statistics		118f-119a
Dieter F. Uchtdorf	A warning about the Internet	May 2008	59b-60a
Thomas S. Monson	His wife calls him a "show-a-holic"	Nov 2008	85a-b
Robert D. Hales	"I'm not old enough to see that film"	May 2010	95d

Music
Related Topics: —

Ezra Taft Benson	Modern , is utterly demoralizing	June 1969	46e-47c
Joseph F. Smith	His testimony of ,	Dec 1969	37f
Robert L. Simpson	A 6-year-old's song brought his inactive father back		40f
	Church , at a cocktail party brought him back —story		42f
Ezra Taft Benson	Some , is utterly demoralizing	Dec 1970	49e-f
Ezra Taft Benson	The six demeaning characteristics of modern ,	Dec 1971	53b-e
	Filth in modern music		55c
	Comments on rock festivals		55d-e
	Different effects of music in Book of Mormon		55e
	The anti-Christ in religious rock ,		55f
	, can sooth or stir the savage beast		56c
	Have good home record library to teach good ,		56d
Sterling W. Sill	Secret of Mozart's success was desire	July 1973	104d
Boyd K. Packer	Entire talk —excellent, excellent	Jan 1974	25a
Gordon B. Hinckley	Origin of hymn "We Thank Thee, O God, for a Prophet"		122a
Vaughn J. Featherstone	Every bird came back when , played —story	Nov 1976	105d-f
Boyd K. Packer	, affects inspiration	Nov 1979	20f
Spencer W. Kimball	Statement about , that belongs in hell —humorous	Nov 1982	4c
Franklin D. Richards	Words of hymns must be in full harmony with gospel		22c
	Origin of "Come, Come Ye Saints"		23a
	Origin and history of "The Spirit of God"		23f-24a
Ezra Taft Benson	Minds can't afford hard , of our day	Nov 1986	84a-b
Elaine L. Jack	Girl obtained peace playing piano —story	Nov 1989	88b
Boyd K. Packer	Influences reverence - must be appropriate	Nov 1991	22d-f
	Many aren't singing - all must		22e
Joe J. Christensen	Teach children to play an instrument	Nov 1993	12a-e
H. David Burton	Youth destroyed their bad ,	May 1994	68a-b
Dallin H. Oaks	Statement of First Presidency on hymns	Nov 1994	9f
	, calms and unifies —2 stories		10a-c
	Use of hymns mentioned in scriptures		10d-e
	How Apostles use hymns in their meetings		10e
	Heavenly beings join choirs in temple dedication		10f
	All in congregation should sing —story		10f-11b
	Appropriate , for sacrament meetings		11b-f
	, can be used to neutralize temptation		11f-12a
	"Singing" at a deaf conference —story		12a-b
Boyd K. Packer	Wholesome , vs. sacred ,		61b

Boyd K. Packer	Do not ever disturb prelude , for others	Nov 1994	61b-c
	Some , is more dangerous than you may suppose		61c
L. Tom Perry	Singing attracted Hinckley's grandfather to Church —story	May 1995	72f-73a
Neal A. Maxwell	Authorities sang to dying child —story	May 1996	70e-f
Gordon B. Hinckley	1895: Tabernacle Choir to be world's greatest		82d-83a
David B. Haight	History of "Come, Come Ye Saints"	Nov 1997	70d-71c
M. Russell Ballard	Avoid , that celebrates the sensual	May 1999	86e
Boyd K. Packer	Calmness and direction come from , —story	Nov 1999	23b-24b
Virginia U. Jensen	Origin of "Lead, Kindly Light" —story	Nov 2000	63c-d
David B. Haight	Sheepherder asked for an "A" on the radio —story	Nov 2001	22b-d
Jeffrey R. Holland	Can't capture a note with Velcro but sings anyway	May 2002	63d-e
Sharon G. Larsen	, at a party hit girl's spirit —story		91f-92c
Russell M. Nelson	A hymn he composed	May 2003	9b-d
Thomas S. Monson	Violin sold to finance mission —story		19e-20c
Coleen K. Menlove	Inspiration and 3 tries to write , —story	May 2005	15a-c
Anne C. Pingree	Answer to prayers came from hymn —story	Nov 2005	112d-114a
James E. Faust	Grandfather sang most of the day —story	Nov 2006	53b-c
Gordon B. Hinckley	Impressed by "Rise Up O Men of God"		59d-60b
Jay E. Jensen	, brings Lord closer than anything but prayer	May 2007	11f
	Seven converts made through , —story		11f-12a
	Church , must not be a performance		12b
	Hymns are a course in doctrine		12b-d
Boyd K. Packer	A calming, defining moment for him		26b-f
	Satan uses , to erase still, small voice		28b
Gordon B. Hinckley	Mormon Tabernacle Choir broadcast 75 years.		43e
Gordon B. Hinckley	Why "School Thy Feelings" was written	Nov 2007	62c-e
Dallin H. Oaks	All should sing. Sacrament , should be appropriate	Nov 2008	19a
Yoon Hwan Choi	Made converts of nine troublemaker Koreans —story	Nov 2009	53b-55b
Thomas S. Monson	The two sides and effects of ,	May 2010	66b-c

Paul H. Dunn	"Can't" is false doctrine. There are no failures among us	July 1972	93f
John H. Vandenberg	How to become a , —short quote	Jan 1973	38b
Marvin J. Ashton	No man a , in kingdom of God	July 1973	24b
	Lord displeased when we call ourselves a ,		24c
	Error to call others , . - Blessings missed.		24f
	Joseph Smith obscure but not a ,		26a
Thomas S. Monson	A , with two General Authorities —story	May 1989	43e-f

LeGrand Richards	2 reactions of , to the Church —stories	Dec 1968	45e-f
	2 more reactions of , to the Church —stories		46d
	A , asked to speak in Church —story		46e
	3 reactions of , to Mormons —stories		46f-47e
Harold B. Lee	Saints and , to be all mixed up in mountain valleys		71d-e

Non-members, cont'd
Related Topics: Missionary Work, Other Churches

Spencer W. Kimball	Observations by a , of our hidden treasures —story	Dec 1968	99b-100b
LeGrand Richards	Statements about Church by , —stories	Dec 1969	54c-55c
Delbert L. Stapley	I hope you can keep Satan out of your Church	Dec 1971	94b
	I believe the Church will save the world		95b
Gordon B. Hinckley	Letter from one crying for help	Nov 1976	95b-c
Hartman Rector, Jr.	Conversion of Lutheran pastor —story		97d-99b
Robert E. Wells	, thought Salt Lake temple was J. Smith's shrine —story	Nov 1982	69c-f
Gordon B. Hinckley	Comments of , from Temple Square	Nov 1989	53f-54c
M. Russell Ballard	Excellent list of facts about Church for ,	Nov 2007	25b-27f
Jeffrey R. Holland	, shouldn't wonder if LDS are Christian		40b-d
L. Tom Perry	Over 50% of , don't know about Church	May 2009	110b

Obedience
Related Topics: Commandments

Loren C. Dunn	Children deserve to be taught ,	June 1969	52e
Harold B. Lee	Survival of Apollo 13 depended upon ,	Dec 1970	28a-d
	Ultimate destiny depends on , to what we already know		30f
Eldred G. Smith	List of scriptures on ,		41f-42d
Harold B. Lee	Proclaim necessity of ,	Jan 1973	60e
N. Eldon Tanner	Walk in , to all the commandments		103e
Harold B. Lee	Obedience to counsel in patriarchal blessings		107f
Delbert L. Stapley	Lord obeys all commandments He gives us	July 1973	100c
N. Eldon Tanner	We demand , of our animals and punish them at times	Jan 1974	93e
Boyd K. Packer	Spiritual Crocodiles —entire talk, —story	May 1976	30a-32b
Spencer W. Kimball	Forceful statements to follow counsel of Brethren		124b-125d
James E. Faust	We must be courageously ,	Nov 1976	59e-f
Marion G. Romney	Disobedience brought flood. , sanctified Enoch's Zion	May 1977	53d
Royden G. Derrick	Best horses, though starved, come to whistle —story		57f-58b
Delbert L. Stapley	The purpose of our mortal life	Nov 1977	18f
	4 ways in which we learn ,		18f
N. Eldon Tanner	Strict , leads to freedom not slavery —Brigham Young	May 1978	15b
J. Richard Clarke	Classic statements by prophets	Nov 1980	83a-b
	Blind , better than disobedience		83b-c
Teddy E. Brewerton	Good men obey because of love - Wicked because of fear	May 1981	68d
	He rules laws who obeys them		68e
Boyd K. Packer	Boy untied horse and looped rope around wrists —story	Nov 1981	32c-f
Carlos E. Asay	, ensures us of the guidance and protection of Holy Ghost		68b
Boyd K. Packer	Some see , only as restraint	May 1983	66c
	Blind obedience? No - Obedient because we see		66d-e
L. Tom Perry	Fruits of , and disobedience	Nov 1984	18b
Robert B. Harbertson	In , "ye shall eat the good of the land" —Isaiah 1:18-19		24d-e
Ronald E. Poelman	Giving enlightened , rather than blind ,		65c
Ezra Taft Benson	You can't do wrong and feel right	May 1985	36e
	Missionaries roughed up because weren't obedient —story		36e-37f
Boyd K. Packer	, comes close to being a cure-all	Nov 1987	18a-b
L. Aldin Porter	A call was rejected - family left Church —story		73e-f

David B. Haight	We learn , by being obedient	May 1988	23d
Boyd K. Packer	Apostates are always irritated by the word ,	Nov 1989	15b-e
Michaelene P. Grassli	When we disobey a rule, the protection is gone		92f-93a
Robert D. Hales	Pilot fatality because training shirked —story	May 1990	39d-40d
	People are sometimes selectively obedient		41b
Glenn L. Pace	Place energy into current ,	Nov 1992	12f
Joseph B. Wirthlin	Sustaining leaders yet shopping on Sunday		35b-c
Joseph B. Wirthlin	The first law of heaven —Benson	May 1994	39d
	Well-trained horses —story		39d-f
	Momentary lapses in , —football story		40f-41f
	Advice to youth —entire talk		39b-42b
Monte J. Brough	Boy stayed on horse 80 miles —story	May 1995	41d-f
M. Russell Ballard	We need to have , like Hyrum Smith	Nov 1995	7f-8d
Carlos E. Asay	The world is drifting - 1916 quote	May 1996	60f
Donald L. Staheli	Disobedient puppy lost life —story	May 1998	82b-c
	"When , ceases to be an irritant..."		82d-e
Athos M. Amorim	You will command. So learn to obey.	Nov 1998	30b-c
James E. Faust	President McKay's horse wanted freedom —story	May 1999	45b-e
	All creation is orderly and obedient		45f-46e
	, becomes a building block not a stumbling block		47a
	, brings peace in decision making		47b
Thomas S. Monson	"Keep Right" to be happy		50e
Vaughn J. Featherstone	A wonderful privilege	Nov 1999	14f-15a
M. Russell Ballard	Girl removed second earrings —story	May 2001	66d
H. Ross Workman	A contrast in , to a simple request —story	Nov 2001	86d-e
	The evils of murmuring		85b-86f
Joseph B. Wirthlin	Leaving our nets to follow Jesus	May 2002	15b-17f
R. Conrad Schultz	Not blind , because we can see		29f-30b
	Every prophet has taught ,		30f-31b
Dieter F. Uchtdorf	Our strength comes from , —G. Hinckley	Nov 2002	12a
Thomas S. Monson	Abraham was the model of ,		60d-e
H. David Burton	, builds strength	May 2003	50b
D. Rex Gerratt	"If all else fails - Please! Follow instructions"		90b-91f
L. Tom Perry	We must have intelligent , not blind ,	Nov 2003	86f
David A. Bednar	, qualifies us for tender mercies of the Lord	May 2005	99b-102b
James E. Faust	Plan of happiness requires ,	Nov 2005	21d
Jeffrey R. Holland	Angels will be your associates —Joseph Smith		28e
Henry B. Eyring	The great test of life is , in trials		38b
Richard G. Scott	The most fundamental purpose of mortality		78d-f
James E. Faust	Meaning of "to carry the cross"	Nov 2006	20d-f
	, makes our crosses lighter		22e-23b
James E. Faust	Reading scriptures but not living them —story		53e-54a
Margaret S. Lifferth	, alone in family worship invites blessings		75b
Joseph B. Wirthlin	Wise men cultivate an obedient spirit	May 2007	47b-d

Obedience, cont'd
Related Topics: Commandments

Robert D. Hales	Selective , killed the pilot —story	May 2007	50a-d
	Unstable as water - Or firm as a rock?		50d-e
	Be There —great counsel		50f-51a
Gordon B. Hinckley	J.F. Smith's dream - I am clean —story		60f-62b
L. Tom Perry	Deacon's president took the challenge —story		85d-f
Joseph B. Wirthlin	, ceases to be a burden when we love the Lord	Nov 2007	30a-c
Richard G. Scott	The relationship between faith, character and ,		92c-e
Dallin H. Oaks	One of two channels to God - Knowledge encourages ,	May 2008	28d-29a
Susan W. Tanner	Youth individually resisted peer temptations		113f-114b
	Girl took self to church - Became General R.S. President		114d
D. Todd Christofferson	Enjoy a continual flow of blessings through ,	May 2009	21a-b
	During times of distress let , be exact		22e
	When obedient we seek more commandments		23a
Quentin L. Cook	Eternal life available only through ,		37d-f
Kevin W. Pearson	Faith requires an attitude of exact ,		39a
Dallin H. Oaks	Cooperative service of members isn't from blind ,		94b-d
Dieter F. Uchtdorf	Becomes a joy rather than a burden	Nov 2009	21e-f
Quentin L. Cook	, to the unenforceable		91b-d
Boyd K. Packer	Priesthood power comes through ,	May 2010	9d-e
Ann M. Dibb	Brings success —H.W. Hunter		115b

Offerings
Related Topics: Fast Offerings, Poor and Needy, Tithing, Welfare Program

Marion G. Romney	Donate liberally to fast funds	Jan 1973	99f
Adney Y. Komatsu	New home resulted from temple sacrifice —story	May 1976	101e
H. Burke Peterson	Give 7 times more than the meals' value	Nov 1976	115a
Marion G. Romney	President Grant's , increased fourfold —story	Nov 1977	41f-42a
Spencer W. Kimball	Generous fast , increases temporal and spiritual prosperity		78f-79a
Victor L. Brown	Artistic boy received artificial limbs —story		82d-e
Spencer W. Kimball	Give many times the value of fasted meals	May 1978	80a
J. Richard Clarke	Surplus should go to fast , —Give 10 times more —Kimball		84d-e
Victor L. Brown	Fast , - Purpose, how much —story	May 1981	37e-38e
	How to reduce financial burdens on members		38f-39f
M. Russell Ballard	Local fast , used to deal with Peruvian slides —story	Nov 1987	80a-81a
	General Mission Fund provides for thousands		81a
Thomas S. Monson	Advice from prophets on proper fast ,	Nov 1988	44f-45d
Joseph B. Wirthlin	Poignant plea for , —story	May 2001	74d-f
	Give yourself into the Kingdom of God		75a-d
Quentin L. Cook	Be careful what you ask of people —story	Nov 2009	93d-e

Opportunity
Related Topics: —

Spencer W. Kimball	Mill can't grind with water that's past	Dec 1970	74f
	"O, that I had" the silent cry of many		74f
	A calling refused and always regretted —story		74f-75a
	The golden , never offered twice —poem		75a
	Four things never come back		75b

Spencer W. Kimball	Quote from Julius Caesar by Shakespeare	Dec 1970	75b-c
	Thyself must make thyself		75e
	What you might have been. What you have been —Maesar		75e
	Opportunities —good poem		75e-f
David B. Haight	We have equal , for exaltation —George Albert Smith	Nov 1979	24a
Robert D. Hales	Opposition may be an , —First Presidency	Nov 2008	72f-73e

Opposition
Related Topics: Satan

Gordon B. Hinckley	, against Church will intensify	June 1970	40a
John H. Vandenberg	, in all things says that sin must exist	Dec 1971	115b
Neal A. Maxwell	Adversary's attention merely cruel form of commendation	Nov 1980	14f
Marvin J. Ashton	Team needed stronger competition		54d-e
	As yet I am strong…give me this mountain —Caleb		60c
Carlos E. Asay	Apostate cited changes in Church publications —story	Nov 1981	67e-f
	9 steps for protection against anti-Christs		67f-68f
	, refines us and testifies of divinity of this work		68f-69a
	Every time you kick the Church you kick it upstairs —Young		69b
Neal A. Maxwell	All prophets were called names and persecuted	Nov 1983	55f
Howard W. Hunter	We should not expect no , in life —story	Nov 1984	33f-35b
Marvin J. Ashton	No peace to those who fight the Church	Nov 1985	69e-f
Gordon B. Hinckley	Enemies of Church chipping at granite with a wooden chisel	May 1986	47c
Ezra Taft Benson	God wants us to be like Him - Satan likewise	May 1988	6b
Boyd K. Packer	More dangerous than in earlier days	Nov 2005	71a
Boyd K. Packer	Different , but will not end	Nov 2006	86e-f
Joseph B. Wirthlin	Adversity leads to happiness. Reason for ,	Nov 2008	28f
Robert D. Hales	, may be an opportunity - How to respond		72f-73e
	, will be a blessing		74f-75b

Other Churches
Related Topics: Atheism, Non-members

LeGrand Richards	411 churches in New Zealand	June 1969	91b
	, held out no hope to bereaved parents at funeral		93a
Gordon B. Hinckley	Those who contend with , will reap persecution	June 1970	40a
Alvin R. Dyer	Lord showed no vindictiveness toward , in First Vision		50d
Harold B. Lee	A liberal church is founded on sand	June 1971	7c-d
Spencer W. Kimball	Attitudes of , toward immorality		18b-d
	Sin never mentioned in some ,		19a
Harold B. Lee	Committing suicide	Dec 1971	28d-e
	What people are looking for in churches		28e-29c
Boyd K. Packer	One Church is not as good as another - all different		40b-e
	, play just one or a few notes of keyboard		41c-e
Theodore M. Burton	Interested more in political activism and psychiatry than God		78b-d
Delbert L. Stapley	"We have failed to keep Satan out of our church."		94b
Hartman Rector, Jr.	We don't write tracts against ,	July 1972	64e
Theodore M. Burton	Falsely secure in their idea of salvation		78a
LeGrand Richards	Only two churches have tenable positions —story		114f

Other Churches, cont'd
Related Topics: Atheism, Non-members

Bernard P. Brockbank	Pharisees religious but not saved	Jan 1973	45c
Howard W. Hunter	Confused because no revelation		64b
	Giving stones, not bread		64e
LeGrand Richards	Don't believe in eternal marriage —story	July 1973	79b
	Preached to convention leaders of ,		79c
LeGrand Richards	No other major church believes marriage is eternal	Jan 1974	57b
	The minister believed marriage is eternal —story		57c
	The minister believed marriage is eternal —story		57d
Joseph Anderson	Some ministers as confused as their flocks	May 1974	9e
John H. Vandenberg	3 creeds from ,		12f
S. Dilworth Young	Why there are so many ,	Nov 1974	91e-f
Thomas S. Monson	Educator says , devoid of revelation	May 1975	17c-d
LeGrand Richards	697 churches in U.S.		95e
	Jesus' pronouncement upon ,		96c-e
	Statements of converted ministers		97b-c
	Protestants don't have a leg to stand on		97c-e
Neal A. Maxwell	The test is not sincerity but truth		101f
L. Tom Perry	Refused to acknowledge God's hand in the affairs of USA	Nov 1975	85e-86c
Boyd K. Packer	His church must show merciful fate for unbaptized dead		97f-98e
N. Eldon Tanner	Roger Williams' and Luther's statements	May 1976	49f
LeGrand Richards	Fallacious concepts of God , have	Nov 1976	65b-66b
Hartman Rector, Jr.	Conversion of Lutheran pastor —story		97d-99b
LeGrand Richards	Parable of talents: One must do more than confess the Lord	Nov 1977	23d-e
Hugh W. Pinnock	Minister: "When we get together we talk about Mormons"	Nov 1979	74b
LeGrand Richards	, pay all missionary expenses but no one goes —story		77a-b
	A church paid its choir members —story		77c-d
Bruce R. McConkie	Prophecy that the barriers of Islam will be broken	May 1980	72c
Bruce R. McConkie	The false gods worshipped by ,	Nov 1980	50f-51a
	No idol ever will save one soul		51c-e
LeGrand Richards	Minister couldn't respond to debate questions —story	May 1982	30f-31d
	Minister wanted to hear the rest —story		31d-e
Marvin J. Ashton	Proper response to anti-Mormons	Nov 1982	63a-e
	None can prosper with fault-finding as their foundation		63e
Vaughn J. Featherstone	Minister missed point in Prodigal Son Parable		72e
Ted E. Brewerton	What Catholic study learned about LDS Church	May 1983	74c-d
Neal A. Maxwell	Joseph Smith's defense of ,	Nov 1983	56d
Bruce R. McConkie	Ministers' reaction to invitation to read B of M —story		72b-73a
Dallin H. Oaks	Those without authority use Lord's name in vain	May 1985	81a
Boyd K. Packer	Can all churches lead to heaven?	Nov 1985	82b-c
Glenn L. Pace	Can't save men temporally, then can't save spiritually —Smith	May 1986	25b
Dallin H. Oaks	We have no right to scare people to repentance	Nov 1986	22d-e
Boyd K. Packer	Preacher chastised parents at funeral for no baptism —story	Nov 1988	18b-d
Dallin H. Oaks	Concepts taught by ,		65b-d
Wm. Grant Bangerter	3 ministers were amazed at his knowledge —story		80f-81a
Russell M. Nelson	Bible calls believers "Saints" 98 times but "Christians" just 3	May 1990	16d-e

Other Churches

David B. Haight	Are not connected up —Electrical story	May 1990	24d-25a
Boyd K. Packer	, have almost abandoned the Old Testament		38a
Lynn A. Mickelsen	Foregone conclusions exclude Spirit	Nov 1990	28d
Dallin H. Oaks	, no longer have fundamental belief in Jesus		31d-f
	"Creator, Redeemer, Sustainer" —non-sexist terms		32a
Gordon B. Hinckley	Joseph Smith willing to die for members of ,		54b
Loren C. Dunn	Joseph Smith helped Catholic priest —story	May 1991	81b-c
Howard W. Hunter	God uses not only His covenant people	Nov 1991	19a-b
Chieko N. Okazaki	She grew up a Buddhist		88d-f
Russell M. Nelson	Keep the truth you have, and come get more	May 1994	70e
Gordon B. Hinckley	Live with respect and appreciation for ,	May 1995	71b-c
Richard C. Edgley	Minister told woman LDS aren't Christian —story	May 1998	11d-12d
M. Russell Ballard	Eliminate "non-member" from vocabulary	Nov 2001	37d-e
Gordon B. Hinckley	Do not persecute Muslims		72e
Gordon B. Hinckley	, say we don't believe in traditional Christ	May 2002	90f-91b
Robert D. Hales	, attach donor's name to contributions	Nov 2002	28b
Russell M. Nelson	Descendants of Ishmael and Isaac could yet work together		40e-41d
Gordon B. Hinckley	Cannot understand why , don't accept Book of Mormon		81a
James E. Faust	No , claim to have keys to bind families	Nov 2003	21a
Gordon B. Hinckley	Retention in , not as great	May 2004	4d
Ronald T. Halverson	What is the reward for following the philosophies of men?	Nov 2004	32b-e
Gordon B. Hinckley	Another church was financed by bingo	May 2005	59f
Gordon B. Hinckley	, based upon Nicaean Creed		80f-81b
L. Tom Perry	A church can't exist without government aid —story		84b-e
Boyd K. Packer	Fate of Tyndale and Wycliffe	Nov 2005	71b-72a
Robert D. Hales	History of coming forth of the Bible		89b-90e
James E. Faust	We have many beliefs in common with ,	May 2006	61d-e
	Mohammed, Confucius, etc. received God's light		68d-e
Boyd K. Packer	Sometimes attack us - Something we never do	Nov 2006	87a
	Hold preposterous opinions of us —story		87b-c
James E. Faust	The Amish and forgiveness —story	May 2007	67b-68a
Gordon B. Hinckley	Most recite the Nicene Creed - Confusing		83b-e
Gary J. Coleman	"Mom, are we Christians?"		92b
Boyd K. Packer	Unlike , we have an inexhaustible supply of leaders	Nov 2007	6f-7b
Jeffrey R. Holland	Notion of Trinity is not true		40d-e
	Harper's Bible Dictionary dismisses Trinity		40e
	History of early councils		40f-41c
	His testimony to , of our Christianity		42b-e
Gordon B. Hinckley	He cannot understand Nicene Creed		84e-f
Douglas L. Callister	Infants can't be saved - Viewpoint of , —story		100e-f
Dieter F. Uchtdorf	"How can you leave our church?" —Wife's story	May 2008	70e-75a
	Faith of our Father goes back to beginning		75a-f
Boyd K. Packer	Odd that , call us non-Christian		85f-86a
Jeffrey R. Holland	Revelation and more scripture make LDS unchristian?		91d-e
	Answer posed to misunderstanding of Rev. 22:18		91e-f

Other Churches, cont'd
Related Topics: Atheism, Non-members

Jeffrey R. Holland	Bible is not common ground for , but a battleground	May 2008	92e-f
Robert D. Hales	Do not contentiously debate ,	Nov 2008	73e-74b
	How to maintain theological high ground		74d-f
Quentin L. Cook	Teach that heaven is closed - no revelation	May 2009	36a-c
	Taught grandfather few would be saved —story		36c-e
	Teach that most will go to hell		36f-37a
	No criticism of , - Live with respect		37b-d
Neil L. Andersen	Others pray, sacrifice and share faith in Church		80d-e
Quentin L. Cook	Jewish leaders' reaction upon visit to Church	Nov 2009	91b-d
D. Todd Christofferson	, don't talk about sin any more		108f
D. Todd Christofferson	What they imagine Jesus to be today	May 2010	34b-d
Dallin H. Oaks	Prayer healed girl —story		47e-48b
	8 in 10 Americans believe in miracles		47f

Parents
Related Topics: Children, Family, Fathers, Home, Motherhood and Mothers

David O. McKay	Strong statement about duties of ,	Dec 1968	37c
Gordon B. Hinckley	The tailors and seamstresses of society		69b-d
Loren C. Dunn	The power of example and correct teaching by ,		78a
David O. McKay	, cannot shift responsibility to train children	June 1969	4b-c
Loren C. Dunn	Godlike , make it easy for child to love God		52e
	Study to hold children's love		52f
Richard L. Evans	, who are bad examples will have children who are worse		80e-f
Marion G. Romney	Blood of untaught children to be upon ,		95d
Spencer W. Kimball	Work of , to build for children	Dec 1969	48b
	Story of two families —story		49c
	Story of posterity of 2 brothers —story		50a
	Resisting communism —story		50c
Richard L. Evans	Your children entitled to best ,		73c
Thomas S. Monson	Love of missionary converts , —story		91d
A. Theodore Tuttle	The roles of , in the home		108d-e
Victor L. Brown	Quote on being an example to children —good	June 1970	46a
Thomas S. Monson	Most powerful emotions in world come because of children		90d-e
Paul H. Dunn	Accent on youth but stress on parents	Dec 1970	38f
Ezra Taft Benson	Successful , greater than successful statesmen		46a-b
	Take nothing for granted about your children		46d-e
Loren C. Dunn	Who will care for a youth who has been given up on?		62b-63b
	Father didn't give up on girl —story		63b-c
	Mother didn't give up on boy —story		63d-64a
	Don't abandon children on thoroughfares of life —story		64a-e
Delbert L. Stapley	, may be responsible for sins of children forever		65d
	Parents love children more than children love ,		65f
Elray L. Christiansen	Short poem on parental example —poem	June 1971	38b
	Never let children hear a cross word		38b
Marion D. Hanks	The type of love , must give children		92d
Paul H. Dunn	How does it feel to have my sins on your hands?		102c-d

Delbert L. Stapley	, cannot give children what they don't possess	June 1971	105a
A. Theodore Tuttle	True parenthood is fast disappearing	Dec 1971	91a
Delbert L. Stapley	Honor thy father and mother applies to God , too		96c
Joseph Fielding Smith	Greatest calling is to be successful ,	Jul 1972	27f
N. Eldon Tanner	Don't prejudice children		36b
H. Burke Peterson	Tribute to his , and how they taught him		47d
Elray L. Christiansen	Set example —short poem		55a
	Must avoid disputations		55b
S. Dilworth Young	Helps for raising sons —entire talk, excellent		76a
Howard W. Hunter	Make children do things on their own —story		85a
Paul H. Dunn	Never let children go —story		93b
David B. Haight	To be held to a strict accounting		108e
A. Theodore Tuttle	Responsibility of , cannot be shifted	Jan 1973	67b
James E. Faust	Still needs his mother's prayers		81b
H. Burke Peterson	Ways , can exert greater efforts with children		114f
	Responsibility of , to teach children —good		115e
Thomas S. Monson	Sacrifice of , for missionary —story		120f
	Hard working father —story		121a
S. Dilworth Young	Prophets are born of goodly ,		123f
N. Eldon Tanner	Discipline your children	July 1973	8d
Spencer W. Kimball	Lord placed , at head of home		15b
O. Leslie Stone	Vanity of , toward children —funny story		59b
James E. Faust	Mothers must never demean fathers before children	Jan 1974	23a
A. Theodore Tuttle	Son was to be in before alarm clock went off		68a
	Don't do genealogy if you don't know where kids are		68a
L. Tom Perry	His , protective shield —story	May 1974	98e-99b
Loren C. Dunn	Love can overcome many parental mistakes	Nov 1974	11a
Neal A. Maxwell	A world full of orphans with parents		12e
Vaughn J. Featherstone	, care for children but children won't care for aged ,		29e
	Don't send , to nursing homes		30d-e
N. Eldon Tanner	Love of , brought hippy son back —story		86e-f
Spencer W. Kimball	Creating positive currents to fight the negative ones		110a-113f
James E. Faust	Parenthood brings greatest joy, privileges and responsibilities	May 1975	27e
H. Burke Peterson	My parents love me but I wish they cared —story		52d-e
Marvin J. Ashton	Threats, procrastination or purchase don't make good ,		86a
Neal A. Maxwell	, must not desert their posts		101e
Marion D. Hanks	Must use example and active teaching	Nov 1975	25b-c
	Judgment of , —a good, short scripture		26a
Gordon B. Hinckley	Influences , should provide in home		39b-d
Spencer W. Kimball	Parenthood - the most holy joy of humanity	May 1976	108a
	Best time of life is grandparenthood		108b-d
Victor L. Brown	The way children should learn from , example		112f
Marion G. Romney	Children, not government, should support aged ,		121d-122a
O. Leslie Stone	What constitutes delinquent , —McKay	Nov 1976	60b-c
Marion G. Romney	We must care for our aged ,		125b-f

Spencer W. Kimball	We must care for our aged , even if senile —story	Nov 1976	127e-f
H. Burke Peterson	A success pattern for raising healthy children	May 1977	68d
J. Richard Clarke	Working mothers and weekend fathers —story		85f-86a
James E. Faust	Marriage greatly enriched through parenthood	Nov 1977	11b
Ezra Taft Benson	The bent over heads are the ones with grain in them —story		31d-e
A. Theodore Tuttle	Teach in home as if isolated from Church	Nov 1979	27f-28a
	Book of Mormon examples of parental teaching		28c-e
N. Eldon Tanner	Dating: Why , need to know who and where —good	May 1980	16f-17a
Jack H. Goaslind, Jr.	When children are most unlovable they need more —story	May 1981	60b-c
H. Burke Peterson	We are to care for our aging , —story		82d-83a
Marion G. Romney	It is an ungrateful child who will not assist ,		90f
	We covenant to care for ,		91b-c
J. Richard Clarke	Caring son wanted father to visit —story	Nov 1981	81f-82b
Ezra Taft Benson	, responsible for acts of children if they have neglected duty		106b
	Counsel to ,		107a-c
H. Burke Peterson	Respond when child earnestly asks - not later	May 1982	43d-e
James E. Faust	Example: Chickens come home to roost and bring chicks too		48b
Marion G. Romney	Some , place children on the dole	Nov 1982	91f
Matthew S. Holland	His , went to his game, not BYU's —story	May 1983	39c-e
Boyd K. Packer	If all your children knew is what you taught them at home..?		66e
Paul H. Dunn	Advantages and treatment of old age	Nov 1983	25b-26f
David B. Haight	Act preventively now or redemptively later —Kimball		40d
Howard W. Hunter	Comfort for , of children that stray —excellent		63d-65b
Ezra Taft Benson	Division of responsibility between , - no inequality	May 1984	6c
A. Theodore Tuttle	The things , have done in the past are no longer sufficient		23f
	, have prime responsibility to teach		24b-d
	Teach by drawing out - not by pouring on		24f
James E. Faust	Caring for the handicapped —entire talk	Nov 1984	54b-60e
Boyd K. Packer	Fatherhood taught him the important lessons		67b
James E. Faust	A Parent's Guide —Church booklet available	May 1987	82b
Richard G. Scott	To Help a Loved One in Need	May 1988	60b-61f
Joseph B. Wirthlin	, know what leads to happiness or sorrow	Nov 1988	34e
L. Tom Perry	How to teach children and prepare them —good		73b-75f
Glenn L. Pace	"I've told you a thousand times"	Nov 1990	8b-9a
James E. Faust	The greatest challenge in the world		32d-33d
	Parental example is paramount		33f-34a
Boyd K. Packer	Caring for handicapped child perfects ,	May 1991	9c-e
Dallin H. Oaks	Elderly , are our responsibility —Benson		15f
	How to care for elderly ,		16d-f
	How honoring , lengthens your days —story		17d-f
Russell M. Nelson	Parents do not own children —story		22b-e
	Girl didn't listen to , and lost life —story		22e-23a
Graham W. Doxey	Children are internship-grandchildren postgraduate education	Nov 1991	25b
Thomas S. Monson	10 suggestions for , —Ezra Taft Benson	May 1992	5b-e
Merrill J. Bateman	, searched diligently for lost son —story	Nov 1992	27d-f

Parents

Neal A. Maxwell	Small equivocations in , lead to large ones in kids	Nov 1992	65f-66a
Richard G. Scott	God has unresponsive children, too	May 1993	34d
Robert D. Hales	Example of , will be followed —stories	Nov 1993	8d-10f
Joe J. Christensen	Counsel on being , in a polluted environment		11b-13b
Boyd K. Packer	We are commanded to become ,		22e-23c
Hugh W. Pinnock	I've never been a father before —story		41b
Gordon B. Hinckley	Straighten the sapling when young —story		59c-f
	Use love, patience, encouragement, prayers		60b-f
Dallin H. Oaks	Parenthood was the first commandment		72f
	Parenthood is the most exalted power		74a
	Have all the children you can care for		75a-c
Albert Choules, Jr.	Children copy examples of ,	May 1994	14e-f
Kenneth Johnson	Imperfect paint job was OK —story		30b-e
Neal A. Maxwell	Gentle beneath firmness - firm beneath gentleness		90d
	Give up one outside thing for family		90f
Howard W. Hunter	Sacred obligation and privilege	Nov 1994	9a
Gordon B. Hinckley	The greatest, most rewarding occupation		54c-d
Rex D. Pinegar	Father's and son's view of day spent fishing —story		82b
Neal A. Maxwell	Failure to visit and care for , breaks commandment	May 1995	68e
Gordon B. Hinckley	Honor , with the goodness of your lives		70d
L. Tom Perry	Aged , don't have to compete or prove, just enjoy		74e-f
Gordon B. Hinckley	Proclamation on the family	Nov 1995	100f-101e
Bruce C. Hafen	A test no hireling would endure —story	Nov 1996	27d-f
Gordon B. Hinckley	Children are the trip I did not take —poem		68c
Richard G. Scott	, have a responsibility to bear children		73f
James E. Faust	Were difficult Sundays worth the effort?		96a-b
Patricia P. Pinegar	No joy equals that of happy parenthood	May 1997	13f
	Yours is a custodial relationship to children		14f
Jeffrey R. Holland	God's basic expectations of ,		36d
Thomas S. Monson	The first calling of a man or woman	Nov 1997	96a-b
Gordon B. Hinckley	What greater thing than to become a ,	May 1998	51b
Margaret D. Nadauld	Young widower helped by Young Women —story		65b-d
Boyd K. Packer	Most important calling —important talk	Nov 1998	22b-24f
Henry B. Eyring	Warnings from , through love, example, testimony		32d-f
Robert D. Hales	Though children wander, they will return	May 1999	34c-d
Henry B. Eyring	Teachings of , last generations —story		74d-75f
M. Russell Ballard	What , should teach children		86e
Ben B. Banks	'Twas a sheep that strayed —poem	Nov 1999	10e-11a
Vaughn J. Featherstone	Children may carry example of , to extreme		14d
James E. Faust	Master pianist put arms around student —story		101b-c
Dallin H. Oaks	Parenthood best suited to prepare for exaltation	Nov 2000	33d
Sharon G. Larsen	Takes an enormous amount of time and energy	Nov 2001	68d
	Overheard comment bound her to , —story		68e
	Harvest time - Worth every sacrifice		68f
Russell M. Nelson	Don't cling to children but to Savior —raft story		69b-e

Russell M. Nelson	, will be accountable before God	Nov 2001	70e
	Devote best efforts to children		70f
	What should , teach?		71a
	What to give highest priority to		71f
Boyd K. Packer	Most valuable lessons are from ,	May 2002	9f-10b
Coleen K. Menlove	No other joy equals happy parenthood —Hinckley	Nov 2002	15d-e
James E. Faust	Parenthood - A schoolmaster to overcome selfishness		19e-f
F. Melvin Hammond	Lashes couldn't have cut so deeply —story		99a-b
Gordon B. Hinckley	Everything in life counts on our being good ,		100c-f
James E. Faust	Some children would challenge any ,	May 2003	61e
	, influence us from other side of veil		67d
	Comfort to , with wayward children		61b-68b
Jeffrey R. Holland	Off-course , will be exceeded by children		86a-d
	Parenthood is like shooting an arrow		87d
Russell M. Nelson	Children follow example of ,	May 2004	27c-e
Thomas S. Monson	Son finally visited mother —story		57d-e
L. Tom Perry	Do not let your children out to specialists		71f-72b
Boyd K. Packer	Don't be afraid to bring children into world		79d-e
Robert D. Hales	, aren't failures if they do their best		88e
	Though children wander they will return —Whitney		91c-d
W. Douglas Shumway	Parenthood: the first commandment		95a-b
	What will matter in 100 years?		95b-d
Boyd K. Packer	Children fulfill dreams of , by being faithful	Nov 2004	87f-88a
H. David Burton	Families need less possessions and more ,		98c-d
Thomas S. Monson	Dad took boys to circus —story	May 2005	20f-21a
	Advice about raising children		20d-21b
M. Russell Ballard	Bar raised for , too		70b
Bonnie D. Parkin	Good advice on parenting children	Nov 2005	109a-b
Richard G. Hinckley	Tribute to his ,	May 2006	48e-49a
Gordon B. Hinckley	Sacrifice , make for children —poem	Nov 2006	116e-f
Gordon B. Hinckley	Treat your children with great kindness	May 2007	105e
Boyd K. Packer	Work as , transcends anything in Church or out	Nov 2007	8f-9a
Mary N. Cook	Our responsibility to break cycle of bad example of ,		13b
Quentin L. Cook	Righteous children can be raised anywhere		72b-d
Julie B. Beck	Commandment to bear children remains in force		76d-e
Dallin H. Oaks	Everything in life counts upon parenthood		106b-d
Julie B. Beck	Commandment to multiply remains in force		110e-f
Russell M. Nelson	How , are to correct children	May 2008	9a-10a
Thomas S. Monson	Never do anything you wouldn't want son to do		66e
M. Russell Ballard	Heed counsel of , —Edsel dealership story	May 2009	31b-e
	God's plan: Teach children to be better than you		33b-34a
Boyd K. Packer	4 grandsons came to announce engagements		52e
Dallin H. Oaks	Couple decided to have a dog instead of child		93e-f
	Church rejoices when children care for aging ,		93f
David A. Bednar	Must frequently express love	Nov 2009	17e-18f

Parents

Dallin H. Oaks	Dealing with wayward children	Nov 2009	28d-29b
M. Russell Ballard	How , see children - Improved versions of selves		47e
Yoon Hwan Choi	Surrogate , made nine converts —story		53b-55b
Henry B. Eyring	Wayward children will return —Whitney		71f-72c
	Blessings for honoring ,		72c-d
D. Todd Christofferson	Make converts of children while still at home		107c
L. Tom Perry	Central cast members in children's lives	May 2010	30c-e
	Most powerful, sustaining force for good		60e
David A. Bednar	Spontaneously bear testimony to children		42b-e
	Read and testify to bless posterity		43f
Richard G. Scott	A calling from which never released		77d-78a
Robert D. Hales	Take advantage of teaching moments		95d-e
	Mealtime interaction is important		95f-96b
Neil L. Andersen	Cannot be casual in teaching		108e
	Testimony of , will distill on children		110e-f

Patience
Related Topics: —

Angel Abrea	Have , in affliction —entire talk	May 1992	25d-27b
Thomas S. Monson	Irritant became loving ritual —story	Nov 1992	99a-e
V. Dallas Merrell	Church will prevail over all difficulty —story	May 1993	29b-f
Marlin K. Jensen	Boy made candy last a year —story	May 1994	48e-f
Russell M. Nelson	Limitless tolerance leads to permissiveness		71a-c
	Must have tolerance —entire talk		69b-71f
Thomas S. Monson	Patience - A heavenly virtue —entire talk	Nov 1995	59b-61f
Neal A. Maxwell	We seek to counsel Him who oversees cosmic clocks	Nov 1998	62f-63a
Thomas S. Monson	Boys, dogs and snake teach , —2 stories	Nov 2002	54e-55b
Thomas S. Monson	Job was the model of ,		60e-f
Anne C. Pingree	Taught disabled son to read - 7 years to read B of M —story		109d-f
Robert C. Oaks	Motorcycles fell like dominoes —story	Nov 2006	16e-f
	The power of patience —entire talk		15d-17b
Dieter F. Uchtdorf	Tried his counsel for a week. It didn't work —story	May 2009	76d-f
Kent D. Watson	Being temperate in all things —entire talk	Nov 2009	38b-39f
Dieter F. Uchtdorf	Experiment of kids eating marshmallows —story	May 2010	56c-e
	A purifying process		56e-f
	Not passive - Requires work		57a-e
	Refines natures		58a
	Never give up on self or others		58b
	Everyone is called to wait		58b-c
	Lord's promises not swift but certain		58d-e
	Trials will only be understood later		58f
	A process of perfection		58f-59b
	The essence of ,		59b-f

Patriarchal Blessings
Related Topics: —

Harold B. Lee	Sacred and never published	Jan 1973	105b
	"Iffy" blessings —story		107f
A. Theodore Tuttle	Fathers' blessings are ,	Jan 1974	67a
Ezra Taft Benson	Personal scripture to you	May 1986	43f-44a
Thomas S. Monson	What , are	Nov 1986	65e-f
	What is a Patriarch? How is he called? —story		65f-66c
	Not to be framed, published or put away		66d-e
	Unreasonable promises given in , fulfilled —story		66f-67b
Ezra Taft Benson	Personal scripture to you		82c-d
	Receive , under fasting and prayer		82c-d
James E. Faust	Discussion on , —excellent	Nov 1995	62f-64f
Thomas S. Monson	, given by man with no hands —story	May 2002	51b-f
Boyd K. Packer	A shield and a protection	Nov 2002	42b
	An evangelist is a patriarch		42d-e
	Three kinds of patriarchs		42f
	Who calls patriarchs and how called		42f-43a
	The training available for patriarchs		43a
	No fixed age for receiving ,		43a
	Should not be read except by family		43b
	Lord designated who should be called —story		43b-44b
	Stake presidents should read some blessings		44b-c
	Blessings come from Spirit, not patriarch —story		44d
	A paragraph from your book of possibilities		44d
	Declaration of lineage in ,		44d-45a
	Which patriarch should give your ,		45a
	Promises in , are not just for mortality		45b
	When patriarchs are excused from service		45b
	Light went through Elder Lee into patriarch —story		45b-d
	Stake president should read some blessings		45d-e
	Patriarchs must live worthy of the Spirit		45e
	A line from his ,		45e-f
Anne C. Pingree	, emphasized missionary work —story	Nov 2005	112d-114a
Gordon B. Hinckley	Remarkable line from his ,	May 2006	82e-f
Julie B. Beck	Good explanations about ,		106b-108f
Boyd K. Packer	Prophetic insight in his , —story	May 2009	50b-c

Patriarchal Order
Related Topics: Fathers

Ezra Taft Benson	Family and , will outlive Church	Dec 1970	46a
James A. Cullimore	Scope of ,	Jan 1973	124b
	No higher authority in home than father		125d

Peace
Related Topics: —

Joseph Fielding Smith	, is not likely soon to be established on the earth	Dec 1968	41f
Harold B. Lee	Peace comes by overcoming the world	June 1970	65e
Marion G. Romney	Peaceful nations will come from peaceful men		67e

Marion G. Romney	No , because we do not know God	June 1970	68a-b
Robert L. Simpson	The only real , is peace of mind	Dec 1970	97e
Theodore M. Burton	Cannot come by legislation or political affiliation	Dec 1971	80b-c
John H. Vandenberg	Peace of mind is the first condition of happiness		116f-117a
Eldred G. Smith	At , with self first then with neighbor	July 1972	117f
	Comes from service, repentance, teaching		117f
	Quote from Isaiah —good		118e
John H. Vandenberg	227 yrs. of , 3130 yrs. of war since 1496 B.C.		128b
Harold B. Lee	Has been taken from earth	July 1973	4b
Marion G. Romney	Possible now if all believed we were children of God		11a
Howard W. Hunter	Peace beyond mere cessation of hostilities		121e
A. Theodore Tuttle	Should be found in 2 places - home and temple	Jan 1974	67b
Harold B. Lee	Can't be won by guns and tanks - only in Church		128c
Theodore M. Burton	People will flock to Church in great numbers if we show ,	Nov 1974	56b
John H. Vandenberg	Earth would be at , without man but would have no purpose		93b-c
Franklin D. Richards	How and where to be a peacemaker		106a-c
	Bishop challenged youth to be , makers in home—results		106c-f
James E. Faust	We need fewer revolutions and more revelations	Nov 1976	58b
Spencer W. Kimball	, in land only if people keep commandments	Nov 1977	4f-5a
Bruce R. McConkie	, will not be gained by diplomats	May 1979	93b
Bruce R. McConkie	Men in our time will never find ,	Nov 1980	51e-f
Gordon B. Hinckley	Nuclear giants and ethical infants	Nov 1982	77d
Marvin J. Ashton	Can only come by refusing to pass judgment	May 1983	32b
Gordon B. Hinckley	, and blessings come by doing these things...		80e
Marvin J. Ashton	No , to a man untrue to his better self	Nov 1985	69d-e
Michaelene P. Grassli	How to have children at ,	Nov 1988	78f-79a
Dallin H. Oaks	His views on world ,	May 1990	71b-73f
James E. Faust	Places of , for Church members		86b
Joseph B. Wirthlin	What it is and how to obtain it —entire talk	May 1991	36d-38f
Robert E. Wells	President Lee avoided a media trap —story		86d-f
	Family scripture study brought , —story		86f-87b
	Ways to achieve personal ,		87e-f
Rex D. Pinegar	Comes not without pain, but in midst of pain	May 1993	66b-d
Neal A. Maxwell	Have inner , though no , in world		79a
Thomas S. Monson	When power of love replaces love of power	May 1994	61b
	, can only come from lives and hearts of men		61d
James E. Faust	Man's basic need: Peace of mind	May 1995	61f
Russell M. Nelson	Inner , cannot be found in affluence	May 1996	14d
Jeffrey R. Holland	Obtaining , —entire talk	Nov 1996	82b-84f
Ronald T. Halverson	True joy is an intense inner , and happiness —entire talk	Nov 1998	78d-79f
Sheri L. Dew	Is , possible when life is hard?	May 1999	67c-d
Patricia P. Pinegar	, came through plan of salvation at son's death —story	Nov 1999	67b-e
Russell M. Nelson	Inner conflict if we compartmentalize lives	Nov 2000	17e-f
Richard G. Scott	Repentance - the path to , and joy —excellent talk		25b-27b
Gordon B. Hinckley	Terrorism, 9/11 and the future	Nov 2001	72b-74f

Peace, cont'd
Related Topics: —

M. Russell Ballard	Make me an instrument of thy , —poem	May 2002	89d-e
	Inner , that comes from God —entire talk		87b-89f
Dieter F. Uchtdorf	Lost everything twice, but found , —story	Nov 2002	10f-11d
	No need to fear —G.B. Hinckley		12a
Russell M. Nelson	Peace and cessation of war is possible		40e-41d
Gordon B. Hinckley	His views on war —entire talk	May 2003	78d-81f
Dale E. Miller	Conversion brings , —entire talk	Nov 2004	12b-14f
Richard G. Scott	, of conscience and , of mind		15b-18b
James E. Faust	A gift of the Holy Ghost	Nov 2005	21d
Joseph B. Wirthlin	Peace comes by drinking deeply of living waters	May 2006	99f-100f
Boyd K. Packer	A , accord with terrorism isn't possible	Nov 2006	87e-f
Don R. Clarke	, came to blind man after prayer —story		98f
Richard G. Scott	Answers to prayer come as feelings of ,	May 2007	9f-10c
Henry B. Eyring	How to be a peacemaker	Nov 2008	70e-71a
Henry B. Eyring	This is not a time of ,	May 2009	63b
Gregory A. Schwitzer	Must be external and internal	May 2010	105b-d

Perfection
Related Topics: Excellence

Delbert L. Stapley	The overcoming of every weakness one by one	Dec 1968	54d
D. L. Stapley	Possible in many respects now	Dec 1969	64b
Richard L. Evans	Is possible, so be improving		74f
Robert L. Simpson	One Man was perfect. Saints are just sinners who try harder	Dec 1970	97c-e
Sterling W. Sill	Whistler wouldn't sell his best work —story	June 1971	44a-b
William H. Bennett	Athletes who reached , despite handicaps	Nov 1976	29e-f
	Letter from athlete who almost reached ,		30c-31b
Bruce R. McConkie	, not necessary at death		107b-d
Spencer W. Kimball	Not mere rhetoric that we can achieve ,	Nov 1978	6b
Neal A. Maxwell	Prophets have never claimed , . That leaves hope for us	Nov 1984	10d-f
Wm. Grant Bangerter	Wife's first husband was perfect —humorous	May 1987	11f-12d
Marvin J. Ashton	We will not reach , in this life	May 1989	20f-21a
	, does not come all at once		21a
J. Richard Clarke	Be as perfect as you can be —Brigham Young	May 1991	42a-c
Russell M. Nelson	A command and a process —entire talk	Nov 1995	86b-88f
Boyd K. Packer	Close enough to mail the letter	Nov 1999	24f-25b
Sheri L. Dew	Not panicked about , but working toward purity		98f-99b
	Identify one thing at a time to do		99e-f
Joseph B. Wirthlin	"Restricted Entrance - Perfect People Only"	May 2008	19b-f
Dieter F. Uchtdorf	Women tend to focus on imperfections	Nov 2008	117d-f
Jorge F. Zeballos	, and eternal life are not impossible	Nov 2009	33b-34f
Boyd K. Packer	Object is , of individual and family	May 2010	9f-10a

Philosophy
Related Topics: —

D. L. Stapley	Man's , not equal to truth	Dec 1969	64c
Harold B. Lee	Suicide victims lacked ,	Jan 1974	6a

Plan of Salvation
Related Topics: —

N. Eldon Tanner	The blueprint of life	Dec 1969	35f
	Promises if lived		36b
Harold B. Lee	All members to preach ,	Jan 1973	60d
Howard W. Hunter	Defined as the gospel	July 1973	120d
Neal A. Maxwell	This is the process	Nov 1982	67d
Neal A. Maxwell	This subject should be studied more than any other —Smith	Nov 1986	52f-53a
Ezra Taft Benson	His testimony of , —Entire talk	Nov 1988	86b-87f
Russell M. Nelson	Other names by which , is known	Nov 1993	33e-f
Dallin H. Oaks	, explained —entire talk		72b-75f
Russell M. Nelson	Three crucial components of ,	Nov 1996	33d
Keith B. McMullin	Definition of the gospel —good	Nov 1997	40f
L. Aldin Porter	Commandments give us the ability to follow the ,	Nov 1999	65b-66f
Patricia P. Pinegar	Peace came through , when son died —story		67b-e
Russell M. Nelson	Various names of , and 3 components of ,	May 2000	84c-e
Richard G. Scott	The plan of protection	May 2004	100f
Earl C. Tingey	World won't determine happiness if , followed	May 2006	74a-b
	Five elements of ,		72b-74b
L. Tom Perry	, outlined	Nov 2006	69d-72b
Henry B. Eyring	As explained by God before our birth	May 2008	123b-d
Gerald Causse	So simple that even children can understand	Nov 2008	32b-34b
Quentin L. Cook	Saves the living, redeems dead, rescues damned	May 2009	37f
Dieter F. Uchtdorf	Many theories for happiness, but only one plan is real		75e-f
Wilford W. Andersen	Does anyone have a problem with , ? —story	May 2010	17f-18a
Richard G. Scott	Atonement made , fully active		76d-f
Thomas S. Monson	Panoramic view of ,		87a-90f
Bradley D. Foster	The end is better than the beginning		100f
Elaine S. Dalton	Dismayed, discouraged, distracted, delayed, disqualified		121b
Dieter F. Uchtdorf	"Your Happily Ever After" —entire talk		124c-127f

Politics
Related Topics: Government, Voting

Harold B. Lee	Evils of controversy in ,	July 1972	29a
	The great danger to society is apathy in ,		32e
	Type of official to be sought		32f
N. Eldon Tanner	Don't indulge in vituperative talk		36a
Ezra Taft Benson	Deficits - inflation - price controls - shortages	Jan 1974	81d
Harold B. Lee	How members were to act during Chilean Turmoil		125f
Spencer W. Kimball	Church does not dictate political affiliation	May 1974	5b-c
	Church members urged to attend mass meetings		5d
Marion G. Romney	Elections turn upon monetary promises	Nov 1976	124c
Gordon B. Hinckley	Church will be involved in few extracurricular causes	May 1983	7f-8a
Jacob de Jager	Politicians —humorous anecdote		75e
Robert S. Wood	On dangerous ground when , bring unkind words	May 2006	95b
	, never justify hatred or ill will —Hinckley		95d-e

Poor and Needy
Related Topics: Fast Offerings, Offerings, Tithing, Welfare Program

John H. Vandenberg	Origin and purpose of fast day - promises to ,	June 1971	66b-67b
Marion G. Romney	Judgment made on care given ,	Jan 1973	97a
	Care for , helps remission of sins		97c
	Care for , and efficacy of prayers		97f
	If you love the Lord, remember the ,		98b
	Zion's Camp to remember the ,		98b
Marion G. Romney	Penalty for not remembering the ,	June 1971	99f
Marion G. Romney	List of scriptures concerning caring for ,	Jan 1974	91d
	Care of , is sole mandate of bishop		91f
Henry D. Taylor	Observe fast offerings and , will have more than enough	Nov 1974	14e
Russell M. Nelson	Graphic examples of poverty in the world	May 1986	25d-e
	Talk on , —entire talk, excellent		25d-27f
Robert D. Hales	Exalting the poor by humbling the rich exalts both		30b-c
James E. Faust	Money-poor but value-wealthy	May 1987	82c
D. Todd Christofferson	God measures societies by their care for ,	Nov 2008	39b-f
Henry B. Eyring	, must help others	May 2009	26a-c

Pornography
Related Topics: Chastity, Homosexuality, Immorality, Sex

Mark E. Petersen	Telling dirty stories is satanic	Dec 1968	91f
Ezra Taft Benson	Few major magazines could be in his home	June 1969	46e-47c
Victor L. Brown	He remembers a dirty story told in his teens	June 1970	46c
	, can make normal 12-year-old become homosexual		46d-e
Gordon B. Hinckley	$500 million per year business in U.S.	Dec 1970	72d-e
Thomas S. Monson	Digging gold from dirt		101a
Harold B. Lee	Our duty is to remove it from communities		105a
Richard L. Evans	Pollution of mind that puts no limits on self	June 1971	74b-c
Robert L. Simpson	An addicting tool of Satan	Jan 1973	112e
	Ways to fight ,		112e
	Effects of , on mind and actions		113b
	Do you have books President Lee wouldn't?		113d
	Statement by First Presidency on ,		113e
Marion D. Hanks	Mining gold from dirt		127f
N. Eldon Tanner	Stomach vomits back filth but mind can't	Jan 1974	7f
Spencer W. Kimball	, has a definite relationship to crime	Nov 1974	7b-c
	, is an approach to homosexuality		8b
	Dirty stories lay bare your mind —poem		83c-d
Vaughn J. Featherstone	Man who healed dead son couldn't have had he read ,—story	May 1975	66f
Gordon B. Hinckley	4 ways to fight , and immorality	Nov 1975	38b-40b
Spencer W. Kimball	Become actively and relentlessly engaged in fight	Nov 1976	5b
	Do not be lulled into inaction		6b
	Resist , with all our might		6c
Marvin J. Ashton	Respected husband became casualty of , —story	Nov 1977	71f-72a
Spencer W. Kimball	Poem about folly of unclean stories —poem	Nov 1978	45d-e
Thomas S. Monson	2 astounding statistics concerning ,	Nov 1979	66e
	Causing America to die from within		67b-c

H. Burke Peterson	Things we should not do - How to cleanse minds	Nov 1980	38d-39e
Dean L. Larsen	Momentary sampling leads to tragedy	Nov 1981	26f-27a
Joseph B. Wirthlin	Men destroy nervous system for tingling pleasures	May 1982	24f-25a
Gordon B. Hinckley	The misery , brought one man —story	May 1983	46f-52e
Ezra Taft Benson	To lust in our heart is to deny the faith	Nov 1983	42d-e
Gordon B. Hinckley	Nullifies effectiveness as priesthood leaders		45c-46c
Wm. Grant Bangerter	To set an age limit on , is hypocrisy —entire talk	May 1984	27b-28f
David B. Haight	Discussion on , —entire talk, excellent	Nov 1984	70b-73b
L. Tom Perry	, can intoxicate and destroy one's mind	Nov 1985	49b
Ezra Taft Benson	Lust denies the faith and the Spirit departs	Nov 1986	46d-e
	A mind is never the same after ,		84a
Russell M. Nelson	Provokes the wrath of God	Nov 1987	89d
Joseph B. Wirthlin	Allow passions to rule: Become a slave	Nov 1991	16b
Gordon B. Hinckley	Letter from an addict	Nov 1992	51d-52a
Neal A. Maxwell	, is better protected than citizens	May 1993	77d
H. Burke Peterson	Powerful farewell address directed against ,	Nov 1993	42d-44b
Gordon B. Hinckley	Pity the man who wallows in the mire	Nov 1994	48c
Howard W. Hunter	, and fantasies erode character		50d
James E. Faust	Brain can't vomit back filth —D.H. Oaks	Nov 1997	45a-d
Gordon B. Hinckley	Destroys self respect and sense of the beautiful		51e
Gordon B. Hinckley	Strong warnings against ,	May 1998	49e-f
Russell M. Nelson	Highly addictive to body and spirit	Nov 1998	87b-c
Russell M. Nelson	Avoid it like the plague	May 1999	39b-c
M. Russell Ballard	The power in ,		86e
Vaughn J. Featherstone	"We don't even own a pornograph" —story	Nov 1999	13f-14b
Joseph B. Wirthlin	Shun , like a deadly contagious disease		41a-b
Richard C. Edgley	Boy walked street to avoid movie —story		42f-43a
James E. Faust	Satan delights in , on the Internet		48a
Gordon B. Hinckley	It will destroy you		54d-f
Richard G. Scott	Take along a picture of your wife when traveling	May 2000	37d
	A warning about addictiveness of ,		37d-38a
H. David Burton	, and priesthood are not compatible		39d-40a
James E. Faust	As addictive as cocaine —letter from addict	Nov 2000	45d-46a
Gordon B. Hinckley	Strong warnings against ,		51b-d
David E. Sorensen	You can't pet a rattlesnake —3 stories	May 2001	41b-42f
Gordon B. Hinckley	Word of Wisdom applies to ,	May 2003	58d-59a
Boyd K. Packer	Unhappiness will follow ,	Nov 2003	25c-26a
Gordon B. Hinckley	Enslaves and destroys		83f-84b
Gordon B. Hinckley	Statistics on use of ,	Nov 2004	61a-b
	A Tragic Evil among Us —entire talk		59d-62f
Joseph B. Wirthlin	, is much like quicksand		102e-f
Dallin H. Oaks	, was the same problem as in Jacob's day	May 2005	87e-88b
	Brain won't vomit back filth		88b-c
	5 temple recommend questions deal with ,		88c-e
	Patrons of , forfeit power of priesthood		88e

Pornography, cont'd

Dallin H. Oaks	Patrons of , lose companionship of Spirit	May 2005	88f-89a
	Hard drug addiction simpler to overcome		89b-d
	No difference between soft and hard ,		89d-f
	How to deal with ,		90b-e
	List of articles on ,		90f
Thomas S. Monson	Alexander Pope's Essay on Man —-poem	May 2006	18e
	Will take you down to destruction —Hinckley		18e-19a
James E. Faust	Avoid every kind of addiction including ,		53b-d
Dallin H. Oaks	Lessons in overcoming an unbelievably difficult addiction	Nov 2006	8b-d
	5 pain-filled years shared with husband		8d-e
Gordon B. Hinckley	We must not partake of ,		60b-d
	Letter from an addict to ,		61b-e
Gordon B. Hinckley	Totally unbecoming to priesthood holders	May 2007	62e-f
L. Whitney Clayton	How to free self from , trap	Nov 2007	52a-b
	Users lose perspective and proportion		52d-e
	Caribbean fish traps —entire talk		51d-53b
Henry B. Eyring	Causes Spirit to withdraw		58b-c
James E. Faust	Mind altering - Destroys agency		123d-124a
	Addiction Recovery Program of Church		124a-c
D. Todd Christofferson	Vicarious immorality	Nov 2008	38f-39b
Richard G. Scott	Would your thoughts benefit from a cleaning		45a-b
Elaine S. Dalton	Consumers of vice, or guardians of virtue		79b-f
Boyd K. Packer	Avoid deadly poison of ,	May 2009	50f
Thomas S. Monson	Will literally destroy the spirit		113a-d
Richard G. Scott	Overpoweringly addictive - Most damning	Nov 2009	8f-9d
Jeffrey R. Holland	3 girls were divorced because of ,	May 2010	44a-e
	Can "blast a crater in their minds forever"		44e
Thomas S. Monson	Avoid , at all costs		65f-66b

Possessions

Victor L. Brown	We didn't come here with these things	Dec 1968	98d-e
N. Eldon Tanner	Material things have no power to raise spirits	June 1970	32d
Paul H. Dunn	In making a living don't forget to make a life	Dec 1970	39b
Ezra Taft Benson	Provide room and board while we're here at school	June 1971	33c
Franklin D. Richards	Thou shalt not covet thine own property		46e
Richard L. Evans	Children pulling brass nails at a party —story		73b-d
Hartman Rector, Jr.	He left it all; he didn't take any with him —story		79a
Spencer W. Kimball	We want the "things" before the kingdom	Jan 1972	38d
Marion D. Hanks	We struggle to exhaustion for more than we need	July 1972	105b
John H. Vandenberg	Most , are hindrances to progression —Thoreau		128a
	Destructive nature of striving for more , than others		128a
L. Tom Perry	Greed for , that never satisfy	July 1973	20a
	Greed for , leading us on age-old course		20c
Rex D. Pinegar	Christianity most valuable , —Patrick Henry	Jan 1974	34c
Loren C. Dunn	Don't expect to get luggage past celestial customs	Nov 1974	12f

Mark E. Petersen	Tis heaven alone that is given away —poem	Nov 1974	51c-d
A. Theodore Tuttle	Thou shalt not covet thine own property	Nov 1976	24a-b
Vaughn J. Featherstone	Mike will come back won't he? —story		104c-e
N. Eldon Tanner	How to manage personal finances -Entire talk	Nov 1979	80b-82f
Boyd K. Packer	Why President Kimball tells us to care for our ,	May 1982	85a-b
	Father got the loan because he took care of , —story		86c-e
Paul H. Dunn	Man valued wife more than car —story	May 1987	74f
Wm. Grant Bangerter	You can't take it with you - then I won't go —story	Nov 1988	81a-b
James E. Faust	Must earn , ourselves to be appreciated	Nov 1990	34e
Joseph B. Wirthlin	Luxuries misdirect. Resources better used to build kingdom		65a-e
Dean L. Larsen	, are both a blessing and a curse	May 1991	10b-12b
	Brigham Young feared saints couldn't handle riches		11a-b
James E. Faust	Persons obsessed with getting can't find God		70e
Janette C. Hales	Prosperity cycle in B of M: Church and youth today		84f-85a
Dallin H. Oaks	You never get enough of what you don't need	Nov 1991	75d
Wm. R. Bradford	Things cause us to squander and pay, and wander and play	May 1992	27f-28a
R.S. Conference	Buying to impress —excellent statement		97c-e
Dean L. Larsen	Book of Mormon cycles of prosperity - Then and today	Nov 1992	40d-42f
Neal A. Maxwell	We are possessed by ,		67a
W. Eugene Hansen	Rather enjoy a good meal than have a million $—Rockefeller	Nov 1993	81f
	Summer's labor bought shoes and joy —story		81f-82a
Dallin H. Oaks	"How much did he leave? - All of it"	May 1994	35e-f
L. Tom Perry	3-car garages with RV's parked beside them	Nov 1995	35e
	Garages so full there is no room for car		36c-d
Russell M. Nelson	Inner peace cannot be found in affluence	May 1996	14d
Richard G. Scott	Children aren't depressed by things they don't have		25b-d
	You may temporarily lack here - but not later		25d-f
Joe J. Christensen	Brigham Young's greatest fear for the Church	May 1999	9c-d
	Luxuries become necessities —story		9e-f
	Overindulging children —excellent advice		9f-11a
	Wealth is accumulations - not level of spending		11b-c
	Resources are a stewardship - not ,		11c-e
Sheri L. Dew	Life must not be a sight-seeing or shopping trip	Nov 1999	97d-f
	If building worldly kingdom, that's what we'll inherit		97f-98a
Angel Abrea	Testimony: a , we can take with us and leave behind	May 2000	42a
Neal A. Maxwell	Transients can't confer that which is lasting	Nov 2000	35f
	Secular heights are small mounds of sand		36e
	Hearts set on things of world may have to be broken		36f
	What does the world really have to offer us?		37f
Dallin H. Oaks	The worldly quartet of property, pride, etc.	May 2001	84b
Jeffrey R. Holland	"How much did he leave?" - "All of it" —story	Nov 2001	34d-e
Joseph B. Wirthlin	May become a net we're unable to leave	May 2002	15b-e
	Some would forsake all for longer life or peace		16d-f
James E. Faust	Family destroyed fighting over inheritance	Nov 2002	19c-d
	Selfishness is how we feel about ,		19f

Possessions

Possessions, cont'd
Related Topics: Wealth

James E. Faust	"Vell den, I vill not go" —story	Nov 2002	20b-c
	Hero gave life - greatest , —story		20f-21f
Quentin L. Cook	Obsession with , cankers and destroys	Nov 2003	95f-96b
H. David Burton	Families need parents more than ,	Nov 2004	98c-d
	Happy with 2 Hot Wheels, unhappy with many —story		98f-99a
Joseph B. Wirthlin	Don't allow , precedence over spiritual things		102d-e
Russell M. Nelson	Ill man relied upon his wealth —story	May 2005	17a-b
L. Tom Perry	Book of Mormon more valuable than ,	Nov 2005	8e-f
Joseph B. Wirthlin	Epitaph of a miser —poem	May 2006	101b-d
Gordon B. Hinckley	Old age doesn't worry about , - only children	Nov 2006	116f
Enrique R. Falabella	Father fixed hole in shoe with shoeshine —story	Nov 2007	14b-e
Silvia H. Allred	Measure of life - Not what we get, but give		113f-114a
Lance B. Wickman	Life is not a time for accumulating	May 2008	105a
L. Tom Perry	Thoreau's simple life at Walden Pond described	Nov 2008	7c-8b
D. Todd Christofferson	Societies that worship , and pleasures		39b-f
Boyd K. Packer	Won't hurt to want something and not have it	May 2009	52b-d
	Take care of your , - Don't be wasteful		52e
Dallin H. Oaks	Choosing values of world over unselfish service		94e-95c

Prayer
Related Topics: Communication

Spencer W. Kimball	Wards off spiritual foes	Dec 1969	50d
Ezra Taft Benson	Supreme court and ,		70e
John H. Vandenberg	Joseph Smith expected a different answer to his ,	June 1970	58f
Robert L. Simpson	"I wasn't talking to you," child said to Dad —story		82f-83a
Henry D. Taylor	Child prayed she wouldn't be spanked —story	Dec 1970	44d-f
Elray L. Christiansen	Pray until you feel like it —Brigham Young	June 1971	38b
Gordon B. Hinckley	The blessings of family ,		72e-f
Bernard P. Brockbank	Explanation of Lord's ,		85d-f
Spencer W. Kimball	Pres. Kimball's description of a good family , —story	Dec 1971	37e-f
Eldred G. Smith	Problems can't be licked without the Lord's help		46b
Harold B. Lee	Leaders to be prayed for —story	July 1972	29c
	Pray for leaders of country		33a
	Feeling of security comes from ,		33c
	Need for , increases with responsibility		33e
Spencer W. Kimball	Youth lax in , —First question to people in trouble		38f
	Sin comes when , neglected		39e
Franklin D. Richards	Do what you can when asking for help —Brigham Young		66d
	Have courage to follow the feeling you receive		66f
	Attitudes in family , —John Taylor		67d
	People who pray will not go wrong —H.J. Grant		67e
Marion D. Hanks	The boy who tried everything but asking —story		104f
	Not enough to know scriptures on , or motions of ,		105e
Marion G. Romney	Efficacy depends on care of poor	Jan 1973	97d
Spencer W. Kimball	If knees knocking, kneel on them	July 1973	16e
	Passport to spirituality		17b

Spencer W. Kimball	Value of family prayer —story	July 1973	17b
	World's potential if families prayed		17d
L. Tom Perry	His home has a closet for ,		21e
Ezra Taft Benson	There is safety in a nation on its knees		41c
Gordon B. Hinckley	Praying wife converts rebellious husband —story		50a
O. Leslie Stone	Prayer is vocalized faith		60f
Marion G. Romney	List of commandments to pray		91a
H. Burke Peterson	Prayer keeps man from sin —Brigham Young	Jan 1974	19b
	How to pray		19d
Howard W. Hunter	In his greatest trial Jesus prayed for others	May 1974	19b-c
Thomas S. Monson	3 great lessons from 3 of Jesus' prayers		49c
N. Eldon Tanner	Lord's Prayer - Pray in this manner, not verbatim		51e-f
	If you want prayers answered, get to work		52e
Henry D. Taylor	Six hours of , brought permission to heal —story	Nov 1974	15d-e
James A. Cullimore	Why all , not answered as we'd like —Kimball		28d-e
Vaughn J. Featherstone	, with old lady brought peace during husband's death —story		29e-30b
Thomas S. Monson	Faith and , of a dying girl answered —story	Nov 1975	20d-22f
N. Eldon Tanner	Columbus prayed to find land before crew mutinied	May 1976	48f-49a
	G. Washington's elegant prayer for America		51d-e
James E. Faust	What is the quality of , when only He listens?	Nov 1976	58e
Ezra Taft Benson	, got him in to see the general —story	May 1977	34a-d
Ezra Taft Benson	No worries about youth that pray twice a day —H.J. Grant	Nov 1977	32c-d
Howard W. Hunter	Prayer only in crisis is selfish		52b-c
	In , we must think first of God - not of ourselves		52e
Thomas S. Monson	Prayer and primary brought man into Church —story	May 1978	20b-c
	Mother's , and work saved son in WWII —story		21b-c
	, kept son in mission field —story		21e-f
George P. Lee	As he prayed; brothers taunted		27e
	A praying young man becomes a praying man		27f
Paul H. Dunn	If it's important to you, it's important to the Lord	May 1979	9f
Spencer W. Kimball	W. Woodruff prayed hard for gospel from boyhood —story		47e-f
Spencer W. Kimball	Not too many , should be silent	Nov 1979	4e
Boyd K. Packer	Train self to hear answers through static —3 stories		19d-20b
	Answers most often come as feelings		20c
	Reasons answers may be slow in coming		21b
	Sage observations on wisdom of telling Lord what to do		21c
	Pilots followed radio beam —analogy		21e-f
Paul H. Dunn	, compared to time out in sports	May 1980	38b
Boyd K. Packer	The man was an answer to , —story		63b-e
H. Burke Peterson	We can literally pray righteous things to happen	May 1981	83a
Angel Abrea	Pray always lest ye enter into temptation	Nov 1981	24c-d
Boyd K. Packer	As missionary, Pres. Woodruff prayed for healing —story		30c-e
H. Burke Peterson	He used a rock to remind him to pray —story		35b
Spencer W. Kimball	, gives stabilizing power in difficulties	May 1982	5e
James E. Faust	A struggle to have family , but pays great dividends	May 1983	40f-41a

L. Tom Perry	Stop praying and God becomes a stranger	Nov 1983	12e
	Use the sacred pronouns rather than "you"		13a
	Family , will bring unity —Brigham Young		13c-d
	Family , must be planned for. It's never convenient.		13e
Vaughn J. Featherstone	Boy nearly drowned during lengthy , —story		37b-c
	Boy committed to pray night and morning —story		37c-e
A. Theodore Tuttle	Family , is key element in righteous children	May 1984	24b-d
Devere Harris	Land was sighted after Columbus' ,	Nov 1984	26f
M. Russell Ballard	Rained every day in Ethiopia because of his , —story	May 1985	41c-d
Marvin J. Ashton	President Kimball learning how to really pray		45b
Russell M. Nelson	His children never gave him the silent treatment	Nov 1986	69a
Boyd K. Packer	Elder Tuttle asked that , in his behalf be given to others	May 1987	22b-23d
Thomas S. Monson	, brought $600 after everything else had been done —story		44b-e
Boyd K. Packer	, gives a transfusion of spiritual strength	Nov 1987	18d
Ezra Taft Benson	Daily family prayer pleases God	May 1988	5d-e
Glen L. Rudd	Apostle was safe because boy prayed —story		28d-29a
Gordon B. Hinckley	, will become a spirit of revelation —W. Woodruff		45e-46b
Robert D. Hales	An alcoholic and a boy with nightmares —2 stories	Nov 1988	10d-f
Howard W. Hunter	Study and , are answers to trials —entire talk		59d-61f
Thomas S. Monson	Family , is the greatest deterrent to sin		69f
	No enmity if couples pray together		70a
Richard G. Scott	If you don't feel worthy to pray…		77f
Michaelene P. Grassli	Things families do at family , time		79a
Thomas S. Monson	I prayed, then went to work —story	May 1989	44f
Joy F. Evans	God meets our needs through others		74a
Henry B. Eyring	, of gratitude brings more gratitude	Nov 1989	12f-13a
Richard G. Scott	Recognizing answers to , —entire talk		30d-32f
Dallin H. Oaks	, will be answered —great scripture		67b
Joanne B. Doxey	I wasn't talking to you —child's prayer		91a
M. Russell Ballard	Prayer in extremity followed by call from Ballard —story	May 1990	7d-8d
Neal A. Maxwell	Doing our Christian calisthenics	Nov 1990	15b
James E. Faust	One family , per day no longer enough		33e-f
Russell M. Nelson	, for Bible yielded Bible and more —story	May 1991	24c-d
Henry B. Eyring	, is a commandment		66e-67a
Janette C. Hales	Example of sister and roommates taught ,		84b-c
Robert E. Wells	"Make me an instrument" prayer		87c
Neal A. Maxwell	We pray for exemption not sanctification		90d
	God cannot always say yes		90e-f
Boyd K. Packer	We are drifting from use of sacred pronouns	Nov 1991	22f-23a
Francis M. Gibbons	Satan cannot hear secret ,		78d-79a
Richard G. Scott	How to receive answers to ,		84b-f
	Receiving asked-for blessings —excellent talk		84b-86b
Gordon B. Hinckley	We don't pray to Mother in Heaven		100a-e
James E. Faust	The best way to obtain truth and wisdom	May 1992	8d
Thomas S. Monson	Grant to handicapped girl an answer to , —story	Nov 1992	70b-d

Prayer

Dallin H. Oaks	The language of , - Use thee, thy, thou, thine	May 1993	15d-18b
David E. Sorensen	The object of , —Bible Dictionary		30e-f
	Injured son recovered through , —story		30f-31a
	Why we must first ask —story		31b-d
	Entire talk		30b-31f
Rex D. Pinegar	, healed him from explosion —story		65d-66b
	, healed him from explosion —story		68a-b
	, brought profound peace from distress —story		67a-b
	, is not like a beggar's upturned hand		67b-c
	Even Jesus' , was not answered as He desired		67d-68a
L. Tom Perry	What daily family , did for Peru —story		90b-e
	What we should pray over —Joseph Smith		91b
	Are your , like grinding of machinery? —J. Taylor		91b-c
	, —poem		91f
	A promise if family , is held daily		92f
Joe J. Christensen	No , is like sending children out into blizzard	Nov 1993	12e-13a
Spencer J. Condie	Long , conquered alcohol —story		16d-f
John H. Groberg	Answer to , required rowing to shore —story		26d-28b
Ben B. Banks	Lost boy prayed and was found —story		28d-f
Dallin H. Oaks	Pray for a good wind, not a tail wind —story	May 1994	99b-e
	Savior's request was denied, but answered		99f-100a
Boyd K. Packer	, is essential to revelation	Nov 1994	59f
	Your personal key to heaven		59f
Joseph B. Wirthlin	Feed soul through ,		75d
Rex D. Pinegar	Family , is simple but yields great blessings		81d-f
Joe J. Christensen	No marriage in serious trouble where couple prays together	May 1995	64e
LeGrand R. Curtis	The value of family ,		82e-83a
	Busy teenager left out of , —story		83a
Richard G. Scott	You will get what you need, not what you want	Nov 1995	17d
Dallin H. Oaks	Little girl was found after , —story		26d-e
Gordon B. Hinckley	We are a praying people		89d-e
Russell M. Nelson	Attitudes are elevated by lowering heads in ,	May 1996	16a
Henry B. Eyring	Family , will touch hearts		63d-e
Thomas S. Monson	"Living What We Pray For" —poem	Nov 1996	18e
Thomas S. Monson	Family paid tithing - then prayed —story		44f-45c
L. Edward Brown	Lord's , begins with simplest title - Father	May 1997	78b-c
	7-year-old found key to door through , —story		78d-e
Bonnie D. Parkin	11-year-old girl left Sweden alone to go to Zion —story		84d-85a
Richard J. Maynes	Very difficult to cram for mission or marriage	Nov 1997	30b-31f
James E. Faust	Boy found cow after prayer —story		59b-d
Janette Hales Beckham	When all deserted her , saved her —story		76d-e
Henry B. Eyring	One of two great keys to inviting Spirit		83f-84a
Virginia U. Jensen	Great list of what , can do		90e-f
Sheri L. Dew	Pray - then go to work —G.B. Hinckley	Nov 1998	96c
Joe J. Christensen	Humorous prayer for help	May 1999	9b-c

Richard G. Scott	He prays for those in spirit world	May 1999	27a
Vaughn J. Featherstone	Boy wanted , more than Thanksgiving dinner —story	Nov 1999	15c-16a
Neil L. Andersen	First Presidency's counsel on , and Family Home Evening		17c-18a
Boyd K. Packer	Airplane engines stopped one by one —story		23b-24b
James E. Faust	The greatest unused power	May 2000	18d
Henry B. Eyring	Young, inexperienced stake president advised to pray —story		66f-67c
	Sleeping congregation was praying for him —story		68d-e
Yoshihiko Kikuchi	The object of , —good statement		79a
Douglas L. Callister	"Teach the members to ," —counsel by Spencer W. Kimball	Nov 2000	31a
Thomas S. Monson	Too proud to pray —A. Lincoln		64f
Sydney S. Reynolds	Twins survived through fasting and , —story	May 2001	12f-13e
Henry B. Eyring	Please tell me who needs me - answers will come		40b
Sharon G. Larsen	Predates every other form of communication		86d
Margaret D. Nadauld	Holy Ghost and , helped her through polio —story		90f-91b
Henry B. Eyring	If casual in study, then become casual in ,	Nov 2001	17b
L. Tom Perry	Continue , habits after mission —story		75d-76b
Richard G. Scott	How answers to , come		88a-b
Gordon B. Hinckley	His , before the closing , of conference		90e-f
Virginia U. Jensen	Lucy Mack Smith prayed in a grove of trees		95b-d
Thomas S. Monson	Tahitians pray and they go	May 2002	49b-c
James E. Faust	, brought ship through storm —story		60e-f
	Family , every night and morning		60f-61a
	Family , with bomb outside door —story		61a-b
	Joseph's , for enemies —story		61b-f
	Entire talk —excellent		59d-62b
Carol B. Thomas	, mentioned 44 times in 3 Ne. 17-20		95d-e
Thomas S. Monson	, answered through chewing gum —story		101b-c
Coleen K. Menlove	Casual or infrequent family , not enough	Nov 2002	14d-e
Keith B. McMullin	"Stop. Wait. Pray." —Brigham Young		94e-f
Russell M. Nelson	How to pray	May 2003	7d-e
	Revelation for surgery came through , —story		7f-8f
	In , don't give counsel but inquire of the Lord		8f
	Entire talk		7b-9f
Kathleen H. Hughes	Constant , finally brought peace —story		13d-e
Gordon B. Hinckley	What we should pray for —drought story		99c-100a
Sydney S. Reynolds	Lost children prayed and were guided —story		113d-e
Gordon B. Hinckley	, on tithing answered through teacher —story		117e-118b
Boyd K. Packer	When temptation comes, use prayer	Nov 2003	25c-26a
Robert D. Hales	Every major event of Restoration was preceded by ,		30e
Russell M. Nelson	Boy knelt on operating table —story		44b-d
Thomas S. Monson	Son saw mother at , —story		69d-e
Henry B. Eyring	Pray with the intent to obey		90e
Susan W. Tanner	Answer to , came as a dream —story	May 2004	106b-107b
Elaine S. Dalton	Answer to , came months later through scripture —story		111d-112a
Gordon B. Hinckley	Nothing too unimportant for ,		114d-e

Thomas S. Monson	Though separate, Apostles united in , —story	May 2005	22b-d
Russell M. Nelson	President Kimball healed through , —story	Nov 2005	85e-86c
	Our , is never ignored or unanswered		86c
Henry B. Eyring	Prayed through night before answer came	May 2006	16c-e
H. Bruce Stucki	Faith and , found boy's arrow —story		96a-f
	Faith and , accomplished brain surgery —story		97a-98b
Robert D. Hales	Speak to God through , He speaks to us through scriptures	Nov 2006	26f-27a
Thomas S. Monson	One of 3 necessities for a deep foundation		67c-f
Gordon B. Hinckley	, located grandmother's lost ring —story		84f-85a
Don R. Clarke	Peace came to blind man after , —story		98f
Richard G. Scott	A supernal gift	May 2007	8b-c
	How to pray		8d-9a
	Answers come in pieces and packets		9b
	Always hears - always answers - but later		9d
	Be thankful for long struggles for answers		9d-e
	Why , doesn't bring desired results		9e
	Answers come as feelings of peace		9f-10c
	Answers come in three ways		10d-f
Henry B. Eyring	Morning prayers are always answered		89f
Charles W. Dahlquist, II	Returned from date - Found mother on knees —story		96b-c
Gordon B. Hinckley	A simple recipe for happiness includes ,		115e&117f
Boyd K. Packer	Easier to get answers to , as testimony matured	Nov 2007	8d-e
Enrique R. Falabella	Boy advised dad to speak on , —story		15b-d
Keith K. Hilbig	Draw-Seek-Ask-Knock-Whatsoever ye ask…		39b-d
Henry B. Eyring	Forget self - Pray for those you serve		57a-b
Robert D. Hales	Experiences in calling 4 stake presidents —story		87a-88b
	David O. McKay's delayed answer to ,		88f-89a
Claudio D. Zivic	Prayed to know - began to cry —story		99b-d
Douglas L. Callister	Testimony came after earnest , —story		100f-101b
Thomas S. Monson	A defense against temptation		119f-120a
David A. Bednar	Girl awoke before death in answer to , —story	May 2008	96e-97a
	Brings Father's and child's wills into correspondence		97a
	Should not be a wish list		97a-b
	Move beyond routine ad checklist ,		97b
Marcos A. Aidukaitis	Absurd to think God can't answer ,	Nov 2008	17a
Jeffrey R. Holland	Rescued by father after , —story		30c-31c
David A. Bednar	Definition and relation of , and revelation		41b-d
	How to use , to improve ourselves		41d-42d
	Express only appreciation for blessings —story		42d-43c
	Revelation comes through , for others		43d-44b
James J. Hamula	A precondition to revelation		52e
Henry B. Eyring	A missionary who was answer to parents' , —story		58f-59a
	"Don't ask me. Go to Him" —story		59a-d
Thomas S. Monson	, and priesthood turned submarine around —story		67d-68b
Keith B. McMullin	Affliction not taken away, but , always answered		76f-77a

Prayer, cont'd

Marion G. Romney	Importance of doctrine of ,	July 1973	11a
Boyd K. Packer	Explaining , to children		51c
Harold B. Lee	Good discussion of ,	Jan 1974	4d
Marion G. Romney	The Great Council in , —poem by Orson Whitney		11b
Eldred G. Smith	We promised ancestors in , that we'd do genealogy		63d
Elray L. Christiansen	Don't undo the work of your prior existence	May 1974	26f
Bruce R. McConkie	Not far away - Our talents received there		73c-e
Joseph Anderson	Wordsworth's poem	Nov 1974	101d
	We lived by sight there		101e
Theodore M. Burton	Foreordination of families and priesthood in ,	May 1975	69f-70a
Marion G. Romney	Our conduct in , earned us two things	Nov 1978	14d
LeGrand Richards	We're ships without rudders without knowledge of ,	May 1982	29e
Boyd K. Packer	Life is unexplainable without knowledge of ,	Nov 1983	16b-18f
Neal A. Maxwell	We rejoice in art, music and scenery because of that in the ,	May 1984	21f
Neal A. Maxwell	Discussion of development of doctrine of ,	Nov 1985	15d-18b
Boyd K. Packer	We waited anxiously to come to earth	Nov 1988	19a
Boyd K. Packer	I don't even know how I got into this town —story	May 1989	53e
Robert D. Hales	We are all winners because of choices in ,	May 1990	39b-d
Thomas S. Monson	Wordsworth's poem		53f
Boyd K. Packer	No beginning to ,	May 1991	9b
Howard W. Hunter	All are of the same spiritual descent	Nov 1991	18c-f
	Literal spirit children of God		19b
Russell M. Nelson	Our , - Life did not begin with birth	May 1992	72e
Marvin J. Ashton	Our glorious , is followed by distractions	Nov 1992	23b-e
Dallin H. Oaks	Explanation of our ,	Nov 1993	72b-e
Carlos E. Asay	Know where we are by knowing where we started —Webster	May 1996	60e
James E. Faust	Youth reserved in , to come now	May 1998	95b
Russell M. Nelson	Young man didn't know who he was —story	Nov 1998	85b
Keith B. McMullin	We knew every nook and garden —B. Young	May 1999	81a
Mary Ellen Smoot	"Our birth is but a sleep" —Wordsworth poem	Nov 1999	92f
Sheri L. Dew	We agreed to be saviors for all mankind	Nov 2000	95d-e
Richard G. Scott	Great anticipation and resolve we had in ,	May 2001	6d-f
Russell M. Nelson	Premortal pillars undergirding the Church	May 2002	75d-76c
David B. Haight	We were there. We chose to come	May 2004	6d-e
Keith B. McMullin	Life does not begin at birth		34b-d
Richard G. Scott	No memory of , to make it a valid test	Nov 2005	79a
Thomas S. Monson	Wm. Wordsworth's poem	May 2007	22e-f
Henry B. Eyring	Felt joy because confident we could pass test		89f-90b
Elaine S. Dalton	Your acts and knowledge in ,	May 2010	120d-121a

President
Related Topics: Apostles, First Presidency, General Authorities, Prophets

David O. McKay	How President McKay gained a testimony —story	Dec 1968	85b-c
	Prophecy that President McKay would lead Church		85d-f
Harold B. Lee	How a new , is chosen	June 1970	28c-f
Spencer W. Kimball	Death of President McKay		92a-e

Spencer W. Kimball	Transition from McKay to Smith	June 1970	92a-e
	Dates of service and ages of all ,		92f-93c
	We may expect the , to always be an older man		92f-93c
LeGrand Richards	McKay—Nearest approximation of Savior, says non-member		108c
Spencer W. Kimball	President Kimball posing for his portrait —story	Dec 1971	36a-39f
Ezra Taft Benson	Judge everything by words of ,	July 1972	61b
Joseph Fielding Smith	Will never lead Church astray		88b
Marion G. Romney	Follow his counsel even if wrong and you'll be blessed		98a
	President will never lead people astray		98a
Harold B. Lee	Trials before calling of ,	Jan 1973	24e
Spencer W. Kimball	Holds keys, calls Apostles		34b
	Will never lead Church astray		35e
Gordon B. Hinckley	President Lee heeded Spirit as boy —story		93d
N. Eldon Tanner	Passing of Pres. Joseph Fielding Smith - a man without guile		100d
	President Lee was foreordained and prepared		101d
	President Smith's testimony of President Lee		101f
	All offices belong to ,		103a
Harold B. Lee	President Lee organizing welfare plan —story		104a
	Denial of false rumor about President Lee		105b
	Don't speculate on next ,		107a
	Don't compare one , with another		107e
	President Lee calling a stake pres. —story		107e
Thomas S. Monson	President Lee ordaining a patriarch —story		121c
S. Dilworth Young	President Lee and his ancestry —great story		122a
Harold B. Lee	President Lee changed by calling		133d
Joseph Anderson	Prophecies that Smith, Grant, and McKay would be ,	July 1973	106f
Harold B. Lee	President Lee's miraculous healing —story		123d
Spencer W. Kimball	Pres. Kimball ordained an apostle 30 yrs ago on this day	Jan 1974	15b
David B. Haight	Follow counsel of , even if wrong and you'll be blessed —Lee		42c
Gordon B. Hinckley	What circumstances made President Lee a prophet		124f
Spencer W. Kimball	Poem in memory of President Lee —poem	May 1974	4c-e
N. Eldon Tanner	President Kimball foreordained —Tanner's testimony		50e
Mark E. Petersen	No man will ever be , unless the Lord wants him		56c
S. Dilworth Young	Prophecies that 3 boys would become ,		60e-f
Bruce R. McConkie	Foreordination and calling of President Kimball		71d-f
N. Eldon Tanner	Early Apostles each held keys, could have been ,		82f
	Why senior Apostle becomes ,		83f-84a
	Prophecy that Brigham would be ,		84a-d
	Each , foreordained - just the man needed		84a-d
	Counselors stepped aside when President Lee died		84d-e
	79 yrs ago an infant of promise was born - Pres. Kimball		84e-f
	Account of the choosing and setting apart of Pres. Kimball		84f-85c
	Spirit is withdrawn when we don't sustain ,		85d-e
Spencer W. Kimball	Pres. Kimball set a goal at age 14 to read the Bible —stories		88a-b
	Kimball set goal in youth to observe Word of Wisdom —story		88b-89a

President

Robert L. Simpson	Insights into President Kimball's life and amazing activity	Nov 1975	13b-e
Spencer W. Kimball	How President Kimball memorized Articles of Faith		79e
Rex D. Pinegar	Incidents from ministry of President Kimball —stories	Nov 1976	67b-69f
W. Grant Bangerter	A new prophet has arisen - President Kimball —whole talk	Nov 1977	26a-27f
Spencer W. Kimball	A portion of President Kimball's patriarchal blessing	May 1978	103c-d
Spencer W. Kimball	Account of W. Woodruff first hearing gospel —story	May 1979	47e-f
N. Eldon Tanner	The death of Pres. Lee and calling of Pres. Kimball —story	Nov 1979	43b-44a
Spencer W. Kimball	Pres. Kimball's activities during previous 6 months —amazing	May 1981	5d-7f
	Pres. Kimball got out of bed to address latecomers —story		45e-46a
Robert D. Hales	The diligence and trials of President Kimball —stories	Nov 1981	19b-21b
Carlos E. Asay	Follow counsel of , even if wrong and you'll be blessed —Lee		68b-c
Spencer W. Kimball	The 10 commandments of President Kimball	May 1982	5b-c
Robert E. Wells	President Kimball reproved swearing man —story	Nov 1982	69f
Gordon B. Hinckley	Be grateful , will always be an older man	May 1983	6e-7a
J. Thomas Fyans	Joseph Fielding Smith read Book of Mormon twice by age 10	May 1984	38d-e
	Pres. McKay failed first time he said sacrament prayer —story		38e
Gordon B. Hinckley	How First Presidency functions when , is infirm	Nov 1984	4f-5e
Marvin J. Ashton	What kind of man is President Kimball —entire talk	May 1985	43d-45f
David B. Haight	Sketch of President Benson's life	May 1986	8f-9f
Gordon B. Hinckley	How the Lord chooses a ,		46f-47a
Richard P. Lindsay	President Kimball visited and blessed fellow patients —story	May 1990	15b-c
J. Ballard Washburn	The life of Ezra Taft Benson	Nov 1990	41d-42f
Gordon B. Hinckley	One , of Apostles and 7 of the Seventy. Why?		48d-f
	Every other president has counselors		48f-49b
	Every , must choose own counselors		49b-d
	A counselor is president's assistant		49d-50c
	His experiences serving as proxy to ,		50c-51b
Rulon G. Craven	President Hunter told he would not walk again —story	May 1991	28f-29d
Gordon B. Hinckley	Worked closely with 7 presidents of Church		92d
Gordon B. Hinckley	10 years in First Presidency	Nov 1991	49b-e
Francis M. Gibbons	Spirit told H.J. Grant he would be , —story		79b-e
Yoshihiko Kikuchi	President J.F. Smith and Hawaiian mother —story	May 1992	11d-12c
Gordon B. Hinckley	Infirm , ? No problem. How Church works	Nov 1992	53b-60b
Gordon B. Hinckley	Lessons he learned as a boy —great talk	May 1993	52b-59b
James E. Faust	Presiding officer has ultimate authority to decide	Nov 1993	37f-38a
Howard W. Hunter	One man should not have all power - Shared by all Apostles	Nov 1994	7f-8b
David B. Haight	3 purposes for solemn assemblies		14d-15c
	The process by which the , is chosen		15d-16d
	Life sketch of President Hunter		16d-17b
L. Tom Perry	What is a seer? What is a prophet?		17f-18e
	Joseph F. Smith showed how to walk in dark —story		18e-19a
Jeffrey R. Holland	His insightful testimony of Pres. Hunter as the prophet		32a-d
James E. Faust	How Brigham became president		72d-f
	There is no mystery about choosing a new ,		72f-73a
	How President Hunter was ordained		73a-b

President, cont'd

Pride

Marion D. Hanks	Watermaster wronged farmer so he took no more water	July 1972	105f
Neal A. Maxwell	Hearts "so set" must first be broken	Nov 1974	13d
Marvin J. Ashton	Egotists never get anywhere—they think they're already there		41f
Spencer W. Kimball	Many think Church can't get along without them	May 1975	78f-79a
Marvin J. Ashton	Personal , is a great motivator	Nov 1976	84b-c
John H. Groberg	Hawaiian overcame insult - returned to Church —story	May 1980	49a-f
Howard W. Hunter	Take , in the good things you've done	Nov 1983	65b
Howard W. Hunter	If there was only one righteous it would be me	May 1984	65e
Ezra Taft Benson	, —excellent discussion	May 1986	6d-7b
Ezra Taft Benson	Beware of Pride —entire talk —excellent	May 1989	4b-7b
Marlin K. Jensen	More interested in finding Lord's sheep than in counting them	Nov 1989	27f
Marvin J. Ashton	Boasting creates resentment, not respect	May 1990	65d-67f
Dallin H. Oaks	Lincoln swallowed , and apologized —story		73b-c
Janette C. Hales	, is vertical - Righteousness is horizontal	May 1991	83f-84a
Neal A. Maxwell	, makes a barrier between us and God	May 1992	38f-39a
Russell M. Nelson	Ladder of success leaned against wrong wall	Nov 1992	6f-7a
Spencer J. Condie	Satan's tools: pride and discouragement	Nov 1993	15f-16d
	, is concerned with who is right - not what		17d
H. David Burton	Captain ordered lighthouse to change course	May 1994	68d-e
Neal A. Maxwell	Strutting celebrities hide inner emptiness	Nov 1994	34f
Rex D. Pinegar	The best people aren't famous		80d-f
M. Russell Ballard	We need to be like Hyrum Smith —story	Nov 1995	7f-8d
James E. Faust	The cause of Oliver Cowdery's apostasy	May 1996	5b-6c
Neal A. Maxwell	The sin of selfishness —entire talk	May 1999	23b-25b
James E. Faust	Church will move forward with or without us	May 2000	18d
Marlin K. Jensen	Arrogance and pleasure of having more than another	May 2001	10d-e
Dallin H. Oaks	The worldly quartet of pride, etc.		84b
Henry B. Eyring	Makes a noise within that drowns the Spirit	Nov 2001	16b-c
Joseph B. Wirthlin	, in scholarly achievements is dangerous	Nov 2004	102b-c
Thomas S. Monson	Cardinal Wolsey served king more than God	Nov 2007	60f-61a
D. Todd Christofferson	Materialism is a manifestation of ,	Nov 2008	39b-f
Henry B. Eyring	The enemy of unity - An example		70e
Robert D. Hales	Don't confuse boldness with overbearance		73e-74b
	Being guileless - Look for own faults first		74b-d
Richard G. Scott	Overpowers Holy Ghost —good example	Nov 2009	8e
Dieter F. Uchtdorf	Center of the universe syndrome	May 2010	57d-e

Priesthood
Related Topics: Aaronic Priesthood, Authority, Foreordination, Keys

S. Dilworth Young	Explanation of the office of Seventy	Dec 1968	76a-77f
Henry D. Taylor	If men live their , they could change the world —McKay	June 1969	64f
Delbert L. Stapley	Holders must be free of personal transgressions		72b
John Longden	The army of the Lord in warfare against evil		113e
S. Dilworth Young	Objectives of quorums 50 years ago and now	Dec 1969	61a-c
David O. McKay	Responsibility to teach 5 items		87a
S. Dilworth Young	How Seventies should function —entire talk	June 1970	54b-57e

N. Eldon Tanner	If , magnified, the holder will be magnified	June 1970	62f
Harold B. Lee	"Elder" means "Defender of the faith"		63b-c
Joseph Fielding Smith	Fullness of , revealed by Elijah		65d-f
	Fullness of , available only in temple		65f-66c
	Elders receive all the blessings any man can get		65f-66c
	We covenant in temple to magnify ,		66c-d
	, holds power to exalt self and loved ones		66e
Joseph Fielding Smith	What magnifying , means	Dec 1970	26f
	One office in , not greater than another		26f-27b
N. Eldon Tanner	One in 1,000 holds the ,		91d-e
Joseph Fielding Smith	What our commission entails	June 1971	49b-d
Dallin H. Oaks	No worldly honor can add to the ,	Dec 1971	110a
Joseph Fielding Smith	Definition of ,	July 1972	87d
Marion G. Romney	Penalty for turning away from , - D&C 84:41		99d
N. Eldon Tanner	Be humbly proud of your ,		100d
Harold B. Lee	Home Teaching and temple work depend on testimony of ,		103b
A. Theodore Tuttle	All Church offices derive authority from ,		119b
	Defined by John Taylor		119d
	No exaltation without ,		119e
	H.P: genealogy, Seventies: missionary work, Elders: welfare		119f
	No power but , can withstand power of adversary		120b
	Day is coming when quorums will assume responsibility		120d
Spencer W. Kimball	Restored through proper channels	Jan 1973	33f
N. Eldon Tanner	Definition of ,		100a
	Obligation of , to heed Prophet		103a
	Expected to live worthy of ,		103b
	Responsibilities as holders of ,		103e
Harold B. Lee	Welfare plan a monument to power of ,		104a
Marion G. Romney	Three requirements in magnifying ,	July 1973	89d
	Few are qualified to even be priests —Joseph Smith		90c
N. Eldon Tanner	Honor your , wherever you are		92b
	Don't ordain to , until worthy —story		94a
	All we need to prepare for exaltation		94d
	Respect of world comes from honoring ,		95c
Harold B. Lee	Acting for Lord - Be careful of appearance		98b
James E. Faust	A wife's gratitude for husband who honored ,	Jan 1974	23f
Spencer W. Kimball	Each ward to have an elders quorum	May 1974	86d
	Seventies to be ordained by stake presidents		86e
Theodore M. Burton	Priesthood lineages were foreordained	Nov 1974	55b-c
Marion G. Romney	Most sacred trust given to man		73d
N. Eldon Tanner	Youth must not be advanced till worthy		77c
	No kindness to advance one in , till worthy		77f
Vaughn J. Featherstone	Pure man was able to heal dead son —story	May 1975	66f
Theodore M. Burton	We are foreordained to receive , through lineages		69b-70a
Spencer W. Kimball	Announcement that First Quorum of 70 to be organized	Nov 1975	4b

Priesthood

W. Grant Bangerter	Use , to administer for spiritual ills	Nov 1975	70a
H. Burke Peterson	A difference between , authority and , power	May 1976	33a
	, receives fulfillment only with happy wife at side		34a
N. Eldon Tanner	Comparison of Church and , to army		44f
Vaughn J. Featherstone	Future "power surge" when , organization is understood	Nov 1976	120e-f
Spencer W. Kimball	Example of how , quorums should serve —story		127b-d
N. Eldon Tanner	Ways to promote quorum brotherhood	May 1977	47e-48a
	Helps from , following accident —story		48d-e
	No full measure of sonship and manhood without ,		48e-f
Spencer W. Kimball	Don't yet have all , keys. Don't have keys of resurrection		49b-d
	We don't yet have keys to give life or organize matter		50b-51a
Bruce R. McConkie	Melchizedek , is a , of equals	Nov 1977	33b-c
	10 blessings of the , listed in italics		33a-35f
N. Eldon Tanner	Announcement that Negroes could hold ,	Nov 1978	16a-e
Carlos E. Asay	, loses savor as salt does when contaminated	May 1980	42d-f
	Definition of , by President Kimball		43b
	We covenanted to be saviors of men		43b-d
	Failure to use , is like salt without savor		44b
Douglas W. DeHaan	Stake's corn harvested when rain stopped by , —story	Nov 1980	87b-88f
Marion G. Romney	, body that counsels together succeeds together		93b-c
Gordon B. Hinckley	Blessings effective conditioned upon faith and will of God	May 1981	20e
Boyd K. Packer	Yours forever unless disqualified by transgression	Nov 1981	32a
	, never given in secret		32b-c
	Power in the , comes through obedience and worthiness		32c & 33b
H. Burke Peterson	Young elder gave a girl her hearing —story		35e-36f
L. Tom Perry	A priesthood quorum is three things		37e
	Priests quorum met at bedside of inactive —story		38d-39c
	Not a static investiture		39d-e
Bruce R. McConkie	, can stay the fall of atomic bombs	May 1982	33a & 34b
Marion G. Romney	, we hold is a delegated power		43d-e
Robert L. Backman	Purposes of quorums	Nov 1982	38b
H. Burke Peterson	, power comes from the righteous pattern of our lives		43b
L. Tom Perry	Boy thanked God for , blessing —story	Nov 1983	13b
Adney Y. Komatsu	Fullness of , obtained by keeping all commandments		28b-d
Jack H. Goaslind Jr.	Men empowered to do all the Savior did		32a
	, conferred as an instrument of service		33f-34a
A. Theodore Tuttle	, is power - to serve	May 1984	25a
Elaine A. Cannon	I love holding the , —joke		25e
Dallin H. Oaks	Service is a covenant obligation of the ,	Nov 1984	12e
Russell M. Nelson	, compared to electrical power		31f-32a
	Couples bear and share ,		32b
Thomas S. Monson	Prospective elders outnumber Melchizedek , holders		41f-42a
Gordon B. Hinckley	One of 4 cornerstones of the Church		51a-d
Don Lind	More anxious to associate with , than any others	Nov 1985	37d-e
Rex D. Pinegar	, is a lifeline to our families		41a-d

Priesthood

Priesthood, cont'd
Related Topics: Aaronic Priesthood, Authority, Foreordination, Keys

Rex D. Pinegar	A , holder is a mediator between God and man	Nov 1985	41f
Thomas S. Monson	You are responsible for those you might have saved —Taylor	May 1986	37f-38a
	Magnify your , that others will gladly follow you		38d-e
	What it means to magnify your ,		38f-39a
Ezra Taft Benson	Announcement discontinuing 70's Quorums	Nov 1986	48e-f
Dallin H. Oaks	, blessing given: no Indians seen —story	May 1987	36b-c
	Types of , blessings and comments thereon		36c-38d
	, blessing given: 1500 babies delivered safely —story		38d-e
	, blessing given: Man escaped train wreck —story		38e
	, blessing given: Boys spy on murderers' meeting —story		38e-39d
Ezra Taft Benson	A , blessing given to general church membership		85e-f
Russell M. Nelson	Definitions of the ,	Nov 1987	37a
Glen L. Rudd	, means service - boys pledged in unison	May 1988	28b
	, is of no value unless we serve		28b-c
Thomas S. Monson	The greatest force in the world today		41f
Joseph B. Wirthlin	Some fathers watch too much TV sports	Nov 1988	35f
Thomas S. Monson	Organization of Second Quorum of Seventy	May 1989	17e-f
Gordon B. Hinckley	Definition of magnify		46f
	When Cowdery magnified calling, he was magnified—story		47d-48d
	How to magnify ,		48f-49f
F. Arthur Kay	, blessing: Down's Syndrome baby wasn't —story	Nov 1989	80b-c
	, blessing: Cystic fibrosis relief promised —story		80d-e
Marion D. Hanks	3 military men set apart a senior officer	Nov 1990	41a-b
Gordon B. Hinckley	One president of Apostles and 7 of Seventy. Why?		48d-f
J. Richard Clarke	The greatest power and honor —Ezra Taft Benson	May 1991	41e
	Remember who you are —stories		42a-c
	Quorum served handicapped boy —story		42c-f
	"Deacons in our church are older men" —story		42f
	The man with 39 brothers —Fire story		42f-43a
	Quorum ran farm of sick brother —story		43a
Thomas S. Monson	Be loyal to the royal within you		47f-48b
Dallin H. Oaks	Men have no greater claim than women on ,	May 1992	36f
Thomas S. Monson	An instrument of service: Must be used		47f-48b
Dean L. Larsen	More prospective elders than elders	Nov 1992	42f
Boyd K. Packer	Fullness of , only obtained in temple	May 1993	20a-b
	Only given in one way		20b-c
	Only mortals can baptize		20d
James E. Faust	Is not gender. How it blesses all		36b-c
Russell M. Nelson	Honoring the , invites revelation		38b
	Proper titles to use when addressing ,		38e-f
	Do's and don'ts concerning , callings		39b-e
	Elders hold same , as President of Church		40a
	First priority of , is to honor wife		40b
	High council has no president or seniority		40e
Boyd K. Packer	Highest , ordinance is given to man and woman together	Nov 1993	21e

Priesthood

Boyd K. Packer	, is entrusted to men by divine decree	Nov 1993	21f-22c
Russell M. Nelson	Men must daily be worthy vessels		35a-c
James E. Faust	The extent of one's , power —Joseph Smith		37a-b
	Significant and beautiful language - D&C 121		39b-c
	No limit to your , power		39d
	May break , covenant by doing nothing		39d
M. Russell Ballard	, is for service, not servitude...		78e-f
David B. Haight	No more angels will come to restore , —story	Nov 1994	15d-16d
Richard C. Edgley	Developing confidence in using ,		39d-41b
	Most important earthly assignment - magnify ,		40c
James E. Faust	How , keys were transferred to Brigham		72d-f
	Keys of , will stay until Second Coming		73b-c
	What are , keys?		73d-f
Howard W. Hunter	A personal , blessing from the prophet		88f
James E. Faust	He neglected his duty and lost his lamb —story	May 1995	46a-d
	Duties of general officers of Church		47a-e
Thomas S. Monson	Be participants not spectators in , service		49b
Janette Hales Beckham	Uses of the , listed	Nov 1995	12d
Robert D. Hales	What if there were no , ?		32b-c
	History of the ,		32c-33c
	How , blesses throughout a typical life		33c-34d
	Admonition to obtain and use ,		34d-e
	, —sonnet composed by Elder Hales		34e-f
Henry B. Eyring	Wear better clothing when performing ordinances		40b-c
James E. Faust	, - the dominant influence in family affairs		62e-f
James E. Faust	No higher authority than President of Church	May 1996	6d-7a
	No angel will ever come again to restore ,		7c
	5 fundamental truths about ,		7c-d
David B. Haight	His account of revelation giving Blacks the ,		23c-f
Thomas S. Monson	The perfect plan of service —S.L. Richards		43e
	Preparation precedes performance		43f
	, is given for the ministry of service		44b
Gordon B. Hinckley	Abusive men are not worthy of ,	Nov 1996	68d-e
Elaine L. Jack	Two purposes of , —J.F. Smith		76f
James E. Faust	Never let , lie dormant within us	May 1997	41b
	Caring for others is essence of , power		41b-c
	Full measure of manhood attainable through ,		43d-e
Russell M. Nelson	Highest and most important , duty is ...		71e
	Magnify , by magnifying wife		71f
James E. Faust	A solemn thing - an honor and responsibility	May 1998	43d
Boyd K. Packer	, functions differently in Church and home		73e-f
D. Todd Christofferson	The purpose of , quorums —entire talk	Nov 1998	40d-42f
James E. Faust	The greatest power source in the world		45d-f
	Officer blessed boy - real authority —story		45f-46a
	Early brethren were tried and tested —story		46a-f

James E. Faust	We will account to prophets for our use of ,	Nov 1998	47d
Gordon B. Hinckley	Abusers are unworthy to hold , of God		72b-c
Virginia U. Jensen	Defined by Joseph Smith		92b-c
Ray H. Wood	No limit to the power of , —Spencer W. Kimball	May 1999	41b
	Our , will exalt or damn us —G.Q. Cannon		41e
Thomas S. Monson	Proclamation on , from First Presidency	Nov 1999	49b-d
	Boy found emerald because of doing duty —story		49e-50d
	, is a gift and a commission		50e
	Letter from excommunicated member		51a-b
	What does it mean to magnify ,		51b-c
Jeffrey R. Holland	New elder healed boy struck by lightning —story	Nov 2000	38c-39b
Thomas S. Monson	Stuttering priest baptized girl —story		47f-48c
Henry B. Eyring	We are the shepherds of Israel —entire talk	May 2001	38b-40f
John H. Groberg	, power limited only by bearer's purity		43b-d
	Tongan cleaned up before healing boy —story		43d-44c
	Don't sell , power for mess of R-rated pottage		44d-f
Sheri L. Dew	Womanhood plus , means exaltation	Nov 2001	12d-14f
Cecil O. Samuelson Jr.	You are on the Lord's errand —Lee		42f-43a
Keith K. Hilbig	We were foreordained to ,		45d-e
	, can't be used to bless self		45e-f
Gordon B. Hinckley	Tyrants and bad examples unworthy of ,		52c-d
Gordon B. Hinckley	Personal worthiness to hold , - No sin, no abuse	May 2002	52b-59b
L. Tom Perry	The most perfect order of government	Nov 2002	7d-e
	Quorums are classes, fraternities, service units —story		7f-8c
James E. Faust	Samuel Brannon failed to honor , —story		50f-51d
	Like a reservoir - not a passive power		52a-b
Thomas S. Monson	The perfect plan of service	May 2003	54b-c
	An agent of the Lord on the Lord's errand		54d
Russell M. Nelson	, blessings are not prayers	Nov 2003	46d
Merrill J. Bateman	How , keys were restored		50b-e
	Who holds , keys		50f
	Back-to-school blessings a tradition —story		51a-52d
L. Tom Perry	A quorum is three things… —S.L. Richards	Nov 2004	24f-26a
Henry B. Eyring	Joseph's statement about sealing keys on Apostles		27f-28b
	Federal official tried to take over meeting —story		28e-29a
	Two necessities: Keys and faith in leaders —stories		26d-29e
James E. Faust	, holds key to the knowledge of God		52c-d
	Magnifying , requires three things		52d-23d
	Essential that a man hold both Melchizedek and Aaronic ,		53b
	Eight promises in oath and covenant of ,		53d-f
Thomas S. Monson	1980 Proclamation - , restored		56e-f
	I want to see , strengthened		56f
	Miracles are everywhere when , magnified		59a-b
Jeffrey R. Holland	The most distinguishing feature of the Church	May 2005	43b-d
	Oliver's statement that they sought the ,		43f-44b

Priesthood

Jeffrey R. Holland	Wesley's poetical rebuke of false authority	May 2005	44c-d
	Kimball blessing family before mission —story		44e-45b
Robert C. Oaks	Many , holders are AWOL		48d-e
Thomas S. Monson	Must be held sacred by the people		54c
	Covenant of , is broken by doing nothing		54d-e
	How , is magnified		54f
	The perfect plan of service		55f-56a
	A , holder is an agent of the Lord		56e
Dallin H. Oaks	Patrons of pornography forfeit , power		88e
James E. Faust	One of 7 "blockbuster" doctrines	Nov 2005	21f
Dallin H. Oaks	Examples of , abuse and misunderstanding		24d-25b
	Differences of , in Church and in family		26b-27b
David A. Bednar	Holders of , are sons of Abraham		46f-47f
James E. Faust	A shield against evils of world		55e-f
Thomas S. Monson	Your duty explained - Smith —good quote		59a
	How is a calling magnified? - by doing		59b
Boyd K. Packer	Curriculum restructured to center on ,		72f
Russell M. Nelson	Foremost , duty is to nurture your marriage	May 2006	37d
L. Tom Perry	His ordination as a deacon		39b-f
Thomas S. Monson	Definition of , by two prophets		55b-d
	His interview when receiving Melchizedek, —story		55d-56b
	2 requirements in oath and covenant of ,		56d-e
	How , is magnified		56e-f
	Miracles are everywhere when , magnified		57f
Dallin H. Oaks	Why some , blessings don't heal	Nov 2006	7d-8b
Henry B. Eyring	One deacon, one teacher in his branch		43b-c
	Presidents are to teach according to the covenants		43e-f
	Service by , is multiplied by more than numbers		44c-d
Stanley G. Ellis	Lord gives us a power of attorney		51b-d
	We and Lord each promise two things		51e
	We should each restudy D&C 121		51f-52b
	We never know when we'll be called upon		52b-c
	How we might be guilty of priestcraft		52c-d
James E. Faust	Every missionary was healed —story		54e-55a
Thomas S. Monson	Duty doesn't end when released as president		57b-c
	Alexander tried to imitate , —story		58c-d
Craig A. Cardon	"Move that mountain, Dad" —story		94d-e
	Priesthood progression —excellent		94d-96f
Joseph B. Wirthlin	Bishop taught that , means service	May 2007	46e-47a
James E. Faust	Reserved for the relatively few		54b
	What the , is		54b-c
	Young priest ordained a teacher		54c-e
Thomas S. Monson	Definition by Joseph F. Smith		57c
	Be careful where you take the ,		57f-58a
	No limit to the power you hold —Kimball		58a

Priesthood, cont'd
Related Topics: Aaronic Priesthood, Authority, Foreordination, Keys

Thomas S. Monson	Blessing a sick sailor —story	May 2007	58b-f
	Blessings given at hard-to-find address —story		58f-60a
Enrique R. Falabella	A father is able to bless and ordain his children	Nov 2007	14f-15a
Thomas S. Monson	Five marks of a true , holder —entire talk		59b-61f
William R. Walker	How First Presidency functions	May 2008	39b-d
	Why a presidency? —entire talk		37d-39f
Dieter F. Uchtdorf	Great trust = great responsibility		59a-b
Henry B. Eyring	The necessity of receiving and honoring ,		61f-b
	Evidence that God has chosen you		61f-62d
	Savior has promised his personal help		62d
	Promise to renew our bodies —example		62d-e
	Given power to bear testimony		62f
	Prepares you to live in eternal families		62f-63e
	Leads us to develop feelings of charity		63d-f
Thomas S. Monson	The greatest force in the world today		65d
D. Todd Christofferson	The Seventy: most profound miracle in Church		76d-77a
Boyd K. Packer	8 quorums of Seventy - Follow Apostles' direction		83f
	Seventy don't hold keys - 308 Seventy		85f
David A. Bednar	Healing came only after prayer of faith —story		96b-e
Richard G. Scott	Definition of , and how power in , is achieved	Nov 2008	44d-45a
	A private , interview with Elder Scott		45a-f
	You shouldn't have to lose , to appreciate it		46f-47a
Henry B. Eyring	When feeling overwhelmed in , duties…		57b-f
	Father selected a few of His sons to hold ,		57f-58b
	When Eyring felt overwhelmed as an Apostle		59a-d
	What we get when we give our all in , service		60a-b
Thomas S. Monson	The perfect plan of service —S.L. Richards		61f-62b
	, made submarine turn around —story		67d-68b
Keith B. McMullin	Miraculous healing of girl —story		77a-d
Barbara Thompson	Angels cannot be restrained as associates —Smith		116c
Michael A. Neider	Quorum: A class, brotherhood and service unit	May 2009	14f
Boyd K. Packer	, is intangible but is real authority and power		50a
Richard C. Edgley	Mobilize quorums to help those in distress		53e-f
	Retired executive helped 12 find jobs —story		53f-54b
	Quorum put mechanic back on feet —story		54b-e
	Enough resources in each quorum to help —Hinckley		55b-c
Claudio R. M. Costa	Each has a fourfold responsibility —Hinckley		56b-c
	Embodies an eternal covenant to serve others		57b-e
	Most , service is accomplished quietly		58b-d
Henry B. Eyring	Duty of , to help the "Man Down" —entire talk		63b-66e
Thomas S. Monson	Keys held by the two priesthoods		67b-c
	Definition of , by two prophets		67c
	If worthy, we cannot fail		67c-d
	Food poisoning healed by two new elders —story		69e-70e
Walter F. Gonzalez	Using Book of Mormon makes powerful , holders	Nov 2009	50d-51a

Priesthood

Henry B. Eyring	Be ready - Be prepared —Healing story	Nov 2009	59b-d
	Be ready —entire talk		59b-62b
Thomas S. Monson	Requirements of the oath and covenant of ,		69b-f
Russell M. Nelson	No , calling is intended for personal benefits		83a-b
Julie B. Beck	A work of salvation, service and holiness		111b
	Requires full dedication and loyalty —Packer		111c-d
Boyd K. Packer	Defined	May 2010	7e
	Difference between authority and power of ,		7f
	President declined to bless boy in favor of father —story		8b-d
	Made father ordain son —story		8d-f
	Many live below their privileges		9b
	, power comes through obedience		9d-e
	Father's , a shield between home and adversary		9e
Dallin H. Oaks	Use , and medical science for healings		47b-e
	Will be needed more in future		48c
	5 parts to a healing blessing		48d
	Scriptures on Biblical anointing		48d-e
	Meaning of sealing		48e-f
	Power passes through administrator		48f
	Avoid too frequent administrations		49b-c
	Words of blessings aren't essential		49c-50b
Ronald A. Rasband	8 Quorums of the Seventy		51b
Dieter F. Uchtdorf	, service refines natures		58a
Henry B. Eyring	Diligence in , brings revelation —B. Young		60a-b
	Old ex-bishop's , service didn't end		60e
	And invitation to become as He is		61d-62a
	Rallying cry when tired: Remember Him		62a-63a
	A man refined by ,		63a-c
	How to serve in the ,		63d
Thomas S. Monson	A sacred trust - Much expected		64b

Priorities
Related Topics: —

A. Theodore Tuttle	Are the things that matter most at the mercy of the least?	Dec 1971	90a-c
James E. Faust	A father's , —a list by H.B. Lee	Jan 1974	23b
Paul H. Dunn	Mission, marriage, schooling and family —Kimball	May 1975	62a
Neal A. Maxwell	Women deserting the home to shape society	May 1978	11a
N. Eldon Tanner	Put first the spiritual side of our lives		14e
Paul H. Dunn	Caught up in the thick of thin things	May 1979	8e
J. Thomas Fyans	Beautiful box overshadowed beauty of pearl —story	Nov 1982	61d-e
M. Russell Ballard	Ways to keep life in balance	May 1987	13d-16b
William R. Bradford	Some things are interesting - others are important	Nov 1987	76d-f
Russell M. Nelson	Mothers' top , are children —poem		88a
Ezra Taft Benson	Put God first. All else falls into place	May 1988	4f
Elaine L. Jack	Spinning spiritual wheels while temporal treads hit the road	May 1994	15d-e
Dallin H. Oaks	Jesus should be our first priority	Nov 1995	26e-27c

Dallin H. Oaks	Avoid pet doctrines - Screwtape Letters	Nov 1995	26e-27c
Richard G. Scott	Don't let good things crowd out essential things	May 1997	53f-54c
	Don't give up what you most want for wants now		54d-59a
Russell M. Nelson	Don't allow 4 "f's" to upset ,		72c
Sheri L. Dew	Busyness crowds out the Spirit	Nov 1998	95f
Richard G. Scott	Distraction - Good things crowd out essentials	May 2001	7d-f
	Periodically check your ,		9a-b
Dallin H. Oaks	God first - family second		83f-84f
Keith B. McMullin	"Keep your dish right side up" —Brigham Young	Nov 2002	94e-f
Joseph B. Wirthlin	He daily writes , on a card for tomorrow	Nov 2003	80b
	Let family come first		81d
Russell M. Nelson	Foremost duty is to nurture your marriage	May 2006	37b
M. Russell Ballard	For mothers: God, husband, children	May 2008	108e
	Don't overschedule - 29 weekly commitments		109d-110a
Thomas S. Monson	Life's purpose is to learn what's important	Nov 2008	85a
	Vietnam prisoner counseled family about ,		86d-e
Dieter F. Uchtdorf	"The Story of the Light Bulb" —story	May 2009	59d-e
	Nehemiah rebuilding walls of Jerusalem —story		61a-c
	Letting the unimportant distract —entire talk		59b-62f
Dallin H. Oaks	Fixing , on standards and values of the world		94e-95c
Elaine S. Dalton	Our , and everything else must be different		122a-f
Thomas S. Monson	Immersed in the thick of thin things?	Nov 2009	85d-f
Quentin L. Cook	Spiritual , more important than material ,		93a-b
Julie B. Beck	The nobler art of leaving things undone		111e-112a

Problems
Related Topics: Trials, Worry

John H. Vandenberg	Everyone either a part of the , or the answer	Dec 1971	117c
Bernard P. Brockbank	Knowing God does not solve life's ,	July 1972	121f
Harold B. Lee	Gospel most beautiful during ,	Jan 1973	133d
James E. Faust	If you don't have , just wait awhile	July 1973	86b
H. Burke Peterson	A mother's typical day of crises	Jan 1974	18a
	Trials evidence the Father's love		19a
O. Leslie Stone	Blessings in disguise		39b
Eldred G. Smith	All progress made by overcoming ,		63a
	Limerick on ,		63b
James E. Faust	Be glad there are big hurdles in life	Nov 1982	89a
Marvin J. Ashton	No one can do anything to us that will last for eternity	May 1984	10f
Marvin J. Ashton	All suffering is not punishment —entire talk	Nov 1984	20b-22f
David B. Haight	Don't underestimate ability to deal with ,	May 1987	60d-e
Marvin J. Ashton	Things that hurt also instruct —Franklin	May 1989	22b
Boyd K. Packer	Be quiet while I untie the knot —poem	Nov 2009	46d
Thomas S. Monson	No fog so dense, no night so dark…	May 2010	113b-d

Joseph Fielding Smith	, is the thief of eternal life	June 1969	37b
N. Eldon Tanner	What if the sun said "Well, I won't do it today?"	Jan 1974	93e
Neal A. Maxwell	"Not yet" usually means "never"	Nov 1974	13e
Eldred G. Smith	Satan's best tool —story		26e-f
Marvin J. Ashton	A little poem about , —poem	May 1983	30d
	, - concentrating on the futility of the problem		31f
	An unwholesome blend of doubt and delay		32d
Marvin J. Ashton	Catchy couplet about ,	Nov 1986	14d
Russell M. Nelson	, must yield to preparation	May 1992	74e
Russell M. Nelson	Now is the time to prepare	May 2005	16b-18f
Henry B. Eyring	Danger in the word "someday"	May 2007	89b-c
	Comes from complacency or feeling overwhelmed		90b-d
Donald L. Hallstrom	Submission of recipe became embarrassment —story	Nov 2007	49d-50a
	Leads to loss of exaltation —Kimball		50f
Thomas S. Monson	Makes empty yesterdays today		59e
Claudio R.M. Costa	"Tomorrow Never Comes" —poem		74f-75e

Rex D. Pinegar	Brother told friend not to swear around brothers —story	May 1974	68f-69a
Spencer W. Kimball	Use name of Lord only in prayers and sermons.	Nov 1974	7a
Spencer W. Kimball	G. Washington condemned , among his officers	May 1976	108a-b
Paul H. Dunn	Hall of Famer fell off his pedestal because of , —story	Nov 1976	55e-f
O. Leslie Stone	Delinquent parents profane in home —McKay		60c
Spencer W. Kimball	Repetition of a few sour notes	May 1978	78d
H. Burke Peterson	The reality of , does not argue for its toleration	Nov 1980	38d
Joseph B. Wirthlin	Good definition of vulgarity	May 1982	24f-25a
Robert E. Wells	Kimball reproved man who took Lord's name in vain —story	Nov 1982	69f
Ted E. Brewerton	Mend your speech lest it mar your fortunes	May 1983	72d
	Scriptures on ,		72e-f
	How to deal with rudeness		72f-73a
	A person is known by his language		73a
	Freedom to swear? Or freedom from listening?		73b-c
	No dominion over others without dominion over self		74e-f
Dallin H. Oaks	, is using sacred names without authority	May 1986	49e-50a
	Woman cautioned boys against , —story		52a-b
Gordon B. Hinckley	Take Not the Name of God in Vain —entire talk	Nov 1987	44d-48b
	Mother washed his mouth out with soap —story		46d-e
Howard W. Hunter	The tragedy of misusing the name of deity	May 1993	64d-e
Joe J. Christensen	One vulgarity used 256 times in a movie	Nov 1993	11d
Lynn A Mickelsen	We take God's name in vain by breaking covenants	Nov 1995	79d
Gordon B. Hinckley	Be clean in language	May 1996	48e-f
Gordon B. Hinckley	Avoid , —soap story and Spencer W. Kimball story		94a-c
Henry B. Eyring	President Kimball's rebuke of , while on gurney —story	May 1998	68c
Vaughn J. Featherstone	A great offense to the Spirit	Nov 1999	13e
H. David Burton	, and priesthood are not compatible	May 2000	39a-d

Profanity, cont'd
Related Topics: —

James E. Faust	Holders of priesthood never use foul language	May 2000	44d-e
H. David Burton	Stand tall against ,	Nov 2001	65f-66b
Gordon B. Hinckley	President Kimball's rebuke of , while on gurney —story	Nov 2006	60d-f
Gordon B. Hinckley	Be clean in language	May 2007	62c-e
Henry B. Eyring	, offends the Spirit	Nov 2007	58c-d
	Officers' , and vulgarity disappeared —story		58d-f
James E. Faust	Son helped dad change —story		123a-d
Elaine S. Dalton	Our language and everything else must be different	May 2009	122a-f
Thomas S. Monson	Counsel about ,	May 2010	65d-f

Progression
Related Topics: Growth

Thomas S. Monson	Pray for powers to equal the tasks	Dec 1968	83f
Thomas S. Monson	People become what they're treated like	Dec 1971	132d-e
John H. Vandenberg	Unless we're better tomorrow we aren't useful	Jan 1973	38b
Robert L. Simpson	Savior does not do what man can do for self	July 1973	22b
Neal A. Maxwell	Following celestial road signs while in telestial traffic jams	Nov 1976	12e
Russell C. Taylor	Progress is not created by contented people	Nov 1984	23e
Boyd K. Packer	Children of God may become like him —entire talk		66b-69f
Hugh W. Pinnock	Minister shown that man could become as God —story		73d-e
Marvin J. Ashton	Not speed that counts, but direction	May 1989	21a-b
Henry B. Eyring	Must expect to become better throughout life	Nov 2009	70b

Prophecy
Related Topics: Prophets

Boyd K. Packer	, of famine for hearing word of Lord by Amos now fulfilled	Dec 1969	57b-f
Harold B. Lee	History in reverse	Dec 1970	28d-f
Marion G. Romney	, of tribulations in last days	Jan 1973	32a
	Restoration fulfills ,		32e
Gordon B. Hinckley	Joseph's and Brigham's prophecies fulfilled	Jan 1974	124b
Ezra Taft Benson	The Stephen A. Douglas ,	Nov 1981	62f-63a
Vaughn J. Featherstone	Patriarch said Thomas Monson would be Apostle	Nov 1987	29b-c
Neal A. Maxwell	Prophecies may have rapid fulfillment	May 1988	7c-d
Neal A. Maxwell	Astonishing prophecies by Joseph Smith	May 1992	38d-f
Dieter F. Uchtdorf	1976 promises to a divided Germany	Nov 1994	42b
Thomas S. Monson	East Germany - Every blessing will be yours	Nov 1995	61a-f
David B. Haight	Church to be greatest power in world —Tolstoi	May 1996	22d-f
L. Aldin Porter	Too many members deny spirit of ,	Nov 1996	10c-f
David E. Sorensen	Church will fill the world — , by Joseph Smith	Nov 1998	64b-c
Gordon B. Hinckley	Brigham Young's , on growth of Utah and Church	May 2002	6d-e
Thomas S. Monson	Millions will die —George Albert Smith	May 2007	41d-e
Walter F. Gonzalez	God cannot lie. Therefore , will be fulfilled	Nov 2009	52d-e
David A. Bednar	Spiritual early warning system	May 2010	40c-41c
Dieter F. Uchtdorf	Lord's promises not swift but certain		58d-e

Milton R. Hunter	All , were foreordained	Dec 1968	59b-60c
Hugh B. Brown	What a , is	June 1969	32e
N. Eldon Tanner	Neither dead nor , can convince	Dec 1969	34c
	All in perfect harmony		35c
LeGrand Richards	Two great events announced by ,		52c
Paul H. Dunn	, are always hard to accept while living		105c-106a
	Many , have been reluctant to accept the call		106b
	Jeremiah and Joseph Smith were 14 when called		106d
	Soldier's diary pled for new revelation to world		106e-f
Mark E. Petersen	Israel without , 400 years before Moses	June 1970	79d
Spencer W. Kimball	Transition from McKay to Smith		92a-e
A. Theodore Tuttle	Things , must be and things he need not be	June 1971	70c-d
Ezra Taft Benson	Brigham Young told man to double walls —story	July 1972	61b
Marion G. Romney	What the governor felt like standing beside , —story		98e
N. Eldon Tanner	People accept historians, not ,	Jan 1973	26e
	Lord favors those who listen to ,		26f
	Reject one , reject all		26f
Ezra Taft Benson	Accept present , as well as past ,		58a
	Needed now as in days of Noah		59a
Howard W. Hunter	Church always has ,		65d
	A , for those who will hear		65f
N. Eldon Tanner	Admonition to listen to ,		101f
	Not go astray if , listened to		103a
Harold B. Lee	Cannot destroy appointment of , —story		107c
Mark E. Petersen	Revealeth his secrets to , —scripture		116b
	Lord always deals through ,		116e
	List of scriptures on ,		117a
N. Eldon Tanner	Cannot go astray if we listen to ,	July 1973	10f
A. Theodore Tuttle	Will never lead people astray		18f
	Current scripture is best of all		19a
	Don't need more , need more ears		19f
	Accept living , or deny past ,		19c
Boyd K. Packer	A little boy's testimony of , —story		53f
S. Dilworth Young	The role of John the Baptist	Jan 1974	49a
Gordon B. Hinckley	Having a prophet, we have everything		122c
	Filipino read of a living prophet - converted —story		122d
	Joined Jews because they believed in , - converted —story		124b
	Young man on plane was reading about , —story		124d
Joseph Anderson	Ancient peoples destroyed for not heeding living ,	May 1974	9d-e
Theodore M. Burton	Who was and what is an Elias?		62d-e
N. Eldon Tanner	Only Lord calls and releases ,		84d
Ezra Taft Benson	No untimely passing of a prophet		104c
S. Dilworth Young	Examples of , called and prepared in youth	Nov 1974	90d-91e
Thomas S. Monson	Churchill's comment upon need for ,	May 1975	17d
LeGrand Richards	Why there must be ,		96a-c

Loren C. Dunn	What modern , say is more important than scriptures	May 1976	65f-66b
Spencer W. Kimball	Powerful counsel to follow ,		124b-125d
John H. Groberg	Follow the , —good sea story	Nov 1976	44b-45c
Henry D. Taylor	Purest scripture comes from lips of living , —H. B. Lee		64b
Victor L. Brown	Follow appearance of present , - no beards —story	May 1977	37e-38d
	Should keep mouth shut about old age assistance —story		38e-f
Gordon B. Hinckley	If you accept the revelation you must accept the revelator		64c-d
Spencer W. Kimball	Revelation to , does not come with awe-inspiring display		78a-c
W. Grant Bangerter	Seem impatient and angry—Lord too—also parents	Nov 1979	9b-c
Bruce R. McConkie	Would you have believed , had you lived 2000 years ago?	Nov 1981	46b-d 48d-f
Ezra Taft Benson	Resist temptation to criticize , —Brigham Young —story	May 1982	64b-e
Marion G. Romney	Refusal to follow , leads to apostasy	May 1983	17e
Loren C. Dunn	Sustaining the , —short talk, good stories		29d-30b
Ted E. Brewerton	From 8 to 500 Brazilian missionaries - They listened to ,		74b
Neal A. Maxwell	, never claimed to be perfect. That leaves hope for us.	Nov 1984	10d-f
Rex C. Reeve	When the Lord wants to change the world he sends a baby	Nov 1985	78d-f
David B. Haight	How , and Brigham Young were called	May 1986	8a-f
James E. Faust	, must warn for they must give account for our souls	Nov 1986	8b-c
Joseph B. Wirthlin	The voices of , are the same as the Lord's	May 1989	8a-b
Glenn L. Pace	How valiant he'd have been following past ,		27a
James E. Faust	Scriptures without , cannot exalt anyone	Nov 1989	10b
Janette C. Hales	The magnificence of President Benson's spirit	May 1991	85b
Gordon B. Hinckley	His testimony of each latter-day ,	May 1992	50d-53f
Gordon B. Hinckley	President Benson's stirring testimony of Jesus	May 1993	93c-e
Joe J. Christensen	Of what value is a , if counsel not heeded	Nov 1993	13a-b
Spencer J. Condie	Man tried to warn that bridge was out —story		17e-f
L. Tom Perry	Our , will never lead us astray —Brigham Young	Nov 1994	19c-d
Robert D. Hales	How each , gained his testimony		20e-21f
L. Aldin Porter	Will never lead Saints astray		62f-63b
	Any document from , is will of the Lord		65a-b
Howard W. Hunter	A personal priesthood blessing from the ,		88f
Boyd K. Packer	Prophet does not ordain successor	May 1995	7c-d
	President Kimball testified he held the keys —story		8b-d
H. David Burton	Sever ties to , and sink self to hell	Nov 1995	43d
	Most important prophet is living prophet		43e-f
Carlos E. Asay	, are a sextant to keep us on course	May 1996	60e-61c
Janette Hales Beckham	You have a living , and don't know what he said? —story		84e-f
Bonnie D. Parkin	"I knew I had seen a , of God" —story		90c-d
Henry B. Eyring	Jacob Haun ignored counsel of , —story	May 1997	24f-25a
	Quote one another and repeat warnings - Law of witnesses		25a-b
	How different men view , —good		25b-26c
Jerald L. Taylor	Presidential summit and arrival of , in same city contrasted		33d-e
Gordon B. Hinckley	Don't look to press for doctrines of Church	Nov 1997	4b-f
James E. Faust	Believing in dead , but not living , -story		54c-d
Virginia U. Jensen	Current , necessary —W. Woodruff	Nov 1998	12d-e

Prophets

Prophets, cont'd

Related Topics: Apostles, General Authorities, President, Prophecy

Virginia U. Jensen	Photographer found a prophet —McKay story	Nov 1998	12f-13a
	Lord will never allow , to lead us astray		13d
Gordon B. Hinckley	What is the role of , - His answer to media		70d
Merrill C. Oaks	Revelation comes day by day to , —Kimball		82d-e
	We need , because conditions change		82f-83b
M. Russell Ballard	Nothing authoritative except that which comes through ,	Nov 1999	62e-f
	Beware of false , and teachers —entire talk		62b-64f
M. Russell Ballard	Sure directions from , —entire talk	May 2001	65b-67b
	Girl removed second earrings —story		66d
L. Tom Perry	Joseph of Egypt —story	May 2002	40c-41f
Sheldon F. Child	Woman asked "Why don't we have , ?" —story	Nov 2003	8f-9d
Joseph B. Wirthlin	One village saved from tsunami —story	Nov 2005	16b-d
	People aren't destroyed unless warned		16d-e
	Some societies listened to , and repented		18d-19a
James E. Faust	One of 7 "blockbuster" doctrines		22a
Richard G. Hinckley	His feelings about his prophet father	May 2006	48e-49a
Jeffrey R. Holland	A hike, General Conference and , —story	Nov 2006	104d-105a
James E. Faust	Will accomplish great things by following ,	May 2007	56e-f
Quentin L. Cook	How Polynesians find water during drought	Nov 2007	71e-72b
Robert D. Hales	Experiences in calling 4 stake presidents —story		87a-88b
Quentin L. Cook	Forewarnings by Presidents Grant and McKay	May 2008	48d-49a
	Our need to valiantly follow counsel of ,		47b-50f
Quentin L. Cook	No more , ? False teachings are stumbling blocks	May 2009	36a-c
F. Michael Watson	Like , horse found way through fog —story		106d-e
	What he learned as secretary to 7 , —entire talk		106d-107f
Thomas S. Monson	Remember General Authorities in your prayers		114b
Boyd K. Packer	His testimony of President Monson's calling	Nov 2009	46e-f
Ann M. Dibb	Part of our safety equipment —Bridge story		79b-81b
Russell M. Nelson	Moses, Lehi and Brigham led arduous travel		82b
Thomas S. Monson	Pray for me and General Authorities		110b
Gregory A. Schwitzer	Avoid problems by listening to ,	May 2010	105b
Neil L. Andersen	His testimony of Monson as prophet		111e
Elaine S. Dalton	Meeting President McKay —story		121d-122b

Purity

Related Topics: Chastity, Immorality, Virtue

David O. McKay	A clean man is a national asset	Dec 1968	37b
Richard L. Evans	Answer to evil come-ons	Dec 1969	74c
Milton R. Hunter	Happiness and , of heart go hand in hand	June 1971	42b
Gordon B. Hinckley	Youth cannot afford filth	Jan 1973	92b
H. Burke Peterson	Brightest light comes from cleanest instrument	Nov 1974	70f
Carlos E. Asay	Not clean, don't think it - etc. —good quote	May 1980	43a
James E. Faust	My strength is as the strength of ten because heart is pure	May 2000	44e-f
Thomas S. Monson	Safety of nation depends on , of home —McKay		54c
James E. Faust	Standing in holy places —entire talk	May 2005	62b-68f
Russell M. Nelson	Happiness is predicated upon personal ,	May 2006	37a

Purity, cont'd
Related Topics: Chastity, Immorality, Virtue

Gordon B. Hinckley	J.F. Smith's dream - I am clean —story	May 2007	60f-62b
David A. Bednar	Clean hands and a pure heart —entire talk	Nov 2007	80d-82b
D. Todd Christofferson	Impurity even in a non-television, non-Internet world	Nov 2008	38f-39b
Barbara Thompson	Angels cannot be restrained as associates —Smith		116c
Elaine S. Dalton	Virtue is ,	May 2009	120b-e
	Sexual , is the core of a virtuous life		120f-121a

Quarreling and Anger
Related Topics: Contention, Forgiveness (has stories of quarrels)

David O. McKay	No man has right to utter cross word in home	June 1969	116b-c
Elray L. Christiansen	The size of a man determined by things that anger him	June 1971	37b
	No good accomplished while angry		37d
	Make no decisions while angry		37d-e
	Good quote on anger		37f
	Absurd to be angry at things		37f-38a
	Children remember , in the home		38a
	Don't get so angry that you can't pray		38b
	He is a weak man who quarrels —McKay		38b
	Quarreling —short poem		38b
	Quarreling —short poem		38e
James A. Cullimore	Compromise everything but truth		94e
Thomas S. Monson	, caused son to leave. Love brought him back —story		96c-e
Boyd K. Packer	Result of a family , —story	Jan 1973	89f
Harold B. Lee	If we knew our brotherhood we wouldn't , so much	Jan 1974	6e
Marion D. Hanks	Walk the second mile to relieve your anger		20f
Henry D. Taylor	Spirit will not be in a home where there is ,		37b
	Joseph couldn't translate until made up with Emma —story		37b
Harold B. Lee	All children of one Father, so stop shouting at each other		97b
O. Leslie Stone	Tolerate abuse rather than retaliate	Nov 1974	32f
Theodore M. Burton	If Satan gets people to , they inevitably destroy themselves		55e-f
	Contention for evil or good both please Satan		56a
O. Leslie Stone	Delinquent parents quarrel in front of children	Nov 1976	60c
John H. Groberg	Hawaiian overcame challenge - family stayed active —story	May 1980	49a-f
F. Enzio Busche	Father's anger cooled before disciplining son —story	May 1982	70e-f
Mark E. Petersen	No man should quarrel with his wife	Nov 1982	17a
Marvin J. Ashton	Those who stir up water create whirlpools	May 1983	31f
Jeffrey R. Holland	An experience when disciplining his son —story		36b-38b
James E. Faust	Let there be no , - settle quickly		42a
Ezra Taft Benson	One who doesn't control temper is not in control of thoughts	Nov 1983	42e
L. Tom Perry	We put God first if we aren't bickering	May 1987	35d-e
Hugh W. Pinnock	, ranchers forgave —story		62e-f
Marvin J. Ashton	I'm an adult now —story		65b-e
Gordon B. Hinckley	Invoke healing power of Christ to stop , in homes	Nov 1988	54c-d
Neal A. Maxwell	Letting off steam produces more heat than light	Nov 1989	84e
H. Burke Peterson	Look for the good - "Your ceiling's really clean"	May 1990	83e
Thomas S. Monson	God counts women's tears	Nov 1990	47a

Russell M. Nelson	, children looked funny to deaf mother —story	May 1991	24e-f
Gordon B. Hinckley	No justification for losing temper	Nov 1991	50f-51b
Marvin J. Ashton	Women's response to outburst of anger —story	May 1992	20c-d
Howard W. Hunter	, will leave us blind and toothless	Nov 1992	18e
Gordon B. Hinckley	Let no bickering cloud spirit of home	Nov 1993	60d
Howard W. Hunter	We should not lose our tempers	May 1994	51b-c
Thomas S. Monson	Numbers of war dead at Normandy		61a-b
	, builds nothing but destroys everything		61c
Joe J. Christensen	Differences in marriage will come. Resolve them	May 1995	65d-e
James E. Faust	Spirit departs regardless of who is at fault	May 1996	41b
Gordon B. Hinckley	Demeans and offends		49a
Gordon B. Hinckley	Abusive men are not worthy of priesthood	Nov 1996	68d-e
Gordon B. Hinckley	Warnings against ,	May 1998	50b-c
Lynn G. Robbins	Recipe for disaster		80b-c
	Player learned anger can be controlled —story		80d-e
	Angry "without a cause" mistranslation		80f
Neal A. Maxwell	No room for , on the straight and narrow way	May 1999	23e
Robert D. Hales	Angry voices cause Spirit to depart home —H. B. Lee		33b
Thomas S. Monson	Worst enemy was best friend —story	Nov 2001	60f-61f
Gene R. Cook	Blinded a man to God's love	May 2002	82d-e
David E. Sorensen	Neighbors' quarrel escalated to murder —story	May 2003	10b-11d
	When bitten by a rattlesnake... —Brigham Young		11d-12a
Thomas S. Monson	Quarrel made boy leave—Apology brought him back —story	Nov 2003	58a-d
Gordon B. Hinckley	We must never be disagreeable		83d
Gordon B. Hinckley	No , in a marriage if …	Nov 2004	84c-d
Joseph B. Wirthlin	, caused inactivity - Kindness activated —story	May 2005	26b-d
Robert S. Wood	Entire talk	May 2006	93d-95f
David A. Bednar	To be offended is a choice we make	Nov 2006	90b-91c
	Dealing with offense —entire talk good		89b-92b
James E. Faust	Healthful benefits of forgiveness	May 2007	68d-e
Julie B. Beck	Ruth May Fox overcame her quick temper		109d-110b
Gordon B. Hinckley	Why "School Thy Feelings" was written	Nov 2007	62c-e
	Railroad man stomped on hat —story		62e
	The mother of many evil actions		62e
	Over half of marriages end before 25th year		62f-63a
	Married 67 years - No quarrel		63a
	Answer to slanderous article —excellent		63a-b
	"A little piece of string" —story		63b-66a
	Old age attributed to fresh air —humor		66a
	Control your tempers		66b
L. Tom Perry	Making peace with God: Not aware we had quarreled	Nov 2008	10b
D. Todd Christofferson	Zion people must be free from contention and strife		38b-e
Robert D. Hales	Jesus endured mocking with silence		72b-e
	Joseph Smith didn't retaliate		72e
	Better to keep distance and simply walk away		74d-f

Quarreling and Anger, cont'd
Related Topics: Contention, Forgiveness (has stories of quarrels)

Richard G. Scott	Anger overcomes influence of Holy Ghost —example	Nov 2009	8e
Dallin H. Oaks	God's anger is evidence of His love		26e-27d
Kent D. Watson	Being temperate in all things —entire talk		38b-39f
Thomas S. Monson	Lead news stories all have , at their base		62d-e
	Marital troubles physically injured child —story		62f-67c
	Builds nothing but can destroy everything		67c
	Heber J. Grant was insulted —story		67c-e
	Can't have Spirit if we're angry		67f
	No one can make us angry. It is a choice		67f-68a
	Thomas B. Marsh's anger led to apostasy —story		68b-f
	Brothers didn't speak for 62 years —story		68f-69a
	Leave harsh and hurtful things unsaid		69a
	School Thy Feelings —poem		69a-b
Julie B. Beck	Spirit distances self when temper is lost	May 2010	11d
Quentin L. Cook	May disagree but don't be disagreeable		84f-85a

Race
Related Topics: —

Bernard P. Brockbank	Japanese from tribe of Joseph	Dec 1970	120d
Harold B. Lee	How we are to treat people of other races	July 1972	103c
Harold B. Lee	Determined by our actions in pre-mortal life	Jan 1974	5b
Robert L. Simpson	Black man found Church in prison —story	Nov 1974	46d-e
Russell M. Nelson	The , of life is an obstacle course	Nov 1987	86c
James E. Faust	We can be different but unified —entire talk	May 1995	61b-63f
Gordon B. Hinckley	Don't be part of any ethnic superiority		71b-c
Gordon B. Hinckley	No disciple of Christ makes racial slurs	May 2006	58b-e
Dallin H. Oaks	Gospel is for everyone - Scripture list		77c-78b
	Gospel is for all men everywhere		77b-80f
Joseph B. Wirthlin	Joseph's kindness to 8 black people —story		100f-101b

Relief Society
Related Topics: Women

Barbara B. Smith	Works with Melchizedek Priesthood like wife with husband	May 1977	91e
Boyd K. Packer	, formation began emancipation of women	Nov 1978	7d
	He hopes the name of , will never be changed		7d
	Uses for , —good analogy to shopping		7e
	As mandatory as priesthood attendance of brethren		8c-e
	Don't get anything from , ? What are you putting in? —story		8e-9a
Barbara B. Smith	Instructions to , and things to be learned from ,	May 1981	84c-85a
Joy F. Evans	The heart of , is visiting teaching and compassionate service	May 1989	73f
Dallin H. Oaks	Relief of poverty, illness, doubt, etc.	May 1992	34f
	The , —entire talk		34b-37b
Thomas S. Monson	Illiterate sister taught to read —story		101a-b
M. Russell Ballard	Each woman may do a great deal —E.R. Snow	Nov 1993	89d
Elaine L. Jack	What a sister learned in ,	Nov 1994	90c
Boyd K. Packer	Belle S. Spafford could not get released from , —story	Nov 1997	8c-e
Mary Ellen Smoot	History of growth of ,		86e-f

Mary Ellen Smoot	Every problem can be solved through devotion to , —story	Nov 1997	87a-e
	Car wreck at Baker, Oregon and devotion to , —story		88c-f
Thomas S. Monson	Statements by Young and Snow about ,		94b-d
Boyd K. Packer	His endorsement of ,	May 1998	72b-74f
Virginia U. Jensen	6 purposes of ,	Nov 1998	92b-94b
Gordon B. Hinckley	Make , foremost —J.F. Smith		97c-d
	Your responsibilities as members of ,		97e-f
Robert D. Hales	Attend , when you reach 18th birthday	May 1999	34a
Mary Ellen Smoot	, declaration - succinct statement of belief	Nov 1999	92f-93b
	World will change - one sister at a time		94d-f
Virginia U. Jensen	Purpose of new Enrichment Meeting		96d-f
	Purpose is to build Christ-centered homes —story		96f-97b
Sheri L. Dew	Energies must be spent bringing people to Christ		98b-c
James E. Faust	Focus of ,		100e-101a
James E. Faust	Joseph turned key for emancipation of womankind	Nov 2002	111a
	The four enduring concepts of ,		111b
Bonnie D. Parkin	How has , blessed your life? - 3 answers	Nov 2004	34d-35d
	, is a fundamental part of gospel		35d
	How , blesses lives —entire talk		34d-36f
Bonnie D. Parkin	How does anyone die without , ? —story		108c-e
Thomas S. Monson	The joy of learning to read —story		113f-114f
Gordon B. Hinckley	Video presentation on history of ,	Nov 2005	105a-106f
James E. Faust	Joseph Smith turned the key for ,		116b-c
	Visiting and befriending the difficult sister		116e-f
M. Russell Ballard	President must not finish others' visiting teaching	Nov 2006	19b-c
Gordon B. Hinckley	, stands for education		116b
	What , does for women		118f
Julie B. Beck	Relief of what? - Definition	Nov 2007	111b-c
	Focus on sociality does not bring relief		112d
Silvia H. Allred	Purposes of visiting teaching		113e
	Walking in heavy rain to visit teach		113f
	Give , precedence —B.K. Packer		114d
	The visit was not delayed —story		114d-f
Thomas S. Monson	Visiting teachers came in time of need —story		121b-d
Julie B. Beck	Similar organization existed anciently	Nov 2008	108f
	Divinely authorized and instituted		108f-109a
	To look after spirituality and salvation of women		109b
	Purpose is to organize, teach, and inspire		109b-c
	The 3 purposes of ,		109d-110b
	"Who will be my mother?" —story		110b-e
	Still a part of , though serving elsewhere		110e-f
	Lord cannot accomplish His work without ,		111b-e
Barbara Thompson	Service in , magnifies and sanctifies		115a
	"I now turn the key to you..." —J. Smith		115b-c
	A refuge - safety and protection —J. Smith		116d-e

Relief Society

Relief Society, cont'd
Related Topics: Women

Julie B. Beck	The threefold purpose of ,	Nov 2009	110d-e
	No hostile nor competitive interests to interfere		110e-f
	Operates after pattern of priesthood		110f-111b
	A work of salvation, service and holiness		111b
	Requires full dedication and loyalty —Packer		111c-d
	Keep business portion of , brief		112a-b
	Policy for additional , meetings		112b-113e
	Visiting teaching is evidence of our discipleship		113f-114c
Silvia H. Allred	The purposes of ,		115c
	How , developed her mother		115f-116c
	How , helped a young couple		116f-117a
	List of what , does for women		117b-e
Barbara Thompson	Not just what you get from , but what you give		119f
Henry B. Eyring	"Charity never faileth" will serve forever		121e
	No organized , for 4 decades		122b
	Began hospital system and other things		122c-e
	His wife always there ahead of bishop		123f
	Visiting teacher inspired to bring yellow tulips —story		124b-f
Julie B. Beck	What , does	May 2010	11e-12a

Religion
Related Topics: —

David O. McKay	Government never gets ahead of , —Coolidge	Dec 1968	37d-e
Alma Sonne	We need a living , not just a history of one —Emerson		102f
Sterling W. Sill	A man's , is the most important thing about him		104d-e
Delbert L. Stapley	Not tried and found wanting—found difficult and left untried	June 1969	69f
Howard W. Hunter	Difference between ethics and ,	Dec 1969	96f
Sterling W. Sill	America will survive if religious —D. Webster	Dec 1970	82c-e
N. Eldon Tanner	If we were arrested for being Christians …	June 1971	13d
Paul H. Dunn	There are two educations …	Dec 1971	119c
Harold B. Lee	Gives courage —Quote from Eisenhower	July 1972	33d
Bruce R. McConkie	Man cannot create a saving ,	Jan 1973	36e
Marion D. Hanks	The value of ,	May 1975	14f
Gordon B. Hinckley	85% of high achieving youth practice ,	Nov 1983	44d-e
Royden G. Derrick	Takes as much study and effort as understanding science	Nov 1984	61f-62b
George R. Hill, III	No conflict between science and ,	May 1988	72e-f
Jeffrey R. Holland	, is a mockery without revelation —John Taylor	Nov 2004	8d-e
M. Russell Ballard	This is an era when , is scoffed at and ridiculed	May 2009	33a

Repentance
Related Topics: Confession, Forgiveness, Sin

Richard L. Evans	You, not the world must change	Dec 1968	64c-d
Joseph Fielding Smith	We are not automatically cleansed in the grave	June 1969	37f-38c
Gordon B. Hinckley	Leopards do change their spots		74f
Robert L. Simpson	Make , unnecessary		90c-d
Harold B. Lee	Teach first principles of gospel first		104f-105a
Alvin R. Dyer	Stressed from beginning	Dec 1969	39a

Alvin R. Dyer	Of greatest worth to man	Dec 1969	39c
	Brings peace of mind		40a
	Anything can be cured by ,		40e
Robert L. Simpson	The road back isn't long - it's just the first step		43a
Loren C. Dunn	Observations on , when daughter broke glass —story		44d-f
Richard L. Evans	Not beyond , don't postpone ,		74f
Richard L. Evans	If we don't change direction, we will arrive...	June 1970	38b
	Sincere , is a miracle		38f
Hartman Rector, Jr.	World will drown in blood if men don't repent		102b
	90% from Lord, 10% from man		103d
Harold B. Lee	Commit same sin after , and former sins return	Dec 1970	29f
Paul H. Dunn	Easier to build a boy than mend a man		39a
	Leopards don't change spots?		41a-c
Hartman Rector, Jr.	No miraculous change in character at death		76d-e
	100 times easier to repent on earth —story		77a-b
	God cannot force repentance		78a-c
Boyd K. Packer	Prevention the best cure for , —poem		107a-b
William H. Bennett	Comparison of , with astronaut's correction		123e-f
Richard L. Evans	If on wrong road, turn back immediately	Dec 1971	58f
James A. Cullimore	Repentance wouldn't be necessary if no forgiveness possible		86e
	Time must be given for sinner to demonstrate ,		87d-e
Marvin J. Ashton	You can't get there from here —story		99a-e
	A prisoner's story —story		99f-101a
Robert L. Simpson	Neglect of opportunity...develops inability to repent	July 1972	49a
	Eternity will not bring a magic change of heart		49b
	Excommunication can be first step back		49e
N. Eldon Tanner	Will save world from destruction	Jan 1973	28a
John H. Vandenberg	Disgrace leaves upon , —short quote		39c
Marion G. Romney	How to retain remission of sins		97c
Harold B. Lee	How to know when , is complete	July 1973	122a
Elray L. Christiansen	What true , entails —Joseph F. Smith	Jan 1974	34f
	You don't know how soon it will be too late		35b
James A. Cullimore	Justice must be satisfied before forgiveness comes	May 1974	29e
	Some men can't repent until turned over to Satan		30b-c
	Not taking action against offenders is very unkind		30d
O. Leslie Stone	If you want to be where God is - repent —Joseph Smith	Nov 1974	32c-e
Bernard P. Brockbank	Well organized talk on ,		56d-58f
Boyd K. Packer	When you know truth you don't mind giving up bad habits		89b-c
N. Eldon Tanner	You can escape from everything but conscience —good	May 1976	44e
Robert D. Hales	8 steps to ,	Nov 1976	26a-f
Boyd K. Packer	Justice, mercy, the Mediator and , —entire talk	May 1977	54b-56f
Wm. R. Bradford	5 steps in ,	Nov 1979	38d
Marvin J. Ashton	Recognizing need for , —good quote		62d
	When we're through changing, we're through		62f
Marion G. Romney	Retaining remission of sins depends on service	Nov 1980	92e-f

Spencer W. Kimball	Repentance explained	Nov 1980	97f-98f
Adney Y. Komatsu	Hard-core prisoner became Elder's Quorum president —story	Nov 1981	21f-22b
Hugh W. Pinnock	Good thoughts on ,	May 1982	12c-f
	8 things to do in , —good ideas		12f-14b
Ronald E. Poelman	Unrepented sin becomes habitual - makes , harder		27d-e
	Hosea and Gomer - modernized story		27e-28e
	God's love transcends our transgressions		28f & 29f
	Good , scriptures		29a-b
Vaughn J. Featherstone	Prodigal son parable retold —good	Nov 1982	71b-72f
F. Burton Howard	Comparison of two crystal glasses	May 1983	58b-e
	Ran from mission call - No peace until confession —story		58f-59e
	Requires time, prayer, effort, help		59e
	Not once in a lifetime but ever recurring		59e-60a
	Not a free gift		60a
Theodore M. Burton	, is a change of behavior which invites forgiveness		70f
Neal A. Maxwell	Discipleship is proving, reproving and improving	Nov 1984	10a
Richard G. Scott	Please Come Back —entire talk	May 1986	10b-12b
Ezra Taft Benson	One is far better off to have never sinned		45a
Boyd K. Packer	Even child abuse yields to sincere ,	Nov 1986	18e-f
Dallin H. Oaks	We have no right to scare people to , —Joseph Smith		22d-e
F. Burton Howard	He forgot which priest had sinned —story		77d-78b
Neal A. Maxwell	We must either suffer as Jesus or overcome as Jesus	May 1987	72f
Henry B. Eyring	Repent daily —George Q. Cannon	May 1988	40d
Thomas S. Monson	Barnacles drop off ships at Portland, Oregon —story		42b-d
Russell M. Nelson	, is best achieved while one still has a body	Nov 1988	8a-b
Neal A. Maxwell	Even God cannot reconcile only one party		33a
Hugh W. Pinnock	4 steps to a changed life	May 1989	11d-12c
Richard G. Scott	Sin is bad: Doing nothing about it is worse		36d-e
	If in a dark tunnel, turn back toward light		36e-f
Boyd K. Packer	It's never too late. , is like soap		59a-b
Royden G. Derrick	The "R's" of ,		77c
Robert L. Backman	God is only interested in our future conditioned on ,	Nov 1989	40a-b
Richard G. Scott	Entire talk —good	May 1990	74b-76b
	Like fixing a tape measure —good analogy		75c-d
M. Russell Ballard	Don't make self sick just to try the remedy	Nov 1990	36e
Boyd K. Packer	, available for abortion and homosexuality		85e-86f
F. Burton Howard	Blaming others doesn't help , —entire talk	May 1991	12d-14a
Neal A. Maxwell	Must sometimes publicly own up to sins		90f-91b
Neal A. Maxwell	Entire talk	Nov 1991	30d-32f
James E. Faust	Turns mourning into joy	May 1992	8d-f
Robert D. Hales	Gratitude is the foundation for ,		63f
Boyd K. Packer	All moral sins are repentable		68e-f
Russell M. Nelson	Opportunity for , is forfeited at death		73a-b
M. Russell Ballard	Letter from former drug addict	Nov 1992	32e-33a
Richard G. Scott	How to heal a damaged life —insightful		60d-62f

Repentance

John K. Carmack	Faith sometimes requires , first	May 1993	42f-43a
Spencer J. Condie	Long prayer conquered alcohol —story	Nov 1993	16d-f
Malcolm S. Jeppsen	Seven steps to ,	May 1994	17b-19b
Thomas S. Monson	Apply a proper-sized bandage to the wound		50e
Hartman Rector, Jr.	A difference between ceasing to sin and ,	Nov 1994	25f-26b
Richard G. Scott	Finding Forgiveness —entire talk good	May 1995	75b-77f
Boyd K. Packer	Sins will be forgotten by Father and us	Nov 1995	18d-21b
Russell M. Nelson	Issue self command to "about face"	May 1996	15b
Gordon B. Hinckley	J.F. Smith's dream - "I am clean" —story		46e-47d
	Account of spring cleaning - do it in lives —story		47d-48a
Carlos E. Asay	"The Land of Beginning Again" —poem		61c-d
James E. Faust	Jesus works his healing miracle through ,	Nov 1996	53b
Boyd K. Packer	10 filthy servicemen felt uncomfortable —story	May 1997	9c-f
	Spiritual pain is called "guilt"		9f-10a
	Why youth feel cornered or rebellious		10b
	We renew baptismal covenants with sacrament		10d
	J.F. Smith's dream. He was clean —story		10d-f
Neal A. Maxwell	Developmental ,	Nov 1997	22d
M. Russell Ballard	Planned sin is a slippery slope		40a-b
James E. Faust	An amazing comeback —story		43d-f
James E. Faust	Letters from W.W. Phelps and Joseph Smith		54f-59b
Dallin H. Oaks	Baptism and sacrament preceded by ,	Nov 1998	37f-38a
Neal A. Maxwell	Little difference between indifferent and indulgent	May 1999	24a
Boyd K. Packer	Foolish to remain in open door prison	Nov 1999	24e
Henry B. Eyring	Procrastinating , —entire talk		33b-35f
Joseph B. Wirthlin	Through , the atonement becomes operative		40f
Richard C. Edgley	Repentant missionary became best —story		43b-44a
L. Tom Perry	Change you by changing environment —S. W. Kimball		77c-d
Sheri L. Dew	Identify one thing per month to work on		99e-f
Boyd K. Packer	"What shall we do?" - repent and be baptized	May 2000	8d-e
Thomas S. Monson	Barnacles drop off ships at Portland —story		46e-47a
Richard G. Scott	, - the path to peace and joy —excellent talk	Nov 2000	25b-27b
	Steps to ,		25f-26a
	Read Kimball's Miracle of Forgiveness		26d
	Mistake to consider self a second-class citizen		26d-e
	Forgive self after complete ,		26e-f
James E. Faust	Premeditated , is a false concept		46a-b
Boyd K. Packer	"The Touch of the Master's Hand" —entire talk	May 2001	22d-24f
Thomas S. Monson	Leopards can't change spots, but men do.		49f
Gordon B. Hinckley	Available for every sin		95a-d
Thomas S. Monson	Hidden Wedges —story	May 2002	18b-e
	"I wish I had a second chance" —story		20e
Dieter F. Uchtdorf	Our safety lies in , —G.B. Hinckley	Nov 2002	12a
Neal A. Maxwell	Must give away our sins - not just make a down payment		18e-f
Richard G. Scott	How to free self of despair		86b-88f

James E. Faust	Wayward children will return after ,	May 2003	62b-f
	, is but the homesickness of the soul		62f
Spencer V. Jones	Skunk smell would not come off —story		88b-89f
Lynn A. Mickelsen	The atonement, repentance and dirty linen	Nov 2003	10d-13b
Boyd K. Packer	You hold the key to ,		26b-c
Dallin H. Oaks	Must exchange national cultures for Church culture		37b-40f
Joseph B. Wirthlin	We can't go back - Begin where you are		79b-c
	Waiting for right time to repent —good quote		79f
	A parable leading a man through ,		78d-81f
Dallin H. Oaks	Why not repent now and be ready for Savior	May 2004	8f-9c
James E. Faust	Steps to ,		52d-e
Bruce C. Hafen	Must yank weeds out by roots - not mow them		97e-f
	Almost repenting is not enough		98d-99a
Richard G. Scott	Not forgiving self is denying Atonement	Nov 2004	17f-18b
	Peace of conscience comes through ,		15b-18b
Boyd K. Packer	, can remove needless burdens of guilt		87d
Henry B. Eyring	"I've been repenting as I went along"	Nov 2005	40d
Boyd K. Packer	What Jesus made, He can fix	May 2006	28a
	Corianton's , —entire talk		25b-28b
Richard G. Hinckley	Investigator wept at opportunity for ,		49f-50b
Jeffrey R. Holland	Change what you can, forgive the rest		70b
Earl C. Tingey	Only way to empty our bag of rocks		72e-f
Shayne M. Bowen	Beautiful park built over a landfill	Nov 2006	33b-34f
Marcus B. Nash	The great enabling principle of the gospel		49b-50f
Boyd K. Packer	Always the remedy of , and forgiveness		86d
Dieter F. Uchtdorf	Point of No Return noted by pilots	May 2007	99b-d
	No principle is more important —McKay		100b-d
	Wipes away anguish and remorse —Kimball		100f
	Peace of conscience will come —Harold B. Lee		101a
	We will remember our sins		101b-d
	There is always a point of safe return		101f
Russell M. Nelson	Appears in 47 of 138 sections of D&C		102d-e
	The prize is worth the price		102e
	The steps to ,		102e
	Offered to the dead as well		104b-d
	72 times in Bible - 360 times in Book of Mormon		104f
	Applies to everything we do in life		105a
Gordon B. Hinckley	"A little piece of string" —story	Nov 2007	63b-66a
Claudio D. Zivic	"Don't touch me. I can't sin" —story		98d-e
	A sense of shame can't be found again		98f
James E. Faust	All need change - Saul's conversion		122b-d
	Brutal alcoholic became convert —story		122e-123a
	Son caused father to repent —story		123a-d
	Mother got off drugs - Brand new —story		124c-f
Russell M. Nelson	King offered to have his people baptized	May 2008	8c-d

Repentance

Richard G. Scott	Easier in this life than in the next	May 2008	43c
Dieter F. Uchtdorf	A 2-degree error caused plane crash —story		57f-58b
	A 1-degree error = 500 miles in 25,000 mile trip		58f-59a
	Make early and decisive corrections		59a
	Willingness to repent shows gratitude		60a-b
	Heaven is filled with the repentant		60b-c
	An elegant plea for people to repent		60d-e
Boyd K. Packer	Nothing from which you cannot be made clean	May 2009	51b
Dieter F. Uchtdorf	It is never too late		77a-78a
Richard G. Scott	A feeling of remorse is fertile soil	Nov 2009	9d
Neil L. Andersen	A "re-turn" toward God		40e
	No sin that cannot be forgiven		40f
	A journey rather than a one-time event		41a-b
	Repeatedly struggling - Don't be discouraged		41f-42a
	Faust regretted letting grandmother get wood —story		42b-d
	Relief will come - A promise		42e
	"We are back, but we are back alone"		42e-f
	Healing through , —entire talk		40b-42f
Quentin L. Cook	All can repent and return		92f-93a
Henry B. Eyring	Downward spiral easily arrested early	May 2010	22a-e
Jeffrey R. Holland	Get help. Much is available		45d
	Makes light shine again		46f
Thomas S. Monson	There is a way back		66f-67a

Harold B. Lee	Heavy , brings greater dependence on Lord	July 1972	33e
Gordon B. Hinckley	Men work harder for duty than for money	Nov 1982	20d-21a
Hugh W. Pinnock	Take , for self-activity, afflictions, testimony	May 1989	10d-12f
Thomas S. Monson	Bishop brought excommunicated man back —story	May 1990	48f-49b
Thomas S. Monson	Boy found King's emerald by doing duty —story	Nov 2006	56e-57b
Quentin L. Cook	Stewards over bodies, minds, families, properties	Nov 2009	91e
	Steward over a spring and virtue —story		91f-92d
Keith B. McMullin	Our path of duty —entire talk	May 2010	13a-15e

Bruce R. McConkie	Proven through testimony, not through scripture	Dec 1970	114e
LeGrand Richards	Remodeling an old house or building a new one	July 1972	115e
N. Eldon Tanner	Second greatest event of world	Jan 1973	28e
Marion G. Romney	Fulfills prophecy		32e
LeGrand Richards	Must be a , not a reformation —story	July 1973	79c
Thomas S. Monson	The contributions of the reformers to the ,	May 1975	15e-16a
LeGrand Richards	Scriptures supporting ,		97e-f
Bruce R. McConkie	Once or twice in a thousand years —entire talk	Nov 1975	15d-18f
LeGrand Richards	Only church meeting terms of restitution spoken of by Peter	May 1980	22f
	Scriptures showing complete apostasy and ,		23f-24a

Restoration, cont'd
Related Topics: —

Mark E. Petersen	Good discussion of angels, revelation, and ,	Nov 1983	29b-31a
Neal A. Maxwell	Nearly 900 pages of scripture added because of ,	May 1986	34e
Russell M. Nelson	The score was 1,143,000,000 to 6	May 1988	33f-34d
Carlos E. Asay	Joseph Smith and the , —excellent talk	May 1990	62d-65b
Gordon B. Hinckley	, was to prepare for second coming	May 1991	91f-92d
M. Russell Ballard	The role of the Reformers in the ,	Nov 1994	66e-f
	The story of the ,		66f-67e
Boyd K. Packer	Came a piece at a time	Nov 1996	6d-f
Thomas S. Monson	The role of the Reformers	May 1997	51c-e
James E. Faust	One of 2 pivotal events in history	May 1999	17b-e
Gordon B. Hinckley	Reformation , and Second Coming —good	Nov 1999	73b-74f
Boyd K. Packer	We owe immense debt to Reformers	May 2000	8a-c
James E. Faust	Also unlocked secular knowledge		18b-c
Gordon B. Hinckley	The wonder of the , —strong message	Nov 2002	80b-81f
Boyd K. Packer	Not remodeled, corrected or a protest	Nov 2003	24d-f
Robert D. Hales	Events of , described		28b-31f
Henry B. Eyring	Eyewitnesses to the ,		89e-90d
Neal A. Maxwell	"Stunners" among the revelations		100b-101a
Gordon B. Hinckley	Light of , breaking over a dark world	May 2004	81b-84b
Thomas S. Monson	1980 Proclamation on ,	Nov 2004	56e
Gordon B. Hinckley	Compare First Vision to Nicaean Creed	May 2005	80f-81b
Merrill J. Bateman	Most dispensations began with a book	Nov 2005	74f-75b
Robert D. Hales	The Reformation and , —entire talk		88d-92b
James E. Faust	Authority and keys that were restored	May 2006	62d-f
	Origin of each Standard Work		67d-68b
	Restored Church - Not a break off		68d
M. Russell Ballard	What we'd be missing without the ,		84b-e
Gary J. Coleman	Three essential restored truths	May 2007	92b-94b
M. Russell Ballard	A , occurred in every dispensation	May 2009	32f
Quentin L. Cook	Salvation as taught before ,		36f-37a
Neil L. Andersen	Fulfills ancient prophecies - list		79f-80b
Tad R. Callister	Four truths learned in sacred grove	Nov 2009	35d-36a

Resurrection
Related Topics: Jesus

N. Eldon Tanner	Review of the Savior's ,	June 1969	34b-37e
Howard W. Hunter	Explanation of 1 Cor. 15:42-44 - Spiritual Body		107e-108c
	Take away doctrine of , and only a code of ethics left		108c
Mark E. Petersen	, will prevent some things	Nov 1974	49e
Franklin D. Richards	No church believes in the , as we do	May 1975	59e-f
LeGrand Richards	Others believe God and Jesus are a spirit. Why then the , ?	Nov 1976	65b-66b
Spencer W. Kimball	We will be ordained to resurrect people	May 1977	49b-d
Marion G. Romney	The , of Jesus —excellent talk	May 1982	6a-9b
James E. Faust	The Atonement and , —entire talk	May 1985	30d-32f
Russell M. Nelson	A listing of the Lord's appearances after his ,	May 1987	8d-9e
Gordon B. Hinckley	The Atonement and , —entire talk	May 1988	65b-68f

James E. Faust	Christ's ,	Nov 1988	13b-14b
F. Melvin Hammond	It's simple, you just sink up —story	May 1990	29b-c
	Reuniting with loved ones will be like Mary seeing Jesus		29b-30b
Russell M. Nelson	, will be a day of judgment	Nov 1990	75c
M. Russell Ballard	Joseph wished to rise beside father	Nov 1991	5e
Marion D. Hanks	Down's boy had empty Easter egg —story	May 1992	11a-b
Russell M. Nelson	He who created life can resurrect us		73f-74a
Russell M. Nelson	, changes bodies to a bloodless form	Nov 1993	34e
Carlos E. Asay	The greatest miracle and fact of history	May 1994	10e-f
	List of all who saw Jesus after the ,		10f-12f
Thomas S. Monson	Letter from Civil War soldier facing death		62f-63b
Gordon B. Hinckley	Best attested event in history		72b-f
Gordon B. Hinckley	Jesus' death and ,	May 1996	66e-67f
Russell M. Nelson	Bodies will function without blood	Nov 1996	34b
Chieko N. Okazaki	Death has no dominion over us		90d
	Christ's , guarantees our own		90e
Thomas S. Monson	Good concise statement about the ,	May 1997	52d-e
Thomas S. Monson	Children to be raised to maturity after ,	Nov 1998	19d-20f
Gordon B. Hinckley	Powerful testimony of Jesus and ,	May 1999	70b-72f
Russell M. Nelson	More references to , in Book of Mormon than in Bible	Nov 1999	70b-e
Dallin H. Oaks	Great discourse on , —entire talk	May 2000	14b-16f
	Prime of life ,		15b
Neal A. Maxwell	Little girl will have her hand in the , —story		74f
James E. Faust	A free gift	Nov 2001	19c-d
Boyd K. Packer	There is no , preacher said —story		62d-63e
Russell M. Nelson	The Lord's consummate act of healing	Nov 2005	87f-88a
Earl C. Tingey	, does not overcome spiritual death	May 2006	73a-d
Joseph B. Wirthlin	We will meet the same identical being there	Nov 2006	29b
	Life at our prime		29b-c
	The core of our beliefs		29d-e
	The darkest day of earth's history		29e-30a
	From despair to joy in an instant		30a
	Thousands witnessed - Disciples renewed		30b-c
	We will embrace loved ones on that day		30d
Russell M. Nelson	Mentioned more in Book of Mormon	Nov 2007	44d & 46a
Russell M. Nelson	Atonement made , a reality	May 2008	8f-9a
Henry B. Eyring	Our spirits will be changed in the ,	May 2009	23f-24b
Quentin L. Cook	All spirits blessed by birth will have ,		37a-b
Tad R. Callister	God's temporary physical manifestation?	Nov 2009	35e-f

Revelation
Related Topics: —

N. Eldon Tanner	Comparison to spaceships and communication	Dec 1968	39d-e
David O McKay	Leaders entitled to ,		84b
	Priesthood holders entitled to ,		84d
Bruce R. McConkie	No man can be saved until he receives ,	Dec 1969	84d

Revelation, cont'd
Related Topics: —

Bruce R. McConkie	Can't receive Holy Ghost without receiving , —J. Smith	Dec 1969	85a
	No limit to , you can receive		85a-c
	High callings are not a prerequisite to ,		85d
	Each of us can receive the vision of degrees of glory		85d-e
Paul H. Dunn	Soldier's diary pled for new , to straighten out world		106e-f
Richard L. Evans	Astute observations on the need for ,	June 1970	38a
Harold B. Lee	How to recognize and handle false ,		63f-64e
	Persecution accompanies , - always		64e-65c
Marion G. Romney	Authenticity of Church and Book of Mormon rest upon ,	Dec 1970	51b-d
Richard L. Evans	He has told us more than we have ever lived up to	June 1971	74f
Bruce R. McConkie	Comparisons to TV and radio		77a-e
	If a man could gaze into heaven 5 minutes...		78b
	Must receive , to be on path to salvation		78f
Theodore M. Burton	After First Vision Joseph knew more than anyone	Dec 1971	80b
N. Eldon Tanner	Science seeks warnings from space	Jan 1973	26a
Ezra Taft Benson	Follow present , or drown		58a
Howard W. Hunter	Rock of , solution to confusion		64b
	Needed now —quote by Emerson		64c
	Feast or famine		65f
Gordon B. Hinckley	You may never hear a voice, but ...		93f
Harold B. Lee	Beware of false ,		105c
	Mighty , given today		108f
Mark E. Petersen	Plan of salvation rests upon ,		116c
	Lord has always used ,		116e
	Lord is speaking to you today		118f
Harold B. Lee	His testimony of ,	July 1973	6f
Marion G. Romney	Reveals man's destiny. Other learning can't		14b
A. Theodore Tuttle	Current revelation is best scripture		19a
	Adam's , did not tell Noah how to build ark		19b
	Accept present , or deny past ,		19c
Marion D. Hanks	To finance mission Lord told father to plant onions —story	May 1975	14d-e
Thomas S. Monson	Educator's comments for world's need for ,		17c-d
Joseph Anderson	The vice of theology is the claim that there is no , —Emerson	May 1976	88b
James E. Faust	We need fewer revolutions and more ,	Nov 1976	58b
Henry D. Taylor	Scripture study brings , —Spencer W. Kimball		62d-e
Spencer W. Kimball	Where there is no ear, there is no voice		111d-f
Gordon B. Hinckley	If you accept the , you must accept the revelator	May 1977	64c-d
Spencer W. Kimball	When people are unreachable the Lord does nothing		76f
	No awe-inspiring display. Day to day , to prophets is written		78a-c
Henry D. Taylor	Foundation of Church	May 1978	38b
	8 ways Lord gives ,		38b-f
	Every person has right to receive , for his calling		39b
Marion G. Romney	Voice told him to bear testimony —story		50d-e
J. Richard Clarke	Lord gave vision of Zion, not of mudholes		83e
Spencer W. Kimball	2 , W. Woodruff received as a non-member youth	May 1979	48a-c

Revelation

Boyd K. Packer	Learn to pick , out of interfering static —good stories	Nov 1979	19d-20b
	Comes more as feeling than sound		20c
	How Word of Wisdom affects ,		20c-e
	Can receive , instantly - especially to help others		20e
	How to identify false ,		20f-21b
	Same inspiration he listened to as a boy - clearer now		21d
	Pilots used to follow radio beam —story		21e-f
James E. Faust	Ridiculous reasons why God has become silent	May 1980	13b-c
	Church could not live 24 hours without , —Woodruff		14f
Howard W. Hunter	Explanation of Rev. 22:18-19	May 1981	64b-65f
Marion G. Romney	He can only guide our footsteps when we move our feet		91b
Thomas S. Monson	Directed to missionary's dying mother at conference —story	May 1982	61d-f
Boyd K. Packer	We are determined to reach the headwaters of ,	Nov 1982	53c-d
Mark E. Petersen	Good discussion of angels , and restoration	Nov 1983	29b-31f
James E. Faust	If First Vision a fraud, would have said Father taught him	May 1984	68c
Ezra Taft Benson	It takes , to perceive ,	Nov 1985	36a
Wm. Grant Bangerter	Many people don't want to hear , —story	Nov 1988	80f-81a
Dallin H. Oaks	Hearing , through a chorus of voices	May 1989	27d-29a
James E. Faust	Continuous Revelation —entire talk	Nov 1989	8d-11b
	Major revelations in 1900s		9d-e
	Adam's , did not instruct Noah to build Ark		9f
	Scriptures alone can't lead us to Celestial Kingdom		10b
	People can't blindly follow Church leaders		11a
Boyd K. Packer	All , does not come from God		14f
	Keep special experiences to yourself		15b-e
Boyd K. Packer	Comes in peaceful settings	Nov 1991	21f-22a
	Cannot survive without personal ,		23a
Graham W. Doxey	Comes as deep impressions - even to prophets		25b-e
David B. Haight	How , is received - , is drawn to us	May 1992	16c-d
	Benson's promise for increased ,		16d
Neal A. Maxwell	Joseph's face was clear when receiving ,		39a
Glenn L. Pace	Need to increase capacity to receive ,	Nov 1992	11e
Marion D. Hanks	The great I Am, not the great He Was		63e-f
Aileen H. Clyde	Don't need , in every choice		88f-89a
Russell M. Nelson	We don't receive , for those higher than us	May 1993	39b-f
Boyd K. Packer	Prayer is essential to ,	Nov 1994	59f
	Comes through feelings from Holy Ghost		60b-f
	For whom may you receive , ?		61d-f
Joe J. Christensen	Want a , ? Ask wife how to be a better husband	May 1995	64e
Joseph B. Wirthlin	, super highway opens universe to view	Nov 1995	75b-78b
James E. Faust	Can't receive , for those higher in authority	May 1996	6d-7a
	Can't receive , for those higher in authority		7c-d
Boyd K. Packer	, promised to those who keep Word of Wisdom		19a
	Will be warned of dangers if live Word of Wisdom		19d-f
L. Aldin Porter	Most important knowledge comes through ,	Nov 1996	11a

Revelation

M. Russell Ballard	Joseph's appearance as he received ,	May 1998	31c-e
	Section 76 took 1 1/2 hours to receive		32a-b
Neal A. Maxwell	Only acceptance of , can save world or people	Nov 1998	62f
Merrill C. Oaks	Church vaults contain day-to-day ,		82d-e
	What is current today may not be tomorrow		82f-83b
Sheri L. Dew	Lord speaks to us constantly		95d
Carol B. Thomas	, may be expected in temple —Widtsoe	May 1999	13d
Boyd K. Packer	The spirit of revelation —entire talk	Nov 1999	23b-25b
Thomas S. Monson	Seek for and enjoy the , of God —G.Q. Cannon		49b-d
James E. Faust	Flexible gristle replaced hip socket —story	May 2000	19a-d
Russell M. Nelson	, of all things in latter days		85e-f
James E. Faust	Idea to invent TV came while plowing —story	Nov 2001	48f-49a
Thomas S. Monson	, for talk came after 1:00 a.m. prayer —story		49d-50b
Russell M. Nelson	, to do surgical procedure came through prayer —story	May 2003	7f-8f
L. Tom Perry	The difference between , and inspiration	Nov 2003	85e-f
	Can't receive , for those higher in authority		85f-86c
	We can't tell God what to do		88d
Neal A. Maxwell	"Stunners" among the revelations		100b-101a
Jeffrey R. Holland	Unreasonable that God wouldn't speak —Jonathon Edwards	Nov 2004	8b
	Principle of , is lost —Ralph Waldo Emerson		8b-d
	Religion is a mockery without , —John Taylor		8d-e
Thomas S. Monson	Every man should seek for ,		56f
Boyd K. Packer	, to Church in recent years	Nov 2005	73a-c
Thomas S. Monson	How does Church differ from others? —McKay	May 2006	54f
Boyd K. Packer	The Word of Wisdom is a key to ,	Nov 2006	87a
Don R. Clarke	Lord told man to help blind friend —story		97b-98b
Jay E. Jensen	Reverence and , are twins	May 2007	12b-d
Boyd K. Packer	You receive , that belongs to that office	Nov 2007	9a-b
Keith K. Hilbig	Temple is a marvelous environment to seek ,		39d-e
Robert D. Hales	Experiences in calling 4 stake presidents —story		87a-88b
	How to receive ,		88f
	6 common types of , that we receive		88f
	David O. McKay's delayed answer to prayer		88f-89a
Richard G. Scott	God's creations revealed through ,		91e-92c
Henry B. Eyring	He is eye witness to President Monson's revelations	May 2008	23d-24a
Thomas S. Monson	All can receive inspiration		88a-c
Jeffrey R. Holland	Continuing , does not make LDS unchristian		91d-e
	Answer to problem posed by Rev. 22:18		91e-f
	Bible not compiled until after 1000 A.D.		91f-92a
	Moses' words not sufficient for all time		92b-c
	Lies at very heart of the Church		93b-f
Jeffrey R. Holland	The ministry of angels —entire talk	Nov 2008	29b-31f
David A. Bednar	Definition and relation of prayer and ,		41b-d
	Revelation is conveyed through Holy Ghost		41d
James J. Hamula	Prayer is a precondition to ,		52e

Revelation

William D. Oswald	Pondering invites personal ,	Nov 2008	97f
Thomas S. Monson	The very lifeblood of the Church is continuous ,		107d
Julie B. Beck	We can't succeed without personal ,		110a-b
	Requires serious mental effort on our part —Maxwell		110b
Allan F. Packer	Notice the first intimation of , —J. Smith quote	May 2009	18b-d
Quentin L. Cook	No more , ? - False teachings are a stumbling block		36a-c
Richard G. Scott	Holy Ghost becomes a principle of , —J. Smith	Nov 2009	6e
Tad R. Callister	Is there a need for current , ? Three questions		35f-36a
	Visions and angels in former times too		36f-37b
Russell M. Nelson	No hardware, software or monthly service fees		81d-e
	Some , is for unique circumstances		82b
	Personal , honed to spiritual discernment		82f-83a
	Preceded by faith, virtue, patience, etc.		83b
	Never contradicts doctrine		83b-d
	May be incremental		83d-f
	Every member may merit ,		84a
Julie B. Beck	Receiving , - Most important skill	May 2010	11b
	How to receive ,		10f-11e
D. Todd Christofferson	Scriptures are , and bring more ,		35c
David A. Bednar	Spiritual early warning system		40c-41c
Henry B. Eyring	Diligence in priesthood brings , —B. Young		60a-b
Francisco J. Viñas	Impart knowledge and facilitate ,		108a

Robert L. Simpson	The need for ushers, greeters and organists	Nov 1976	100d-e
Howard W. Hunter	In moral decline , is the first virtue to go	Nov 1977	52f
	Reverence is the atmosphere of heaven		53f
	Entire talk		52b-54b
Gordon B. Hinckley	Instructions for , in sacrament meetings	May 1987	45b-46e
Thomas S. Monson	Interview ended Primary , problem —story	Nov 1987	69b-f
M. Russell Ballard	Definition of ,	May 1988	57e-f
Boyd K. Packer	Spiritual communications may be lost if no spirit of ,	Nov 1988	20d-21b
Russell M. Nelson	, for Lord, earth, leaders, others, law, life and chapels	May 1990	17a
L. Tom Perry	, is an attitude —entire talk	Nov 1990	70d-72f
	Two area conferences contrasted		71b-e
Boyd K. Packer	We are drifting	Nov 1991	22a
	World grows increasingly noisy		22a
	Lack of , disrupts spiritual channels		22b-c
	Fathers should take toddlers out		22c-d
	How music affects ,		22d-f
	Troubles will decrease with more ,		23a-b
M. Russell Ballard	The bishop was the , problem —story	May 1994	25d-f
Boyd K. Packer	, is essential to revelation - prelude music	Nov 1994	61b-c
Harold G. Hillam	Have respect for your elders, your body and sacred things	May 2000	10d-f
L. Lionel Kendrick	Discussion of , —excellent	May 2001	78c-f

Reverence, cont'd

Rome

Sabbath

James E. Faust	A sure protection against plagues of day	Nov 1991	35c
	A perpetual covenant forever		35c
Rex D. Pinegar	What would Jesus want you to do? - , campout —story		41a-b
Joseph B. Wirthlin	Shop on , and then ask Lord to bless food?	Nov 1992	35b-c
H. David Burton	Team declined to play on , —story	Nov 1995	44c-e
Lynn A. Mickelsen	Don't need rules for , when purpose understood		79d
Earl C. Tingey	The , day and Sunday shopping —excellent	May 1996	10b-12b
Thomas S. Monson	Father walked rather than gas up on , —story	Nov 1997	18b-e
Gordon B. Hinckley	We are like mainstream America in , observance		69b
H. David Burton	President Smith used stores that kept , holy —story	Nov 1998	9d-10a
Thomas S. Monson	Father walked rather than gas up on , —story	Nov 1999	19b-e
H. Aldridge Gillespie	Abstinence from work is insufficient	Nov 2000	79e
	If you have doubts about , just observe it		79f
	, divides righteous from wicked —McConkie		80b
	Blessings of , —Lev. 26:2-12		80b
Richard G. Scott	Young man would not compete on , —story	May 2001	8c-f
L. Tom Perry	Appropriate activities for the ,	May 2003	42e
L. Tom Perry	The , at a busy resort	May 2006	42a-b

Sacrament
Related Topics: —

A. Theodore Tuttle	Replaces animal sacrifice	June 1971	69d-e
Gordon B. Hinckley	Administer , with clean hands	Jan 1973	92b
Henry D. Taylor	Points to remember in , prayers	July 1973	47b
Vaughn J. Featherstone	Should be prepared before meeting begins	May 1975	68c
Spencer W. Kimball	When the Apostles attend to the ,		79e-f
Marion G. Romney	Renew baptismal covenant weekly	Nov 1975	73d-e
Angel Abrea	Can't maintain Spirit without partaking of ,	Nov 1981	24a-c
Boyd K. Packer	, replaced sacrifice. Both point to Christ.		31a-b
Mark E. Petersen	Can we take , if we have ill feelings?	Nov 1982	18a
Gordon B. Hinckley	, meetings must be spiritual		47b-f
David B. Haight	The Sacrament —whole talk	May 1983	12b-14f
J. Thomas Fyans	D.O. McKay failed first time he said , prayer —story	May 1984	38e
L. Tom Perry	We renew baptismal covenants during ,	Nov 1984	19c-d
Thomas S. Monson	Day saved by priest who memorized the , prayers —story		42c-f
Gordon B. Hinckley	Deportment of Aaronic Priesthood during ,	May 1987	46a-c
Boyd K. Packer	The Passover is commemorated as the ,	May 1988	72b
John H. Groberg	The importance of the ,	May 1989	38b-40a
	If we desire to improve, we're worthy to partake		38e-f
David B. Haight	Jesus' sacrifice and significance of ,	Nov 1989	59e-61b
Dallin H. Oaks	Jesus was not mentioned in , meeting	Nov 1990	30a
Boyd K. Packer	, is a covenant		84b
Jack H. Goaslind	, meeting depends on your attitude —story	May 1991	46d-f
James E. Faust	Purposes of , meeting	May 1992	7f-8b
Gordon B. Hinckley	We covenant anew each time we take ,	May 1994	53c
Henry B. Eyring	Blessings that come from always remembering Him	May 1995	25b-26b

Sacrament, cont'd
Related Topics: —

Jeffrey R. Holland	The , is the purpose of our most holy meeting	Nov 1995	67b-69f
	White shirts and worthy lives in ,		68c
Boyd K. Packer	The ordinance we shall keep forever	May 1996	19c-d
L. Tom Perry	Replaced law of sacrifice —J.F. Smith		54b-c
	The obligations we assume when taking ,		54e-59a
Dallin H. Oaks	Renews covenants and cleanses from sin	Nov 1996	61c-f
Boyd K. Packer	, renews baptismal covenants	May 1997	10d
Dallin H. Oaks	Should be preceded by repentance	Nov 1998	37f-38a
	Renews the cleansing effect of our baptism		38a-f
	Principle of non-distraction during ,		39c-40b
Dallin H. Oaks	Renews the cleansing effect of baptism	May 2002	34a-d
D. B. Neuenschwander	Spiritual renewal at , won't exceed preparation and desire	May 2003	72d-e
Thomas S. Monson	Administering , to 5000 scouts	Nov 2005	56d-e
L. Tom Perry	Administering , in glass cups	May 2006	39b-f
	A sacred moment in a holy place		39f
	We renew all covenants when taking ,		41b
	Music used to be played during ,		41d
	Lifts loads. Brings comfort		41d-e
	Administering , at a busy resort		42a-b
James E. Faust	Reverence of older men when passing ,		50d-51a
Thomas S. Monson	Handicapped priest blessed , —story	May 2006	56f-57f
Gordon B. Hinckley	Most important item in our meetings	May 2007	117d-f
Christoffel Golden Jr.	Most holy of all meetings —J.F. Smith	Nov 2007	79d-80a
Dallin H. Oaks	The most sacred and important meeting	Nov 2008	17f
	Be seated well before meeting begins		18b-d
	How to dress for , meeting		18f
	Not a time to visit or text message		18f-19a
	All should join in singing		19a-b
	A solemn time. Not a time for amusement		19b
	, replaced blood sacrifices of Mosaic law		19d-f
	Administrators must be worthy and well-groomed		19f-20d
	Deacons should wear white shirts		20d-e
	Administered only when authorized by holder of keys		20e-f
Jay E. Jensen	People take , hoping to hear "Your sins are forgiven"		48b-e
	Appearance of those administering , must not distract		48e-49a
Boyd K. Packer	Is a renewing of the covenant of baptism	May 2009	51a-b
David A. Bednar	Points toward temple		97e-98e
Dale G. Renlund	Zeal waned when not taking , —story	Nov 2009	98e-99d
David L. Beck	An experience taking , to a sick man —story	May 2010	55a-b
Henry B. Eyring	Administering , - Same job given Apostles		61a-d
Quentin L. Cook	Most sacred and holy of all meetings		84c-d

Sacrifice
Related Topics: —

Joseph F. Smith	Fate of Jesus' disciples	Dec 1969	37c
Thomas S. Monson	Class gave party fund to needy family —story	June 1970	91d-f

John H. Vandenberg	We love that for which we , —Mothers and Christ	June 1971	63b
Spencer W. Kimball	Missionary gave blood to stay on mission —story	Dec 1971	39a-d
Hartman Rector, Jr.	Excerpts from sixth lecture on faith		64f-65c
Ezra Taft Benson	Appeasement - the , of principle	July 1973	38f
Gordon B. Hinckley	Sacrifice attending conversion of an Asian		48b
	Only churches requiring , are growing		48f
J. Thomas Fyans	, of Mexican saints to get to conference —stories	Nov 1974	64a-c
Bruce R. McConkie	Be ready and able to , anything — Joseph Smith	May 1975	50d
Hartman Rector, Jr.	Through , we know we please God —Joseph Smith		56b
Victor L. Brown	Youth will be converted only as they ,	Nov 1975	66b-68f
Ezra Taft Benson	2 statements from Lectures on Faith	May 1979	32b&d
	Great blessings are preceded by great , —Lee		34e
Adney Y. Komatsu	New stake president made , in employment —story	Nov 1979	69a-c
LeGrand Richards	, some General Authorities made to accept calling —story		76c-77a
	, made by Tabernacle Choir and Regional Representatives		77c-d
James E. Faust	When you give, your circumstances improve		91e
Thomas S. Monson	Letter from A. Lincoln to mother who lost 5 sons	Nov 1981	16d-e
Gordon B. Hinckley	3 boys earned place in Celestial Kingdom by one , —story		42d-f
Dallin H. Oaks	Forced , is a tax rather than an offering	Nov 1984	14d
Russell M. Nelson	His wife supported him and gave her blood —story		31b-c
	No true worship without ,		32f
Thomas S. Monson	Mission call came the day after marriage		41e
Gordon B. Hinckley	The , of men called as mission presidents	Nov 1985	83f-84f
	Living commandments is hardly a ,		85b-f
Glenn L. Pace	A religion must require , of all things or can't save —J. Smith	May 1986	25b
L. Tom Perry	Cannot give to the Church and be any poorer —Romney		32d-e
L. Tom Perry	Kimball and Young leaving on mission —story	May 1987	34f-35c
Gordon B. Hinckley	H.C. Kimball left family destitute to serve mission		53b-e
M. Russell Ballard	A religion must require the , of all things —Joseph Smith	Nov 1987	78e
Thomas S. Monson	3 young men carried pioneers across river —story	May 1990	46f-47a
	Man gave street cleaner his coat —story		47a-b
	Anonymous donation sent family to temple —story		47b-48a
	Samaritans bought room and food —story		48a-e
Gordon B. Hinckley	Brigham's call to rescue handcart companies —Unthank story	Nov 1991	52d-59b
M. Russell Ballard	Ward members raised $30,000 —story	May 1992	75f-76e
Neal A. Maxwell	Some are reluctant to give their all	Nov 1992	66d
James E. Faust	The , of handcart pioneers —entire talk		84b-86b
David B. Haight	Because of , family would never lack bread —story	Nov 1993	61b-d
Jeffrey R. Holland	Muscular dystrophy sisters and grandmother caregiver —story	Nov 1994	32f-33f
Neal A. Maxwell	We must , the animal within us	May 1995	68f
Gordon B. Hinckley	The , of his grandfather —story		69f-70b
Harold G. Hillam	"I have never slept in a sleeping bag" —story	Nov 1995	41b-c
Thomas S. Monson	Alaskan flight diverted to save boy —story	May 1996	51b-d
Bruce C. Hafen	A test no hireling would endure —parent story	Nov 1996	27d-f
Russell M. Nelson	Animal , pointed toward Atonement		34f-35a

Sacrifice

Aileen H. Clyde	Mary F. Smith letter recounting her trials	Nov 1996	87e-88c
	Attending meeting in pouring rain —story		88f-89b
Thomas S. Monson	A donated child's walker —story	Nov 1997	19c-20a
Neal A. Maxwell	Do we , and wait around for a receipt?		23b
James E. Faust	, for temples was not a , but a joy —story	Nov 1998	59f-60b
	, provides extra defense against evils		60c-e
Stephen A. West	Woman gave coins and slice of bread —story	May 1999	28e-f
Robert J. Whetten	7-year-old girl gave her shoes —story		30f-31a
James E. Faust	Man left comforts to save handcart people —story		47b-f
Jeffrey R. Holland	Money saved for house addition donated —story	May 2000	76b-f
	22-mile walk on wooden leg —story		76f-77a
L. Tom Perry	Converts gave up ship's passage —story	Nov 2000	61e-62b
Carol B. Thomas	"If that girl comes home, the sheep are yours" —story	May 2001	63d-e
	Teach your child to deny himself		63f
	Not a , when you get more than you give —Hinckley		64f
Robert K. Dellenbach	, through tithing, fasting, and family history	Nov 2002	33b-e
	, of Joseph Smith		33f-34e
	, of Jesus		34e-35e
Jeffrey R. Holland	His , compared to earlier missionaries'		36b-d
	The , of early missionaries and their families		36d-37a
	Bishop's , in answering phone —great story		37a-38d
	His thanks to all who , in their callings		38d-f
Thomas S. Monson	Violin sold to finance mission —story	May 2003	19e-20c
D. B. Neuenschwander	, means "to make sacred"		71e-f
Quentin L. Cook	, is the crowning test of the gospel	Nov 2003	96c-d
Jeffrey R. Holland	, made by 3 missionaries to go —stories	May 2004	30d-e
	, of Chile Saints to go to temple		31b-d
L. Tom Perry	Young and Kimball leaving on mission —story	Nov 2004	23f-24c
Elaine S. Dalton	We did this for you - Two way exchange		89b-91e
Thomas S. Monson	, of his pioneer ancestors —story	May 2005	21b-22b
Lynn G. Robbins	Tithing and , —excellent talk		34b-36b
Dieter F. Uchtdorf	Hasn't seen family since his calling		36d-e
Jeffrey R. Holland	Kimball blessing family before mission —story		44e-45b
C. Scott Grow	, of members and Mexico's amazing growth	Nov 2005	33b-e
James E. Faust	Two martyrs in early Mexico —story	Nov 2006	21f-22b
	Martyrdom of Edward Partridge —story		22b-d
D. Todd Christofferson	A year without lunch to buy an Ironrite —story		46b-d
Gordon B. Hinckley	, made by parents for child —poem		116e-f
Neil L. Andersen	Examples of ,	May 2007	75b-f
Enrique R. Falabella	15-day journey to temple —story	Nov 2007	14b-e
Dieter F. Uchtdorf	His ancestors didn't cross plains, but legacy is his	May 2008	70b-d
D. Todd Christofferson	Man cut his table in half —story	Nov 2008	39f-40d
Boyd K. Packer	Won't hurt to want something and not have it	May 2009	52b-d
Dallin H. Oaks	Unique unselfish , made by Latter-day Saints		93b-94b
	Unique cooperative , of Latter-day Saints		94b-d

Sacrifice

Dallin H. Oaks	A time when , is out of fashion	May 2009	95c-96f
D. Todd Christofferson	Far superior to self serving interests	Nov 2009	107b
Gregory A. Schwitzer	Good decisions help to learn about ,	May 2010	104f

Salvation
Related Topics: Celestial Kingdom, Eternal Life, Exaltation, Heaven

Bruce R. McConkie	Salvation defined	Dec 1968	103e-f
Hugh B. Brown	Folly of predestination and damnation of unbaptized infants	June 1969	32f-33a
	Heaven or hell vs. degrees of glory doctrine		33a-e
	, is an eternal quest for knowledge		34c
Bruce R. McConkie	Full , depends on continuation of family unit	June 1970	44e
Harold B. Lee	Saved by grace after all we can do	Dec 1970	29e-f
Theodore M. Burton	Other churches' view of ,	July 1972	78a
Marion G. Romney	Meaning of the word "saved"	Nov 1974	38c
Ezra Taft Benson	Definition of , by Joseph Smith		67e
Marion G. Romney	Difference between , and eternal life	May 1975	84f-85a
William R. Bradford	Laws must be known and applied —good example	Nov 1977	64e-f
Jack H. Goaslind, Jr.	Working for , of others is essential to our own	Nov 1983	33f-34a
Dallin H. Oaks	The various meanings of ,	May 1998	55b-57f
Dallin H. Oaks	Not for a chosen few. Gospel is for all	May 2006	77c-78b
Russell M. Nelson	Meaning of salvation	May 2008	8a-b
	Salvation is an individual matter		8c-d
	An individual matter - Exaltation a family matter		10d
Russell M. Nelson	, is an individual matter - Exaltation is not	Nov 2008	92d
Quentin L. Cook	Convert wanted a more liberal , for man —story	May 2009	36c-e
	False teaching that Atonement won't bring , to most		36f-37a
Tad R. Callister	Can be found only in one place	Nov 2009	37f

Satan
Related Topics: Opposition

Harold B. Lee	Ever present in our midst with his hordes	Dec 1968	71d
Thomas S. Monson	His lures are like octopus traps		82d-f
David O. McKay	, will tempt you in your weakest point	June 1969	28c-d
	, has power today that he hasn't had before		31c
Gordon B. Hinckley	Opposition against Church will intensify	June 1970	40a
Sterling W. Sill	, has no power over us except as we give it to him		45d
Harold B. Lee	How to recognize and handle revelations from ,		63f-64e
	How to make the power of , begin to cease		64e
Hartman Rector, Jr.	, one of 3 independent principles —Joseph Smith		102f
Eldred G. Smith	How Satan is to be bound		104b-d
	2 scriptural examples where , was bound		104e-f
Marion G. Romney	Satan lives	June 1971	35b
	Makes an attack at opening of every dispensation		36c-d
	His program will gain in tempo as end nears		36f
Bernard P. Brockbank	We owe , nothing yet many pay him tribute		85c
Eldred G. Smith	We have the power to resist ,	Dec 1971	45d-e
	We can't lick , alone		46b

Satan, cont'd
Related Topics: Opposition

Ezra Taft Benson	Working to destroy a generation of youth	Dec 1971	53a-b
Delbert L. Stapley	Non-member - "I hope you can keep , out of your Church"		94b
	There is only one way for , to be bound		94f
Harold B. Lee	Made boy prove his convictions —story	July 1972	102a
A. Theodore Tuttle	Priesthood is the only power that can withstand ,		120b
Bernard P. Brockbank	Don't permit , to come into your home		123a
LeGrand Richards	Mixes truth with error	Jan 1973	110a
Harold B. Lee	Has power over his dominion now	July 1973	4b
David B. Haight	People do not understand power of ,		55a
	The "very elect" includes our children		56b
	Satan takes charge of lives —story		56c
Harold B. Lee	His hosts now among us	Jan 1974	4f
	If we lose self respect , has gained a victory		5f
Elray L. Christiansen	Satan works carefully without jerks		35e
Bernard P. Brockbank	, now has power over his dominion —Lee	May 1974	113e-f
Elray L. Christiansen	, had knowledge but not intelligence	Nov 1974	22f
	Satan lives		23c-e
	Keep , out by keeping Holy Ghost in		24e
Delbert L. Stapley	There are but 2 parties on the earth —Brigham Young	May 1975	21d-e
Ezra Taft Benson	, mindful of youth too	Nov 1977	30d-e
Marvin J. Ashton	, has no power over us unless we let him in	May 1978	9d
Spencer W. Kimball	Would pay no attention to us if this were not the Lord's work	May 1981	79a
Charles Didier	A well defined line between Lord's territory and Satan's	Nov 1981	52f
Carlos E. Asay	1 devil for a wicked city but 7 for a righteous man —story		67b-c
Boyd K. Packer	Confuses the careless with false doctrine	Nov 1984	66d
David B. Haight	Step to his side and lose power to reason		73b
James E. Faust	Avoid witchcraft, sorcery, voodooism, black magic	Nov 1987	33e-f
	, sought to divert Elder Faust from his mission		34a
	Powers oppose us the nearer we approach the Lord —Smith		35e
	Cannot know our thoughts unless spoken		35e
	We have more power over , than we realize		35e-f
Ezra Taft Benson	We are meeting , daily		85d-e
Ezra Taft Benson	God wants us to be like Him - Satan likewise	May 1988	6a-b
Boyd K. Packer	, cannot destroy us without our consent		71b-c
James E. Faust	, carefully leads us - Boiling frog story	May 1989	32b-e
Richard G. Scott	If we hide sins, Satan will reveal them		37a-b
Boyd K. Packer	Don't toy with , worship		54f
Michaelene P. Grassli	How , works on us		92e-93a
M. Russell Ballard	Focuses us on present - a dirty fighter	Nov 1990	36a-b
Dallin H. Oaks	Misery encouraged by , comes from losses	Nov 1991	73d-e
Francis M. Gibbons	, cannot hear secret prayer		78d-79a
	Can convey thoughts but doesn't know if they lodge		79b-e
	Patriarch dared not reveal Grant would be president —story		79b-e
Spencer J. Condie	His two tools - Pride and discouragement	Nov 1993	15f-16d
Boyd K. Packer	Purpose is to corrupt most pure experiences		21c

Satan

Dallin H. Oaks	Directs best efforts at most important aspects of God's plan	Nov 1993	72e-f
Boyd K. Packer	Ultimate purpose of , is to disrupt family	May 1994	19e-f
Richard G. Scott	Can't please God without upsetting ,	Nov 1994	37d
Dallin H. Oaks	His whole study is to destroy	Nov 1995	26f-27c
Joseph B. Wirthlin	Many try to serve the Lord without offending the devil	May 1997	16a
Richard B. Wirthlin	, confuses location of joy	Nov 1997	10a
Vaughn J. Featherstone	Giving up and hoping the wolf will have enough	Nov 1999	13d
Richard C. Edgley	Whose man is the boy who begins smoking?		42e
Virginia U. Jensen	Ultimate purpose is to destroy family —Packer		95e
Boyd K. Packer	Uses same channels of mind and heart as does Holy Ghost	May 2000	9b
James E. Faust	Power of , rises in proportion to rise of Church		17d
	Spirit of darkness prevails now as in Jesus' day		17e
	Employs great discoveries to his advantage		17e-f
James E. Faust	Unable to reason if you cross to devil's side	Nov 2000	45a-d
Richard G. Scott	Distraction - good things crowd out essentials	May 2001	7d-f
Richard G. Scott	What , cannot do	Nov 2001	88d-e
James E. Faust	His problem was selfishness	Nov 2002	19d-e
James E. Faust	The arch imitator, deceiver, counterfeiter	May 2003	51e-52a
	More subtle, open, blatant and sophisticated		52d-e
M. Russell Ballard	Family is the main target of ,	Nov 2003	18b-d
Boyd K. Packer	Tries to capture our thoughts		25c-26a
L. Tom Perry	Working overtime	May 2004	69b-c
Dallin H. Oaks	Ways , uses to deceive us	Nov 2004	43f-45b
Elaine S. Dalton	Tries to discourage, distract and disqualify		90d
Joseph B. Wirthlin	No one is immune from influence of ,		102f-103a
	H.J. Grant's prayer in old age		102f-103a
Neil L. Andersen	Beware of evil behind smiling eyes —story	May 2005	46b-e
Robert D. Hales	Can't have happiness unless we sin	May 2006	6b-c
	Cannot make us do anything		6d
Boyd K. Packer	, harvests his crop and binds them down		27f
Marcus B. Nash	Works to set the hook —entire talk	Nov 2006	49b-50f
John B. Dickson	Can't tempt with things you never touched	May 2007	14e-f
Boyd K. Packer	Uses his music to cover still, small voice		28b
James E. Faust	Can't make us do anything we don't choose		55a
Charles W. Dahlquist, II	Can't come on Lord's side of line —G.A. Smith		96e
James E. Faust	His tool - Find ways to control us	Nov 2007	124a
Richard G. Scott	Leads into blind alleys where solutions can't be found	May 2008	41b-c
Elaine S. Dalton	Directs all attacks to body		117b
Henry B. Eyring	You are a target		125c-e
James J. Hamula	Focus of his war is you	Nov 2008	51b
	How , was overcome in war in heaven		51f-52d
Robert D. Hales	Knows us extremely well	May 2009	7f
Boyd K. Packer	Tempts to do, say and think destructive things		51a
	Beings with bodies have power over those who don't		51a
Henry B. Eyring	The war against , intensifies		63b

Satan

Satan, cont'd
Related Topics: Opposition

Thomas S. Monson	Neglecting study and prayer opens door to ,	May 2009	67f-68a
Dallin H. Oaks	Desires to sift us as wheat or make us common		94e-f
	Taught that we could be our own god - Selfish		95a-b
Richard G. Scott	Extremely good at blocking spiritual communication	Nov 2009	8f
Thomas S. Monson	To be angry is to yield to ,		67f-68a
D. Todd Christofferson	Is a vigorous multimedia advocate of selfishness		107d
Boyd K. Packer	Attacks home not Church meetings	May 2010	9f
L. Tom Perry	More subtle and brazen than ever		31f
Elaine S. Dalton	Dismays, discourages, distracts, delays, disqualifies		121b

Scouting
Related Topics: Aaronic Priesthood, Youth

Vaughn J. Featherstone	21 Eagle Scouts in one year —story	Nov 1976	103d-f
Spencer W. Kimball	Award to Kimball. Affirmation of Church's commitment to ,	May 1977	35a-36e
Gordon B. Hinckley	Church was first , partner - 1913	Nov 1982	20d-e
	Boy's life was spared because he was Scout —story		21d-f
Vaughn J. Featherstone	1150 committed to missions including one Catholic —story	Nov 1983	37a
	How , developed his leadership qualities —story		37e-39a
Ezra Taft Benson	All 24 of his scouts married in temple -story	Nov 1984	46d-47f
Marvin J. Ashton	Teaches tenacity	May 1987	66a
Vaughn J. Featherstone	Life is a process of tying knots that will hold	Nov 1987	28f-29a
Thomas S. Monson	Reaffirmation of Church support for ,	Nov 1991	47a-c
BSA Executives	Bronze Wolf award given to President Monson	Nov 1993	46b-47b
Thomas S. Monson	Reaffirmation of Church's support of ,		47e
	Scout master bailed out —story		47f
	Norman Rockwell paintings of ,		47f-48b
	Cub buried in uniform with awards —story		50b-e
Robert D. Hales	Earn Duty to God and Eagle awards	Nov 2001	38d-39a
	What Duty to God award entails		39b-d
Cecil O. Samuelson Jr.	Earn Duty to God and Eagle awards		41d-43b
James E. Faust	Opportunities open because of Eagle award		49a
Thomas S. Monson	Passing sacrament to 5000 scouts	Nov 2005	56d-e
Robert D. Hales	Most meaningful activities are talks with scouts	May 2010	95d-e

Scriptures
Related Topics: See names of individual books

Alvin R. Dyer	Location of Tower of Babel	Dec 1968	43a
Sterling W. Sill	Never becomes outdated - Bible		104d
N. Eldon Tanner	The central theme of all the , is ..	June 1969	34d
A. Theodore Tuttle	The results when a family read , 15 min. each day	Dec 1969	108a
Harold B. Lee	I accept the rest on faith —A. Lincoln	June 1971	8a
Henry D. Taylor	We must study , daily —Lee		109c-e
Vaughn J. Featherstone	Observations on , and prophets —whole talk	Jan 1973	94a
Marion G. Romney	We to be judged by modern ,		97f
A. Theodore Tuttle	Greatest , is present	July 1973	19a
	Accept present , or deny past		19c
LeGrand Richards	Teaching non members from own Bibles —story		79a

Author	Description	Date	Page
LeGrand Richards	Two passages other churches can't explain —story	July 1973	79c
Marion G. Romney	List of commandments to search the ,		90c
Spencer W. Kimball	Scriptures are all rewards and promises	Jan 1974	17d
L. Tom Perry	One of the bare essentials of life		51b
Sterling W. Sill	Scriptures don't work unless we do		61d
Spencer W. Kimball	Kimball set a goal at age 14 to read Bible and did	May 1974	88a-b
Boyd K. Packer	Composed of revelations and the history surrounding them		93d
S. Dilworth Young	Why there are errors in the Bible	Nov 1974	91e-f
John H. Vandenberg	Those who don't use , will dwindle in unbelief and perish		94c-e
H. Burke Peterson	The blessings of reading , daily as a family	May 1975	53c-54f
J. Thomas Fyans	If spirituality is low, immerse yourself in the , —Kimball		88e
L. Tom Perry	The Bible is this country's foundation	Nov 1975	86d
L. Tom Perry	Suppose the Bible was a nation's only law?	May 1976	64c-e
LeGrand Richards	Explains parts of Isaiah		82e-84b
Joseph Anderson	Vice of theology is claim that Bible is closed book —Emerson		88b
Mark E. Petersen	Less difficult to believe Bible than to disbelieve it —Lincoln	Nov 1976	48d
James E. Faust	Spirituality returns when immersed in scriptures —Kimball		58f-59a
Henry D. Taylor	Any message from God through Holy Ghost is , —McConkie		62d
	Study of , will bring revelation —S.W. Kimball		62d-e
	Testimonies grow thinner unless , are studied daily —Lee		62e
	Official statements by leaders are ,		63a
	Resolution making two additions to Pearl of Great Price		64a-b
	Purest , comes from lips of living prophets		64b
Delbert L. Stapley	He who reads it oftenest will like it best —J. Smith	Nov 1977	19b
Robert E. Wells	Study , to come to know Christ —Benson	Nov 1980	12e
Howard W. Hunter	Discussion of Rev. 22:18-19	May 1981	64b-65f
J. Richard Clarke	He gained his testimony by reading , —story	Nov 1982	13b-e
	President Kimball read Bible at age 14 —story		13e-14e
	Value of reading , to children —story		14e-15a
	The value of the ,		15a-f
Boyd K. Packer	Story of printing of LDS Bible —story		51c-53f
Neal A. Maxwell	The moral memory of mankind	May 1983	10e
Victor L. Brown	Arrogant man could not understand , until humble —story		62a-c
Boyd K. Packer	Learn to use them with diligence		67a-f
Hugh W. Pinnock	Girl kept from leaving Church by studying , —story	Nov 1984	73e-74a
Ezra Taft Benson	Admonitions from prophets to read the ,	May 1986	80f-81f
Neal A. Maxwell	Record of Lost Tribes will make a "Triad of Truth"	Nov 1986	52c-e
L. Aldin Porter	He who reads oftenest will like it best —Joseph Smith	Nov 1987	73f
Hugh W. Pinnock	No substitute for ,	May 1989	12d
James E. Faust	Scriptures without revelation can't exalt	Nov 1989	10b
Boyd K. Packer	New additions and translations of , - amazing	May 1990	36b-37f
Ruth B. Wright	Specific examples of how , strengthen her	Nov 1990	78d-79f
Janette C. Hales	Girl read , with feet in sink	May 1991	84d-e
Robert E. Wells	Family study of , brought peace —story		86f-87b
Jayne B. Malan	Girl likened herself to , —story	Nov 1991	94b-d

Scriptures, cont'd
Related Topics: See names of individual books

Neal A. Maxwell	Joseph Smith gave more pages of , than any other man	May 1992	38c
Merrill J. Bateman	Search , like parents searched for son —story	Nov 1992	27d-f
	Accomplish far more with daily study		27f-28a
Jay E. Jensen	Importance of studying , —Benson and Kimball		80d
	Filled with promises —entire talk		80b-81f
Russell M. Nelson	Ignorance of , cost lives —story of infection		7a-f
L. Lionel Kendrick	Search the , daily —J. Smith and S.W. Kimball	May 1993	14d-f
	Necessity of , and how to use them		13b-15b
L. Tom Perry	What daily study of , did for Peru —story		90b-e
	Recommit to , —E.T. Benson		92e-f
	A promise if , are studied daily		92f
Joe J. Christensen	Read , daily as a family	Nov 1993	12e-13a
Richard G. Scott	Daily study of , a necessity —Benson and Kimball		86d-f
	Testimonies will dim without study of ,		88b
Carlos E. Asay	, are a sextant to keep us on course	May 1996	60e-61c
Henry B. Eyring	Read , aloud as a family		63c-d
Virginia H. Pearce	Study , or you may not stay	Nov 1996	12b-c
Anne G. Wirthlin	Read , to children —G.B. Hinckley	May 1998	11a-b
L. Tom Perry	History of Articles of Faith		23a-d
Russell M. Nelson	The "standards" by which we should live	Nov 2000	17a-b
	How they conducted family , study		18c-d
	, don't have the answer to every question		18f
Boyd K. Packer	Old Bible returned to family —story	Nov 2001	64a-c
Sharon G. Larsen	, are the best washing machine for thoughts	May 2002	93b
D. Todd Christofferson	Few in ancient times had ,	May 2004	13d
W. Rolfe Kerr	The , are our personal Liahona		36b-37f
Clate W. Mask, Jr.	Grandparents' , affected grandkids —story		93f-94b
Julie B. Beck	The worth of and how to study ,		107d-109f
Donald L. Staheli	Immerse self in , —S.W. Kimball	Nov 2004	39c
Thomas S. Monson	President Lee's note to daughter on flyleaf of ,		67f
	J. Reuben Clark Jr.'s favorite ,		68d-e
Gordon B. Hinckley	Bible was composed 4 times systematically	May 2005	81b-82b
Boyd K. Packer	Tyndale's and Wycliffe's contributions	Nov 2005	71b-72a
	Preparation of LDS edition		71b-72f
	Curriculum restructured to center on ,		72f
Robert D. Hales	History of the coming forth of the Bible		89b-90e
James E. Faust	Origin of each Standard Work	May 2006	67d-68b
Dallin H. Oaks	More , to come forth		80d-f
Robert D. Hales	God speaks to us when we search the ,	Nov 2006	26f-27a
James E. Faust	Reading , but not living them —story		53e-54a
Boyd K. Packer	Pearl of Great Price became , in 1880	May 2007	27f
	LDS version of Bible introduced in 1979		28a
M. Russell Ballard	Companionship of Bible and Book of Mormon —good		82b-c
	Explanation of the three testaments		82c-d
	Bible quoted nearly 200 times in general conference		82e-f

Scriptures

M. Russell Ballard	The miracle of the Bible —entire talk	May 2007	80b-82f
Gordon B. Hinckley	What he recommends for reading the ,		116b-d
Jeffrey R. Holland	Why Rev. 22:18 does not prevent more ,	May 2008	91e-f
	Bible not compiled until after A.D. 1000		91f-92a
	Revelations to Moses weren't forever sufficient		92a-c
	Early Christians only had gospel of Mark		92d-e
	Bible is a battleground for other churches		92e-f
	, are not the ultimate source of knowledge		92f-93a
Henry B. Eyring	A , to put on your mirror	Nov 2008	58b-e
Claudio R. M. Costa	A father's sacred duty to lead in , study	May 2009	56c-e
	In case of fire, 7-year-old wanted , —story		56f
Thomas S. Monson	Prophet's promise if , studied daily		68a-e
Ann M. Dibb	Part of our safety equipment —Bridge story	Nov 2009	79b-81b
Jeffrey R. Holland	Travelers held continually and tenaciously to ,		88c-e
Quentin L. Cook	As important as food		93a-b
Julie B. Beck	Accumulates over time - Need to study	May 2010	11b
D. Todd Christofferson	Life and work of William Tyndale —story		32a-e
	Great debt owed to writers of ,		32f
	What , do		32f-33b
	We weren't present to see Red Sea part		33b-d
	When no , people forget		33d-f
	Ignorance of , abounds today		33f
	Discredits Korihor's and today's philosophy		33f-34b
	Touchstone for measuring truth		34d
	Moral core of society decays without ,		34d-e
	Central purpose of , is faith		34f-35b
	Written and accompanied by Holy Ghost		35b-c
	Are revelation and bring more		35c
	How much , we have		35c
	Never a people with such quantity		35d-e
Ann M. Dibb	Testimonies grow thinner if no daily study		115f

Second Coming
Related Topics: Jesus, Last Days

LeGrand Richards	One of two greatest events	Dec 1969	52c
Alvin R. Dyer	Turbulence today is preliminary to devastation of ,	June 1970	51c
Harold B. Lee	Signs to precede , . The Peru earthquake	Dec 1971	31b-e
Harold B. Lee	Not far away	July 1973	124e
LeGrand Richards	Explanation of Malachi 3:1-2	May 1974	116d-e
Spencer W. Kimball	Missionary work by members can hasten ,	Nov 1976	4e
Marion G. Romney	Our course will end in a cataclysmic disaster	Nov 1977	14b
Spencer W. Kimball	Time of , depends on our righteousness	May 1978	80f-81a
Robert D. Hales	If you knew what I knew... —Spencer W. Kimball story	Nov 1981	20f-21a
Boyd K. Packer	There is time and to spare to prepare for a long life	May 1989	59b-c
Gordon B. Hinckley	Restoration preparatory for ,	May 1991	91f-92d
Gordon B. Hinckley	Not far distant —sobering	Nov 1992	4d-f

Second Coming, cont'd
Related Topics: Jesus, Last Days

M. Russell Ballard	Statistics on increase in earthquakes	Nov 1992	31b-e
Robert E. Wells	Restoration of Church essential to ,	Nov 1995	66d-f
Jeffrey R. Holland	United Order may not be until ,	May 1996	30e-f
Gordon B. Hinckley	Assembly Hall - "Building for the long term"	May 1997	4c
Gordon B. Hinckley	Announcement to build Assembly Hall	Nov 1997	4b
James E. Faust	Assembly Hall is expression of hope	Nov 1999	59b
Gordon B. Hinckley	Reformation - Restoration and , —good		73b-74f
Gordon B. Hinckley	All-consuming calamity is not here yet	Nov 2001	74a
Dallin H. Oaks	Four indisputable matters for saints	May 2004	7c-d
	Signs preceding ,		7d-f
	Increasing earthquakes and disasters		7f-8a
	The gathering and temples are signs of ,		8a-b
	Parable: Only half of Saints will be ready		8b-d
	Why not repent now and be prepared		8f-9c
	Entire talk		7b-10f
Keith B. McMullin	Our duty is to prepare for ,	Nov 2005	12d
Russell M. Nelson	Moses, Elias and Elijah came on Easter at Passover	Nov 2006	82b
Neil L. Andersen	Jesus' , is sure	May 2010	111f

Self-Mastery
Related Topics: —

Ezra Taft Benson	All evils must be overcome by suppression	June 1969	46e
David O. McKay	Earthly existence a test of ,	Dec 1969	31b
	Equated with spirituality		31c
Alvin R. Dyer	Individual control the key		38b
Loren C. Dunn	Makes a man or woman —McKay		44b
Ezra Taft Benson	Anything impairing , is sin - John Wesley's mother—good	Dec 1970	49f-50a
Gordon B. Hinckley	Conquest of self is only satisfying conquest		72c-d
Richard L. Evans	Habits - "I won't count it this time"		90d
Milton R. Hunter	We're never sorry for the word unspoken	Dec 1971	69d
Delbert L. Stapley	No man is safe unless he is master of himself		96b
Paul H. Dunn	Bob Feller the pitcher and control —story	July 1972	95a
Gordon B. Hinckley	Permissiveness never produced greatness	July 1973	49b
Boyd K. Packer	How to control thoughts	Jan 1974	27e
N. Eldon Tanner	Height of success or failure depends on , —quote	Nov 1974	85f
N. Eldon Tanner	Quotes from Plato, da Vinci, Solomon	May 1975	75a-c
	Largely a matter of will power		75c
Neal A. Maxwell	Not enough policemen for those who won't restrain selves		101d
Neal A. Maxwell	Jesus' grip on himself was our hold on eternity	May 1976	26e
William H. Bennett	Athletes who overcome great handicaps —story	Nov 1976	29e-f
	Letter from athlete who worked and fell short		30c-31b
James E. Faust	Emerson quote. People who need no outside control	May 1982	47c-d
Boyd K. Packer	The best control is self-control	May 1983	66d-e
	Control of tongue, eyes and thoughts most difficult		66f-67a
Ted E. Brewerton	No dominion over self, then no dominion over others		74e-f
Ezra Taft Benson	Patience is the ability to postpone gratification	Nov 1983	42f

Self-Mastery, cont'd

Related Topics: —

Russell M. Nelson	, —entire talk , good	Nov 1985	30b-32f
Dallin H. Oaks	The redemption of Zion is ,		62d
Ezra Taft Benson	Patience is composure under stress	Nov 1986	47d-e
Howard W. Hunter	Suffering teaches , and makes saints of people	Nov 1987	54f
Robert L. Backman	Never give in —W. Churchill quote	Nov 1989	39e-f
Kenneth Johnson	A 100 MPH motorcycle ride - never again —story	May 1990	42c-e
Russell M. Nelson	Self esteem comes from self control	May 1996	15a-b
James E. Faust	Good definition of self mastery	May 2000	44b
	Not restrictive - It is liberating		44e-f
	3 stories of H.J. Grant's , —stories		44f-45c
James E. Faust	No great role in eternity if no , now	May 2007	55b-d
Jeffrey R. Holland	Things to have self control over	May 2010	45d-e

Self-Respect

Related Topics: Love

Harold B. Lee	Excellent thoughts on importance of ,	Jan 1974	2a
	If we have not , Satan has won a victory		5f
Marvin J. Ashton	Personal pride is a great motivator	Nov 1976	84b-c
	, does not mean we have risen above our problems		84f
	Difficult to make a man miserable who has ,		85a
	Avoid self pity, judgment, and indulgence. Have ,		85a
Vaughn J. Featherstone	The desire to be important is a deep human urge		103d-f
Hartman Rector, Jr.	Conceit a strange disease - Makes everyone else sick	May 1979	29e
Marvin J. Ashton	I know I'm somebody cause God don't make no junk	Nov 1981	89b
Paul H. Dunn	Children hear 100,000 negative messages and few positive	May 1987	73b-c
	Thomas Moore's song restored his wife's , —story		74b-e
Marvin J. Ashton	A sad day for God when we lose our ,	Nov 1987	20b
Neal A. Maxwell	Some judge their worth by the size of their audience	May 1989	63c
James E. Faust	Man's basic need: Self-esteem	May 1995	61f
Jeffrey R. Holland	Don't speak or think negatively of self	May 2007	17f-18a
Boyd K. Packer	Don't fall into trap of envying others	May 2009	50e-f

Seminary and Institute

Related Topics: —

Boyd K. Packer	320,000 enrolled - some in humble classes	May 1983	67f-68a
	, holds together the foundation of all learning		67a-f
	Student didn't realize Mom had to get up first —story		68a
Boyd K. Packer	What you learn in ,	May 1990	37f-38c
	Temple marriages double among , graduates		38d
	President Kimball's endorsement of , —humorous		38e
Gordon B. Hinckley	Report on , and encouragement to attend	Nov 1995	54c
L. Tom Perry	History, statistics, and promises about ,	Nov 1997	60b-62b
Henry B. Eyring	Students voted with their feet —story	May 2004	18d-e

Service

Related Topics: Welfare Program

Richard L. Evans	Wise counsel for , we can render	Dec 1968	66e
David O. McKay	Casting bread upon waters —poem		84f

Victor L. Brown	What one serviceman learned about ,	Dec 1968	98d-e
John H. Vandenberg	The Mansion —story by Henry Van Dyke	June 1969	48c-d
Eldred G. Smith	Make me an instrument of thy peace —poem		87c-e
Joseph F. Smith	Interest in others required	Dec 1969	37e
Richard L. Evans	Prove love for Church by ,		74e
David O. McKay	Spirit of gospel comes from ,		88e
	Failure in duty stops progress		88f
Mark E. Petersen	Pretenses accomplish nothing		100d
David O. McKay	Man does not live for self		111c
N. Eldon Tanner	Who is our neighbor - anyone needing help	Dec 1970	32d
Paul H. Dunn	It doesn't matter to me at all —story		37b
John H. Vandenberg	You get no closer to God than you do to fellowmen	June 1971	68e
Thomas S. Monson	Service of 3 boys to 3 widows —story		95f-96c
S. Dilworth Young	, rendered by those not having callings —stories	Dec 1971	66e-67c
Marvin J. Ashton	Show the person that he can get there from here —story		99a-e
	Build yourself by stooping to help someone		101d-e
Thomas S. Monson	Bread cast upon the waters returns —poem		132b
	Treat people as you would like them to be		132d-e
Harold B. Lee	Many are calling for help	July 1972	103c
Eldred G. Smith	Peace comes from ,		117f
A. Theodore Tuttle	It is service that saves		120b
Robert L. Simpson	We're our brother's keeper	July 1973	22d
	We'll be judged by our , rendered		22e
	Joy comes from ,		23b
	Savior gave not money, but other things		23b
	, justifies and sanctifies		23c
	Be a friend through ,		23d
	Judgment to be on , not high callings		23e
Vaughn J. Featherstone	Sugar beet story —story		36c
Robert L. Backman	3 examples of youth , projects		85b
James E. Faust	Turns wounds into muscles for living		87b
Harold B. Lee	Must call ourselves to new ,		98e
Harold B. Lee	Qualities one must have to help others		123c
	If you want to love God...serve the people		124d
Hartman Rector, Jr.	Service is vain unless we love the people	Jan 1974	107d
	Don't care how much you know until know you care		107f
Marvin J. Ashton	The more we lift, the more we're able to lift		104e
	In order to lift, you must step to higher ground		104e
Vaughn J. Featherstone	Stake president wanted the lonely, heartsick and inactive	Nov 1974	30f-31a
O. Leslie Stone	No better exercise than to lift someone up		32b
Marvin J. Ashton	We learn to live abundantly through ,		42c
Sterling W. Sill	We are all the products of ,		61d
Ezra Taft Benson	Overcome gloom by helping someone worse		66b-d
L. Tom Perry	A tribute to his wife —entire talk —story	May 1975	31d-33f
Robert D. Hales	We must give and accept help	Nov 1975	92b-93d

Service

Neal A. Maxwell	I wore out my life in helping…	Nov 1976	12d
Jacob de Jager	Man he went to rescue turned out to be his brother —story		56f-57e
James E. Faust	Selfish people are corrupted by the company they keep		58f
Royden G. Derrick	Happiness is a by-product of ,	May 1977	58f
Thomas S. Monson	One stood at crossroads to help youth decide —poem		72b-d
	Boy gave train cars to another —story		72d-73b
Thomas S. Monson	Help came to a 60-year-old crippled man —story	Nov 1977	9a-b
Boyd K. Packer	We all need "somebody to do for" - a basic need —story	Nov 1978	7f-8a
Vaughn J. Featherstone	Missionaries gave away food - found groceries —story		26d-e
Jacob de Jager	No limit to good you do, if you don't care who gets credit		68f
Thomas S. Monson	Willingness must overflow obligation —good quote	May 1979	35f
Boyd K. Packer	Inspiration comes quicker when needed to help others	Nov 1979	20e
James E. Faust	When you give , your circumstances improve		91e
	Best way to help someone is to lead him into , of others		93a
Boyd K. Packer	How a man felt performing a , —story	May 1980	63b-e
M. Russell Ballard	Helped girl translate to Braille - Church published —story	Nov 1980	23a-b
Robert L. Backman	, increases our capacity and opportunity for ,		41a
Thomas S. Monson	Ward prepared old apartment for German family —story		91a-e
Marion G. Romney	Retaining remission of sins depends on ,		92e-f
	Can't give yourself poor - Give crust to Lord, receive loaf		93c
	Efficacy of prayers depends on our ,		93d-e
Marvin J. Ashton	We learn to love that which we serve	May 1981	24b-d
Thomas S. Monson	Sunday dinner and a house for old Bob —story		47f-48c
F. Burton Howard	Parable of the desert travelers —entire talk		71b-72f
L. Tom Perry	Quorum organized to help farm widow —story	Nov 1981	37e-38c
J. Richard Clarke	Woman walked miles each day to care for infant —story		81c-e
	Woman sat with invalid each Sunday —story		81e-f
Barbara B. Smith	Work becomes , when given gladly		84e
JoAnn Randall	Ideas for , - a family's experiences —entire talk		85c-86f
Nyle Randall	The lessons the family learned from a foster child		87b-88f
Marvin J. Ashton	Woe to him that is alone when he falleth —Eccl.		89c
	The closest helping hand is ours		90b
Marion G. Romney	Welfare: Lord could do it but we need experience		92b-d
	, will hasten advent of the Millennium		93f
Gordon B. Hinckley	Men work harder for duty than for money	Nov 1982	20f-21a
Robert L. Backman	Most inactives will respond to invitation to help someone		40f
Marvin J. Ashton	Happiness is bound up with helpfulness		65a
	Ways to give , without being called		65b-c
Marion G. Romney	The very fiber of Celestial life		93d-e
Thomas S. Monson	Jewels are substitutes for gifts —Emerson	May 1983	56b
	Father and sons shoveled driveways anonymously —story		56c
	Boy secretly maintained missionary's grave —story		56d-e
	Henry Van Dyke's "The Mansion" —story		56e-57f
Jack H. Goaslind, Jr.	Not what we receive but what we give that enriches lives	Nov 1983	32f-33a
	Priesthood conferred as an instrument of ,		33f-34a

Service, cont'd

Marvin J. Ashton	Effectiveness of , is the difference between want and will	Nov 1983	63b
Richard G. Scott	, provides channels of inspiration and power		70e
Dallin H. Oaks	, is a covenant obligation of Church members	Nov 1984	12e
	6 reasons people serve		13b-15b
Russell C. Taylor	, is the rent we pay for our room on earth		23b
	Joy and blessings follow ,		23b-c
H. Burke Peterson	A few forget themselves into immortality	May 1985	66b
	Definition of selfish		66e
Robert L. Backman	Happiness is a by-product of ,	Nov 1985	13d-f
	Examples of , projects rendered by youth —stories		13f-15b
Robert E. Wells	Act of , by missionaries softened a professor —story		28d-f
Hartman Rector, Jr.	Some , we must do whether we want to or not		74e-75b
Glenn L. Pace	The more the , the greater the sanctification	May 1986	23e
	He passed by a chance for , because of assignments —story		23f-24a
	A disposition for , comes from understanding principles		24e
Robert D. Hales	Examples of , families rendered		29f-30b
Thomas S. Monson	You are responsible for those you might have saved—Taylor		37f-38a
	Men work hardest when dedicated to a cause		38b-c
	Where shall I work today? —poem		39d-e
Thomas S. Monson	Ward prepared old apartment for German family —story		64e-65e
George I. Cannon	Hindu proverb about ,	Nov 1986	25f
Howard W. Hunter	A man wrapped up in himself makes a small bundle		35a
Russell M. Nelson	Another General Authority shined his shoes —story		68b-c
Howard W. Hunter	No one should serve more than you —H.J. Grant	May 1987	18d
William R. Bradford	Money raised for trip donated to miss. fund —story	Nov 1987	75b-e
	Selfless service projects or self service projects?		75f
	The evil of praise and popularity		75f-76c
	The only way to become sanctified is through ,		76c-d
	Interesting things vs. important things		76d-f
Glen L. Rudd	Priesthood means ,	May 1988	28b
	As in tennis, if we don't serve well, we don't win		28b
	Priesthood is of no value unless we serve		28b-c
Thomas S. Monson	His father took crippled uncle for drives —story	Nov 1988	71a-b
Joy F. Evans	God meets our needs through others	May 1989	74a
	, during her bedridden pregnancies —story		74a-b
	I needed you, I couldn't find you, I don't need you anymore		74b
	I've come to clean your shoes —story		74d-e
	We've never done enough		75b
Ezra Taft Benson	, elderly can render	Nov 1989	4b-6d
	The key to overcoming aloneness		6c
Thomas S. Monson	Description of dinner by youth for widows —story		46b-d
Dean L. Larsen	We cannot have spirituality without ,		63e-f
Thomas S. Monson	Computer plant built in poverty area —story		69a-c
	The bottom line of living is giving		69c
Jayne B. Malan	The Summer of the Lambs —story		78b-79f

Service

Elaine L. Jack	Girl helped less popular girl - made friend	Nov 1989	88a
Derek A. Cuthbert	10 aspects of , —entire talk	May 1990	13b-14f
Russell M. Nelson	What? I do care!		17f
Joseph B. Wirthlin	Service rendered to single mother of 8 —story		32f-33a
Neal A. Maxwell	We ought to be at the foot of someone else's cross		34b-c
Thomas S. Monson	3 young men carried handcart pioneers across river —story		46f-47a
	Man gave street cleaner his coat —story		47a-b
	Anonymous donation sent family to temple—story		47b-48a
	Samaritans bought room and food —story		48a-e
	Bishop redeemed excommunicated man —story		48f-49b
Thomas S. Monson	Doctors and the Church in 3rd World nations		54b-d
Howard W. Hunter	Yoke: a device linking two together for ,	Nov 1990	18a-b
Thomas S. Monson	Laurels took Christmas to widow —story		99a-f
Boyd K. Packer	Class helped handicapped classmate —story	May 1991	8e
	, to handicapped builds our accounts		9c-e
J. Richard Clarke	Quorum's , to handicapped boy —story		42c-f
	Held woman's hand two hours —story		43a-b
Henry B. Eyring	Win God's heart through kindness to His children		67d
Janette C. Hales	Man's most significant , was performed as a youth —story		84e-f
Rex D. Pinegar	Man helped stranded family —story	Nov 1991	39e-f
Russell M. Nelson	Mormon Tabernacle Choir's European tour		59d-61f
Chieko N. Okazaki	"I'm a little pencil in the hands of God"		89d-f
	Our chance to be His hands		89f
Marion D. Hanks	Must help and give in order to inherit kingdom with Savior	May 1992	9a-11b
Vaughn J. Featherstone	We are instruments of a divine purpose		44d-e
Thomas S. Monson	Sunday school class gave party money —story		59d-60a
Stephen D. Nadauld	Girl with cerebral palsy rendered , —story		83b-f
Chieko N. Okazaki	Kigatsuku - Act without being told		95d-96f
Robert L. Backman	What to do with the golden years	Nov 1992	13d-15b
C. Max Caldwell	We love those best whom we serve most		30e-f
Thomas S. Monson	, rendered in wake of Hurricane Andrew —story		48f-49f
James E. Faust	3 men carried handcart company over river —story		84d
Howard W. Hunter	Visibility does not equate to value		96f-97a
F. David Stanley	9,000 of 12,000 volunteers were LDS —story	May 1993	45b-d
Thomas S. Monson	17th letter got a response —story		49f-50d
	2 letters saved a man and a family —story		50f-51f
Carlos H. Amado	Donated corneas give girl her eyesight —story	Nov 1993	44d-45a
James E. Faust	People with few talents can serve thousands	May 1994	5d
Richard G. Scott	Our needs are usually met through another mortal —Kimball		9a
Elaine L. Jack	Bishop taught convert to read —story		16d-e
Kenneth Johnson	Our , is not for God's benefit		29f
	The very fiber of an exalted life		29f-30a
Thomas S. Monson	All had been blessed by stake president —story		52c-d
Jeffrey R. Holland	Doing the best things in the worst times	Nov 1994	33f-34a
Thomas S. Monson	Don't leave anyone in loneliness		70d-e

Thomas S. Monson	Truckload of fruit donated —story	Nov 1994	70e-f
	Widow allowed to sit in president's chair —story		71a-b
	, to widow and widower —2 stories		71b-e
Rex D. Pinegar	Life is made of little Christ-like acts		80f-81a
James E. Faust	He neglected his duty and lost his lamb —story	May 1995	46a-d
Thomas S. Monson	Soldier gave water to wounded enemy —story		54c-59a
Gordon B. Hinckley	He doesn't feel old		70e
Thomas S. Monson	Friends carried girl up mountain —story		98e-f
W. Craig Zwick	You are the instrument God uses	Nov 1995	13f
Henry B. Eyring	Assignment from deacon's president saves boy —story		38a-c
Thomas S. Monson	Boy saved drowning girl —story		48e-49b
	Youth helped elderly man find page —story		49f
Gordon B. Hinckley	96,484 volunteers now serving		54b-c
Elaine L. Jack	Sweet the voice of a friend when imprisoned —J. Smith		91d
	Woman met water moccasins and alligators —story		92a
Richard G. Scott	God meets our needs through others	May 1996	26b
Jeffrey R. Holland	Give time and love when money runs out		31b
	We're to help all - not just members		31b-c
	Starving family saved —story		31c-f
	A handful of meal and a little oil —entire talk		29b-31f
Joseph B. Wirthlin	A debt that is best paid in ,		34b-c
Thomas S. Monson	Priesthood: The perfect plan of service		43e
	Priesthood is given for the ministry of ,		44b
David B. Haight	Enthusiasm—the difference between duds and live grenades	Nov 1996	15d
Thomas S. Monson	"Living What We Pray For" —poem		18e
Gordon B. Hinckley	Rescue of handcart pioneers —story		85d-86f
James E. Faust	, to one brought ward together —story		95a-b
Joseph B. Wirthlin	Many try to serve the Lord without offending the devil	May 1997	16a
Jack H. Goaslind	, rendered by 20 young pioneers —story		39d-40f
M. Russell Ballard	Rescue of handcart company like Jesus' rescue of us		61e-f
Gordon B. Hinckley	Our pioneer heritage gives a duty for ,		65b-67f
Russell M. Nelson	Service lifts - Spool and card demonstration		70f-71a
H. David Burton	Examples of ,		76e-77f
Thomas S. Monson	Friends carried girl up mountain —story		94b-d
Boyd K. Packer	Baptism is a call to lifelong ,	Nov 1997	6c
	Two kinds of , - callings and caring		6d
	Call if you need help or Here I am, what can I do? —story		6d-e
	Called to go about doing good		6f
	Other ways we serve		6f-7a
Thomas S. Monson	Story of a donated child's walker —story		19c-20a
James E. Faust	He insensitively let grandmother fill wood box —story		59d-e
Dallin H. Oaks	Two million hours of ,		73b
Mary Ellen Smoot	Every problem solved through , —promise and story		87a-e
	Car wreck at Baker, Oregon followed by , —story		88c-f
Boyd K. Packer	, by call in Church - by choice in home	May 1998	73f

Service

Henry B. Eyring	Man didn't join because of , but son did —story	Nov 1998	33e-34b
D. Todd Christofferson	Sugar beet —story		40d-41a
Thomas S. Monson	, mission most spiritually rewarding —story		50d-51f
Gordon B. Hinckley	60,000 missionaries - 137,629 volunteers	May 1999	4c-d
Robert J. Whetten	Why are missionaries happy?		31d
James E. Faust	Man went to save handcart people —story		47b-f
Thomas S. Monson	"You're God aren't you?" —story		50e-f
Thomas S. Monson	Man built two chapels and chartered a train —story		55d-f
	One who was helped relit his candle —poem		56a
M. Russell Ballard	Governed by covenants or convenience		86d
Vaughn J. Featherstone	Boy cleaned kitchen for 3 hours —story	Nov 1999	15a-c
Thomas S. Monson	Family lost 4 sons in WWII —story		20c-e
Dallin H. Oaks	Love of God and man is highest reason for ,		79c
Thomas S. Monson	Act of , healed animosity —story	May 2000	47d-48c
	President G.A. Smith sent his own coat —story		53d-f
Henry B. Eyring	Sleeping congregation was praying for him —story		68d-e
James E. Faust	Noblest , is within family		96d
Sheri L. Dew	Ultimate , is to lead someone to Christ	Nov 2000	96a
Thomas S. Monson	If we don't serve why are we here? —rescue story	May 2001	48d-f
	Reaching people through friendship and , —stories		49f-50e
Keith K. Hilbig	It's not where you serve but how	Nov 2001	46b
James E. Faust	Oliver Cowdery and Hyrum Smith contrasted		46f-48b
	George R. Hill's quiet , —story		48c-e
Robert F. Orton	Love is a natural consequence of ,		82b
Mary Ellen W. Smoot	1,000 quilts for Albania —story	May 2002	14a-b
Thomas S. Monson	Former friends reunited through , —story		20f-21b
Gayle M. Clegg	Man made frozen girl run —story		68e-69a
James E. Faust	Following Savior is commitment to ,	Nov 2002	19e-f
	Korean boy helping another —story		20e-f
	Hero gave life at World Trade Center —story		20f-21f
James E. Faust	Most rewarding are "extra mile" hours		52d-e
Dallin H. Oaks	Purpose of , is to develop us		70a-b
Thomas S. Monson	Priesthood: the perfect plan of ,	May 2003	54b-c
Thomas S. Monson	Helping Louis take sacrament —story	Nov 2003	56f-57b
	Inactives brought back by , assignments —story		58f-59d
Thomas S. Monson	"The Bridge Builder" —poem		67c-e
	Do something for someone somewhere		69a
	Blessing requested before death —story		69a-c
Gordon B. Hinckley	Don't nag yourself with a sense of failure —story		113e-114b
Thomas S. Monson	Party fund given to family —story	May 2004	20f-22b
Susan W. Tanner	God meets our needs through others		105f-106a
	Youth rallied to help deaf girl —story		106b-107b
Thomas S. Monson	Miracles occur when doing Lord's work	Nov 2004	56d
	Miracles are everywhere when we serve		59a-b
Thomas S. Monson	Grandson helped dying woman —story		69c-70a

Service

Joseph B. Wirthlin	Talmage cared for diphtheria family —story	May 2005	28b-d
Dieter F. Uchtdorf	Pumped air-driven organ for church		36f-37d
Thomas S. Monson	Men work harder for a cause than for money		54e
	Priesthood is the perfect plan of ,		55f-56a
	Widow's home renovated —story		56a-e
Kathleen H. Hughes	Loaned stranger a spare tire —story		74f-75b
M. Russell Ballard	There is no happiness without , —Smith	Nov 2005	42f-43a
Bonnie D. Parkin	Aged mother started rest home branch		109b-d
Henry B. Eyring	A call to , is a call to come to love the Lord	May 2006	16f-17a
Thomas S. Monson	, by humble couple to missionaries —story		21b-e
David F. Evans	Hinckley's mission: Forget yourself		32f-33d
Joseph B. Wirthlin	Epitaph of a miser —poem		101b-d
	No greater joy than relieving distress of others		101d
Susan W. Tanner	Differing outlooks on , by 2 literary characters		103e-f
David S. Baxter	What we give is what enriches us —quote	Nov 2006	14b-d
Henry B. Eyring	Priesthood , is multiplied by more than numbers		44c-d
James E. Faust	Young man gave collected food away —story		54b-e
Thomas S. Monson	One of 3 necessities for a deep foundation		68c-69a
Don R. Clarke	Helped blind man —story		97b-98b
	Blind man was patriarch 32 years		98f
	Carries a book to write impressions in		99a-b
Gordon B. Hinckley	LDS stands for love, devotion, service		115f
Joseph B. Wirthlin	Bishop taught that priesthood means ,	May 2007	46e-47a
Henry B. Eyring	Aged people have not yet earned a rest		90d-e
	Being the answer to someone's prayer		90f-91a
	Two promises if you serve		91a-b
Elaine S. Dalton	Man carried 5 packs for others —story		114b-d
Richard C. Edgley	, rendered by ward to family in tragedy —story	Nov 2007	9d-10a
Michael J. Teh	Screwtape's advice about ,		35f-36b
	Rock thrower becomes convert because of , —story		36f-37b
Keith K. Hilbig	, determines how much Holy Ghost influences us		38e-39b
Walter F. Gonzalez	Priesthood went out at night after earthquake		53d-54b
Henry B. Eyring	Forget self - Start praying for those you serve		57a-b
Steven E. Snow	"I wish I had served more" —story		102b-d
	God meets needs through others —Kimball		103d
	Don't get too busy for quiet , —Kimball		103d
	The rent we pay for our place on earth		103f
	Boy shared one piece of candy among friends —story		103f-104b
Silvia H. Allred	Measure of life - Not what we get, but give		113f-114a
Thomas S. Monson	Neighbor watched tired mother's children —story		121a
Joseph B. Wirthlin	Counsel to those who are weary	May 2008	18e-19b
Carlos H. Amado	A different kind of leadership		35d
	Insightful list of blessings that come through ,		36d-37a
Henry B. Eyring	President of U.S. called Hinckley to thank for ,		63d-e

Service

Boyd K. Packer	Life is like shoes - to be worn out in ,	May 2008	86d
Dieter F. Uchtdorf	Noble servant or self-serving noble?	Nov 2008	54f-55a
	Walking 22 miles on artificial leg —story		55d-56a
Henry B. Eyring	There is help from Spirit World when we serve		58b-e
	We will have help when we give , —story		58f-59a
Thomas S. Monson	Priesthood: The perfect plan of , —S.L. Richards		61f-62b
	Adage: "Do your duty, that is best…"		62e
Keith B. McMullin	"…ranges through world anxious to bless…" —Smith		75f
Russell M. Nelson	Must surrender ego to , of fellow man		94d
Quentin L. Cook	Comforted by perpetrator's family —story		105a-d
Dieter F. Uchtdorf	By lifting others we rise higher		119d-120a
	Bringing sunshine to others brings it to self		120b
	Small acts of , are all that's required		120c
	The prayers we answer are most meaningful		120d-e
D. Todd Christofferson	Service begets joy	May 2009	21a-b
Henry B. Eyring	Widows visiting each other		25f-26a
Claudio R. M. Costa	Priesthood is an eternal covenant of ,		57b-e
	40-minute walk to church - Handicapped —story		57f-58b
	Most priesthood , is accomplished quietly		58b-d
Henry B. Eyring	Rangers lost lives saving downed pilot —story		63c-f
	Duty of priesthood to help the "Man Down"		63b-66e
Barbara Thompson	Needs are met through others —Spencer W. Kimball		85a
	Mess cleaned up by others —story		85a-b
Dallin H. Oaks	LDS are unique in , - List of unselfish , rendered		93b-94b
	Selfish wither and die. Unselfish blossom —Hinckley		93d
	Unique cooperative , of Latter-day Saints		94b-d
	Foregoing unselfish , for values of the world		94e-95c
	The "me" generation - Entitlement vs. ,		95c-96f
	A great example of , - Mother Teresa		95f-96a
Yoon Hwan Choi	Nine Korean troublemakers joined Church —story	Nov 2009	53b-55b
Thomas S. Monson	What did you do for someone today? —story		84d-85a
	Lose self in , or little purpose to life		85b-c
	Man's greatest happiness comes from , —McKay		85d
	No regrets for being too kind —poem		85f-86a
	Services done for his birthday		86a-f
	The loneliness of old age —R.L. Evans		86e-f
Quentin L. Cook	Talmud: Two reasons for giving ,		91b-d
	"Bishop, come quick! Save Sarah" —story		93d-e
	We can't do everything we'd wish		93e
D. Todd Christofferson	Far superior to self-serving interests		107b
Julie B. Beck	Never suppress a generous thought		114c-d
Silvia H. Allred	How Relief Society helped a young couple		116f-117a
Koichi Aoyagi	We are the Lord's hands on earth —Monson	May 2010	37f
David L. Beck	Taking sacrament to shut-in —story		55a-b

Service, cont'd
Related Topics: Welfare Program

Henry B. Eyring	How to perform priesthood ,	May 2010	63d
Dieter F. Uchtdorf	Statue lost hands. You are my hands —story		68a-c
James B. Martino	Serve during trials and save self		102f-103a

Sex
Related Topics: Chastity, Homosexuality, Pornography, Sex Education

Mark E. Petersen	Sex is spiritual	June 1969	78c
Gordon B. Hinckley	, is a river of fire that must be restrained	Dec 1970	72c-d
	, has emerged as a new religion		72d-e
Spencer W. Kimball	Continence as practiced by Paul	June 1971	17b-c
	Attitudes of other churches toward ,		18b-d
Victor L. Brown	Man is expected to have dominion over self		55f-56a
Boyd K. Packer	A subject of reverence not jokes	July 1972	111a
	Excellent discussion on , —entire talk		111d
Spencer W. Kimball	A wonderful servant but a terrible master	May 1974	7d-8d
	No masturbation		7e
Paul H. Dunn	No , of any kind prior to marriage	May 1975	62e
Vaughn J. Featherstone	Sex urge doesn't have to be satisfied		66f
	Dad told son never to masturbate and he never did —story		66f-67a
	Sexual impurities discussed—pornography, masturbation, etc.		66d-67a
Spencer W. Kimball	Full discussion of all sexual sins	Nov 1980	94a-98f
Boyd K. Packer	The gift of procreation —poem by Elder Packer	May 1981	15e-f
Richard G. Scott	Healing the tragic scars of abuse	May 1992	31d-33f
Boyd K. Packer	Our polluted moral environment —entire talk		66b-68f
Neal A. Maxwell	A river of fire that must have restraints	May 1993	77a-b
Boyd K. Packer	Gender did not begin at birth	Nov 1993	21b
	Part of most beautiful experiences of life		21c
	Man is not preferred above woman		21e
Dallin H. Oaks	Gender existed before birth		72e-f
	Church opposes homogenization of gender		73f-74a
	Power to procreate is most exalted power		74a
	Nothing unholy about sexuality		74b-d
Boyd K. Packer	Sexual powers must be protected until marriage	May 1994	19d-e
Richard G. Scott	Straight talk to young men about ,	Nov 1994	37b-39b
James E. Faust	Lose something sacred when , is abused	Nov 1995	47b
Lynn A. Mickelsen	A celestial power that if abused, will be taken away		79f
Russell M. Nelson	Destruction to come to those whose God is ,	May 1996	15b
Boyd K. Packer	Consummate purpose of , is begetting children		19d-f
Richard G. Scott	Gender existed before coming to earth	Nov 1996	73d
	Procreation is a holy privilege		73f
James E. Faust	Sexual purity is most precious possession	May 1998	95d
Boyd K. Packer	Gender was premortal - Sex is good	Nov 2000	73b-c
	Good discussion on homosexuality		73c-74f
Sheri L. Dew	The united roles of gender	Nov 2001	12d-14f
Gordon B. Hinckley	A power that can build or destroy	May 2003	58d-59a
James E. Faust	Source of greatest joy or great misery		109a-b

M. Russell Ballard	75% of TV and music is sex-based	Nov 2003	17f-18b
Boyd K. Packer	Essential to happiness and exaltation		25b
	Words we would rather not say		25c-26a
Gordon B. Hinckley	The sanctity of , is destroyed by pornography		83f-84b
Russell M. Nelson	A divine, sacred gift in marriage	May 2006	37a
Boyd K. Packer	Only between husband and wife	Nov 2006	86d-e
James E. Faust	Safeguard the great powers of procreation	May 2007	55b-d
Richard G. Scott	Healing the consequences of abuse	May 2008	40b-43f
Elaine S. Dalton	Only one opposed to premarital sex —story		116e-117a
	All Satan's attacks directed to body		117b
Boyd K. Packer	Gender was determined in premortal existence	May 2009	50f
Elaine S. Dalton	Safeguard the sacred power to create life		121a-b
M. Russell Ballard	Fathers must have the "big talk" with sons	Nov 2009	49d-50a
D. Todd Christofferson	Mere wanting is no guide for moral conduct		107f
M. Russell Ballard	Talk to daughters frequently about ,	May 2010	20e-f
Thomas S. Monson	Is sacred. Requires self-control and purity		66d-e

Sex Education
Related Topics: Sex

Alvin R. Dyer	The evils of ,	June 1969	40a-e
Ezra Taft Benson	, whets curiosity and augments appetite		44c-e
Mark E. Petersen	Afraid the next generation won't know how to reproduce?		78a-b
	Any , must be coupled with teaching chastity		78b-c
	Schools unqualified to teach , since can't teach spiritual things		78c
	, belongs in the home		78d
Harold B. Lee	Does not promote chastity	July 1972	32c
	How a father must teach it		102f
Gordon B. Hinckley	The effectiveness of , in schools	May 1987	47e-48a

Sin
Related Topics: Confession, Forgiveness, Temptation

John H. Vandenberg	Like weeds	Dec 1968	57d-f
Richard L. Evans	Why do you play so much in the rough?		64b
	Be angry about evil		64b
	You, not the world must change		64c-d
John H. Vandenberg	"The Calf-Path" —poem	June 1969	47b-f
	All paths needn't be tried to know they're wrong		48b
Robert L. Simpson	Cases of the faithful being led away gradually		89d-90c
	Thin ice eventually gives way		90c
	Just open the door and we're led quietly away		90e-f
Alvin R. Dyer	Repentance of , brings peace	Dec 1969	40a
Loren C. Dunn	Don't yield to peer pressure. Time will prove you right		44d
LeGrand Richards	Fable about error —funny		54e
Ezra Taft Benson	Forbear sinner but not sin		69b
Richard L. Evans	Learn from the first ,		74f
	Firmly decide what you won't do		76a
	If not right, don't do it		76c

Richard L. Evans	Learn from others' errors. Need not repeat their mistakes	June 1970	38c-f
Boyd K. Packer	Life is a mountain. The easy trails lead downward.		51b-e
John H. Vandenberg	Error: If we called the tail a leg would a sheep have 5?		57f-58a
Ezra Taft Benson	How to recognize , - John Wesley's mother's advice —good	Dec 1970	49f-50a
N. Eldon Tanner	Those who , have no happiness		92c
Boyd K. Packer	Prevention the best cure —poem		107a-b
Spencer W. Kimball	First endure, then pity, then embrace —poem	June 1971	18d-19a
	Never mentioned in some churches		19a
Richard L. Evans	No guilty man is acquitted by his conscience		74a
	The heaviest burden in all the world is , —Lee		74c
Paul H. Dunn	How does it feel to have all my sins...		102c-d
Ezra Taft Benson	You cannot do wrong and feel right	Dec 1971	55c
Richard L. Evans	There are no successful sinners —Lee		58c
Sterling W. Sill	One vice can overcome 10 virtues —Luther		93d-e
Delbert L. Stapley	Life begins like pure stream then , enters		97b-d
John H. Vandenberg	Saying there is no , runs counter to laws of opposition		114b
Harold B. Lee	Positive teachings greatest weapons against ,	July 1972	32b
Spencer W. Kimball	Comes when prayer neglected		39f
	Accepted as a way of life - today worst		39f
Gordon B. Hinckley	Short, humorous story	Jan 1973	91a
Marion D. Hanks	The way in is easy, the way out is hard		128f
Hartman Rector, Jr.	Don't see how close you can come - set rules		131b
O. Leslie Stone	The greatest faith destroyer	July 1973	60f
N. Eldon Tanner	Bishops' responsibility to deal with ,		94d
Harold B. Lee	How to know when you have been forgiven of a ,		122a
H. Burke Peterson	Sin keeps man from prayer —Brigham Young	Jan 1974	19b
Delbert L. Stapley	Cannot mix good with evil		44d
N. Eldon Tanner	Halfway down a cliff you might say 'All is well'		93d
Harold B. Lee	Nothing sadder than losing Spirit through ,		101e
Elray L. Christiansen	Satan knows little sins don't stay little	Nov 1974	24b-c
H. Burke Peterson	There is no right way to do something wrong		68f
N. Eldon Tanner	No progress or happiness until , repented of		78b-f
Victor L. Brown	Avoid appearance of evil. Don't even walk on same street		104f
Joseph Anderson	People work harder to reach hell than heaven	May 1975	30b
Marion G. Romney	Hide your , from the public gaze —Brigham Young	Nov 1980	48a-c
Angel Abrea	Little butterflies stopped his car —story	Nov 1981	23d-24a
James E. Faust	Sins repented of may strengthen commitment —story	May 1982	48f-49f
Neal A. Maxwell	Sadness and badness are mutually reinforcing	May 1983	9d
Howard W. Hunter	Errors of judgment less serious than errors of intent	Nov 1983	64e
Elaine A. Cannon	Tell them don't do it —S.W. Kimball —joke	May 1984	26b
M. Russell Ballard	Do missionary work and our sins are more readily forgiven	Nov 1984	16b-d
James E. Faust	The ultimate evil is closing one's mind against truth	Nov 1985	7e
Robert D. Hales	Spiritual vertigo - a degree at a time —story		21b-c
Jack H. Goaslind	Why is sin sin?	May 1986	53b
James E. Faust	The knowledge of , tempteth to its commission	Nov 1987	33e-f

James E. Faust	The safest road to hell is the gradual one	Nov 1987	35d
Ezra Taft Benson	Full cursing for , does not come immediately	May 1988	6b-d
Thomas S. Monson	Barnacles drop off ships at Portland, Oregon —story		42b-d
James E. Faust	Satan leads us carefully —Boiling frog story	May 1989	32b-e
	We first endure , then pity, then embrace —poem		32e
Richard G. Scott	No one today will avoid serious , without Lord's help		36c-d
	Not good to , : Worse to do nothing about it		36d-e
	Self pity - gross selfishness - depression		36e-f
	If you hide sins, Satan will reveal them		37a-b
Russell C. Taylor	, stuns the conscience —McKay		41f
Thomas S. Monson	If where you shouldn't be - Get Out!		44e
Boyd K. Packer	Dual alarm system: Pain and guilt		54f-59a
Robert L. Backman	Description of feelings caused by , —excellent	Nov 1989	39a-b
Joanne B. Doxey	Ideas about avoiding appearance of ,		90f
Derek A. Cuthbert	, is for one's own ends - Service is the opposite	May 1990	12e-f
Marvin J. Ashton	There are no successful sinners	Nov 1990	21b-c
M. Russell Ballard	Former , returns when done again		38a-b
Joseph B. Wirthlin	Sin: good things done to excess—sports, TV, movies, homes		65a-e
F. Burton Howard	Blaming others for , —entire talk	May 1991	12d-14b
Russell M. Nelson	Opportunity to repent is forfeited at death	May 1992	73a-b
Gordon B. Hinckley	Only dispensation in which , will not prevail	Nov 1992	4d-f
Marvin J. Ashton	We are far too easily pleased - distraction		23b-e
James E. Faust	Bishops will bear , if not dealt with	Nov 1993	37c-e
Hugh W. Pinnock	Never feed the foxes		41d-f
Dallin H. Oaks	The difference between transgression and ,		73b-e
W. Eugene Hansen	Pleasure is Satan's counterfeit happiness		82b-f
Elaine L. Jack	Catch the vision of eternity: leave world behind	May 1994	15d
Thomas S. Monson	Apply a proper-sized bandage to the wound		50e
Russell M. Nelson	A strain of sin-resistant souls	May 1995	33f
Thomas S. Monson	Lord will give maximum reward and least punishment		59b-c
Neal A. Maxwell	Boulders, loose gravel and small stones		66f-67a
	David dealt greater blow to Goliath or to himself?		68d
	Small sins spread		68d-e
Boyd K. Packer	No sin is exempt from complete forgiveness	Nov 1995	18d-21b
Neal A. Maxwell	Sins of omission may prevent exaltation		23a-c
James E. Faust	Avoid appearance of , - No mixed overnighters		47a
Richard G. Scott	Can be a growth experience	May 1996	26b-c
W. Eugene Hansen	He who picks up one end of stick...		39b-d
Carlos E. Asay	The world is drifting - 1916 quote		60f
James E. Faust	The grand key is to stay free from ,	Nov 1996	53d
Boyd K. Packer	10 filthy servicemen felt ashamed —story	May 1997	9c-f
	Youth: cornered when they don't know how to erase mistake		10b
M. Russell Ballard	A slippery slope upon which you lose footing	Nov 1997	40a
James E. Faust	Wanting to belong - An amazing comeback —story		43d-f
James E. Faust	He insensitively let grandmother fill wood box —story		59d-e

Sin, cont'd
Related Topics: Confession, Forgiveness, Temptation

Neal A. Maxwell	They seek to erase emptiness by sensations	May 1999	23b
	Willing to break covenants to fix appetites		24b-c
Keith B. McMullin	All , falls under one of three classes —D.O. McKay		80b-c
Vaughn J. Featherstone	Giving up and hoping the wolf will have enough	Nov 1999	13d
Boyd K. Packer	"All the water in the world" —poem		24b-c
David R. Stone	Spiritual hurricanes —entire talk		31b-32f
Henry B. Eyring	Atonement washes away all effects of , —story		35b-f
James E. Faust	Peter's denials led to strength		61a-d
L. Tom Perry	, is intensely habit forming —Spencer W. Kimball		77c-d
Thomas S. Monson	Barnacles drop off ships at Portland —story	May 2000	46e-47a
Neal A. Maxwell	We may not be in transgression but in diversion	Nov 2000	36f-37a
Boyd K. Packer	"The Touch of the Master's Hand" —entire talk	May 2001	22d-24f
Keith B. McMullin	3 deadly , nullified by living covenants		62a-e
Russell M. Nelson	Yielding to any , puts family at risk	Nov 2001	71a-c
Thomas S. Monson	Hidden wedges —story	May 2002	18b-e
R. Conrad Schultz	Sneaker wave nearly capsized boat —story		29d-f
Kenneth Johnson	Cannot , without overruling a warning	Nov 2002	90c
Spencer V. Jones	Skunk smell would not come off —story	May 2003	88b-89f
Dallin H. Oaks	Used to be localized and covered	May 2004	9c-10a
James E. Faust	, is , even if everyone does it		53d-f
Boyd K. Packer	Best protection against , is stable home		79a
Clate W. Mask, Jr.	Missionaries sloshed through mudslides —story		92b-f
Richard G. Scott	Effort used to be required to seek evil		100d-e
Gordon B. Hinckley	Player dropped ball - Never forgotten —story		114e-115b
James E. Faust	Instant punishment for , would destroy agency	Nov 2004	19a-c
Neil L. Andersen	Beware of evil behind smiling eyes —story	May 2005	46b-e
Gordon B. Hinckley	"He was against it" —C. Coolidge		58d
Robert D. Hales	Satan can't have happiness unless we ,	May 2006	6b-c
Thomas S. Monson	Alexander Pope's Essay on Man —poem		18e
Earl C. Tingey	Life is spent gathering rocks		72e-f
Marcus B. Nash	Like setting the hook —entire talk	Nov 2006	49b-50f
James E. Faust	We have to guard against , all our lives	May 2007	55a-b
Dieter F. Uchtdorf	The willful transgression of divine law		99e
	We should and will remember our ,		101b-d
L. Whitney Clayton	Caribbean fish traps	Nov 2007	51d-e
Thomas S. Monson	, is preceded by thoughts		61a-b
Richard G. Scott	Heavy man ordering doughnuts —humor		92b-c
Claudio D. Zivic	"Don't touch me. I can't sin." —story		98d-e
	A sense of shame can't be found again		98f
Joseph B. Wirthlin	"Restricted Entrance - Perfect People Only"	May 2008	19b-e
Dieter F. Uchtdorf	A 2-degree error caused plane crash —story		57f-58b
	Lessons from Saul's ,		58c-e
	A 1-degree error makes one 500 miles off course		58f-59a
D. Todd Christofferson	Retaining some disposition to do evil		78f
Quentin L. Cook	Ingratitude ranks close to unpardonable ,	Nov 2008	104f

Rafael E. Pino	No tragedy in death, but only in , —S. W. Kimball	May 2009	41e-f
Dieter F. Uchtdorf	It is never too late to repent		77a-78a
Richard G. Scott	Addictive, deadening, contagious, corrosive…	Nov 2009	8e
Neil L. Andersen	No , that cannot be forgiven		40f
Henry B. Eyring	Choose , and Holy Ghost becomes faint		60e
D. Todd Christofferson	Has been branded a "value judgment"		106d-e
	Can only be overcome by moral discipline		106f-107a
	Satan a multimedia advocate of , and selfishness		107d
	Mother put early end to life of crime —story		107e
	Other churches don't talk about , any more		108f
Henry B. Eyring	Downward spiral easily arrested early	May 2010	22a-e
Jeffrey R. Holland	Our , hurts family and Jesus		46b-c
Donald L. Hallstrom	Atonement has broader purpose than just ,		80f

Single Adults
Related Topics: —

James E. Faust	Loneliness and discouragement of ,	July 1973	86b
	Divorce is harder than death for ,		86c
	Should be organized into home evening groups		87d
James E. Faust	Don't be upset about all the talk about families	Jan 1974	23c
Harold B. Lee	The Special Interest program - letters from women		97d
	No marriageable man who is single lives his religion		99d
	Men who date and never marry - their duty is to marry		100b
Thomas S. Monson	Helping widows —good stories	May 1981	47b-49b
Marvin J. Ashton	Counsel to single women —entire talk	May 1984	9b-11f
Gene R. Cook	Even , are part of a family - Practice the principles		31a
Robert D. Hales	President Lee had to lose his wife so he could understand ,	May 1985	29a
Russell M. Nelson	I'm lonely, but I'm not lonesome —service	Nov 1985	32c-d
Gordon B. Hinckley	1/3 of LDS adult women in U.S. are ,		89b
Dallin H. Oaks	The dilemma of ,	May 1988	31f-32c
Ezra Taft Benson	To the single brethren of the Church		51b-53b
Joseph B. Wirthlin	Advise to , brethren to marry	Nov 1988	35f
Dallin H. Oaks	Surprised that his mother was a widow —story	Nov 2005	27d-f
Russell M. Nelson	No blessings will be withheld from ,	May 2006	36d-e
Barbara Thompson	Her unfulfilled goals as a ,	Nov 2009	119b-f
Neil L. Andersen	Promise to single mothers	May 2010	110a

Speaking
Related Topics: —

Spencer W. Kimball	Wisdom in remaining silent on the things you are ignorant of	June 1970	93d
Wendell J. Ashton	Elder Hinckley frightened of , in General Conference	June 1971	57b
Gordon B. Hinckley	Heber C. Kimball - a man of stammering tongue	Dec 1971	124b-c
Marion D. Hanks	Fright about , —humorous anecdote	Jan 1973	127a
Hartman Rector, Jr.	Short talk by the Spirit better than long one without	Jan 1974	106d
Theodore M. Burton	Don't base talks on one isolated scripture —Lee	Nov 1974	55a
Henry D. Taylor	Arrogant youth spoke without Holy Ghost —story	Nov 1975	62f
Marvin J. Ashton	Say what needs to be said, not all that can be said	Nov 1976	86b

Speaking, cont'd

Spirit

Russell M. Nelson	Development of , may never reach a limit	Nov 1997	14f
Russell M. Nelson	Provides body with animation and personality	Nov 1998	86e-f
	The active , is the responsible component of the soul		87d
Dieter F. Uchtdorf	Your , is a masterpiece	Nov 2008	118e-119d
Henry B. Eyring	Our , will be changed in the resurrection	May 2009	23f-24b

Spirit World
Related Topics: —

Joseph Fielding Smith	We are not automatically cleansed in the ,	June 1969	37f-38c
Harold B. Lee	A great deal to be learned in ,		104f
Hartman Rector, Jr.	Paradise and spirit prison are one place	Dec 1970	76f
	Same desires in , as here —story		77a-b
Ezra Taft Benson	Where is it? - "It is here" —Brigham Young	June 1971	33d
LeGrand Richards	Misunderstanding about thief on cross	Jan 1973	110b
Spencer W. Kimball	The meaning of the Lord's "rest"	Nov 1975	80c-d
LeGrand Richards	Unseen powers operate on minds of men	May 1977	63d
Thomas S. Monson	One great program on both sides of veil	May 1993	5d-f
David B. Haight	Same grand work on each side of veil		25f
Robert D. Hales	Many of us held in reserve in , —Woodruff	May 1995	16f
Richard G. Scott	Progress more rapidly with body on earth than in spirit world	May 1997	54f
Richard G. Scott	He prays for those in ,	May 1999	27a
Henry B. Eyring	Ancestors looking at us with hope	May 2005	78d-80b
M. Russell Ballard	Most pressing need in , is finding family	Nov 2005	41b-d
James E. Faust	Ministering angels are often family members	May 2006	51b-52d
Gordon B. Hinckley	Reception in , for woman doing 20,000 endowments	May 2007	85a-b
Russell M. Nelson	Repentance is offered in ,		104b-d
Henry B. Eyring	Help will come from ,	Nov 2008	58b-e
	Angels will bear us up		60a-b
Quentin L. Cook	Description of 2 parts of ,	May 2009	37a-b

Spirituality
Related Topics: —

David O. McKay	Defined as victory over self	Dec 1969	31c
Spencer W. Kimball	Spiritual reservoirs		48b
David O. McKay	Communion with Deity		110a
Harold B. Lee	Activity is the soul of ,	Dec 1971	114c
Harold B. Lee	Greater trials, the greater the ,	Jan 1973	25e
Spencer W. Kimball	Born in home	July 1973	17a
Bruce R. McConkie	Cannot survive spiritually with one foot in world	Nov 1974	34b
J. Thomas Fyans	If , is low, immerse self in scriptures —Kimball	May 1975	88e
LeGrand Richards	Earth's crammed with Heaven but few see —poem	May 1976	82d
Boyd K. Packer	We hear what we're trained to hear —3 stories	Nov 1979	19c-20b
	Inspiration comes more as feelings than sound		20c
	How Word of Wisdom affects ,		20c-e
	How music affects ,		20f
Robert E. Wells	Actor knew 23rd Psalm—Old man knew Jesus —story	Nov 1980	12b-e
	Know Jesus through study, prayer, revelation		12e

Spirituality, cont'd
Related Topics: —

Robert E. Wells	Am I loving, studying and serving enough to know Jesus	Nov 1980	13f
Spencer W. Kimball	Temple attendance best builder of ,	May 1982	4f-5a
Marion G. Romney	, is the highest acquisition of the soul —McKay	Nov 1982	92f
Henry B. Eyring	Ears to hear: An undiminished heritage	May 1985	77b-f
Robert E. Wells	Well-worded examples of spiritual experiences	Nov 1985	29e-f
Dallin H. Oaks	A spiritual man is happiest of all —Widtsoe		62b
	, is the consequence of a series of right choices		63d-f
J. Thomas Fyans	Develop , and see Jesus		90d-e
Howard W. Hunter	Jesus restored physical and spiritual sight	May 1989	16d-17a
Dean L. Larsen	Must be frequently renewed by 5 things	Nov 1989	62b-f
	No , without service —Kimball		63e-f
Jeffrey R. Holland	Beautiful talk on the need for Savior	Nov 1997	64d-66f
Russell M. Nelson	Spiritual fitness as important as physical fitness	Nov 1998	87a-c
Mary Ellen Smoot	Oil for our lamps comes drop by drop —Kimball		90a
Henry B. Eyring	Spiritual preparedness —entire talk	Nov 2005	37d-40f
James E. Faust	Spiritual oil cannot be shared	May 2006	113f
	How to fill your lamps —Spencer W. Kimball		113f-114e
Russell M. Nelson	Revelation hones to spiritual discernment	Nov 2009	82f-83a

Standards
Related Topics: Appearance, Dress Standards

Ezra Taft Benson	Music, dances, dress, literature	June 1969	46f-47c
Delbert L. Stapley	Church's , can never be lowered	Dec 1969	64c
Delbert L. Stapley	Miniskirts have affected morals	Dec 1970	65c-d
Robert L. Simpson	What does hair length have to do with worthiness?		96d-e
Boyd K. Packer	We can't dilute Lord's , to suit others	Nov 1974	87f
	Only problem , cause Church is fast growth		88f-89a
Gordon B. Hinckley	Today's test: live in the world without surrendering ,		100c-d
Paul H. Dunn	Baseball player compromised , kicked off team —story	Nov 1976	54d-55c
Victor L. Brown	Follow appearance of present leaders - no beards	May 1977	37e-38d
L. Tom Perry	He left Marine buddies to go to LDS dance —story	Nov 1979	35c-36a
	Girl required each date to agree to her , —story		36a-c
L. Tom Perry	Actions follow the type of clothing we wear	Nov 1984	18f-19b
Don Lind	Keep self right side up even when world looks upside down	Nov 1985	39d-e
Gordon B. Hinckley	Statistics on America's deteriorating ,	May 1992	69f-70b
Joe J. Christensen	Say "no" to children - Set ,	Nov 1993	11e-12a
Sharon G. Larsen	Girl could choose popular people or , —story	May 2002	91f-92c
Dieter F. Uchtdorf	For the Strength of Youth a gem for any age	May 2006	44a-b
	Promises if , in For the Strength of Youth are lived		44d
James E. Faust	Joan of Arc maintained her , —story		112b-f
Boyd K. Packer	Not free to alter or ignore ,	Nov 2006	86b
	High , are a magnet and don't repel growth		87d
	A worthy LDS family is a , to the world		87f
	Individuals are to be ,		87f
Larry W. Gibbons	We must stop drifting		102f-103a
W. Craig Zwick	Do I lower , to keep friends?	May 2008	97e-98d

W. Craig Zwick	We cannot yield —Boyd K. Packer	May 2008	98e
Dallin H. Oaks	Foregoing unselfish service for , of the world	May 2009	94e-95c
Elaine S. Dalton	Focus on , changes during a mission		120b-e
	Lord's , are absolute, not relative		121a-b
Richard G. Scott	, and commitment prevent being led astray	Nov 2009	9d

Hugh B. Brown	Our concept of God changes as we , and learn	June 1969	33e-34a
N. Eldon Tanner	The way to know God	Dec 1969	34e
Joseph F. Smith	Good books and gospel to be studied		37e
Sterling W. Sill	I was born just after I finished a book	June 1971	44f
	Sill read every article in his Improvement Era		44f-45a
Dallin H. Oaks	Spirit needs nourishing as often as body	Dec 1971	109f
Thomas S. Monson	Missionary who didn't develop mind —story	July 1972	70c
Sterling W. Sill	Thoughts on , and reading —entire talk, good		124a
	A doctor wrote prescriptions for books —story		124b
Bruce R. McConkie	Obligation to , and bear testimony	July 1973	28f
	Obligation to , and bear testimony		29d
Spencer W. Kimball	20 years of worldly , but just hours for God	May 1974	119a
Sterling W. Sill	"…I had a mother who read to me" —poem	May 1975	41f
	Born at age 25 after reading a good book		42a
Robert L. Simpson	He who doesn't read has no advantage over him who can't	Nov 1975	13f
Spencer W. Kimball	Everyone should memorize Articles of Faith —story		77d-79e
James E. Faust	Spirituality returns when immersed in scriptures—Kimball	Nov 1976	58f-59a
Spencer W. Kimball	Read the conference talks	May 1978	77f
	We must , to enable Lord to inspire us		102d-e
William R. Bradford	The amount you could read if TV was cut out - amazing	Nov 1979	37e-38a
Howard W. Hunter	Method of ,		64d-65a
Robert E. Wells	, scriptures and testimony of those knowing Jesus —Benson	Nov 1980	12e
LeGrand Richards	12 years preparing for life. How about eternal life?	Nov 1981	28d
Gordon B. Hinckley	Challenge to read daily chapter from gospels	May 1983	80d-e
Boyd K. Packer	, brings to light sacred things hidden from the insincere	Nov 1983	17a
A. Theodore Tuttle	Family , is key element in righteous children	May 1984	24b-d
J. Thomas Fyans	Spiritually exercise each day		39b
Boyd K. Packer	, of gospel improves behavior	Nov 1986	17f
Ezra Taft Benson	Leaders must immerse themselves in the scriptures		47b-c
Ezra Taft Benson	Daily family scripture reading pleases God	May 1988	5d
Howard W. Hunter	, and prayer are answers to trials —entire talk	Nov 1988	59d-61f
Hugh W. Pinnock	Go directly to the scriptures - no substitute	May 1989	12d
F. Enzio Busche	, makes it possible to avoid suffering		72d
Neal A. Maxwell	, accesses a divine data bank	May 1991	90b
Merrill J. Bateman	Be diligent in , like parents were searching for son —story	Nov 1992	27d-f
	Accomplish far more with daily ,		27f-28a
Jay E. Jensen	Importance of studying scriptures —quotes		80d
L. Lionel Kendrick	Search scriptures daily —J. Smith and S. W. Kimball	May 1993	14d-f

L. Lionel Kendrick	Necessity of scriptures and how to , them	May 1993	13b-15b
L. Tom Perry	What daily family , did for Peru —story		90b-e
	A promise if daily family , occurs		92f
Richard G. Scott	Testimonies will dim without , of scriptures	Nov 1993	88b
Jeanne Inouye	Scripture , more important. Don't slight it —story		97d-f
Joseph B. Wirthlin	Feed soul through daily ,	Nov 1994	75d
Chieko N. Okazaki	Seek learning by study and faith —entire talk		92b-94b
Bonnie D. Parkin	Lord doesn't expect us to diet	May 1995	90b
3 Young Women	Experiences of young women with the scriptures —stories		93b-95e
Thomas S. Monson	Advice on flyleaf of scriptures from a father		97f-98a
Gordon B. Hinckley	Counsel to , saved family of single mother —story	Nov 1995	99f-100e
Susan L. Warner	Son was listening with eyes closed —story	May 1996	79b-c
Virginia H. Pearce	Continue to , or you may not stay	Nov 1996	12b-c
	, of doctrine will change behavior		14b
Boyd K. Packer	, of doctrine will improve behavior	May 1997	9b
Richard J. Maynes	Very difficult to cram for mission or marriage	Nov 1997	30b-31f
L. Tom Perry	Decades to learn spiritual - eternity for secular		60d-e
Henry B. Eyring	One of two great keys to inviting Spirit		83f-84a
Anne G. Wirthlin	Pondering moves the word from mind to heart	May 1998	10f
Thomas S. Monson	Priest memorized sacrament prayers —story	May 1999	49b-e
Neil L. Andersen	Presidency's counsel on family , and Family Home Evening	Nov 1999	17c-18a
Richard G. Scott	Memorize scriptures - paraphrasing loses power		87f-88c
James E. Faust	Scriptures are a washing machine for unclean thoughts	May 2000	44d
Douglas L. Callister	How J.R. Clark and Thomas Jefferson studied	Nov 2000	31a
Henry B. Eyring	If casual in , then become casual in prayer	Nov 2001	17b
Boyd K. Packer	You have everything crossed out —story		64c
L. Tom Perry	Continue , habits after mission		76b-e
Coleen K. Menlove	Casual or infrequent , not enough	Nov 2002	14d-e
D. Todd Christofferson	How to really ,	May 2004	11e-f
Julie B. Beck	The worth of and how to , scriptures —good		107d-109f
Donald L. Staheli	Immerse self in scriptures —Kimball	Nov 2004	39c
Thomas S. Monson	Children must , gospel themselves —H.J. Grant		115b
Boyd K. Packer	Insights come in next readings	May 2005	7c-e
Paul K. Sybrowsky	The 2-year-old knew the answer —story	Nov 2005	35d-e
Henry B. Eyring	Go to scriptures early and consistently		39b-f
Robert D. Hales	God speaks to us when we , the scriptures	Nov 2006	26f-27a
Thomas S. Monson	One of 3 necessities for a deep foundation		67f-68c
Marlin K. Jensen	Church historian speaks of value of remembering	May 2007	36d-38f
Keith B. McMullin	Flunked chemistry class —story		51d-f
Gordon B. Hinckley	A simple recipe for happiness includes ,		115e&117f
	What we should , in the scriptures		116b-d
Keith K. Hilbig	, expands influences of Holy Ghost in our lives	Nov 2007	39b
Thomas S. Monson	Neglecting , and prayer opens door to Satan	May 2009	67f-68a
	Prophet's promise if you , diligently		68a-e
Vicki F. Matsumori	Pray and , daily to invite the Spirit	Nov 2009	11c

Study

Vicki F. Matsumori	Provide a daily quiet time for Spirit	Nov 2009	11d
David A. Bednar	Consistency in family , most important		19d-20e
Quentin L. Cook	As important as food		93a-b
Dale G. Renlund	He analyzed why his zeal waned and fixed it —story		98e-99d
Julie B. Beck	Scripture accumulates over time	May 2010	11b
D. Todd Christofferson	Faith matures as we feast upon word		35a
Richard G. Scott	Energetically encourages a , plan		77d
Francisco J. Viñas	Prophets ask parents and children to ,		107f
Neil L. Andersen	Open scriptures. Read book of John		109f
	Young Dallin Oaks spent evenings reading		112b
Ann M. Dibb	Testimony grows thinner without , —Lee		115f

Hugh B. Brown	"When is , a failure" —poem	June 1969	98e-f
Paul H. Dunn	Vince Lombardi's formula for ,	Dec 1970	37f-38e
Sterling W. Sill	Story of the Artist Whistler and his roses	June 1971	44a-b
Spencer W. Kimball	Man's 8 children all married in temple —story	Dec 1971	36c-37a
Sterling W. Sill	Formula for , - decide in advance what you won't do		92a-c
Alvin R. Dyer	To say no and stand by it is first element of ,		122b
N. Eldon Tanner	Which way you are headed is most important	July 1972	35b
Paul H. Dunn	There isn't a failure among us		93f
	Babe Ruth - success and failure —story		94a
	Getting up once more than you fall down is ,		95a
	Rules for , don't work unless you do		95a
Sterling W. Sill	Best way to succeed is to be a good man	Jan 1973	82f
Hartman Rector, Jr.	You can complain about sour lemon or make lemonade		130b
Robert L. Simpson	Savior concerned with our , more than we are	July 1973	22b
Ezra Taft Benson	During greatest , is greatest danger		40f
Thomas S. Monson	Our business is to get ahead of ourselves		42f
David B. Haight	Short poem by Henry Van Dyke		54f
Hartman Rector, Jr.	Many definitions - 2 humorous ones		57b
	Different measurements of , —quote		57b
	No one is really successful who is not happy		57c
	Success is full of promise till men get it		57e
Sterling W. Sill	Desire comes first —Socrates and Mozart stories		104c
Vaughn J. Featherstone	Noble saying about work and ,	Jan 1974	84a
	A modern version of 'The Little Red Hen'		84b
	Doing the impossible $5 job —story		84e
Sterling W. Sill	Jack Dempsey's formula for , —story	Nov 1974	62d-f
Spencer W. Kimball	Abe Lincoln failed and failed but kept trying —story		80c-e
N. Eldon Tanner	How great men achieve , —short poem	May 1975	76b
H. Burke Peterson	Obedience, enthusiasm and positive thinking equal ,	Nov 1976	116d
Paul H. Dunn	British at Waterloo were brave 5 minutes longer	May 1979	9b-c
Rex D. Pinegar	Man on mountain top didn't fall there	Nov 1980	72f
David B. Haight	, depends upon preparation —funny story	May 1981	42d-e

M. Russell Ballard	Develop attitude of , and you'll be successful	May 1981	87b
R. LaVell Edwards	Wait for opportunity to come, or prepare for opportunity?	Nov 1984	44f
Thomas S. Monson	President Truman was a sissy —story	May 1987	68f
Richard G. Scott	We are here to succeed gloriously	Nov 1989	30e
Marvin J. Ashton	W. Churchill's statement on war		37b-c
Joseph B. Wirthlin	, results when preparation meets opportunity		74b
Russell M. Nelson	Ladder of , leaned against wrong wall	Nov 1992	6f-7a
Jacob de Jager	, is a journey, not a destination	Nov 1993	32c
Claudio R. M. Costa	What is true , —story	Nov 1994	27b-c
	All of the man's children married in temple —story		27e-f
Richard C. Edgley	Developing confidence —entire talk great —story		39d-40b
Boyd K. Packer	We cannot always expect , but we must try	Nov 2004	86b-e
Dieter F. Uchtdorf	Desire makes the impossible possible —story	Nov 2006	37b-f
Henry B. Eyring	Measure , by how your service changes hearts	Nov 2007	57d-e
Quentin L. Cook	All descendants born in the covenant		70f-71a
Rafael E. Pino	No , is right if not Christ-centered —H.W. Hunter	May 2009	42e
Julie B. Beck	How women can measure ,	May 2010	12c-d
Ann M. Dibb	Obedience brings , —H.W. Hunter		115b

Sustaining
Related Topics: Voting

Loren C. Dunn	Meaning of the action of sustaining	July 1972	43a
Russell M. Nelson	Sustaining makes known who has authority	Nov 1989	20b
Jeffrey R. Holland	Meaning of sustaining		25c
Marlin K. Jensen	He made his leaders look good		28c
Neal A. Maxwell	Have confidence in leaders who keep confidences		82f
James E. Faust	Not popular to be , Apostles and prophets	May 1992	8b-c
Gordon B. Hinckley	The principle of sustaining	May 1994	53d-f
David B. Haight	, means we agree and will follow	Nov 1994	14d-15c
Gordon B. Hinckley	The meaning of sustaining	May 1995	51b-d
James E. Faust	W. Woodruff decided not to board boat —story	May 1997	42d-e
	Great safety and peace in , leaders		42f-43a
Boyd K. Packer	A commitment to support	Nov 1997	7d-e
David B. Haight	Recounting of 3 important , events in history —story	Nov 1998	36a-e
Thomas S. Monson	Farmer , President Hinckley in barn —story	Nov 2000	49d-f
Boyd K. Packer	A great protection to the Church	May 2001	22d
Gordon B. Hinckley	The sustaining of Uchtdorf and Bednar	Nov 2004	4b-c
Boyd K. Packer	Unique to the Church	Nov 2007	6b-f
Dieter F. Uchtdorf	Solemn assembly to sustain President Monson	May 2008	4b-7b

Talents
Related Topics: Gifts

George I. Cannon	A bee is not an eagle but makes honey	Nov 1991	14c
Chieko N. Okazaki	"I'm a little pencil in the hands of God"		89d-f
Boyd K. Packer	Mission callings issued to learn the arts	May 1993	19f
Joe J. Christensen	Each child should develop a skill or ,	Nov 1993	12a-e
James E. Faust	People with few , can feed thousands	May 1994	5d

James E. Faust	, are augmented by Holy Ghost many fold	May 2002	47e-48a
Dieter F. Uchtdorf	Indulge your desire to create	Nov 2008	118e-119d
Quentin L. Cook	Teach children they're accountable for ,	Nov 2009	93a-b
Julie B. Beck	Receiving revelation - Most important ,	May 2010	11b

Teachers
Related Topics: Teaching

David O. McKay	5 things a , must be and do	Dec 1968	109a-b
Richard L. Evans	A teacher affects eternity...	June 1969	80b
	, must be what they teach		80b
David O. McKay	The army of , in the Church	Dec 1969	111c
	Necessary attributes of ,		111d
Thomas S. Monson	Only a teacher —story of boyhood argument	June 1970	90a-b
	, can never tell where influence stops		90b
Paul H. Dunn	Old priest's adviser gave gem thought each day —story	Dec 1971	117b-118e
	What is a teacher? —good list		119a-c
	You can't teach anybody anything...		119c
Boyd K. Packer	Very few , are unworthy of support	May 1983	67f
Dwan J. Young	Everyone is a teacher - by example	May 1988	78e-f
Virginia H. Pearce	Convert called to be ,	Nov 1996	14a
	Every , can be a better , —G.B. Hinckley		14a
Thomas S. Monson	, who truly cares makes the difference	May 1997	46a-b
Harold G. Hillam	Methods are replaced - but not need for good ,	Nov 1997	62d-64b
Dallin H. Oaks	Have you ever really had a , ? —good quote	Nov 1999	78b
Harold G. Hillam	Some , somewhere is teaching future prophet	May 2000	11c-d
Thomas S. Monson	, had students give away party fund —story	May 2004	20f-22b
James E. Faust	Experience and others' mistakes are good ,		52c-e
Julie B. Beck	Mothers are ,	Nov 2007	77b-d
Dallin H. Oaks	Don't substitute your own lesson		107f-108a
William D. Oswald	Every position requires an effective ,	Nov 2008	96b
	Jesus was the Master Teacher		96d-e
	A good , calls students by name		97a-d
Richard G. Scott	An inspiring , and a learned , —story	Nov 2009	7b-8d
Russell T. Osguthorpe	Got him to give talk —story		15f-16b
	Encouraged him to aim high —story		16b-c
	Laundress helped him learn Tahitian —story		16d-f
Henry B. Eyring	Taught until 90 at own request	May 2010	23b-d
L. Tom Perry	His mother as a , —story		29d-30c

Teaching
Related Topics: Education, Teachers

Alvin R. Dyer	Sensitivity training is inconsistent with gospel principles	June 1969	40e-41a
Ezra Taft Benson	Sensitivity training breaks down personal standards		44e-46e
Eldred G. Smith	Can't wait for perfection before you teach		86a
Harold B. Lee	Teach first principles of gospel—Don't jump to top rung		104f-105a
Joseph F. Smith	Duty of Zion's watchmen	Dec 1969	37b
Spencer W. Kimball	Results on children —story		49c

Teaching, cont'd
Related Topics: Education, Teachers

Spencer W. Kimball	Results in 2 families —story	Dec 1969	50a
	By parents behind iron curtain		50c
David O. McKay	Opportunity for , in Church		111c
	Opportunities and obligations		111d
Boyd K. Packer	What if youth are not warned of pitfalls? —story	June 1970	51f-52c
Thomas S. Monson	Molding souls —good poem		90c-d
Joseph Fielding Smith	Teach in plainness - not theory or philosophy	Dec 1970	2f
Thomas S. Monson	Purpose of , is to change lives		101b-c
	Hear and forget, see and remember, do and learn		103a
Howard W. Hunter	Customers are influenced by the packaging	June 1971	51a
	Specifications for the meetinghouse library		52a-b
David B. Haight	Explanation of Teacher Development Program		53a-54f
A. Theodore Tuttle	, in the home by example	Dec 1971	91c-f
Paul H. Dunn	Beggar shown worth - begged no more —poem		120e
Harold B. Lee	Honesty not taught by , burglary	July 1972	32c
	"I teach them correct principles…" —Joseph Smith		32c
	Don't overemphasize unrighteous philosophies		32d
H. Burke Peterson	Parents taught him by example		47d
Howard W. Hunter	The bird who taught its young —story		85a
N. Eldon Tanner	Parents to teach discipline	July 1973	8d
Spencer W. Kimball	Must be done in infancy		16e
	If children taught well, they can't go wrong		16f
Robert L. Simpson	Helps us progress when we teach		22c
Paul H. Dunn	Teach toward individual - red schoolhouse —story		30b
David B. Haight	Bishops and teachers can't do it all		56e
Harold B. Lee	Warning against sensationalism —Ivins		97b
Paul H. Dunn	You can't go back to where you ain't been	May 1974	15a
	To mom: "How does it feel to have all my sins on you?"		15a
	Couplet on , by example —good		15b-c
David B. Haight	The wind still whips the leaves, but the roots are down	May 1975	12b
Vaughn J. Featherstone	Teach self worth—you'll have class in the palm of your hand	Nov 1976	103d-f
	Every bird came back —story		105d-f
Spencer W. Kimball	Later , is done to compensate for early failure	May 1978	5f-6a
Jacob de Jager	Savior taught using simple illustrations —poem	Nov 1978	68d
Spencer W. Kimball	Improve the quality of ,	May 1981	45d-e
Paul H. Dunn	Teach the why	Nov 1981	71c-d
Marion G. Romney	A good reason for repetition	May 1982	87e-f
Boyd K. Packer	Strength of , determines how temptations will be handled	May 1983	68b
M. Russell Ballard	How Church lesson manuals are prepared		68d-f
	Use scriptures and words of General Authorities as sources		69d-f
A. Theodore Tuttle	Church cannot assume prime responsibility for ,	May 1984	24b-d
	Draw out instead of pouring on		24f
Ezra Taft Benson	Repetition is a key to learning	Nov 1985	36b
Dallin H. Oaks	Failure to teach basics permits misunderstanding —story	Nov 1988	65d-e
L. Tom Perry	Father held on to doorknob to keep son in class —story		73b-74a

Teaching

L. Tom Perry	, children to be good missionaries and people —story	Nov 1988	73b-75f
Thomas S. Monson	The noblest profession —D.O. McKay	Nov 1991	67e-f
Dallas N. Archibald	Pouring a bucketful into a glass	Nov 1992	26c-f
Boyd K. Packer	Ultimate purpose of every ,	May 1994	19e
Ruth B. Wright	She taught children while changing diapers		85b-d
	Mother had children repeat statement —story		85f
Chieko N. Okazaki	Spoke in Spanish, Korean and Tongan	May 1996	13d-f
Henry B. Eyring	How to teach families sacred truths		62b-d
Virginia H. Pearce	Where can you learn , ?	Nov 1996	12c-d
	Two classes contrasted —inactivity story		12d-f
	There are three parts to a lesson		13a
	An effective lesson demonstrated —story		13b-14a
Boyd K. Packer	Study of doctrine will improve behavior	May 1997	9b
Henry B. Eyring	Law of witnesses: Prophets quote one another		25a-b
Thomas S. Monson	Father walked rather than gas up on Sabbath —story	Nov 1997	18b-e
Janette Hales Beckham	Children must be moved - not titillated —good		76b-c
Virginia U. Jensen	Law of harvest most evident in homes		90d-e
Jeffrey R. Holland	Entire talk - good quotes	May 1998	25b-27f
	Theological Twinkies and fried froth		26f-27a
Thomas S. Monson	Children may not listen or understand —story	Nov 1998	49b-c
L. Tom Perry	History of organization of Sunday School	May 1999	6b-e
	Flannel board presentation swayed board —story		8c-f
	The noblest profession —D.O. McKay		8f
Henry B. Eyring	, of parents lasts generations —story		74d-75f
Vaughn J. Featherstone	A precious or damaging work	Nov 1999	14d-f
Dallin H. Oaks	Teach doctrine - not rules		79f
	Teach the prescribed lesson		80a-b
	Teach by the Holy Ghost		80c-d
	Marble and brass perish - minds don't		80e
James E. Faust	Master pianist put arms around student —story		101b-c
Jay E. Jensen	In teaching, we teach ourselves	May 2000	28b
Thomas S. Monson	Teacher's grave decorated each year —story	Nov 2001	100d-f
Coleen K. Menlove	Held Primary for just one child —story	Nov 2002	13f-14b
Susan W. Tanner	Learned all gospel principles at home first	May 2003	73c-e
Gordon B. Hinckley	, by Spirit - Boy's prayer answered —story	May 2003	117e-118b
Henry B. Eyring	Six things to teach those you love	Nov 2003	89b-92f
Thomas S. Monson	, is best done in home —McKay	Nov 2004	115a
	Wife converted husband —tender story		115b-116a
Thomas S. Monson	First years are critically important	May 2005	19e-f
Boyd K. Packer	Curriculum restructured to center on 4 things	Nov 2005	72f
Daniel K. Judd	Giving dirt to horses rather than grain	Nov 2007	93b-d
	People come to church to be nourished		93d-e
	Possible to feed without nourishing		94b-c
	Spirit teaches with greatest effect		94d-95a
Dallin H. Oaks	Don't substitute your own lesson		107f-108a

Teaching, cont'd
Related Topics: Education, Teachers

Russell M. Nelson	How to best teach and correct children	May 2008	9a-10a
Gerald Causse	Take a great subject and make a child understand	Nov 2008	32d-e
	The goal of , is the conversion of hearts		34b
William D. Oswald	How 3 tiny girls learned to jump rope —story		95d-96b
	, is the center of all we do		96b
	Make your students ponder		97f
Silvia H. Allred	Symbolic , in temple means Spirit teaches us		113b-c
M. Russell Ballard	God's plan: Teach children to be better than you	May 2009	33b-34a
Richard G. Scott	Inspirational , and show-off , —story	Nov 2009	7b-8d
Vicki F. Matsumori	Help students recognize Spirit —Blanket story		11d-f
Russell T. Osguthorpe	Teach doctrine, invite to do, then promise blessings		15b-f
	Goal is not just information but to do —Monson		15c&e
	Questions to ask about your ,		17a
	Saves lives —entire talk		15b-17f
D. Todd Christofferson	Must be constant , in home		107c
L. Tom Perry	No such thing as overpreparing	May 2010	31a-b
	, in home: Another layer of insulation		31f
Richard G. Scott	Must be done primarily in home		77d-78a
Francisco J. Viñas	Make converts of children by ,		106a-108b
Neil L. Andersen	Cannot be casual in our ,		108e
	Are stories of Jesus embedded in children?		109b-e
	Every morning without fail —story		110f-111e

Temple Marriage
Related Topics: Marriage, Temples

David O. McKay	Do not go to temple unless you will keep covenants	June 1969	28e-29a
S. Dilworth Young	Brings a taste of eternal life		84f-85a
Eldred G. Smith	Cause of greatest happiness	Dec 1969	60d
Marion D. Hanks	Statistics of , among youth		93f
Boyd K. Packer	The loftiest mountain youth will climb	June 1970	51b-e
Neal A. Maxwell	95% of institute graduates have a ,	Dec 1970	94c-d
Spencer W. Kimball	All 8 children married in temple —story	Dec 1971	36c-37a
Harold B. Lee	Testimony of mother whose husband became active		114a-e
O. Leslie Stone	His wife wouldn't marry till he became worthy	Jan 1973	80b
Hartman Rector, Jr.	No promise to family ties without ,	July 1973	59a
N. Eldon Tanner	How some parents taught ,		92f
Gordon B. Hinckley	Conversation with non-member couple about , —story	May 1974	22e-23c
	When , is understood, no distance is too great —story		23f-24a
	I want you only for a little while —funny story		24d-e
Mark E. Petersen	Willing to make yourself a widow for eternity? —Kimball	Nov 1974	51d-e
Ezra Taft Benson	Decision on , affects generations	May 1979	33d-e
Paul H. Dunn	Why temple marriage —story	Nov 1981	71d-72b
James E. Faust	One of 7 "blockbuster" doctrines	Nov 2005	21f
Dallin H. Oaks	Surprised that his mother was a widow —story		27d-f

Joseph Fielding Smith	Fullness of priesthood available only in ,	June 1970	65f-66c
	What the covenants in , entail		66c-d
LeGrand Richards	, will dot Europe —J.F. Smith	Dec 1970	70f
LeGrand Richards	Salt Lake Temple to stand through Millennium —story	Dec 1971	81d-f
H. Burke Peterson	How parents taught him importance of ,	July 1972	47d
Harold B. Lee	How to increase attendance at ,		103b
Eldred G. Smith	Will be found all over earth	Jan 1973	56f
LeGrand Richards	Will be thousands of , —Pres. Young and Woodruff	Nov 1974	54b
William H. Bennett	What occurs there	Nov 1975	46d-47b
A. Theodore Tuttle	Work done in , keeps earth from being smitten	May 1980	40b-c
Loren C. Dunn	Inspiration for Widtsoe's experiment came in , —story	May 1981	25e
James E. Faust	We can't build , without bells of hell ringing	May 1983	40c
Adney Y. Komatsu	Exaltation not obtainable without ,	Nov 1983	28b-d
Gordon B. Hinckley	The bells of hell begin to ring each time , built	Nov 1985	54b
	, work comes nearest the vicarious work of the Savior		60e-f
Joseph B. Wirthlin	Lutheran bishop's thoughts on Sweden temple	Nov 1986	60e-f
	Dedication of GDR and Freiburg Temple —story		60f-61b
Boyd K. Packer	Elder Tuttle's crowning service was in ,	May 1987	23d-e
Ezra Taft Benson	A promise for increased personal revelation		85f
J. Richard Clarke	I'm no longer the only member in my family	May 1989	61d
F. Enzio Busche	, bring gospel into sharper focus		71d-e
Russell M. Nelson	Highest ordinances received together or not at all	Nov 1989	20f
Gordon B. Hinckley	What constitutes worthiness for a recommend	May 1990	49d-52f
	Recommends used to be signed by Church President		50e-f
	Will you let a cup of coffee stand between you and , —story		51b-c
	Why sustaining leaders is prerequisite		51c-e
	Why paying taxes is prerequisite		51e-f
	Why paying child support is prerequisite		51f-52c
	Do not use , language outside ,		52d-e
David B. Haight	Answers to problems come because of , attendance-Widtsoe	Nov 1990	61b-c
Gordon B. Hinckley	44 operating ,	May 1991	52d-e
David B. Haight	Clear heart of disharmony before going	May 1992	15b-f
	Brigham Young's definition of the endowment		15f-16a
	How to receive revelation in ,		16c-d
	Understand endowment by seeing beyond symbols		16d
	President Benson's promise for increased revelation		16d
Russell M. Nelson	, sealings - His most important accomplishment		74c-d
Gordon B. Hinckley	Nine , announced or reported on	Nov 1992	21b
Thomas S. Monson	What gift do you want? - A temple sealing —story		99a-e
Thomas S. Monson	One great program on both sides of veil	May 1993	5d-f
Boyd K. Packer	3 Missouri temples never built		18e
	, ordinances carried West in Apostles' minds		19a
	16 inverted granite arches under Salt Lake ,		19e
	History of , building in Church		18d-21b
	Fullness of priesthood only obtained in ,		20a-b

David B. Haight	San Diego Temple open house - observations	May 1993	23d-f
	, worship available since Adam		24b-d
	, work done by 83-year-old woman —story		25b-c
Gordon B. Hinckley	45 operating ,		73f
	Temples are built to stand through Millennium		74a
	Square footage of temples compared		74b
	Capstone laying and dedication of Salt Lake , —story		72b-75f
Howard W. Hunter	The great symbol of our membership	Nov 1994	8e-f
	Every adult should be temple-worthy		8e-f
Claudio R. M. Costa	Family sold everything to go to , —story		27d-e
Joseph B. Wirthlin	Feed soul through , attendance		75d
Lance B. Wickman	The temple is in me		83b-d
	The , is the key to all holy places		82d-83f
Russell M. Nelson	, work and missionary work are the same		84b
	The necessity of baptism for dead		84c-85a
	, work before Christ was only for living		85a
	Kirtland , Nauvoo , and baptism for dead		85a-b
	"They without us cannot be made perfect"		85c-d
	How the Nelson family does , work		85f-86a
	For whom do we do , work?		86b-d
Howard W. Hunter	Our ultimate earthly goal - crucial ordinances		87d-88e
J. Ballard Washburn	Do family history and take children to , for baptisms	May 1995	11d-f
	Going to , a greater highlight than mission call —Hunter		12b
	Preventing childbirth is breaking temple covenant		12c-d
	We go to , to make covenants but go home to keep them		12d-e
L. Tom Perry	Young father died working on temple —story		73b-d
Gordon B. Hinckley	47 , and more announced	Nov 1995	52c-53b
Gordon B. Hinckley	Building , to serve through Millennium	May 1997	5a
James E. Faust	Brigham Young worked late into night at Nauvoo ,		18b-f
	Salt Lake Temple announced 2nd day after arrival.		18b-f
	Hundreds to be built —prophecy		18b-f
	Deepest questions of existence answered in ,		19b-f
	All are equal in ,		20b-c
	Paramount reasons for pioneers' willingness to suffer		20c-f
	President Hinckley dedicated 24 of 49 operating ,		20d
Russell M. Nelson	Selection of Ecuador , site —story	Nov 1997	16c
Gordon B. Hinckley	50 operating ,		49c
	How smaller , will work		49d-50b
David B. Haight	The great moment of his life - in a sealing room		71d-f
Gordon B. Hinckley	Announcement of 30 small temples	May 1998	87f-88e
James E. Faust	Sacrifice for , was not sacrifice but joy	Nov 1998	59f-60b
David E. Sorensen	Statistics on numbers of temples		64c-e
	Every , lessens power of Satan —G.Q. Cannon		65b
	Man was no longer only member following , work —story		65e-f
	A gate to heaven —L. Snow		65f

Temples

Carol B. Thomas	A place where revelation may be expected	May 1999	13d
	Adversary resists , because place of power		13d-e
	Things to do in lieu of , attendance		13f-14b
Richard G. Scott	Preparing for first , visit —entire talk		25d-27f
	Greatest joys have their roots in , ordinances		25e
	Limit those who accompany you to ,		26d
	Don't abandon hope for , marriage —story		27b-c
Thomas S. Monson	, work releases from bondage and darkness		56d-e
Gordon B. Hinckley	Announcement to rebuild Nauvoo ,		89b
Gordon B. Hinckley	15 , dedicated in 1999	Nov 1999	4b-c
	New , offer every ordinance Salt Lake Temple offers		5b-6a
	May dedicate 42 , in 2000		6b
	3 prerequisites to build , in an area		6b
James E. Faust	Sisters enter solely on worthiness - brethren need priesthood		102c-e
Statistical Report	68 in operation, 15 dedicated in 1999	May 2000	22e
Glenn L. Pace	Wasatch Front - A , always in sight		25e
	Necessity for nearby , - 700 unendowed missionaries		25f-26d
Gordon B. Hinckley	76 in operation - 36 new this year		87f-88a
D. Todd Christofferson	Work for dead testifies of Jesus —entire talk	Nov 2000	9d-12b
Gordon B. Hinckley	81 dedicated in 20 years - 100th last Sunday		68b-d
Gordon B. Hinckley	103 dedicated and 18 more announced	May 2001	5d-6a
Statistical Report	34 dedicated in 2000		22b
Russell M. Nelson	Everything we do in Church points toward ,		32e-f
	Breaking , covenants is worse than not making them		32f
	Recommend questions are spiritual separators		33b-d
	, dress standards		33d-e
	, teachings are simple yet lofty		33e-f
	List of required reading before going first time		33f-34a
	How and when , garment should be worn		35a-b
Gordon B. Hinckley	103 , dedicated		67d
David B. Haight	6 day buggy trip to be married —story		70b-d
L. Lionel Kendrick	Reverence in the ,		78c-f
	Enhancing our , experience —entire talk		78b-79f
Thomas S. Monson	Family sold car and quit job to go to , —story	May 2002	49f-50c
Russell M. Nelson	Special foundation under , in Mexico City		75b-c
Gordon B. Hinckley	The building and rebuilding of Nauvoo ,	Nov 2002	4d-6e
	114 temples		6e
	I urge you to utilize the temples		6e-f
Robert D. Hales	Paying tithing got family to , —story		27c-e
Gordon B. Hinckley	Recommends to be renewed every two years		56f-57a
Robert D. Hales	We need , endowment to get through trials	May 2003	17e
Statistical Report	114 temples		25e
L. Tom Perry	Our families are not yet ours —Brigham Young		42d-e
Anne C. Pingree	18-mile walk for recommends in Africa —story	Nov 2003	13d-f
Gordon B. Hinckley	Isaiah 2:2-3 refers to Salt Lake Temple		82e-f

F. Michael Watson	116 operating ,	May 2004	26e
Gordon B. Hinckley	130 announced or dedicated	Nov 2004	4f-5d
Elaine S. Dalton	There will be thousands of , —Brigham Young		89f-90d
	The , is the reason for everything we do		90e
	Youth serving in , work: an untapped resource		90f-91e
Gordon B. Hinckley	Go to , a little more frequently		104f-105a
	We become saviors on Mount Zion		105b-c
	Ponder and pray in God's living room		105d-f
Gordon B. Hinckley	47 in 1995 - 119 to 122 today	May 2005	5d
Russell M. Nelson	The reason for the Restoration and creation		16f
F. Michael Watson	119 temples in operation		25c
James E. Faust	87 , during President Hinckley's administration		53a
Gordon B. Hinckley	What temple attendance will do		102f
Gordon B. Hinckley	122 temples in operation	Nov 2005	4d-f
	32 million ordinances last year		4f
	Other , announced and under construction		4f-5f
James E. Faust	One of 7 "blockbuster" doctrines		21f
James E. Faust	Only a few places where life's questions answered	May 2006	67a-d
David R. Stone	Manhattan temple is silent inside		92a-b
Gordon B. Hinckley	123rd temple dedicated	Nov 2006	4d
Richard H. Winkel	Love for family increases by attendance at ,		9d-f
	Sealed wayward children will return —quote		10d-f
	Dust and distraction settle out in ,		10f
	A place of personal revelation		10f-11a
	A place to experience divine presence		11b
	Everything in , testifies of Jesus Christ		11b
Robert D. Hales	Covenants made in , more important than mission	May 2007	49e-f
Gordon B. Hinckley	Woman did 20,000 endowments		85a-b
Yoshihiko Kikuchi	Rain came because of tithing, fasting and , —story		97e-98d
Enrique R. Falabella	15-day journey to temple —story	Nov 2007	14b-e
Keith K. Hilbig	A marvelous environment to seek revelation		39d-e
Octaviano Tenorio	Father joined Church - Family sealed —story		95f-96e
	Happy - even when children died —story		96e-97f
Russell M. Nelson	Sealing ordinances are essential to exaltation	May 2008	10b
	What about those who cannot be sealed?		10b-c
F. Michael Watson	124 in operation		25c
Thomas S. Monson	Report on dedications and cultural events of 3 ,	Nov 2008	4b-6a
	Announcement of 5 new ,		6b
Silvia H. Allred	The most holy places on earth		112b-c
	1976 trip to , required crossing 6 borders —story		112c-e
	Good explanation of ordinances in ,		113a-b
	In , are our credentials for admission to God		113b
	Symbolic teaching in , means Spirit must teach us		113b-c
	How to prepare to go to ,		113d-114a
	6 things we must do in relation to ,		114b

Temples

Temples, cont'd
Related Topics: Temple Marriage, Work for Dead

D. Todd Christofferson	Obtain all God's divine possibilities through ,	May 2009	20d
Statistical Report	128 in operation at end of 2008		30e
Richard G. Scott	Sacrifice to go far, but neglect nearby , - Set goals		43d
	He's attended every week for 14 years		43d-e
	What is more important than , attendance?		43e
	Suggestions to improve , experience		43e-44b
	Ordinances in Nauvoo prepared pioneers - Journal		44f-45a
	Sustained by covenants after family deaths —story		45a-f
Dallin H. Oaks	Love and service are only motives for work in ,		93c
David A. Bednar	Stake president's focus would have been on ,		97b-d
	Baptism and sacrament point toward ,		97e-98f
	Bells of hell ring when , are built —Brigham Young		98f-99a
	A difference in those who consistently worship in ;		99b
	The protecting power of , ordinances and covenants		99b-100a
	Covenants of , gave Nauvoo refugees strength		100b-d
	Plea to young, old, and inactive to come to ,		100e-f
Gary E. Stevenson	Never lost when you can see the , —story		101b-e
	Replace some leisure activities with , service		101e
	Make your home like a ,		101f-102e
	The ultimate purpose of all we teach —B.K. Packer		103a-b
	Grandfather had girl touch the ,		103d-f
Thomas S. Monson	Admonition to go often		113f-114a
Ann M. Dibb	Dad took girl 2500 miles to , to complete goals —story		116b-f
Elaine S. Dalton	Never allow the goal of , to be out of your sight		122f-123a
Thomas S. Monson	83% of members are within 200 miles of ,	Nov 2009	4d
	5 new , announced		4d-f
M. Russell Ballard	Everything including , focuses on families		47b-c
L. Tom Perry	Manti Temple built without power tools		73e-f
	Settling Sanpete County and building Manti Temple		74a-75c
Joseph W. Sitati	Marriage in , eliminates tradition of a dowry		105a-b
Statistical Report	130 in operation at end of 2009	May 2010	28c
Jeffrey R. Holland	Arms us with power, glory and angels		46a
Elaine S. Dalton	Dismayed, discouraged, distracted, delayed, disqualified		121b

Temptation
Related Topics: Sin

David O. McKay	Satan will tempt you in your weakest point	June 1969	28c-d
	Virtues are negative until tested —poem		29a-b
Delbert L. Stapley	Sometimes hard to stay up there with high standards		72f
Richard L. Evans	When you flee , don't leave forwarding address	June 1970	38d-e
Sterling W. Sill	There are , upward as well as downward		45c-d
	, without imply desires within		45d
Eldred G. Smith	Resist , and thereby bind Satan in your life		104b-d
N. Eldon Tanner	I am happy for having , —Brigham Young	Dec 1971	34e
	Determine your course before , comes		34f
Richard L. Evans	We gain the strength of the , we resist —Emerson		58b

Temptation, cont'd
Related Topics: Sin

Richard L. Evans	Don't tempt , . Stay away from the precipice	Dec 1971	58e
Elray L. Christiansen	We won't have , beyond our abilities to overcome		60a-b
Sterling W. Sill	Decide in advance what you definitely won't do		92a-c
	I won't know how I'll react until I know what the , is		92f-93a
Alvin R. Dyer	Idlers have trouble resisting ,		120f
Harold B. Lee	Know how to meet a , before it comes	July 1972	102f
Delbert L. Stapley	Decide your course before , comes	Jan 1974	44c
N. Eldon Tanner	As a youth the General Authority fled from the girl —story	Nov 1975	75f-76c
Howard W. Hunter	Jesus victorious over , as a man, not as a God	Nov 1976	19a
	3 categories of , —D.O. McKay		19c-e
N. Eldon Tanner	Make up mind early how you will react	May 1979	45b-c
Marvin J. Ashton	Those who yield to , become weaker	Nov 1980	60e
Dean L. Larsen	Some recover from these excursions - Others are tragic	Nov 1981	26f-27a
Marvin J. Ashton	Never give in, never give in ... —Churchill		89f
Dean L. Larsen	, will increase, stigmas will disappear	May 1983	34a-f
Gordon B. Hinckley	When , comes name him "Goliath" and slay him		46f-52e
Neal A. Maxwell	Jesus gave no heed to his temptations	May 1987	71b-c
	If we entertain , soon it begins to entertain us.		71b-c
	He will make a way to escape or a way to bear it.		71b-c
Robert D. Hales	Coyotes entice lambs by frolicking pups —story		75e-f
Richard G. Scott	No one today will avoid serious sin without Lord's help	May 1989	36c-d
Boyd K. Packer	There are , now that didn't exist yesterday		54a-c
	Gareth and the Black Knight —story		54c-e
	Run away from ,		54f
	Dual alarm system: Pain and guilt		54f-59a
Neal A. Maxwell	Entertaining , sets stage for succumbing	May 1990	34b
Joseph B. Wirthlin	Good activities done to excess are sin - sports, TV, homes	Nov 1990	65a-e
Spencer J. Condie	All , comes from pride or discouragement	Nov 1993	15f-16d
Joseph B. Wirthlin	If we entertain , it begins entertaining us	May 1994	40e
Dallin H. Oaks	Music may neutralize ,	Nov 1994	11f-12a
Boyd K. Packer	Following false spirits causes great injury		61c-d
James E. Faust	Living on edge is perilously close to bottomless pit —story	Nov 1995	45d-46c
Boyd K. Packer	Land mines on the way to maturity have increased	May 1996	17b-c
	King chose driver who would stay away from edge		18b
Rulon G. Craven	The purpose of and dealing with ,		76b-77f
James E. Faust	Refrain - the next abstinence will be easier	May 2000	44f
Boyd K. Packer	If you don't act on , you need feel no guilt	Nov 2000	74c-d
R. Conrad Schultz	Sneaker wave nearly capsized boat —story	May 2002	29d-f
James E. Faust	Trials and , - No one invincible —Titanic story		46d-47b
Thomas S. Monson	No , when on Lord's side of line —G.A. Smith		99d-e
James E. Faust	Selfishness is the strongest ,	Nov 2002	19f
James E. Faust	Iguacu Falls and staying on Lord's side	May 2003	51b-e
Boyd K. Packer	We are not condemned for , or tendencies	Nov 2003	26b
Gordon B. Hinckley	Yielding to , creates unhealing wounds	May 2004	114b
Thomas S. Monson	Octopus traps are all around us	May 2006	18b-d

Temptation

Thomas S. Monson	Grasping , causes loss of greatest desires	May 2006	20b
	Cardinal Wolsey's fall		20d-f
Marcus B. Nash	Hooks are set suddenly —entire talk	Nov 2006	49b-50f
Joseph B. Wirthlin	Tempted to move ball 2 inches —story	May 2007	46b-e
James E. Faust	We must guard against , all our lives		55a-b
Walter F. Gonzalez	Cut off every bad influence	Nov 2007	54f-55a
Richard G. Scott	Heavy man ordering doughnuts —humor		92b-c
Thomas S. Monson	Prayer is a defense against ,		119f-120a
Dieter F. Uchtdorf	"The Story of the Light Bulb" —story	May 2009	59d-e
	Nehemiah building walls of Jerusalem —story		60a-c
	Letting the unimportant distract —entire talk		59b-62f
Thomas S. Monson	Daily scripture study increases power against ,		68a-e
Boyd K. Packer	Mind needs a delete key during , - Use music	Nov 2009	46a
Dale G. Renlund	Identify , and put , way out of reach		99b
D. Todd Christofferson	Mere wanting is no guide for moral conduct		107f
Jeffrey R. Holland	Separate self from , - proximity can be fatal	May 2010	45c-d
Thomas S. Monson	You can bear it - 1 Cor. 10:13		66e-f

Loren C. Dunn	How to gain a ,	Dec 1968	78e-f
David O. McKay	How President McKay gained a , —story		85b-c
Robert L. Simpson	Obtain , by practicing doctrines		89a
Spencer W. Kimball	How to gain a , —good		100f
Hugh B. Brown	Vivid sense of own divinity	Dec 1969	32e
Bruce R. McConkie	First revelation a person must receive is a ,		84f
	Must be kept current		86c
Thomas S. Monson	Power of , makes convert —story		91b
Robert L. Simpson	Manifestations confirm but don't create , —McKay story	Dec 1970	96e-97a
Bruce R. McConkie	Restoration proven through , not through scripture		114e
Franklin D. Richards	A , alone will not save us	June 1971	47c
Loren C. Dunn	How to gain a , —story of 2 boys		81f-82e
	The power of a , —Brigham Young		82e-f
Henry D. Taylor	We will not be able to endure on borrowed light — Kimball		108b
	, gained through clean living and prayer —McKay		108b-c
	Must be fed by daily study —Lee		109c-e
Marvin J. Ashton	Possessors of , have obligation to bear witness	July 1972	63a
N. Eldon Tanner	He had the visitor's friend bear , —story		101b
Harold B. Lee	We must see the power of God rest upon leaders		103e
Bruce R. McConkie	I Believe in Christ —poem		109c-e
Harold B. Lee	More powerful than sight	Jan 1973	25f
Bruce R. McConkie	A gift		36b
	A strong , by McConkie		36b
Loren C. Dunn	Church's strength in individual , —Lee		84a
	All entitled to a ,		84a
	Bearing of , brings spirit of ,		85e

Testimony, cont'd
Related Topics: —

Vaughn J. Featherstone	He gained his , from 3 Nephi 17	Jan 1973	95d
Harold B. Lee	Sacrifice of convert because of ,		108e
A. Theodore Tuttle	Must go down into heart like fire	July 1973	18f
	Bear , shift responsibility		20a
Bruce R. McConkie	Obligation to study and bear ,		28f
	Obligation to study and bear ,		29d
	You can't argue with a ,		29e
	Present reasoning then bear ,		30a
Gordon B. Hinckley	Nothing else matters —Asian convert story		48b
	Strength of Church lies in individual ,		49e
	The wonder of this work is that each may know		50c
Robert L. Simpson	Testimony of First Vision is basis of service	Jan 1974	87b
Franklin D. Richards	Formula for obtaining a ,	May 1974	57f
Rex D. Pinegar	Father's , saved daughter from bad marriage —story		68a-d
Boyd K. Packer	Testimony of humble men vs. academic giants		95b-c
Hartman Rector, Jr.	What is a testimony?		109c
Bruce R. McConkie	What is a , - Who can have one	Nov 1974	35a
	What is "being valiant in , of Jesus?"		35a-e
A. Theodore Tuttle	We gain , as we bear , —story		72c-e
O. Leslie Stone	What is a , ?	May 1975	8b
	Things to do to gain a ,		8f
	A , must be recaptured every day —Lee		9e
Neal A. Maxwell	Powerful , of Jesus —entire talk	May 1976	26a-27e
	Bear , to others - they become accountable for it		27e
Gene R. Cook	Woman bore , and touched a heart —story		103d-e
James E. Faust	His stirring ,	Nov 1976	59e-f
Henry D. Taylor	, grows thinner without daily scripture study —Lee		62e
Marion G. Romney	If you have , no storm could drive you from work —story		70b-d
Loren C. Dunn	A more certain way of knowing than seeing	May 1977	31a-c
	Warm spot in heart gave man a , —story		31c-32b
Gordon B. Hinckley	Don't go to Xerox Co. for information about IBM—story		64e-f
George P. Lee	We aren't born fully grown. Neither is a ,	May 1978	27f
Thomas S. Monson	Action must stem from desire more than duty	May 1979	35f
Rex C. Reeve, Jr.	Sacred obligation to bear ,	Nov 1980	27f
Marion G. Romney	How his wife gained a , —story	Nov 1981	15b-f
Ezra Taft Benson	What a , is	May 1982	62d-63e
	Won't be able to endure on borrowed light —H.C. Kimball		63e-64b
J. Richard Clarke	He gained his , by reading the scriptures —story	Nov 1982	13b-e
Ezra Taft Benson	A , is to have current inspiration	May 1983	54f
James E. Faust	Basis for all , is a , of the Book of Mormon	Nov 1983	9f-10a
	A way to know more surely than seeing		11b
Angel Abrea	Our , is more important than our life	May 1984	71a
Henry B. Eyring	He received a , as a very young boy	May 1985	76b-f
Thomas S. Monson	Men work hardest when dedicated to a cause	May 1986	38b-c
Robert L. Simpson	The formula for obtaining a , of anything	May 1987	42a-b

Testimony

Thomas S. Monson	Bus driver asked if anyone could tell about Mormons —story	May 1988	43a-c
James E. Faust	No one need depend continually on another's ,	Nov 1988	14e
John K. Carmack	Desire must precede ,		26a-b
	3 ways people lose ,		27a-d
David B. Haight	Is our , as great as the pioneers' - Yes		82f-83a
Ezra Taft Benson	His , of the Plan of Salvation —entire talk		86b-87f
Joseph B. Wirthlin	The effect President Benson's , had in Moscow —story	May 1989	9d-10a
Hugh W. Pinnock	4 steps to a strengthened ,		11d-12c
Richard G. Scott	Like a fire a , initially requires outside energy		35b-c
Helvecio Martins	Opens our eyes, minds, and hearts —story	Nov 1990	26b-27b
Dallin H. Oaks	Jesus not mentioned in 17 testimonies		30a
	Preceded by witness of Holy Ghost		30b-d
Boyd K. Packer	Comes when sought - Can't be forced	Nov 1991	21b-d
Charles Didier	Cannot endure on borrowed light —H.C. Kimball		62c-d
	Strength of Church is in individual testimony — Lee		62d
	What constitutes a ,		62e-f
	Steps to obtain a ,		62f-63b
	Hold on to , by bearing it		63f-64a
	One of few possessions we can keep		64b
James E. Faust	Benefits of bearing ,	May 1992	8b
Carlos E. Asay	E.T. Benson bore , in Moscow		41d-f
R.S. Conference	, of 5 women from 5 continents		93a-95b
Glenn L. Pace	Time to develop own ,	Nov 1992	11e
	Our light must be original - not reflected		12b
Joseph B. Wirthlin	Signs of a weak ,		35b-c
Gordon B. Hinckley	President Benson's stirring , of Jesus	May 1993	93c-e
Robert D. Hales	What a , is —excellent	Nov 1994	20b-e
	How each prophet received his ,		20e-21f
	A , develops like a photograph		22a-b
	How to gain a , —excellent		22b-d
L. Aldin Porter	, comes when we do His will		64d-65a
Loren C. Dunn	The law of witnesses —entire talk	Nov 1995	28b-29f
Keith B. McMullin	The law of witnesses —entire talk	May 1996	8b-9f
David B. Haight	His , of giving Blacks the priesthood —story		23d-f
Henry B. Eyring	How to give families a , and the Holy Ghost		62b-d
	Use , in family home evening		63b
	Tragedy shows one's , —story		64a-d
Henry B. Eyring	What a , is and isn't	Nov 1996	32e
	His powerful apostolic ,		33b
Thomas S. Monson	Czech girl's , converted dozens —story	May 1997	94a-b
Sheri L. Dew	"Grandma, what if the gospel isn't true?" —story	Nov 1997	91d-f
	Responsibility for , and how to gain one		91f-92e
Gordon B. Hinckley	Discussion on , —excellent	May 1998	69e-71f
Susan L. Warner	Holy Ghost bears , when we bear ,	Nov 1998	66e
	Taught , with fingers of his hand		67e-f

Testimony

Dallin H. Oaks	The law of witnesses —very good	May 1999	35b-36b
	The history of Martin Harris —story		36b-37f
Thomas S. Monson	"It is springtime and I am blind" —story		54b-e
	Blind man led him through darkness —story		54e-f
	One who he helped relit his candle —poem		56a
Boyd K. Packer	You can bear , to your grandchildren	Nov 1999	24f-25b
Angel Abrea	The highest type of knowledge —Widtsoe	May 2000	41f
	A possession we will both take with us and leave behind		42a
	Nephi's steps to receiving a ,		42b-d
	Results of having a ,		42e-f
Gordon B. Hinckley	His testimony —entire talk		69b-71f
Joseph B. Wirthlin	How John Taylor received his , —story	Nov 2000	22e-23a
	McKay's , came through performance of duty —story		23e-f
	, is to be found in the bearing of it		24b-c
Dallin H. Oaks	Conversion is far more than , —entire talk		32b-34f
James E. Faust	His growing , —entire talk excellent		53d-59f
L. Aldin Porter	, of Jesus comes from reading testimonies	May 2001	30b-32b
Boyd K. Packer	Student bore , to class —story	Nov 2001	63f-64a
Richard G. Scott	How to fortify a ,		87b-89b
James E. Faust	New, young stake president didn't have absolute , —story	May 2002	48a-e
Carlos H. Amado	A gift God gives to those who seek		80f
Joseph B. Wirthlin	Dramatic , came though Holy Ghost —story	May 2003	28d-f
Sydney S. Reynolds	Her , on one hand		114d
Sheldon F. Child	Shallow-rooted trees fell —story	Nov 2003	8b-c
	Some left Church during "The freeze" in Ghana —story		9f-10b
James E. Faust	A , begins with Jesus and Joseph Smith		19f
	A , comes by doing each principle		22d-f
Henry B. Eyring	, of eyewitnesses to Restoration		89e-90d
Keith B. McMullin	Have , and all else will come together	May 2004	33b-e
	Four prerequisites to gaining a ,		33f-34b
Boyd K. Packer	A , can immunize your children		78f
	Will change behavior		79b-d
Ronald T. Halverson	You know a thing when you live it	Nov 2004	32f-33a
Donald L. Staheli	Steps to a , - from Alma		38a-39a
M. Russell Ballard	Having a , is a rare thing		40b-c
	, meetings need to center on Savior		41a
	The basic things of which we need ,		41f
	Elder's tongue loosed when he testified as he should—Young		42a-c
	Fruits of Hyrum's , are immeasurable		42c-f
	, changes hearts —examples		42f-43b
Dallin H. Oaks	We must act upon our beliefs		46e-f
Cecil O. Samuelson, Jr.	What eyewitnesses said of Jesus	Nov 2004	51b-c
Thomas S. Monson	Apostles' , in 1980 Proclamation		56e
H. David Burton	Slow missionary had great , —story		100a-b
Joseph B. Wirthlin	Can't endure on borrowed light —H.C. Kimball		103f-104a

Testimony

Boyd K. Packer	No special spiritual experience came to him	May 2005	6f-7c
	, does not burst upon us suddenly		8b-d
Richard C. Edgley	African's chest was throbbing —story		10b-f
	A still small voice and a throbbing heart		10b-12f
Robert J. Whetten	Most inactives still have a ,		92f-93a
Thomas S. Monson	Rejected elder returned to testify of Joseph —story	Nov 2005	69b-f
James E. Faust	Alma's , came from Holy Ghost - not from angel	May 2006	51b-52d
Gordon B. Hinckley	His powerful benedictory ,		83b-f
Dieter F. Uchtdorf	Desire motivated learning English —story	Nov 2006	37b-f
	What is a , ?		37f-38c
	How a , is not acquired		38c-d
	How do we get a , ?		38c-39d
	What a , does		39d-f
Thomas S. Monson	Like Canadian roads, our foundation must be deep		62b-69b
A. Roger Merrill	, came while reading Book of Mormon		92d-93b
Boyd K. Packer	LeGrand Richards' , as a 12-year-old ,	May 2007	27b-d
Glenn L. Pace	Gained his , when reading Joseph Smith's story		78b-d
	, from Holy Ghost more certain than angels		78f-79f
Boyd K. Packer	, of Apostles no different than ours —story	Nov 2007	7f-8d
	President Romney's , as strong when just a missionary		8d-e
Mary N. Cook	, of missionary brought his family's sealing —story		12f-13b
Enrique R. Falabella	Why he's a member of the Church		14b-15f
Jeffrey R. Holland	His , of our Christianity		42b-e
Quentin L. Cook	Most important qualification for callings		70b-c
Douglas L. Callister	None can endure on borrowed light		100b-c
	New stake president didn't know —H.J. Grant story		100d-e
	"We do have the truth, don't we?" —story		100e-f
	, came after fasting and prayer —story		100f-101b
	No proxies for acquisition of a ,		101b
	Brigham's , cried out to be borne		101b-c
	Must be borne to family		101d
	What if family can't light lamps from ours?		101d-f
Henry B. Eyring	His , came before age 8 in a tiny branch	May 2008	23d-24a
Dallin H. Oaks	Not a travelogue, health log, or expression of love		26b
	How we know things		26d-27a
	How to gain a ,		27a-d
	Our obligation to bear ,		27d-28b
	Don't allow misrepresentations of Church		28b-e
	One of our two channels to God		28e-29a
	His model ,		29b
D. Todd Christofferson	Meaning of "born again" - How it's done		77a-78e
Boyd K. Packer	Apostles have that witness		87a
Susan W. Tanner	Holy Ghost bore , of Jesus to convert —story		113b-d
	Youth bore , through courageous actions		113f-114b
Elaine S. Dalton	Only one opposed to premarital sex —story		116e-117a

Testimony

Testimony, cont'd
Related Topics: —

Marcos A. Aidukaitis	A promise without reservation —G.B. Hinckley	Nov 2008	15f-16c
	If Book of Mormon is true, so are many other things		16c-d
Dieter F. Uchtdorf	His , of hope		24b-e
Robert D. Hales	The most powerful answer to accusers is ,		74b-d
	Mormon's , is his		75b
Carlos A. Godoy	Nothing dramatic happened to give him his ,		100d-102b
Allan F. Packer	To know and to feel —definition by D.H. Oaks	May 2009	17f
M. Russell Ballad	Comes by desire, study, prayer, obedience, service		34a-b
David A. Bednar	A difference in temple-going members		99b-100a
L. Tom Perry	"Open your mouths" - What to testify of		111a-e
David A. Bednar	Frequently bear , in family	Nov 2009	18f-19e
Robert D. Hales	Invitation to gain a personal ,		32b-f
Jeffrey R. Holland	Joseph's and Hyrum's dying ,		88f-89d
	Hostile witnesses to Book of Mormon wouldn't deny ,		89f-90c
	His powerful , of Book of Mormon		90c-f
	Amazing , of Church and Book of Mormon		88b-90f
Dale G. Renlund	Physical and spiritual heart transplants		97d-98e
	He analyzed why his , waned and fixed it —story		98e-99d
Michael T. Ringwood	Increases as we do seemingly insignificant things		102b-f
David A. Bednar	Spontaneously bear , to children	May 2010	42b-e
	Bear , and bless future posterity		43f
Thomas S. Monson	, of a dying boy —story		89f-90e
Neil L. Andersen	Your , will never leave your children		110c-e
	Your , will keep you safe —Monson		112b
Ann M. Dibb	Grow thinner if no daily scripture study —Lee		115f
Dieter F. Uchtdorf	Incorrect advice couldn't fool him		126f-127a

Thoughts
Related Topics: Meditation, Mind

Mark E. Petersen	Dirty stories: Satanic to promote evil ,	Dec 1968	91f
Sterling W. Sill	Mind is what it feeds upon	Dec 1969	46c
	Mind is colored by what it holds		46e
Paul H. Dunn	We just sit and think, mostly sit —story	Dec 1970	37d
Alvin R. Dyer	Man is what he thinks and does	Dec 1971	122a
Boyd K. Packer	How to banish evil thoughts - sing a hymn	Jan 1974	27e
Bruce R. McConkie	How , lead to actions		48a
	How to banish evil thoughts - preach a sermon		48d
Sterling W. Sill	The man decided to get out of the junk business —story		60d
Delbert L. Stapley	Thoughts - actions - habits - character	Nov 1974	20b-c
Spencer W. Kimball	, make the man —J. Edgar Hoover	May 1975	80d-e
	One's life and , register in face —story		80e-81b
J. Thomas Fyans	Your thoughts are like which type of river?		89b-c
Boyd K. Packer	Put up a "No Dumping" sign in your mind —good	Nov 1977	59e-60a
Marion G. Romney	We gravitate toward the subject of our ,	May 1980	66d
	We first endure, then pity, then embrace —poem		66f
Joseph B. Wirthlin	When will and imagination are in conflict will usually loses	May 1982	24d

Joseph B. Wirthlin	All we achieve or fail to achieve is the result of ,	May 1982	24d-e
Royden G. Derrick	A man becomes what he thinks about all day	May 1983	24c
	We select our type of life by our ,		24d
Ted E. Brewerton	We should be incurable optimists		73c-74a
Ezra Taft Benson	To lust in our heart is to deny the faith	Nov 1983	42d-e
	One who cannot control temper is not in control of ,		42e
Angel Abrea	Actions are fruits of either ignorance or knowledge	May 1984	70d
Russell M. Nelson	, precede deeds	Nov 1985	30e-f
Boyd K. Packer	, can lead to unworthy behavior	Nov 1986	17f
Ezra Taft Benson	Lust denies the faith and the Spirit departs		46d-e
Gordon B. Hinckley	Jesus commanded that we control our ,	May 1987	47b-c
Thomas S. Monson	Every action is preceded by a thought	Nov 1990	47a
Russell M. Nelson	Everyday , have not been lost - judgment		75d-e
Francis M. Gibbons	Patriarch dared not say that Grant would be president —story	Nov 1991	79b-e
Howard W. Hunter	Fantasies and pornography erode character	Nov 1994	50d
Neal A. Maxwell	According to our desires it shall be done	Nov 1995	23c-d
Joseph B. Wirthlin	We have a word of wisdom for the mind, too		76f-77d
Gordon B. Hinckley	Mind dwelt on sin before transgression	May 1996	48c
Rulon G. Craven	Visualize exit, stop, and wrong way signs		76e-f
Gordon B. Hinckley	We cannot even think about immorality		92c-d
Russell M. Nelson	Do not provide brain with unclean memories	Nov 1998	87b-c
Boyd K. Packer	"All the water in the world" —poem	Nov 1999	24b-c
	Rub thumb on wedding ring to dispel ,		24d-e
	Conquering the kingdom within —poem		24f
James E. Faust	Scriptures are a washing machine for unclean ,	May 2000	44d
James E. Faust	Unable to reason if you cross to devil's side	Nov 2000	45a-d
L. Tom Perry	Clean out the corners of our ,		60b-e
Boyd K. Packer	Fighting unworthy , may be a lifelong struggle		74c-d
L. Lionel Kendrick	Lord knows every ,	May 2001	79b
Wayne S. Peterson	Sow , reap a destiny —quote	Nov 2001	84b
Sharon G. Larsen	Are you in good company with your , ?	May 2002	91d
	Scriptures are best washing machine for ,		93b
James E. Faust	Succumb to tempter and lose reason	May 2003	51d
Charles W. Dahlquist, II	Hymn automatically replaced bad , —story	May 2007	94c-e
Gordon B. Hinckley	A magnificent promise if , are virtuous		115c-d
Donald L. Hallstrom	Addicts to mental indolence	Nov 2007	50f
Thomas S. Monson	Sin is always preceded by ,		61a-b
Dieter F. Uchtdorf	Outer acts and inner , must be close to Spirit	May 2008	60a
Richard G. Scott	Would your , benefit from a housecleaning?	Nov 2008	45a-f
Elaine S. Dalton	Desensitized by degrees —good		79b-f
Elaine S. Dalton	Safeguards through purity of , and actions	May 2009	121a-b
Boyd K. Packer	Mind needs a delete key - Use music	Nov 2009	46a
Jeffrey R. Holland	Throw out unworthy ,	May 2010	45f
Thomas S. Monson	Every action is preceded by ,		66d-e

Time

Tithing

Victor L. Brown	Ditch digger paid excessively large ,	June 1969	61e
	Unorthodox way of paying , —G.A. Smith story		61f-62e
	We only return 10% of what is already His		62e
A. Theodore Tuttle	People pay , because they have faith (not money)	June 1970	80f-81a
Franklin D. Richards	9/10 goes farther than untithed money	June 1971	46f
Gordon B. Hinckley	Will make a happy home		72c-e
Bernard P. Brockbank	Do you love God as much as you love the grocer?		86c-d
Marion G. Romney	Part of welfare obligation	Jan 1973	99f
Marion G. Romney	God does not fellowship non-tithers —Brigham Young	Jan 1974	91a
N. Eldon Tanner	The man who couldn't pay , that year —story		94f
Henry D. Taylor	A test of our loyalty and faithfulness	May 1974	107d
	What is a tithe? - 1/10 of net income		107d-e
	No one is forced to pay ,		107e-f
	Mary Fielding Smith and , —story		108a-b
	A Maori sister paying , —story		108b-e
Boyd K. Packer	The man who couldn't accept , —story	Nov 1974	88a-e
Marion G. Romney	A lesser law	Nov 1975	125c
Marion G. Romney	, is an opportunity to implement law of consecration	May 1977	94f-95c
James E. Faust	, is an excellent insurance against divorce	Nov 1977	11a
Marion G. Romney	Soil can be sanctified by , its products —Talmage	May 1979	40f
	Only people who could have made Utah productive —Young		40f
	Crop insurance		40f-41a
	H.J. Grant rewarded four-fold —story		41a-b
	Insurance against burning		41b-c
Spencer W. Kimball	Failure to pay , is a weighty transgression	Nov 1980	78f
Loren C. Dunn	President Lee sought a blessing but forgot , —story	May 1981	25f-26a
David B. Haight	Never be in debt to the Lord - pay it now		42c
Marion G. Romney	Promises associated with ,		44b-d
Mark E. Petersen	, is to protect us against hard times		63c-e
Angel Abrea	Refund , out of own pocket if blessings didn't come —story	Nov 1981	24e-25a
Robert L. Simpson	Mismanaged money cause windows of heaven to stick a little	May 1982	22a-f
Gordon B. Hinckley	Couplet on , —cute		40d
	Blessings coming from , —story		40e-41a
Hartman Rector, Jr.	No exaltation, roots, or branches without ,	May 1983	27a-b
Gordon B. Hinckley	Contrast D&C 119:4 with complex tax codes	May 1984	47b-c
Russell C. Taylor	Some expect windows of heaven to open before , is paid	Nov 1984	23b-d
Gordon B. Hinckley	, one's life through serving a mission	May 1985	49b
Russell M. Nelson	Defends against dishonesty	Nov 1985	32b
L. Tom Perry	Cannot give to Church and be any poorer —M.G. Romney	May 1986	32d-e
Russell M. Nelson	Tithing wife's blood money —story	Nov 1987	88e-f
Gordon B. Hinckley	An indicator of faithfulness in other matters	May 1990	51b
Gordon B. Hinckley	, compared to taxation and other methods		95c-d
	One-tenth of interest or income		96c-d
Dean L. Larsen	Only a small percent of members pay ,	Nov 1992	42e
	, may be only way to escape poverty		42e

Russell M. Nelson	Not temporary - An everlasting principle	Nov 1993	35d-e
Gordon B. Hinckley	His testimony of ,		52f-53b
Dallin H. Oaks	Not a remote Old Testament practice	May 1994	33b-c
	Promise of peace, prosperity and financial success —Grant		33d-e
	Testimonies of two widows on , —story		33f-34b
	Lord is grieved when poor do not pay ,		34b-c
	Tithe payers bless their nations		34d-e
	Others besides LDS pay , —examples		34e-35a
	Paying interest on Lord's loan to us		35a
	One-tenth of our annual income		35a
	Contributions to charity come from our funds		35b
	What Church does with , funds		35b
	, in kind was excellent way to teach ,		35b-e
	A test of priorities		35e-f
	One of most important laws revealed		35f
Gordon B. Hinckley	35 words in contrast to tax codes	Nov 1995	53f-54b
Joseph B. Wirthlin	Blessings from , are not just financial		76d-e
Thomas S. Monson	Dying woman left a note with , —story	Nov 1996	18f-19d
Thomas S. Monson	Inspired to give meat to family —story		44f-45c
	Insures Church activity		45d-e
Gordon B. Hinckley	Reporters can't believe we pay 10%	Nov 1997	69c
Ronald E. Poelman	Pay , or get baby bed? Bed was gifted —story	May 1998	79a-d
James E. Faust	Grandfather tithed with best hay —story	Nov 1998	54d-f
	"A full tithe and a little bit more"		54f
	Fundamental to personal happiness		54f-59a
	Possible to break out of poverty through ,		59b
	Do not lose membership, only blessings		59b
	Prosperity promised —story		59b-d
	Large family at , settlement —story		59d-e
	How , funds are allocated		59e-f
	Provides extra defense against evil		60c-e
Gordon B. Hinckley	What happens to , and how Church is financed		72c-e
Joe J. Christensen	Give more than we can spare - offerings	May 1999	11c-e
Jeffrey R. Holland	Five reasons for paying , —entire talk	Nov 2001	33b-35b
Gordon B. Hinckley	Set forth in few words in D&C 119		74a-b
Earl C. Tingey	How he paid , as a child	May 2002	10d-f
	What is a tithe? Is , equitable?		11a-b
	Law of , came at inopportune time		11c-f
	Counsel to converts to pay ,		11f-12b
	The blessings received by Widow Smith		12b-e
	No income? Pay a goose egg —story		12e
	Fears concerning finances and family will diminish		12e-f
Dallin H. Oaks	Teaches unimportance of pride, prominence, property, power		34f
Gordon B. Hinckley	A miracle for student after , was paid —story		73c-74d
Robert D. Hales	Unfit to be baptized for dead if , not paid	Nov 2002	26d-27a

Tithing

Robert D. Hales	Preparatory law for law of consecration	Nov 2002	27b-c
	Couple paid , and saved for temple —story		27d-e
	Would you intentionally reject outpouring of blessings?		27e-28a
	Other churches attach donor's name to donations		28b
	How Counsel on Disposition of Tithes works		28b-f
	Teach children to pay , - Won't be easier later		28f-29a
	Payment of , blesses ancestors and posterity		29b-c
	Poor investigators needed to be taught , —story		29c-e
Gordon B. Hinckley	Payment of , is increasing in Church	May 2003	5b-d
Gordon B. Hinckley	Lord didn't take boy's , —story		117e-118b
Gordon B. Hinckley	African measles vaccinations not from ,	Nov 2003	6b-f
Sydney S. Reynolds	Eyesight restored because , paid —story		76f-78a
Russell M. Nelson	How to enroll name among people of God	May 2005	18b
Lynn G. Robbins	Sacrifice and , —excellent talk		34b-36b
Gordon B. Hinckley	Another church was financed by bingo		59f
L. Tom Perry	A church can't exist without government aid —story		84b-e
Henry B. Eyring	Qualifies us for the blessing of protection	Nov 2005	40a-b
Thomas S. Monson	Why is Church so wealthy? —story	May 2006	54d-e
James E. Faust	Great are the blessings upon tithe payers		62f-67a
Daniel L. Johnson	Deny ourselves the promises? - Not inconsequential	Nov 2006	35b-c
	What is a , ? —H.W. Hunter		35c-d
	Break out of poverty by paying , —Faust		36b-c
Gordon B. Hinckley	Wife refused to spend , for food —story		117d-118b
Robert D. Hales	A mission is , on first 20 years of life	May 2007	49e-f
Yoshihiko Kikuchi	All 10 apples belong to the Lord		97b-d
	Rain came because of , fasting and temple —story		97e-98d
	Statements on , by President Hinckley		98d-e
	A token of gratitude and obedience		98e
Gordon B. Hinckley	A simple recipe for happiness		115e&117f
Sheldon F. Child	Paid tithing on $20 calf —story	May 2008	79d-e
	The promise		79f-80b
	Breadfruit drops in front of family —story		80b-d
	Lord will bless us financially —H. J. Grant		80d-f
	Brings spiritual blessings —Widtsoe		80f-81a
	Testimony of an African mother		81a
	Opens doors of the temple		81b
	The best investment you will ever make		81b
Robert D. Hales	Primary purpose of , is to develop faith	May 2009	9b-d

N. Eldon Tanner	Now is most crucial time in history	Dec 1968	38a-b
Gordon B Hinckley	Improve , without waiting for tomorrow		68b-d
Theodore M. Burton	Men must have a hope for solution to ills of ,	Dec 1969	55b-c
Franklin D. Richards	The value of , —good short quote		101b
Sterling W. Sill	Today, the best and the worst of times	June 1970	44b-d

Sterling W. Sill	We are in the approaches of the final cleansing	June 1970	45a
Alvin R. Dyer	Today's turbulence is preliminary to devastation		51c
Harold B. Lee	Be grateful for one more day	Dec 1970	30e
Richard L. Evans	, is a part of eternity	June 1971	73f
Joseph Fielding Smith	Needn't be troubled by world , if we're walking in light	Dec 1971	26b
Ezra Taft Benson	, noble words define ignoble things		55b-c
Harold B. Lee	Mighty revelations given ,	Jan 1973	108f
	Greatest problems and promises		133a
L. Tom Perry	Old Testament prophet saw ,	July 1973	20a
James A. Cullimore	Day here when light of heaven to fill earth —Woodruff	Jan 1974	121e
	All prophets have longed for , —Joseph Smith		121f
Spencer W. Kimball	If ye are prepared ye shall not fear	May 1974	6b
Spencer W. Kimball	We are facing a trial of our faith	Nov 1974	8d
Bruce R. McConkie	Conditions won't be getting better		35e
Marvin J. Ashton	The best of life is not in the future but ,	May 1975	85d-e
Spencer W. Kimball	, put in perspective to eternity	Nov 1978	71f-72a
Hartman Rector, Jr.	The spirit of our work must be urgency —Kimball	May 1979	31b-c
Spencer W. Kimball	If ye are prepared ye shall not fear		83b
Ezra Taft Benson	Challenges of , will rival any of the past	Nov 1987	85d-e
George I. Cannon	"I've never lived this day before"	Nov 1991	13b-d
James E. Faust	Description of an overloaded society	May 1992	6b-d
Russell M. Nelson	A few precious moments left to be kind		74e
David B. Haight	Biggest prejudice is anti-Christian	Nov 1992	74b-75b
Carlos E. Asay	The world is drifting —1916 quote	May 1996	60f
Harold G. Hillam	A century of changes in communication	Nov 1997	63a-b
Gordon B Hinckley	A season of a thousand opportunities		67c-d
Virginia U. Jensen	Influence of righteous women is tenfold ,		89d-e
James E. Faust	Advances of 3 centuries compared —amazing	May 1999	17b-e
	People lived happily without computers		17f
	Technology vs. spirituality		18a-19f
Gordon B Hinckley	The focal point - The summit of the ages	Nov 1999	73b-74f
James E. Faust	Life more complicated	May 2000	17d
	We are entitled to greater blessings —Joseph Smith		17e
Gordon B Hinckley	The world's amazing progress and wickedness	Nov 2001	4b-6f
Thomas S. Monson	Don't just live for tomorrow		60c
Gordon B Hinckley	Terrorism, 9/11 and the future		72b-74f
Gordon B Hinckley	"O that I were an angel..." - We can do it	Nov 2002	4b-d
Gordon B Hinckley	The most wonderful of all ages - spiritually, too		80e
Thomas S. Monson	, is a special occasion - don't wait	May 2003	20f-21b
Thomas S. Monson	Do it now before it's too late —poem and story		21b-22b
Russell M. Nelson	Our dispensation will not be limited in time or place	Nov 2003	45d-f
Keith B. McMullin	A wonderful time to be alive —Hinckley	May 2004	33b
Boyd K. Packer	Don't be afraid of future		77d-80f
Gordon B. Hinckley	Perilous times of , are culmination of what has always been		81b-84b
Richard G. Scott	Unprecedented evil and opportunity		100b-d

James E. Faust	Difficult days ahead - but optimistic	Nov 2004	55d-e
Gordon B. Hinckley	Gen. Conf. could reach 95% of members	May 2005	102d
Keith B. McMullin	"Now is the time to …" —G. Hinckley	Nov 2005	12d-e
Joseph B. Wirthlin	Calamities are going to happen		18b-d
Boyd K. Packer	Terrible days but he's positively optimistic		70d-e
	Different more dangerous trials ,		71a
Thomas S. Monson	A lot of empty yesterdays if nothing done ,	Nov 2008	85a-b
Dieter F. Uchtdorf	A day of change, challenges and checklists		117f
M. Russell Ballard	There has never been such remarkable progress	May 2009	32f-33a
Richard C. Edgley	Economic clouds are fully upon us —R.D. Hales		53d-e
Neil L. Andersen	Ancient prophecies being fulfilled , - List		79f-80b
Elaine S. Dalton	Nothing exceeds depravity and wickedness of ,		120e-f
Thomas S. Monson	Technology of his day and , compared		123d-124a
L. Tom Perry	Want past way of facing future		73f-74a
Boyd K. Packer	Greatest array of sin, vice and evil	May 2010	6d
Dieter F. Uchtdorf	Trials only to be understood in future		58f
Neil L. Andersen	A glorious but troubled time		108d-e
Thomas S. Monson	World has slipped from moorings		113b-d

Trials
Related Topics: Affliction, Problems

David O. McKay	Virtues are negative until tested —poem	June 1969	29a-b
Elray L. Christiansen	Faith must be tested in adversity and serenity		66b
	What Joseph and Hyrum suffered in Liberty Jail		66d-f
	Each trial will have its compensation		66f
	Trials are our greatest blessings —Brigham Young		67a
Hugh B. Brown	We'll be tested as never before		99f
Hugh B. Brown	There is an explanation for suffering	Dec 1969	33d
Loren C. Dunn	Trials shape us for higher things		44a
Marion G. Romney	Men have to suffer		66b
	Intensity of Lord's suffering		67a
	Man must suffer to prove self		67b
	Saints' , equal to Abraham's		67d
Gordon B. Hinckley	A pioneer story of suffering —story	June 1970	40f-41e
William H. Bennett	Opportunities. Learned humility through inferiority complex	Dec 1970	123b
N. Eldon Tanner	Most suffering caused by not keeping commandments	Dec 1971	34a
Franklin D. Richards	Nothing worthwhile comes except by , and work		50a
	Each has his Gethsemane —poem		50b
	Great men became great through ,		50c
Elray L. Christiansen	We won't have opposition beyond what we can endure		60a-b
Harold B. Lee	, precede calling of prophet	Jan 1973	24e
	Rolling stone quote of Joseph Smith		25c
	Meaning in his ,		25d
	Greater , the closer to Lord		25e
Marvin J. Ashton	Stay with us in ,		41b
	Lord's friends were tried		41f

Harold B. Lee	God will wrench heartstrings	Jan 1973	62d
S. Dilworth Young	Suffering of Christ is beyond comprehension	July 1973	114d
David B. Haight	The gem cannot be polished without friction…	Jan 1974	41a
Harold B. Lee	The veil grows thinner as the , grow greater		129f
Loren C. Dunn	Wind blew one tree over but not another —story	May 1974	27d-e
	Three reasons for ,		28b-c
Thomas S. Monson	We cannot go to heaven in a feather bed		49b
James A. Cullimore	Why we can't do without suffering —Kimball	Nov 1974	28d-e
O. Leslie Stone	No strong, noble, generous people without suffering		31f-32a
Spencer W. Kimball	Abe Lincoln's incredible string of failures —story		80c-e
	Be grateful for numerous big hurdles		80e
	Every David has his Goliath. Every Goliath can be whipped		80e-82d
	Adverse winds lift some kites and crash others		82d-e
Gordon B. Hinckley	A test, a test, a test is coming —H.C. Kimball		100c-d
Marion D. Hanks	Savior not spared most intense suffering —story	May 1975	13a-c
Bruce R. McConkie	Life never was intended to be easy	Nov 1976	106e-f
	Why we have ,		107d-108a
James E. Faust	Amazing blessings came from , of handcart company —story	May 1979	53b-e
	We listen to spirit better during ,		53f
	Having suffered you're able to console and comfort		54c
	Thorns must be plucked with the roses		59a-c
Marvin J. Ashton	Root bound plant couldn't grow until roughed up —story	Nov 1979	61b
	In repairing the cottage God makes a palace —good		61e
	Thomas Edison's beginnings —story		62b&f
Adney Y. Komatsu	No , that we experience are wasted —Orson F. Whitney		69d-e
John H. Groberg	Hawaiian overcame challenge - family stayed active —story	May 1980	49a-f
Boyd K. Packer	Everyone's , are different but very equal	Nov 1980	21d-e
Marvin J. Ashton	Mother's suffering was so she could measure herself		60a
	Joseph's and Jesus' characters developed by suffering		60b
Gordon B. Hinckley	Caroline Harman —story of trials and service	May 1982	45c-46c
G. Homer Durham	Hole in the Rock —Church history story		67b-68a
J. Richard Clarke	Church taken through fiery furnace - came out refined		77d-e
Neal A. Maxwell	Most , caused by ignorance of or non-compliance with plan	May 1984	21c
Yoshihiko Kikuchi	Suffering can make saints of people —Kimball		73e
	Story of a quadriplegic —story		73e-74a
Marvin J. Ashton	All suffering is not punishment —entire talk	Nov 1984	20b-22f
Howard W. Hunter	Master, the Tempest is Raging —story		33f-35b
Robert D. Hales	Lee had to lose wife so he could understand single adults	May 1985	29a
	8 years of paralysis so that she and he could learn patience		29a-b
Neal A. Maxwell	God causes or permits some suffering		72d-e
Marvin J. Ashton	The Lord knows the reason for , —story	Nov 1985	69b&d
Glenn L. Pace	50% unemployment increased spirituality	May 1986	24d-e
Thomas S. Monson	He shot for the wrong basket —story	May 1987	68d-e
	Editor rejected Robert Frost's poems		68f-69a
	Handicapped boy finishes race —story		69c-f

Adney Y. Komatsu	Suffering makes saints of people	May 1987	79c-f
Howard W. Hunter	Trials and suffering —excellent talk	Nov 1987	54d-60b
Howard W. Hunter	Turn to prayer and study during , —entire talk	Nov 1988	59d-61f
David B. Haight	Our , are as great as the pioneers'		82f-83a
Joseph B. Wirthlin	, make us able to endure hard or evil times	May 1989	7d-8a
F. Enzio Busche	Study makes it possible to avoid suffering		72d
Neal A. Maxwell	Unwise to end some trials early	May 1990	33f
	Our race is a marathon, not a dash		34c
Helio R. Camargo	Accident changed life but was great blessing	Nov 1990	80c-d
Boyd K. Packer	Handicaps are not because of sin	May 1991	7f-8a
	Girl making fun of handicapped —story		8b-e
	Caring for handicapped perfects you		9c-e
Russell M. Nelson	Testimony of deaf mother —story		24e-f
James E. Faust	The purpose of thorns and thistles		68b-70f
Gordon B. Hinckley	"I can come to you" —single mother story		73d-f
Neal A. Maxwell	Chastisements are for our good —W. Woodruff		88e
	"Lord, give me experience, but not grief"		88e
Robert L. Backman	No , Jesus didn't experience more intensely	Nov 1991	8e-f
Julio E. Davila	Growth only comes through , —E.T. Benson		24d-e
James E. Faust	Four children lost to diphtheria —story	May 1992	6d-7a
Angel Abrea	Have patience in , —entire talk		25d-27b
Richard G. Scott	Healing the tragic scars of abuse		31d-33f
Thomas S. Monson	Interviewed both missionary and dying mother —story		102c-e
Glenn L. Pace	Used to jar us loose from apathy	Nov 1992	12b-e
	Used to sanctify the righteous		12f-13b
M. Russell Ballard	Righteousness doesn't preclude adversity		32f
John B. Dickson	Having only one arm is greatest blessing —story		45c-e
	The Oyster —poem		45e-f
Marion D. Hanks	We will have , but also help —story		64b-65b
Neal A. Maxwell	Hard times necessary when we grow soft		66e
Thomas S. Monson	Blinded, injured man becomes patriarch —story		69d-70b
	Smile that shines through tears —poem		70b
	No fingers but plays violin —story		70b-d
	Entire talk		68b-70f
Howard W. Hunter	The path to joy lies through ,	May 1993	63d-e
Gordon B. Hinckley	13-year-old quadriplegic paints with mouth —story	Nov 1993	54b-e
Thomas S. Monson	We'd take our own , from a common store —Socrates		70d
	"It's easy enough to be pleasant…" —poem		71a-b
	Bearing our , —excellent talk and stories		68d-71f
James E. Faust	Girl's murder blessed many lives —story	May 1994	6f-7b
Lloyd P. George	Blessings in disguise		28f
Thomas S. Monson	Before Easter, there must be a cross		91f
Jeffrey R. Holland	Muscular dystrophy girls and caregiver grandmother —story	Nov 1994	32f-33f
Thomas S. Monson	Widow in Europe walked 1,000 miles —story		68d-69b
Lance B. Wickman	Gloom turned to hope —story		82d-f

Trials, cont'd
Related Topics: Affliction, Problems

Eduardo Ayala	Suffering can make saints of people —Kimball	May 1995	29d-e
Richard G. Scott	Multiple doses are evidence of God's love	Nov 1995	16f-17a
	Comforting thoughts about , —entire talk		16d-18b
Neal A. Maxwell	Jesus felt our pains before we did		24a
	Why , come —good		24b-d
Richard G. Scott	In a sea of , be a cork, not a rock	May 1996	24e-25a
	There are purposes and blessings in ,		25d-f
	General Authorities' wives learned to paint		25f-26b
	Don't become absorbed in a single event		26d-f
Carlos E. Asay	Winds slightly opposed to the ship make it go		61d-e
James E. Faust	All , will be fully compensated	Nov 1996	52d-f
	Woman's pioneer husband died in night —story		54c-d
	All tears shall be wiped away		54d-e
Aileen H. Clyde	Mary F. Smith letter recounting her ,		87e-88c
Neal A. Maxwell	No lines in front of fiery furnaces	May 1997	11f-12a
James E. Faust	All must pass through a refiner's fire		63f
Neal A. Maxwell	Customized ,	Nov 1997	22d-e
	Partaking of a bitter cup without becoming bitter		22f
	One of our , is irony		23c-d
	Passing big tests while failing small quizzes		23f
Richard D. Allred	Crippled girl's condition blessed lives —story		28a-b
Jeffrey R. Holland	We shall emerge from , better and purer		66c-e
W. Eugene Hansen	Farm taught , in school of hard knocks	May 1998	63b
Robert D. Hales	Girl relearned how to swallow and walk —story		76a-b
Robert D. Hales	The purpose of pain —excellent talk	Nov 1998	14d-17b
Val R. Christensen	Overcoming Discouragement —excellent talk		31b-32b
Richard G. Scott	Loss of his children resulted in father joining Church —story	May 1999	27b-c
Jeffrey R. Holland	Jesus is the light at the end of the tunnel	Nov 1999	36b-37c
	Young couple stranded on highway —story		37d-38b
James E. Faust	Good things from missionary's shooting —story		59d-60e
	Faith casts burden's shadow behind us		60e
Richard G. Scott	How Holy Ghost can help you through ,		87b-89f
Coleen K. Menlove	Things will straighten out —B.K. Packer	May 2000	12e-f
Joseph B. Wirthlin	Would we shield a child from learning to walk?		60b-61c
James E. Faust	What one young woman endured —story		97a-c
Dallin H. Oaks	Sanctification achieved more readily through ,	Nov 2000	33f-34a
Sheri L. Dew	The ultimate burden: walking without light		95b
Joseph B. Wirthlin	Blind man climbed Everest —story	Nov 2001	25d-26a
Steven E. Snow	Hole-in-the-Rock and Comb Ridge		44e-f
Mary Ellen W. Smoot	Handcart woman became a different person —story	May 2002	13c-e
Joseph B. Wirthlin	Convert persecuted by father —story		17b-c
R. Conrad Schultz	Sneaker wave nearly capsized boat —story		29d-f
James E. Faust	, and temptation - No one invincible —Titanic story		46d-47b
Richard C. Edgley	, are for our good —entire talk		65b-66f
Russell M. Nelson	God prepared woman for husband's death		77b

Trials

Russell M. Nelson	Missionary grateful for cancer —story	May 2002	77c-d
Dieter F. Uchtdorf	His family lost everything twice but found gospel —story	Nov 2002	10f-11d
Joseph B. Wirthlin	Lack of light may stem from within —story		85b-d
Claudio R. M. Costa	Life without a leg is still happy —story		93c-94a
Anne C. Pingree	Mother taught disabled son to read —story		109d-f
Robert D. Hales	Faith through , brings peace and joy	May 2003	15d-18f
Richard G. Scott	Superior blessings are preceded by ,		77b
	Righteousness prevents most calamities		77f-78a
Dallin H. Oaks	Be thankful for ,		96c-97f
Gayle M. Clegg	Crack is where light comes through —story		111d-112f
Sheldon F. Child	"The freeze" in Ghana —persecution story	Nov 2003	9f-10b
W. Craig Zwick	Blessing a premature son —story		34f-35e
	Blind man ran marathon —story		36d-f
Richard C. Edgley	Enduring missionary accidents —2 stories		97b-e
Gayle M. Clegg	One step after another —excellent talk	May 2004	14b-16b
Henry B. Eyring	Why we have ,		16d-17f
	How to endure ,		17f-19f
Neal A. Maxwell	Don't let bitter cups make you bitter		44e-f
Robert D. Hales	, may soften, strengthen and sanctify		91b
Bruce C. Hafen	Cannot understand sweet without bitter		97c-d
Susan W. Tanner	Deaf girl helped by ward —story		106b-107b
Elaine S. Dalton	Father's death became great trial —story		111d-112a
James E. Faust	, harden some and soften others —story	Nov 2004	20a-c
	Blind man pulled handcart —story		20d-f
	Every , is necessary for your salvation		21d-f
L. Tom Perry	Young and Kimball leaving on mission —story		23f-24c
James E. Faust	Bone cancer one of greatest blessings —story		55b-c
Russell M. Nelson	Try prayer, fasting, and mission to solve family problem		81a
Joseph B. Wirthlin	Pioneer children died of diphtheria —story		103c-f
Anne C. Pingree	Lessons learned from a dying friend		111d-113b
Adhemar Damiani	, are opportunities for our growth	May 2005	94f-95b
Keith B. McMullin	Tragedies never triumph over righteousness	Nov 2005	12f
Henry B. Eyring	The great test of life is obedience in ,		38b
Boyd K. Packer	Different more dangerous , now		71a
Russell M. Nelson	Real joy awaits on the other side of sorrow		87f-88a
Dieter F. Uchtdorf	Hard boyhood job became a blessing —story	May 2006	42f-43b
Jeffrey R. Holland	The need to "Come unto Jesus"		69b-f
James E. Faust	Had it made at graduation?	May 2007	56a
James E. Faust	Every , is necessary for your salvation —Brigham Young		68c-d
Susan W. Tanner	Abraham didn't know there'd be an angel and a ram	May 2008	82f-83a
	Jesus didn't come until the fourth watch		83a
Elaine S. Dalton	No matter the preparation, there are hills —story		117d-118b
Dieter F. Uchtdorf	Train left with children aboard —story	Nov 2008	21b-e
M. Russell Ballard	Our , contrasted to pioneers'		83f-84b
Quentin L. Cook	Things that are best for us are often bitter —H.B. Lee		102f-103d

Trials, cont'd
Related Topics: Affliction, Problems

Dieter F. Uchtdorf	Work and service will cure your grief	Nov 2008	119d-120a
Henry B. Eyring	, are invitations to grow	May 2009	25a
	Former bishop smilingly endured , —story		26c-27a
Steven E. Snow	The , of a pioneer and his attitudes —story		82e-83b
Thomas S. Monson	Scottish converts immigrated despite , —story		89d-90b
	German refugee woman lost all but faith —story		91a-92f
Dieter F. Uchtdorf	, build character	May 2010	58f
Donald L. Hallstrom	Babies' deaths affected families differently —story		78c-79e
	Never let , disable you spiritually		80d-e
Quentin L. Cook	Recued children from tsunami —story		85f-86c
James B. Marino	We can grow from the experience		101c-d
	Small pains now protect from larger ones		101f-102a
	Make us more earnest, sincere and faithful		102d-f
	Serve during , and save your life		102f-103a
	Don't pass the blame		103a
Dieter F. Uchtdorf	Why we must have , and opposition		125d-f
	Reaction to , determines life's story		126d-e
	"Your Happily Ever After" —entire talk		124c-127f

Truth
Related Topics: —

David O. McKay	Be of good cheer for , will triumph	June 1969	117b-c
Hugh B. Brown	Faith not a substitute for ,	Dec 1969	33e
Joseph F. Smith	God upholds those who sustain truth		37d
LeGrand Richards	Fable about , —funny		54e
Delbert L. Stapley	Philosophy no substitute for ,		64c
John H. Vandenberg	People cannot change , but , can change people	June 1970	59a
Harold B. Lee	Positive teachings greatest weapon against error	July 1972	32b
Marvin J. Ashton	Joy in walking in ,		62f
Ezra Taft Benson	No compromise with ,	July 1973	38f
John H. Vandenberg	, forever on scaffold and wrong on the throne	Nov 1974	93d
Mark E. Petersen	I know it is right because Christ teaches it —Lincoln	Nov 1976	49b
James E. Faust	Beautiful description of , by President Kimball		59c
Royden G. Derrick	Some has little to do with exaltation while other , is essential	Nov 1984	62f
James E. Faust	The ultimate evil is closing one's mind against ,	Nov 1985	7e
Ezra Taft Benson	All , is not of the same value		36a
	Children need to hear the , repeated		36b
Robert L. Simpson	A testimony of the , of anything is obtained in the same way	May 1987	42a-b
Glenn L. Pace	Legalizing an act does not make it moral	Nov 1987	40e-f
Wm. Grant Bangerter	Many people don't want to hear , —story	Nov 1988	80f-81a
Dallin H. Oaks	Hearing , in a confusion of voices	May 1989	27d-29a
	, is better served by silence than by a bad argument		28b
Richard G. Scott	You can't change ,	Nov 1992	60f-61f
Marion D. Hanks	All , comes from the fountain of ,		63d-e
Russell M. Nelson	Part of gospel whether coming from laboratory or revelation	Nov 1993	35e
Richard G. Scott	Unbelief does not alter reality	Nov 2001	87b

Kenneth Johnson	Holy Ghost: the consummate courier of ,	Nov 2002	91b
Richard G. Scott	Two ways to discover , - Science and inspiration	Nov 2007	90b-e
Marcos A. Aidukaitis	Absurd notion that God does not know where , is	Nov 2008	17a
Elaine S. Dalton	World filled with relative , - Standards are absolute	May 2009	120a-b
Neil L. Andersen	Time and , are on your side	May 2010	110c-e

United Order
Related Topics: —

Harold B. Lee	Welfare plan forerunner of ,	Jan 1973	63c
Marion G. Romney	Welfare program preliminary to ',	May 1977	92e
	Explanation of ,		92f-95f
J. Richard Clarke	Welfare plan not , but is evolving	May 1978	84a

United States
Related Topics: America, Constitution, Freedom, Government, Rome

David O. McKay	He denounces any ideology that would change ,	Dec 1968	35b-e
Ezra Taft Benson	Created 50% of world's wealth in 160 yrs.		52f
David O. McKay	, has forgotten God —A. Lincoln		109b-c
N. Eldon Tanner	20 other similar civilizations have fallen	June 1971	12c-13c
Spencer W. Kimball	There will be no centuries for a leisurely decay		17a
	Toleration of sexual anarchy endangers survival		19a
Mark E. Petersen	3 civilizations have been here - 2 are extinct		47a
	Warnings from leaders in , concerning religion		48b-c
Ezra Taft Benson	Stand by the , not its leader —T. Roosevelt	July 1972	60c
	Wake up or have a change of government		60d
	Godless conspiracy greatest threat		60e
Bruce R. McConkie	Take affirmative attitude about local and world affairs	Jan 1974	46b
L. Tom Perry	The story of Ben Franklin		52d
Charles A. Didier	, has done more than any other nation	May 1976	89c-e
Ezra Taft Benson	Nation must be righteous to be free		92f-93c
Marion G. Romney	Money will be taken from the "haves" and given to others		120d-e
	Blood shall run before , corrects welfare system		121b-c
	, cannot support groups in idleness and remain free		121d-122a
Mark E. Petersen	But we have forgotten God —Lincoln	Nov 1976	50a-b
Spencer W. Kimball	Peace in land only if commandments are kept	Nov 1977	4f-5a
	Same vices that wrecked empires are among us in the ,		6a-f
Marion G. Romney	Our course will end in a cataclysmic disaster		14b
	We are approaching the end of the Jaredite-Nephite cycle		14f-15a
Joseph B. Wirthlin	They who choose evil are more numerous	May 1989	9a-c
Neal A. Maxwell	Founding Fathers the most remarkable generation ever	Nov 2002	17d-18a

Unity
Related Topics: —

Theodore M .Burton	Saints must show , to give troubled world hope	Dec 1969	55b-c
James A. Cullimore	Holy Ghost is catalyst bringing , in Church	July 1972	56f
Marion G. Romney	If ye are not one —scripture	Jan 1973	98a
Harold B. Lee	, of General Authorities		133b
Marion D. Hanks	You can cry with me —story	July 1973	112d

Unity, cont'd

Harold B. Lee	We're all children of one Father so let's get along	Jan 1974	97b
J. Thomas Fyans	4 nations demonstrated , at Stockholm Conference	Nov 1974	64f
N. Eldon Tanner	One battery cell was foaming and fuming —story	Nov 1976	74e-75b
N. Eldon Tanner	Trees growing alone produce knots —story	May 1977	46f-47b
	Help received after car accident —story		48d-e
Ezra Taft Benson	Why men with divergent views reach accords in the Church	May 1979	87a
James E. Faust	In councils humble selves until , reached	Nov 1980	36c
L. Tom Perry	Family prayer will bring , —Brigham Young	Nov 1983	13c-d
Gordon B. Hinckley	Perfect , among First Presidency and Apostles	May 1984	51d-e
Hugh W. Pinnock	Canal built and valley saved through , —story	May 1987	63d-64b
	Unity is power —Joseph Smith		64d
	We show Savior our gratitude through ,		64e-f
Henry B. Eyring	The story of Orderville and pants —story	Nov 1989	11f-13c
Howard W. Hunter	Total unanimity among Apostles	Nov 1994	7e
	All Apostles share in responsibility		7f-8b
Joe J. Christensen	Couple makes bed together in under one minute	May 1995	66a-b
Thomas S. Monson	Apostles united in prayer —story	May 2005	22b-d
James E. Faust	Stick with the Brethren - Harmony	Nov 2005	53d-f
Susan W. Tanner	Reading by combined light of glowworms	May 2006	104f-105a
Henry B. Eyring	Changes how a quorum plays basketball	Nov 2006	44f-45b
D. Todd Christofferson	Zion people must be free from contention and strife	Nov 2008	38b-e
	Moldovan youth split up to cover all classes —story		38e-f
Dieter F. Uchtdorf	Moving a piano - Lift where you stand —story		53d-f
	Sons of Helaman couldn't do it alone		56a
	You shouldn't lift a piano by yourself		56f
Henry B. Eyring	A great day of , is coming		68d-e
	Cannot come to us individually		69d
	Pride is the enemy of ,		70e
	Entire talk		68d-71f
David A. Bednar	Individual brushstrokes make a painting or a family	Nov 2009	19f

Virtue

Ann M. Dibb	Her experiences working on , projects	May 2009	115c-116a
Mary N. Cook	Definition of ,		117b-d
	Steps to , - Youth is a defining time		117d-e
	Atonement makes , possible		118c
	86-year-old mother working on , projects		119d-f
Elaine S. Dalton	Virtuous men are attracted to virtuous women		120b-e
	Banner unfurled on mountain one year ago		120e-f
	Moral excellence, power and strength		120f-121a
	The strength of Zion is in , —Brigham Young		121a-b
	If we don't stand for , who will?		120b-d
	Raising banners of , around world		121d-e
	A hike compared to a virtuous life —story		122a-f
	President Monson gave her a white rose		123b

Virtue, cont'd

Elaine S. Dalton	One virtuous woman can change the world	May 2009	123b
Thomas S. Monson	A plea for ,		125b-126a
H. David Burton	The "ity" virtues —entire talk	Nov 2009	76d-78f
Quentin L. Cook	Steward over a spring and , —story		91f-92d
Elaine S. Dalton	Can't accomplish mission without ,	May 2010	120f
	I was born to be a king —story		121d
	Deep beauty stems from ,		122b-d
	Girl realized she was beautiful —story		122e-f
	You are golden. You are the banner		122f-123a

Voting

Richard L. Evans	Good men should prepare selves for public service	June 1969	80d-e
Harold B. Lee	Counsel about how to vote —excellent	July 1972	32b
	Type of man to be , for		32f
Ezra Taft Benson	A sin to vote for wicked men		60c
	Who to support - First Presidency directive		60d
N. Eldon Tanner	Proceedings of Solemn Assembly 1974	May 1974	38a-45b
	Sustaining is a solemn covenant with Lord		38f
Mark E. Petersen	Solemn Assembly held as was done in Israel		56a
Ezra Taft Benson	Goodness, wisdom and honesty: 3 qualities of statesmanship	May 1976	93c-d
N. Eldon Tanner	How he handled a negative vote	Nov 1977	18b
N. Eldon Tanner	What happens when there is a dissenting vote	May 1978	19a
N. Eldon Tanner	What happens when there is a dissenting vote	Nov 1979	45e-46a

Weakness

David O. McKay	Only thing stopping progress	Dec 1969	88f
Hartman Rector, Jr.	Where do weaknesses come from?	June 1970	102c-e
	Lord expects us to excel where we have a ,		103b-c

Wealth

Hugh B. Brown	Can't buy faith —story	Dec 1969	33b
Paul H. Dunn	In making a living don't forget to make a life	Dec 1970	39b
N. Eldon Tanner	Rich man got a hut in heaven —story	June 1971	14d
Franklin D. Richards	Increased , promised to the faithful		45d
	We are trustees of , to be used for poor		46a-b
Richard L. Evans	Little brass nails gathered by children —story		73b-d
Harold B. Lee	As people gain , they forget God	Dec 1971	29e-f
Thomas S. Monson	Purchasing , of eternity by abandoning , of time	July 1972	68f
Rex D. Pinegar	An entire talk comparing earthly and eternal ,	Jan 1974	32a
Elray L. Christiansen	He wouldn't go to heaven because he couldn't take , —story		35b
Sterling W. Sill	Earthly and heavenly , —entire talk, great		60a
Sterling W. Sill	A disadvantage to have too many advantages	May 1975	41e
Bruce R. McConkie	Rich man wouldn't give - died 10 days later —story		50e
LeGrand Richards	No rich friends ever shed tears of joy over their purchases	Nov 1976	64e-65a
Vaughn J. Featherstone	Mike will come back won't he? —story		104c-e

Wealth, cont'd
Related Topics: Possessions

Marion G. Romney	We are to use , to build the kingdom, not personal security	May 1977	95d-e
Franklin D. Richards	Lord ready to give us , if we use it properly —B. Young	May 1979	39d-e
Spencer W. Kimball	W. Woodruff's dream of a miser who died —story		48a-b
James E. Faust	Many have not known the blessings of economic adversity	Nov 1982	87d
	Difference between recession and depression		87d
Hartman Rector, Jr.	Worthy poor and unworthy wealthy. One gets reward now	May 1983	26e-27a
Victor L. Brown	16-year-old won car - used it to finance mission —story		61e
Robert B. Harbertson	If obedient "ye shall eat the good of the land"	Nov 1984	24d-e
L. Tom Perry	If you wish to get rich, save what you get —B. Young	Nov 1986	63a-b
Wm. Grant Bangerter	Wealthy rancher ended with 6' x 3' plot —story	May 1987	12f-13b
Howard W. Hunter	One could have the world and yet be poor —P. Henry		18b
L. Tom Perry	Lord condemns those who feel deprived of , also		33e-34a
	Lord does not say we should not be prosperous		34b-c
Joseph B. Wirthlin	Easy living prevents deep roots	May 1989	7d-8a
Russell M. Nelson	Comes at expense of spiritual development	Nov 1992	6f-7a
Joseph B. Wirthlin	, causes some to harden their hearts	Nov 2005	16e-17a
	The course chosen by Solomon and Jereboam		17b-f
C. Scott Grow	Early Mexican members had nothing		33b-e
Thomas S. Monson	Why is Church so wealthy? —story	May 2006	54d-e
Henry B. Eyring	Remembering is hardest for those with much	Nov 2007	67f-68d

Welfare Program
Related Topics: Fast Offerings, Food Storage, Idleness, Offerings, Poor & Needy, Service, Tithing, Work

Ezra Taft Benson	Government cannot set up ,	Dec 1968	52d-e
	Welfare state is reversible - tells how		53d-e
Henry D. Taylor	Joy of being able to work shown by D. I. worker —story	Dec 1969	104b
	Care of needy has first call on funds of Church —Grant		104d
	More people are spiritually hungry than physically		104e
Henry D. Taylor	Who has responsibility for the needy - Priority	June 1970	60b-c
	How to make preparations to care for selves		60c-d
	Responsibility to provide for kin		60d-e
	2 major resources for the bishop		60f-61a
Harold B. Lee	Will be the master plan for Christian living	Dec 1971	30b
Ezra Taft Benson	Lord wants Church independent	Jan 1973	59d
Harold B. Lee	Purpose to abolish idleness		61e
	Forerunner of United Order		63c
Victor L. Brown	Social services activities		68f
	Roger and Janey helped at Welfare Square —story		69b
	Accomplishments, purposes, embodiments of ,		69f
Marion G. Romney	Remember the poor and needy		97a
	World's 3 , - numbers		98a
	Two principles in ,		98d
	Obligation to labor and give		98d
	The earth is full —scripture		99e
	Our 3 contributions to the ,		99f
Harold B. Lee	Origin of , —story		104a

Harold B. Lee	Teaches people to care for selves	July 1973	6a
Vaughn J. Featherstone	Essence of the Church		35a
	Charity in purest form		35e
	Sugar beet story		36c
Ezra Taft Benson	Basic principles of , —J.R. Clark	Jan 1974	69c
	Have a cash reserve		81d
Vaughn J. Featherstone	How the Bishop's Storehouse works		82b
Marion G. Romney	An approach to the Law of Consecration		89a
	Those who can must work —story of mice		89d
	Don't give anything without work —Brigham Young		89f
	Church cares for needy only if kin can't		91a
	Dignity of receiver must be preserved		92c
	Purpose is not temporal help but to save souls		92c
Henry D. Taylor	We must increase our fast offerings	Nov 1974	14b
	How fast offerings used to be given		14e
Robert D. Hales	Be self sufficient but not independent of help of others	Nov 1975	91f
Victor L. Brown	Purpose of , to prepare for Law of Consecration		113f-114a
	Welfare problems in the typical ward		114b-115a
H. Burke Peterson	Become as self-sufficient as possible		116e-f
	Purpose and extent of production projects		116f-117e
	Fast Offerings increased 47% last year		117e
	Church has a year's supply for current needy		117f
	Needy must work for what they get - only 25% currently		117f-118a
	Main purpose of Deseret Industries to employ handicapped		118a-b
Marion G. Romney	Pres. Grant's statement introducing ,		125c-127a
	Each ward must have a production project		127d-f
Spencer W. Kimball	You can nearly feed your family from your own lot	May 1976	4e-5a
	Don't waste a thing —Brigham Young		6a-c
Victor L. Brown	Church cannot provide a great reservoir for needy		110e
	Individual efforts is "Church Preparedness"		110f
	We'll see day when we live on what we produce —Romney		111a
	Church's ability to handle 3 possible economic conditions		111b-112b
	5 basic elements of family preparedness		112d-e
	Parents are to teach children welfare principles by examples		112f
Marion G. Romney	Nation taking from "haves" and giving to "have nots"		120d-e
	Blood will flow before U.S. corrects welfare system		121b-c
	Children are to support aged parents, not government		121d-122a
	Babylon's , will be destroyed, but not Zion		123d-f
Spencer W. Kimball	Work or get nothing - 2 Thess. 3:8, 10-12 and 1 Tim. 5:8		125e
Victor L. Brown	, is bishop's duty alone. No one may question his actions	Nov 1976	112d-e
	Use storehouse commodities first		113e
H. Burke Peterson	Souls can be destroyed by the dole		115a
	Use storehouse commodities first		115b
	Purposes of production projects		115b-d
	How to acquire a production project		115d-116c

Welfare Program, cont'd

Welfare Program

Marion G. Romney	Role of bishop in , —entire talk	Nov 1979	94b-96f
Harold G. Hillam	The , and all its aspects - how it works	May 1980	84d-86b
Victor L. Brown	Number of production projects, storehouses, etc.		88f
	Church can't care for everyone - just a few		89c-d
	Survey on family preparedness		89d
Ezra Taft Benson	Don't shift burden of your support elsewhere	Nov 1980	32b-c
Victor L. Brown	Two stakes: One prepared - one not		79b-f
	Young couple canceled health insurance —story		79f-80a
J. Richard Clarke	Have life and health insurance		84d
Douglas W. DeHaan	Corn harvested when priesthood stopped rain —story		87b-88f
Thomas S. Monson	Bishop called family to paint elderly parents' home —story		91a
	Ward prepared old apartment for German family —story		91a-e
Marion G. Romney	Important to labor together, not just give money		92f-93a
Thomas S. Monson	House purchased for widow and invalid daughters —story	May 1981	48f-49b
H. Burke Peterson	Disgrace to not care for poor kin. Report refusals to bishops		82d-e
	Mother given a blanket each year - example for son —story		82f-83a
L. Tom Perry	Statistics showing increase in welfare assistance		87e-f
	Teach preparedness and self reliance —story		87f-88b
Marion G. Romney	Not a program - The gospel in action		91d
Marvin J. Ashton	We don't give lifts when we give free rides	Nov 1981	91b
Marion G. Romney	Objective of , is to build our character		92b-d
Marion G. Romney	Sad day when man figures out how to keep from working	May 1982	87f-88d
	A history of the various welfare programs		88d-89e
Marion G. Romney	Gulls starved amidst plenty —story	Nov 1982	91d-e
Gordon B. Hinckley	List of disasters Church helped with in 1983	Nov 1983	51d-f
Ezra Taft Benson	Christ takes slums out of men—they take selves out of slums	Nov 1985	6e-f
James E. Faust	Entire talk —good	May 1986	20b-22f
Glenn L. Pace	Passed opportunity for service because of assignment—story		23f-24a
	Self reliance, service, personal responsibility the basis of ,		24b
	Local needs should be solved using local resources		24d-e
	Local needs should be solved using local resources		24e
	A church that can't save temporally can't save spiritually		25a-b
Robert D. Hales	Exalting poor by humbling rich sanctifies both — Romney		30b-c
	Concise summation of ,		30e-f
L. Tom Perry	Tithing in place of offerings used only as last extremity		31f
Thomas S. Monson	Nation's , is creating poverty		64b
	President Reagan's praise for Church's ,		64b-d
M. Russell Ballard	How Peruvian slides were dealt with —story	Nov 1987	80a-81a
Thomas S. Monson	Chickens quit laying when boys cleaned farm —story	Nov 1988	45d-f
	Storehouse includes time, talents, finances of members		47a
	Proper administration of , —coal shed story		47b-f
Thomas S. Monson	Doctors and the Church in 3rd World nations	May 1990	54b-d
Glenn L. Pace	Who are we to help? Everyone —quotes	Nov 1990	9d-e
Thomas S. Monson	Report on worldwide , efforts	May 1991	48b-49c
Thomas S. Monson	Humanitarian aid since 1985	Nov 1994	43f-44f

Welfare Program

Welfare Program, cont'd
Related Topics: Fast Offerings, Food Storage, Idleness, Offerings, Poor & Needy, Service, Tithing, Work

Thomas S. Monson	, at work in Europe after WWII —stories	Nov 1994	44f-46b
Thomas S. Monson	Project threw chickens into molt —story	Nov 1996	47a-b
H. David Burton	Help sent to other countries	May 1997	76c-d
Joe J. Christensen	Advice about overindulging children —excellent	May 1999	9f-11a
	Grinding debt —H.J. Grant quote		11b-c
Joseph B. Wirthlin	Scope of , - number of facilities		76d-f
	Can't save spiritually if can't save temporally		76f
	, committee helped addicted man —story		77b-c
	Amount of humanitarian effort in decade		77d-f
	How to be self reliant		78b-79a
Gordon B. Hinckley	African measles vaccinations not from tithing	Nov 2003	6b-d
Dallin H. Oaks	Some gifts promote dependency		40b-d
Gordon B. Hinckley	More noteworthy than pioneer trek	May 2004	58b-e
	Scope of Church ,		58b-61b
Gordon B. Hinckley	Calamities are coming - Be prepared	Nov 2005	60b-62f
H. David Burton	List of recent humanitarian aid	May 2006	8d-11b
H. David Burton	President Grant's inauguration of ,	May 2007	33b
H. David Burton	Amazing list of humanitarian aid in 2007	May 2008	51b-52f
Keith B. McMullin	Chinese visitor gave his fast offering —story	Nov 2008	76b-d
	Welfare principles do not change		76d-e
Robert D. Hales	We can't afford it - Where would I wear it —story	May 2009	8b-9b
Richard C. Edgley	Preparation, organization, empathy, charity		53b-c
	Economic clouds are fully upon us —R.D. Hales		53d-e
	Quorum got mechanic on feet —story		54b-e
	Employment resources provided by Church		54e-f
	Enough resources in each quorum to help —Hinckley		55b-c
	Brigham Young's call to help handcart companies		55d-f
Quentin L. Cook	Talmud: Two reasons for generosity	Nov 2009	91b-d
	Martin Luther King III's reaction to ,		93e-f
	Over $900 million in assistance		94f
Thomas S. Monson	25 years of humanitarian program	May 2010	4e-f
Wilford W. Andersen	Haitian earthquake		16e-17a

Women
Related Topics: Motherhood and Mothers, Relief Society, Young Women

Joseph Fielding Smith	Every gift and blessing is available to , too	June 1970	66d-e
N. Eldon Tanner	The role of , —entire talk, excellent	Jan 1974	7a
	Men have no greater strength than wives and mothers		8d
	Not the weaker instruments		8d
	Satan trying to destroy , because of their potential		8e
Rex D. Pinegar	Helping husband is worshipping God	May 1974	67f-68a
Howard W. Hunter	, should prepare for employment before marriage	Nov 1975	124f
Barbara B. Smith	Have perspectives that elude men —story	May 1977	91f-92a
Spencer W. Kimball	Later teaching to compensate for failure of teachings in home	May 1978	5e-6a
Neal A. Maxwell	, deserting home to shape society		11a
Boyd K. Packer	LDS more blessed than any other , —G.A. Smith	Nov 1978	7d

Boyd K. Packer	Place of , is beside the man —John A. Widtsoe	Nov 1978	7e-f
William R. Bradford	Most important role is motherhood but maybe a mission first	Nov 1981	50e-f
Ezra Taft Benson	Exaltation of , predicated on faithfulness as mother		105b-c
	Leaving home for education misguided idea		105d-e
Gordon B. Hinckley	The need for , to receive educations	Nov 1983	81f-82a
	Counsel to , who have not had temple marriage		82d-e
	Talents required of a housewife		82e
	Counsel to unmarried ,		82f-83b
	Counsel to , who work outside the home		83b-f
	Equality between men and , - responsibilities of each		83f-84a
Ezra Taft Benson	No inequality between sexes - just division of responsibilities	May 1984	6c
Marvin J. Ashton	Don't compare yourself to others		9f-10b
Gordon B. Hinckley	The opportunities open to ,	Nov 1985	86d-89f
Ezra Taft Benson	Full-time motherhood - Life's greatest career	Nov 1986	84f-85a
Vaughn J. Featherstone	Coarseness and vulgarity are contrary to nature of ,	Nov 1987	28e-f
James E. Faust	, have borne more than half the burdens	May 1988	38e-f
Ezra Taft Benson	Advice to single , about marriage	Nov 1988	96e-97a
	Don't be so self-reliant that you decide against marriage		97a-b
Russell M. Nelson	Women - Of Infinite Worth —entire talk	Nov 1989	20b-21f
	When you teach a girl, you teach a generation		21c
Gordon B. Hinckley	, counseled to get an education		96e-97b
Elaine L. Jack	Growth of Church depends upon ,	May 1990	78e-f
Thomas S. Monson	God counts their tears	Nov 1990	47a
Gordon B. Hinckley	Letters from his "Unhappy Women" file	Nov 1991	50a-b
	Domineering, unfaithful husbands inexcusable		51c-f
M. Russell Ballard	Major growth of Church coming because of ,		96f-97a
Gordon B. Hinckley	Are men more important than , ?		97d-100a
Dallin H. Oaks	, and authority - how they hold it	May 1992	35b-36e
R.S. Conference	Testimonies of 5 , from 5 continents		93a-95b
Howard W. Hunter	List of , in Jesus' life	Nov 1992	95e-96b
	A woman's sphere —poem		97b
Thomas S. Monson	Church's , are a testimony of our integrity		97d
James E. Faust	God's greatest creation	May 1993	35b
	The "golden mean" in status of , —E.R. Snow		35f-36b
Boyd K. Packer	Complementing differences between men and ,	Nov 1993	21f
	Worst effect of WWII was , entering work force		22e
	Role of , is the highest and holiest service		22e-23c
James E. Faust	Invite , leaders to participate in councils		38f
	Lord values daughters as much as sons		38f-39a
	An especially noble calling		39a
Gordon B. Hinckley	A woman's greatest blessing, mission, happiness		60b
M. Russell Ballard	Each may do a great deal —E.R. Snow		89d
Howard W. Hunter	Allow mothers to stay in home	Nov 1994	51c-d
Gordon B. Hinckley	Girls need all the education they can get	May 1996	92b
Gordon B. Hinckley	Counsel to single ,	Nov 1996	68e-f

Women

Women, cont'd
Related Topics: Motherhood and Mothers, Relief Society, Young Women

Gordon B. Hinckley	Counsel to working ,	Nov 1996	69c-e
	A tribute to older ,		69f-70b
Richard G. Scott	Mothers need to be in the home		74e-75a
	A tribute to complementary role of ,		75b-c
Patricia P. Pinegar	Not fulfilled? Where feeling comes from?	May 1997	14e
Gordon B. Hinckley	Relatively few young , should serve a mission	Nov 1997	52b-e
Virginia U. Jensen	Influence of righteous , is tenfold today		89d-e
Sheri L. Dew	The influence of righteous , is enormous		92e-93f
Thomas S. Monson	No blessing to be withheld from single ,		96b-c
Gordon B. Hinckley	, are twice blessed if able to stay at home	May 1998	50d-e
Boyd K. Packer	Every need will be fulfilled if family is first		73a
	No fullness of priesthood without ,		73d-e
James E. Faust	God's noblest creation		95e
	Most important occupation is homemaking		96a-b
	Mother's death taught girl homemaking —story		96b-e
	You can have it all sequentially		96e-f
	Get an education		96f-97b
Virginia U. Jensen	No blessing will be denied faithful , —D.H. Oaks	Nov 1998	93d-e
	"We are not ordinary , "		93f
Gordon B. Hinckley	The history of Mary Fielding Smith —story		97f-98f
	Cautions to , in the workplace		99b-c
	Guard your children, marriage and home		99d-f
Sheri L. Dew	Gave up magazines - became more content —story	Nov 1999	98b-c
	LDS , must lead , of world —J.F. Smith		98c-e
	Growth of Church depends on , —Spencer W. Kimball		99b-e
James E. Faust	What being a daughter of God means		100d
	Cannot imagine potential, gifts, and influence		101f-102a
Richard G. Scott	God's crowning creation —G.B. Hinckley	May 2000	36b-c
	A plea for proper treatment of ,		36d-37c
Earl C. Tingey	The specialness of widows and our responsibility		62b-63f
James E. Faust	The highest place of honor in human life		95f-96b
	Young , requirements in 1916		96b-d
	A mistake to want to be like men		96d-e
	The precious gift of femininity		96e-f
	, boxers and wrestlers demean womanhood		96f-97a
Margaret D. Nadauld	, were feminine before birth	Nov 2000	14e-f
	World needs more tender and refined ,		15f
	Womanhood —excellent talk		14d-16b
Sheri L. Dew	Endowed premortally with motherhood	Nov 2001	96e-f
	Role of , —excellent talk		96b-98b
Thomas S. Monson	, urged to pursue educations		99b
Gordon B. Hinckley	Unfortunately, most wives work - costly	Nov 2002	100c-f
James E. Faust	Joseph turned key for emancipation of ,		111a
	Single , will be compensated		112e
L. Tom Perry	Allow wife to stay at home	May 2004	72b-e

Women

Julie B. Beck	The exalted role of mothers —good talk	May 2004	75d-77b
Gordon B. Hinckley	Girls to get all the education they can		113b-f
Bonnie D. Parkin	Jesus and Joseph turned to , when in distress	Nov 2004	35d-e
Gordon B. Hinckley	The preeminence of women		83d-84a
	When a man gets old he'd better have daughters about him		85b
	The women in our lives —entire talk		82d-85e
Thomas S. Monson	A , feels for you more keenly than you do for self		116a-b
James E. Faust	More opportunities have come to , since 1842	Nov 2005	22a-b
Jeffrey R. Holland	Nobility of , and advice		28b-30f
James E. Faust	A stream paralleling the priesthood line		114f
	Let go of the hurt - forgive		115b-d
	, do incalculable good - especially as mothers		115d-e
	, supported Nauvoo Temple workers		116c-d
	First and foremost in all good words		116d
	Women need women —Marjorie Hinckley		117d-e
Gordon B. Hinckley	Women must get all the education they can	Nov 2006	116b
	Not second-class citizens		118d
	What Relief Society does for ,		118f
Julie B. Beck	Should be nurturers and homemakers	Nov 2007	76f-77a
	Education avails nothing if , can't make a home		77a
	, who are strong and immovable		78a-b
	"Mothers Who Know" —entire talk		76b-78b
Thomas S. Monson	Urged to pursue educations		119d-f
	God planted within , something divine —Hinckley		121d-e
Susan W. Tanner	Meaning of "nurture"	May 2008	82b-d
Richard G. Scott	Leaders must be sensitive to needs of ,	Nov 2008	46b-c
	, are not to be owned or dominated		46d-e
	Most inspiring of all creations —Hinckley		46e
	Some , can be overly compassionate		46e-f
Dieter F. Uchtdorf	Tend to focus on imperfections		117d-f
Mary N. Cook	Satan succeeds in confusing roles of ,	May 2009	117f
	All , invited to complete Young Women values		119d-f
Elaine S. Dalton	Call for , to arise and be a standard to the world		120e-f
Silvia H. Allred	Church growth will come because of , —Kimball	Nov 2009	115d-e
Barbara Thompson	Your duty to be holy , —E.R. Snow		120a-c
Henry B. Eyring	His wife always there ahead of bishop		123f
Julie B. Beck	What , need to be and do —Eliza R. Snow	May 2010	12b
	Should not need petting and correction		12b
	How , can measure success		12c-d
	Church growth will come because of ,		12d-e
M. Russell Ballard	LDS , must lead , of the world		18d
	Nothing as life changing as influence of righteous ,		18d-e
	Inherent talents and stewardship of all		18f
	Silly , slinking across movie screens		19b-c
	Have a nature to nurture		20d

Women, cont'd

Word of Wisdom

Gordon B. Hinckley	The , is a "miracle"	May 1977	64d
Carlos E. Asay	Alcoholic reformed life —story	Nov 1978	52b-d
Marion G. Romney	Explanation of destroying angels and promise in ,	May 1979	40b-e
N. Eldon Tanner	The experience of Daniel and his friends —story		45c-46a
Gordon B. Hinckley	Executive died on skid row —story		65e-f
	Convert went back to his tobacco —story		66a
Boyd K. Packer	How , affects spirituality and revelation	Nov 1979	20c-e
L. Tom Perry	As a boy President Kimball decided he'd obey ,		36c-e
Marvin J. Ashton	Married taxi driver had money to lend to single peers —story	May 1981	22f-23a
David B. Haight	No pangs from quitting tobacco —story	Nov 1981	59c-e
Ezra Taft Benson	Health statistics for Church		63d-e
Ezra Taft Benson	History of ,	May 1983	53b-d
	Use meat sparingly means no unnecessary killing of animals		54b
	Knowledge will come by keeping all commandments		54c-e
Gordon B. Hinckley	89% of high achieving youth have never smoked	Nov 1983	44d-e
Peter Vidmar	Winner had to drink wine —story	May 1985	40b-d
Russell M. Nelson	Addictions reduce time available for repentance	Nov 1985	31b-e
Marion D. Hanks	Friends drugged sailor and led him into iniquitous acts—story	Nov 1986	12a-13a
Dallin H. Oaks	Stores and magazines that refuse to sell harmful substances		21f-22d
Russell M. Nelson	Alcohol produces growth-retarded infants		69c
	Tobacco is the #1 preventable cause of death		69d
	Addictive disorders cause 1/4 of U.S. deaths		69d
L. Tom Perry	At social hours, he asked for milk - others did too —story	May 1988	14b-f
Boyd K. Packer	The Passover symbol reappears in ,		72b
Russell M. Nelson	Addiction and freedom —excellent talk	Nov 1988	6d-9b
	Statistics on tobacco and alcohol		6f-7b
	Living , is a sign that we are Lord's covenant people		8e
Joseph B. Wirthlin	Satanic advertising on TV		36a-b
Boyd K. Packer	Anything addictive is dangerous	May 1989	54e
Boyd K. Packer	A key to revelation. Addiction disrupts channel	Nov 1989	14c-e
Robert L. Backman	"I, Spencer Kimball, will never..." —story		39c-e
Gordon B. Hinckley	Diving into empty pool not mentioned in ,		49d-51b
	A South American country closed because of drugs		49d-51b
Kenneth Johnson	Never again will I let someone else control my life —story	May 1990	42c-e
Malcolm S. Jeppsen	Friends start most people using alcohol and tobacco		44e
	In U.S., 6,000/day kick the habit or kick the bucket		44e-f
	A doctor's printed warning on advertising		44f-45a
	1 in 6 in U.S. dies from smoking		45a
Gordon B. Hinckley	Let a cup of coffee stand between you and temple? —story		51b-c
Eduardo Ayala	Microneurosurgeon's success due to , —story	Nov 1990	10d-11f
Gordon B. Hinckley	Study showed longer life if , lived		53b-f
Boyd K. Packer	Drugs are a spiritually dangerous life-style		84c
	Arsenic not warned against in ,		84e-f
Thomas S. Monson	Woman loved cigarettes more than son —story		98b-c
James E. Faust	, fortifies against destroying agents	May 1992	7d-f

Russell M. Nelson	Indifference to , brings death and financial burden	Nov 1992	8b-d
James M. Paramore	Deliverance from a 20-year prison —story		10e-f
Spencer J. Condie	Long prayer conquered alcohol —story	Nov 1993	16d-f
Boyd K. Packer	Substances that interfere with the Spirit	Nov 1994	61a
Joseph B. Wirthlin	Smoking and cancer first linked 117 years after ,	Nov 1995	76e-f
	We have a , for the mind, too		76f-77d
Boyd K. Packer	Must live , to lead, teach, be baptized, go to temple	May 1996	17d-e
	, now a commandment		17e
	The principle behind the ,		17e-18b
	Teaches moderation. Avoid extremes and fads		18b-d
	Promises health. His personal blessing		18d-19a
	Escape spiritual death by obeying ,		19b-c
Gordon B. Hinckley	Don't injure the miracle that is your body		48a-c
	Pleads to avoid drugs like poison		92e
L. Tom Perry	How , came about	Nov 1996	36d-f
	Creed Haymond refused wine - won races —story		36f-38d
	He refused beer and lost friend —story		38d-f
Gordon B. Hinckley	Warning against alcohol and drugs	Nov 1997	51f-52a
	LDS live 10 years longer		69b-c
Richard C. Edgley	Smoke to prove they're men - try to quit for same reason	Nov 1999	42e
Gordon B. Hinckley	Warning about drugs and alcohol		54d-f
H. David Burton	Drugs as dangerous as reptile's venom	May 2000	40a-b
James E. Faust	Don't experiment with addictive substances—Mr. Hyde story	Nov 2000	44d-e
	Man refused wine and won race —story		44f-45a
Boyd K. Packer	Addictive things relieve craving they caused in the first place		72e
F. Enzio Busche	Man could not drink because of sacred covenants —story		83d-f
Gordon B. Hinckley	20% introduced to drugs by parents		99e
James E. Faust	Just one won't hurt?	May 2002	47b-e
Gordon B. Hinckley	, applies to pornography	May 2003	58d-59a
James E. Faust	Moderation - stay in the center —story		109f-110b
Gordon B. Hinckley	BYU named most "stone-cold sober"	Nov 2003	84b-c
James E. Faust	Officer declined vodka toast —story	May 2004	53a-d
Gordon B. Hinckley	Drugs are a foul disease		114d
David E. Sorensen	Commander made him assistant because of , —story	May 2005	72b-73b
Susan W. Tanner	Ate too many sweet rolls —story	Nov 2005	15c-d
Benjamin De Hoyos	Convert quit job in cigarette factory —story		31e-f
Thomas S. Monson	The maka-feke of drugs	May 2006	19b-c
James E. Faust	Avoid every kind of addiction		53b-d
Dallin H. Oaks	The meaning of bond and bondage		77e-78b
Paul B. Pieper	A man's small choice affected thousands	Nov 2006	12e-f
Boyd K. Packer	, is a key to revelation		87a
Larry W. Gibbons	God cares what I have for lunch - Rabbi		102c-d
Boyd K. Packer	Became binding on Church in 1908	May 2007	28a-b
Julie B. Beck	Faithful member drank coffee and lost children —story		110b-e
Donald L. Hallstrom	Addicts to pursuit of pleasure	Nov 2007	50f

Word of Wisdom

James E. Faust	Brutal alcoholic became convert —story	Nov 2007	122e-123a
	Addictions are mind-altering - Destroy agency		123d-124a
	Addiction Recovery Program of Church		124b-c
	Mother got off drugs - Brand new —story		124c-f
Susan W. Tanner	Called as Laurel advisor while smoking —story	May 2008	114f-115d
L. Tom Perry	Best counsel on , is in For the Strength of Youth	Nov 2008	8b-9a
Richard G. Scott	Avoid stimulants that conflict with intent of ,		45a-b
D. Todd Christofferson	Wisdom, health, control, and greater capacities	May 2009	21a-b
Boyd K. Packer	Take nothing into your body that will harm it		50c-e
Dieter F. Uchtdorf	Why did runners pass him? —story	May 2010	58d-e
Thomas S. Monson	Destroy physical, mental, spiritual well-being		66b

Work
Related Topics: Idleness, Welfare Program

Thomas S. Monson	Pray for powers to equal the tasks	Dec 1968	83f
Hugh B. Brown	Man: fellow worker with God	Dec 1969	33a
Franklin D. Richards	Work is a privilege and blessing —D.O. McKay		101d
	Two guidelines for developing love of ,		102a
	Do humble tasks as if they were great —Helen Keller		102d
	Extra mile brought 3 referrals —story		102e-f
	Stake president's motto was "Be there"		103a
Henry D. Taylor	Joy of being able to , shown by D. I. worker —story		104b
Franklin D. Richards	Benefits of , - letter of father to son	Dec 1970	83d-e
Richard L. Evans	A physical and spiritual necessity		88d-f
Franklin D. Richards	Nothing worthwhile comes except through , and trials	Dec 1971	50a
Harold B. Lee	What if everything came without effort?	July 1972	31d
Thomas S. Monson	Effort must be coupled with goals		69e
	Finish what you begin —good poem		69f
Harold B. Lee	Man must , and earn what he needs	Jan 1973	61e
A. Theodore Tuttle	A commandment but not an end in itself		67d
Sterling W. Sill	Religion is not an idea - it is an activity		82f
Gordon B. Hinckley	Work of world not done by geniuses		91f
LeGrand Richards	More than confession required		110f
O. Leslie Stone	Rich rewards come only to those who ,	July 1973	60d
Robert L. Backman	Not a Church of organized sitters —E.T. Benson		85e
Sterling W. Sill	What it takes to be a Socrates or Mozart —story		104c
	If we don't enjoy , then repent		104e
	There is usually more said than done		104f
Vaughn J. Featherstone	Noble sayings about , and success	Jan 1974	84a
	A modern version of "The Little Red Hen"		84b
	Doing the impossible $5 job —story		84e
Marion G. Romney	Ground cursed for Adam's sake		89b
	The idle mice became a mob —story		89d
	Never give things free if needy can work —B. Young		89f
Loren C. Dunn	Short work week brings stress and tension	Nov 1974	11b
	I'm raising boys and not cows —story		11b-c

N. Eldon Tanner	Beware of vocational involvement leading you off path	Nov 1975	76c-e
Marion G. Romney	The dole will ruin a community or state —Young		126f-127a
	If we honored , most of our ills would be solved		127a-c
Spencer W. Kimball	Give children assignments in the home and yard	May 1976	5b
Marion G. Romney	If heaven's streets paved gold we'll have to do it—Young		123a-b
	Workers live to a good old age —H.J. Grant		123b-d
Spencer W. Kimball	, or get nothing from Church —2 Thess. 3:8, 10-12		125e
Ezra Taft Benson	Man shall live by the sweat of his brow	Nov 1976	34f-35a
Marion G. Romney	Hippy collected benefits then demonstrated —story		123d
	Gullible gulls forgot how to , —story		123d-e
	Grace vs. ,		124e-125a
	Adam's ground cursed for his sake		125a
Spencer W. Kimball	My boys never going to have to , like that — didn't —story		128a-c
N. Eldon Tanner	Rewards come to those who do extra —story	May 1978	44b-c
N. Eldon Tanner	A great antidote for many things —good quote		44e
Spencer W. Kimball	Tames wilderness in nature and in man		78a
Victor L. Brown	Old man was no longer a vegetable because of ,		90f
Marion G. Romney	We are saved after all we can do	May 1979	94d-e
Neal A. Maxwell	Called not to admire but to perspire	Nov 1980	15a
Rex. D. Pinegar	Rise early, work late, and strike oil —J. Paul Getty		72e
	, at my music until it , for me —Isaac Stern story		72e-f
	Man on mountain top didn't fall there		72f
Spencer W. Kimball	, is a spiritual as well as economic necessity	May 1981	80a
L. Tom Perry	All play and no , makes Jack a useless boy		88d
Barbara B. Smith	, becomes service when given gladly	Nov 1981	84e
J. Richard Clarke	Put a Mormon in a hopper and out comes a tycoon	May 1982	77c
	Church rose from nothing with no outside help		77d-e
	The happiness of pursuit —3 good quotes		77e-f
	The antidote for many ills and deficiencies		77f-78b
	In our jobs , like we owned the enterprise		78c
	If at first you do succeed, try something harder		78c
	Don't label jobs strictly male or female		78e
Boyd K. Packer	Give more than you're paid for		86f-87a
Barbara B. Smith	Divorced mother put kids to , - paid bills —story	Nov 1982	84b-85a
Dean Jarman	Teaching children to work —stories, excellent		85d-87b
Marion G. Romney	Gulls starved amidst plenty —story		91d-e
Boyd K. Packer	Learning piano, language or gospel requires ,	May 1983	67a-f
Marvin J. Ashton	There is genius, power and magic in beginning	Nov 1983	62b
Joseph B. Wirthlin	Unless we get the job done, it is not enough	May 1984	40a
Angel Abrea	The prize goes to those who are ready to do the impossible		71b-c
Russell M. Nelson	One can be anxiously engaged in a meaningless cause	Nov 1984	30e-f
Dallin H. Oaks	I'm raising boys, not cows —story	Nov 1985	62a
Robert D. Hales	God won't send angels to do what man can do for himself	May 1986	30f
Thomas S. Monson	I know what pleasure is, for I have done good ,		38f
L. Tom Perry	His job was to pull and straighten nails —story	Nov 1986	62c-e

L. Tom Perry	His job was to pull and straighten nails —story	Nov 1986	63b-64a
	Happy is the man who has work he loves to do		62f
Thomas S. Monson	Lord sent $600 only after all the people could do —story	May 1987	44b-e
Ezra Taft Benson	Mothers should not , outside the home	Nov 1987	48e-49d
Joseph B. Wirthlin	Growth comes only from ,	May 1989	8d-e
Richard G. Scott	A rudder won't control a drifting boat	May 1990	75f
James E. Faust	, fascinates me. I can look at it for hours.	Nov 1990	34c
Joseph B. Wirthlin	Fruits of gospel only worthy of full effort		66e
L. Tom Perry	The Lord helps those who help themselves —Nephi's story	Nov 1991	64d-f
	You will have 3 to 5 career paths		65a
	Selecting a child's vocation at age one —story		65b-c
Joseph B. Wirthlin	Seeking is not passively waiting	May 1992	86d
Russell M. Nelson	Ladder of success leaned against wrong wall	Nov 1992	6f-7a
F. David Stanley	The principle of , —entire talk	May 1993	44b-45f
Joe J. Christensen	A 13-year-old's idle day - Give kids work	Nov 1993	12a-e
John H. Groberg	Answer to prayer required , —rowboat story		26d-28b
Janette Hales Beckham	Woman would have liked to clean oven —story	Nov 1995	12f-13b
James E. Faust	The secret of missionary , is ,	May 1996	40e-f
	I can't enjoy what I don't do		40f
Russell M. Nelson	President Hinckley's quote on praying and ,	Nov 1997	16b
James E. Faust	, will serve you better than brilliance		43a-b
Neal A. Maxwell	His teen years as a swineherd	May 1998	37b-f
	, is a spiritual necessity		37f-38a
	Latter-day Saints' , should be preferred		38f
Gordon B. Hinckley	Description of his ,		69b-e
M. Russell Ballard	W. Woodruff's vision of Joseph and others hurrying	Nov 1998	6d-e
Sheri L. Dew	Busyness crowds out the Spirit		95f
	Pray and then get on feet and go to work —Hinckley		96c
Thomas S. Monson	Tahitians pray and they go	May 2002	49b-c
Thomas S. Monson	A necessity. There is no other way		101a
James E. Faust	"I , harder than the average man" —Roosevelt	Nov 2002	50b
James E. Faust	Knowledge with labor is genius	May 2003	67a
Gordon B. Hinckley	General Conference: "It's all over but the , "		99b
Donald L. Staheli	Do the very best you can —Hinckley	Nov 2004	37e-f
Thomas S. Monson	Men , harder for a cause than for money	May 2005	54e
	Life is , Work is joy —poem		54e
	Pleasure is good , —R. L. Stevenson		54f-55a
Dieter F. Uchtdorf	Hard boyhood job became a blessing —story	May 2006	42f-43b
Gordon B. Hinckley	The man is an infidel if he won't ,		58e-f
Thomas S. Monson	Boy found King's emerald by doing duty —story	Nov 2006	56e-57b
Keith B. McMullin	Flunked chemistry class —story	May 2007	51d-f
Donald L. Hallstrom	Photo of a sloth became a lesson	Nov 2007	50d-e
	Easy Street was a dead end —story		50f-51a
Henry B. Eyring	Advice for new calling: Go to work		57b-d
	Jesus' life was never easy		57e-f

Thomas S. Monson	Runner lost shoe, continued, finished third	Nov 2007	59e-f
Joseph B. Wirthlin	Counsel to those who are weary	May 2008	18e-19b
Dieter F. Uchtdorf	, to create something beautiful —Brigham Young	Nov 2008	118e-119d
	, will cure your grief —G. Hinckley		119d-120a
Boyd K. Packer	Learn to , and to support	May 2009	52b-d
Dieter F. Uchtdorf	Discipleship is not a spectator sport		76f-77a
L. Whitney Clayton	A curse given for our sake (benefit)	Nov 2009	13d-e
Boyd K. Packer	Girl prayed, then kicked trap to pieces —story		46a-b
Dieter F. Uchtdorf	Physical , turned out to be a blessing		56b-d
	Not expected to , harder than we are able		56d-e
	An antidote, an ointment and a doorway		56f
	Lord helps the man who prays and goes to ,		56f-57a
	Don't work for that which cannot satisfy		57a-c
	Retirement is not a part of Lord's plan		57c-e
	Working in kingdom upgrades your resume		57e

Work for Dead
Related Topics: Elijah, Family History, Temples

Howard W. Hunter	Explanation of 1 Cor. 15:29	June 1969	107c-d
Eldred G. Smith	Our chance to be saviors	Jan 1973	55f
	Keys of Elijah explained		56a
	Ancestors were promised we'd do ,		56f
LeGrand Richards	To be thousands of temples —Young and Woodruff	Nov 1974	54b
Gordon B. Hinckley	Jesus' sacrifice an example of vicarious work	May 1975	93e
Boyd K. Packer	True church shows how dead to be given justice and mercy	Nov 1975	97f-98e
	, impossible in scope? We'll do it anyway		99b
Robert L. Simpson	Savior provided immortality. We work for one at a time	Nov 1980	11f
Derek A. Cuthbert	Minister wanted to know why baptism for dead —story	Nov 1985	25e-f
Gordon B. Hinckley	Must be universal opportunity if to be universal justice		59d-e
Boyd K. Packer	Christ's Atonement was vicarious too	May 1987	24e-f
Vaughn J. Featherstone	Those worked for shall embrace our knees —J. Smith	Nov 1987	28b-c
Henry B. Eyring	Few if any will reject work done for them —W. Woodruff	May 2005	78e
	Entire talk motivational and good		77b-80b
Gordon B. Hinckley	32 million ordinances last year	Nov 2005	4f
	Duplication of work is troublesome		5f-6a
Richard H. Winkel	Saviors enabling dead to advance —Hinckley	Nov 2006	11a
Russell M. Nelson	Gathering of Israel on both sides of veil		80b & 80f
Gordon B. Hinckley	Woman did 20,000 endowments	May 2007	85a-b
Russell M. Nelson	Repentance is offered to the dead		104b-d
Richard G. Scott	His vision of waiting spirits	May 2009	44d-e
Thomas S. Monson	We are saviors - Dead can't move forward		113f-114a
Thomas S. Monson	Chains fall and darkness clears —J.F. Smith	Nov 2009	4f-5d
Tad R. Callister	Not an invention of a creative mind		36b-d

Worry

Harold B. Lee	Don't try to live too many days ahead	Dec 1970	30f
Sterling W. Sill	Ulcers are caused by what's eating us —neat quote	July 1972	124b
Boyd K. Packer	Worry helps. The things I , about never happen	Nov 1977	60a
Richard G. Scott	Do not waste energy on useless ,	May 1988	60f
George I. Cannon	Don't , about unchangeable things —poem	Nov 1991	14c-d
Neal A. Maxwell	Anxieties are not part of being anxiously engaged	Nov 2002	17d
Richard G. Scott	Most calamities don't happen	May 2003	77f-78a
Boyd K. Packer	Lord not pleased with needless ,	Nov 2004	87d
Quentin L. Cook	Every cloud doesn't result in rain	Nov 2008	104d

Worship
Related Topics: —

Bruce R. McConkie	No salvation in worshipping a false god	Dec 1971	129e-f
	What true worship consists of		130b-e
Russell M. Nelson	No true , without sacrifice	Nov 1984	32f

Young Women
Related Topics: Aaronic Priesthood, Virtue, Women, Youth

Marion D. Hanks	Temple marriage statistics of youth	Dec 1969	93f
N. Eldon Tanner	What a girl may expect from a man bearing the priesthood	June 1970	62f-63a
Delbert L. Stapley	Undesirable friends cause you to lower your standards	Dec 1970	65b
Neal A. Maxwell	95% of institute grads marry in temple		94c-d
Ezra Taft Benson	Satan's thrust	Dec 1971	53a-b
Victor L. Brown	Special spirits reserved for this day	July 1972	90e
Harold B. Lee	Activity leaves no time for evil	Jan 1973	62a
Boyd K. Packer	Not nourished by activity programs		89d
Victor L. Brown	Never a finer generation of youth	July 1973	83f
Victor L. Brown	Today's youth some of most valiant	May 1974	75f-76a
H. Burke Peterson	Some left, some stayed at the filthy movie —story	Nov 1974	69b-d
Spencer W. Kimball	Youth of Church must not be just average		83f
Victor L. Brown	These spirits were held for this day		104c
Franklin D. Richards	Results when youth became peacemakers in home		106c-f
Paul H. Dunn	Proper list of priorities for youth	May 1975	62a
	Proper dating age		62c
Theodore M. Burton	This is an elect generation reserved for today		69f-70a
Thomas S. Monson	Man stood at crossroads to help youth decide —poem	May 1977	72b-d
Ezra Taft Benson	Many have been reserved for 6000 years	Nov 1977	30b-c
	No worries about , who prays twice a day —Grant		32c-d
	Satan mindful of , too		30d-e
George P. Lee	Today's , choice. Lived and now live with exactness	May 1978	27b-d
Spencer W. Kimball	Talk to youth about sexual sins —special talk	Nov 1980	94a-98f
Victor L. Brown	75% of the daughters got home in time —story	May 1982	34f
Boyd K. Packer	Revelations will be opened to this generation as to no other	Nov 1982	53b
Dean L. Larsen	Here not by accident. Most counted on generation	May 1983	33c-f
	Say "I am everything," then prove it		35f
David B. Haight	Act preventively now or redemptively later —Kimball	Nov 1983	40d
Gordon B. Hinckley	Nation's high achievers are moral and religious —survey		44d-e

Young Women, cont'd

Related Topics: Aaronic Priesthood, Virtue, Women, Youth

Elaine A. Cannon	Tell them don't do it. —Spencer W. Kimball joke	May 1984	26b
Ezra Taft Benson	Reserved to be born today	May 1986	43b-c
Ezra Taft Benson	Counsel to young women —entire talk, excellent	Nov 1986	81b-85b
Vaughn J. Featherstone	Church , one of most powerful forces for good on earth	Nov 1987	27f
	Youth will face trials exceeding those of pioneers		27f-28a
	Our youth will rescue an entire generation		28b-c
	Won't be beaten down by storms - Alma 26:6-7		28c
	Older brother was girl's best friend —story		28c-d
	Will perform most important work of this dispensation		29f-30a
Glenn L. Pace	Difference between telestial pleasure and celestial joy		39d-41b
James M. Paramore	Girl refuses marriage except in temple - converts boy	May 1988	11e-f
Dwan J. Young	God has saved most valiant children for today		78d
Joseph B. Wirthlin	What would your unborn children ask you to do?	May 1989	8f
Marvin J. Ashton	Finest and strongest , ever		36e-37a
Boyd K. Packer	To Young Women and Men —entire talk		53d-59f
Ezra Taft Benson	Today's , some of most valiant		83b-c
Robert L. Backman	Only young once: Old a long time	Nov 1989	38f-39a
Victor L. Brown	5 examples of , of faith		76e-77a
Elaine L. Jack	3 inspiring letters from girls		88a-c
Thomas S. Monson	Principles governing budgeting of activities	May 1990	93b-d
M. Russell Ballard	The necessity of chastity among ,	Nov 1990	35d-38b
Thomas S. Monson	Reserved for this day		45d-f
	"For the Strength of Youth" pamphlet reviewed		45b-48b
Ardeth G. Kapp	Today's trials harder than pioneers' —excellent talk		93b-95b
Thomas S. Monson	Repeat of talk given in Ensign, Nov. 1990, pg. 45b-48b		95d-99f
Richard G. Scott	Advice to , —entire talk	May 1991	34b-36b
Jack H. Goaslind	Yagottawanna youth conference		45d-47a
	Young woman turned off movie —story		47a-b
Thomas S. Monson	Be loyal to the royal within you		47f-48b
Janette C. Hales	Man's most significant service was in youth —story		84e-f
	Teens must deal with Book of Mormon cycle		84f-85a
Gordon B. Hinckley	The finest generation ever	May 1992	69e
	A call to youth to be a royal generation		69b-71f
M. Russell Ballard	Counsel to read and carry For The Strength of Youth	May 1993	7f-8d
L. Tom Perry	What Book of Mormon will do for ,		92d-e
Thomas S. Monson	Youth at crossroads —poem	Nov 1993	48e
W. Eugene Hansen	Explaining to youth why we worry so much about them		83b-d
Joseph B. Wirthlin	Advice to youth on obedience —entire talk	May 1994	39b-42b
Neal A. Maxwell	Sobering statistics about youth		88f-89a
Russell M. Nelson	Meaning of "a peculiar people"	May 1995	34b-c
Jeffrey R. Holland	Having walked the path we give encouragement and warning		38d-f
Thomas S. Monson	Modern Pied Pipers leading youth away		49a
Thomas S. Monson	Young want to change world - old change young		97c
Gordon B. Hinckley	There is divinity and potential in each ,		99d-e
James E. Faust	No young single overnight mixed groups	Nov 1995	47a

Young Women

Speaker	Topic	Date	Pages
Boyd K. Packer	Advice to youth about word of wisdom	May 1996	17b-19f
W. Eugene Hansen	Life in 40's determined by actions in teens		39f
Thomas S. Monson	Service project: Dinner for elderly —story		44e-f
Bonnie D. Parkin	Personal Progress program became positive —story		90d-91a
Boyd K. Packer	Feel cornered when they don't know how to erase mistakes	May 1997	10b
Thomas S. Monson	Most influenced by teachers who care		46a-b
Gordon B. Hinckley	Advice to youth on how to live lives		48e-50b
4 speakers	Choices young women made —many examples and stories		88b-92f
Thomas S. Monson	Clean , will have joy unspeakable		93c
	Effect a leader had on her young women		95c-e
Gordon B. Hinckley	Advice to best generation we have ever had	Nov 1997	51d-52b
Margaret D. Nadauld	Young women helped young widower —story	May 1998	65b-d
	Service by 12-year-old girl when mom was sick —story		89e-f
James E. Faust	Reserved for this time		95b
	How glorious and near to the angels is youth		95d
Boyd K. Packer	When you schedule a youth, you schedule a family	Nov 1998	22b-24f
Carol B. Thomas	Ward youth prepared 10,000 names for temple	May 1999	13e-f
Joseph B. Wirthlin	The greatest generation in the Church —Hinckley	Nov 1999	41d
Gordon B. Hinckley	Warning to youth about drugs and pornography		54d-f
James E. Faust	Young Women requirements in 1916	May 2000	96b-d
	Great happiness and endless joy if ...		96d
Sharon G. Larsen	Church publications available to help ,	Nov 2001	67d-e
Thomas S. Monson	How glorious and near to the angels is clean youth	May 2002	100f
Spencer V. Jones	8 youth at fireside had poor countenances —story	May 2003	88e-f
Richard G. Scott	Our youth excel the capacity of forebears	Nov 2003	41b-d
	A singular generation with exceptional potential		42b
Gordon B. Hinckley	The best generation we have ever had		84d-e
Gordon B. Hinckley	Our refreshing and inspirational youth	May 2004	4d-f
Earl C. Tingey	Following the standards		49b-51b
Boyd K. Packer	Better than previous generations		79a
Boyd K. Packer	Better and stronger than previous generations	Nov 2004	87b
Elaine S. Dalton	An untapped resource for temple work		90f-91e
Thomas S. Monson	The very best ever	May 2005	19b
Gordon B. Hinckley	Book studied religious lives of teenagers		61b-e
M. Russell Ballard	Colt resisted being pushed and pulled —story		71b-d
David A. Bednar	Leader memorized names of youth —story		100b-e
Jeffrey R. Holland	The nobility of women and advice to girls	Nov 2005	28b-30f
Dieter F. Uchtdorf	For the Strength of Youth a gem for any age	May 2006	44a-b
	Promises if standards in For the Strength of Youth are lived		44d
Ronald A. Rasband	Finest generation ever —G.B. Hinckley		46e-f
	Testing of , will become more severe		46f
Elaine S. Dalton	Finest generation of youth ever —Hinckley		109d
	Mary Goble's pioneer experience —story		109f-110d
James E. Faust	Rollins girls saved D&C pages —story		111f-112a
	Joan of Arc —story		112b-f

James E. Faust	Smiling girl at bus stop made converts —story	May 2006	113a-d
Elaine S. Dalton	Why it's important to be clean and pure	Nov 2006	31b-32f
Robert D. Hales	Your 20's - The Decade of Decision	May 2007	48d-e
James E. Faust	Will accomplish great things if prophet followed		56e-f
Henry B. Eyring	Peers' future shaped by what you do		90c-d
Charles W. Dahlquist, II	Really a chosen generation —Hinckley		94e
Gordon B. Hinckley	There is no limit to your potential		115d-e
L. Tom Perry	Isolating themselves in technology	Nov 2007	48e-f
Dean R. Burgess	"Do you know who you are?"	May 2008	53b-55b
John M. Madsen	Reserved for this day —J.F. Smith and S.W. Kimball		56b-d
Thomas S. Monson	A network of influence for , in Church		66e-f
Susan W. Tanner	2 Laurels activate advisor and 14 girls —story		114f-115d
Elaine S. Dalton	Only one opposed to premarital sex —story		116e-117a
Mary N. Cook	, are like water lilies —analogy		120b-d
Henry B. Eyring	You are remarkable - Pre-earth standouts		123d-e
	You are a target		125d-e
	You will influence thousands		125f
	True servants and angels will help you		125f
Ann M. Dibb	This talk completes one of her , values	May 2009	114d
	Did not understand magnitude of her , experiences		114d-115a
	Her experience working on virtue value		115d-116a
	Girl completed 79 of 80 goals —story		116b-f
Mary N. Cook	A mother's greatest hope is virtuous daughter		117b-d
	Steps to virtue - Youth is a defining time		117d-e
	Peer pressure: Satan's strategy		118a-b
	Three daily habits: Prayer, Study, Smile		118d-e
	, are not alone		118e-119b
	How girl handles mocking of standards		119b-c
	All women invited to complete values		119d-f
Elaine S. Dalton	Virtuous young men are attracted to virtuous ,		120b-e
	Virtue banner unfurled on mountain one year ago		120e-f
	You are not common or ordinary		121a-b
	Raising banners of virtue around world		121d-e
	Choose a symbol representing your life		121f-122a
	One virtuous , can change the world		123b
Thomas S. Monson	Strongest , saved for this time		127e-f
Barbara Thompson	No leave of absence between , and Relief Society	Nov 2009	118f-119a
M. Russell Ballard	Mothers are first line of defense for ,	May 2010	19f-20a
Robert D. Hales	Mothers: Do Personal Progress with daughter		96d-e
Ann M. Dibb	4 guidelines to , from Joshua		114a-116f
Mary N. Cook	Mother should do Personal Progress with daughter		119a-b
	Life compared to hike. Advice to ,		117b-119f
Elaine S. Dalton	Works and knowledge in premortal life		120f-121b
	Can't be content to just fit in		121b-c
	Born to be a queen - Meeting Sister McKay —story		121d-122b

Young Women

Elaine S. Dalton	Remember who you are	May 2010	122f-123a
	Counsel to , —great talk		120b-123a
Dieter F. Uchtdorf	"Your Happily Ever After" —entire talk		124d-127f

Youth
Related Topics: Aaronic Priesthood, Scouting, Young Women

David O. McKay	The most sheltered generation is most exposed	Dec 1968	36f-37a
	Get involved in young people's lives		37a
John H. Vandenberg	Spirituality of ward depends on , —McKay		58b
	Set goals higher for selves than would adults		58e
Richard L. Evans	Easier to be excited over social reform than character reform		64d-e
	Comments on protesting movement —good		64e-65a
Loren C. Dunn	The gaining of a testimony by ,		78a-f
David O. McKay	Curious horse compared to , —story		85f-86c
Ezra Taft Benson	Communists seek to destroy a generation of our ,	June 1969	46e-47c
Loren C. Dunn	Don't yield to pressure. Time will show error of others	Dec 1969	44d
Spencer W. Kimball	Today's , as faithful as before		47b
Boyd K. Packer	, fulfill prophecy of famine for hearing words of the Lord		57b-f
	Invitation to wandering , —entire talk		57b-59e
Ezra Taft Benson	Part played in communist plot		69d
	Communists aim to destroy ,		69f
Marion D. Hanks	Want to "teach before they learn, retire before they work"		93b
	Temple marriage statistics of ,		93f
Gordon B. Hinckley	Better than their parents		98e
Victor L. Brown	A group of , deeply touched by lesson on eternal life —story		108f-109a
Boyd K. Packer	The hills and mountains , must climb	June 1970	51b-e
	What if , are not warned of pitfalls? —story		51f-52c
John H. Vandenberg	Your life is not really your own		59c-e
N. Eldon Tanner	What a girl may expect from a , bearing the priesthood		62f-63a
Paul H. Dunn	Accent on , but stress on parents	Dec 1970	38f
	Easier to build a boy than mend a man		39a
Loren C. Dunn	Who will care for abandoned , ? - Don't give up		62b-63b
Delbert L. Stapley	Undesirable friends cause you to lower your standards		65b
Marion D. Hanks	Will children of rebellious , be able to thank them?		67b
Gordon B. Hinckley	Peace and freedom or enslavement and debauchery?		71b-72c
	Don't dismiss the wisdom of generations past		72c-d
	As with the bud, so with the blossom		72f
Neal A. Maxwell	95% of institute grads marry in temple		94c-d
Alvin R. Dyer	His father reactivated 12 rebellious , —story		124c-d
Paul H. Dunn	We want to help you , in the worst way	June 1971	102e
	Boys are the only things from which men are made		103b
Loren C. Dunn	Problems of , arise from false ideals of today	Dec 1971	47e-48a
Ezra Taft Benson	Satan's thrust		53a-b
	The most vulnerable age		55a
	Confused definitions in language of ,		55b-c
Marvin J. Ashton	A self-motivated missionary —story		101a-b

Youth, cont'd
Related Topics: Aaronic Priesthood, Scouting, Young Women

Marion D. Hanks	Joseph Smith organizing the young people —story	Dec 1971	104e-105c
	Some problems of , —stories		105d-f
	Five needs of ,		106a-e
	Drugs led to suicide —story		106c
Victor L. Brown	Special spirits reserved for this day	July 1972	90e
Harold B. Lee	Activity leaves no time for evil	Jan 1973	62a
Boyd K. Packer	Not nourished by activity programs		89d
Gordon B. Hinckley	Most dedicated, most capable		91a
	God has plans for each ,		91b
	Brethren were formerly boys		92f
N. Eldon Tanner	Great men must be great boys		103c
Marion D. Hanks	Many have no guidance - must not be abandoned		128a
Victor L. Brown	Never a finer generation of ,	July 1973	83f
Robert L. Backman	A spiritual day for Utah Valley ,		84a
Victor L. Brown	Services performed by ,	Jan 1974	108e
Victor L. Brown	Today's , some of most valiant	May 1974	75f-76a
Spencer W. Kimball	Goals each , should make		86f-87c
	Each young man should fill a mission		87c
James E. Faust	A , who was much better than parents —story	Nov 1974	60c-d
H. Burke Peterson	Youth who are unusually dedicated —story		68b-e
	Some left, some stayed at the filthy movie —story		69b-d
N. Eldon Tanner	Don't advance , in priesthood till worthy		77c
Spencer W. Kimball	One , defeated an army —story of David retold		80e-82d
	Every , begins with all that the great have had		83a-c
	Senseless destructive acts of , denounced		83d-e
	, of Church must not be just average		83f
S. Dilworth Young	Examples of prophets called and prepared in ,		90d-91e
Victor L. Brown	These spirits were held for this day		104c
Franklin D. Richards	Results when , became peacemakers in home		106c-f
William H. Bennett	Remember God in , or maybe not at all	May 1975	58e
Paul H. Dunn	Proper list of priorities for ,		62a
	Proper dating age		62c
Theodore M. Burton	This is an elect generation reserved for today		69f-70a
Spencer W. Kimball	Early Church leaders were but youths		80c
	How do you make a boy a man? —J.E. Hoover		80d-e
Victor L. Brown	, will be converted only as they sacrifice	Nov 1975	66b-68f
Thomas S. Monson	Man brought boy back from planned inactivity —story	May 1977	71f-72b
	Man stood at crossroads to help , decide —poem		72b-d
Thomas S. Monson	Boisterous , threw hens into molt —story	Nov 1977	7e-f
Ezra Taft Benson	Many have been reserved for 6000 years		30b-c
	No worries about , who prays twice a day —Grant		32c-d
	Satan mindful of , too		30d-e
Marion D. Hanks	, worked to pay mother's bill and converted druggist —story		37b-f
George P. Lee	Today's , choice. Lived and now live with exactness	May 1978	27b-d
Spencer W. Kimball	Talk to , about sexual sins —special talk	Nov 1980	94a-98f

Youth

Victor L. Brown	75% of the daughters got home in time —story	May 1982	34f
	Fun and games will not save any boy —story		36d-f
C. Frederick Pingel	How to build young men —entire talk	Nov 1982	35b-36f
Michael Nicholas	What Young Men program does for him —entire talk		37b-f
Robert L. Backman	Caring advisors can have huge impact on ,		38f
	Quorum activities should be weekly		39f-40a
	Discussion of various activities for ,		40a-e
	Importance of service projects		40f
	Be judicious not stingy with cost for programs		40f-41d
	Challenge to activate 3 per quorum per year		41d-f
Boyd K. Packer	Revelations will be opened to this generation as to no other		53b
Dean L. Larsen	Here not by accident—Most counted on generation	May 1983	33c-f
	, who premeditate their sins and repentance.		34f-35f
	Say "I am everything," then prove it		35f
Vaughn J. Featherstone	Keep your eyes open where , are concerned —story	Nov 1983	37b-c
	Boy took challenge to pray regularly —story		37c-e
	How scouting developed his leadership ability		37e-39a
David B. Haight	Opposite extremes because of teachings in homes —story		39d-40b
	Act preventively now or redemptively later —Kimball		40d
Gordon B. Hinckley	Nation's high achievers are moral and religious —survey		44d-e
Elaine A. Cannon	Tell them don't do it. —Spencer W. Kimball joke	May 1984	26b
Thomas S. Monson	Bishop found priest hiding in grease pit —story	Nov 1984	43e-f
R. LaVell Edwards	Do missions and college athletics mix?		44b-46b
Ezra Taft Benson	Reserved to be born today	May 1986	43b-c
	Advice to young men —entire talk		43b-46b
Ezra Taft Benson	Counsel to young women —entire talk, excellent	Nov 1986	81b-85b
Thomas S. Monson	President Truman was a sissy —story	May 1987	68f
Vaughn J. Featherstone	Don't give up on wayward , - God loves them	Nov 1987	27d
	Million dollar facility worth it if 1 boy saved —story		27d-e
	Church , one of most powerful forces for good on earth		27f
	, will face trials exceeding those of pioneers		27f-28a
	Our , will rescue an entire generation		28b-c
	, won't be beaten down by storms - Alma 26:6-7		28c
	Older brother was girl's best friend —story		28c-d
	Will perform most important work of this dispensation		29f-30a
Glenn L. Pace	Difference between telestial pleasure and celestial joy		39d-41b
William R. Bradford	Funds raised for a trip donated to missionary fund —story		75b-e
James M. Paramore	Girl refuses marriage except in temple - converts boy	May 1988	11e-f
Dwan J. Young	God has saved most valiant children for today		78d
	Boy left when TV show made him feel dark inside —story		79b-c
Thomas S. Monson	Sportsmanship in Church sports —funny stories	Nov 1988	44b-f
Joseph B. Wirthlin	What would your unborn children ask you to do?	May 1989	8f
Marvin J. Ashton	Finest and strongest , ever		36e-37a
Boyd K. Packer	To Young Women and Men —entire talk		53d-59f
	Temptations are greater now		54b-c

Youth, cont'd
Related Topics: Aaronic Priesthood, Scouting, Young Women

Boyd K. Packer	Gareth and the Black Knight —story	May 1989	54c-e
	Some , may not have found themselves but they are not lost		59f
Ezra Taft Benson	Today's , some of most valiant		83b-c
Robert L. Backman	Only young once: Old a long time	Nov 1989	38f-39a
Joe J. Christensen	Never had to worry what he'd done Saturday night —story		42f-43d
Victor L. Brown	5 examples of , of faith		76e-77a
Elaine L. Jack	3 inspiring letters from girls		88a-c
Thomas S. Monson	Principles governing budgeting of activities	May 1990	93b-d
M. Russell Ballard	The necessity of chastity among ,	Nov 1990	35d-38b
Marion D. Hanks	Do they do this to make it fun for , ? —story		38e-f
Thomas S. Monson	Reserved for this day		45d-f
	"For the Strength of Youth" pamphlet reviewed		45b-48b
Ardeth G. Kapp	Today's trials harder than pioneers' —excellent talk		93b-95b
Thomas S. Monson	Repeat of talk given in Ensign, Nov. 1990, pg. 45b-48b		95d-99f
Richard G. Scott	Advice to , —entire talk	May 1991	34b-36b
J. Richard Clarke	Can handle men's jobs when 12 years old		42f
Jack H. Goaslind	Yagottawanna youth conference		45d-47a
	Young woman turned off movie —story		47a-b
Thomas S. Monson	Be loyal to the royal within you		47f-48b
Janette C. Hales	Man's most significant service was in , —story		84e-f
	Teens must deal with Book of Mormon cycle		84f-85a
Joseph B. Wirthlin	, is time to master bodily appetites	Nov 1991	16b
Thomas S. Monson	Nobody knows what a boy is worth —poem		46d
	Be understanding of youthful mistakes —story		46d-e
	How to organize Church sports teams		46f-47a
Gordon B. Hinckley	The finest generation ever	May 1992	69e
	A call to , to be a royal generation		69b-71f
Janette C. Hales	Learn the names of ,		80f
Glenn L. Pace	Place energy into current obedience	Nov 1992	12f.
Virginia H. Pearce	How to conquer our fears —good advice		90b-92b
M. Russell Ballard	Counsel to read and carry "For The Strength of Youth"	May 1993	7f-8d
L. Tom Perry	What Book of Mormon will do for ,		92d-e
Joe J. Christensen	A 13-year-old's idle days - They need work	Nov 1993	12a-e
Hugh W. Pinnock	What Joseph Smith did in teenage years		40e
	I've never been a teenager before —story		41b
	Direction you're flying as , determines where you land		41f
	A flight checklist for ,		40b-42b
Thomas S. Monson	Youth at crossroads —poem		48e
W. Eugene Hansen	Explaining to , why we worry so much about them		83b-d
Joseph B. Wirthlin	Advice to , on obedience —entire talk	May 1994	39b-42b
Neal A. Maxwell	Sobering statistics about ,		88f-89a
Richard G. Scott	Straight talk to young men about sexuality	Nov 1994	37b-39b
Russell M. Nelson	Meaning of "a peculiar people"	May 1995	34b-c
Jeffrey R. Holland	Having walked path, we shout encouragement and warnings		38d-f
Thomas S. Monson	Modern Pied Pipers leading , away		49a

Youth

Thomas S. Monson	Young want to change world - old change young	May 1995	97c
Gordon B. Hinckley	There is divinity and potential in each ,		99d-e
Harold G. Hillam	"I have never slept in a sleeping bag" —story	Nov 1995	41b-c
James E. Faust	No young single overnight mixed groups		47a
Thomas S. Monson	Priest helped elderly man find page —story		49f
Boyd K. Packer	Advice to , about word of wisdom	May 1996	17b-19f
W. Eugene Hansen	Life in 40's determined by actions in teens		39f
Thomas S. Monson	Service project: Dinner for elderly —story		44e-f
Bonnie D. Parkin	Personal Progress program became positive —story		90d-91a
Boyd K. Packer	, feel cornered when they don't know how to erase mistakes	May 1997	10b
Thomas S. Monson	, most influenced by teachers who care		46a-b
Gordon B. Hinckley	Advice to , on how to live lives		48e-50b
4 speakers	Choices young women made —many examples and stories		88b-92f
Thomas S. Monson	Clean , will have joy unspeakable		93c
	Effect a leader had on her young women		95c-e
Keith B. McMullin	Manhood begins with ordination, not age	Nov 1997	41c-d
Gordon B. Hinckley	Advice to best generation we have ever had		51d-52b
Thomas S. Monson	What scouting does for ,	May 1998	47f-48a
	Must have leader's membership record before issuing calls		48c
Margaret D. Nadauld	Young women helped young widower —story		65b-d
Margaret D. Nadauld	Service by 12-year-old girl when mom was sick —story		89e-f
James E. Faust	Reserved for this time		95b
	How glorious and near to the angels is ,		95d
Boyd K. Packer	When you schedule a youth, you schedule a family	Nov 1998	22b-24f
Carol B. Thomas	Ward , prepared 10,000 names for temple	May 1999	13e-f
Vaughn J. Featherstone	Boy wanted prayer more than Thanksgiving —story	Nov 1999	15c-16a
Joseph B. Wirthlin	"You'll grow into it" —story		38d-39b
	The greatest generation in the Church —Hinckley		41d
Richard C. Edgley	Boys smoke to be men - quit for same reason		42e
Gordon B. Hinckley	Warning to , about drugs and pornography		54d-f
James E. Faust	Young Women requirements in 1916	May 2000	96b-d
	Great happiness and endless joy if …		96d
Gordon B. Hinckley	Warnings about Rave parties and choking	Nov 2000	50f-51a
Richard G. Scott	Young man would not compete on Sabbath —story	May 2001	8c-f
James E. Faust	, and their patriarchal blessings most promising		45b-c
Robert D. Hales	Earn Duty to God and Eagle awards	Nov 2001	38d-39a
Sharon G. Larsen	Church publications available to help ,		67d-e
Thomas S. Monson	How glorious and near to the angels is clean ,	May 2002	100f
Thomas S. Monson	Boys, dogs and a snake teach patience —2 stories	Nov 2002	54e-55a
James E. Faust	Being a good boy requires practice	May 2003	52c
Spencer V. Jones	8 , at fireside had poor countenances —story		88e-f
Richard G. Scott	Our , excel the capacity of forebears	Nov 2003	41b-d
	A singular generation with exceptional potential		42b
Thomas S. Monson	"The Bridge Builder" —poem		67c-e
Gordon B. Hinckley	The best generation we have ever had		84d-e

Youth

Henry B. Eyring	You are remarkable - Pre-earth standouts	May 2008	123d-e
	You are a target		125d-e
	You will influence thousands		125f
	True servants and angels will help you		125f
James J. Hamula	Most valiant and noble sons and daughters	Nov 2008	50e-f
	Must do again what you did before		50f-51b
	Focus of Satan's war is you		51b
James J. Hamula	Counseled to be sober - Definition		51d-f
	Three qualities needed to overcome Satan		52d-f
Boyd K. Packer	, speak of future because they have no past ...	May 2009	49d
	Samuel, David, Mormon, Joseph, Jesus called in ,		49f
	Teach , the same as adults		49f-50a
	Counsel to young men —entire talk		49d-52f
Ann M. Dibb	Did not understand magnitude of experiences in ,		114d-115a
	Girl completed 79 of 80 Young Women goals —story		116b-f
Mary N. Cook	Satan's strategy: Peer pressure		118a-b
	, are not alone		118e-119b
	How a girl handles mocking of standards		119b-c
Elaine S. Dalton	Choose a symbol representing your life		121f-122a
	You are being tapped on the shoulder —Churchill		123a
	One virtuous , can change the world		123b
Thomas S. Monson	How glorious and near to angels is clean ,		125b-126a
	Strongest children saved for this time		127e-f
M. Russell Ballard	Three ways to improve relations with father	Nov 2009	47f-50e
Walter F. Gonzalez	Read Book of Mormon looking for peer pressure		51f-52c
Yoon Hwan Choi	Nine Korean troublemakers joined Church —story		53b-55b
Henry B. Eyring	Bishop's policy: No lights out		61a-d
	Better than we are		62a-b
Brent H. Nielson	Encouragement to serve missions —great		95b-97b
D. Todd Christofferson	Should not have to learn by sad experiences		107d
Henry B. Eyring	Downward spiral easier to arrest at first	May 2010	22a-e
	Lost child and rescuers —story		23d-24b
	Personal Progress and Duty to God programs		24b-e
	Can only succeed with Spirit of God		25a-d
Ronald A. Rasband	The most important work , can do		53b-f
David L. Beck	Non-member describes his friend		54b
	2 , made Book of Moron possible		54c-e
	New Duty to God program		54e-55a
	Lord: "I have a work for you"		55d
	Impact a , has on his family		55d-e
	We look to , like Nephites looked to Mormon		55f
	Will change people and the world		56a-b
Robert D. Hales	Duty to God and Personal Progress to be done with parents		96d-e
Bradley D. Foster	Distractions don't have to be evil —story		99b-f
Gregory A. Schwitzer	Adults should read For the Strength of Youth		105a-b

Youth, cont'd
Related Topics: Aaronic Priesthood, Scouting, Young Women

Neil L. Andersen	"The very best ever" —Monson	May 2010	108d-e
	Their preparation cannot be casual		108e
	Each needs own conversion and light		108f
	Study. Read book of John		109f
	You will have to defend your faith —Monson		112a
	Your testimony will keep you safe —Monson		112b
Ann M. Dibb	Teacher attacked girl's faith —story		116d-e
	4 guidelines from Joshua —entire talk		114a-116f
Elaine S. Dalton	I was born to be a king —story		121d
Dieter F. Uchtdorf	"Your Happily Ever After" —entire talk		124c-127f

Zion
Related Topics: —

Harold B. Lee	Saints and non members to be all mixed up in ,	Dec 1968	71d-e
	Safety to be had not merely in Utah but in stakes		72c-d
	Meanings of ,		72d-e
	Does not matter where we live		73c
Marion G. Romney	Babylon will fall but , will not go down with it	May 1976	123d-f
Spencer W. Kimball	What is required to establish ,	May 1978	80a-81f
Robert D. Hales	Definition of , —excellent	May 1986	30d-e
David R. Stone	Creating our , in the midst of Babylon	May 2006	90d-92b
D. Todd Christofferson	Ancients looked forward to , —Joseph Smith	Nov 2008	37b
	Both a place and a people		37b-d
	Babylon is the antithesis and antagonist of ,		37d-f
	Why early Saints failed to establish ,		37f-38b
	Residents of , can't keep summer cottages in Babylon		39b
	Building of , is our greatest object —Joseph Smith		40d-f
Elaine S. Dalton	The strength of , is in virtue —Brigham Young	May 2009	121a-b

My Favorite Talks
Related Topics: —

Ezra Taft Benson	"The Proper Role of Government"	Dec 1968	51a-53f
Hartman Rector, Jr.	"Repentance Makes Us Free" —Spirit and Body	Dec 1970	76a-78e
Gordon B. Hinckley	"Except the Lord Build the House" —Marriage	June 1971	71a-72f
Spencer W. Kimball	"Glimpses of Heaven" —Heaven on earth	Dec 1971	36a-39f
Sterling W. Sill	"Thou Shalt Not" —10 Commandments		92a-94e
Boyd K. Packer	"Inspiring Music" - Worthy Thoughts	Jan 1974	25a-28f
Ezra Taft Benson	"Prepare Ye" —Food Storage		68b-82e
Vaughn J. Featherstone	"The Gospel of Jesus Christ is the Golden Door" —Work		84a-86e
H. Burke Peterson	"Mother, Catch the Vision of Your Call" —Working Moms	May 1974	31d-33b
Theodore M. Burton	"Salvation for the Dead" —Family History, Missionary	May 1975	69a-71f
Bruce R. McConkie	"Once or Twice in a Thousand Years" —Restoration	Nov 1975	15d-18f
Boyd K. Packer	"Spiritual Crocodiles" —Holy Ghost, Obedience	May 1976	30a-32b
Boyd K. Packer	"The Mediator"	May 1977	54b-56f
H. Burke Peterson	"The Daily Portion of Love"		68d-69f
Boyd K. Packer	"Judge Not According to the Appearance"	May 1979	79d-81f
Boyd K. Packer	"Prayers and Answers"	Nov 1979	19d-21f

Youth | Zion | My Favorite Talks

Bruce R. McConkie	"The Coming Tests and Trials and Glory" —Last Days	May 1980	71a-73f
Vaughn J. Featherstone	"Forgive Them I Pray Thee" —Confession	Nov 1980	29d-31f
F. Burton Howard	"In Saving Others We Save Ourselves" —Parable of travelers	May 1981	71b-72f
Marion G. Romney	"The Resurrection of Jesus"	May 1982	6a-9b
J. Richard Clarke	"My Soul Delighteth in the Scriptures"	Nov 1982	13b-15f
Robert L. Backman	"Revitalizing Aaronic Priesthood Quorums"		38a-41f
Dean Jarman	"The Blessings of Family Work Projects"		85d-87b
Jeffrey R. Holland	"Within the Clasp of Your Arms" —Being a Father	May 1983	36b-38b
Mark E. Petersen	"The Angel Moroni Came" —Revelation, Book of Mormon	Nov 1983	29b-31f
Boyd K. Packer	"The Pattern of Our Parentage"	Nov 1984	66b-69f
John H. Groberg	"The Power of Keeping the Sabbath Day Holy"		79d-81f
Russell M. Nelson	"Reverence for Life" —Abortion	May 1985	11c-14b
Glenn L. Pace	"They're Not Really Happy" —Youth, Happiness and Joy	Nov 1987	39d-41a
Ezra Taft Benson	"To the Fathers in Israel"		48c-51b
Ezra Taft Benson	"Beware of Pride"	May 1989	4b-7b
Carlos E. Asay	"One Small Step For A Man. One Giant Leap for Mankind"	May 1990	62d-65b
M. Russell Ballard	"The Family of the Prophet Joseph Smith"	Nov 1991	5d-7f
Chieko N. Okazaki	"Spit and Mud and Kigatsuku"	May 1992	95d-96f
Dallin H. Oaks	"Tithing"	May 1994	33b-35f
Richard C. Edgley	"That thy Confidence Wax Strong"	Nov 1994	39d-41b
Gordon B. Hinckley	"Don't Drop the Ball"		46d-49b
Gordon B. Hinckley	"Be Ye Clean"	May 1996	46d-49f
Boyd K. Packer	"Parents in Zion"	Nov 1998	22b-24f
Val R. Christensen	"Overcoming Discouragement"		31b-32b
Charles Didier	"Building A Bridge of Faith"	Nov 2001	10b-12b
Sheri L. Dew	"It is Not Good For Man or Woman to be Alone"		12d-14f
James E. Faust	"Some Great Thing" - Diligent service		46d-49b
Joseph B. Wirthlin	Leaving our nets to follow Jesus	May 2002	15b-17f
Robert D. Hales	The Reformation and Restoration	Nov 2005	88d-92b
Joseph B. Wirthlin	"The Abundant Life"	May 2006	99b-102b
Joseph B. Wirthlin	"Sunday Will Come"	Nov 2006	28b-30f
Jeffrey R. Holland	"The Only True God" - LDS are Christian	Nov 2007	40b-42f
Julie B. Beck	"Mothers Who Know"	Nov 2007	76b-78b
Joseph B. Wirthlin	"Come What May, and Love It" - Adversity	Nov 2008	26b-28f
Dieter F. Uchtdorf	We're Doing a Great Work and Cannot Come Down	May 2009	59b-62f
Jeffrey R. Holland	Powerful testimony of Book of Mormon	Nov 2009	88b-90f
Dieter F. Uchtdorf	"Your Happily Ever After"	May 2010	124c-127f

ABOUT THE AUTHOR

James E. Kerns is a sixth generation Oregonian farm boy who was given a Book of Mormon in 1966 at the age of nineteen. Reading the book was for him a Lamoni experience that "infused such joy into his soul, the cloud of darkness having been dispelled . . . that the light of everlasting life was lit up in his soul" (Alma 19:6). He finished the book, read the Doctrine and Covenants, knocked on the missionaries' door, and told them he needed to hear their discussions so he could be baptized.

James served in the U.S. Navy as a Russian linguist, obtained a BS degree from Brigham Young University, and married Marjorie Hunt in the Salt Lake Temple. He and his wife have raised ten children and have thirty-seven grandchildren.

James has served as a bishop and in a stake presidency and currently serves as a temple ordinance worker in the Boise Idaho Temple.

NOTES

NOTES

NOTES

NOTES